Investment Analysis and Portfolio Management

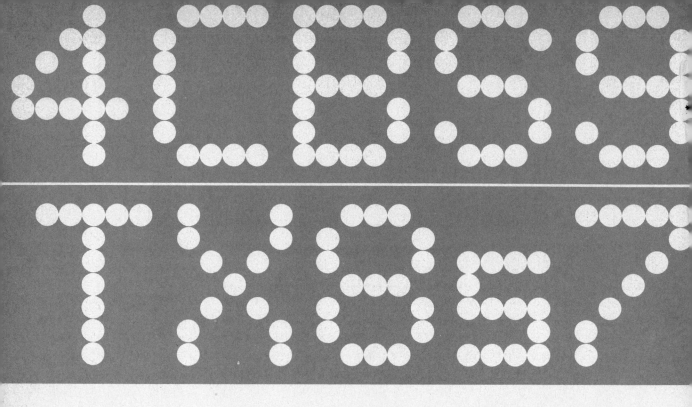

**Investment Analysis and
Portfolio Management**

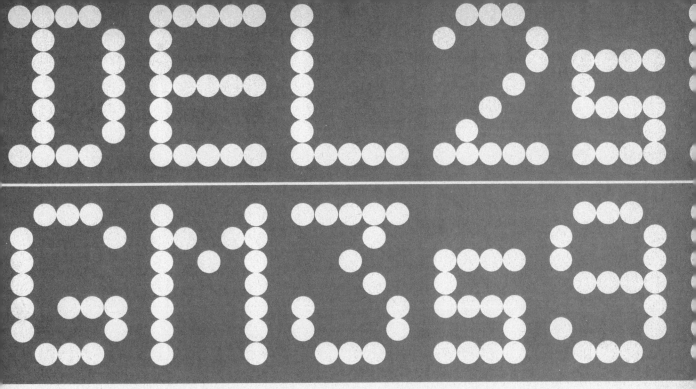

Frank K. Reilly
University of Illinois

The Dryden Press
Hinsdale, Illinois

To
My wonderful wife Therese
And our four fantastic children
Frank K. III
Clarence R. II
Therese B.
Edgar B.

Preface

An author usually decides to write a textbook because he wants to include some material not generally available in existing texts or because he feels that it is possible to present the material in a better manner or sequence. Both of these reasons prompted the writing of this text.

The material added includes an extensive discussion of changes that have taken place in the securities markets and their implications for the future; a consideration of the extensive empirical work done in the area of efficient capital markets; and a lengthy look at the analysis and management of fixed income securities, an area which has excited growing interest. The discussion of international diversification and stock options is more complete than that generally available elsewhere. Throughout the text, a concerted effort has been made to discuss the relevant empirical studies related to an area and to consider the implications of the results of these studies.

During the past decade, there have been two major theoretical advances in the investments area. One is portfolio theory and its subsequent evolution into capital market theory. The second is the efficient market hypothesis. Both of these have had major implications for the field of security analysis and portfolio management. Because of the importance of these theories, they are introduced early in the text so that they can be used in the analysis and management sections.

The text can be used for a beginning course in investments by undergraduate or graduate students who have had a basic financial management course and prerequisites in accounting and economics. The book can also be used, with supplementary readings, for a course in security analysis or portfolio management.

Obviously it is not possible to write a text like this without substantial help and support from a number of individuals. Special thanks is due to Michael D. Joehnk of Texas Tech, who sparked my interest in the area of bonds and helped write the three chapters on them (Chapters 16, 17, 18). I am also grateful to my associate at the University of Illinois, Kenneth J. Carey, who helped write the two chapters on portfolio theory and capital market theory (Chapters 19 and 20).

In addition, I had the benefit of some excellent reviewers who commented extensively on all parts of the text, including Robert Angell, East Carolina University; Kenneth J. Carey, the University of Illinois; Eugene F. Drzycimski, University of Wisconsin at Oshkosh; Joseph E. Finnerty, University of Massachusetts; Mary Lindahl-Stevens, University of Tennessee; and George Pinches, University of Kansas.

During the time when the text was being written and used in classes, I received many excellent suggestions from students, but I especially appreciated the help of Rupinder Sidhu, who cheerfully carried out numerous projects as the text neared completion. I have been very fortunate to have a number of friends in the investment community whom I refer to as my "contacts with reality": Ray Dixon, Goldman Sachs and Company; Phil Hummer, Wayne Hummer and Company; John Maginn, Mutual of Omaha; Richard McCabe and Barry Schnapel, Merrill Lynch, Pierce, Fenner and Smith; Robert Murray, First National Bank of Oregon; and Thomas V. Williams, Kemper Financial Services.

I cannot help but acknowledge the contribution of my good friend Jere Calmes, who helped me initiate the project one fateful night in Laramie, Wyoming, and of Paul Jones, the developmental editor, who kept the project moving. The final copy editing was done by Madelyn Roesch, who was both competent and a delight to work with. I was fortunate to have Daniel Tomcheff as the production editor to carry the project to completion.

Finally and most important is my family. This includes my own loving parents, who sacrificed for me, and my in-laws who raised my wonderful wife and encouraged me in my education. My greatest debt is to my wife and children, who understood my desire to do the book and helped me continue although it meant a loss of time with them.

Frank K. Reilly
University of Illinois at Urbana-Champaign
Urbana, Illinois
August 1978

Contents

Contents

ix

Part 1   *The Investment Background*

Introduction to Part 1

The chapters in this section are meant to give the reader a background in the total area of investments by answering the following questions:

Why do people invest?

What are some of the investments available?

How do securities markets function?

How and why are these securities markets changing?

How can you determine what common stocks are doing?

Where do you get relevant information on various potential investments?

In the first chapter we will consider why individuals invest and discuss in detail the factors that determine a person's required rate of return on an investment. The latter point will be very important in subsequent analyses. Because one of the most important tenets of investment theory is the need to diversify, in the second chapter we will discuss a number of alternative investment instruments and consider several studies of the rates of return and risk some of them involve.

In Chapter 3, we examine the function of markets in general, and of the securities markets specifically, concentrating on the markets for bonds and common stocks. There have been significant changes in the operation of the securities market since 1965, that are dealt with in Chapter 4, where we will also consider what the future may hold for these markets, and the implications for investors.

The behavior of the stock market is often measured in terms of changes in various stock market series. Because these series are used in a number of ways, in Chapter 5 we will examine them in depth, and compare several of them. The final chapter in this section contains a description of sources of information on various aspects of investments.

Before any analytical study can be attempted, a theoretical framework must be established. This is as true for the analysis of investments as it is for any other academic discipline. In the area of investments, several major theories that affected the way in which the entire subject is approached have been developed in the last 20 years. It is with these that Part Two is concerned.

Chapter 1   *The Investment Setting*

The Concept of Investment[1]

For most of our lives, we will be earning money. And we will want to purchase certain things. Usually, though, there will be an imbalance between our current money income and our consumption desires at any given point in time, and also in the future. We will have more money than we want to spend, or we will want more things than we can afford. In most cases, these imbalances will cause us to save either negative or positive amounts in order to maximize the benefits (utility) from our income.

When your current money income exceeds your current consumption desires, you will save the excess. You can put the savings under your mattress or bury it in the back yard until some future time when your consumption desires exceed current income. Or you may feel that it is worthwhile to give up the immediate possession of these savings for a future larger amount of money that will be used for consumption. This trade off of *present* consumption for a higher level of *future* consumption is the essence of saving and investment. In contrast, when your current money income is less than your current consumption desires, you will attempt to trade part of your *future* money income stream for a higher level of *current* consumption. Where current consumption desires exceed current money income, you engage in *negative saving,* commonly referred to as *borrowing.* The funds

---

[1]The discussion in this section draws heavily on Irving Fisher, *The Theory of Interest* (New York: Macmillan, 1930: reprinted Augustus M. Kelley, 1961); J. Hirshleifer, "Investment Decision Under Uncertainty: Choice—Theoretic Approaches," *Quarterly Journal of Economics,* Vol. 79, No. 4 (November, 1965), pp. 509–536; and Eugene F. Fama and Merton H. Miller, *The Theory of Finance* (New York: Holt, Rinehart and Winston, 1972), Chapter 1.

borrowed can be used for consumption *or* invested at rates of return above the cost of borrowing.

Obviously the individual who foregoes part of his current money income stream, and thereby defers current consumption, will want more than the same amount in the future. At the same time, the individual attempting to consume or invest more than his current income is willing to pay back more than a dollar in the future for a dollar today. The rate of exchange between *certain* future consumption (future dollars) and *certain* current consumption (current dollars) is the *pure rate of interest* or the *pure time value of money.* The rate of exchange between current and future consumption is established in the capital market and is influenced by the supply of excess income available to be invested at a point in time and the demand for excess consumption (borrowing). If the cost of exchanging 100 dollars of certain income today is $104 of certain income one year from today, the pure rate of exchange on a risk-free investment is said to be 4 percent (104/100 − 1).

The pure value of money is a "real" rate in that it indicates the increase in "real" goods and services desired. The investor is giving up 100 dollars of consumption today in order to consume $104 of goods and services *at today's prices.* If investors expect a change in prices, they will adjust their required rate of return to compensate for this change. If they expect prices to increase at the rate of 2 percent during the period of investment, one would expect them to increase their rate of exchange by this 2 percent (from 4 percent to 6 percent).

Finally, if an individual feels that the future payment is not certain, he will require a return which exceeds the pure time value of money plus the inflation rate. The amount required in excess of the pure time value of money plus the inflation rate is called a *risk premium.* Extending the example, when the investor is not certain about future repayment, he would require something in excess of $106 one year from today, possibly $110. In this example, the investor is requiring a 4 dollar, or 4 percent, risk premium.

Investment Defined

Following from the previous discussion, an investment is defined as *the current commitment of funds for a period of time in order to derive a future flow of funds that will compensate the investing unit for the time the funds are committed, for the expected rate of inflation, and also for the uncertainty involved in the future flow of funds.* This encompasses all types of investments, whether they be corporate investments in machinery, plant and equipment, government investments in flood control, or investments by individuals in stocks, bonds, commodities, or real estate. In all cases the investor is trading a *known* dollar amount today, for some *expected* future stream of payments or benefits that will exceed the current outlay by an amount which will compensate the investor for the time the funds are committed, for the expected changes in prices during the period, and the uncertainty involved in expected future cash flows.[2] The alternative investments that are considered by various investing units (corporations, governments, and individuals) noted above only differ with regard to the institutional characteristics of the investment and some unique factors which must be considered in the analysis (e.g., differential taxes).

Measures of Return and Risk

In our discussion we referred to the return derived from an investment and contended that this return is influenced by the uncertainty or risk involved. Prior to discussing specific factors that determine the required rate of return, it is necessary to briefly discuss how the return is measured. In addition, it is important to generate an operational definition of risk and determine how it is measured.

Measure of Return

The purpose of investing is to defer current consumption and thereby add to our wealth so that it will be possible to consume more in the future. Therefore, when we talk about a return on an investment, we are concerned with the increase in wealth resulting from this investment. As an example, if an investor commits 100 dollars to an investment at the beginning of a year and gets back 110 dollars at the end of the year, it can be said that the return on the investment (i.e., increase in wealth) was ten dollars. Because the actual dollar amount committed to alternative investments differs, it is typical to express a rate of return in terms of a relationship between the amount invested and the amount returned:

$$\text{Rate of Return} = \frac{\text{Ending Wealth} - \text{Beginning Wealth}}{\text{Beginning Wealth}}$$

$$= \frac{\$110 - \$100}{\$100} = \frac{\$10}{\$100} = 10\%$$

Many investments provide the investor with a flow of cash in addition to changing value while the funds are invested. These cash flows must also be considered an addition to wealth. And, because a particular investment may only be a portion of an investor's wealth, it is appropriate to consider

---

[2] It is recognized that the uncertainty involved is a function of the asset's unique uncertainty and also its relationship with all other assets in the investing unit's portfolio. The exact nature of this uncertainty is considered in detail in a later chapter. At this point it is only necessary to recognize that the investor requires that the expected cash flows compensate him for this uncertainty, however defined.

ADDITIONAL
FLOW OF CASH
WOULD BE
DIVIDENDS PAID

the rate of return on each investment. Therefore, a more general specification of rate of return is:

$$\text{Rate of Return} = \frac{\text{Ending Value} - \text{Beginning Value} + \text{Cash Flows}}{\text{Beginning Value}}$$

If we consider the prior example and add a 3 dollar cash flow to it, the rate of return would be:

$$\text{Rate of Return} = \frac{\$110 - 100 + 3}{100}$$

$$= \frac{10 + 3}{100} = \frac{13}{100} = 13\%$$

The rate of increase in wealth for this portion of the investor's portfolio would therefore be 13 percent. This *total* rate of return of 13 percent can be broken down into capital appreciation (the change in price) which was 10 percent, and dividend income, which was 3 percent.

Risk and Uncertainty

Although in a formal sense, there is a difference between risk and uncertainty, in the discussion that follows such a distinction will not be made since, in fact, there is a tendency to use the terms interchangeably or to use one term to explain the other. Risk is thought of as *uncertainty regarding the expected rate of return from an investment.* When an investor is considering an investment it is possible to ask what rate of return he "expects." The answer might be 10 percent, which is really a point estimate of his total expectation. If you were to press him further he might acknowledge that he is not certain of this return and he recognizes that, under certain conditions, the return might go as low as a minus 10 percent or as high as plus 25 percent. The point is, the larger the range of possible returns, the more uncertain the investor is regarding the actual return, and, therefore, the greater the risk.

It is possible to determine how certain an investor is regarding the expected rate of return on an investment by analyzing the probability distribution of expected returns. A probability distribution indicates the *possible* returns and assigns probabilities to each of them. The probabilities of a specified return range from zero (no chance of this return) to one (complete certainty). The probabilities that can be assigned to a particular return are either subjective estimates by the investor or are based upon past frequencies (e.g., about 30 percent of the time the return on this particular investment was 10 percent). Let us begin with an example of perfect certainty, i.e., the investor is supposedly certain of a return of 5 percent.

This can be envisioned as:

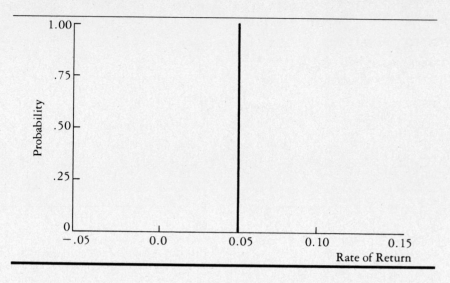

In the case of certainty there is only one possible return and the probability of receiving that return is 1.0. The *expected* return from an investment is defined as:

$$\text{Expected Return} = \sum (\text{Probability of Return})\,(\text{Possible Return})$$
$$= \sum (Pi)\,(Ri)$$

In this case it would be:

$$\text{Expected Return} = (1.0)\,(.05) = .05$$

An alternative example would be a case in which an investor felt several rates of return were possible under different conditions. If there is a strong economic environment with high corporate profits and little or no inflation, the investor may feel that his return on common stock could be as high as 20 percent. In contrast, if there is an economic decline and a higher than average rate of inflation similar to what happened during 1974, he might feel that the return on common stock could be a negative 20 percent. Finally, the investor may feel that, if there is no major change in the economic environment, the return on common stock will approach the long run average of 10 percent. The investor's estimated probabilities for each of these potential states based upon past experience are as follows:

State of Nature	Probability	Rate of Return
Strong Economy—No Inflation	.15	.20
Weak Economy—Above Average Inflation	.15	−.20
No major change	.70	.10

This set of potential outcomes can be visualized as follows:

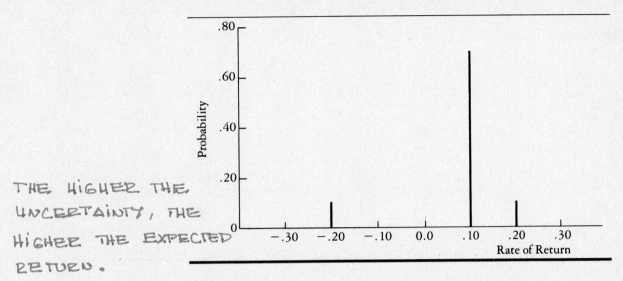

THE HiGHER THE
UNCERTAINTY, THE
HiGHER THE EXPECTED
RETURN.

The computation of the expected rate of return is as follows:

$$\text{Expected Rate of Return} = (.15)(.20) + (.15)(-.20) + (.70)(.10)$$
$$= (.03) + (-.03) + (.07)$$
$$= .07$$

Obviously, the investor is more uncertain regarding this investment than he was with the prior investment with a single possible return. One can visualize an investment with ten possible outcomes ranging from minus 40 percent to plus 50 percent with equal probabilities for each rate of return. A graph of such a set of expectations would look like this:

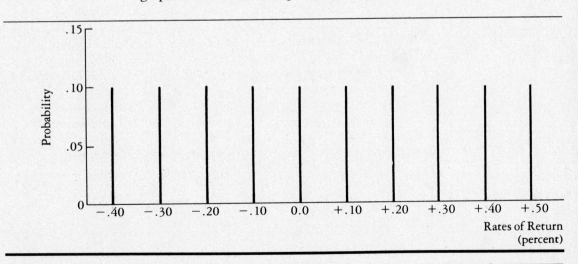

In this case there are numerous outcomes from a wide range of possibilities. The expected return would be:

$$
\begin{aligned}
\text{Expected Rate of Return} &= (.10)(-.40) + (.10)(-.30) + (.10)(-.20) \\
&\quad + (.10)(-.10) + (.10)(0.0) + (.10)(.10) + \\
&\quad (.10)(.20) + (.10)(.30) + (.10)(.40) + (.10) \\
&\quad (.50) \\
&= (-.04) + (-.03) + (-.02) + (-.01) + \\
&\quad (.00) + (.01) + (.02) + (.03) + (.04) + (.05) \\
&= .05
\end{aligned}
$$

Note that the expected rate is the same as it was in the certainty case, but the investor is obviously not very certain about what the actual return will be. This would be considered a high risk investment.

Measure of Risk

The prior discussion indicated that the uncertainty or risk of an investment can be derived by determining the range of possible outcomes and the probability of each occurring. What is needed now is a *measure* of the dispersion of returns. There are several possible measures, including simply the range of the distribution. Another possible measure that has received support in some theoretical work on portfolio theory is *the variance* of the estimated distribution of expected returns, or the square root of the variance, i.e., *the standard deviation* of the distribution. These statistics are meant as indicators of deviations of possible returns from the expected return and are computed as follows:

$$
\begin{aligned}
\text{Variance } (\sigma^2) &= \sum(\text{Probability})(\text{Possible Return}-\text{Expected Return})^2 \\
&= \sum(Pi)(Ri-\bar{R})^2
\end{aligned}
$$

The larger the variance, everything else remaining constant, the greater the dispersion of expectations and the greater the uncertainty or risk of the investment.

The variance for the perfect certainty example would be as follows:

$$
\begin{aligned}
(\sigma^2) &= \sum Pi(Ri-\bar{R})^2 \\
&= 1.0(.05-.05)^2 = 1.0(0.0) = 0
\end{aligned}
$$

Note that in the case of perfect certainty there is *no variance of return* because there is *no deviation from expectations* and, therefore, *no risk or uncertainty*.

The variance for the second example would be:

$$
\begin{aligned}
\sigma^2 &= \sum Pi(Ri-\bar{R})^2 \\
&= [(.15)(-.20-.07)^2 + (.15)(.20-.07)^2 + (.70)(.10-.07)^2]
\end{aligned}
$$

$$= (.15) (-.27)^2 + (.15) (.13)^2 + (.70) (.03)^2$$
$$= (.15) (.0729) + (.15) (.0169) + (.70) (.0009)$$
$$= .010935 + .002535 + .00063$$
$$= .0201$$

As noted, the standard deviation is the square root of the variance and so is equal to:

$$\text{Standard Deviation} = \sqrt{\sum P_i(R_i - \overline{R})^2}$$

In some cases, an unadjusted variance, or standard deviation, can be misleading if all else is not held constant, i.e., there are major differences in the mean rate of return. In such cases, a popular measure of *relative variability* is the Coefficient of Variation:

$$\text{Coefficient of Variation} = \text{Standard Deviation of Returns/Expected Returns}$$

$$CV = \frac{\sigma_i}{\overline{R}_i}$$

It is generally assumed that investors are *risk averse.* This means that if they are given a choice between two investments that both have an expected return of 5 percent, and for one the standard deviation of the probability distribution is .001, while the standard deviation for the second distribution is .1, the investor would choose the investment with the smaller standard deviation (smaller risk).

Determinants of Required Rates of Return

Once an individual has excess income (savings), and decides that he wants to invest it, the rate of return for the investment instrument selected (savings account, bond, stock, real estate, etc.) becomes a crucial question. There are two important points to consider regarding required rates of return. First, *the overall level of required rates of return for all investments changes dramatically over time.* An example of such changes can be seen in what happened to the promised yield on Moody's Aaa corporate bonds (the highest grade corporate bonds), which was over 5 percent during the 1930's, declined to about 3 percent in the 1940's, and rose to over 9 percent in the mid-1970's.[3] Obviously, it is important to understand why the required rate on a security changes over time. The second point regarding required returns is that *there is a wide range of required returns for alternative*

---

[3] For a graph of the long-term rates extending back to the 1920's see *Historical Chart Book* (Board of Governors of the Federal Reserve System, 1978).

investments. As an example, Table 1–1 contains a list of promised yields on alternative bonds:

Table 1–1
Promised Yields on Alternative Bonds

Type of Bond	1974	1975	1976	1977
U.S. Govt.—3 month Treasury Bills	7.84	5.80	4.98	5.27
U.S. Govt.—long-term	6.99	6.98	6.78	7.06
Aaa Utility	9.34	9.41	8.49	8.19
Aaa Corporate	8.57	8.83	8.43	8.02
Baa Corporate	9.50	10.61	9.75	8.97

Source: *Federal Reserve Bulletin*, various issues

The point is, all of these are bonds and yet the yields differ significantly. One could detect even greater differences in expected returns if one could observe promised yields on common stock, real estate, etc.

Because the required returns on all investments change over time, and because of the large differences in required rates of return for alternative investments, investors should be aware of what determines the required return.

The Risk-Free Rate[4]

The risk-free rate (RFR) is the basic exchange rate assuming no uncertainty of future flows, i.e., the investor knows with certainty what cash flows he will receive and when he will receive them. There is no probability of default on the investment. Earlier this was referred to as the pure time value of money because the only sacrifice on the part of the lender was that he gave up the use of the money (consumption) for a period of time. This rate of interest is the price charged for the exchange between current goods (consumption) and future goods. There are two factors, one psychological and one objective, that influence this price. The subjective factor is the *time preference of individuals for the consumption of income.* When individuals give up 100 dollars of consumption this year, how much consumption do they want a year from now to compensate for this sacrifice? The level of this human desire for consumption influences the rate of compensation required. The time preference will vary among individuals with a composite rate determined by the market. While this composite time preference rate will change over time, one would expect any aggregate changes to be gradual and slow.

The objective factor that influences the risk-free rate is *the investment opportunities available in the economy.* The investment opportunities are a function of the long-run real growth rate of the economy. Therefore, a

---

[4] This subsection draws heavily from Irving Fisher, *The Theory of Interest,* chapters 4, 7, and 16.

change in the long-run growth rate causes a change in all investment opportunities and a change in the returns on all investments. The factors that influence the growth rate of the economy are similar to those that determine the growth rate of any economic unit: the resources invested in the unit, and the returns derived from these resources. For an economy, the major resources invested are capital, population growth, and natural resources. As any or all of these increase, there should be an increase in the growth of the economy, other factors being held constant. Further, the productivity of the capital and resources invested is affected by the education of the population and changes in labor productivity due to technological advancement. An increase in the level of education or technology will increase the marginal productivity of the resources retained by individuals or business firms and thereby increase the long-run real growth rate of the economy. As the investment opportunities in an economy increase or decrease due to changes in the long-run real growth rate, the risk-free rate of return should likewise increase or decrease, i.e., there is a *positive* relationship between the investment opportunities in an economy and the RFR. Again, while investment opportunities and, therefore, the RFR can change over time, one would expect these changes to be slow and gradual.

① EASE OR TIGHTNESS IN THE CAPITAL MARKET.
② EXPECTED RATE OF INFLATION.

Factors Influencing the Nominal (Money) Rate on Risk-Free Investments

Because the factors that determine the level of the risk-free rate are long-term variables that change only gradually, one might expect the required rate on a risk-free investment to be quite stable over time. As noted previously, this has *not* been true for long-term government bonds over the period from 1930 through 1977. A more specific example can be derived from an analysis of the average yield on U.S. Government Treasury Bills for the period 1967–1977. This analysis is appropriate because Government T-Bills are a prime example of a default-free investment, owing to the government's unlimited ability to derive income from taxes or the creation of money.

Table 1–2
Average Yields on U.S. Government Three Month Treasury Bills

1967	4.29	1972	4.07
1968	5.34	1973	7.03
1969	6.67	1974	7.84
1970	6.39	1975	5.80
1971	4.33	1976	4.98
		1977	5.27

Source: *Federal Reserve Bulletin,* various issues

Especially notable is the steady increase in 1968 and 1969 followed by a sharp decline in 1971 and a mammoth increase (75 percent) in 1973. The nominal (money) rate of interest on a default-free investment is definitely *not* stable in the long-run or the short-run, even though the underlying determinants of the RFR *are* quite stable. Therefore, it is important to consider the other factors that influence the *nominal* risk-free rate. Recall that these nominal rates are also referred to as money rates or market rates. The two factors that influence the *market* rates are relative ease or tightness in the capital market, and the expected rate of inflation.

Relative Ease or Tightness

This is a short-run phenomenon that is caused by a temporary disequilibrium in the supply and demand of future income streams or capital. As an example, starting from a point of equilibrium in the capital market, one can visualize a disruption caused by a change in monetary policy as evidenced by a sharp decrease in the growth rate of the money supply. In the short-run, assuming no immediate adjustment in demand, there would be relative tightness and interest rates would increase. If one assumes a relatively stable supply of funds and a sudden increase in the government's demand for capital because of an increase in the deficit, there would also be an increase in money rates reflecting the relative tightness. Therefore, the market rate on risk-free investments can change in the short-run because of temporary ease or tightness in the capital market. One would expect this to be a short-term effect because in the long-run the higher or lower rates would affect supply and demand.

Expected Inflation[5]

Up to this point the discussion has been in "real" terms, unaffected by changes in the price level. In discussing the rate of exchange between current consumption and future consumption it was assumed that the 4 percent required return meant that the investor was willing to give up one dollar of consumption today in order to consume $1.04 worth of goods and services one year from now. The exchange rate assumed *no change in prices,* so a 4 percent increase in money wealth would mean a 4 percent increase in potential consumption of goods and services. If the price level is going to increase during the period of investment, investors should increase their required rate of return by the rate of inflation to compensate. Assume that an investor wants a 4 percent rate of return on a risk-free investment. The 4 percent required return is a "real" required rate of return. Assuming the investor expects prices to increase by 3 percent during the period of the investment, we would expect him to increase his required rate of return by approximately the same amount, to about 7 percent $[(1.04 \times 1.03) - 1]$. If the investor does not increase his required return he will receive 104 dollars at the end of the year. But because prices have increased by 3 percent during the year, what cost 100 dollars now costs 103 dollars and the investor can only consume about one percent more at the end of the year ($104/103 - 1$). His ability to consume "real" goods and services has only increased by about

---

[5] This section draws heavily on Fisher, *The Theory of Interest,* chapter 2.

one percent, and his "real" return is only one percent, not 4 percent. If he had required a 7 percent nominal return (in current dollars), his real consumption would have increased by 4 percent (107/103 − 1). Therefore, an investor's *nominal* required rate of return (in current dollars) on a risk-free investment is:

$$\text{Nominal RFR} = (1 + \text{RFR}) (1 + \text{Expected Rate of Inflation})$$

The nominal (market) rate of interest on a risk-free investment is not a good estimate of the "real" RFR because it can be changed dramatically in the short-run by temporary ease or tightness in the capital market and in the long-run by expected inflation. Albert Burger of the St. Louis Federal Reserve developed a model to explain short-term interest rates that included growth of the monetary base (a proxy for the supply of funds); state of economic activity (demand for funds), and actual and expected rate of inflation.[6] The model did an excellent job of explaining past movements in short-term rates. Prior to the Burger study, Yohe and Karnosky examined the relation between interest rates and past inflation and derived preliminary estimates of a "real" rate of interest of between 3 and 3.5 percent for the period 1952–1969.[7]

The Common Effect

Note that all the factors discussed thus far regarding the required rate of return *affect all investments equally.* Irrespective of whether the concern is with stocks, bonds, real estate, or machine tools, if the expected rate of inflation increases from 2 percent to 6 percent, the required return on all investments should increase by 4 percent. On the other hand, if there is a general easing in the capital market because of an increase in the rate of growth of the money supply that causes a decline in the market RFR of one percent, then the required return on all investments will decline by one percent.

TYPES: { 1 - BUSINESS 2 - FINANCIAL 3 - LIQUIDITY.

A Risk Premium

A risk-free investment was defined as one for which the investor is certain of the amount and timing of his income stream. In contrast, an actual investor is not certain of the income he will receive, when he will receive it, or if he will receive it. Not only is there uncertainty involved in most investments, but there is a wide spectrum of uncertainty running from basically risk-free

---

[6] Albert E. Burger, "An Explanation of Movements in Short-Term Interest Rates," St. Louis Federal Reserve *Review,* Vol. 58, No. 7 (July, 1976), pp. 10–22.

[7] William P. Yohe and Denis S. Karnosky, "Interest Rates and Price Level Changes, 1952–69," St. Louis Federal Reserve *Review,* Vol. 51, No. 12 (December, 1969), pp. 18–38.

items such as government T-Bills to highly uncertain items like the common stock of small companies engaged in speculative operations such as oil exploration. Because most investors do not like uncertainty, they will require an additional return on an investment to compensate for the uncertainty. This additional required return is referred to as a *risk premium* that is added to the nominal RFR. While the risk premium is a composite of all uncertainty, it is possible to consider several major sources of uncertainty. The three major ones discussed most frequently are: business risk, financial risk, and liquidity risk.

Business Risk is uncertainty of income flows caused by the nature of the firm's business. When someone, a firm or an individual, borrows money, his ability to repay the loan and pay interest on it is a function of the certainty of his income flows. As the income flows of the borrower become more uncertain, the uncertainty of the flows to the lender increases. Therefore, the lender will consider the basic pattern of income flows he receives and assign a risk premium on the basis of this distribution of flows. An example of a borrower with no uncertainty of income flows is the U.S. Government because of its power to tax. In contrast there is the small oil drilling firm which has a potential range of returns from a large probability of no income to a small probability of a very large income. This uncertainty of income caused by the basic business of the firm is typically measured by the distribution of the firm's operating income over time; i.e., the more volatile the firm's operating income over time relative to its mean income, the greater the business risk.[8]

In turn, the firm's operating income volatility is a function of its sales volatility and its operating leverage. Assuming a constant profit margin, if sales fluctuate over time, operating income will fluctuate. Hence, one can consider sales volatility the prime determinant of operating earnings volatility (business risk). One must also consider the production function of the firm; if all production costs are variable costs, then operating income will vary according to sales variability. In contrast, if some costs are fixed, (e.g., depreciation, administration, research), then operating income will be more volatile than sales. Depending upon where the firm is operating relative to its break-even point, its earnings can increase by more than sales during good times and decline by more than sales during bad times. This effect of fixed costs on the volatility of operating earnings is referred to as *operating leverage*.[9] Therefore, a firm's business risk is measured in terms of

---

[8] For a more detailed discussion of the measure see J. Fred Weston and Eugene F. Brigham, *Managerial Finance,* 5th Ed. (Hinsdale, Ill.: The Dryden Press, 1975), pp. 314–320; and James C. Van Horne, *Financial Management and Policy,* 4th Ed. (Englewood Cliffs, N.J.: Prentice-Hall, Inc., 1977), pp. 114–124.

[9] For a general discussion of operating leverage see Eugene Brigham, *Financial Management* (Hinsdale, Ill.: The Dryden Press, 1977), pp. 557–561. For an analysis of the effects see

the coefficient of variation of operating earnings. In turn, operating earnings volatility is a function of sales volatility and operating leverage.

Business Risk = f(Volatility of Operating Earnings)

Operating Earnings Volatility = f(Sales Volatility; Operating Leverage)

Financial Risk is the uncertainty introduced by the method of financing an investment. If a firm uses equity to finance a project, there is only business risk involved; the variability of income to the ultimate owner is the same as the variability of operating income (assuming a constant tax rate). If, in addition to using equity, a firm borrows money to help finance an investment, it introduces fixed financing charges (interest) that must be paid prior to paying the owners (the equity holders). As a result, the uncertainty of returns (variability) increases because of the method of financing the investment. This increase in uncertainty due to fixed cost financing is referred to as *financial risk* and causes investors to increase their risk premium.[10]

Liquidity Risk is the uncertainty introduced by the secondary market for an investment. When an investor gives up current consumption (commits funds) by investing, there is an expectation that, at some future time, the investment will mature (as with a bond), or that the investor will be able to sell it to someone else (convert it into cash) and use the proceeds for current consumption or other investments. Given a desire to liquidate an investment (convert it into the most liquid of all assets—cash) the investor is faced with two uncertainties: (1) how long will it take to make the conversion?; and (2) what price will be received? There is similar uncertainty for a buyer: how long will it take to acquire the asset and what will be the price? *The ability to buy or sell an investment quickly without a substantial price concession is known as liquidity.*[11] The greater the uncertainty regarding whether the investment can be bought or sold or the greater the price concession required to buy or sell it, the greater the liquidity risk. An example of an asset with almost no liquidity risk would be a United States Government Treasury Bill. A treasury bill can be bought or sold in minutes at a price almost identical to the quoted price. Purchase or conversion into cash is almost instantaneous and the price is known with almost perfect

---

Frank K. Reilly and Roger Bent, "A Specification, Measurement and Analysis of Operating Leverage," Financial Management Meeting (October, 1974), University of Illinois Working Paper No. 257.

[10] For a detailed discussion of financial leverage and financial risk see Weston and Brigham, *Managerial Finance,* chapter 18 and Van Horne, *Financial Management and Policy,* pp. 725–730.

[11] For a discussion of a measure of liquidity applied to common stocks, see Michael D. Hirsch, "Liquidity Filters: Tools for Better Performance," *Journal of Portfolio Management,* Vol. 2, No. 1 (Fall, 1975), pp. 46–50.

certainty. In contrast, an example of an illiquid asset would be a specialized machine or a parcel of real estate in a remote area. In both cases it might take a considerable period of time to find a potential seller or buyer and the expected selling price could vary substantially from expectations; i.e., the selling price is uncertain because it is a "unique" investment.

The risk premium on an investment is, therefore, determined by the basic uncertainty of income flows to the investor. The specific factors influencing this uncertainty are sales volatility and operating leverage (business risk), any added uncertainty of flows caused by how the investment is financed (financial risk), and the uncertainty involved in buying or selling the investment (liquidity risk).[12]

Risk Premium = f(Business Risk; Financial Risk; Liquidity Risk)

Risk Premium and Portfolio Theory

An alternative view of risk has been derived based upon extensive work in portfolio theory and capital market theory by Markowitz, Sharpe, and others, which is dealt with in greater detail later, but should be mentioned briefly. Their work indicated that investors should use an external market measure of risk. It has been shown that all rational, profit maximizing investors want to hold a completely diversified portfolio of risky assets, called the market portfolio, and they borrow or lend to arrive at the desired risk level. Under such conditions, the relevant risk measure for an individual asset is its *comovement with the market portfolio*. This covariance with the market portfolio of risky assets is referred to as an asset's *systematic risk*. It is that portion of an individual asset's total variance that is attributable to the variability of the total market portfolio. In addition, individual assets have variance that is due to unique features called *unsystematic* variance. This is not generally considered to be important because it is eliminated in any large portfolio composed of different earning assets. At the same time, if an investor's portfolio is not large and well diversified this unsystematic variability will be important. Still, it is typically assumed that investors can become diversified by acquiring shares of an investment company that owns a portfolio of assets.

Therefore, under these assumptions *the risk premium for an individual earning asset is a function of the asset's systematic risk with the aggregate market portfolio of risky assets.*

Risk Premium = f(Systematic Market Risk)

---

[12] For an empirical analysis of factors influencing the risk premium on bonds see Lawrence Fisher, "Determinants of Risk Premiums on Corporate Bonds," *Journal of Political Economy*, Vol. 67, No. 3 (June, 1959), pp. 217–237. For an application to common stock see Fred D. Arditti, "Risk and the Required Return on Equity," *Journal of Finance*, Vol. 22, No. 1 (March, 1967), pp. 19–36.

For those concerned with an apparent conflict between the two views, a number of studies have examined the relationship between the market measure of risk (systematic risk) and numerous corporate accounting variables used to measure business risk, financial risk, and liquidity. These studies have generally concluded that there is a significant relationship between the two measures.[13] Therefore, the two definitions of risk are not contradictory, but are parallel and complementary. It seems logical that, in a properly functioning capital market, the market measure of risk will reflect all the risk characteristics of the asset, not only internal risk but also external liquidity characteristics.

Therefore, one can say:

Risk Premium = f(Business Risk; Financial Risk; Liquidity Risk)

or

Risk Premium = f(Systematic Market Risk)

Summary of Required Return

The overall required rate of return on alternative investments is determined by three major sets of variables. The first is the economy's RFR which is influenced by the investment opportunities in the economy (i.e., the long-run real growth rate) and investors' time preferences for consumption. These factors are generally quite stable and change only gradually. The second set of variables influences the market rate on risk-free investments and includes short-run ease or tightness in the capital market and expected changes in the price level (inflation). *The first two sets of variables are the same for all investments.* The final set are those variables that influence the risk premium on investments, which is the factor that causes differences among investments. One can visualize the risk premium as being affected by business risk, financial risk, and liquidity risk. One can also envision the risk premium as a function of a composite market risk variable derived from portfolio theory and referred to as systematic risk. Therefore:

1 — Required Rate of Return
    Risk-Free Rate
        Time Preference for Consumption
        Investment Opportunities (Long-run real growth rate)

2 — Factors Influencing the Market RFR
    Ease or Tightness of Capital Market
    Expected Rate of Inflation

---

[13] This will be discussed more fully in later chapters. A brief review of several of these is contained in Donald J. Thompson II, "Sources of Systematic Risk in Common Stocks," *Journal of Business,* Vol. 49, No. 2 (April, 1976), pp. 173–188.

3 — Risk Premium
  Business risk
  Financial Risk
  Liquidity Risk
  or
  Systematic Risk

Relationship between Risk and Return

To better illustrate the foregoing material, this section contains a graph of the relationship between risk and return with an emphasis on what causes changes in required returns over time. The basic relationship is shown in Figure 1–1.

Figure 1–1
Relationship between Risk and Return

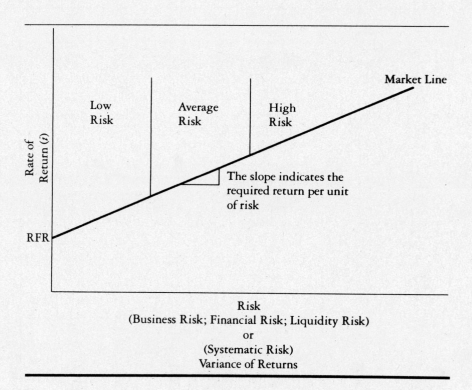

This graph indicates that investors want the risk-free return on riskless investments and that they increase their required return as perceived uncertainty increases. As noted, the slope of the market line indicates the composite return per unit of risk required by all investors. Investors who are more risk averse would have a steeper line, while others would be willing to accept a lower slope.

Given the market line indicating the average relationship, investors select investments that are consistent with their risk preferences. Some will only consider low risk, while others will welcome high risk investments.

Figure 1–2 indicates what happens to the market line when the notion of ease or tightness in the capital market or expected inflation is considered.

Figure 1–2
Effect of Capital Market on Investment Risk

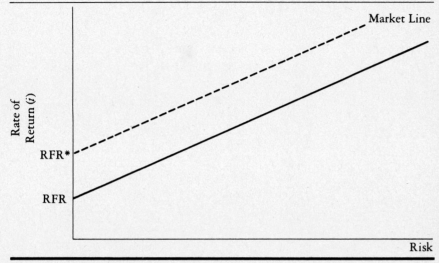

RFR* = nominal risk-free rate

The dotted line indicates a parallel shift in the market line that is caused by either temporary tightness in the capital market or an increase in the expected rate of inflation. The parallel shift in the line reflects the fact that these changes affect all investments, irrespective of their level of risk.

Summary

Individuals have expected income streams and patterns of desired consumption. Except in rare cases, these streams of income and desired consumption do not match. Therefore, there are certain economic units that have more income than they want to consume (savings) and they are willing to trade current consumption for a larger amount of future consumption. In contrast, others have more current consumption desires than income and want to dis-save (borrow future income). The rate of exchange between current and future consumption, assuming no risk, is the time value of money.

Because the required rate of return differs substantially between alternative investments and the required return on specific investments changes over time, it is important to examine the factors that influence the required rate of return on investments. The three major variables affecting it are the RFR, factors that influence the market rate on risk-free investments (most notably inflation), and the risk premium. The required rate of return on all investments is changed by changes in the RFR, by market ease or tightness, or by changes in the expected rate of inflation. Therefore the factor causing all differences *between* investments at a point in time is the risk premium.

Questions

1. Why do people invest? Be specific regarding when they are willing to invest and what they are looking for in the future.

2. Define an investment.

3. Why do people engage in negative saving, i.e., dis-save? Be specific.

4. As a student are you saving or dis-saving? What do you expect to derive from this activity?

5. Divide a person's life from ages 20 to 70 into ten-year segments and discuss what the saving or dis-saving patterns during each of these periods are likely to be and why.

6. Would you expect the saving–dis-saving pattern to differ by occupation, e.g., for a doctor versus a plumber? Why or why not?

7. It was reported in the Wall Street Journal that the yield on common stocks is about 4 percent, while a study at the University of Chicago contends that the rate of return on common stocks has averaged about 9 percent. Reconcile these statements.

8. The variance of the distribution of expected rates of return has been suggested as a good measure of uncertainty. What is the reasoning behind this measure, i.e., what is its purpose? Discuss.

9. What are the three *major* determinants of an investor's required rate of return on an investment? Discuss each of these briefly.

10. Discuss the two major factors that determine the market's risk-free rate (RFR). Which of these factors would you expect to be more volatile over the business cycle? Why?

11. Discuss the three factors that contribute to the risk premium of an investment.

12. You own stock in the Edgar Company and you notice that after a recent bond offering their debt/equity ratio has gone from 30 percent to 45 percent. What effect will this change have on the variability of the net income stream, other factors being constant? Discuss. Would you change your required rate of return on the common stock of the Edgar Company? Discuss.

13. You are told that the rate of return on bonds is below that on stocks. Also, the average return on the stock of small companies is above the return on the stock of large firms. Do these revelations surprise you? Why or why not? Discuss.

14. Discuss in nontechnical terms why you would change your nominal required rate of return if you expected the rate of inflation to go from zero rate (no inflation) to a 7 percent rate.

15. Assume the long-run growth rate in the economy increased by 1 percent and the expected rate of inflation increased by 4 percent. What would happen to the required rate of return on government bonds; common stocks; and real estate? How would the effect differ? Show this graphically.

References

Arditti, Fred D. "Risk and the Required Return on Equity." *Journal of Finance*, Vol. 22, No. 1 (March, 1967).

Brigham, Eugene F. *Financial Management*. Hinsdale, Ill.: The Dryden Press, 1977.

Burger, Albert E. "An Explanation of Movements in Short-Term Interest Rates." St. Louis Federal Reserve *Review*, Vol. 58, No. 7 (July, 1976).

Fama, Eugene F. and Miller, Merton H. *The Theory of Finance*. New York: Holt, Rinehart and Winston, 1972.

Fisher, Irving. *The Theory of Interest*. New York: Macmillan, 1930; reprinted Augustus M. Kelley, 1961.

Fisher, Lawrence. "Determinants of Risk Premiums on Corporate Bonds." *Journal of Political Economy*, Vol. 67, No. 3 (June, 1959).

Hirsch, Michael D. "Liquidity Filters: Tools for Better Performance." *Journal of Portfolio Management*, Vol. 2, No. 1 (Fall, 1975).

Hirshleifer, J. "Investment Decision under Uncertainty: Choice—Theoretic Approaches." *Quarterly Journal of Economics*, Vol. 29, No. 4 (November, 1965).

Historical Chart Book, Board of Governors of the Federal Reserve System.

Reilly, Frank K. and Bent, Roger. "A Specification, Measurement and Analysis of Operating Leverage." Working Paper No. 257, University of Illinois (June, 1975).

Thompson, Donald J. II. "Sources of Systematic Risk in Common Stocks." *Journal of Business*, Vol. 49, No. 2 (April, 1976).

Van Horne, James C. *Financial Management and Policy*. 4th Ed. Englewood Cliffs, N.J.: Prentice-Hall, Inc., 1977.

Weston, J. Fred and Brigham, Eugene F. *Managerial Finance*. 5th Ed. Hinsdale, Ill.: The Dryden Press, 1975.

Yohe, William P. and Karnosky, Denis S. "Interest Rates and Price Level Changes, 1952–1969." St. Louis Federal Reserve *Review*, Vol. 51, No. 12 (December, 1969).

Chapter 2   *Alternative Investments—*
A Brief Overview

In any book on investments, the emphasis is usually on common stocks. Although this is also true, to a great extent, of the book in your hands, at the outset you should be aware that *there are numerous investment instruments available and the astute investor should consider a broad range of alternatives.* The principles of valuation and portfolio management discussed here are applicable to a variety of investments, with which we will deal. In some cases there may be problems in deriving inputs for the valuation models, but the concept will be the same.

One of the main reasons that investors should consider numerous different investments is that they can derive substantial benefits from *diversification.* In the context of investments diversification means *owning alternative investments with different return patterns over time* such that when one investment is yielding a low or negative rate of return, another investment will hopefully be enjoying above normal returns. The overall result is relatively stable earnings for the collection of investments (also referred to as the portfolio). Several subsequent chapters contain a discussion of the principle of diversification in greater detail. At this point it is important only to recognize that proper diversification results in less variability in the rates of return for a portfolio over time and, therefore, helps reduce the uncertainty or risk of the portfolio. Investors should consider a variety of investment instruments in order to diversify their portfolio so that the rates of return for the total portfolio will yield a relatively stable earnings pattern over time. The intent is obviously to find investments with different earnings patterns (hopefully almost exactly opposite to one another) such that when one earnings stream is down the other is up and vice versa.

Types of Investments

The purpose of this chapter is to briefly discuss some of the major investment alternatives that all investors should consider for their portfolios. It will become apparent that some are not appropriate for particular investors given their individual risk or liquidity preferences. Hopefully, though, exposure to the numerous alternatives will ensure that an investor considers the full range and does not miss some very worthwhile and interesting investment opportunities. We will begin our discussion with the most obvious alternatives, bonds and stocks, but will eventually consider some rather unusual possibilities, as well as the rates of return on a number of the investments.

Fixed Income Investments

Within this category are investments that have a *fixed payment schedule*. With securities of this type, the owner is guaranteed specific payments at predetermined times, although the legal force behind the guarantee varies. At one extreme, if the contractual payment is not made at the appointed time, the firm can be declared bankrupt. In other cases, the payments must be made only if earned (an income bond), while in some instances the payment does not have to be made unless the board of directors votes for it (preferred stock).

Savings Accounts

It is probably not necessary to describe savings accounts except to indicate that they are an example of a fixed income investment. When an individual deposits funds in a savings account at a bank or savings and loan association, he is really lending money to the institution in order to derive a fixed payment. Such investments are considered very low risk, convenient, and liquid. Therefore, the rate of return is generally low compared to other alternatives.

Debentures (Bonds)

A debenture is a financial instrument that the government or a private institution uses to borrow money from investors, promising to make stipulated payments (interest payments) for a number of years and to pay the face amount of the loan at some maturity date. Typically, there is no collateral put up and the lender is dependent upon the success of the borrower to receive the promised payments. Debenture owners usually have first call on the earnings and assets of a firm. If an interest payment is not made, the debenture owners can declare the firm bankrupt and claim the assets of the firm to pay off the bonds. The reader should recognize that a bond can take an almost unlimited variety of potential forms.

Mortgage Bonds These bonds are similar to debentures except that there are specific assets pledged as backing for them in case of bankruptcy. Railroad bonds that are backed by specific pieces of rolling stock, e.g., boxcars, are an example.

Income Bonds Income bonds have a stipulated coupon and interest payment schedule, but the interest is only due and payable *if the company earns the interest payment* prior to the stipulated date. If the required amount is not earned, the interest payment does not have to be made and the firm cannot be declared bankrupt. Instead, the interest payment is considered in arrears and, if subsequently earned, it must be paid off. Given the lack of legal guarantees, an income bond is not considered as safe as a debenture or a mortgage bond.

Municipal Bonds Municipal bonds are similar to the bonds mentioned earlier, except that they are issued by municipalities (states, cities, towns, etc.). Municipal bonds can be general obligation bonds that are comparable to corporate debentures since the full taxing power of the municipality is used to pay for them. There are municipal revenue bonds for which the revenue comes from a particular project (e.g. sewer bonds for which the revenue comes from water taxes).

A major distinguishing feature of municipal bonds is that *they are tax-exempt* which means that the interest earned is exempt from taxation by the federal government, and also by the state that issued the bond, if the investor is a resident of that state. This feature is important to investors in high tax brackets. Assume that an individual has an income such that his marginal tax rate is 60 percent. If he buys a regular bond with an interest rate of 8 percent, because he must pay 60 percent tax on this income, his net return after taxes is only 3.2 percent ($.08 \times [1 - .60]$). Such an investor would be better off with a tax-free bond that had a yield of 5 percent. As a result, yields on municipal bonds are below yields on comparable taxable bonds (the yield is generally about 60–70 percent of the yield on taxable bonds).[1]

Convertible Bonds Convertible bonds have all the characteristics of other bonds with the added feature that *they can be converted into the common stock of the company that issued the bond.* A firm could issue a 1,000 dollar face value bond and stipulate that owners of the bond could, at their discretion, convert the bond into 40 shares of common stock. Such bonds are considered very attractive, especially when issued by growth firms. In this case, investors acquire an investment with a fixed income feature, but also have the potential opportunity to convert the bond into the common stock of the firm and become an owner if the company does well. The interest rates on convertible bonds are generally lower than those on comparable straight

[1] A recent and readable article on the subject is "Investing in Tax-Exempts," *Business Week* (July 25, 1977), pp. 127–129.

debentures of the firm. The greater the growth potential of the company, the greater the yield differential because the conversion potential is of greater value.[2]

Preferred Stock

Preferred stock is a fixed income security because a payment for each year, based upon a coupon (e.g., 5 percent of the face value) or a stated dollar amount (e.g., 5 dollars preferred), is stipulated. The major difference between preferred stock and bonds is that the payment stipulated on the former is not legally binding and, for each period, must be voted on by the firm's board of directors as is a common stock dividend. Even if the firm earned enough money to pay the dividend, the board of directors could vote to withhold it and, because most preferred is cumulative preferred, the dividend would accumulate and no common stock dividends could be paid until this accumulated dividend payment was eliminated.

Although preferred dividends are not legally binding, they are considered binding in a practical sense because of the credit implications of a missed dividend. Also the payments are not tax deductible expenses like the interest on bonds. As a consequence, preferred stock has not been a very popular source of financing for corporations except utilities. Ignoring the latter category, they constitute less than 3 percent of all new corporate financing. At the same time, because of the law which allows corporations to exclude 85 percent of dividends from taxable income, preferred stocks have become popular investments for some financial corporations. The demand by these corporations has been such that, during many periods, the yield on high-grade preferred stock has been *below* the yield on high-grade bonds.[3]

Equity Instruments

Common Stock

When considering investing, many persons think of common stock. Such stock represents ownership of a firm and, therefore, an investor who buys shares in a company is basically buying part of the company. Like any owner of a business, he will share in the company's successes and problems. If, like IBM or Xerox, the company does very well, the value of his common stock will increase tremendously and the investor can become very wealthy. As an example, 200 shares of Xerox stock at the end of 1960 cost a total of

---

[2] For further discussion of bonds see chapters 16–18 and David M. Darst, *The Complete Bond Book* (New York: McGraw–Hill Book Co., 1975).

[3] For a detailed analysis of trends regarding preferred stock, see Donald E. Fischer and Glenn A. Wilt, Jr., "Non-Convertible Preferred Stock As a Financing Instrument, 1950–1965," *Journal of Finance,* Vol. 23, No. 4 (September, 1968), pp. 611–624.

$14,800. At the end of 1976 the investor would have owned 3,000 shares worth $175,500 because of stock splits. This figure does not even include the dividends received during the 17 year period.

In contrast to such a success story, one can think of investments in many common stocks that ended in disaster. Most readers are aware of the Penn Central case: common stock investors could have acquired Penn Central stock for $11.50 a share in 1960 and sold it in 1976 for about $4.00. Common stock entails all the advantages *and* disadvantages of ownership. It is a relatively risky investment compared to the fixed income securities.

Other Investment Considerations

In addition to classifying equity investments according to the risk involved, the nature of the firm invested in should also be considered, both in terms of the type of business it represents and in terms of its earnings potential.

Classification by Business Line

Common stocks can be categorized in a number of ways. An obvious broad classification is by function or general business line: industrial firms, utilities, transportation, financial.

The best known firms are the industrial companies such as General Motors, General Electric, and IBM, a category which includes a wide variety of specific industries. In fact, Standard & Poor's has constructed a stock price index of 400 industrial firms and has broken these 400 firms down into about 80 separate industries including autos, electrical equipment, retail stores, and computers. Clearly, the industrial category includes a wide variety of different economic groups.

The utility category includes companies providing telephone service, electricity, gas, etc. Major factors differentiating these firms from industrial companies are their monopoly position, the regulation involved, and their geographical limitations.

The transportation group includes the railroads that at one point were the only companies in this category. In recent years airlines have been added along with trucking companies and shipping firms.

Finally, the financial category includes banks, savings and loan companies, loan companies, and insurance firms.

Classification by Operating Performance

Another technique for classifying companies is in terms of their performance as growth companies, cyclical companies, and defensive companies. Such a classification helps the investor analyze the companies and subsequently make a valuation of the stock.

A growth company is a company that has opportunities to invest capital at rates of return that exceed the required cost of the capital. As a result of these opportunities, such firms retain a large amount of earnings (have low dividend payments), and their earnings grow rapidly—almost certainly faster than the average firm's. Growth firms can provide outstanding opportunities, but can also be very risky if their growth rate decreases.

Cyclical companies are closely tied to cyclical fluctuations in the economy and typically experience changes in earnings over the business cycle that are *greater* than the earnings changes for the aggregate economy. The industries that fall into this category are automotive, steel, and industrial machinery.

COUNTERCYCLICAL COMPANIES.

Defensive companies are firms whose sales and earnings are expected to move countercyclically to the economy, especially during recessions. These firms are not expected to feel the effects of a recession. Typically these are companies that produce or sell products that are considered necessities. A prime example is retail food stores. These firms are also generally defensive during expansions, which means that they do not feel the full benefits of an expansion because consumers generally reduce the proportion of income spent on necessities during expansions.

Commodities Trading

1 — SPOT CONTRACTS
2 — FUTURE CONTRACTS.

Almost all individuals who have excess funds to invest will consider buying either stocks or bonds. In contrast, very few potential investors ever consider trading commodities. While some characteristics of commodities trading probably justify this attitude, there are many aspects of commodities trading that are very similar to buying and selling stock.[4] Investors should be aware of the similarities between stocks and commodities and not be intimidated by some of the unique characteristics of commodity trading.

Spot Contracts

In one sense, the commodity exchanges function like any other market, simply dealing in the purchase and sale of commodities (corn, wheat, etc.) for current delivery and consumption. This is obviously a very necessary function: bringing together those who produce commodities (farmers), and those who consume them (food processors). When someone wants to buy a commodity for current delivery, he goes to a "spot" market and acquires the available supply. There is a spot market for each commodity and prices fluctuate depending upon currently available supply and demand.

Future Contracts

The bulk of trading on the commodity exchanges is in future contracts, which are contracts for the delivery of a commodity at some future date,

---

[4] For a discussion of some of these similarities see Charles V. Harlow and Richard J. Teweles, "Commodities and Securities Compared," *Financial Analysts Journal,* Vol. 28, No. 5 (September–October, 1972), pp. 64–70.

usually within nine months. The price reflects what the participants feel the future will be for the commodity. In July of a given year one could speculate on the future prices for wheat on the Chicago Board of Trade in September, December, March, and May of the next year. If investors expected the eventual price to rise, they could buy a contract now and sell it later; if they expected the prices to fall, they could sell a contract now and buy a similar contract later to cover the sale when the price declines. The number of commodities available for trading is quite large and increasing over time as shown by the quotations in the *Wall Street Journal*.

There are several factors that distinguish investing in commodities from investing in stocks.[5] One of these is the greater use of leverage which increases the volatility of returns. Another unique aspect is the term of the investment. While stocks can have an infinite maturity, commodity contracts are almost never for more than a year.[6]

Real Estate

Real estate investments are somewhat like commodities in that most investors consider this area "interesting" and probably profitable, but feel that it is limited to a select group of experts with large capital bases. The fact is, there are real estate investments that are feasible for all investors because they do not require large capital commitments. We will begin our discussion by considering low capital alternatives.

Real Estate Investment Trusts (REIT)

An REIT is basically a closed-end mutual fund designed to invest in various real estate properties. The idea is similar to a common stock mutual fund except that the purpose is to invest in property and buildings rather than in stocks and bonds. There are several types.

Construction and Development Trusts and Mortgage Trusts Construction and development trusts lend money required during the initial construction of a building, shopping center, etc. Mortgage trusts are involved in long-term financing of various properties; they acquire the long-term mortgage once the construction is completed.

Equity Trusts Equity trusts own various income producing properties such as office buildings or apartment houses. As a result, an investor who buys an equity trust is buying a portfolio of income producing properties.

REITs were very popular during the period 1969–1970 and grew sub-

---

[5] For a detailed discussion of these differences, see Richard J. Teweles, Charles V. Harlow, and Herbert L. Stone, *The Commodity Futures Trading Guide* (New York: McGraw–Hill Book Co., 1969). Also the discussion in Chapter 24.

[6] For a further discussion of some of the risks involved, see "The Dangerous Bull in the Commodity Market," *Fortune* (July, 1973), pp. 65–66 ff.

stantially. They experienced problems during 1973–1974 due to general economic and money market conditions. While they are subject to unique risks, it appears that the concept is viable for investors interested in real estate investments.[7]

Direct Real Estate Investments

The most common type of direct real estate investment is the purchase of a home. It is often said that this will be the largest investment you will make in your career. This is certainly possible when you consider that the purchase of a single family house will probably cost a minimum of over 30,000 dollars. This is an investment because a homeowner is committing a sum of money for a number of years and he hopes to get that money back along with some excess return. The commitment includes a down payment and specific payments over the next 20 to 30 years.

Raw Land Another form of direct real estate investment is the purchase of raw land with the intent of selling it in the future at a profit. From purchase to sale it is necessary to make payments on the mortgage and pay all taxes until the time at which someone will want to buy the lot. Obviously, a major risk in such an investment is the general lack of liquidity of such an asset compared to that of most stocks and bonds.[8]

Apartment Buildings It is possible to acquire a building with rental apartments with a low down payment. Once the initial down payment is made, the intent is to derive enough from the rents to pay the expenses of the building, including the mortgage payments. For the first few years following the purchase, there is generally no reported income from the building because of deductible expenses. Subsequently, there is a cash flow and an opportunity to profit from the sale of the building after the equity has been increased.

Land Development The idea of buying raw land, splitting it into individual lots and building houses on it is feasible but such an undertaking requires a substantial commitment of capital and time, and also extensive expertise. Clearly, the returns from a successful development can be significant.[9]

---

[7] For a general description of REITs, see Peter A. Schulkin, "Real Estate Investment Trusts," *Financial Analysts Journal,* Vol. 27, No. 3 (May–June, 1971), pp. 33–40. A discussion of some of the problems is contained in "New Lows for the Once Mighty REITs," *Business Week* (April 20, 1974), pp. 82–84. A more recent appraisal is contained in James Grant, "Amid the Rubble," *Barron's* (April 5, 1976), p. 3.

[8] Some indication of the returns on this form of investment can be derived from Frank K. Reilly, Raymond Marquardt, and Donald Price, "Real Estate as an Inflation Hedge," *Review of Business and Economic Research,* Vol. 12, No. 3 (Spring, 1977), pp. 1–19.

[9] For a general review of studies on returns on real estate see Stephen E. Roulac, "Can Real Estate Returns Outperform Common Stocks?" *Journal of Portfolio Management,* Vol. 2, No. 2 (Winter, 1976), pp. 26–43.

Special Equity Instruments

In addition to straight common stock investments, it is also possible to invest in *options* to acquire common stock at a specified price. The two major option instruments available are warrants and puts and calls.

Warrants

A warrant is an option issued by a corporation that gives the holder the right to acquire the common stock of the company, from the company, at a specified price within a designated time period. The warrant does not constitute ownership of the stock, only the option to buy the stock.

Warrants are generally issued by corporations as part of fixed-income instruments (bonds) to increase the appeal of the bonds. A firm with common stock selling at 45 dollars a share can issue a 1,000 dollar bond with ten warrants attached that will allow the bond holder to buy shares of the company's common stock from the company at 50 dollars a share for the next five years. Assuming that investors have confidence in the growth prospects of the firm, these common stock warrants could become very valuable.

Large amounts of warrants are currently available from large, well-known firms. We will deal in depth with the valuation of warrants in a subsequent chapter. For now, the reader should merely be aware of their availability and their usefulness in a well-rounded portfolio.[10]

Puts and Calls

A call option is somewhat similar to a warrant in that it is an option to buy the common stock of a company at a specified price (referred to as the striking price) within a certain period. The difference is that the call option is not issued by the company but by another investor willing to "write" such an option and stand behind it. It also differs because it is typically for a much shorter period, less than a year compared to an initial term of over five years for warrants.

A put is an option that allows the holder to sell a given stock at a specified price during a designated time period. It is used by investors who expect the stock price to decline during the period, or by investors who own the stock and want to have downside protection.

Prior to 1973, the put and call market was very small and was not used by the typical individual investor nor by institutions because it did not have enough volume and liquidity. In April 1973, this changed dramatically

---

[10] For further discussion of the topic, see "Warrants: Risks with Rewards," *Financial World* (November 29, 1972), p. 4; and Ira U. Cobleigh, "Warrants: Who? How? Where?" *Commercial and Financial Chronicle* (August 9, 1973), p. 4. Both articles are included in F. K. Reilly (ed.), *Readings and Issues in Investments* (Hinsdale, Ill.: The Dryden Press, 1975). See also the discussion and references in Chapter 24.

with the establishment of the Chicago Board Options Exchange (CBOE). The CBOE introduced many features that helped to standardize this market.

As can be seen from the numerous articles and books on the subject, the options market is certainly a viable investment alternative and allows a wide range of risky investments for those who want to buy or sell options.[11] We will discuss options trading more fully in Chapter 23.

Initial Stock Issues

In contrast to buying shares of a new issue of American Telephone and Telegraph, an investor can occasionally acquire shares in an initial public offering of a stock that was not public prior to the sale (an example was Coor's Brewing in 1975). Note that because there is no public market the initial pricing is uncertain so the risk on these stocks is quite high. The new issue market was very active during 1968 and 1969 and almost disappeared during 1974. There was some recovery during 1976–1978 and that may continue.[12] If it does, investors should be aware of the risks and returns of this investment alternative.[13]

Foreign Securities

American citizens think nothing of buying TV sets and automobiles produced by companies in Japan, Germany, and France, but seldom consider the common stock of these firms. This is a mistake because the earnings of many foreign firms have grown substantially as a result of increasing sales to the U.S. market.

In addition to the potential rates of return, foreign securities are attractive because of the diversification possibilities. Specifically, foreign companies have sales and earnings patterns substantially different from those of

---

[11] "The New Thrust in Call Options," *Business Week* (August 11, 1973), p.90; Gerald Appel, "Big Levers for Small Investors," *Money* (December, 1973), pp. 60–65; Jonathon R. Laing, "Chicago Options Mart Attracts Big Volume, Exceeds Expectations," *Wall Street Journal* (April 22, 1974), p. 1; "New Look in Calls," *Barron's* (August 6, 1973), p. 9; J. R. Laing, "It Takes Good Timing and Nerves of Steel to Trade in Options," *Wall Street Journal* (May 3, 1976), p. 1; Peter C. DuBois, "In the Money," *Barron's* (March 15, 1976), p.3.

[12] For a discussion of the revivals, see Peter C. DuBois, "Hot-and-Cold Issues," *Barron's* (July 19, 1976); John C. Boland, "Avantek to Xidex," *Barron's* (October 30, 1978).

[13] For a more detailed analysis of the historical short-run returns on initial stock issues see Dennis E. Logue, "On the Pricing of Unseasoned Equity Issues, 1965–1969," *Journal of Financial and Quantitative Analysis,* Vol. 8, No. 1 (January, 1973), pp. 91–103; J. G. McDonald and A. K. Fisher, "New Issue Stock Price Behavior," *Journal of Finance,* Vol. 27, No. 1 (March, 1972), pp. 97–102; Frank K. Reilly and Kenneth Hatfield, "Investor Experience with New Stock Issues," *Financial Analysts Journal,* Vol. 25, No. 5 (September–October, 1969), pp. 73–80; Frank K. Reilly, "Further Evidence on Short-Run Results for New Issue Investors," *Journal of Financial and Quantitative Analysis,* Vol. 8, No. 1 (January, 1973), pp. 83–90; Frank K. Reilly, "New Issues Revisited," *Financial Management,* Vol. 6, No. 4 (Winter, 1977), pp. 28–42.

U.S. firms. Hence, there is a much lower correlation between the returns on foreign stocks and those on U.S. stocks, than there is among alternative U.S. stocks. Therefore, even leaving aside the possibility of superior returns from the stocks of fast growing foreign companies, there are diversification advantages to be derived from foreign stocks.[14]

Low Liquidity Investments

All of the investment alternatives mentioned thus far are generally traded on national markets and have good liquidity. The investments briefly discussed in this section are certainly viable alternatives for individual investors, but they have never been considered by financial institutions because they have low liquidity and high transaction costs. Many of these assets are sold at auctions and there is substantial uncertainty regarding the expected price under such conditions. It may take a long time to get the "right" price for some of them. The transaction cost on these investments is usually very high compared to that on bonds and stocks. This is because there is no national market for these investments so local dealers must be compensated for the added carrying costs and the cost of searching for buyers or sellers. Given these two attributes, many observers consider these investment alternatives to be more in the nature of hobbies, although the returns have often been substantial.

Antiques

The most obvious antique investors are antique dealers who specifically acquire antiques in order to refurbish them and sell them at a profit. From the few specific instances in which the value of antiques can be established based upon sale prices at large public auctions, it can be estimated that returns to serious collectors may be substantial.[15]

Art

There are many examples of paintings that have substantially increased in value and the implied rates of return would be significant.[16] These returns

---

[14] For a more detailed and rigorous discussion of the diversification possibilities, see Tamir Agmon, "The Relations Among Equity Markets: A Study of Share Price Co-Movements in the United States, United Kingdom, Germany and Japan," *Journal of Finance,* Vol. 27, No. 4 (September, 1972), pp. 839–856; Herbert G. Grubel, "Internationally Diversified Portfolios: Welfare Gains and Capital Flows," *American Economic Review,* Vol. 51, No. 5 (December, 1968), pp. 1299–1314; Donald R. Lessard, "International Portfolio Diversification: A Multivariate Analysis of a Group of Latin American Countries," *Journal of Finance,* Vol. 28, No. 3 (June, 1973), pp. 619–633. Chapter 21 contains a discussion of these studies and further justification of the concept.

[15] Richard H. Rush, *Antiques as an Investment* (New York: Bonanza Books, 1968).

[16] Richard H. Rush, *Art as an Investment* (Englewood Cliffs, New Jersey: Prentice–Hall, 1961). Also, James Winjum and Joanne Winjum, "The Art Investment Market," *Michigan Business Review* (November, 1974), pp. 1–5.

---

are generally realized on the works of well-known artists which enjoy some liquidity. Therefore, art can be used as an investment vehicle but it typically requires a large capital base to acquire the work of known artists.[17]

Coins and Stamps

The market for coins and stamps is fragmented compared to the stock markets but is more liquid than most of the market for art and antiques. The reason is that the volume of coins traded has prompted the publication of several price lists on a weekly and monthly basis.[18] These areas are therefore much more amenable for investing because the investor can determine the correct market price on most coins given a grading specification, and, once graded, a coin or stamp can usually be disposed of quite quickly through a dealer.[19]

Historical Returns on Alternative Investments

During the past two decades a number of studies have been done on the rates of return available on common stocks. These studies were prompted by the interest in common stocks as an investment and because the data on stocks, as compared to other investments, were readily available.

The Fifty-Year Fisher–Lorie Study[20]

The most famous work in this area involved the Fisher–Lorie studies done at the University of Chicago.[21] These studies were substantially more complete than all prior studies. They included *all* common stocks listed on the NYSE since 1926 and considered all capital changes such as splits and mergers. In addition, they included taxes and commissions as well as showing the effect of reinvesting dividends. The results were widely publicized and became a new bench mark for all portfolio managers.

---

[17] For a further discussion see "Investing in Art and Antiques," *Business Week* (October 27, 1973), pp. 105–107.

[18] There are several monthly coin magazines including *Coinage* (Encino, Calif.: Behn–Miller Publishers, Inc.).

[19] For a discussion of grading stamps, see Richard Cabeem, *Standard Handbook of Stamp Collecting* (New York: Thomas Y. Crowell Company, 1957). For a discussion of a stamp auction see Myron Keller, "Above Catalog," *Barron's* (April 12, 1976), p. 11.

[20] Lawrence Fisher and James H. Lorie, *A Half Century of Returns on Stocks and Bonds* (Chicago: The University of Chicago Graduate School of Business, 1977).

[21] James H. Lorie and Lawrence Fisher, "Rates of Return on Investment in Common Stock," *Journal of Business,* Vol. 37, No. 1 (January, 1964), pp. 1–17; Lawrence Fisher and James H. Lorie, "Rates of Return on Investment in Common Stock: The Year-by-Year Record, 1926–1965," *Journal of Business,* Vol. 40, No. 3 (July, 1968), pp. 219–316; Lawrence Fisher, "Outcomes for Random Investments in Common Stocks Listed on the New York Stock Exchange," *Journal of Business,* Vol. 38, No. 2 (April, 1965), pp. 149–161.

Recently, the authors updated the returns through 1976.[22] The recent study expanded the earlier work in three ways: (1) in addition to computing rates of return for an equal weighted portfolio (there is an equal dollar amount invested in each stock), the authors computed rates of return for a value weighted portfolio (the amount of stock in the portfolio is proportional to its market value); (2) besides computing rates of return on a current dollar basis, the rates of return are adjusted for changes in the price level (inflation); (3) this study includes rates of return for long-, intermediate-, and short-term government securities.

The rates of return reported in Table 2–1 were taken from over 20 tables and were limited to three time intervals considered to be of interest: the longest period available (12/25 to 12/76); the latest 20-year period (12/56 to 12/76); and the latest 10 year period (12/66–12/76).

An analysis of the first block of returns, which are based on the assumption that all dividends are reinvested and that the portfolio is held at the end of the period, allows for several interesting observations. The first figure in the upper left hand corner (9.0) is of prime interest since it is widely quoted as the long-run rate of return on common stocks. This figure does not take into account any taxes, the effects of inflation, or commissions or taxes entailed in selling the portfolio. The long-run effect of inflation over the 50 year period was about 2.5 percent, but this increased to about 4 percent for the last 20 years, and to almost 6 percent in the last 10 years. Because of this increase Fisher and Lorie felt compelled to report both sets of returns. The effect of taxes indicates that the difference between tax exempt and lower tax rates was about one percent, with another one percent due to higher tax rates. Finally, the effect of weighting the stocks in the portfolio also had a changing impact. For the longest period (51 years) there was *very little difference* in returns due to the weighting. In contrast, during the last 20 years and 10 years the rates of return differed by at least one percent. This indicates that stocks with a higher market value did not do as well as other stocks.

A comparison of the rates of return in the first and second blocks indicates the effect of reinvesting dividends compared to consuming dividends. Finally, the last set of returns indicates the effect of dividends on the total rates of return. In general the impact was significant. Between 4 and 5 percent a year and over 50 percent of the total return is due to the dividend return.

The total listing of common stock results clearly shows that investors in common stock listed on the NYSE have received positive rates of return during the great majority of periods since 1926. Also investors have received fairly substantial positive returns during most periods, even when considering commissions and taxes.

---

[22] Fisher and Lorie, *A Half Century of Returns*.

Table 2–1 **Long-Run Rates of Return for Common Stocks Listed on the New York Stock Exchange under Various Assumptions**

	12/25 to 12/76		12/56 to 12/76		12/66 to 12/76	
	Equal Weighted	Value Weighted	Equal Weighted	Value Weighted	Equal Weighted	Value Weighted
Dividend Reinvested; Cash to Portfolio:						
Tax Exempt; Current Dollars	9.0	9.1	9.6	8.5	8.4	7.4
Tax Exempt; Deflated Dollars	6.5	6.6	5.6	4.5	2.4	1.4
Lower Tax Rate; Current Dollars	8.3	8.3	8.7	7.5	7.4	6.2
Lower Tax Rate; Deflated Dollars	5.8	5.9	4.7	3.6	1.5	0.3
Higher Tax Rate; Current Dollars	7.2	7.1	7.4	6.1	6.2	4.9
Higher Tax Rate; Deflated Dollars	4.7	4.7	3.5	2.2	0.4	−0.9
Without Dividend Reinvested; Cash to Portfolio:						
Tax Exempt; Current Dollars	7.3	7.9	9.9	8.6	8.4	7.1
Tax Exempt; Deflated Dollars	5.8	6.7	6.4	5.1	2.5	1.3
Lower Tax Rate; Current Dollars	7.0	NA[a]	9.0	NA	7.5	NA
Lower Tax Rate; Deflated Dollars	5.4	NA	5.4	NA	1.6	NA
Higher Tax Rate; Current Dollars	6.4	6.8	7.6	6.2	6.3	4.8
Higher Tax Rate; Deflated Dollars	4.6	5.3	3.9	2.6	0.4	−0.9
Rates of Change in Prices; Cash to Portfolio:						
Tax Exempt; Current Dollars	4.6	4.3	5.9	4.5	4.9	3.4
Tax Exempt; Deflated Dollars	2.2	1.9	2.0	0.7	−0.9	−2.3

[a] Not available

Source: Lawrence Fisher and James H. Lorie, *A Half Century of Returns on Stocks and Bonds* (Chicago: The University of Chicago Graduate School of Business, 1977). Reprinted by permission.

Table 2–2 contains selected annual rates of return on U.S. Treasury securities of different maturities for different time intervals (51 years, 20 years, 10 years). All these securities are considered to be risk-free in the sense that there is no probability of default.

An analysis of the rates of return *across* a line indicates the influence of maturity on rates of return. (The long-term bonds have a maturity of at least ten years, the intermediate bonds have maturities of between five and ten years, and it was assumed that the short-term bonds were acquired when they had about a year left to maturity and were sold after six months). For the 51 year period the intermediate securities consistently provided the highest rates of return. The effect of taxes on bond returns was similar to the effect on stock returns, about one percent for lower taxes and an additional one percent for the higher tax rates. The most important impact was due to inflation. For the total period the effect was about 2 percent. For the last 20 years, the "real" returns (returns adjusted for inflation, i.e., deflated dollars) were only about one percent without taxes and were negative after taxes. During the last ten years, almost all the deflated returns were

Table 2–2 **Long-Run Rates of Return on U.S. Treasury Securities For Different Maturities Under Various Assumptions**

Interest Reinvested	12/25 to 12/76			12/56 to 12/76			12/66 to 12/76		
	Long	Inter-mediate	Short	Long	Inter-mediate	Short	Long	Inter-mediate	Short
Tax Exempt; Current Dollars	3.4	3.6	3.0	4.2	4.7	5.3	5.4	5.7	7.0
Tax Exempt; Deflated Dollars	1.1	1.2	0.7	0.4	0.8	1.4	−0.4	−0.1	1.0
Lower Tax; Current Dollars	2.7	2.9	2.4	2.8	3.3	3.9	3.5	3.8	5.0
Lower Tax; Deflated Dollars	0.4	0.6	0.1	−1.0	−0.5	0.1	−2.2	−1.9	−0.8
Higher Tax; Current Dollars	1.7	2.0	1.6	1.0	1.5	2.1	1.3	1.6	2.7
Higher Tax; Deflated Dollars	−0.6	−0.3	−0.7	−2.7	−2.2	−1.6	−4.3	−4.0	−3.0

Source: Lawrence Fisher and James H. Lorie, *A Half Century of Returns on Stocks and Bonds* (Chicago: The University of Chicago Graduate School of Business, 1977). Reprinted by permission.

negative. Therefore, individuals who invested in government securities during the last ten years were not able to increase their consumption of goods and services as a result of this investment.

The rates of return on U.S. Treasury securities have generally been consistent with expectations over the long-run (51 years). In contrast, recent experience has been unique because of the effect of inflation on relative returns and, more important, the effect on deflated returns. This indicates the importance of considering the effect of inflation when analyzing investments and constructing portfolios.

Ibbotson–Sinquefield Study[23]

A second major study dealing with the nominal and real rates of return on common stocks, bonds, and bills for the period 1926–1974 was done by Ibbotson and Sinquefield at the University of Chicago. The authors present year-by-year historical rates of return for five major classes of assets in the United States: 1) common stocks, 2) long-term U.S. government bonds, 3) long-term corporate bonds, 4) U.S. Treasury bills, and 5) consumer goods (inflation). For each asset the authors present total rates of return which reflect dividend or interest income as well as capital gains or losses. None of the returns are adjusted for taxes or transaction costs. In addition to the five basic series, the authors present seven derived series. These represent the component parts of asset returns, including real inflation adjusted returns, for the first four basic series. They also derived series that measure the net return from investing in common stocks rather than U.S. Treasury bills, from investing in long-term government bonds rather than short-

[23] Roger G. Ibbotson and Rex A. Sinquefield, "Stocks, Bonds, Bills and Inflation: Year-by-Year Historical Returns (1926–1974)," *Journal of Business*, Vol. 49, No. 1 (January, 1976), pp. 11–47.

term government bills, and from investing in long-term corporate bonds rather than long-term government bonds. All returns are annual for the period January 1926–December 1974.

The common stock total return index is based upon the Standard & Poor's Composite Index. The Standard & Poor's series includes 500 of the largest stocks in the United States, and is referred to as a market value weighted series.

The long-term government bond series is derived from data gathered at the Center for Research in Security Prices (CRSP) at the University of Chicago. The objective of the Ibbotson–Sinquefield series was to maintain a 20-year term bond portfolio the returns from which do not reflect potential tax benefits and are not influenced by special redemptions, call privileges, or other unique characteristics.

The long-term corporate bond series was basically derived using the same principle as the Salomon Brothers high-grade long-term corporate bond index.[24] Ibbotson and Sinquefield used the Salomon Brothers index for 1969–1974 and then attempted to generate a similar index for earlier periods using Moody's and other individual bond series. To derive an index of U.S. Treasury bills, the authors used the data in the CRSP U.S. Government Bond File in order to construct one that included the shortest-term bills available with not less than a one-month maturity. To derive an index of inflation, the authors utilized the Consumer Price Index (CPI) which is the rate of change of consumer goods' prices.

Given the monthly and annual rates of return, they computed geometric mean returns over longer periods and the arithmetic mean returns. In addition to the five basic series, the authors computed seven monthly returns series derived from the basic series. The first three of these were net returns reflecting different premiums. The first was a net return from investing in common stocks rather than in U.S. Treasury bills. This net return is referred to as the *risk premium* involved in investing in a risky alternative, rather than in something basically risk-free like Treasury bills. The second net return was the difference in investing in long-term government bonds and U.S. Treasury bills. This is referred to as a *maturity premium* because in both cases the securities are considered default-free and the only difference between them is their maturity dates. Finally, the difference in net returns from long-term corporate bonds and long-term government bonds was determined. This is referred to as a *default premium* since the difference between the two long-term bond series is that the corporate bonds involve a possibility of default. The final four series derived are basically inflation adjusted returns for the initial four. The authors ascertained the real rates of return on common stocks, Treasury bills, long-term government bonds, and long-term corporate bonds.

---

[24] The Salomon Brothers index indicates the realized rates of return on a representative sample of long-term corporate bonds. The construction and computation of the series is discussed in detail in the section on bonds.

A summary of the results for the basic and derived series is contained in Table 2–3. The geometric mean returns are always lower than the arithmetic returns, and the difference increases with the standard deviation of returns.[25]

Table 2–3 **Basic and Derived Series: Historical Highlights (1926—1974)**

Series	Annual Geometric Mean Rate of Return	Arithmetic Mean of Annual Returns	Standard Deviation of Annual Returns	Number of Years Returns are Positive	Number of Years Returns are Negative	Highest Annual Return (and year)	Lowest Annual Return (and year)
Common Stocks	8.5%[a]	10.9%	22.5%	32	17	54.0% (1933)	−43.3 (1931)
Long-Term Government Bonds	3.2	3.4	5.4	37	12	16.8 (1932)	− 9.2 (1967)
Long-Term Corporate Bonds	3.6	3.7	5.1	39	10	18.4 (1970)	− 8.1 (1969)
U.S. Treasury Bills	2.2	2.3	2.1	48	1	8.0 (1974)	− 0.0 (1940)
Consumer Price Index	2.2	2.3	4.8	39	10	18.2 (1946)	−10.3 (1932)
Risk Premiums on Common Stocks	6.1	8.8	23.5	31	18	53.5 (1933)	−43.7 (1931)
Maturity Premiums on Long-Term Govt. Bonds	1.0	1.1	5.6	25	24	15.7 (1932)	−12.8 (1967)
Default Premiums on Long-Term Corp. Bonds	.3	.4	3.2	28	21	10.5 (1933)	− 7.2 (1974)
Common Stocks– Inflation Adjusted	6.1	8.8	23.5	31	18	53.3 (1954)	−37.4 (1931)
Long-Term Government Bonds–Inflation Adjusted	1.0	1.3	8.0	29	20	30.2 (1932)	−15.5 (1946)
Long-Term Corporate Bonds–Inflation Adjusted	1.4	1.7	7.7	31	18	23.5 (1932)	−13.9 (1946)
U.S. Treasury Bills– Inflation Adjusted	0.1	0.2	4.6	29	20	12.6 (1932)	−15.2 (1946)

[a]The annual geometric mean rate of return for capital appreciation exclusive of dividends was 3.5 percent over the entire period.

Source: Roger G. Ibbotson and Rex A. Sinquefield, "Stocks, Bonds, Bills, and Inflation: Year-by-Year Historical Returns (1926–1974)," *Journal of Business,* Vol. 49, No. 1 (January, 1976). Copyright © 1976 by The University of Chicago Press. Reprinted by permission of The University of Chicago Press.

Over the period 1926–1974, common stocks returned 8.5 percent a year, compounded annually. Excluding dividends, stocks increased at a rate of 3.5 percent a year. For the total period, the risk premium on common

[25] There is a discussion in the appendix to this chapter of the difference between the arithmetic and geometric mean. Readers not familiar with the difference are encouraged to read this before proceeding further.

Part 1
The Investment Background

40

stocks and the inflation adjusted "real" returns were 6.1 percent per year. Although common stocks outperformed the other assets in the study, the returns on stocks were also far more volatile as measured by the range and the standard deviation of returns.

Long-term U.S. government bonds experienced a 3.2 percent annual return over the period 1926–1974. During the same period, the real return on these bonds was one percent and the maturity premium for these bonds, compared to treasury bills, was also one percent. The returns on these bonds were far less volatile than the annual returns on common stocks.

The annual compound rate of return on long-term corporate bonds was 3.6 percent over the total period. The default premium on these bonds, compared to that on long-term government bonds, was only 0.3 percent. The inflation adjusted return was 1.4 percent. The volatility of these bonds was similar to the volatility on government bonds. In fact, the standard deviation was slightly smaller.

During the entire period, U.S. Treasury bills returned 2.2 percent a year, which is about equal to the rate of inflation for the total period. As a result, the inflation-adjusted return on T-bills for the entire period was 0.1 percent. The return on T-bills was not very volatile; the standard deviation was the lowest for all of the series examined. In contrast, the inflation-adjusted T-bill series was much more volatile.

This study generally confirmed the results of the Fisher–Lorie studies and extended the analysis to other alternatives. The returns were as expected and were generally consistent with the uncertainty as measured by the standard deviation of annual returns.

Robichek–Cohn–Pringle Study[26]

The R–C–P Study deals with the rates of return on a number of investments, including stocks, bonds, commodities, real estate, and foreign securities. It computes *ex post* rates of return and correlation coefficients for 12 investment media for the period 1949–1969, inclusive, and analyzes the implications of the results for portfolio construction. The alternative investment media included common stocks in the United States and two other countries, U.S. government and corporate bonds, real estate, and commodity futures. The purpose of the study was to show the difference in returns for alternative investments and is considered illustrative since the authors recognize that not all media were considered. The specific media considered were: 1) the Standard & Poor's Industrial Common Stock Index, 2) S&P Utility Index, 3) U.S. Government 2½ percent bonds of 1970–65, 4) Bethlehem Steel 2¾ percent bonds due in 1970, 5) Canadian

---

[26] Alexander A. Robichek, Richard A. Cohn, and John J. Pringle, "Returns on Alternative Media and Implications for Portfolio Construction," *Journal of Business,* Vol. 45, No. 3 (July, 1972), pp. 427–443.

Pacific Perpetual 4 percent bonds, 6) farm real estate, 7) cotton future contracts, 8) wheat future contracts, 9) copper future contracts, 10) Japanese common stocks, 11) Australian common stocks, and 12) Treasury bill yields. A summary of the mean returns and the standard deviation of returns for the total period 1949–1969 is contained in Table 2–4.

Table 2–4
Mean Rates of Return and Variability of Annual Returns for Alternative Investment Media: 1949–1969

	Arithmetic Mean	Geometric Mean	Standard Deviation[a]	Coefficient of Variation[b]
S&P Industrials	12.97	11.63	17.55	1.51
S&P Utilities	9.31	8.60	12.43	1.45
Japanese Stocks	24.07	18.94	41.30	2.18
Australian Stocks	7.80	6.82	14.22	2.09
Treasury Bill Yields	3.01	3.00	1.60	0.53
U.S. Government 2 percent bonds, 1970–65	2.48	2.37	4.68	1.97
Bethlehem Steel, 2¾ percent bonds (maturity 1970)	2.06	2.00	3.40	1.70
Canadian Pacific Perpetual 4 percent bonds	1.56	1.40	5.71	4.08
Farm Real Estate	9.56	9.47	4.50	0.48
Cotton Futures	17.10	3.80	66.77	17.57
Wheat Futures	− 0.49	−22.88	64.07	2.80
Copper Futures	121.02	26.60	244.02	9.17

[a]Standard deviation about geometric mean
[b]Coefficient of Variation = Standard Deviation ÷ Geometric Mean
Source: Alexander A. Robichek, Richard A. Cohn, and John J. Pringle, "Returns on Alternative Investment Media and Implications for Portfolio Construction," *Journal of Business,* Vol. 45, No. 3 (July, 1972). Copyright © 1972 by The University of Chicago Press. Reprinted by permission of The University of Chicago Press.

The authors felt that the returns on U.S. equities were as expected. Industrials had a higher mean return and a higher standard deviation than did utilities. The returns on Japanese stocks indicated that the mean annual return for the 20, one-year periods was a surprising 18.9 percent. The holding period return over the entire time was 21.1 percent. The coefficient of variation of returns for Japanese stocks was higher than it was for U.S. stocks. Returns from Australian common stocks, at 6.8 percent, were considerably lower than returns from other groups. On the other hand, the relationship between the instability of returns and the mean return was about the same for Australian stocks as for Japanese issues and somewhat higher than it was for American stocks.

The *ex post* compound rates of return over the 20-year period for the three bonds studied were 2.4 percent for the U.S. government 2½ percent bonds, 2.0 percent for the Bethlehem Steel bonds, and 1.4 percent for the Canadian Pacific Perpetual 4 percent bonds. All of these ex post returns exhibited a high degree of variance in relation to the mean return, and all three bonds produced negative returns in a large number of years. The *ex post* returns on these bonds were lower than the average rate of return on treasury bills, which was 3 percent.

The most notable thing about the return on farm real estate was the apparent stability of returns over time. The geometric mean rate of return was 9.47 percent and the standard deviation was only 4.5 percent resulting in a coefficient of variation of only .48. This relative measure of volatility was considerably lower than that of any other long-term investment media.

Returns on commodity futures showed very large year-to-year variations. Comparison of the returns on long contracts in the three different commodities shows that wheat provided a high negative mean return (minus 22.88 percent), copper a high positive rate of return (26.60 percent), and cotton a very low mean return (3.8 percent).

The authors examined the correlation among the rates of return over time for the alternative investment media (for a discussion of covariance and correlation, see Appendix B). The correlation coefficients among the various media were generally low and the signs of the coefficients were almost equally divided between positive and negative values. The common stock returns for the alternative countries had very low correlation coefficients. Further, the returns from real estate were very stable and not significantly correlated with any other media. Commodity futures, on the other hand, were extremely volatile year-to-year and variability among the commodities was quite different than that among other media. These general findings indicate that enlarging the universe of investment alternatives would benefit portfolio construction in terms of the risk-return opportunities. Given the correlation coefficients, the authors specifically constructed a number of portfolios and found that there was a significant improvement in their risk-return characteristics based upon the multimedia diversification. The authors contended that *the results support the arguments that investors should look beyond common stocks and treasury bills in constructing investment portfolios.*

Summary

The purpose of this chapter was to briefly describe some of the major investment alternatives available to individuals. In addition, a major intent was to help the reader become aware of *the vast variety of these alternatives.*[27]

[27] One of several areas not specifically mentioned is rare books. For a discussion of this area see Phillip Corwin, "No Volume Discounts," *Barron's* (May 17, 1976), p. 11. Another alternative is diamonds. A discussion of some of the risks involved in this area is contained in Jonathan Kwitny, "Average Diamond Buyer May Find that Gains are Elusive Even as Prices on Stones Increase," *Wall Street Journal* (April 10, 1978), p. 38.

The reader should be aware of *all* the alternatives for two reasons. The first is that they provide a wide variety of risk and return choices that may be of interest to different investors. One man's garbage may be another man's feast. As an example, one reader, after becoming familiar with commodities trading, may decide that it is much too speculative for him and would not consider it at all, while another reader may feel that it is very exciting and decide to commit a large share of his resources to this area.

In addition, it is widely acknowledged that considering several areas in terms of risk can benefit the investor's portfolio. Assuming that the alternatives are not highly correlated, it can be shown that the variance of returns for an investor's total portfolio can be substantially reduced through diversification.

The chapter finished with a discussion of three studies concerned with the historical rates of return on common stocks and a number of other investment alternatives including bonds, commodities, and real estate. The results of these studies pointed toward two generalizations:

1. There was typically a positive relationship between the rates of return on an investment medium and the variability of the rate of return over time. This is consistent with expectations in a world of risk averse investors who require a higher return to assume more uncertainty.

2. The correlation of the rates of return for alternative investments were typically quite low, which indicates that there are definite benefits to diversification among investments in order to reduce the variability of the investor's total portfolio.

Questions

1. What are the major advantages to investing in the common stock, compared to corporate bonds, of the same company? What are the major disadvantages?

2. Discuss briefly why an investor might prefer utility common stocks to industrial common stocks.

3. Would you expect the returns on industrial common stocks to have the same pattern over time as the common stock of financial firms? Why or why not?

4. Assume that the returns from transportation stocks are not correlated with the returns from financial stocks. Will this benefit an investor who has both types of stock in his portfolio? Why or why not?

5. How does a bond differ from a common stock in terms of the certainty of returns over time? Draw a simple time series graph to demonstrate the pattern of returns you might imagine.

6. Assume that you had the opportunity to acquire a convertible bond from a growth company or a utility. Both firms have straight debentures that yield 9 percent. Given the conversion feature, which convertible bond would have the lower yield? Why?

7. Define a spot commodity contract and a future commodities contract.

8. A contract involves 5,000 bushels of wheat. Assuming wheat is selling for $3.50 a bushel, the total value of the contract is $17,500. Given a margin of 15 percent, an investor would have to put up $2,625 to purchase such a contract. Ignoring commissions, if the price of wheat increases to $3.75 a bushel, what is the percent of change in the value of the contract and what is the investor's return on his investment? Assuming a decline in price to $3.35, what is his return? Show all calculations.

9. Define an REIT and briefly discuss the alternative types.

10. Discuss the difference in liquidity between an investment in raw land and an investment in common stock. Be specific as to why there is a difference and how they differ. (Hint: begin by defining liquidity).

11. Define a stock warrant.
Define a call option.
Discuss how a warrant differs from a call option.

12. What has the CBOE contributed to the call option market that has caused significant growth in the market since 1973? Be specific.

13. Would you expect the price of an initial public offering to fluctuate more when it is first offered than would the price of a listed stock involved in a new offering? Why or why not?

14. It is contended that the returns on foreign stocks should have low correlation with the returns on U.S. stocks. What is the rationale behind such an assumption?

15. Why is it contended that antiques and art are generally illiquid investments? Be specific in your discussion. Why are coins and stamps considered to be more liquid than antiques and art? Again be specific and consider what it would require to sell the various assets.

16. Look up in the *Wall Street Journal* the current *maturity premium* on U.S. Government securities. The long-term security should have a maturity of at least 20 years.

17. Each week in *Barron's* on the last two or three pages there is a set of stock indexes for foreign countries. For a recent week, determine the percent of change in the index for Japanese and Australian stock and compare this to the percent of change in the DJIA for the same period. Do the results of the comparison indicate any benefits to diversification among securities from these countries? Why or why not?

References

Agmon, Tamir. "The Relations Among Equity Markets: A Study of Share Price Co-Movements in the United States, United Kingdom, Germany and Japan." *Journal of Finance,* Vol. 27, No. 3 (September, 1972).

Appel, Gerald. "Big Levers for Small Investors." *Money* (December, 1973).

Barnes, Leo and Feldman, Stephen (eds.). *Handbook of Wealth Management.* New York: McGraw–Hill Book Co., 1977. This book contains numerous articles on alternative investments by a variety of authors.

The Bond Book. New York: Merrill, Lynch, Pierce, Fenner and Smith, Inc., 1975.

Cabeem, Richard. *Standard Handbook of Stamp Collecting.* New York: Thomas Y. Crowell Company, 1957.

Corwin, Phillip. "No Volume Discounts." *Barron's,* May 17, 1976.

"The Dangerous Bull in the Commodity Market." *Fortune* (July, 1973).

Darst, David M. *The Complete Bond Book.* New York: McGraw–Hill Book Co., 1975.

DuBois, Peter C. "Hot-and-Cold Issues." *Barron's,* July 19, 1976.

Fisher, Lawrence and Lorie, James H. "Rates of Return on Investments in Common Stock: The Year-by-Year Record, 1926–1965." *Journal of Business,* Vol. 40, No. 3 (July, 1968).

Grubel, Herbert G. "Internationally Diversified Portfolios: Welfare Gains and Capital Flows." *American Economic Review,* Vol. 58, No. 5 (December, 1968).

Harlow, Charles V. and Teweles, Richard J. "Commodities and Securities Compared." *Financial Analysts Journal,* Vol. 28, No. 5 (September–October, 1972).

Ibbotson, Roger G. and Sinquefield, Rex A. "Stocks, Bonds, Bills and Inflation: Year-by-Year Historical Returns (1926–1974)." *Journal of Business,* Vol. 49, No. 1 (January, 1976).

"Investing in Art and Antiques." *Business Week,* October 27, 1973.

Keller, Myron. "Above Catalog." *Barron's,* April 12, 1976.

Lessard, Donald R. "International Portfolio Diversification: A Multivariate Analysis of a Group of Latin American Countries." *Journal of Finance,* Vol. 28, No. 3 (June, 1973).

Logue, Dennis E. "On the Pricing of Unseasoned Equity Issues, 1965–1969." *Journal of Financial and Quantitative Analysis,* Vol. 8, No. 1 (January, 1973).

McDonald, J. G. and Fisher, A. K. "New Issue Stock Price Behavior." *Journal of Finance,* Vol. 27, No. 1 (March, 1972).

"New Lows for the Once Mighty REITS." *Business Week* April 20, 1974.

Reilly, Frank K. "Further Evidence on Short-Run Results for New Issue Investors." *Journal of Financial and Quantitative Analysis,* Vol. 8, No. 1 (January, 1973).

Reilly, Frank K. "New Issues Revisited." *Financial Management,* Vol. 6, No. 4 (Winter, 1977).

Reilly, Frank K. and Hatfield, Kenneth. "Investor Experience with New Stock Issues." *Financial Analysts Journal,* Vol. 25, No. 5 (September–October, 1969).

Reilly, Frank K., Marquardt, Raymond, and Price, Donald. "Real Estate as an Inflation Hedge." *Review of Business and Economic Research,* Vol. 12, No. 3 (Spring, 1977).

Robichek, Alexander A., Cohn, Richard A., and Pringle, John J. "Returns on Alternative Investment Media and Implications for Portfolio Construction." *Journal of Business,* Vol. 45, No. 3 (July, 1972).

Roulac, Stephen E. "Can Real Estate Returns Outperform Common Stocks?" *Journal of Portfolio Management,* Vol. 2, No. 2 (Winter, 1976).

Rush, Richard H. *Antiques as an Investment.* New York: Bonanza Books, 1968.

Rush, Richard H. *Art as an Investment.* Englewood Cliffs, New Jersey: Prentice–Hall, 1961.

Schulkin, Peter A. "Real Estate Investment Trusts." *Financial Analysts Journal,* Vol. 27, No. 3 (May–June, 1971).

Appendix 2–A
Geometric Mean Returns

When examining the average returns on an investment over an extended period of time, the typical measure used is the arithmetic average of annual rates of return. As will be shown, the arithmetic average return can be biased upward if there is substantial variability in the returns over time. An alternative measure of the central tendency is the geometric mean of the annual returns. This measure is considered superior by some investigators because it is the same formulation that is used to derive compound interest and provides a proper measure of the true ending wealth position for the investment involved.

Arithmetic Mean Bias

As is known, the arithmetic mean (designated $\bar{X}$) is the sum of each value in a distribution divided by the total number of values.

$$\bar{X} = \sum X/n$$

A problem occurs if there are large changes in the annual returns over time. Consider the example in which a nondividend paying stock goes from 50 to 100 dollars during year one and back to 50 dollars during year two. The annual returns would be:

Year 1: 100%
Year 2: −50%

Obviously, during the two years there was *no* return on the investment. Yet the arithmetic mean return would be:

$$(+100) + (-50)/2 = 50/2 = 25\%.$$

In this case, although there was *no* change in wealth and, therefore, no return, the arithmetic mean return is computed as 25 percent.

Geometric Mean The geometric mean (designated G) is the nth root of the product arrived at by multiplying the values in the distribution times each other. Specifically, it is

$$G = \prod X^{1/n}$$

where $\prod$ stands for "product." When calculating the geometric mean returns, it is customary to use holding period returns, which are the yield plus 1.0 (e.g., a positive 10 percent return is designated 1.10; a negative 15 percent return is designated 0.85). This is done because a negative yield causes the geometric mean calculation to be meaningless. As an example, consider the extreme example used in the prior discussion of the arithmetic mean:

	Yield	Holding Period Return
Year 1:	100%	2.00
Year 2:	−50%	0.50

$$G = (2.00 \times 0.50)^{1/2} = (1.00)^{1/2} = 1.00 - 1.00 = 0\%$$

To get the yield, 1.00 is subtracted from the geometric holding period return. As can be seen, this answer is consistent with the ending wealth position of the investor. He ended where he began and had a 0 percent return during the period.

Extended Example
Consider the following more complete example using actual rounded percent of price changes for the DJIA during the period 1970–1977:

	Percent of Price Change	Holding Period Change
1970	5.00	1.05
1971	6.00	1.06
1972	15.00	1.15
1973	− 17.00	0.83
1974	− 28.00	0.72
1975	38.00	1.38
1976	18.00	1.18
1977	− 17.00	0.83

$$\overline{X} = \sum X/n = 37/8 = 4.625\%$$
$$G = (1.05 \times 1.06 \times 1.15 \times 0.83 \times 0.72 \times 1.38 \times 1.18 \times 0.83)^{1/8}$$
$$= (1.155692)^{1/8} = 1.01825 - 1.0 = .01825 = 1.825\%$$

As shown, the arithmetic mean price change is more than twice as large as the geometric mean price change. Because of the upward bias in the arithmetic mean, it will *always* be larger (except where all returns are equal) and the discrepancy will be wider with a more volatile series. If there is a large difference between the arithmetic mean and the geometric mean, it can be inferred that the returns were very volatile.

Appendix 2–B
Covariance and Correlation

Covariance

It is assumed that almost all students have been exposed to the concept of covariance, so the following discussion is set forth in intuitive terms with an example that will, hopefully, help the reader recall the concept.[1]

Covariance is an absolute measure of the extent to which two sets of numbers move together over time, i.e., move up or down together. In this regard "move together" means they are generally above their means or below their means at the same time. Covariance between i and j is defined as:

$$Cov_{ij} = \frac{\sum (i-\bar{i})\,(j-\bar{j})}{N}$$

If we define $(i-\bar{i})$ as i' and $(j-\bar{j})$ as j', then

$$Cov_{ij} = \frac{\sum i'\, j'}{N}$$

Obviously, if both numbers are consistently above or below their individual means at the same time, their products will be positive and the average will be a large positive value. In contrast, if the i value is below its mean when the j value is above its mean or vice versa their products will be large negative values and you would find negative covariance. The following example should make this clear.

---

[1]For a more detailed, rigorous treatment of the subject the reader is referred to any standard statistics text including Ya-lun Chou, *Statistical Analysis* (New York: Holt, Rinehart, and Winston, Inc., 1975), pp. 152–156.

Obs.		i	j	i−$\bar{\text{i}}$	j−$\bar{\text{j}}$	i'j'
1		3	8	−4	−4	16
2		6	10	−1	−2	2
3		8	14	+1	+2	2
4		5	12	−2	0	0
5		9	13	+2	+1	2
6		11	15	+4	+3	12
$\sum$	=	42	72			34
Mean	=	7	12			

$$\text{Cov}_{ij} = \frac{34}{6} = +5.67$$

In this example the two series generally moved together, so there was positive covariance. As noted, this is an *absolute* measure of their relationship and, therefore, can range from $+\infty$ to $-\infty$. Note that the covariance of a variable with itself is its *variance.*

Correlation

To obtain a relative measure of a given relationship we use the correlation coefficient (r_{ij}) which is a normalized measure of the relationship:

$$r_{ij} = \frac{\text{Cov}_{ij}}{\sigma_i \, \sigma_j}$$

The reader will recall from introductory statistics courses that $\sigma_i = \dfrac{\sqrt{\sum(i-i)^2}}{N}$ so, if the two series move *completely* together, then the covariance would equal $\sigma_i \sigma_j$ and

$$\frac{\text{Cov}_{ij}}{\sigma_i \, \sigma_j} = +1.0.$$

The correlation coefficient would equal unity and we would say the two series are perfectly correlated. Since we know that

$$r_{ij} = \frac{\text{Cov}_{ij}}{\sigma_i \, \sigma_j}$$

we also know that $\text{Cov}_{ij} = r_{ij}\sigma_i\sigma_j$, which is a relationship that may be useful when computing the standard deviation of a portfolio because, in many instances, the relationship between two securities is stated in terms of the correlation coefficient rather than the covariance.

Continuing the example given in Table 2B–1, the standard deviations are computed in Table 2B–2 as is the correlation between i and j. As shown, the two standard deviations are rather large and similar but not the same. Finally, when the positive covariance is normalized by the product of the two standard deviations, the results indicate a correlation coefficient of .898 which is obviously quite large and close to 1.00. Apparently these two series are highly related.

Table 2B–2
Calculation of Correlation Coefficient

Obs.	$i-\bar{i}$[a]	$(i-\bar{i})^2$	$j-\bar{j}$[a]	$(j-\bar{j})^2$
1	−4	16	−4	16
2	−1	1	−2	4
3	+1	1	+2	4
4	−2	4	0	0
5	+2	4	+1	1
6	+4	16	+3	9
		42		34

$$\sigma_i^2 = 42/6 = 7.00 \qquad\qquad \sigma_j^2 = 34/6 = 5.67$$
$$\sigma_i = \sqrt{7.00} = 2.65 \qquad\qquad \sigma_j = \sqrt{5.67} = 2.38$$
$$r_{ij} = Cov_{ij}/\sigma_i\sigma_j = \frac{5.67}{(2.65)(2.38)} = \frac{5.67}{6.31} = .898$$

[a] from Table 2B–1

Chapter 3

Organization and Functioning of Securities Markets

The stock market, Wall Street, the Dow Jones Industrials are part and parcel of our everyday experience. Each evening we find out how they fared on the television news broadcasts; each morning we read about their prospects for a rally or decline in the pages of our daily newspaper. Yet the operation of the securities market remains a given to most investors. What this market is, how it functions, and who is involved in it are imperfectly understood at best. It is the purpose of this chapter to define the securities market, both primary and secondary, and to indicate those persons who are key to its operation, especially the specialists.

Financial Markets

What Is a Market?

Prior to discussing the organization and functioning of the stock and bond markets, it seems appropriate to consider the general question of what a market is, or, more specifically, what is its purpose. Most people have been exposed to numerous markets in their lives, without really being aware of what they do and why they exist. Basically, we take markets for granted. *A market is the means through which buyers and sellers are brought together to aid in the transfer of goods and/or services.* Several aspects of this general definition seem worthy of emphasis. First, it is not necessary for a market to have a physical location. It is only necessary that the buyers and sellers can communicate regarding the relevant aspects of the purchase or sale.

Second, the market does not necessarily own the goods or services involved. When we discuss what is required for a "good" market, the reader will note that ownership is not involved; the basic criterion is the smooth, cheap transfer of goods and services. In the case of most financial markets, those who establish and administer the market do not own the assets, but they simply provide a location for potential buyers and sellers to meet and they help the market to function by providing information and transfer facilities.

Finally, a market can deal in any variety of goods and services. For any commodity with a diverse clientele a market should develop to aid in its transfer and both buyers and sellers will benefit from its existence.

Factors That Determine a "Good" Market

A buyer or seller of goods or services enters a market in order to buy or sell the commodity quickly, at a price justified by the prevailing supply and demand in the market. So he would like to have timely and accurate information on past transactions in terms of volume and price, and on all currently outstanding bids and offers. Therefore, one attribute of a good market is *availability of information regarding price and volume for past transactions and current market conditions.*

Another prime requirement is a liquid market, where we define liquidity as *the ability to buy or sell an asset quickly, at a known price,* i.e., a price not substantially different from the prior price, assuming no new information is available. Therefore, there are two aspects of liquidity: *the time involved to complete the transaction* and *the certainty of the price.* An instance in which a broker can assure the owner of a specified price, but indicates that it might take six months to sell the asset at that price would not be considered a very liquid market because the time involved is excessive. In contrast, if a broker tells an owner that he can sell an asset very quickly, but at a substantial discount from the prior market price for a comparable asset, this, likewise, is not a very liquid market because of the significant price change that accompanies a quick transaction. The latter case, in which it is possible to sell *quickly* is sometimes referred to as *marketability,* i.e., *the asset can be turned into cash quickly,* but there is nothing certain about price. Therefore, marketability is a necessary, but *not* a sufficient, condition for liquidity.

One of the factors that contributes to liquidity is *price continuity.* Continuity refers to prices which do not change much from one transaction to the next, unless substantial new information becomes available. Given a case in which new information is not forthcoming, and the last transaction was at a price of 20 dollars, if the next trade was at 20⅛[1] it would probably be considered a reasonably continuous market. Obviously, *it is necessary to have a continuous market without large price changes between trades in order to have a liquid market.*

A continuous market also requires *depth.* There must be numerous

---

[1] The reader should be aware that common stocks are sold in increments of eighths which are equal to $0.125. Therefore, 20⅛ means the stock sold at $20.125 per share.

potential buyers and sellers who are willing to trade at figures above and below the current market price. These buyers and sellers enter the market when there are price changes and thereby ensure that there are no major price moves.

Another factor contributing to a good market is the *cost of a transaction.* The lower the cost of the transaction (in terms of the percentage of the value of the trade), the more efficient the market. Assuming that an individual is comparing two markets, if the cost of a transaction on one was 2 percent of the value of the trade, while the other market charged 5 percent, the individual would trade in the 2 percent market. Most micro-economic textbooks define an "efficient" market as: *one in which the cost of the transaction is minimized.* Papers by West and Tinic define this attribute of a market as "internal" efficiency.[2]

Finally, a buyer or seller would want the prevailing market price to adequately reflect all the available supply and demand factors in the market. If supply and demand conditions change as a result of new information, participants would want this information to be reflected in the price of the commodity. Therefore, another requirement for a good market is that *prices adjust quickly to new information regarding supply or demand.* This attribute is referred to as "external" efficiency.

In summary, a good market for goods and services would have the following characteristics:

1. Timely and accurate information on the price and volume of past transactions and similar information on prevailing supply and demand.

2. Liquidity—a buyer or seller of a good or service can buy or sell the asset quickly, at a price which is close to the price of previous transactions, assuming no new information has been received. In turn, a liquid market requires price continuity, i.e., prices do not change very much from transaction to transaction. Price continuity itself requires depth. There must be a number of buyers and sellers willing and able to enter the market at prices above and below those prevailing.

3. Low transaction cost. This "internal" efficiency means that all aspects of the transaction entail low costs, including the cost of reaching the market, the actual brokerage cost involved in the transaction, as well as the cost of transferring the asset.

4. Rapid adjustment of prices to new information. This "external" efficiency ensures that the prevailing price reflects all available information regarding the asset.

---

[2] Richard R. West and Seha M. Tinic, "Corporate Finance and the Changing Stock Market," *Financial Management,* Vol. 3, No. 3 (Autumn, 1974), pp. 14–23; Richard R. West, "On the Difference Between Internal and External Market Efficiency," *Financial Analysts Journal,* Vol. 31, No. 6 (November–December, 1975), pp. 30–34.

Seasoned and Initial Primary Offerings

The primary market for corporate offerings is the one in which new issues, bonds, preferred stock, or common stock, are sold by companies to acquire new capital. The proceeds of the sale of securities goes to the firm as new capital. These new issues are typically broken down into two groups. The first and largest group are *seasoned* new issues offered by companies with existing public markets for their securities. An example would be General Motors selling a new issue of common stock. There is an existing public market for General Motors common stock and the company is increasing the number of outstanding shares to acquire new equity capital.[3]

The second major category in the new issues market is generally referred to as *initial* public offerings. An example would be a small company selling common stock to the public for the first time. In this case, there is no existing public market for the stock, i.e., the company has been closely held.[4]

New issues (seasoned or initial) are typically underwritten by investment bankers who acquire the total issue from the company and, in turn, sell the issue to interested investors. The underwriter gives advice to the corporation on the general characteristics of the issue, its pricing, and the timing of the offering. He also accepts the risk of selling the new issue after acquiring it from the corporation.

Alternative Relationship with Investment Banker

Arrangements made by the company and the underwriter typically take one of three forms. The first is the most common: an existing corporation negotiates with a specific underwriter or investment banker, usually one with whom it has worked on a continuous basis. When the firm decides to sell a new issue of securities (stocks or bonds), the investment banker advises the firm on what type of issue to sell, the price of the issue, and when the firm should come to the market with the issue, and forms an underwriting syndicate and selling group for the sale of the issue.[5]

A corporation may also specify the type of securities to be offered (common stock, preferred stock, or bonds) and then solicit competitive bids from investment banking firms. This is typically done by utilities, which, in many cases, are *required* to submit their issues for competitive bids. It is contended that the cost of the issue is reduced in this manner,

---

[3] An extensive analysis of this segment of the new issues market is contained in I. Friend, J. R. Longstreet, M. Mendelson, E. Miller and A. P. Hess, Jr., *Investment Banking and the New Issues Market* (Cleveland: The World Publishing Co., 1967).

[4] A popular example of an initial public offering was that made by Coor's Brewing Company, in June, 1975. The company had a history of very successful operation, but had been privately held, prior to this time.

[5] For a detailed discussion of the underwriting process see J. Fred Weston and Eugene F. Brigham, *Managerial Finance,* 5th ed. (Hinsdale, Ill.: The Dryden Press), Chapter 12.

although it is also acknowledged that there is a commensurate reduction in the services provided by the investment banker. He will give the issuing firm less in terms of advice, but will still underwrite the issue.

Finally, an investment banker can agree to become involved with an issue and sell it on a "best efforts" basis. This is usually done with speculative new issue. The point is, the investment banker does *not* really underwrite the issue, since he does *not* buy it. The stock is owned by the company, and the investment banker is acting as a broker trying to sell what he can at a stipulated price. The investment banker's commission on such an issue is less than on an issue he underwrites.

Secondary Markets

Importance of Secondary Markets

In secondary markets there is trading in outstanding issues. In this case, an issue has already been sold to the public, and it is traded between current and potential owners. Again, there are secondary markets for bonds, preferred stock, and common stock. The proceeds from a sale in the secondary market do *not* go to the company but to the current owner of the security.

Prior to discussing the various segments of the secondary market, we must consider its overall importance. As noted, the secondary market involves trading securities initially sold in the primary market. Therefore, the secondary market provides *liquidity* to individuals who acquired securities in the primary markets. After an individual has acquired securities in the primary market, he wants to be able to sell the securities at some point in the future in order to acquire other securities, buy a house, or go on a vacation. Such a sale takes place in the secondary market. The investor's ability to convert the asset into cash (his liquidity) is heavily dependent upon the secondary market. *The primary market would be seriously hampered in its function of helping firms acquire new capital without the liquidity provided by the secondary market.* Investors would be hesitant to acquire securities in the primary market if they felt they would not subsequently have the ability to sell the securities quickly at a known price in the secondary market.

Secondary markets are also important to a corporation because the prevailing market price of the security is determined by action in the secondary market. Therefore, any new issue of that security sold in the primary market will necessarily be priced in line with the current price in the secondary market. As a result, the firm's capital costs are determined in the secondary market.

Secondary Bond Markets

Types of Bonds
When considering the secondary market for bonds, the first distinction that should be made is the division between corporate bonds issued by indi-

vidual business firms and the vast group of bonds issued by the federal government or state and local governmental units. Corporate bonds are issued by industrial companies, railroads, and utilities. There can be a large difference in the quality of these bonds depending upon the firm that issued them. Quality in this case refers to the ability of the firm to meet all required interest payments and the face value at maturity.

Government bond issues can likewise be divided into several groups. The first group are those issued by the federal government and include long-term bonds and notes that have maturities of from one year to 25 years. In addition, there are short-term treasury bills that have maturities, at the time of issue, of from 90 to 180 days. There are a number of governmental agencies that likewise are authorized to issue their own bonds. Examples would include the Federal Home Loan Bank; the Federal Land Bank; the Federal National Mortgage Association (FNMA); and the World Bank. There is a more detailed discussion of these bonds in later chapters.

Secondary Corporate Bond Market

The secondary market for corporate bonds has two major segments, the exchanges and the over-the-counter market. The major exchange for bonds is the New York Stock Exchange (NYSE). As of the end of 1977 there were 2,837 bond issues listed on the NYSE with a par value of 497 billion dollars and a market value of 480 billion dollars.[6] On a typical day about 1,000 of the issues trade and the volume of trading is about 30 million dollars. In addition, there are about 200 issues listed on the American Stock Exchange (ASE) which has a typical daily volume of about 2 million dollars. All corporate bonds not listed on one of the exchanges are traded over-the-counter by dealers who buy and sell for their own account.

Secondary Government Bond Market

All government bonds are traded on the over-the-counter market by bond dealers specifically concerned with government bonds. These dealers are typically distinguished by the type of government bonds they handle. Some deal almost wholly in federal bonds, others are involved in agency bonds, and there is a virtually completely separate group of municipal bond dealers. Some of the most active government bond dealers are large banks in major cities like New York and Chicago and some of the large investment banking firms.

Banks are likewise active in municipal bonds because a large part of their investment portfolio is committed to them. Many large investment brokerage firms also have a municipal bond department.

---

[6] 1978 *Fact Book* (New York: New York Stock Exchange, 1978), p. 77.

Secondary Equity Markets

Secondary equity markets are usually broken down into three major groups: the major national exchanges, including the New York Stock Exchange and the American Stock Exchange; what are usually called "regional exchanges" in cities like Chicago, San Francisco, Boston, Philadelphia, and Washington; and the over-the-counter market trading in securities not listed on an organized exchange. The first two groups are similar in that they are referred to as listed securities exchanges; they differ in terms of size and geographic emphasis.

The listed securities exchanges are formal organizations that have a specified group of members that may use the facilities of the exchange and a specified group of securities (stocks or bonds) that have qualified for "listing." In addition to limitations on membership and the securities eligible for trading, these exchanges are similar in that the prices of securities listed on them are determined via an auction process, whereby interested buyers and sellers submit bids and asks for a given stock to a central location for that stock. The bids and asks are recorded by a "specialist" assigned to that stock. Shares of stock are then sold to the highest bidder and bought from the investing unit (individual, institution, etc.) with the lowest asking price (the lowest offering price).

National Securities Exchanges

Two securities exchanges are generally referred to as national in scope: the New York Stock Exchange (NYSE) and the American Stock Exchange (ASE). They are considered national because of the large number of securities listed, the geographic dispersion of the issuing firms, and their clientele of buyers and sellers.

The New York Stock Exchange (NYSE) is the largest organized securities market in the United States. The initial constitution that formally established the exchange was adopted in 1817. The NYSE was originally named the "New York Stock and Exchange Board." This was changed to the New York Stock Exchange in 1863.

As of the end of 1977, there were 1,575 companies with stock listed on the NYSE, and 2,177 stock issues (common and preferred) with a total market value of 797 billion dollars. The specific listing requirements for the NYSE as of 1978 are contained in Table 3–1.

The average number of shares traded on the exchange has increased steadily as has the number of issues listed and the turnover of shares. The average daily volume in recent years is contained in Table 3–2. These figures indicate that prior to the 1960's, the average daily volume was less than three million shares. Daily volume increased to about five million shares in the early 1960's, increased again to about ten million shares in the second half of the 1960's, and averaged about 15 million during the period 1970–1974. From 1975 on, there was another increase to about 18–20

Table 3–1
**Listing
Requirements
for NYSE**

	NYSE
Pre-Tax Income Last Year	$ 2,500,000
Pre-Tax Income Last 2 Years	$ 2,000,000
Net Income Last Year	—
Net Tangible Assets	$16,000,000
Shares Publicly Held	1,000,000
Market Value Publicly Held Shares	$16,000,000
Number of Round lot holders	2,000

Source: *Fact Book* (New York: New York Stock Exchange, 1978). Reprinted by permission.

million shares a day. During 1978 the exchange experienced its busiest day and volume subsequently consistently exceeded 30 million shares.

The domination of other listed exchanges by the NYSE is shown in Table 3–3, which contains the percentage breakdown of share volume and the value of trading.

Table 3–2
**Average Daily
Reported Share
Volume Traded on
the NYSE
(thousands)**

1940	751	1966	7,538
1945	1,422	1967	10,080
1950	1,980	1968	12,971
1955	2,578	1969	11,403
1960	3,042	1970	11,564
1961	4,085	1971	15,381
1962	3,818	1972	16,487
1963	4,567	1973	16,084
1964	4,888	1974	13,904
1965	6,176	1975	18,551
		1976	21,186
		1977	20,936

Source: *Fact Book* (New York: New York Stock Exchange, various years). Reprinted by permission.

The NYSE has consistently accounted for about 75 percent of all shares traded on listed exchanges compared to about 10 to 20 percent for the ASE, and about 10 percent for all regional exchanges combined (the "other" category). Because the price of shares on the NYSE tends to be higher than that of shares on the ASE, the percentage of value of trading on the NYSE has averaged from 80 to 85 percent with lower figures for the ASE, while the regional exchanges are comparable in shares and value.

Based upon this clearly dominant position and the history of the NYSE

Table 3–3
Shares Sold on Registered Exchanges

	Number of Shares Traded (Percent of Total)			Market Value of Shares Traded (Percent of Total)		
	NYSE	ASE	Other	NYSE	ASE	Other
1935	77.6	12.8	9.6	87.3	7.9	4.8
1940	76.0	12.9	11.1	85.3	7.7	7.0
1945	66.6	20.5	12.9	83.0	10.6	6.4
1950	76.5	13.4	10.1	86.0	6.8	7.2
1955	67.7	20.1	12.2	86.5	6.8	6.7
1960	69.0	21.6	9.3	83.9	9.2	6.8
1965	69.9	22.5	7.5	82.0	9.7	8.3
1970	70.8	19.4	9.8	78.7	10.9	10.4
1971	72.1	17.7	10.2	79.5	9.6	10.9
1972	71.4	17.5	11.1	78.3	10.0	11.7
1973	75.7	12.9	11.4	82.3	5.9	11.9
1974	79.0	9.8	11.2	83.9	4.3	11.9
1975	81.1	8.7	10.2	85.2	3.6	11.2
1976	80.3	9.1	10.7	84.4	3.8	11.8
1977	79.9	9.3	10.8	84.0	4.6	11.4

Source: *Annual Report* (Washington, D.C.: Securities and Exchange Commission); *NYSE Fact Book* (New York: New York Stock Exchange, various years). Reprinted by permission.

and other exchanges, the exchange has been called a monopolist.[7] The volume of trading and dominant position is also reflected in the price of membership on the exchange (referred to as a "seat"). As shown in Table 3–4, the price of membership has fluctuated in line with trading volume and other factors that influence the profitability of membership.

The American Stock Exchange (ASE) was begun by a group of persons who traded unlisted shares at the corner of Wall and Hanover Streets in New York and was referred to as the Outdoor Curb Market. It made several moves along the streets of the financial district and, in 1910, formal trading rules were established and the name was changed to the New York Curb Market Association. The members moved inside a building in 1921 and continued to trade mainly in unlisted stocks. The predominance of unlisted stocks continued until 1946, when listed stocks finally outnumbered unlisted stocks. The current name was adopted in 1953.

The ASE is distinct because of its desire to be different from the NYSE. A major factor in this uniqueness was that, prior to August, 1976, no stocks

---

[7] Robert W. Doede, "The Monopoly Power of the New York Stock Exchange," unpublished dissertation, University of Chicago (June, 1967).

Table 3–4
Membership Prices on the NYSE and the ASE (in thousands of dollars)

	NYSE High	NYSE Low	ASE High	ASE Low		NYSE High	NYSE Low	ASE High	ASE Low
1925	150	99	38	9	1966	270	197	120	70
1935	140	65	33	12	1967	450	220	230	100
1945	95	49	32	12	1968	515	385	315	220
1955	90	80	22	18	1969	515	260	350	150
1960	162	135	60	51	1970	320	130	185	70
1961	225	147	80	52	1971	300	145	150	65
1962	210	115	65	40	1972	250	150	145	70
1963	217	160	66	53	1973	190	72	100	27
1964	230	190	63	52	1974	105	65	60	27
1965	250	190	80	55	1975	138	55	72	34
					1976	104	40	68	40

Source: *Fact Book* (New York: NYSE, 1977); *Databook* (New York: ASE, 1976). Reprinted by permission of the NYSE and the ASE.

were listed on the NYSE and ASE at the same time. This lack of dual listing on the two exchanges located in New York was part of an arrangement formalized in May, 1910, when the brokers who organized the New York Curb Market Association drew up a constitution that specifically prohibited members from trading stocks listed on the NYSE. As a consequence, as soon as a stock listed on the ASE was accepted for listing on the NYSE, it was automatically dropped by the ASE. This changed in August, 1976, when the ASE proposed that the "New York Rule" be abolished and that dual listing (trading of the same stock on both exchanges) be permitted. The change was approved by the Securities and Exchange Commission on August 22, 1976,[8] and Varo, Incorporated became the first dual listed stock, beginning trading on August 23, 1976.[9] During the next three months, four other firms likewise became listed on the NYSE, but retained their ASE listing.[10]

The ASE has been quite innovative in listing foreign securities over the years. There were 69 foreign issues listed in 1976 and trading in these issues constituted almost 10 percent of total volume.[11] Further, there were warrants listed on the ASE for a number of years before the NYSE would list them. The most recent innovation by the ASE has been the trading of call options on listed securities, introduced after option trading became wide-

[8] "SEC Clears Trading on Amex of Stocks Listed on Big Board," *Wall Street Journal,* August 23, 1976, p. 3.

[9] *Wall Street Journal,* August 24, 1976, p. 5.

[10] *Wall Street Journal,* September 17, 1976, p. 7.

[11] *Databook* (New York: American Stock Exchange, 1976), p. 20.

spread with the establishment of the Chicago Board Options Exchange (CBOE). Again, because options are not traded on the NYSE (as of 1978) almost all options traded on the ASE are for stocks listed on the NYSE.

At the end of 1978, there were approximately 1,400 stock issues listed on the ASE.[12] As can be seen from the figures in Table 3–5 average daily trading volume has fluctuated substantially over time as the demand for smaller and younger firms has changed. Prior to 1955, average daily volume was below 500,000 shares. Average daily volume reached one million shares in 1959, almost two million in 1961, and exceeded two million in 1965 and 1966. In 1967, the average daily volume increased to 4.5 million and reached its highest level of 6.3 million shares a day in 1968. Trading volume declined to between three and four million shares a day during 1970–1973 and has declined further to about two million shares a day since 1974. This decline in volume is also reflected in the percent of trading as reported in Table 3–3. During 1978, though, the exchange has enjoyed an increase in trading volume similar to the NYSE and daily volume has consistently exceeded four million shares.

Table 3–5
Average Daily Reported Share Volume Traded on the American Stock Exchange (thousands)

Year	Volume	Year	Volume
1940	171	1966	2,741
1945	583	1967	4,544
1950	435	1968	6,353
1955	912	1969	4,963
1960	1,113	1970	3,319
1961	1,948	1971	4,233
1962	1,225	1972	4,454
1963	1,262	1973	3,003
1964	1,479	1974	1,908
1965	2,120	1975	2,150
		1976	2,565
		1977	2,514

Source: *Databook* (New York: American Stock Exchange, 1976). Reprinted by permission.

The American Stock Exchange is national in scope and, although also located in New York, is distinct from the NYSE. The companies listed on the ASE are almost completely different from those listed on the NYSE. In addition, ASE firms are generally smaller and younger than the firms listed on the NYSE consistent with the difference in listing requirements. To prosper and compete against the NYSE, the ASE has had a history of

---

[12] The requirements for listing on the ASE are contained in Table 3–6. The reader will note that the requirements are clearly less stringent than those for listing on the NYSE. The difference is reflected in the fact that the average firm on the ASE is substantially smaller than a firm on the NYSE in terms of sales, earnings, and assets.

innovation including the listing of foreign stocks, warrants, and, most recently, the trading of stock options.

Table 3–6
Listing Requirements for ASE

Pre-Tax Income Last Year	$ 750,000
Pre-Tax Income Last 2 Years	—
Net Income Last Year	$ 400,000
Net Tangible Assets	$4,000,000
Shares Publicly Held	400,000
Market Value Publicly Held Shares	$3,000,000
Number of Round lot holders	1,200

Source: *Databook* (New York: American Stock Exchange, 1976). Reprinted by permission.

Regional Securities Exchanges

Regional Exchanges have basically the same operating procedures as the NYSE and ASE but differ in terms of their listing requirements and the geographic distribution of the firms listed. There are two main reasons for the existence of regional stock exchanges: they provide trading facilities for local companies that are not large enough to qualify for listing on one of the national exchanges. To accommodate these companies, the listing requirements are typically less stringent than are those of the national exchanges as set forth in Tables 3–1 and 3–6. Their second purpose is that they list national firms that are also listed on one of the national exchanges for local brokers who are not members of a national exchange. As an example, American Telephone and Telegraph and General Motors are both listed on the NYSE, but they are *also* listed on several regional exchanges. This dual listing allows a local brokerage firm that is not large enough to purchase a membership on the NYSE (for $55,000 or more) to buy and sell shares of dual listed stock (e.g., General Motors) using his membership on a regional exchange. As a result, the broker will not have to go through the NYSE and give up part of his commission. Currently, between 65 and 90 percent of the volume on regional exchanges is attributable to trading in dual listed issues.[13]

The major regional exchanges are:

Midwest Stock Exchange (Chicago)

Pacific Stock Exchange (San Francisco–Los Angeles)

PBW Exchange (Philadelphia–Pittsburgh)

Boston Stock Exchange (Boston)

---

[13] For an extended discussion of the regional exchanges see James E. Walter, *The Role of Regional Security Exchanges* (Berkeley: University of California Press, 1957).

Spokane Stock Exchange (Spokane, Washington)

Honolulu Stock Exchange (Honolulu, Hawaii)

Intermountain Stock Exchange (Salt Lake City)

The first three exchanges (Midwest; Pacific; PBW) account for about 90 percent of all regional exchange volume. In turn, total regional volume is about 11 percent of total exchange volume as shown in Table 3–3. Table 3–3 shows that the fortunes of the regional exchanges have fluctuated substantially over time. The regional exchanges prospered during the late 1960's, when there was widespread interest in small, young firms. Their recent growth has been influenced by institutional interest in stocks dual listed on national and regional exchanges.

The Over-the-Counter Market (OTC)

The over-the-counter market includes trading in all stocks not listed on one of the exchanges. It can also include trading in stocks that are listed. This latter arrangement, referred to as the "third market," is discussed in the following section. The OTC market is not a formal market organization with membership requirements or a specific list of stocks deemed eligible for trading. In theory, it is possible to trade *any* security on the OTC market as long as someone is willing to "take a position" in the stock. This means an individual or firm is willing to buy or sell, make a market, in the stock.

Size The OTC market is the largest segment of the secondary market in terms of the number of issues traded and is also the most diverse in terms of quality. As noted earlier, there are about 2,000 issues traded on the NYSE, and about 1,400 issues on the ASE. In terms of active issues, there are about 2,500 traded on the OTC quotation system (NASDAQ), inclusion in which requires certain size and at least two active market-makers. In addition, there are at least another 3,000–4,000 stocks that are traded fairly actively, but are not on NASDAQ. Therefore, there are between 5,500 and 6,500 issues traded on the OTC market—more than on the NYSE and ASE combined. While the OTC is dominant in terms of the numbers of issues, the NYSE is still dominant in terms of the total *value* of the stocks.

There is tremendous diversity in the OTC because there are no minimum requirements for a stock to be traded. Therefore, it is possible for OTC listings to range from the smallest, most unprofitable company, to the largest, most profitable firm. On the upper end, all U.S. government bonds are traded on the OTC market, as are the vast majority of bank stocks and insurance stocks. Finally, the 150 listed stocks that are *also* traded on the OTC (the third market), includes AT&T, General Motors, IBM, Xerox, and a host of other stocks with active third markets.

Operation of the OTC As noted, any stock can be traded on the OTC as long as someone indicates he is willing to "make a market" in the stock, i.e., buy or sell for his own account. Therefore, *participants in the OTC market act as dealers because they buy and sell for their own account.*[14] This is in contrast to the situation on the listed exchanges where the specialist is generally acting as an agent for other investors. The specialist keeps the book and attempts to match the buy and sell orders left with him. Because of this, the OTC market is referred to as a *negotiated* market in which investors directly negotiate with dealers. Exchanges are *auction* markets with the specialist acting as the intermediary (auctioneer).

The NASDAQ System NASDAQ is an acronym that stands for National Association of Securities Dealers Automatic Quotations. It is an electronic quotation system that serves the vast OTC market. Because any number of dealers can elect to make a market in an OTC stock, it is possible to have 10, 15, or more market-makers for a given stock, and it is common to have three to five. A major problem has always been determining the current quotations by specific market-makers. Prior to the introduction of NAS-DAQ, it was necessary for a broker to make phone calls to three or four dealers to determine the prevailing market and then, after such a "survey," go back to the one with the best market for his client (i.e., the one with the highest bid or lowest asking price). This process was very time consuming and frustrating, and when there were 10 or 15 dealers making a market for a stock, even after three or four phone calls a broker was not certain he had found the best market. With NASDAQ, all quotes by market-makers are available immediately and the broker can make one phone call to the dealer with the best market, verify that the quote has not changed, and make the sale or purchase. The National Association of Securities Dealers (NASD) has specified three levels for the NASDAQ system to serve firms with different needs and interests.[15]

Level 1 is for firms that want current information on OTC stocks, but do not consistently buy or sell OTC stocks for their customers and are not market-makers. For these brokerage firms, a current quote on alternative OTC stocks is most important. Level 1 provides a single *median quote* ("representative") for all stocks in the system that considers all the market-makers (half the quotes are higher and half the quotes are lower). This composite quote is changed constantly to adjust for any changes by individual market-makers.

Level 2 is for firms that seriously trade in OTC stocks for themselves or their customers. For this clientele, Level 2 provides *instantaneous current*

---

[14] Dealer and market-maker are synonymous.

[15] A detailed description of the NASDAQ system is contained in "NASDAQ and the OTC," National Association of Securities Dealers, Inc. Reprinted in Frank K. Reilly (ed.) *Readings and Issues in Investments* (Hinsdale, Ill.: The Dryden Press, 1975). For a discussion of NASDAQ and its use in a centralized market, see Lawrence A. Armour, "Central Marketplace," *Barron's* (February 28, 1972), p.3.

quotations by all market-makers in a stock. Given a desire to buy or sell, the broker simply calls the market-maker with the best market for his purpose (highest bid if he is selling, or lowest offer if he wants to buy) and consummates the deal.

Level 3 is for investment firms that make markets in OTC stocks. Such firms want to know what everyone else is quoting (Level 2), but they also need the capability to enter their own quotations and the ability to *change* their quotations. This is what Level 3 provides, everything in Level 2 plus the ability to enter and change quotes.

A Sample Trade Assume an investor is considering the purchase of 100 shares of Anheuser Busch. Although Anheuser Busch is large enough and profitable enough to be eligible for listing on either of the national exchanges, the company has never applied for listing because it enjoys a very active market on the OTC (daily volume is typically above 50,000 shares and often exceeds 100,000 shares). Therefore, when the individual contacts his broker, the broker will consult the NASDAQ electronic quotation machine to determine the current markets for ABUD (the trading symbol for Anheuser Busch).[16] The display screen on his Level 2 machine would indicate that about 20–25 dealers are making a market in ABUD. An example of differing markets might be as follows:

Dealer	Bid	Ask
1	24¼	24¾
2	24⅜	24¾
3	24¼	24⅝
4	24½	25
5	24⅛	24¾

If we assume for the moment that these are the best markets available from the total group, the investor's broker would then call dealer number 3 because he had the lowest offering price, i.e., he was willing to sell at the lowest price. He would verify the quote and then tell dealer number 3 that he wants to buy 100 shares of ABUD at 24⅝ ($24.625 a share). Because the investor's firm was not a market-maker in the stock, the firm would act as a broker for the customer and charge $2,462.50 plus a commission for the trade. If the customer had been interested in selling 100 shares of Anheuser Busch, the broker would have contacted dealer number 4 because he had the highest bid, i.e., was willing to pay the most to buy the stock. If the broker was also a market-maker in ABUD and had the quote of 24¼–24⅝, then he

---

[16] Trading symbols are one- to four-letter codes used to designate stocks. Whenever a trade is reported on a stock ticker the trading symbol is used. Many are obvious, like GM (General Motors, F (Ford Motors), GE (General Electric), ATT (American Telephone and Telegraph).

would have sold the stock to the customer at 24⅝ "net" (without commission).

Changing Dealer Inventory It seems useful at this point to consider the quotation an OTC dealer would give if he wanted to change his inventory on a given stock. For example, assume dealer number 2 with a current quote of 24⅜–24¾ decides that he wants to *increase* his holdings of ABUD. An examination of the quotes on his NASDAQ quote machine indicates that the highest bid is currently 24½. He can increase his bid to 24½ and get some of the business currently going to dealer number 4, or, if he wants to be very aggressive, he can raise his bid to 24⅝ and buy all of the stock that is offered, including some from dealer number 3 who is offering it at 24⅝. In this example, the dealer raises his bid but does not change his asking price, which was above another dealer's. Thus he is going to buy stock, but probably will not sell any. If the dealer had more stock than he wanted, he would keep his bid below the market (lower than 24½) and reduce his asking price to 24⅝ or less. Dealers are constantly changing their bid and/or their asking price, depending upon their current inventory or the outlook for the stock.

The Third Market
The term "third market" is used to describe *over-the-counter trading of shares listed on an exchange.* When a stock is listed on an exchange, members of that exchange are generally required to execute all buy and sell orders through the exchange. Further, assuming that most investors are aware that the stock is listed on an exchange, they will likely consider it the best place to go to transact business in this stock. Therefore, one would expect most of the transactions in listed stocks to take place on an exchange. At the same time, an investment firm that is not a member of an exchange can make a market in a listed stock in the same way that it would make a market in an unlisted stock. The success or failure of such a venture will obviously depend upon whether the OTC market is as good as the exchange market and/or the relative cost of the transaction compared to the cost on the exchange. Based upon the relative growth of the third market since 1965, as shown in Table 3–7, it appears that there have been advantages to third market trading for some investors.

The figures in Table 3–7 indicate that the relative volume of trading on the third market, compared to NYSE volume, grew consistently and dramatically from 1965 through 1972, but has declined steadily since 1973. To understand this growth pattern, which will be discussed in Chapter 4, two points must be clarified. First, *almost all trading on the third market is done by institutions.* Most individuals are not aware of this market and, if they know about it, they generally do not know how to use it. Second, *trading in the third market was concentrated in a limited number of stocks.* Almost all third market trading is in less than 200 stocks. According to the NYSE *Fact Book,* during 1976 about 40 percent of third market volume was

Table 3–7
Third Market Volume in NYSE Stocks as a Percent of Volume on the NYSE

	Share Volume (%)	Value of Volume (%)		Share Volume (%)	Value of Volume (%)
1965	2.7	3.4	1971	7.0	8.4
1966	2.6	2.9	1972	7.3	8.5
1967	2.9	3.3	1973	5.8	7.0
1968	3.6	4.2	1974	5.3	7.0
1969	4.9	5.5	1975	4.6	6.0
1970	6.5	7.8	1976	3.8	5.5
			1977	3.3	4.6

Source: *Statistical Bulletin* (Washington, D.C.: Securities and Exchange Commission, various issues).

in 50 stocks.[17] An investment firm considering establishing a market in a listed stock will select a stock that is of interest to the major customers of the third market, the institutions. Therefore, the principal third market stocks are institutional stocks like AT&T, General Motors, IBM, and General Electric.

The Fourth Market The term fourth market is used to describe *the direct trading of securities between two parties* with no broker intermediary. In almost all cases, both parties involved are institutions. When you think about it, a direct transaction is really not that unusual. If an individual owns 100 shares of AT&T and decides to sell it, there is nothing wrong with simply asking his friends or associates if any of them would be interested in buying the stock at a mutually agreeable price and making the transaction directly. Investors typically buy or sell stock through a broker because it is faster and easier. Also, the sale may be better executed because the investor has a good chance of finding the "best" buyer through a broker. The investor is willing to pay a fee for these services, which is the brokerage commission.

The fourth market evolved because the brokerage fee charged institutions with large orders is substantial. At some point it becomes worthwhile for institutions to attempt to deal directly with each other and save the brokerage fee. Consider an institution that decides to sell 40,000 shares of AT&T. Assuming that AT&T is selling for about 50 dollars a share, the value of the 40,000 shares is 2 million dollars. The average commission on such a transaction, prior to fully negotiated rates, was about one percent of the value of the trade which, for this trade, would be *$20,000*. Given this cost, it becomes attractive for the selling institution to spend some time and effort finding another institution interested in increasing its holding of AT&T and attempt to negotiate a direct sale. Because of the diverse nature of the fourth market and the lack of reporting requirements, there are no

---

[17] *Fact Book* (New York: New York Stock Exchange, 1976), p. 17.

data available regarding its specific size or growth, although it is generally conceded that it has grown, especially in trading of the large institutional favorites, such as IBM and AT&T.[18]

Detailed Analysis of the Exchange Market

Because of the importance of the listed exchange market, it must be dealt with at some length. In this section we will discuss the several types of membership on the exchanges, the major types of orders used, and finally the function of the specialist who is considered the main determinant of a "good" exchange market.

Exchange Membership

Listed securities exchanges typically have five major categories of membership: (1) specialist, (2) odd-lot dealer, (3) commission broker, (4) floor-broker, and (5) registered trader.

Specialists constitute about 25 percent of the total membership on exchanges. They are considered by some observers to be the most important group because, as will be discussed, they are responsible for maintaining a fair and orderly market in the securities listed on an exchange.

Odd-lot dealers stand ready to buy or sell less than a round lot of stock (a round lot is typically a multiple of 100 shares). When an individual wants to buy fewer than 100 shares, his order is turned over to an odd-lot dealer who will buy or sell from his own inventory. Note that the dealer is *not* a broker, and that he is buying and selling from his own inventory. Prior to 1976, all odd-lot transactions were handled by an odd-lot house. Since then, the NYSE has taken over the function. On most other exchanges, the specialist in a stock is also the odd-lot dealer for the stock. Some large brokerage firms (most notably Merrill Lynch, Pierce, Fenner and Smith, Inc.) have been acting as odd-lot dealers for their own customers.

Commission Brokers are employees of a member firm who buy or sell for the customers of the firm. When an investor places an order to buy or sell stock through a registered representative of a brokerage firm, and the firm has a membership on an exchange, it will contact its commission broker on the floor of the exchange and he will go to the appropriate post on the floor and buy or sell the stock as instructed.

---

[18] For a further description of the third and fourth markets and a discussion of what might happen if a national market were established, see Donald M. Feuerstein, "Toward a National System of Securities Exchanges: The Third and Fourth Markets," *Financial Analysts Journal*, Vol. 28, No. 4 (July–August, 1972), pp. 57–59.

Floor Brokers are members of an exchange who act as brokers on the floor for other members. They are typically not connected with a member firm but own their own seat. When the commission broker for Merrill Lynch becomes too busy to handle all of his orders, he will ask one of the floor brokers to help him. At one time they were referred to as "two dollar brokers" because that is what they received for each order. Currently they receive about four dollars per 100 share order.

Registered Traders are allowed to use their membership to buy and sell for their own account. They therefore save the commission on their own trading and observers feel they have an advantage because they are on the floor. The exchanges and others feel they should be allowed these advantages because registered traders provide the market with added liquidity. Because of possible abuses, there are regulations regarding how they trade and how many registered traders can be in a trading crowd around a specialists' booth at a point in time.

Types of Orders

The reader should have a full understanding of the different types of orders used by individual investors and by the specialist in his dealer function. The most frequent type is a market order. A *market order* is an order to buy or sell a stock at the best price currently prevailing. An investor who wants to sell some stock using a market order indicates that he would be willing to sell *immediately* at the highest bid available at the time the order reaches the specialist on the exchange. A market buy order indicates the investor is willing to pay the lowest offering price available at the time the order reaches the floor of the exchange. Market orders are used when an individual wants to effect a transaction *quickly* (wants immediate liquidity), and is willing to accept the prevailing market price. Assume an investor is interested in American Telephone and Telegraph (AT&T) and called his broker to find out the current "market" on the stock. Using a quotation machine, the broker determines that the prevailing market is 52 bid–52¼ ask. This means that currently the highest bid on the books of the specialist, i.e., the most that anyone has offered to pay for AT&T, is 52. The lowest offer is 52¼, which is the lowest price someone is willing to accept for selling the stock. If an investor placed a market buy order for 100 shares, he would buy 100 shares at $52.25 a share (the lowest ask price) for a total cost of $5,225 plus commission. If an investor submitted a market sell order for 100 shares, he would sell the shares at 52 dollars each and receive 5,200 dollars, less commission.

The second major category is a *limit order,* which means that the individual placing the order has specified the price at which he will buy or sell the stock. An investor might submit a bid to purchase 100 shares of stock at 48 dollars a share, when the current market is 52 bid–52¼ ask, with the expectation that the stock will decline to 48 dollars in the near future. Such an order must also indicate *how long* the limit order will be outstanding. The alternatives, in terms of time, are basically without bounds—they can be instantaneous ("fill or kill"—fill instantly or cancel it), for part of a day, for a full day, for several days, a week, a month, or open-ended, which means the order is good until cancelled (GTC). Rather than wait for a given price on a stock, a broker will give the limit order to the specialist, who will put it in his book and act as the broker's representative. When and if the market reaches the limit order price, the specialist will execute the order and inform the broker. The specialist receives a small part of the commission for rendering this service.

While most investors purchase stock with the expectation that they will derive their return from an increase in value, there are instances in which an investor believes that a stock is overpriced, and wants to act in order to take advantage of an expected decline in the price. The way to do this is to *sell the stock short*. A *short sale* is the sale of stock that is not owned with the intent of purchasing it later at a lower price. The investor *borrows* the stock from another investor through his broker and sells it in the market. He will repurchase the stock (hopefully, at a price lower than the one at which he sold it) and thereby replace it. The investor who lent the stock has the use of the money paid for it, because it is left with him as collateral on the stock loan. While there is no time limit on a short sale, the lender can indicate that he wants to sell his shares, in which case the broker must find another investor to make the loan.

Two technical points in connection with short sales are important. First, a short sale can only be made on an uptick trade (the price of the sale must be higher than the last trade price). The reason for this restriction is that the exchanges do not want traders to be able to *force* a profit on a short sale by pushing the price down through continually selling short. Therefore, the transaction price for a short sale must be an uptick or, if there is no change in price, the previous price must have been higher than its previous price (a zero uptick). An example of a zero uptick is a transaction at 42, 42¼; you could sell short at 42¼ even though it is no change from the previous trade at 42¼. Second, the short seller is responsible for the dividends to the investor who lent the stock. The purchaser of the short sale stock receives the dividend from the corporation, so the short seller must pay a similar dividend to the lender.

In addition to these general orders, there are several special types of orders. One is a *stop loss order,* which is a conditional market order, whereby the investor indicates that he wants to sell a stock *if* the stock drops to a given price. Assume an individual buys a stock at 50 and expects it to go up. If he's wrong, he wants to minimize or limit his losses. Therefore, he would put in a stop loss order at 45, in which case, *if* the stock dropped to 45, his stop loss order would become a *market sell order,* and the stock would be sold at the prevailing market price. The order does not guarantee the investor will get the 45 dollars; he can get a little bit more or a little bit less. Because of the possibility of market disruption caused by a large number of stop loss orders, exchanges, on occasion, have cancelled all stop loss orders on certain stocks and have not allowed brokers to accept further stop loss orders on the issues involved.

Another type of stop loss, but on the other side, is a *stop buy order*. An investor has sold stock short and wants to minimize any loss if a stock begins to increase in value. This order makes it possible to place a conditional buy order at a price above the price at which he sold the stock short. Assume an individual had sold a stock short at 50, expecting it to decline to 40. To protect himself from an increase, he could put in a stop buy order to purchase the stock if it reached a price of 55. This would hopefully limit any loss on the short sale to approximately five dollars a share.

The Specialist[19]

With justification, the stock exchange specialist has been referred to as the center of the auction market for stocks. As noted, three requirements for a "good" market are depth, price continuity, and liquidity. The existence of these characteristics is heavily dependent upon how the specialist does his job.

The specialist is a member of the exchange who applies for his position by asking the exchange to assign stocks to him. The typical specialist will handle about seven stocks. He must possess substantial capital to carry out this function, either 500,000 dollars or enough to purchase 5,000 shares of the stock, whichever is greater. He must also have the knowledge to fulfill the functions of a specialist.

Functions of the Specialist

The specialist has two major functions. The first is that of a *broker* who handles the limit orders or special orders placed with member brokers. An individual broker who receives a limit order to purchase a stock at five dollars below the current market does not have the time or inclination to constantly watch the stock to see when and if the decline takes place. Therefore, he leaves the limit order (or a stop loss or stop buy order) with the specialist who enters it in his book and executes it when appropriate. For this service the specialist receives a portion of the broker's commission on the trade.

The second major function is to act as a *dealer* in the stocks assigned to him in order to maintain a "fair and orderly market." He is expected to buy and sell *for his own account* when there is insufficient public supply or demand to provide a continuous, liquid market. In this function he is acting like a dealer on the OTC market. If a stock is currently selling for about 40 dollars per share, one could envision a situation in an auction market in

---

[19] An excellent booklet describing the specialist function is "The Specialist" (New York: New York Stock Exchange, 1975). The booklet is reprinted in Frank K. Reilly (ed.), *Readings and Issues in Investments* (Hinsdale, Ill., The Dryden Press, 1975).

which the current bid and ask (without the intervention of the specialist) might be a 40 bid—41 ask. Assuming the specialist does not intercede, and market orders to buy and sell the stock come to the market in a random fashion, the price of the stock would fluctuate between 40 and 41 constantly—a movement of 2.5 percent between trades. Most investors would probably consider such a price pattern to be too volatile; it would not be considered a very continuous market. The specialist is expected to provide an alternative bid and/or ask that will narrow the spread and thereby provide greater price continuity over time. In the above example this would entail either entering a bid of 40½ or 40¾ or an ask of 40½ or 40¼ to narrow the spread to one-half or one-quarter point. The specialist can enter either side of the market. Which side he enters will depend upon several factors. The first is *the trend of the market.* Since he is committed to being a stabilizing force in the market, he is expected to buy or sell *against* the market when prices are clearly moving in one direction; i.e., he is expected to buy stock for his own inventory when there is an excess of sell orders and the market is definitely declining, or to sell stock from his inventory or sell it short when there is an excess of buy orders and the market is rising. He is not expected to prevent the price from rising or declining, but only to ensure that the price changes in an orderly fashion.

Another factor is *his current inventory position in the stock.* If a specialist already has a large inventory position in a given stock, all other factors being equal, he would probably enter on the ask (sell) side in order to reduce his heavy inventory. In contrast, if previous market action had prompted a number of sales from his inventory or short sales, the specialist would tend toward the bid (buy) side in order to accumulate stock to rebuild his inventory or close out his short positions.

Finally, *the position of his book* (i.e., the specialist's information on all limit orders for a stock) will influence his actions, assuming no current trends to which he must react. If the specialist notes a large number of limit buy orders (bids) close to the current market, and very few limit sell orders (asks), he might surmise that the most likely future move for the stock, in the absence of any new information, is toward a higher price because there is apparently heavy demand and limited supply. Under such conditions, one would expect the specialist to attempt to accumulate some stock in anticipation of an increase.

Income
The specialist derives income from both of his major functions. The actual breakdown between income from acting as a broker for limit orders, and income from acting as a dealer to maintain an orderly market will depend upon the specific stock. In the case of a very actively traded stock (e.g., American Telephone and Telegraph), there is not much need for the specialist to act as a dealer because substantial public interest in the issue creates a tight market. The major concern of the specialist (and his main source of income for this stock) is maintaining the limit orders for the stock.

In contrast, in the case of a stock with low trading volume and substantial price volatility, the specialist would be an active dealer and his income would depend upon his ability to profitably trade in the stock. A major advantage for the specialist in his trading of the stock is his access to the "book" that contains all limit orders for the stock in question. The specialist is the only one who is supposed to see the book, which means that he has a monopoly source of very important information. One can visualize the specialist's book containing the full set of limit orders as representing the current supply and demand curve for the stock. Therefore, it should provide the specialist with significant information regarding the probable direction of movement for the stock, at least in the short-run.

Therefore, although specialists may be forced to buy or sell against the market for short periods of time, over longer periods they should make substantial profits on their dealer transactions because of the monopoly source of information contained in the specialist's book.[20] In addition, the income derived from acting as a broker can be substantial and is basically without risk. Most specialists attempt to balance the stocks assigned to them between the two types: they will have some strong broker stocks that provide a steady riskless source of income, and some stocks that require an active dealer role.

Given the capital committed to the specialist function and the risk involved in acting as a dealer, one might wonder about the rate of return that specialists receive on their capital. Because most individual investors typically have received about 10 percent on common stock investments, one might expect a return to specialists of 20 percent. The fact is that a study by the Securities and Exchange Commission (SEC) indicated that there is substantial variation in the monthly income of specialist units, with the greatest variability experienced by units that have high inventory activity, i.e., among those specialists that are most active in market-making. An analysis of gross income per month relative to the average dollar of investment indicated that the annual rate of return for high activity units was *over 80 percent,* the return for the medium activity group was about *110 percent,* while the low activity group had an average rate of return of almost *190 percent.*[21] Besides indicating returns that seem clearly excessive for the risk involved, it is notable that the *least* active specialist units receive the *greatest* return.

The value of being able to trade using the monopoly information contained in the specialist's book should not be underrated. The specialist

---

[20] There is evidence that the specialists do not fare too badly even in instances in which they are forced to trade against the market. In this regard see Frank K. Reilly and Eugene F. Drzycimski, "The Stock Exchange Specialist and the Market Impact of Major World Events," *Financial Analysts Journal,* Vol. 31, No. 4 (July–August, 1975), pp. 27–32.

[21] United States House Committee on Interstate and Foreign Commerce, subcommittee on Commerce and Finance. *Securities Industry Study: Report and Hearings.* 92nd Congress, 1st and 2nd sessions, 1972, Chapter 12.

performs a very useful function on the exchange, but it also appears that the rate of return he receives is excessive for the risk involved. These excess returns seem to be the result of the very strong position of the NYSE in the secondary exchange market and the monopoly position of the specialists in terms of information regarding their respective stocks. The service is useful, but the returns are excessive. Because of these excess returns, one of the stated goals of the SEC is to introduce more competition into the market making function. The idea is to maintain the basic structure, but introduce more competition in order to reduce the costs to the investor. In Chapter 4, we will consider some of the changes that have taken place in the securities markets during the past decade and their effect on the specialist and other members of the securities market.

Summary

The chapter has been concerned with what a market is, why markets exist, and what constitutes a "good" market. It also included a discussion of the division of the securities market into primary and secondary markets and why secondary markets are important for primary markets. We then considered the major segments of the secondary markets, including listed exchanges (the NYSE, the ASE, and regional exchanges); the over-the-counter market; the third market; and the fourth market. The final section included a detailed analysis of the exchange market and a discussion of the membership on an exchange, a consideration of the types of orders used on the exchange and an in-depth look at the specialist function.

Questions

1. Define a market.

2. You own 100 shares of General Motors stock and you want to sell it because you need the money to make a down payment on a car. Assume there is *absolutely no secondary market system* in common stocks—how would you go about selling the stock? Discuss what you would have to do to find a buyer, how long it might take, and the price you might receive.

3. Briefly discuss the major characteristics of a "good" market.

4. Define liquidity and discuss what factors contribute to liquidity. Give an example of a liquid asset, an illiquid asset, and discuss why they are considered liquid and illiquid.

5. Define a primary market for securities.

6. Give an example of an initial public offering in the primary market. Give an example of a seasoned issue in the primary market. Which would involve greater risk to the buyer? Why?

7. What is a secondary market for securities? How does it differ from the primary market?

8. Some observers would contend that without a good secondary market for securities, the primary market would be less effective. Discuss the reasoning behind this contention.

9. In the section of the *Wall Street Journal* on government bonds entitled "Treasury Bonds and Notes," what is the current bid and yield on the 8¼ of 1990?

10. How do the two national stock exchanges differ from each other?

11. What are the major reasons for the existence of the regional exchanges? How do they differ from the national exchanges?

12. How does the OTC market differ from the listed exchanges?

13. Which market segment of the secondary market (listed or OTC) is larger in terms of the number of issues? In terms of the value of the issues traded?

14. Which segment of the secondary market has more diversity in terms of the size of the companies and the quality of the issues? Why is this so?

15. What is the NASDAQ system? Discuss the three levels of NASDAQ in terms of what they provide and who would subscribe to each.

16. What are the benefits derived from NASDAQ? What has it done for the OTC market?

17. Define the third market. Give an example of a third market stock.

18. Why is there a limited number of stocks that are actively traded on the third market?

19. Define the fourth market. Why would a financial institution use the fourth market?

20. What is the major advantage of the fourth market? What is its major disadvantage?

21. Define a market order and give an example for a person selling 100 shares of a stock.

22. Briefly define each of the following terms and give an example:
   A. limit order
   B. short sale
   C. stop loss order.

23. What are the two major functions of the specialist?

24. Over a long-run period (e.g., six months), would you expect the specialist to make money in his dealer function? Why or why not?

25. What are the two main sources of income for the specialist?

26. Other than the example in the chapter, give an example of a stock that would be a broker stock for the specialist. Why is it a broker stock?

27. What is the high risk segment of the specialists' dealer function? Why is it high risk? What aspect of the specialist position reduces the risk involved and also increases potential return? Be specific.

References

Armour, Lawrence A. "Central Marketplace." *Barron's* (March, 1972).

Doede, Robert W. "The Monopoly Power of the New York Stock Exchange." Unpublished dissertation, University of Chicago (June, 1967).

Eiteman, W. J., Dice, C. A., and Eiteman, D. K. *The Stock Market.* 4th ed. New York: McGraw–Hill, 1966.

Fact Book. New York: New York Stock Exchange, published annually.

Friend, Irwin and Winn, W. J. *The Over-the-Counter Securities Markets.* New York: McGraw–Hill, 1958.

Leffler, George L. and Farwell, Loring. *The Stock Market.* 3rd ed. New York: The Ronald Press, 1963.

Loll, Leo M. and Buckley, Julian G. *The Over-the-Counter Securities Markets.* 3rd ed. Englewood Cliffs, N.J.: Prentice-Hall, 1967.

NASDAQ and the OTC. New York: National Association of Securities Dealers, 1974.

Reilly, Frank K. and Drzycimski, Eugene F. "The Stock Exchange Specialist and the Market Impact of Major World Events." *Financial Analysts Journal,* Vol. 31, No. 4 (July–August, 1975).

Robbins, Sidney. *The Securities Markets: Operations and Issues.* New York: The Free Press, 1966.

Sobel, Robert. *The Big Board.* New York: The Free Press, 1965.

"The Regional Stock Exchange's Fight for Survival," *Fortune* (November, 1973).

Walter, James E. *The Role of Regional Security Exchanges.* Berkeley: University of California Press, 1957.

West, Richard R. and Tinic, Seha M. *The Economics of the Stock Market.* New York: Praeger Publishers, 1971.

West, Richard R. "On the Difference Between Internal and External Market Efficiency." *Financial Analysts Journal,* Vol. 31, No. 6 (November–December, 1975).

West, Richard R. and Tinic, Seha M. "Corporate Finance and the Changing Stock Market." *Financial Management,* Vol. 3, No. 3 (Autumn, 1974).

Chapter 4

The Securities Market: Past and Future Changes

The previous chapter was concerned with a general description of securities markets—what they are intended to do and how they function. In textbooks written prior to 1970, such a discussion would have completed the analysis of securities markets. In 1965, however, a series of changes began which, by 1970, had profoundly affected the securities markets. It is necessary, therefore, to add a specific consideration of *what* these changes were and *why* the markets have changed. This analysis will also provide the reader with an insight into possible future developments.

Changes in the Securities Markets

Why the Market Is Changing

Prior to discussing the specific changes in the securities markets that have transpired over the past 13 years, the reader should fully appreciate *why* these changes have occurred. The answer is that *almost all the changes have been prompted by the significant and rapid growth of trading by large financial institutions* like banks, insurance companies, pension funds, and investment companies. As the figures show, the amount of trading by these institutions (in both absolute and relative terms) has grown dramatically since 1965. The trading patterns and requirements of institutions are different from those of individual investors. The market mechanism was basically developed and shaped to serve individuals who were the main customers of the securities exchanges. When a mechanism developed to serve individual investors was faced with completely different customers whose trading patterns were significantly different, there were problems.

Therefore, regarding the question of why the market changed, the answer is simply that *the changes were prompted by a new dominant clientele with substantially different requirements from the original clientele.*

Evidence of Institutionalization

An indication of the growing impact of large financial institutions can be derived from data on size of trades, block trades, and overall institutional trading. It is assumed, because of the size of institutional portfolios, that the institutional portfolio managers buy and sell large quantities ("blocks") rather than 100–200 share lots. (A "block" is defined as a transaction involving at least 10,000 shares.)

Average Size of Trades One indication of increased institutional trading, therefore, is an increase in the average size of trades as reflected in the average number of shares per sale printed on the NYSE ticker tape. As shown in Table 4–1, the size of an average trade has grown steadily and has more than doubled during the last 15 years. Note especially the rapid growth since 1967.

Table 4–1
Average Shares Per Sale Printed on the NYSE Tape

1961—197	1967—257	1973—449
1962—204	1968—302	1974—438
1963—213	1969—356	1975—495
1964—218	1970—388	1976—559
1965—224	1971—428	1977—641
1966—240	1972—443	

Source: *Fact Book* (New York: New York Stock Exchange, various issues). Reprinted by permission.

Growth of Block Trades Because financial institutions are the main source of large block trades, further evidence of institutional involvement can be derived from the data on block trades contained in Table 4–2. The number of large block trades grew steadily at a very high rate from 1965 through 1972. There was a slight leveling off in 1973 and a definite decline in 1974 coincident with a decline in stock prices. The growth resumed in 1975 and has continued into 1978. One can derive an appreciation for the tremendous growth in block trades by considering the average number of block trades per day. As recently as 1965 there were only nine block trades *a day*; obviously they were a relatively rare occurrence. Since 1971, the average has generally exceeded *100* such trades a day. This means that in a six hour trading day there are currently *at least* 16 block trades *an hour*. A block trade is no longer rare. In fact, such trades constitute a major part of the volume on the exchange, about 18–20 percent.

Value of Trading by Institutions Institutional interest in common stock is also indicated by the value of purchases and sales of common stock by major

Table 4–2	Year	Total Number of Transactions	Total Number of Shares (000)	Percent of Reported Volume	Average number of Block Transactions per Day
Block Transactions on the NYSE (10,000 Shares or More)	1965	2,171	48,262	3.1	9
	1966	3,642	85,298	4.5	14
	1967	6,685	169,365	6.7	27
	1968	11,254	292,680	10.0	50
	1969	15,132	402,063	14.1	61
	1970	17,217	450,908	15.4	68
	1971	26,941	692,536	17.8	106
	1972	31,207	766,406	18.5	124
	1973	29,233	721,356	17.8	116
	1974	23,200	549,387	15.6	92
	1975	34,420	778,540	16.6	136
	1976	47,632	1,001,254	18.7	188
	1977	54,275	1,183,924	22.4	215

Source: *Fact Book* (New York: New York Stock Exchange, various issues). Reprinted by permission.

financial institutions as shown in Table 4–3. The financial institutions included are noninsured private pension funds, open-end investment companies, life insurance companies, and fire and casualty companies.

The total value of purchases and sales has grown steadily except for periods in which aggregate stock prices declined, which, in turn, will affect the value of transactions. Even so, the overall growth during the period from 1962 through 1977 has been 463 percent which represents an average rate of growth in excess of 12 percent per year.

A rough measure of the *relative* amount of trading by institutions can be derived by comparing the dollar value of purchases and sales by institutions with the total value of shares sold on registered exchanges during the year. While the total value figure is lower than the true total of all transactions in the United States because it does not include the OTC market or the third market, the series is internally consistent and so should indicate relative growth. The figure has increased substantially to a ratio of about 40 percent. At the same time, the decline in the ratio since a peak during the period 1970–1972 may be an indication that the relative growth is leveling off. Even so, these figures clearly indicate that the impact of institutions on U.S. equity markets has substantially increased since the middle 1960s.

Public Transactions Studies As shown in Table 4–4, prior to 1963, the individual sector accounted for about 70 percent of all trading. The environment began to change in 1965 and 1966, when trading by the individual sector dropped below 60 percent. The trend continued and is quite

Table 4–3 Purchases and Sales of Common Stock by Major Financial Institutions: Total Dollar Value and Relationship to the Value of Stock Transactions on Registered Exchanges

Year	Value of Purchases and Sales by Institutions (000)	Market Value of Total Shares Sold on Registered Exchanges (000)	Institutional Purchases and Sales as Percent of Total Value of Shares Sold
1962	12,555	47,341	.265
1963	14,805	54,887	.269
1964	17,895	60,424	.296
1965	23,160	73,200	.316
1966	33,120	98,565	.336
1967	48,645	125,329	.388
1968	67,245	144,978	.463
1969	79,960	129,603	.616
1970	68,435	103,063	.664
1971	92,340	147,098	.627
1972	101,575	159,700	.636
1973	85,910	146,451	.586
1974	51,546	99,178	.519
1975	66,430	133,819	.496
1976	73,694	164,545	.447
1977	70,650	187,198	.377

Source: *Annual Report* (Washington, D.C.: Securities and Exchange Commission, 1977).

noticeable in the 1971 figures which show that *the majority of public trading on the NYSE at that time was done by institutions (62 percent).* The most recent studies, done during the first quarters of 1974 and 1976, indicate that institutions accounted for about 58 percent of public trading volume. A study by Freund and Minor suggests that institutional influence will continue to grow. In fact, they project the proportion of institutional trading at about 72 percent by 1980.[1] These expectations of continued growth in institutional trading were generally echoed by Soldofsky.[2]

Proportion of Ownership In addition to examining the proportion of *trading* by institutions, one can also consider the percent of common stock *owned* by institutions. Data on this are contained in Table 4–5. The figures

---

[1] William C. Freund and David F. Minor, "Institutional Activity on the NYSE: 1975 and 1980," *Perspectives on Planning* (New York: New York Stock Exchange, Inc., June, 1972).

[2] Robert M. Soldofsky, *Institutional Holdings of Common Stock, 1900–2000* (Ann Arbor, Michigan: University of Michigan Bureau of Business Research, 1971).

Table 4–4
**Public Volume
Shares Bought and
Sold on the NYSE**[a]

	Percentage Distribution	
	Individuals	Institutions[b]
September, 1952	69.2	30.8
March, 1953	75.0	25.0
March, 1954	69.7	30.3
December, 1954	78.7	21.3
June, 1955	75.5	24.5
March, 1956	75.0	25.0
October, 1957	71.1	28.9
September, 1958	71.4	28.6
June, 1959	70.6	29.4
September, 1960	68.6	31.4
September, 1961	66.7	33.3
October, 1963	69.1	30.9
March, 1965	60.7	39.3
October, 1966	57.0	43.0
First Half, 1969	44.6	55.4
Second Half, 1969	43.5	56.5
First Quarter, 1971	42.6	57.4
Second Quarter, 1971	37.6	62.4
First Quarter, 1974	41.1	58.9
First Quarter, 1976	42.7	57.3

[a] Prior to 1959, data are daily averages for two days (the 1958 data are a projection from a 10 percent sample); for 1959–1966 studies, data are for one day; for 1969 study data are daily averages for the year.

[b] Institutions and intermediaries consist of closed-end investment companies, educational institutions, foundations, guardianships, investment clubs, life and other insurance companies, mutual funds, nonbank administered estates, nonfinancial corporations, nonprofit organizations, partnerships, pension funds, personal holding companies, personal trusts, profit sharing plans having legal ownership of the shares bought and sold, religious groups, savings banks, commercial banks and trust companies, and nonmember broker-dealers.

Source: *Fact Book* (New York: New York Stock Exchange, 1977), p. 56. Reprinted by permission.

indicate substantial growth in absolute value and relative to the total value of all stocks on the NYSE in the period from 1949 to 1965. There was further growth from 1965 to 1973, such that institutions currently own about one-third of the stocks on the NYSE. These data indicate that currently institutions own a substantial proportion of these stocks and, again, there is some evidence that the percentage has stabilized.

These figures on ownership are presented not only to demonstrate the growth of the impact of institutions on the markets, but also because some observers refer to them as evidence that institutions are not a dominant force since they "only" own one-third of the stocks on the NYSE. One

Table 4–5 **Estimated Holdings of**
NYSE-Listed Stocks by Selected Institutional Investors

Type of Institution	Year End (Billion Dollars)				
	1949	1965	1973	1974	1975
U.S. Institutions:					
Insurance Companies (Life and Non-Life)	$ 2.8	$ 16.4	$ 36.4	$ 26.7	$ 33.2
Investment Companies (Open and Closed-End)	3.0	34.7	44.4	31.1	40.6
Noninsured Pension Funds	0.5	37.3	101.7	74.1	105.0
Nonprofit Institutions	4.6	30.0	38.7	29.0	38.0
Common Trust Funds	a	3.2	5.8	4.7	6.1
Mutual Savings Banks	0.2	0.5	2.1	1.7	2.3
Foreign Institutions	—	—	—	3.3	5.1
Total	$11.1	$122.1	$229.7	$171.0	$230.5
Market Value of NYSE Stocks	$76.3	$537.5	$721.0	$511.1	$685.1
Estimated Percent Held By Institutions	14.5	22.7	31.8	33.4	33.6

a Less than $50 million

Source: *Fact Book* (New York: New York Stock Exchange, various years). Reprinted by permission.

should be aware of the substantial *growth* in this ratio when discussing *changes* in the impact of institutions. More important, although institutions only own one-third of the stocks, it is the proportion of *trading* that is important for the functioning of the market. If someone owns a security but never trades it, they have little effect on how the market operates. The difference between the proportion of *ownership* and proportion of *trading* is caused by *the difference in trading turnover*.[3] It appears that institutions trade their portfolios more actively than individuals do. During 1977, the average turnover of all stocks on the NYSE was 21 percent. In contrast, trading turnover by institutions has generally been between 25 and 30 percent and turnover by investment companies has typically exceeded 30 percent.

Effects of Institutional Investments on the Securities Markets

The prior discussion indicated that institutions currently dominate the total equity capital market and they differ in how they trade (e.g., 2,000–20,000 shares versus 200–1,000 shares for individuals). This difference in trading patterns has had a profound effect on the functioning of the market in several areas.

---

[3] Trading turnover is defined as the ratio of the dollar value of trading to the dollar value of holdings.

Fixed Commission Schedule

Because the securities markets were designed for the individual investor, the system was established to handle transactions involving less than 1,000 shares and the pricing of trading services was developed to compensate for the handling of small orders. The NYSE developed a *minimum* fixed commission schedule that all exchange members had to abide by. A major effect of heavy institutional trading came in the area of the fixed commission structure. The initial commission structure compensated members for handling many relatively small orders; it made no allowance for the substantial economies of scale involved in trading large orders. The increased cost of trading 10,000 shares as opposed to 300 or 400 shares is relatively small. If it costs 20 dollars to sell 300 shares, it probably costs no more than 30 or 40 dollars to sell 10,000 shares, and possibly less. These economies of scale were not adequately allowed for in the commission structure. The commission charged for a 10,000 share block was approximately five times as much as the charge for a 1,000 share trade.[4]

When institutions began trading heavily, they recognized that, because of the fixed minimum commission schedule, they were required to pay substantially more in commissions than the cost of transactions when trading large blocks. The first reaction to this excess pricing was the introduction of "give-ups."

Give-ups

The practice of "give-ups" evolved because brokers acknowledged that they received more for large transactions than was justified by the costs involved. Brokers consequently agreed to pay part of their commissions to other brokerage houses or research firms designated by the institution making the trade. If a brokerage house received $2,000 for a trade by a mutual fund, they were instructed to "give up" some portion of this commission (sometimes as much as 80 percent) to another brokerage house that had been selling the mutual fund, or to a research firm that had provided research to the mutual fund. As a consequence, institutions used part of their excess commission dollars to pay for services other than brokerage (these commission dollars were referred to as "soft" dollars). Although "give-ups" were quite common in the early and middle 1960s, the SEC attempted to outlaw the practice of splitting commissions and the ruling was especially effective on the NYSE and ASE.

Growth of the Third Market

Following the prohibition on give-ups, institutional use of the third market increased. One of the advantages of trading in the third market was

---

[4] Using the commission schedule in effect in 1970, the commission charge for selling 1,000 shares of a 30 dollar stock would be $262; the commission charge for selling 10,000 shares of this stock would be $1,342.

that commissions were not fixed and regulated as they were on the NYSE. Therefore, institutions could negotiate commissions for trades in the third market. Trading costs on the third market for large block trades were therefore generally substantially less than they were for a comparable trade on the NYSE or ASE. The typical arrangement was that the stock was acquired for one-quarter point above the last trade on the NYSE *net,* meaning no additional commission. Growth in third market volume can be seen in the figures in Table 4–6. There was a steady growth in absolute terms and in terms of percent of total volume from 1965 through 1972. There was an absolute decline in shares and value in 1973 and 1974 that could be attributed to the market decline. More notable is the decline in the percent of volume that began in 1973 and continued through 1977. The relationship between this and the change in the commission structure is discussed in a subsequent section dealing with the future of secondary markets. The main point is, the third market grew substantially since 1965 because it was a viable trading market for large blocks of stock and it allowed institutions substantial savings in commissions as compared to the costs involved in trading on the NYSE.

Table 4–6
Third Market Volume in NYSE Common Stocks

Year	Shares (Thousands)			Value (Millions)		
	Third Market	NYSE	Per Cent	Third Market	NYSE	Per Cent
1965	48,361	1,809,350	2.7	2,500	73,200	3.4
1966	58,198	2,204,761	2.6	2,873	98,565	2.9
1967	85,081	2,885,748	2.9	4,152	125,329	3.3
1968	119,730	3,298,664	3.6	5,983	144,978	4.2
1969	155,437	3,173,565	4.9	7,128	129,603	5.5
1970	210,067	3,213,069	6.5	8,021	103,063	7.8
1971	297,850	4,265,279	7.0	12,383	147,098	8.4
1972	327,031	4,496,187	7.3	13,581	159,700	8.5
1973	249,387	4,336,581	5.8	10,186	146,451	7.0
1974	203,384	3,821,942	5.3	6,960	99,178	7.0
1975	228,273	4,942,562	4.6	7,910	121,009	6.0
1976	212,533	5,577,007	3.8	9,106	164,606	5.5
1977	194,690	5,913,329	3.3	7,276	157,250	4.6

Source: *Statistical Bulletin* (Washington, D.C.: Securities and Exchange Commission, various issues).

Fourth Market

In addition to the increase in popularity of the third market, the fixed commission structure also fostered the development and use of the fourth market. In the fourth market two institutions deal directly with each other without an intermediary broker and, therefore, *save the full cost of the commission*. This obviously is the ultimate in reducing commission costs. While most observers believe there has been growth in the fourth market, it is difficult to document because there are no public figures available on this trading.

Institutional Membership on Exchanges

A further response to the excessive commission costs was an attempt by large financial institutions to gain membership on one of the exchanges to save on commission costs. Initially institutions applied for membership on the NYSE and ASE but were rejected because the exchanges did not want their major customers to become members and thereby cause other members to lose the business generated by institutional trading. The institutions then applied for membership on the regional exchanges, and were granted memberships by some that hoped to increase their volume. After several institutions joined, some of the exchanges became concerned that they would eventually be run by the institutions and, therefore, tightened their requirements. Also, the SEC attempted to reduce the impact of the institutions by requiring any institutional member to have at least 50 percent of their brokerage business done by nonaffiliated customers. This meant that an institution could not carry out all of its business through its own membership.

Imposition of Negotiated Commissions

All of the aforementioned ploys to offset or avoid commissions were attempted because the institutions felt there was little chance of changing the fixed minimum commission structure. Beginning in 1970, however, the SEC considered the implementation of negotiated commissions: for certain specified trades, the fixed commission structure would not hold and the broker and customer would negotiate the commission involved. The NYSE and almost all member firms vehemently opposed the concept, arguing that negotiated commissions would bring about the demise of the NYSE auction market because members would have no reason to remain on the exchange. Members were supposedly willing to accept the rules, regulations, and responsibilities of membership because they were able to charge a fixed commission which most of them recognized was a form of monopoly pricing. Therefore, with negotiated commissions, the major member firms would drop off the exchange and the concept of a central auction market for stock would crumble.[5]

---

[5] A very insightful discussion of some potential effects of negotiated rates written prior to their imposition is contained in Chris Welles, "Who Will Prosper? Who Will Fail?" *Institutional Investor,* Vol. 5, No. 1 (January, 1971), pp. 36–40.

This argument was eventually rejected by the SEC, which began a program of allowing negotiated commissions on large transactions and finally allowed negotiated commissions on all transactions. In April, 1971 it was ruled that the commission on that part of an order exceeding 500,000 dollars could be negotiated between the broker and the customer. On April 24, 1972, the commission on that part of an order exceeding 300,000 dollars became subject to negotiation. Finally, all commissions became fully negotiated on May 1, 1975 ("May Day").[6] Some of the actual and potential effects of negotiated commissions are discussed in the section on the future of the secondary equity market.

Block Trades and Liquidity

A major change in the market caused by the increase in institutional trading was an increase in block trading. There is a twofold relationship between block trades and liquidity.[7] First, block trades are a major test of the market's liquidity since it is obviously difficult to sell a block of 10,000 shares quickly without a major price change. Therefore block trades are *the ultimate test of market liquidity*. Second, seemingly small price changes due to liquidity are obviously very important for an institution that wants to buy or sell a major position. A half point price change on a 10,000 share order entails a cost of 5,000 dollars; on a 50,000 share order it would constitute a cost of 25,000 dollars. Because of the money and costs involved, one can see why liquidity is of prime concern to institutional portfolio managers.

Block Trades and the Specialist

Since there are currently over 200 block trades a day, they are a common occurrence that must be handled in the secondary market. The effect of numerous block trades has been greatest on the specialist because the specialist system was derived and prospered when trades of more than 1,000 shares were considered large, and transactions of over 10,000 shares were typically sold away from the market and treated as a special offering similar to a new primary issue. The environment changed in 1965 when institutions began to feel that it was their right and, in some cases, their obligation to quickly buy or sell a block of stock. This put tremendous strains on the specialists because the specialist system had three problems with regard to block trading: *capital, commitment,* and *contacts* (the three C's).

The first and most obvious problem was that the specialists were *undercapitalized* when it came to dealing in large blocks. In the early 1960s, the exchanges required that specialists have enough capital to acquire 1,000

---

[6] A brief review of the recent history of commission rates is contained in Thomas T. Murphy, ed., *Fact Book* (New York: New York Stock Exchange, 1977), p. 59.

[7] Recall that we defined liquidity as the ability to convert an asset into cash *quickly* at a known price—i.e., at a price similar to the prior market price.

shares of the particular stocks they dealt with. This was usually adequate in a market dominated by individual investors with relatively small orders. As institutional trading increased, capital requirements also increased, but not nearly as fast as block trading. Currently, the specialist must have capital to acquire 5,000 shares of each stock. Even with this higher capital requirement, it is questionable whether the specialist has adequate capital to deal in 10,000 share lots or to handle the numerous cases in which the block trades exceed 20,000 shares.

Second, in some cases, even when a specialist has adequate capital to finance a significant position in a block, *he will not commit himself.* Some specialists do not want the risk involved in accepting a large position in a stock. There is more risk in holding 5,000 shares of a stock than in holding 500 shares, and many specialists will not expose themselves to this sort of risk. The specialists contend that they are not required to provide complete liquidity for the institutions, especially for stocks with relatively thin markets. They feel that in many instances an institution has taken several months to build a significant position, but wants to sell the total position in one day. Such an attitude is considered unfair by the specialists who feel their main obligation is to provide liquidity to the small investor. In contrast, institutions contend that the specialist is *obligated* to take a position and that such an obligation comes with the job.[8]

A study by Reilly and Nielsen indicated that, based on the price pattern surrounding a block trade, a specialist, on the average, would make a profit from participating in block trades.[9] It was assumed that, for a block sale of stock by an institution, the specialist participated in the trade by acquiring some part of the block and sold his position by the close of the trading day. Under these conditions, the figures indicate that the specialist would have derived a profit on most of the trades and had a profit on average. Irrespective of the evidence, the debate continues over how much the specialist should be involved in block transactions.

The third problem of *contacts* is quite serious. Rule 113 of the New York Stock Exchange states that a specialist cannot deal directly with a customer who is not a broker. This rule was intended to insure that customers must deal through a broker. The specialist would be serving the public by serving the broker. Previously, this rule was reasonable because it was not necessary for specialists to deal directly with customers in the transfer of 500 or 1,000 shares. Currently, a major customer of a specialist through a member broker might be an institution attempting to sell a block of 50,000 shares. It is clear that the specialist, if he does not buy the whole block himself, will find it difficult to sell the block to a number of individuals. The obvious

---

[8] For a discussion of the alternative views see Heide Fiske, "Can the Specialist Cope with the Age of Block Trading?" *Institutional Investor,* Vol. 3, No. 8 (August, 1969), pp. 29–34.

[9] Frank K. Reilly and James Nielsen, "Specialists and Block Trades on the NYSE," University of Wyoming Research Paper No. 61 (January, 1975).

solution would be for the specialist to contact another institution with an interest in the block. Unfortunately, because of Rule 113, the specialist cannot make such a contact. He is therefore cut off from the major source of demand for blocks and he is reluctant to take a large position in a thinly traded stock; to whom is he going to sell it?

This lack of capital, commitment, and contacts on the part of specialists created a vacuum in the trading of blocks that caused the development of a new institution on Wall Street called block houses.

Block Houses

Block Houses evolved because many institutions felt that specialists in particular stocks were not doing their job. Therefore, some of these institutions asked various institutional brokerage firms to help them locate other institutions with an interest in buying or selling given stocks. This practice of helping in the movement of a block eventually became rather widespread.

Block houses are brokerage firms, either members of an exchange or nonmembers, that stand ready to help buy or sell blocks for institutions. A good block house has the requisites mentioned before in connection with the specialist: it must have the *capital* required to position a large block; it must be willing to *commit* this capital to an individual block; and, finally, it must have *contacts* among other institutions.

The following example may help clarify what transpires. Assume a mutual fund owns 250,000 shares of Ford Motors and decides that it wants to sell 50,000 shares of this position so that it can establish a position in another stock. Assume further that the fund decides to attempt the sale through Goldman Sachs & Company, one of the larger, more active block houses which is a lead underwriter for Ford and knows institutions with an interest in the stock. The trader for the mutual fund would contact a block trader at Goldman Sachs and tell him that he wants to sell the 50,000 share block and ask what GS&Co. can do about it. At this point, several traders at Goldman Sachs would contact some of the institutions that currently own Ford to see if any of them would have an interest in adding to their position and determine the price the institutions would be willing to bid. After several phone calls, let us assume that GS&Co. received commitments from four different institutions for a total of 40,000 shares at an average price of 49⅝ (the last sale of Ford on the NYSE was 49¾). At this point Goldman Sachs might go back to the mutual fund and bid 49½ minus a negotiated commission for the total 50,000 shares. The fund can reject the bid and try another block house. Assuming they accept the bid, Goldman Sachs now owns the block, and will immediately sell 40,000 shares to the four institutions that made prior commitments while positioning 10,000 shares themselves. The fact that they positioned 10,000 shares means that they own it and must eventually sell it at the best price possible. Because GS&Co. is a member of the NYSE, the block will be processed ("crossed") on the exchange as one transaction of 50,000 shares at 49½. In the process, a specialist may take some of the stock to fill limit orders on his book at prices between 49½ and 49¾. For working on this trade, Goldman Sachs has received a negotiated commission, but has committed almost 500,000 dollars to position the 10,000 shares. The major risk to GS&Co. is the possibility of a subsequent price change on the 10,000 shares. If they can sell the 10,000 shares for 49½ or more, they will just about break even on the position and have the commission as income. If the price weakens, they may have to sell the position at 49¼ and take a loss on it. This loss of about 2,500 dollars will offset the income from the commission.

Such an example indicates the importance of having the contacts to quickly find institutions with an interest, the capital to position a certain portion of the block, and the willingness to commit that capital to the block trade. Without all three, the transaction would not have taken place.

Development of Tiered Trading Market

In addition to the creation of specific trading mechanisms to accommodate the institutions, the dominance of trading by institutions has resulted in a distinction among individual stocks based upon their appeal to institutions. Such a distinction results in a situation known as a *tiered market*. There have been many instances of tiered markets occurring over time. The two-tiered market that developed in the early 1970s is a recent example that will probably be more long-term than past tiered markets have been. For our purposes, it is important to define a tiered market in a general way. A tiered market occurs when *investors are willing to pay different price-earnings ratios for alternative stocks with basically the same characteristics in terms of risk and growth.* Typically, such differences in valuation have been short-run.

Pre-1970 Tiered Markets

Using this definition, one can see that there have been tiered markets over the years because of the existence of numerous "hot" groups. Examples would include electronic stocks, mobile homes, and fast food franchisers. In all these cases investors paid substantial premiums beyond what one would expect based upon growth and risk for stocks within these industry groups. Typically, the period of popularity did not exceed nine months to a year. A major difference between previous tiered markets and the recent tiered market is the broad specification of favored stocks and the length of time they were popular.

Early 1970s Tiered Market

The two-tiered market in the early 1970s was different from previous markets of this type because it included a major *class* of stocks—i.e., the top tier stocks were large growth firms. As discussed in a *Fortune* article, the institutions became interested in growth companies because of their desire for performance and preference for low portfolio turnover.[10] The difference between prior interest in growth stocks and the recent interest is that previously the growth stocks considered were not only *large* growth companies, but in many cases *small* growth companies, many of which were traded OTC, as well. The difference in attitude in the 1960s as compared to that in the 1970s resulted from the institutional experience during the 1969–1970 market decline when institutions found they had a substantial liquidity problem in attempting to sell the small growth companies and realize their profits. The institutions learned the hard way that liquidity was as important as growth. A gain on a small illiquid stock derived over a long period could be quickly lost or reduced at the time of sale.

During the 1971–1972 bull market, institutions felt substantial pressure to perform in line with evolving performance measures and this prompted a return to the growth stock syndrome because of the belief that growth companies would perform well in a rising market. In addition, institutions wanted to acquire stocks with immunity from business cycle pressures that they could hold for long periods without being concerned with trading. The solution was to acquire strong growth companies that were not expected to be greatly influenced by an economic downturn. These two factors (stock price performance and a noncyclical business) led to the popularity of growth stocks during the early 1970s.

A second reason for investing in large companies is a logical consequence of institutional portfolio management. Institutions want to maximize return for a given level of risk or minimize risk for a given level of return. A major tool for minimizing risk is *diversification* which is intended to eliminate all unique or unsystematic risk from the portfolio. A common belief is that a portfolio with more securities is more diversified. Unfortunately, *there is a cost to diversification* because of the costs of administration and research. The more stocks in a portfolio, the higher the administrative costs, the higher the research costs, and, other factors being equal, the lower the net returns. Therefore, a portfolio manager should not overdiversify if he can avoid it.

In terms of overdiversification, several studies have shown that it is possible to derive most of the benefits of diversification with a portfolio consisting of from 12 to 18 stocks.[11] To be adequately diversified does *not*

---

[10] C. J. Loomis, "How the Terrible Two Tier Market Came to Wall Street," *Fortune* (July, 1973), pp. 82–89.

[11] John L. Evans and Stephen H. Archer, "Diversification and the Reduction of Dispersion: An Empirical Analysis," *Journal of Finance,* Vol. 23, No. 5 (December, 1968), pp. 761–767; Lawrence Fisher and James H. Lorie, "Some Studies of Variability of Returns on Investments of Common Stock," *Journal of Business,* Vol. 43, No. 2 (April, 1970), pp. 99–134; Jack E. Gaumnitz, "Maximal Gains from Diversification and Implications for Portfolio Management," *Mississippi Valley Journal of Business and Economics,* Vol. 6, No. 3 (Spring, 1971), pp. 1–14.

require 200 stocks in a portfolio. Moreover, at some point the costs of further diversification exceed the additional benefits. Therefore, managers should attempt to minimize the number of different issues in a portfolio while still being properly diversified. Although most large institutions would probably need more than the minimum 20 stocks, a number much over 100 is probably excessive. Given a portfolio with a large dollar value and a self-imposed limit on the number of stocks included, *the value of each holding must be substantial*. Assume an institutional portfolio has a value of one billion dollars (this size is not at all unusual). In such a portfolio containing 50 stocks, each holding must have *an average value of 20 million dollars;* if the portfolio contains 100 stocks each holding must have *an average value of 10 million dollars.*

In order to insure the liquidity of the holdings institutions will limit their ownership of an issue. The usual limit set by portfolio managers is 5 percent of the outstanding issue (this is a legal limit for mutual funds). Assuming the self-imposed limit is 5 percent and the average value of each holding is 10 million dollars, the market value of each firm's total outstanding stock must be 200 million dollars (\$10 million ÷ .05). If each holding by the institution averages 20 million dollars and the limit is set at 5 percent, the average total market value of each company in the portfolio must be 400 million dollars.

Therefore, when institutions again became interested in growth companies for performance reasons, they *also* required that the growth companies be *large*. Because of these two contraints, *the large institutions concentrated their attention on a universe of less than 700 stocks.* [12] Many observers contend that they concentrated on a substantially smaller number; some felt it was less than 100, and some talked about the 70 "vestal virgins." Because of this concentration, the institutional favorites were bid up and the growth companies became growth stocks because of the attention of institutions. At the same time, other stocks not in this large, growth company group were, on balance, sold by the institutions and they suffered in terms of relative performance during the period 1969–1972. [13]

Future Developments in Secondary Markets

It appears that four factors will influence the future operation of the secondary markets. First is the continued dominant influence of institutional trading on the secondary markets. The second factor is the continuing influence of fully negotiated commissions. Third, the SEC is fully committed to the development of a central market. The question is not

---

[12] Frank K. Reilly, "A Three Tier Stock Market and Corporate Financing," *Financial Management,* Vol. 4, No. 3 (Autumn, 1975), pp. 7–15.

[13] Subsequent discussions of the two-tier market are contained in Daniel Seligman, "The Terrible Two-Tier Market (cont.)," *Fortune* (October, 1973), pp. 105–111; and "The Two-Tier Market Lingers On, Sort Of," *Fortune* (February, 1974), pp. 41–45.

whether there will be a central market, but *when* it will be completely implemented and *what form* it will take. Finally, the tiered market, initiated by institutional investors, will also have a future effect on the markets.

Future Influence of Institutional Traders

As a percentage of total trading, institutional trading will be constant or grow. A NYSE study projected continuing growth from about 60 percent of trading in 1971 to almost 72 percent by 1980.[14] These projections were echoed by Soldofsky in a separate study.[15] At the time these projections were made (1971 and 1972 respectively) there had been steady and rapid growth in institutional trading. Such trading decreased during the severe market decline in 1973 and 1974 and caused some to question whether institutional trading would continue to grow rapidly. Still, virtually no one expects a reversal of growth. The consensus is that *the proportion of trading by institutions will either stabilize at a high figure in excess of 60 percent, or continue to grow slowly over time.*

Impact of Fully Negotiated Rates

As noted earlier, many of the changes in the market that occurred during the 1960s and 1970s were a result of the growth of institutional trading in large blocks and of the existence of fixed trading commissions.[16] The subsequent discussion considers the effect of negotiated commissions on major participants.[17]

Effect on Commissions

One would expect total commissions to be lower and the charge on individual trades to approximate the cost of carrying out the trade. During the first months after May Day, the practice was to quote commission rates in terms of "discounts" from the fixed commission schedule that previously prevailed. Although most observers had expected discounts of 30 to 40 percent, some discounts ran higher, in the range of 50 percent, and by 1978, discounts on some trades were higher than that. Part of this chaos in commission rates was due to a lack of price leadership in the brokerage industry. In an industry with a generally homogeneous product, a price

---

[14] Freund and Minor, "Institutional Activity on the NYSE."

[15] Soldofsky, *Institutional Holding of Common Stock.*

[16] For a further discussion of this topic see Richard R. West, "Institutional Trading and the Changing Stock Market," *Financial Analysts Journal,* Vol. 27, No. 3 (May–June, 1971), pp. 17–24.

[17] An article that considered this question several years before the fact is Chris Welles, "Who Will Prosper? Who Will Fail?" *Institutional Investor,* Vol. 5, No. 1 (January, 1971), pp. 36–40. A more recent discussion is contained in Chris Welles, "Discounting: Wall Street's Game of Nerves," *Institutional Investor,* Vol. 11, No. 11 (November, 1976), pp. 27–33.

leader will emerge, usually one of the low cost producers in the industry. Because such leadership did not emerge and because of strong competition for institutional business, the *customers* (financial institutions) began dictating prices. Initially they would not accept anything less than a 30 percent discount on any trade, and required a 40 percent discount on "no brainers" (a relatively small trade on a very liquid stock, e.g., 2,000 shares of AT&T). Eventually, the discounts drifted higher, to a minimum of 40 percent, and the overall average discount was about 50 percent. One analysis indicated that the average discount ranged from 43 percent for one firm to almost 64 percent for another.[18] The large average discounts emerged because a totally new pricing practice came into existence for the "no brainers." Rather than a discount from the old rate, brokers began to quote commissions on these trades in terms of cents per share, e.g., 8 cents per share, irrespective of the price of the share. To appreciate how drastic this is, consider a 40 dollar stock for which the fixed commission averaged about one percent of the value, or 40 cents. Under such a condition, the 8 cent price constitutes an 80 percent discount, and it would be even larger for a higher priced stock. Clearly, the effect of negotiated commissions on the commission paid by institutions has been significant and there are few signs of any reversal.[19]

While a decline in the rates paid by institutions was expected, it was questionable whether individual investors would receive such treatment. In fact, many felt that the rates on small trades might increase to reflect the relatively high cost of these orders. Shortly after May Day, there was some tendency to charge high rates on small orders and clearly no consideration of lower rates was made. Again, after a period of time to allow for an adjustment, discount houses for individual traders did emerge.[20] These firms only offer execution and do not offer research advice or information, but they typically will charge only about 50 to 70 percent of the commission charged by full service firms. The size of the savings will vary depending on the size of the trade. These firms advertise extensively in financial publications such as *The Wall Street Journal*.

Effect on Research Firms
During the period of fixed minimum commissions, the institutions used soft dollars to pay for research and it was cheaper for most institutions to buy research from external sources than to establish extensive in-house

---

[18] Charles J. Elia, "Study Shows Severe Broker Competition Yields Huge Stock-Trade Discounts for Banks," *Wall Street Journal,* July 1, 1977, p. 1; Charles J. Elia, "Brokerage Firms Continue Heavy Discounting in Fight for Commission Dollars, Data Show," *Wall Street Journal* (October 6, 1977), p. 43.

[19] This trend is discussed extensively in Welles, "Discounting: Wall Street's Game of Nerves."

[20] For a discussion of this development see Linda Snyder, "Wall Street's Discount Houses are Selling Hard," *Fortune* (March, 1977), pp. 117–118.

research staffs. Therefore, numerous research firms were established to serve the large institutions, which were paid in soft dollars. When give-ups were formally outlawed, a few of the research houses went out of business, but many remained and were paid soft dollars in more circular ways. With fully negotiated rates, there are almost no soft dollars left. Any excess available will go to the firm that does the trade and also provides research because the firms with trading capability either already had research facilities or could develop them. Therefore, the alternatives available for pure research houses became:

1. sell research for hard dollars (cash)

2. develop trading capability or merge with a trading firm in order to get paid directly through commission dollars

3. merge with an institution that wanted to set up more in-house research facilities

4. go out of business.

The first alternative was only available to a few highly regarded firms. Institutions dislike paying cash for research because the hard dollars come from the management fee, while the commission dollars come from the customer's account. So paying for research would be a last resort for most and they would only pay for extremely good research. The second option requires developing a trading capability by finding the traders and establishing the capital base to trade or merger.[21] Merging with an institution is the same as going out of business and is an acknowledgement that the first two alternatives are not possible. It was a feasible alternative only because many institutions wanted to build up their in-house research staffs.

Although there are no specific numbers available, it is clear from reading the papers after May Day that many research firms either disbanded or merged with full-line brokerage firms and very few survived as pure research companies.

Effect on Block Houses and Block Trades

The problem for block houses was that lower commission charges increased the risk involved with the portion of a block positioned. With fixed minimum commissions, the block trader had the excess "commission cushion" as a partial offset to any loss on the part of the block positioned. A block trader would position 5,000 shares in a 40,000 share block and attempt to sell the 5,000 shares shortly after the trade. If he lost money on the 5,000 share position, he would always have the big commission to use as a partial offset. In an era of negotiated commission, the cushion is gone. Two possibilities arise: get out of the business, or be more realistic in

---

[21] An example of such a merger is given in Richard E. Rustin, "Baker Weeks Set to Join Reynolds Securities Unit," *Wall Street Journal,* September 15, 1976, p. 7.

bidding for blocks. Given the higher risk and lower commissions involved, many firms that entered the block trading business in the late 1960s and early 1970s got out during 1973 and 1974.[22]

The second alternative was to bid the blocks more realistically rather than depend upon the commission cushion. The result would be *larger discounts from the current market and, therefore, more price volatility for block trades.* As an example, assume a stock was recently traded at 50 dollars per share and a block house was offered a block of 30,000 shares. With fixed commissions, the block house might bid 49¾ for the whole block. After May Day, one might hypothesize that they would bid a more realistic 49½ or 49⅜ so they hopefully would not lose as much on the stock positioned. Such a change in the bidding would be an increase in the volatility of the stock price surrounding the trade, e.g., from 50 to 49½ rather than from 50 to 49¾. The empirical evidence regarding what has happened to block trades since May Day is quite limited although the amount of block trading has generally grown and currently represents about 20 percent of volume on the NYSE with over 200 such trades a day. The empirical evidence regarding concessions on block trades since May Day[23] indicated no significant difference.[24] Indirect evidence derived from an analysis of the relationship between block trading and stock price volatility suggests a significant *negative* relationship between these variables which would not support this expectation of more volatility.[25]

Effect on Regional Exchanges

Regional exchanges flourished during the early 1970s for two reasons. They made it possible to distribute soft dollars and they allowed institutional membership.[26] The regional exchanges allowed multiple tickets on a trade, through which it was possible to distribute the order among several members and accomplish "give-ups." Therefore, many institutions traded some of their blocks on the regional exchanges.[27] Also, some of the regional

---

[22] For a very bearish discussion of the block trading business see John Thackray, "Is Time Running Out for the Big Block?" *Institutional Investor,* Vol. 8, No. 6 (June, 1974), pp. 57–61, 142.

[23] The concession on a block trade is defined as the percent of price change from the trade prior to a block trade in relation to the price for the block. As an example, if the trade before the block trade was made at 50 and the block price was 49, this would be a 2 percent concession.

[24] Frank K. Reilly and David Wright, "Block Concessions and May Day," mimeo.

[25] Frank K. Reilly, "Block Trades and Stock Price Volatility," *Financial Analysts Journal,* forthcoming.

[26] A discussion of the problems and opportunities for regional exchanges is contained in "The Regional Exchanges Fight for Survival," *Fortune* (November, 1973), pp. 118–127.

[27] For a detailed discussion of fee-splitting on the regional exchanges see Chris Welles, "The War Between the Big Board and the Regionals," *Institutional Investor,* Vol. 4, No. 12 (December, 1970), pp. 21–27.

exchanges welcomed institutions as members because they brought added volume to the regional exchange.

With fully negotiated commissions, both of these reasons lost some of their importance. Negotiated commissions generate few excess dollars so distribution of soft dollars became of little concern to institutional investors. Further, the major reason for joining an exchange was to save on fixed commissions. Negotiated commissions are about as low as they can get and institutions are probably happy to avoid the problems of membership.

In consequence, during this period, the regional exchanges developed some unique capabilities. First, in many instances, the cost of clearing a trade, in terms of both specific charges and avoidance of the New York transfer tax, is lower on a regional exchange. In addition, there is a significant negative relationship between the size of the spread and the number of markets in which a stock is traded. This indicates that added competition results in better markets for the dual listed stocks. Finally, it appears that the regional exchanges provide some real alternatives for block traders and block houses attempting to cross a block on an exchange. In many cases, a specialist on one of the regional exchanges is easier to work with and the trade will go more smoothly. Therefore, block volume on regional exchanges has remained quite strong.

The ultimate effect of the competitive commission structure on regional exchanges is best described as undecided. Reilly and Perry analyzed what happened to relative trading volume for the principal regional exchanges following the commission changes.[28] The study indicated that the effect on different exchanges clearly was not consistent. As an example, the Detroit Exchange eventually went out of business, while the Cincinnati Exchange experienced significant growth. Overall, though, the best generalization is that *there was little or no effect on the relative trading on regional exchanges*. Figure 4–1 contains a time series plot of the percentage of trading on the four largest regional exchanges. As shown, the proportion during 1976 was *very similar* to the proportion that prevailed prior to May, 1975. Apparently the regional exchanges have been able to survive in spite of competitive rates.

Effect on the Third Market

The third market expanded rapidly in the late 1960s and early 1970s because it was heavily used by institutions to save on commissions. Third market trades were not reported to the public on an exchange ticker tape or in newspapers. This was considered an advantage by some institutions. Also third market dealers had developed good markets (in terms of depth and liquidity) in many of the strong institutional stocks and they could compete on an equal footing with the exchange markets. Therefore, the

---

[28] Frank K. Reilly and Gladys Perry, "Negotiated Commissions and Regional Exchanges," University of Illinois Working Paper (August, 1978).

Figure 4–1

**Monthly Time Series Plot of Dollar Value of Trading on
Boston, Midwest, Pacific Coast, and PBW Stock Exchanges as
a Percentage of Total Dollar Value of Trading on All
Registered Exchanges January, 1970–March, 1976**

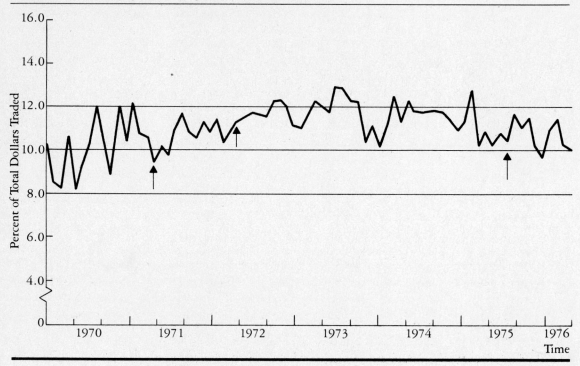

outlook for the third market was somewhat uncertain depending upon how
one felt about its market making capability.

An analysis by Reilly of the data through 1977 generally supported the
prophets of doom.[29] As shown in Figure 4–2, the proportion of trading on
the third market grew steadily through 1971 and into 1972. A change
became evident after the second alteration in the commission structure and,
since the latter part of 1972, *there has been almost a steady decline in the proportion
of trading in the third market.* This relative decline was also reflected when
third market volume was compared to the volume of block trading or total
institutional trading.

Effect on The Fourth Market
This market was likewise born and nurtured by a desire to save on the
excessive commission costs during the fixed commission era. With

---

[29] Frank K. Reilly, "Negotiated Commissions and the Third Market," University of
Illinois Working Paper No. 429 (revised September, 1978).

Figure 4–2
Time Series Plot of Third Market Volume as a Percent of NYSE
Volume Quarterly: 1965–1977

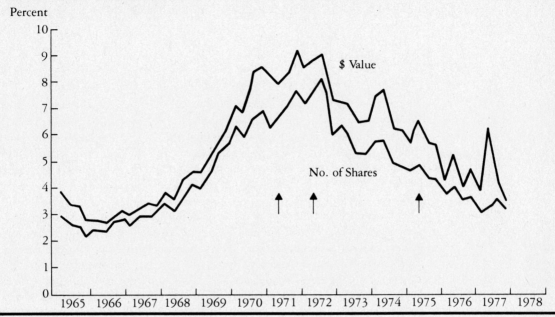

Source: *SEC Statistical Bulletin,* several issues.

negotiated commissions, the advantage is reduced somewhat, but *there is still a cost advantage even with negotiated commissions.* Therefore, while the growth rate may have been reduced, there is no reason to expect the demise of the fourth market. It was contended that business increased after May Day, but there was no solid documentation for this and the observation was made by a fourth market dealer.

Legal Problems

In a fixed commission situation, everyone charged the same price and institutions did not have to worry about the price paid, only about executing the sale or purchase. In a world of negotiated commissions, they have to be concerned with price and execution because a client could theoretically bring suit for not getting the best price. Institutions contended that low commissions with poor executions are not worthwhile. As an example, on a 30,000 share block you may save 2,000 dollars in commissions, but if the sale is made at ¼ point below another dealer's price, the loss in value ($7,500) will more than offset the savings in commissions. In addition, many of the large investment houses still provide research support for their institutional customers and this is obviously worth some difference in commission. The initial feeling was that the SEC would not allow any price difference for such help. Subsequent statements indicated that the SEC would allow a slightly higher price for "service," including research. Although the legal problem has diminished somewhat, there is still major concern over the question of "best execution" which involves the analysis of price changes that accompany a block trade. There are systems developed by several investment firms that consider specific liquidity measures for each stock and then judge transactions accordingly.[30]

Summary of Effects of Negotiated Commissions

Negotiated Commissions substantially reduced total commissions paid to brokers and had a significant effect on the overall structure of the brokerage industry because many high cost firms could no longer compete.[31]

The independent research firms had to sell research for hard dollars, develop trading capability internally or by merger, or go out of business. Most selected one of the latter two alternatives. The number of block houses declined and will remain limited. One might also expect an increase in the price volatility of block trades. Regional exchanges lost some advantages when negotiated commissions were introduced, but apparently had developed some meaningful capabilities in market making because relative trading volume held up well on most of them and the overall average was very similar to the pre-May Day period. This is of benefit to the total system because several studies have indicated that the markets for individual stocks are better when there are competing markets.

The third market lost its cost advantage with negotiated commissions and relative trading on the third market has declined steadily through 1977. The outlook for the fourth market is difficult to assess because of the lack of available data.

Finally, there are added legal problems because of price competition. It is now necessary to determine the "best execution," aside from price. Also, how can an institution pay for other services?

A National Market System

In addition to suggesting that negotiated commissions be introduced, the Institutional Investor Report strongly recommended the creation of a national, competitive market. Although there is not one generally accepted definition of what a national market would constitute, there appear to be three major characteristics that are included:

---

[30] For a discussion of this area and some of the systems see James R. Roscow, "The Jackpot Question, For Hundreds of Billions of Dollars, Define 'Best Execution'," *Financial World* (September 10, 1975), pp. 11–13. For a detailed discussion of one of the better-known measures, see Michael D. Hirsch, "Liquidity Filters: Tools for Better Performance," *Journal of Portfolio Management,* Vol. 2, No. 1 (Fall, 1975), pp. 46–50.

[31] For a brief overview of this restructuring see A. Gary Shilling, "The Brokerage House Shakeout," *Wall Street Journal,* December 13, 1977, p. 26.

1. centralized reporting of all transactions
2. a centralized quotation system with a centralized limit order blank
3. free and open competition among all qualified market-makers.

A Composite Tape

A central market must include *centralized reporting of transactions,* i.e., a composite tape on which all transactions in a stock would be reported irrespective of where the transactions took place. As one watched the tape he would see a trade in GM on the NYSE, another on the Midwest, and a third OTC. The idea is to report all the trades completed on the tape and thereby provide full disclosure. During 1975 the NYSE began operating a central tape for a few stocks, and eventually (June 16, 1975) the tape included all NYSE stocks traded on other exchanges and the OTC.[32] This aspect of a National Market System (NMS) has already been accomplished and is working nicely.

Centralized Quotations

The second requirement for an NMS is a centralized quotation system which contains the quotes for a given stock from all market-makers including those on the national exchanges, the regional exchanges, and the OTC. With a centralized quotation system, a broker who requested the market for GM would be provided with the prevailing market on the NYSE, the Midwest Stock Exchange, the quotes from other regional exchanges on which GM is listed, and the several markets made by OTC dealers. The broker would complete the trade on the market with the best quote for his client.[33] Such a system would provide visible competition for the NYSE specialist. There is some empirical evidence suggesting that such competition results in better markets for investors. A study by Reilly and Slaughter examined what happened to prices when the third market quotations for a number of NYSE stocks were put on the NASDAQ system.[34] The results showed that both the NYSE market and the OTC markets improved.

Problems with CLOB

The technology required to give centralized quotations is currently available, as indicated by the NASDAQ system. The major obstacle to the implementation of the system is the political and technological conflict

---

[32] Thomas T. Murphy, ed., *Fact Book* (New York: New York Stock Exchange, 1976), p. 7.

[33] For a further discussion of the idea see Lawrence A. Armour, "Central Marketplace," *Barron's,* February 28, 1972, p. 3.

[34] Frank K. Reilly and William C. Slaughter, "The Effect of Dual Markets on Common Stock Marketmaking," *Journal of Financial and Quantitative Analysis,* Vol. 8, No. 2 (March, 1973), pp. 167–182.

regarding a central limit order book (CLOB). Assuming centralized quotations are available, *what happens to the limit orders?* Currently, most limit orders are placed with the specialist on the NYSE and, when a transaction *on the NYSE* reaches the stipulated price, the order is filled. What happens when you have numerous markets and a transaction on the Midwest Exchange would fill a limit order, but no comparable transaction takes place on the NYSE? To avoid such inequities, it is proposed that the industry develop an electronic CLOB in which *all* limit orders would be stored and be *automatically* filled when transactions on *any* market reached the appropriate price.

To put it mildly, the NYSE has vehemently opposed a CLOB because most limit orders are placed on the NYSE and the NYSE specialists do not want to give up this very lucrative business. There are also some small technical problems involved in automatically filling limit orders. In fact, two versions of CLOB have been proposed. One is a "soft" CLOB that would only be accessible to specialists and specified market-makers which would probably not entail automatic execution. In contrast, a "hard" CLOB would be available to all market-makers and there would be automatic execution of orders. Again, staunch advocates of an NMS support the "hard" CLOB with rigid time and price guarantees built into the system.

Competition between Market-Makers

The notion of competing market-makers has always prevailed on the OTC market, but has been vigorously opposed by the NYSE. The argument in favor of competition among market-makers is that it will force dealers to make better markets or they will not do any business. Assume dealer A quotes 49–50 for a stock and dealer B makes a quote of 49¼–49¾. Dealer B should do all the business in the stock because he has a higher bid and a lower ask. If dealer A wants to do any business he must at least match the quote by the other market-maker or improve on it by bidding 49⅜ and/or offering stock at 49⅝. If competition works to improve the market for a stock (i.e., reduces the bid–ask spread), this improvement should be reflected in market data. Several studies that examined the relationship between the spread on a sample of stocks and the number of dealers trading those stocks, holding other relevant variables constant, indicated that competition, as represented by the number of dealers, was a significant negative variable; i.e., the more competition (dealers), the smaller the spread.[35]

---

[35] Seha M. Tinic and Richard R. West, "Competition and the Pricing of Dealer Service in the Over-the-Counter Stock Market," *Journal of Financial and Quantitative Analysis,* Vol. 7, No. 3 (June, 1972), pp. 1707–1727; George J. Benston and Robert L. Hagerman, "Determinants of Bid-Asked Spreads in the Over-the-Counter Market," *Journal of Financial Economics,* Vol. 1, No. 4 (December, 1974), pp. 353–364.

In contrast, the NYSE argues that a *central* auction market provides the best market because, under such an arrangement, all orders are forced to the one central location and this concentration of orders will ensure the best auction markets. The NYSE has attempted to create a concentrated market with the following regulations:

1. the New York Rule, no stock can be traded on the ASE and the NYSE at the same time;

2. specialists on the NYSE are noncompeting;

3. Rule 394 (subsequently modified and called Rule 390), making it difficult for a member of the NYSE to trade a NYSE listed stock off the exchange.

The New York Rule

The New York Rule was an agreement that whenever an ASE stock applied for listing on the NYSE, it would *automatically* be delisted on the ASE the day it became listed on the NYSE. Although other regional exchanges might list such a stock, this agreement blocked competition between the specialists on the two national exchanges in New York.[36]

This rule was basically eliminated in 1976 when Varo, Inc. applied for listing on the NYSE but also indicated that it wanted to continue to be listed on the ASE.[37] Since then, several other stocks have made a similar change. The ultimate impact on the stocks involved is unknown at present.[38] There were some indications that spreads were reduced initially, but returned to the prior levels as trading became concentrated on one of the exchanges. Although the markets quoted by the specialists on the two exchanges were quite comparable, brokerage firms tended to settle on one as the "primary" market and subsequently route all orders automatically to this exchange without checking both markets. Typically, the primary market was determined by which exchange was getting the majority of volume. Although there was a period of strong competition, the NYSE was eventually designated the primary market and over 95 percent of all trading was done on the NYSE. Some of the firms involved gave up their ASE listing because of the lack of volume.

---

[36] For a more detailed discussion of the history of the New York Rule, see Robert W. Doede, "The Monopoly Power of the New York Stock Exchange," unpublished dissertation, University of Chicago (June, 1967).

[37] Richard E. Rustin, "Amex Proposes to Let Trading Continue in Issues That Shift Listings to Big Board," *Wall Street Journal*, July 9, 1976, p. 3; Richard E. Rustin, "Varo Consents to Dual Listing on Amex, Big Board as Marts Move to Lift Bar," *Wall Street Journal*, August 4, 1976, p. 6; "Dual Trading in Varo, Inc. Shares Begins with Big Board Getting 58% of Volume," *Wall Street Journal*, August 24, 1976, p. 5.

[38] For a very preliminary analysis of the effect, see Frank K. Reilly, "The Effect of Dual Listing," University of Illinois, Working Paper No. 417 (July, 1977).

Therefore, although the elimination of the New York Rule has not permanently changed the way business is done on Wall Street, there are currently no remaining legal barriers to such competition. While the initial attempt to create competition has not had any permanent effects, the opportunity for it to develop in the future exists.

Competing Specialists on the NYSE

Although there is nothing in the by-laws of the NYSE prohibiting specialists from competing, from 1967 to 1976, there were no competing specialists on the exchange. This was not true prior to 1967, and the decline in number is briefly described by Hamilton as follows:

First, the rate of decline in competition was greatest during 1957–63. During 1933 there were 203 specialist units, and 466 stocks had competing specialists. Each specialist in a unit functions independently on the exchange floor.
Through the next 24 years, the number of stocks with competing specialists declined to 228, while the number of specialist units declined to 136. Then, in only seven years, 1957–63, the number of such issues fell from 228 to 37. The number of specialist units declined from 136 to 109, while the number of competing units dropped from 60 to 13. By 1967 no stock issue had competing specialist units.[39]

One factor contributing to the decline is the fact that the exchange discouraged competition. A reversal in policy occurred in 1976 when the NYSE formally endorsed the concept of competing specialists on the trading floor.[40] Apparently, the SEC's pressure for more competition in the securities markets influenced the policy change. Shortly after the announcement, Mitchum, Jones and Templeton, a member, applied to the exchange for permission to compete with Gaines, Reis and Company as a specialist in 23 stocks.[41] Apparently Mitchum Jones had attempted to merge with Gaines Reis prior to the application. This initial attempt at competition was aborted when Gaines Reis decided to dissolve and their 23 stocks were allocated to Mitchum Jones and Company and two other specialist units.[42] A specialist unit headed by Robb, Peck, McCooey and Company indicated they wanted to compete with Kingsley, Boye and Southwood, in making markets in 18 issues.[43] This application was upheld by the SEC over an

[39] James L. Hamilton, "Competition, Scale Economies, and Transaction Cost in the Stock Market," *Journal of Financial and Quantitative Analysis,* Vol. 11, No. 5 (December, 1976), p. 789.
[40] "Competing-Specialist Idea Is Endorsed by Big Board in a Reversal of Policy," *Wall Street Journal,* May 14, 1976, p. 2.
[41] Richard E. Rustin, "Mitchum Jones Seeks to Compete as Specialist Firm," *Wall Street Journal,* June 24, 1976, p. 2.
[42] Richard E. Rustin, "Big Board Specialist Facing Competition to Dissolve, Giving New Plan False Start," *Wall Street Journal,* June 30, 1976, p. 2.
[43] Richard E. Rustin, "Specialists Ask Big Board Nod on Competition," *Wall Street Journal,* July 30, 1976, p. 2.

application to defer the competition. There was some discussion of whether this application was made in response to Kingsley Boye's campaign to enter the retail brokerage business and offer substantial commission discounts. For whatever reason, there was competition on the floor between specialists for the first time in ten years. A year later Spear, Leeds and Kellogg, the largest specialist firm on the NYSE, applied to compete in all of the 19 issues in which Blair S. Williams and Company specialized.[44] This was a major move since the Williams issues included General Motors, Caterpillar Tractor and St. Joseph Minerals Corp. In response to this application, Blair Williams merged with M. J. Meehan and Company, a larger NYSE market-making firm that had a much larger capital base than Blair Williams did and was also considered an astute market-maker.[45] As a result of the merger, competition was quite strong and Spear Leeds subsequently withdrew as a competing specialist in all but one of the 19 issues (General Motors common).[46]

Therefore, as of 1978 there was direct specialist competition in 19 issues on the NYSE. Again, although the number is not large, the opportunity for competition does exist and is encouraged by the SEC and the exchange. This is important because several studies have indicated that when market-makers compete, the market quotations are better. Further, a study by Hamilton has indicated that, based upon the relationship between volume and number of dealers on the OTC, most stocks on the NYSE would justify three or four specialists dealing in them.[47]

Rule 394/390[48]

A major point of controversy in the discussion of a central market is NYSE Rule 390 which states that unless specifically exempted by the exchange, members must obtain the permission of the exchange before carrying out a transaction in a listed stock off the exchange.

The rule goes on to indicate how, and under what conditions, a member can take an order off the exchange. The initial purpose of the rule was to ensure that all orders for listed stocks came to the exchange because such a requirement is necessary if the exchange auction market is to be as complete as possible. If all the orders come to one central location, you will have the perfect market in which *all* supply and demand will meet and the ideal price for all concerned will be determined. This is the NYSE's view of the central

---

[44] Spear Leeds Files Big Board Bid to Vie with Blair S. Williams in Market-making," *Wall Street Journal,* June 15, 1977, p. 20.

[45] Richard E. Rustin, "Blair S. Williams Plans Meehan Merger to Boost Competition with Spear Leeds," *Wall Street Journal,* June 30, 1977, p. 10.

[46] Richard E. Rustin, "Spear Leeds Drops Most Competition with M. J. Meehan," *Wall Street Journal,* December 14, 1977, p. 7.

[47] Hamilton, "Competition, Scale Economies, and Transaction Costs."

[48] The initial proclamation was referred to as Rule 394. This rule was modified in 1976 and renamed Rule 390. All current references are to the modified Rule 390.

market as stated by James Needham in October, 1975 when he was chairman of the exchange.[49]

The exchange contends that Rule 390 is necessary to protect the auction market and, if it is eliminated, there will be a gradual erosion of this very valuable market mechanism. Allowing members to trade on or off the exchange will result in a "fragmented" dealer market, which, it is contended, is not as good as the central auction market.[50]

The alternative view is that market-making should be on a *free competitive basis* similar to that prevailing on the OTC market. The idea is that anybody who wants to make a market in a stock and can meet specified basic capital requirements should be allowed to do so. In addition, members of the exchange could and *should* trade with the market-maker offering the best market. Advocates of this competitive market contend that such a structure has performed well for decades in the over-the-counter market. It is also felt that the several competing dealers would have more capital than a single specialist.[51]

Abolition Now or Later? The SEC has always contended that its mandate from Congress under the Investment Act of 1975 is to aid in establishing an open, competitive securities market which requires an NMS without restrictions like Rule 390. In contrast, the NYSE and a number of brokerage firms have suggested a modified form of Rule 390 *until* the central market is established because they feel that, until the NMS is working, participants will need a strong auction market such as exists on the exchange.

The alternative view is expressed by Donald Weeden who contends that the abolition of Rule 390 is necessary now if the central market is to become a viable reality.[52] Weeden contends that a central market cannot be firmly established as long as Rule 390 requires about 80 percent of the business in large, active stocks to be carried out on the exchange. He feels that under these restrictive conditions, there is no reason why a firm should consider becoming a market-maker in one of the NYSE stocks because without the elimination of Rule 390 it is not worthwhile to commit the time and capital to develop a market in a stock for which 80 percent of the trading is confined to the NYSE. Therefore Weeden contends that it is not possible to develop a central market until Rule 390 is eliminated.

---

[49] James Needham, "Rule 394 and the Public Interest," *Wall Street Journal,* October 16, 1975, p. 24.

[50] This is the implication derived from a panel reported in Shelby White, "The New Central Marketplace: The Debate Goes On," *Institutional Investor,* Vol. 10, No. 8 (August, 1976), pp. 30–31.

[51] For a further discussion of this view, see Seymour Smidt, "Which Road to an Efficient Stock Market?" *Financial Analysts Journal,* Vol. 27, No. 5 (September–October, 1971), pp. 18–20.

[52] Donald E. Weeden, "Testimony Before the SEC in Respect of Eliminating Rule 394." (October 15, 1975).

Although the SEC contends that Rule 390 must be eliminated progress has been slow because of the controversy between OTC dealers like Weeden, the regional stock exchanges, and the two national exchanges, especially the NYSE. To force the issue, the SEC initially indicated that Rule 390 would be eliminated as of January 1, 1978. There was a last minute deferral of this ruling in December, 1977, following a torrent of protests by numerous brokerage firms. Chairman Williams of the SEC asked for further cooperation from the securities industry,[53] and indicated that the industry should create the elements necessary for an NMS by September 30, 1978.[54]

National Market System Without Rule 390

It is almost certain that at some point in time the SEC will eliminate Rule 390 or modify it drastically. Therefore, it seems appropriate to consider the overall effect on specific major elements of the securities markets. Assume that there is a central tape (which already exists), a central quotation system with a hard CLOB, and no Rule 390. The basic result should be a completely open and competitive market place where all quotations from any registered market-maker are available to all interested investors and any market-maker can trade with any other. Further, all trades are reported to all interested parties.

Dealer Markets One major effect of eliminating Rule 390 would be that any interested market-maker could become a dealer in any stock. Prior to the elimination of Rule 390, a member firm of the NYSE obviously could not make a market in AT&T or GM because all such trades are required to go to the exchange, even the large block trades that are matched "upstairs" (away from the floor of the exchange) by block houses like Goldman Sachs and Solomon Brothers. Member firms like G.S.&Co. and Solomon Brothers will probably not bring the blocks to the exchange but will simply trade them as dealers off the exchange.

A greater effect would be the creation of dealer markets for smaller trades by firms such as Merrill Lynch which could decide to begin making dealer markets in stocks like AT&T and GM and make trades for smaller orders in these stocks for their many individual investors. If a number of large brokerage firms did this for a large number of stocks, one could imagine little or no activity going to the NYSE. Carrying this scenario to its extreme, one observer has contended that without Rule 390, the NYSE would cease to exist in three years.[55]

---

[53] "SEC Chairman Tells Securities Industry to Stop Bickering," *Wall Street Journal,* January 30, 1978, p. 12.

[54] "Securities Industry Must Devise Elements of National Market By September 30, SEC Says," *Wall Street Journal,* January 27, 1978, p. 3.

[55] Letter from John C. Whitehead of Goldman Sachs & Company to Chairman Williams of the SEC, dated August 4, 1977.

This line of reasoning appears to be rather drastic and implies that there is practically no value to the NYSE auction market. The fact is, the major firms that have discussed establishing dealer markets when Rule 390 is eliminated have made it quite clear that they will only become dealers in stocks with reasonable spreads from which there is a potential for reasonable returns.[56] These firms have no desire to compete with the NYSE specialists in stocks like AT&T and GM for which the typical spread is ⅛ or ¼ point at best, because such stocks are not worth their time and effort. They will become dealers in stocks with spreads of ⅜ or ½ point, because the returns will justify the effort and capital required. Some have contended that these dealer markets off the exchange will be inferior to the auction markets. This is questionable because the quotes are available to everyone and one would expect competition to reduce the spread. Also, all trades must be reported on the composite tape, so any broker could be held liable for poor execution (not going to the best market-maker).

Effect on the Specialist Clearly the position of the specialist will change dramatically after Rule 390 is abolished. First, he will lose his protected position as the lone market-maker in many stocks and will be forced to compete with numerous potential dealers. In some cases, the specialist may choose to stop being the market-maker in less active issues. Assuming that the major order flow for stocks like AT&T and GM will continue to come to the NYSE, the specialist could continue to make this market, but he would lose the easy income that previously came from running the limit book because of the existence of a hard CLOB. Therefore, it would be possible to generate respectable returns as a market-maker in a very active stock, but the returns will clearly be less than those reported in the late 1960's. One beneficial change that is contemplated is the elimination of Rule 113 that prohibits the specialist from dealing with institutions. This may allow the specialist to be more active in block transactions, although they will no longer be involved in the block trades that are matched upstairs.

Effect on NYSE There will be substantially less overall volume because there will no longer be block crosses, the off-exchange dealer markets in stocks with large spreads will increase, and the limit order book will be replaced by the hard CLOB. The NYSE has responded by suggesting an intermarket quotation system (IMS) that will list stocks on all major exchanges, including the ASE and the large regional exchanges. This system will allow an investor to determine all the available quotes in all of these markets and automatically consummate a market order with the best market. This system does not include a hard CLOB; the limit order book would remain at

---

[56] For a discussion of this point and the future without Rule 390, see Chris Welles, "The Showdown Over Rule 390," *Institutional Investor,* Vol. 11, No. 12 (December, 1977), pp. 33–38, 125–130.

the NYSE and be run by the specialist. The intent is to keep the exchanges as the central focus for most markets and thereby discourage the establishment of dealer markets, but also to avoid the establishment of a hard CLOB.

Effect on Block Houses The block houses will have everything they had before the change, but will not be forced to take their trades to an exchange to be crossed. This should save money and make the trades easier, although they will not have the benefit of the specialist in some issues. Still, because most blocks are in the large active stocks, and these are the ones that the specialist will stay active in, the specialist may begin to offer some competition to the block houses once Rule 113 is eliminated.

Effect on Regional Exchanges The regional exchanges should benefit from wider exposure of their markets on the consolidated quotation machine and the ability to participate in the limit orders that were formerly restricted to the NYSE. At the same time, they could be seriously affected by the loss of the block trading business. Currently a large number of blocks are crossed on the regionals but this may be lost when block houses are not required to cross blocks on an exchange.

Summary of Effects of NMS Without Rule 390

Without Rule 390, one should expect the creation of more dealer markets than currently exist and an attempt by the large brokerage firms to match the orders by their own customers (this is referred to as "internalization"). At the same time, most of these dealer markets will be in stocks that have only marginal markets on the NYSE (those with large spreads). The specialist will retain the very active stocks in very competitive markets. Clearly, if the hard CLOB is developed and implemented, the specialists will be greatly affected. The NYSE will be affected in terms of overall volume, but should continue to exist because of the demand for auction markets in a large number of active stocks. At the same time, it will lose substantial portions of block business and be affected by the dealer markets in less active stocks away from the exchange. Block houses will be as well off as before, or better, although they will lose some liquidity provided by specialists in certain of their issues. Finally, the regional stock exchanges will lose most of the block crosses but should benefit from more exposure of their markets and a chance to work on the hard CLOB.

Future Tiered Market

Recall that a tiered market developed in the early 1970s because of institutional performance requirements and liquidity constraints. We will probably continue to have tiered markets in the future, concentrated in large companies, irrespective of other characteristics. Size will continue to be an important characteristic for the basic economic reasons indicated previously. While tiers in the trading market will recur, the size requirement will continue and the top tier will be a general class of stocks. Even assuming changing industry popularity, within an industry the concentration will be on the stocks of large companies.

Effect on Corporate Capital Needs

The previous discussion indicated that the primary market for securities, in which companies sell stock or bonds to get new outside capital, is heavily dependent upon the liquidity provided by the secondary market. In the future, we will probably face a substantial problem in the secondary market because of the liquidity requirements of institutions; i.e., they will concentrate their investments in a limited number of large companies. A generous estimate of the number of companies that qualify for most institutional portfolios is about 700 total, while the number of public companies that will not qualify for investment by institutions likely exceeds 8,000.[57] Because institutions are looking at a relatively small number of companies, the secondary market for the remaining stocks traded by individuals will deteriorate. Institutions are concentrating their attention on a smaller group of companies while a shrinking segment of the trading market, the individual investor, is left with a growing number of stocks. Therefore, the secondary markets for the large institutional stocks will improve substantially and be very viable.[58] The secondary market for the great bulk of medium to small firms will continue to deteriorate and will seriously affect the primary market for these companies.[59]

Summary

This chapter was concerned with the many changes that have taken place in our securities markets since 1965, including a consideration of why the changes transpired and a discussion of future changes.

The initial section indicated that the many drastic changes in the markets mainly resulted from the rapid and substantial growth of institutional trading. The rest of the section presented empirical evidence for this growth.

The second section contained a detailed discussion of the several effects of

[57] For a detailed estimate of the number of companies in the alternative tiers, see Frank K. Reilly, "A Three Tier Market and Corporate Financing," *Financial Management,* Vol. 4, No. 3 (Autumn, 1975), pp. 7–15.

[58] For a discussion of how market changes will benefit some corporations, see Richard R. West and Seha M. Tinic, "Corporate Finance and the Changing Stock Market," *Financial Management,* Vol. 3, No. 3 (Autumn, 1974), pp. 14–23.

[59] This problem is discussed in, "Are the Institutions Wrecking Wall Street?" *Business Week,* June, 2, 1973, pp. 58–64.

the fixed commission schedule. Eventually, negotiated commissions were imposed on the exchanges. Heavy institutional trading prompted an increase in block trading which caused major problems for stock exchange specialists and subsequently resulted in the evolution of block houses. Finally, we discussed how a tiered trading market evolved because of the unique portfolio needs of large institutional portfolio managers.

The second half of the chapter was concerned with subsequent changes expected on the basis of what has happened in the markets. We considered the ultimate effects of negotiated commissions on the structure of the industry.

As of 1978, the secondary market has moved about half-way to an NMS (National Market System) in which all quotations and transactions will be reported on a central system. The central tape is a reality and a central quotation system without Rule 390 is inevitable. The effects of such a market will be most pronounced on the exchange specialist and the regional exchanges, with a smaller impact on block houses.

Finally, we discussed the tiered market, why it will continue, and the effects it will have on the top tier and bottom tier firms. The changing market will benefit the large institutions and the large companies they trade, but the impact on many small firms will be rather dismal.

Questions

1. The secondary equity market has experienced major changes since 1965. What is the overall reason for these changes?

2. Discuss three pieces of empirical evidence that attest to the growth in institutional trading in an absolute sense; in a relative sense.

3. Briefly discuss *why* trading by financial institutions has grown dramatically since 1965. Why do the institutions own more stock and trade more stock?

4. Would you expect the large financial institutions to continue to dominate trading in the secondary equity market in the future? Why or why not?

5. Describe the fixed commission schedule. Why did it exist and whom did it protect? Why was it a problem for large financial institutions?

6. What were "give-ups" and why did they exist in the fixed commission world?

7. Why did the third market grow so rapidly from 1965 to 1972?

8. Why do you feel the fourth market grew during the period 1965–1974?

9. Why did institutions want to become members of an exchange? Why did some of the exchanges not allow it? Why did some of the exchanges welcome the institutions?

10. What is meant by the term "negotiated commissions"? When was "May Day"?

11. Discuss why block trades are considered the ultimate test of the liquidity of a market.

12. In the discussion of block trades and the specialist, it was noted that the specialist is hampered by the three C's. Discuss each of the three C's as they relate to block trading.

13. Describe block houses and why they evolved.

14. Describe what is meant by "positioning" part of a block. What is the risk involved?

15. Define a tiered trading market.

16. What were the main characteristics of the tiered trading market that developed in the early 1970s? Why did it develop and what sort of companies were in the top tier?

17. It is contended that the tiered market of the mid-1970s is heavily concerned with the *size* of the companies involved. Why is size important to an institutional portfolio manager? Discuss the logic of this contention.

18. The value of an institutional portfolio is 2 billion dollars. The portfolio managers decide they do not want more than 100 issues in the portfolio and they do not feel they should own more than 4 percent of any firm. What will be the average value of each holding and what must be the average market value of each firm? Show all computations.

19. What would you expect the impact of institutions to be in the future? Discuss the reasoning behind your expectation.

20. Discuss the impact of fully negotiated rates on each of the following segments of the securities industry. Indicate what you think will happen *and why* you believe it will happen.
   a. research firms
   b. block houses
   c. block trades
   d. regional exchanges
   e. the third market
   f. the fourth market.

21. Describe the major attributes of a central market.

22. Briefly discuss Rule 390. What is its purpose?

23. Discuss why the NYSE feels Rule 390 should not be eliminated, i.e., what are the supposed benefits of this rule to the participants (buyers and sellers of stock)?

24. Discuss the free competition argument against Rule 390. What are the supposed advantages of eliminating 390 in terms of market-making and capital?

25. Briefly give the arguments for and against eliminating Rule 390 before the establishment of the central market.

26. What segment of the securities industry will be *most* affected by a central market without Rule 390? Why?

27. What will be the effect of a tiered market on firms in the top tier? Why?

28. What will be the effect of a tiered market on firms in the bottom tier? Why?

References

Archbold, Pamela. "What Weeden Is Doing to Survive." *Institutional Investor,* Vol. 8, No. 11 (November, 1974).

"Are the Institutions Wrecking Wall Street?" *Business Week,* June 2, 1973.

Baker, G. "The Martin Report: Blueprint for Constructive Reform." *Financial Analysts Journal,* Vol. 27, No. 6 (November–December, 1971).

Black, Fischer. "Toward a Fully Automated Stock Exchange." *Financial Analysts Journal,* Vol. 27, No. 4 (July–August, 1971); Vol. 27, No. 6 (November–December, 1971).

Bostian, David B., Jr. "The De-Institutionalization of the Stock Market in American Society." *Financial Analysts Journal,* Vol. 29, No. 6 (November–December, 1973).

Carey, Kenneth J. "Nonrandom Price Changes in Association with Trading in Large Blocks: Evidence of Market Efficiency in Behavior of Investor Returns." *Journal of Business,* Vol. 50, No. 4 (October, 1977).

Demsetz, Harold. "The Cost of Transacting." *Quarterly Journal of Economics,* Vol. 82, No. 1 (February, 1968).

Doede, Robert W. "The Monopoly Power of the New York Stock Exchange." Unpublished Ph.d. dissertation, University of Chicago, 1967.

DuBois, Peter C. "Upstairs, Downstairs." *Barron's,* October 20, 1975.

Elia, Charles J. "Study Shows Severe Broker Competition Yields Huge Stock-Trade Discounts for Banks." *Wall Street Journal,* July 1, 1977.

Farrar, Donald E. "The Coming Reform on Wall Street." *Harvard Business Review,* Vol. 50, No. 5 (September–October, 1972).

Farrar, Donald E. "Toward a Central Market System: Wall Street's Slow Retreat into the Future." *Journal of Financial and Quantitative Analysis,* Vol. 9, No. 5 (November, 1974).

Farrar, Donald E. "Wall Street's Proposed 'Great Leap Backward'." *Financial Analysts Journal,* Vol. 27, No. 5 (September–October, 1971).

Fiske, Heide. "Can the Specialist Cope with the Age of Block Trading?" *Institutional Investor,* Vol. 3, No. 8 (August, 1969).

Freund, William C. "The Historical Role of the Individual Investor in the Corporate Equity Market." *Journal of Contemporary Business,* Vol. 3, No. 1 (Winter, 1974).

Freund, William C. and Minor, David F. "Institutional Activity on the NYSE: 1975 and 1980." *Perspectives on Planning No. 10,* New York Stock Exchange, Inc., June, 1972.

Gaumnitz, Jack E. "Maximal Gains from Diversification and Implications for Portfolio Management." *Mississippi Valley Journal of Business and Economics,* Vol. 6, No. 3 (Spring, 1971).

Grier, Paul C. and Albin, Peter S. "Nonrandom Price Changes in Association with Trading Large Blocks." *The Journal of Business,* Vol. 46, No. 3 (July, 1973).

Hamilton, James L. "Competition, Scale Economies, and Transaction Cost in the Stock Market." *Journal of Financial and Quantitative Analysis,* Vol. 11, No. 5 (December, 1976).

Hirsch, Michael D. "Liquidity Filters: Tools for Better Performance." *Journal of Portfolio Management,* Vol. 2, No. 1 (Fall, 1975).

James, Ralph and James, Estelle. "Disputed Role of the Stock Exchange Specialists." *Harvard Business Review,* Vol. 40, No. 3 (May–June, 1962).

Jones, L.D. "Some Contributions of the Institutional Investor Study." *Journal of Finance,* Vol. 27, No. 2 (May, 1972).

Klemkosky, Robert C. "Institutional Dominance of the NYSE." *Financial Executive,* Vol. 41, No. 11 (November, 1973).

Klemkosky, Robert C. and Scott, David F., Jr. "Withdrawal of the Individual Investor from the Equity Markets." *MSU Business Topics,* Vol. 21, No. 2 (Spring, 1973),

Kraus, Alan and Stoll, Hans R. "Parallel Trading by Institutional Investor." *Journal of Financial and Quantitative Analysis,* Vol. 7, No. 5 (December, 1972).

Kraus, Alan and Stoll, Hans R. "Price Impact of Block Trading on the New York Stock Exchange." *Journal of Finance,* Vol. 27, No. 3 (June, 1972).

Laing, Jonathon R. "Fiduciary Grants: Huge Sums Managed by Bank Trust Units Stir Up Controversy." *Wall Street Journal,* January 7, 1975.

Leuthold, Steven C. "The Causes (and Cures?) of Market Volatility." *Journal of Portfolio Management,* Vol. 2, No. 2 (Winter, 1976).

Loomis, Carol J. "How the Terrible Two-Tier Market Came to Wall Street." *Fortune* (July, 1973).

Lorie, James H. "Public Policy for American Capital Markets." Department of the Treasury, Washington, D.C. (February 7, 1974).

Lyons, John F. "What Happens When Liquidity Disappears?" *Institutional Investor,* Vol. 3, No. 11 (November, 1969).

Marcial, Gene G. "Block Traders Capture Bigger Share of Market, But They Pay a Price." *Wall Street Journal,* February 9, 1978.

Martin, William McChesney, Jr. *The Securities Markets: A Report with Recommendations.* Submitted to the Board of Governors of the New York Stock Exchange (August 5, 1971).

McClintick, David. "Illiquid Stocks—Lack of Ready Buyers and Sellers Imperils the Stock Market." *Wall Street Journal,* December 10, 1971.

Mendelson, Morris. *From Automated Quotes to Automated Trading: Restructuring the Stock Market in the U.S.* Bulletin of the Institute of Finance, Graduate School of Business Administration, New York University (March, 1972).

Merrill Lynch, Pierce, Fenner, and Smith, Inc. "Merrill Lynch's Views on the National Market System," (September, 1977).

Murray, Roger F. "Institutionalization of the Stock Market to Be Feared or Favored?" *Financial Analysts Journal,* Vol. 30, No. 2 (March–April, 1974).

National Bureau of Economic Research. "Regional Stock Exchanges in a Central Market System." *Explorations in Economic Research,* Vol. 2, No. 3 (Summer, 1975).

Nielsen, James F. and Joehnk, Michael D. "Further Evidence on the Effects of Block Transactions on Stock Price Fluctuations." *Mississippi Valley Journal of Business and Economics,* Vol. 9, No. 2 (Winter, 1973–1974).

Officer, Robert R. "The Variability of the Market Factor of the New York Stock Exchange." *The Journal of Business,* Vol. 46, No. 3 (July, 1973).

Reilly, Frank K. "Block Trades and Stock Price Volatility." *Financial Analysts Journal,* forthcoming.

Reilly, Frank K. "Institutions on Trial: Not Guilty." *Journal of Portfolio Management,* Vol. 3, No. 2 (Winter, 1977).

Reilly, Frank K. "Negotiated Commissions and the Third Market," University of Illinois Working Paper No. 429 (revised, September, 1978).

Reilly, Frank K. "A Three Tier Stock Market and Corporate Financing." *Financial Management,* Vol. 4, No. 3 (Autumn, 1975).

Reilly, Frank K. and Drzycimski, Eugene F. "The Stock Exchange Specialist and the Market Impact of Major World Events." *Financial Analysts Journal,* Vol. 31, No. 4 (July–August, 1975).

Reilly, Frank K. and Perry, Gladys. "Negotiated Commissions and Regional Exchanges." University of Illinois Working Paper (August, 1978).

Reilly, Frank K. and Slaughter, William. "The Effect of Dual Markets on Common Stock Marketmaking." *Journal of Financial and Quantitative Analysis,* Vol. 8, No. 2 (March, 1973).

Reilly, Frank K. and Wachowicz, John. "More on the Effect of Institutional Trading on Stock Price Volatility." *Journal of Portfolio Management,* forthcoming.

Robertson, Wyndham. "A Big Board Strategy for Staying Alive." *Fortune* (March, 1977).

Rosenberg, Marvin. "Institutional Investors: Holdings, Prices and Liquidity." *Financial Analysts Journal,* Vol. 30, No. 2 (March–April, 1974).

Scholes, Myron S. "The Market for Securities: Substitution Versus Price-Pressure and the Effects of Information of Share Prices." *The Journal of Business,* Vol. 45, No. 2 (April, 1972).

Seligman, Daniel. "The Terrible Two-Tier Market (Cont.)." *Fortune* (October, 1973).

Shilling, A. Gary. "The Brokerage House Shakeout." *Wall Street Journal,* December 13, 1977.

Smidt, Seymour. "Which Road to an Efficient Stock Market?" *Financial Analysts Journal,* Vol. 27, No. 5 (September–October, 1971).

Snyder, Linda. "Wall Street's Discount Houses Are Selling Hard." *Fortune* (March, 1977).

Soldofsky, Robert M. *Institutional Holdings of Common Stock, 1900–2000.* Ann Arbor, Michigan: Bureau of Business Research, University of Michigan, 1971.

Thackray, John. "Is Time Running Out for the Big Block?" *Institutional Investor,* Vol. 1, No. 6 (June, 1974).

Tinic, Seha M. and West, Richard R. "Competition and the Pricing of Dealer Service in the Over-the-Counter Market." *Journal of Financial and Quantitative Analysis,* Vol. 7, No. 2 (June, 1972).

"The Two-Tier Market Lingers On, Sort Of," *Fortune* (February, 1974).

United States House of Representatives. *Securities and Exchange Commission, Institutional Investor Study Report.* H. Doc. 92–64, 92nd Congress, 1st session. Washington, D.C.: U.S. Government Printing Office, 1971.

Walter, James E. *The Role of Regional Security Exchanges.* Berkeley: University of California Press, 1957.

Weeden, Donald E. "Competition: Key to Market Structure." *Journal of Financial and Quantitative Analysis,* Vol. 7, No. 2 (March, 1972).

Welles, Chris. "Discounting: Wall Street's Game of Nerves." *Institutional Investor,* Vol. 20, No. 11 (November, 1976).

Welles, Chris. "The Showdown Over Rule 390." *Institutional Investor,* Vol. 11, No. 12 (December, 1977).

Welles, Chris. "The War Between the Big Board and the Regionals." *Institutional Investor,* Vol. 4, No. 12 (December, 1970).

Welles, Chris. "Who Will Prosper? Who Will Fail?" *Institutional Investor,* Vol. 5, No. 1 (January, 1971).

West, Richard R. "Institutional Trading and the Changing Stock Market." *Financial Analysts Journal,* Vol. 27, No. 3 (May–June, 1971).

West, Richard R., and Tinic, Seha M. "Corporate Finance and the Changing Stock Market." *Financial Management,* Vol. 3, No. 3 (Autumn, 1974).

West, Richard R., and Tinic, Seha M. *The Economics of the Stock Market.* New York: Praeger Publishers, 1972.

White, Shelby. "The New Central Marketplace: The Debate Goes On." *Institutional Investor,* Vol. 10, No. 8 (August, 1976).

Wood, C. V., Jr. "Why It's Hard to Raise Capital Today." *Financial Executive,* Vol. 41, No. 11 (November, 1973).

Chapter 5

Stock Market Indicator Series

A fair statement regarding stock market indicator series is that everybody talks about them, but few people know how they are constructed and what they represent. Although portfolios are obviously composed of individual stocks, there is a tendency on the part of investors to ask, "What happened to the market today?" The reason for this question is that, if an investor owns more than a few stocks, it is cumbersome to follow each stock individually in order to determine the composite performance of the portfolio. Also there is an intuitive notion that most individual stocks move with the aggregate market. Therefore, if the overall market rose, an individual's portfolio probably also increased in value. To supply investors with a composite report on market performance, some financial publications have developed market indicator series. The general purpose of a market indicator series is to provide an overall indication of aggregate market changes or market movements.

In this chapter we will consider some specific uses of market indicator series, discuss the factors determining what a market indicator series can tell us, and examine some of the major types of indicator series. Finally, we will analyze long- and short-run price movements for some well-known series.

Uses of Market Indicator Series

There are at least four specific uses for stock market indicator series. A primary application is in examining total market returns over a specified time period and using derived returns as a benchmark *to judge the performance of individual portfolios*. A basic assumption is that any investor should be able to derive a rate of return comparable to the "market" return by randomly selecting a large number of stocks from the total market. Hence, it is reasoned that a superior portfolio manager should consistently do better than the market. Therefore, the indicator series are used to judge the performance of professional money managers. In addition to examining the rates of return on the portfolios, one should analyze the differential risk for the institutional portfolios as compared to the market indicator series; i.e., the evaluation of performance should be on a risk-adjusted basis.

Securities analysts, portfolio managers, and others use the series to examine the *factors that influence aggregate stock price movements.* Studies of the relationship between economic variables and aggregate stock market movements require some measurement of overall stock market movements, i.e., a composite stock market indicator series.

Another group interested in an aggregate market series are "technicians," who believe past price changes can be used to predict future price movements. Technicians interested in aggregate market forecasting would obviously want to examine past movements of different market indicator series.

Finally, recent work in portfolio theory has shown that the relevant risk for an individual security is its "systematic" risk with the market. The systematic risk for a stock is determined by the relationship between the rates of return for the security and the rates of return for a market portfolio of risky assets.[1] Therefore, it is necessary for an analyst or portfolio manager attempting to determine the systematic risk for an individual security to relate its returns to the returns for an aggregate market indicator series.

Differentiating Factors in Constructing Market Indicator Series

Because indicator series are intended to indicate the overall movements of a group of stocks it is necessary to consider which factors are important in computing any average intended to represent a total population.

Sample

Our initial concern is with the sample used to construct the series. When talking about samples, three factors must be considered: *the size of the sample, the breadth of the sample,* and *the source of the sample.*

A small percent of the total population will provide valid indications of the behavior of the total population if the sample is properly selected. In fact, at some point the costs of taking a larger sample will almost certainly outweigh any benefits in terms of generating information that is closer to total market performance. The sample should be *representative* of the total population or the size of the sample will be meaningless; a large biased sample is no better than a small biased sample. The sample can be generated

---

[1] William F. Sharpe, "Capital Asset Prices: Theory of Market Equilibrium Under Conditions of Risk," *Journal of Finance,* Vol. 19, No. 3 (September, 1964), pp. 425–442.

by completely random selection or by a nonrandom but well-designed selection process in which the characteristics desired are taken into consideration. The *source* of the sample becomes important if there are any differences between alternative segments of the population, in which case samples from each segment are required.

Weighting

Our second concern is with *the weight given to each member in the sample.* In computing stock market indicator series, three principal weighting schemes are used: (1) a price-weighted series, (2) a value-weighted series, and (3) an unweighted series, or what would be described as an equally-weighted series.

Computational Procedure

Our final consideration is with *the computational procedure used.* One alternative is to take a simple arithmetic average of the various members in the series. Another is to compute an index and have all changes, whether in price or value, reported in terms of the basic index. Finally, some prefer using a geometric average.

Alternative Indicator Series

Price-Weighted Series

A price-weighted series is an arithmetic average of current prices which means that, in fact, movements are influenced by differential prices.

Dow-Jones Industrial Average

The best-known price series is also the oldest and certainly the most popular market indicator series, the Dow-Jones Industrial Average (DJIA). The DJIA is a price-weighted average of 30 large, well-known industrial stocks that are generally the leaders in their industry (blue-chips) and are listed on the New York Stock Exchange. The index is derived by totaling *the current prices* of the 30 stocks and dividing the sum by a divisor that has been adjusted to take account of stock splits and changes in the sample over time.

$$DJIA_t = \sum_{i=1}^{30} P_{it} / D_{adj}$$

where:

$DJIA_t$—the value of the DJIA on day t

P_{it}—the closing price of stock i on day t

D_{adj}—the adjusted divisor on day t.

The example in Table 5–1 uses three stocks to demonstrate the procedure used to derive a new divisor for the DJIA when a stock splits. When stocks split, the divisor becomes smaller. An idea of the cumulative effect of splits can be derived from the fact that the initial divisor was 30 but, as of June, 1978, it was 1.443.

Table 5–1
Example of Change in DJIA Divisor When A Sample Stock Splits

	Before Split	After 3-for-1 Split by Stock A	
	Prices	Prices	
A	30	10	
B	20	20	
C	$\overline{10}$	$\overline{10}$	
	$60 \div 3 = 20$	$40 \div X = 20$	X = 2 (New Divisor)

The idea is to derive a new divisor that will ensure that the new value for the series is the same as it would have been without the split. In this case, the presplit index value was 20. Therefore, after the split, given the new sum of prices, the divisor is adjusted downward to maintain this value of 20.

Because the series is price-weighted, a high-priced stock carries more weight in the series than does a low-priced stock—i.e., as shown in the example below, a 10 percent change in a 100 dollar stock (10 dollars) will cause a larger change in the series than a 10 percent change in a 30 dollar stock (3 dollars). In Case A, the 100 dollar stock increases by 10 percent, which causes a 5 percent increase in the average; in Case B, the 30 dollar stock increases by 10 percent and the average only rises by 1.8 percent.

		Period T + 1	
	Period T	Case A	Case B
A	100	110	100
B	50	50	50
C	$\overline{30}$	$\overline{30}$	$\overline{33}$
Sum	180	190	183
Divisor	3	3	3
Average	60	63.3	61
Percent of Change		5.0	1.8

The DJIA was created in the late 1800's by Charles Dow, publisher of *The Wall Street Journal*. Initially, there were only 15 stocks included in the average, but it was later expanded to 30. The initial computation was the sum of the prices of the stocks, divided by 15 to generate an average price. When stocks split, the after-split price was multiplied by the split factor and divided by the initial 15. It was later determined that using current prices but changing the divisor was an easier method of supposedly achieving the same effect. As will be discussed, the effect is *not* the same because the weighting changes.

The DJIA has been criticized over time on several counts, the first of which is that the sample used for the series is limited. It is difficult to conceive of how 30 nonrandomly selected blue-chip stocks can be representative of the 1,800 stocks listed on the NYSE. In addition to the fact that their number is limited, the stocks included are, by definition, offerings of the largest and most prestigious companies in various industries. Therefore, the DJIA probably reflects price movements for large, mature blue-chip firms rather than for the "typical" company listed on the NYSE. Several studies have pointed out that price movements on the DJIA have not been as volatile as they have been on other market indicator series and that the long-run returns on the DJIA are not comparable to those implied by more representative price indicator series.

In addition, the stocks in the DJIA are weighted on the basis of their relative prices. Therefore, when a high-priced stock such as DuPont moves even a small percent, it has an inordinate effect on the overall index. In contrast, when companies have a stock split their prices decline and, therefore, their weight in the DJIA is reduced, even though they may be large and important. Therefore, the weighting scheme causes a downward bias in the DJIA because the stocks that have higher growth rates will have higher prices and such stocks tend to consistently split, and thereby consistently lose weight within the index.[2] Irrespective of the several criticisms made of the DJIA, a comparison of short-run price movements of the DJIA and of other NYSE indicators shows a fairly close relationship between the daily percentages of price changes for the DJIA and comparable price changes for other NYSE indicators.

In addition to a price series for industrial stocks, Dow-Jones also publishes an average of 20 stocks in the transportation industry and an average

---

[2] For an extensive discussion of these problems see the following studies: H. L. Butler, Jr. and M. B. Decker, "A Security Check on the Dow-Jones Industrial Average," *Financial Analysts Journal,* Vol. 9, No. 1 (February, 1953), pp. 37–45; R. B. Shaw, "The Dow-Jones Industrials vs. the Dow-Jones Industrial Average," *Financial Analysts Journal,* Vol. 11, No. 5 (November, 1955), pp. 37–40; Lawrence Fisher, "Some New Stock Market Indexes," *Journal of Business,* Vol. 39, No. 1, Part II (January, 1966 Supplement), pp. 191–225; W. F. Balch, "Market Guides," *Barron's,* September 19, 1966, p. 7; R. D. Milne, "The Dow-Jones Industrial Average Re-examined," *Financial Analysts Journal,* Vol. 22, No. 6 (December, 1966), pp. 83–88; E. E. Carter and K. J. Cohen, "Bias in the DJIA Caused by Stock Splits," *Financial Analysts Journal,* Vol. 22, No. 6 (December, 1966), pp. 90–94; Paul Cootner, "Stock Market Indexes—Fallacies and Illusions," *Commercial and Financial Chronicle,* September 29, 1966, pp. 18–19; Lewis L. Schellbach, "When Did the DJIA Top 1200?" *Financial Analysts Journal,* Vol. 23, No. 3 (May–June, 1967), pp. 71–73; E. E. Carter and K. J. Cohen, "Stock Averages, Stock Splits, and Bias," *Financial Analysts Journal,* Vol. 23, No. 3 (May–June, 1967), pp. 77–81.

for utilities that includes 15 stocks. Detailed reports of the averages are contained in *The Wall Street Journal* and *Barron's,* including hourly figures.[3]

National Quotation Bureau Average

Another price-weighted series, in contrast to the DJIA, is probably one of the least-known of all stock market indicator series, the National Quotation Bureau (NQB) Average of 35 over-the-counter industrial stocks. The NQB index, like the DJIA, is composed of only industrial stocks and also includes the large, well-established, blue-chip companies traded on the OTC market.

The DJIA and the NQB Industrial Averages are similar in computational procedure and also in their sample selection procedure. Because its sample is limited, some observers have criticized the NQB average as not being representative of the vast OTC market. A distinct difference between the DJIA and the NQB is the number of sample changes. The stocks used in the DJIA were constant for the 17 year period from June, 1959 to August, 1976, when Minnesota Mining and Manufacturing (3M) replaced Anaconda. In contrast, the NQB average has had substantial turnover in its sample.[4]

Value-Weighted Series

A value-weighted index is generated by deriving the initial total market value of all stocks used in the series (market value equals number of shares outstanding times current market price). This figure is typically established as the base and assigned an index value of 100. Subsequently, a new market value is computed for all securities in the index and this is compared to the initial value to determine the percentage of change which, in turn, is applied to the beginning index value of 100.

$$\text{Index}_t = \frac{\sum P_t Q_t}{\sum P_b Q_b} \times \text{Beginning Index Value}$$

where:

Index_t = Index value on day t

P_t = Ending prices for stocks on day t

Q_t = Number of outstanding shares on day t

P_b = Ending prices for stocks on base day

Q_b = Number of outstanding shares on base day.

---

[3] For a further discussion of the series and extensive historical data for all the averages, see Maurice L. Farrell (ed.), *The Dow-Jones Investor's Handbook* (Princeton, New Jersey: Dow-Jones Books, 1978).

[4] Since the creation of the NASDAQ price indicator series in 1971 (to be discussed in the next section) it is very difficult to get figures for the NQB series. Apparently they are

Table 5–2
Example of Value-Weighted Index

Stock	Share Price	Number of Shares	Market Value
December 31, 1977			
A	$10.00	1,000,000	$ 10,000,000
B	15.00	6,000,000	90,000,000
C	20.00	5,000,000	100,000,000
Total			$200,000,000 —

Base Value equal to
an Index of 100

Stock	Share Price	Number of Shares	Market Value
December 31, 1978			
A	$12.00	1,000,000	$ 12,000,000
B	10.00	12,000,000[a]	120,000,000
C	20.00	5,500,000[b]	110,000,000
Total			$242,000,000

$$\text{New Index Value} = \frac{\text{Current Market Value}}{\text{Base Value}} \times \text{Beginning Index Value}$$

$$= \frac{\$242,000,000}{200,000,000} \times 100$$

$$= 1.21 \times 100$$

$$= 121$$

[a] Stock split 2-for-1 during year
[b] Company paid 10 percent stock dividend during the year

A simple example for a three stock index is shown in Table 5–2.

As can be seen, there is an *automatic adjustment* for stock splits and other capital changes in a value-weighted index because the decrease in the stock price is offset by an increase in the number of shares outstanding. In a value-weighted index, the importance of individual stocks in the sample is determined by their relative market value. A given percentage of change in the value of a large company has a greater impact than a comparable percentage change for a small company.

Standard & Poor's Indexes

The first company to widely employ a market value index was Standard & Poor's Corporation. They developed an index using 1935–1937 as a base period and computed a market value index for 425 industrials stocks. They also computed an index of 50 utilities and 25 transportation firms. Finally, they developed a 500 stock composite index. The base period was sub-

available daily only in the NQB "pink" sheets; weekly in the *OTC Market Chronicle;* and monthly in the *OTC Securities Review.*

sequently changed to 1941–1943 and the base value to 10. All the S&P series were again changed significantly on July 1, 1976 when they went from 425 industrials, 60 utilities, and 15 rails, to 400 industrials, 40 utilities, 20 transportation, and 20 financial. A number of stocks added were listed on the OTC which was necessary because, as noted in Chapter 3, most of the major banks and insurance companies are traded on the OTC market. Therefore, in order to construct a relevant financial index, it was necessary to break with the tradition of only including NYSE stocks.[5]

In addition to their major market indicators, S&P has constructed over 90 individual industry series that include from 3 to 11 companies within an industry group. Daily figures for the major S&P indexes are carried in *The Wall Street Journal* and other newspapers and weekly data are contained in *Barron's*. Standard & Poor's has a weekly publication entitled *The Outlook* that contains weekly values for all the industry groups. Extensive historical data on all these indexes and other financial series is contained in Standard & Poor's *Trade and Securities Statistics*.

New York Stock Exchange Index

Following the example set by Standard & Poor's and the general acceptance of its procedure for computing its market value, several other market indicators have been created employing the value-weighted index concept. In 1966, the NYSE derived a market value index with figures available back to 1940. In contrast to other indexes, the various NYSE series are not based upon a sample of stocks, but include all stocks listed on the exchange. Therefore, questions about the number of stocks in the sample or the breadth of the sample do not arise. However, because the index is value-weighted, the issues of large companies still control major movements in the index. The 500 stocks in the Standard & Poor's Composite Index represent 74 percent of the market value of all stocks on the exchange although they are only about 28 percent of exchange listings in terms of numbers.[6]

NASDAQ Series

These constitute a comprehensive set of price indicator series for the OTC market developed by the National Association of Securities Dealers (NASD). The NASDAQ–OTC Price Indicator Series were released to the public on May 17, 1971, with figures available from February 5, 1971 (the index value was 100 as of February 5). Through NASDAQ, the NASD

---

[5] For a further discussion of the specific changes see "S&P 500 Stock Index Adds Financial, Transportation Groups," Standard & Poor's Corporation (July 1, 1976). For a detailed discussion of the computation of all the series and all the potential adjustments, see *Trade and Securities Statistics* (New York: Standard & Poor's Corp., 1978).

[6] For a detailed discussion of the index, written shortly after its inception, and including an historical chart, see Stan West and Norman Miller, "Why the New NYSE Common Stock Indexes?" *Financial Analysts Journal,* Vol. 23, No. 3 (May–June, 1967), pp. 49–54.

provides daily, weekly, and monthly sets of stock price indicators for OTC securities in different industry categories. All domestic OTC common stocks listed on NASDAQ are included in the indexes, and new stocks are included when they are added to the system. The 2,337 issues contained in the NASDAQ–OTC Price Indexes have been divided into seven categories:[7]

1. composite (2,337 issues)
2. industrials (1,584 issues)
3. banks (53 issues)
4. Insurance (125 issues)
5. other finance (449 issues)
6. transportation (51 issues)
7. utilities (75 issues).

The indexes are value-weighted series similar to the S&P series and the NYSE series. Because they are value-weighted, they are heavily influenced by the largest 100 stocks on the NASDAQ system. The NASDAQ series differs from the NQB–OTC series in terms of size of the samples (35 blue-chip stocks versus over 2,000 issues) and method of computation. An analysis of daily percentage of price changes indicated that the correlation between the two series during the period February, 1971 to June, 1973 was about .60, which was significant, but not as high as one might expect. Regarding long-run price movements, the series were relatively consistent during periods of consistently declining or rising stock prices, but were not similar during long periods of mixed movements. During the latter periods, the NASDAQ series were more consistent with the various NYSE series.[8]

Most of the NASDAQ series are reported daily in *The Wall Street Journal* and are contained in *Barron's* on a weekly basis. The daily figures for all years since 1975 are contained in *Barron's Market Laboratory.*[9]

American Stock Exchange

The ASE developed a market indicator series in 1966. As originally developed, it was a price change series in which the price changes during a given day were added and then divided by the number of issues on the

---

[7] As of April, 1978. Securities on the NASDAQ system not included in any of the indexes are warrants, preferred stocks, foreign stocks, and common stocks listed on an exchange traded OTC (third market stocks).

[8] For an extended discussion of the series and an empirical comparison with the NQB series see Frank K. Reilly, "A Report on the NASDAQ Over-the-Counter Stock Price Indicators," University of Wyoming Research Paper No. 1 (August, 1973).

[9] Maurice L. Farrell (ed.), *Barron's Market Laboratory* (Princeton, New Jersey: Dow-Jones Books, 1978).

exchange. This average price change was then added to or subtracted from the previous day's index to arrive at a new index value.[10] As pointed out in two studies published in *Barron's,* this procedure eventually caused a substantial distortion in the value of the series, because the price changes were influenced by the absolute value of the series. The absolute price level declined over time because of stock splits so eventually the absolute price changes seriously underrepresented the percentage of price changes.[11] As a result, the ASE index went from the most volatile to the least volatile market indicator series. Because of severe criticism of the series, the ASE subsequently commissioned the creation of a value-weighted series similar to that used by the NYSE and the NASD. This new series was released in October, 1973. The exchange later made figures available for the new series back to 1969. A comparison of the old and new series indicated a substantial difference in volatility between the two.[12] As the figures in Tables 5–3 and 5–4 show, for the year 1969, the new ASE series was somewhat more volatile than was the original series (it increased more during bear markets). More important, the difference in volatility increased over time. A comparison of daily percentage of price changes in the old and new series indicated that volatility in the new series was 33 percent greater during 1969 and that it increased steadily to the point that the new series was 258 percent more volatile in 1974.[13]

Unweighted Price Indicator Series

In an unweighted index, all stocks carry equal weight irrespective of their price and/or their value. A 20 dollar stock is as important as a 40 dollar stock, and the total market value of the company is not important. Such an index can be used by an individual who randomly selects stocks for his portfolio. One way to visualize an unweighted series is to assume that equal dollar amounts are invested in each stock in the portfolio (e.g., an equal 1000 dollar investment in each stock). Therefore, the investor would own 50 shares of a 20 dollar stock, 100 shares of a 10 dollar stock, and 10 shares of a 100 dollar stock.

The best-known unweighted or equal-weighted stock market series are

---

[10] An extended discussion of the original series, including an historical chart, is contained in B. Alva Schoomer, Jr., "The American Stock Exchange Index System," *Financial Analysts Journal,* Vol. 23, No. 3 (May–June, 1967), pp. 57–61.

[11] S. C. Leuthold and C. E. Gordon II, "Margin for Error," *Barron's,* March 1, 1971, p. 9, and S. C. Leuthold and K. F. Blaich, "Warped Yardstick," *Barron's,* September 18, 1972, p. 9.

[12] Frank K. Reilly, "The Original and New American Stock Exchange Price Indicator Series," University of Wyoming Research Paper No. 68 (March, 1975).

[13] The comparison ends in 1974 because the ASE stopped computing figures for the original series.

Table 5-3
Annual Percentage of Price Changes for the Original and New ASE Series and Other Representative Series

	Original ASE	New ASE	NYSE Composite	DJIA
1969	(19.71)[a]	(28.98)	(12.51)	(15.19)
1970	(13.40)	(18.00)	(2.52)	4.82
1971	12.48	18.86	12.34	6.11
1972	3.01	10.33	14.27	14.58
1973	(17.68)	(30.00)	(19.63)	(16.58)
1974	(10.14)	(33.22)	(30.28)	(27.57)
Average of Annual Changes	(7.57)	(13.50)	(6.39)	(5.64)
Total Change 1969–1974	(40.40)	(64.31)	(38.66)	(34.70)
Compound Annual Change 1969–1974	(5.75)	(8.62)	(5.57)	(5.10)

[a] ( ) indicates price decline.

Table 5-4
Total Percentage of Price Changes for Original and New ASE Series and Representative Series During Major Market Swings

Period From	To	Original ASE	New ASE	NYSE Composite	DJIA
1/2/69[a]	–5/26/70	(41.16)[b]	(57.28)	(36.05)	(33.40)
5/26/70	–4/28/71	37.86	68.61	53.25	50.65
4/28/71	–11/23/71	(12.44)	(17.93)	(14.13)	(16.08)
11/23/71	–1/11/73	14.16	30.60	32.02	31.80
1/11/73	–12/31/74[a]	(11.84)	(35.24)	(27.01)	(25.13)

[a] The beginning and ending dates are not peaks or troughs.
[b] ( ) indicates price decline.

those constructed by Lawrence Fisher at the University of Chicago.[14] Fisher and Lorie carried out several studies examining the performance of stocks on the NYSE assuming that an investor bought equal amounts of each stock on the exchange.[15]

---

[14] Lawrence Fisher, "Some New Stock Market Indexes," *Journal of Business,* Vol. 39, No. 1, Part II (January, 1966 Supplement), pp. 191–225.

[15] Lawrence Fisher and James H. Lorie, "Rates of Return on Investments in Common Stock," *Journal of Business,* Vol. 37, No. 1 (January, 1964), pp. 1–21; L. Fisher and J. H. Lorie, "Rates of Return on Investments in Common Stock: The Year-By-Year Record, 1926–65," *Journal of Business,* Vol. 41, No. 3 (July, 1968), pp. 291–316; Lawrence Fisher, "Outcomes for 'Random' Investments in Common Stock Listed on the New York Stock Exchange," *Journal of Business,* Vol. 38, No. 2 (April, 1965), pp. 149–161.

Another unweighted price indicator series that has gained in prominence is the *Indicator Digest* index of all stocks on the NYSE. It is contended that the *Indicator Digest* series is more representative of all stocks on the exchange compared to value-weighted series that are heavily influenced by large firms. In several instances it reached a trough earlier than other indicator series, and continued to be depressed after some of the "popular" market indicator series resumed rising during a bull market. Such a difference indicates that the market increase only included the large popular stocks as contained in the DJIA or the Standard & Poor's market indicator series which are heavily influenced by the large, well-known companies.[16]

Comparison of Indicator Series Changes Over Time

In this section we will discuss price movements in the different series with an emphasis on *source* of the samples as opposed to size or selection process. We will also consider price movements for the series in the short-run (daily) and over more extended periods (yearly and over market cycles). Our emphasis will be on the difference in results for segments of the total equity market, the NYSE, the ASE, and OTC.

Daily Percentage of Changes

Table 5–5 contains a matrix of the correlation coefficients of the daily percentage of price changes for alternative market indicator series during the period January 4, 1972 through December 31, 1977 (1,512 observations). This recent six-year period was selected because data were available for all the major series including the new ASE Market Value Series and the NASDAQ series initiated in February, 1971.

Table 5–5 **Correlation Coefficients Between Daily Percentage of Price Changes for Alternative Market Indicator Series January 4, 1972–December 31, 1977 (1,512 Observations)**

	DJIA	S&P 400	S&P 500	NYSE Composite	ASE Value Index	NASDAQ Industrials	NASDAQ Composite
DJIA	—						
S&P 400	.878	—					
S&P 500	.909	.877	—				
NYSE Composite	.922	.886	.916	—			
ASE Value Index	.731	.693	.733	.758	—		
NASDAQ Industrials	.665	.637	.661	.683	.625	—	
NASDAQ Composite	.810	.776	.807	.839	.769	.739	—

---

[16] Carol J. Loomis, "How the Terrible Two-Tier Market Came to Wall Street," *Fortune* (July, 1973), pp. 82–89.

The results are notable because *almost all of the differences in the correlations of daily percentage of price changes are apparently attributable to differences in the sample of stocks,* i.e., differences in the types of firms listed on the alternative segments. All the major series except the DJIA are now total market value indexes that include a large number of stocks. Therefore, the computational procedure is the same, the sample sizes are all quite large (from 400 to 2,400), and the samples represent either a large segment of the total population in terms of value or all members of the population. Thus the only notable difference between several of the series is the members of the population; i.e., the stocks are from different segments of the aggregate stock market.

The results reported in Table 5–5 are quite comparable to those produced in a prior study that examined daily stock price changes during the period 1960–1970,[17] and indicate that there is *very high positive correlation* between the alternative series that include almost all NYSE stocks (the DJIA; S&P 400; S&P 500; and the NYSE composite). Although there has been criticism of the DJIA because of its sample size and weighting, its correlation with the other major NYSE series ranged from about .88 to .92. This indicates that, on a short-run basis, the DJIA is a very adequate indicator of price movements on the exchange.

In contrast to the very high correlations among alternative NYSE series, there is a significantly lower correlation between each of these series and the ASE series, from an average of about .69 to .76. These results indicate the possibility that the market is segmented between the two exchanges (segmentation being indicated by significant differences in stock price movements).

The correlation of results with the NASDAQ industrial index indicates a further difference in price movements. The average correlation is about .66, which is likewise significantly lower than the correlation among alternative NYSE series. In addition, the relationship between the NASDAQ and the ASE series is actually *lower* than the NASDAQ relationship with any of the NYSE series. This can probably be explained by the fact that some very large firms are included in the NASDAQ system, such as Anheuser Busch, Coors Company, Tampax Company, and Roadway Express. Several of these companies, and some financial firms that will be discussed later, are larger than the largest firms on the ASE. Therefore, in some respects this index is more closely related to the NYSE than to the ASE.

The final row in the table is initially a surprise because it indicates a fairly strong correlation between the NASDAQ composite index and the alternative NYSE series. Upon reflection this can be explained by the differential sample. The NASDAQ composite series, as of April, 1978, contained

---

[17] Frank K. Reilly, "Evidence Regarding a Segmented Stock Market," *Journal of Finance,* Vol. 27, No. 3 (June, 1972), pp. 607–625.

1,584 industrial issues, 53 bank stocks, 125 insurance stocks, 449 financial company stocks, 51 transportation stocks, and 75 utility stocks. The 753 nonindustrial stocks obviously have a substantial impact on the composite index because they make up a third of the sample in terms of number of issues, but have a much greater effect because of size. The NASDAQ series are value-weighted and some of the very largest OTC companies are in the nonindustrial group including American International Group, Connecticut General Insurance, General Reinsurance, St. Paul Company, Security Pacific Corporation, and First Bank System. These insurance and financial firms obviously have a large impact on the series and are also, in many cases, similar to NYSE listed companies. All of these firms would qualify for listing on the NYSE but have chosen to remain on the OTC. The effect of size and the difference in stock price movement can be seen from the correlation of .71 between the NASDAQ industrial and the NASDAQ composite series.

Annual Price Changes

The annual percentage of price changes for the alternative price indicator series are contained in Table 5–6. The comparison between market segments cannot be made for all the years from 1960 through 1977 because the series for the ASE is not available before 1969 while the OTC series was not available prior to February, 1971.

The results for the four NYSE series can be analyzed for the full 18 year period. One would expect the DJIA series to be generally less volatile and also to experience lower average returns. The average returns were basically consistent with the expectation and the average annual compound rate of change for the DJIA was also lower than it was for the other three NYSE series. In contrast, all the standard deviations were similar, with a tendency for the DJIA to be the largest.

For the nine year period 1969–1977 it is possible to compare the results for the NYSE series to the ASE series. One would expect a higher return and a higher risk for the ASE series because of the smaller, more volatile companies listed on this exchange. The total period returns confirmed this, since the risk was higher as indicated by a higher standard deviation of annual changes. The average price changes were larger, as expected, but they were larger *negative* changes because, during this period, the compound rate of change for all segments was negative. One would expect a higher risk segment to have larger negative returns.

The results for the six-year period 1972–1977 included all three market segments. The risk measure results were consistent with expectations since the four NYSE series all had lower standard deviations than either the ASE or the OTC market. Further, the ASE series was more volatile than the NASDAQ composite series, which can be explained by the fact that there are additional companies in the NASDAQ series.

The average of the annual changes was consistent with the risk because

Table 5–6 **Percentage of Changes in Stock Price Indicator Series 1960–1977**

Year	DJIA	S&P 400	S&Pª 500	NYSE Composite	ASEᵇ Values Index	NASDAQᶜ Industrials	NASDAQ Composite
1960	− 9.34	− 4.67	− 2.97	− 3.89			
1961	18.71	23.14	23.13	24.08			
1962	−10.91	−13.00	−11.81	−11.95			
1963	17.12	19.37	18.89	18.07			
1964	14.57	13.96	12.97	14.35			
1965	10.88	9.88	9.06	9.53			
1966	−18.94	−13.60	−13.09	−12.56			
1967	15.20	23.53	20.09	23.10			
1968	5.24	8.47	7.66	10.39			
1969	−15.19	−10.20	−11.36	−12.51	−28.98		
1970	4.82	− 0.58	0.10	− 2.52	−18.00		
1971	6.11	11.71	10.79	12.34	18.86		
1972	14.58	16.10	15.63	14.27	10.33	13.63	17.18
1973	−16.58	−17.38	−17.37	−19.63	−30.00	−36.38	−31.06
1974	−27.57	−29.93	−29.72	−30.28	−33.22	−32.44	−35.11
1975	38.34	31.92	31.55	31.86	38.40	43.38	29.76
1976	17.86	18.42	19.15	21.50	31.58	23.68	26.10
1977	−17.27	−12.35	−11.50	− 9.30	16.43	9.30	7.33

Average of Annual Changes

1960–1977	2.65	4.16	2.96	4.27			
1969–1977	0.57	0.86	0.81	0.64	0.60		
1972–1977	1.56	1.13	1.29	1.40	5.59	3.45	2.37

Standard Deviation of Annual Changes

1960–1977	17.65	17.33	16.82	17.52			
1969–1977	21.28	20.01	19.88	20.56	28.21		
1972–1977	25.77	24.33	24.14	24.73	30.54	31.80	28.56

Total Percent Change

1960–1977	22.40	62.34	58.79	62.30			
1969–1977	−11.93	− 7.35	− 8.43	−10.87	−24.31		
1972–1977	− 6.63	− 7.11	− 6.86	− 6.96	9.35	− 6.09	− 8.59

Average Annual Compound Rate of Change

1960–1977	1.13	2.73	2.60	2.73			
1969–1977	− 1.42	− 0.85	− 0.98	− 1.29	− 2.48		
1972–1977	− 1.15	− 1.24	− 1.19	− 1.21	1.50	− 1.05	− 1.51

ª S&P 425 prior to July, 1976.
ᵇ Market Value Index started on August 31, 1973 with data back to January 1, 1969.
ᶜ Index started on February 5, 1971 with no prior data available.

the returns to the ASE and the OTC had larger positive values. In contrast, the average compound rate of change results were not consistent. Given that all the NYSE series experienced negative changes, one would expect larger negative values for the higher risk ASE and OTC series. In fact, the ASE series had a positive rate of change and the rate for the NASDAQ industrial, though negative, was smaller. These results were almost wholly caused by the fact that during 1977, all the NYSE series experienced relatively large *declines* (9–17 percent), while the ASE and the OTC experienced relatively large *increases* (7–16 percent). According to most observers, this unusual pattern was due to strong demand for the small secondary stocks that had become underpriced because they had been ignored by institutions. Assuming that this demand corrected any disequilibrium in prices, one would expect the long-run pattern, in which the returns in rising and declining markets are consistent with the underlying risk of the securities, to re-emerge.[18]

Market Period Results

Table 5–7 contains price changes for the alternative series during major market swings since October, 1962. The market swings are determined by major peaks and troughs in the DJIA. Prior to 1977, the use of other series for the dating of peaks and troughs would have had little or no effect.

As before, one would expect the low risk series to be less volatile on the upswing and decline. Prior to 1970, only the NYSE series were available and the results for the alternative series were generally equal during market swings with small changes in rankings. During the two market swings in 1970 and 1971 that included the ASE series, the results for the ASE were consistent with expectations; i.e., the ASE series increased more than the NYSE series did during the market rally and declined more as the market fell. During the bull market from November, 1971 to January, 1973, all segments increased but the ASE fell behind, possibly due to the tiered trading market that became rather prominent during this period. During the 1973–1974 decline, the results were again consistent, with the ASE and OTC experiencing larger declines. Finally, during the 1975–1976 rally, the increases were as hypothesized except that the DJIA did better than one might expect. The table does not include 1977 because price changes at that time followed a very unusual pattern. It appears that the DJIA reached a peak in December, 1976, while the ASE and OTC continued to new highs. Again, one can only assume that the "normal" relationship will be re-established.

---

[18] For an earlier analysis of long-run price changes for the three segments see Frank K. Reilly, "Price Changes in NYSE, AMEX and OTC Stocks Compared," *Financial Analysts Journal,* Vol. 27, No. 2 (March–April, 1971), pp. 54–59.

Table 5–7 Price Changes on the NYSE, the ASE, and OTC During Periods of Rising and Falling Stock Prices October 1, 1962–December 31, 1976

Dates	Number of Months		Percent of Change in Stock Price Indicator Series						
	Rising	Declining	DJIA	S&P 400	S&P 500	NYSE Composite	ASE Value Index[b]	NASDAQ Industrials[c]	NASDAQ Composite[c]
10/1/62[a]–2/9/66 (P)[d]	40.0		73.2	73.3	69.5	N/A			
2/9/66 –10/7/66 (T)[e]		8.0	–24.9	–22.4	–22.2	–22.7			
10/7/66 –12/3/68 (P)	26.0		32.4	51.2	47.6	55.2			
12/3/68 –5/26/70 (T)		18.0	–35.9	–35.8	–35.9	–38.3			
5/26/70 –4/28/71 (P)	11.0		50.2	53.1	51.2	52.9	68.6		
4/28/71 –11/23/71 (T)		7.0	–15.8	–14.1	–13.9	–13.9	–17.9		
11/23/71–4/28/71 (P)	14.0		31.8	35.4	33.4	32.0	30.6	39.6	36.4
1/11/73 –12/6/74 (T)		24.0	–45.1	–46.2	–45.9	–47.4	–54.7	–59.8	–57.5
12/6/74 –12/31/76[a]	25.0		73.9	65.1	65.3	68.0	85.8	82.2	68.2

[a] The beginning and ending dates are neither troughs nor peaks but were selected on the basis of availability of data.
[b] Figures available beginning on January 1, 1969.
[c] Figures available beginning on February 1, 1971.
[d] Peak
[e] Trough

Summary

Given the several uses of stock market indicator series, it is important to know how they are constructed and the differences among them in terms of computational and sampling procedures. Since new series for the ASE and OTC have been introduced, the computational differences are slight. A comparison of short-run and long-run price changes for the alternative series indicates that the computational differences are not nearly as important as the differences in the sample of stocks used, i.e., whether the stocks are from the NYSE, the ASE, or the OTC market. Finally, the results were generally consistent with expectations regarding risk and return. The ASE and OTC typically had higher risk (more volatility) and higher returns (larger negative and positive price changes).

Questions

1. Set forth and discuss briefly the several uses that can be made of stock market indicator series.

2. What are the major factors that must be considered when constructing a market indicator series? Put another way, what characteristics differentiate indicator series?

3. What is meant when it is stated that a market indicator series is price-weighted? In such a case, would you expect a 100 dollar stock to be more important than a 25 dollar stock? Why?

4. What are the major criticisms made of the Dow-Jones Industrial Average?

5. Describe the procedure used in computing a value-weighted series.

6. Describe how a price-weighted series adjusts for stock splits. How a value-weighted series adjusts for splits.

7. How does the new ASE Market Value series differ from the original ASE price change series in terms of percentage of price change during major market swings? What would explain this difference: sample size, source of sample, or method of computation?

8. What is meant by an unweighted price indicator series? How would you construct such a series?

9. The correlation results between the daily percentage of price changes for the alternative NYSE price indicator series indicated substantial correlation among the series. What would explain this similarity: size of sample, source of sample, or method of computation?

10. Regarding daily percentage of price changes, what would explain the significantly lower correlation between price changes for the NASDAQ Industrial Index and the various NYSE series? Would it be size of sample, source of sample, or method of construction?

11. Why are the NASDAQ composite results with the NYSE series much better than the NASDAQ industrial results?

12. Regarding the historical price movements for the various NYSE price indicator series, how did they differ in terms of price changes and variability of price changes? Were the differences generally consistent with what you would expect based upon economic theory?

13. For the period 1972–1977 all three market segments can be compared. During this period, were the results in terms of return (price change) and risk (variability of returns) consistent with expectations based upon economic theory? Discuss specifically why or why not.

References

"Amex Introduces New Market Value Index System." *American Investor,* September, 1973.

Balch, W. F. "Market Guides." *Barron's,* September 19, 1966.

Butler, H. L., Jr. and Decker, M. G. "A Security Check on the Dow-Jones Industrial Average." *Financial Analysts Journal,* Vol. 9, No. 1 (February, 1953).

Carter, E. E. and Cohen, K. J. "Bias in the DJIA Caused by Stock Splits." *Financial Analysts Journal,* Vol. 22, No. 6 (December, 1966).

Carter, E. E. and Cohen, K. J. "Stock Average, Stock Splits, and Bias." *Financial Analysts Journal,* Vol. 23, No. 3 (May–June, 1967).

Cootner, Paul. "Stock Market Indexes—Fallacies and Illusions." *Commercial and Financial Chronicle* (September 29, 1966).

Farrell, Maurice L. (ed.) *Barron's Market Laboratory.* Princeton, N.J.: Dow-Jones Books, published annually.

Farrell, Maurice L. (ed.) *The Dow-Jones Investor's Handbook.* Princeton, N.J.: Dow-Jones Books, published annually.

Fisher, Lawrence. "Outcomes for 'Random' Investments in Common Stock Listed on the New York Stock Exchange." *Journal of Business,* Vol. 38, No. 2 (April, 1965).

Fisher, Lawrence. "Some New Stock Market Indexes." *Journal of Business,* Vol. 39, No. 1, Part II (January, 1966 Supplement).

Fisher, Lawrence and Lorie, James H. "Rates of Return on Investments in Common Stock." *Journal of Business,* Vol. 37, No. 1 (January, 1964).

Fisher, L. and Lorie, J. H. "Rates of Return on Investments in Common Stock, The Year-by-Year Record, 1926–65." *Journal of Business,* Vol. 41, No. 3 (July, 1963).

Latane, Henry A., Tuttle, Donald L., and Jones, Charles P. *Security Analysis and Portfolio Management.* 2nd ed. New York: The Ronald Press Company, 1975, Chapter 25.

Latane, Henry A., Tuttle, Donald L., and Young, William E. "Market Indexes and their Implications for Portfolio Management." *Financial Analysts Journal,* Vol. 27, No. 5 (September–October, 1971).

Leuthold, S. C. and Blaich, K. F. "Warped Yardstick." *Barron's,* September 18, 1972.

Leuthold, S. C. and Gordon, C. E., II. "Margin for Error." *Barron's,* March 1, 1971.

Lorie, James H. and Hamilton, Mary T. *The Stock Market: Theories and Evidence.* Homewood, Ill.: Richard D. Irwin, Inc., 1973, Chapters 2 and 3.

Milne, P. D. "The Dow-Jones Industrial Average Re-examined." *Financial Analysts Journal,* Vol. 22, No. 6 (December, 1966).

Molodovisky, Nicholas. "Building a Stock Market Measure—A Case Story." *Financial Analysts Journal,* Vol. 23, No. 3 (May–June, 1967).

Reilly, Frank K. "Evidence Regarding a Segmented Stock Market." *Journal of Finance,* Vol. 27, No. 3 (June, 1972).

Reilly, Frank K. "The Original and New American Stock Exchange Price Indicator." University of Wyoming Research Paper No. 68 (March, 1975).

Reilly, Frank K. "Price Changes in NYSE, AMEX and OTC Stocks Compared." *Financial Analysts Journal,* Vol. 27, No. 2 (March–April, 1971).

Reilly, Frank K. "A Report on the NASDAQ Over-the-Counter Stock Price Indicators," University of Wyoming Research Paper No. 1 (August, 1973).

Schellbach, Lewis L. "When Did the DJIA Top 1200?" *Financial Analysts Journal,* Vol. 23, No. 3 (May–June, 1967).

Schoomer, B. Alva, Jr. "The American Stock Exchange Index System." *Financial Analysts Journal,* Vol. 23, No. 3 (May–June, 1967).

Shaw, R. B. "The Dow-Jones Industrials vs. the Dow-Jones Industrial Average." *Financial Analysts Journal,* Vol. 11, No. 5 (November, 1955).

West, Stan and Miller, Norman. "Why the New NYSE Common Stock Indexes?" *Financial Analysts Journal,* Vol. 23, No. 3 (May–June, 1967).

Chapter 6   *Sources of Information on Investments*

In the chapters that follow, we will discuss the factors that influence aggregate security prices, the prices for securities issued by various industries, and the "unique" factors that influence the returns on individual securities. It is important for the reader to know where to get relevant information to carry out these analyses. To aid in this task, this chapter briefly describes some of the major sources of information needed for aggregate economic and market analysis, industry analysis, and individual firm analysis. The outline of the presentation is as follows:

Aggregate Economic Analysis
    Government Sources
    Bank Publications
Aggregate Stock Market Analysis
    Government Publications
    Commercial Publications
    Brokerage Firm Reports
Industry Analysis
    S&P Industry Survey
    Trade Associations
    Industry Magazines
Individual Stock Analysis
    Company Generated Information
    Commercial Publications
    Brokerage Firm Reports
    Investment Magazines
    Academic Journals

Sources for Aggregate Economic Analysis

This first section is concerned with data used in estimating overall economic changes as contrasted to data regarding the aggregate securities markets (stocks, bonds, etc.).

Government Sources

It should come as no surprise that the main source of information on the economy is the federal government, which issues a variety of publications on the topic.

Federal Reserve Bulletin This is a monthly publication issued by the Board of Governors of the Federal Reserve System. The magazine contains extensive economic data with thorough coverage of such areas of monetary concern as: monetary aggregates; factors affecting member bank reserves; member bank reserve requirements; Federal Reserve open market transactions; and loans and investments of all commercial banks. It is the primary source for almost all monetary data. In addition, it contains figures on financial markets, including interest rates and some stock market statistics; data for corporate finance including profits, assets, and liabilities of corporations; extensive nonfinancial statistics on output, the labor force, and the GNP; and an extensive section on international finance.

Survey of Current Business A monthly publication issued by the United States Department of Commerce that gives details on national income and production figures. It is probably the best source for current, detailed information on all segments of the Gross National Product and national income. It also contains an extensive listing of industrial production for numerous segments of the economy. The survey is an excellent secondary source for labor statistics (employment and wages), interest rates, and statistics on foreign economic development.

Economic Indicators A monthly publication prepared for the Joint Economic Committee by the Council of Economic Advisers, it contains monthly and annual data on output, income, spending, employment, production, prices, money and credit, federal finance, and the international economic situation.

Business Conditions Digest (BCD) A monthly publication issued by the Department of Commerce's Census Bureau containing data and charts relating to economic indicators derived by the National Bureau of Economic Research (NBER). The NBER has developed a set of economic time series that has consistently indicated future trends in the economy. These series are referred to as leading indicators. There is also a set of series that turn with the general economy and are used to define business cycles (referred to as coincident series). Finally, there are economic series that tend to turn up or down *after* the general economy does, and are referred to as lagging indicators.[1] Basic data for the major series and analytical charts are provided in the BCD. In addition, it contains composite and analytical measures such as diffusion indexes and rate of change series.

The Quarterly Financial Report (QFR) is prepared by the Federal Trade Commission and contains up-to-date aggregate statistics on the financial position of U.S. corporations. Based upon an extensive quarterly sample survey, the QFR presents estimated statements of income and retained earnings, balance sheets, and related financial and operating ratios for all manufacturing corporations. Since the third quarter of 1974, the publication has also included data on mining and trade corporations. The statistical data are classified by industry and, within the manufacturing group, by size.

Business Statistics A biennial supplement to the *Survey of Current Business* that contains extensive historical data for about 2,500 series contained in the survey. The historical data is usually monthly and covers the past four or five years, and quarterly for the previous ten years. Annual data typically go back to 1947 if available. A notable feature is a section of explanatory notes for each of the series that describes the series and indicates the original source for the data.

Federal Reserve Monthly Chart Book is a publication of the Federal Reserve Board that presents graphs depicting many of the monetary and economic series contained in the *Federal Reserve Bulletin.* It emphasizes the short-run changes in these series.

Historical Chart Book A supplement to the *Federal Reserve Monthly Chart Book* that contains long-range financial and business series not included in the monthly book. At the back of the publication is an excellent section on the various series that indicates the source of the data for further reference.

Economic Report of the President Each year in January, the President of the United States prepares an economic report that he transmits to the Congress indicating what has transpired during the past year and including a discussion of what he considers to be the major economic problems during the coming year.

   This message is published by the federal government and also contains an extensive document entitled, "The Annual Report of the Council of Economic Advisers." The Report generally runs over 150 pages and contains a detailed discussion of developments in the domestic and international economies gathered by the council (the group that advises the

---

[1] These series are discussed more extensively in chapter 10 where they are related to stock market movements.

president on economic policy). An appendix contains statistical tables relating to income, employment, and production. Many of the tables provide annual data from the 1940's, in some instances from 1929, to the present.

The Statistical Abstract of the United States This book, which has been published annually since 1878, is the standard summary of statistics on the social, political, and economic organization of the United States. Prepared by the Bureau of the Census, it is designed to serve as a convenient statistical reference and as a guide to other statistical publications and sources. This volume, which currently runs over 900 pages, includes a selection of data from many statistical publications, both government and private.

Bank Publications

In addition to the material issued by the government, there are data and comments on the economy published by a number of banks. Almost all of these appear monthly and are sent free of charge to an individual requesting them. They can be categorized as publications of Federal Reserve Banks or of commercial banks.

Federal Reserve Banks

The Federal Reserve System is divided into 12 Federal Reserve Districts with a major Federal Reserve Bank in each as follows:[2]

1. Boston
2. New York
3. Philadelphia
4. Cleveland
5. Richmond
6. Atlanta
7. Chicago
8. St. Louis
9. Minneapolis
10. Denver
11. Dallas
12. San Francisco

Each of the Federal Reserve district banks has a research department that issues periodic reports. Although most of the publications generated by the various banks differ, monthly reviews, which are available to interested parties, are published by all district banks. These reviews typically contain one or several articles of interest to those in the region as well as statistics. A major exception is the St. Louis Federal Reserve Bank which publishes numerous statistical releases weekly, monthly, and quarterly containing

---

[2] Specific addresses for each of the district banks and names of major personnel are contained in the *Federal Reserve Bulletin,* published monthly by the board.

extensive national and international data and comments in addition to its monthly review.[3]

Commercial Banks

A number of large banks prepare a weekly or monthly letter that is available to interested individuals. These "letters" are generally a comment on the current and future outlook of the economy. Therefore, they typically contain only limited data. Some of the banks publishing letters are:

Chase Manhattan (New York)
Continental Illinois (Chicago)
Harris Trust and Savings (Chicago)
Manufacturers Hanover Trust Company (New York)

Aggregate Stock Market Analysis

There are several government publications that provide useful data on the stock market, but the bulk of detailed information is provided by private firms. Several of the government publications discussed earlier (*Federal Reserve Bulletin; Survey of Current Business*) contain financial market data, such as interest rates and stock prices.

Government Publications

The main source of data in this area is the Securities and Exchange Commission (SEC). The SEC is the federal agency responsible for regulating the operation of the securities markets and collects data in this regard.

Statistical Bulletin A monthly publication of the SEC that contains data on securities trading in the United States with an emphasis on common stocks. This includes volume of trading on all exchanges and the OTC market; prices on these exchanges; volatility and liquidity measures; and information on new issue registrations.

Annual Report of the SEC This is an annual publication of the SEC for the fiscal year ending in June. It contains a detailed discussion of important developments during the year and comments on the SEC's disclosure system and regulation of the securities markets. Finally, it includes a statistics section containing historical data on many of the items in the *Statistical Bulletin* as well as other annual series.

---

[3] An individual can request to be put on the mailing list for any of these publications (free) by writing to:
Federal Reserve Bank of St. Louis
P.O. Box 442
St. Louis, MO 63166

Commercial Publications

Considering the numerous advisory services in existence, a section dealing with their publications could become voluminous. Therefore, our intent is to list and discuss the *major* services and allow the reader to develop his own list of "other available sources." An excellent source of advertisements for these services is *Barron's*.

New York Stock Exchange Fact Book An annual publication of the New York Stock Exchange. The book is an outstanding source of current and historical data on activity on the NYSE, but it also contains comparative data on the ASE, the OTC, institutional trading, and investors in general.

Amex Databook This is a comparable data book for the American Stock Exchange. The first book was published in 1969, with subsequent editions in 1971, 1973, and 1976. It contains pertinent information on the exchange, its membership, administration, and trading activities.

Wall Street Journal Published by Dow-Jones and Company, it is the only daily national business newspaper in the United States. It is published five days a week and is clearly the most complete source of daily information on companies and security market prices. It contains complete listings for the NYSE, the ASE, the NASDAQ-OTC market, bond markets, options markets, and commodities quotations. It is recognized world-wide as a primary source of financial and business information.

Barron's This is a weekly publication of Dow-Jones and Company that typically contains four articles on topics of interest to investors. In addition, this newspaper has the most complete weekly listing of prices and quotes for all financial markets. It provides weekly data on individual stocks, and the latest information on earnings and dividends, as well as including columns on commodities and stock options. Finally, toward the back (typically the last three pages), there is an extensive statistical section with detailed information on stock market behavior for the past week.

Dow-Jones Booklets

Because of the interest in the statistics contained in Dow-Jones publications, the company has begun publishing several annual "handbooks."

The Dow-Jones Investor's Handbook contains the complete DJIA results for each year, along with earnings and dividends for the series since 1939. Individual reports on common and preferred stocks and bonds listed on the NYSE and ASE, including high and low prices, volume, dividends, and the year's most active stocks, are also included.

The Barron's Market Laboratory is an annual compilation of many of the figures contained in the weekly statistics page of *Barron's*. It contains extensive stock and bond averages (foreign and domestic), and volume of sales, among other items.

The Dow-Jones Commodities Handbook contains a review of price action during the past year for every major futures market and a discussion of the outlook for these markets. In addition, there are tables of key supply-demand statistics and cash prices for major markets.

The Dow-Jones Stock Options Handbook contains concise financial sketches of every company whose common stocks underlie options traded on any of the listed options markets. Tables show how options premiums moved during the year in relation to prices of underlying securities and to the overall stock market.

S&P Trade and Security Statistics This is a service of S&P that includes a basic set of historical data on various economic and security price series and a monthly supplement that updates the series for the recent period. There are two major sets of data: (1) business and financial, and (2) security price index record. Within the business and finance section are long-term statistics on trade, banking, industry, price, agriculture, and financial trends.

The security price index record contains historical data for all of the Standard & Poor's indexes. This includes 500 stocks broken down into 88 individual groups, of which the four main groups, industrial composite, rails, utilities, and the 500 composite are composed. There are also four supplementary group series: capital goods companies, consumer goods, high grade common stocks, and low priced common stocks. In addition to the stock price series, Standard & Poor's has derived a quarterly series of earnings and dividends for each of the four main groups. The earnings series includes data from 1946 to the present.

The booklet also contains data on daily stock sales on the NYSE from 1918 on and historical yields for a number of bond series, both corporate and government.

Brokerage Firm Reports

As a means of competing for the investor's business brokerage firms provide, among other services, information and recommendations on the outlook for securities markets (bonds and stocks). These reports are typically prepared monthly and distributed to customers (or potential customers) of the firm, free of charge. In the competition for institutional business, some of these firms have generated reports that are quite extensive and sophisticated. Among the brokerages issuing these reports are: Goldman Sachs & Company; Merrill Lynch, Pierce, Fenner & Smith; and Salomon Brothers.

Industry Analysis

There is only one publication containing information on a number of industries, the *Standard & Poor's Industry Survey*. Beyond this, the major source of data on a given industry is trade associations or trade magazines.

Standard & Poor's Industry Survey This is a two-volume reference work that is divided into 34 segments dealing with 69 major domestic industries. Coverage in each area is divided into a current analysis and a basic analysis. The latter begins with an examination of the prospects for that particular industry, followed by an analysis of trends and problems presented in historical perspective. Major segments of the industry are spotlighted and a comparative analysis of the principal companies in the industry is also included. The current analysis provides information on the latest developments in the industry and available industry, market, and company statistics, along with appraisals of the investment outlook for the specific area covered.

Trade Associations are organizations set up by those involved in an industry or a general area of business to provide information for others in the area on such topics as: education, advertising, lobbying for legislation, and problem solving. Trade associations gather extensive statistics for the industry. Examples of such organizations include:[4]

Iron and Steel Institute
American Railroad Association
National Consumer Finance Association
Institute of Life Insurance
American Banker's Association
Machine Tool Association

Industry Magazines are an excellent source of data and general information. Depending upon the industry, there can be several publications—the computer industry has spawned at least five such magazines. Examples of industry publications include:

Computers
Real Estate Today
Chemical Week
Modern Plastics
Paper Trade Journal
Automotive News

---

[4] For a more extensive list see *Encyclopedia of Associations* (Detroit: Gale Research Company, 1977).

Company Generated Information

An obvious source of information about a company is the company itself. In the case of some small firms, it may be the *only* source of information because there is not enough activity to justify its inclusion in studies issued by commercial services.

Annual Reports

All firms with publicly traded stock are required to prepare and distribute to their stockholders an annual report of financial operations and current financial position. In addition to basic information, most reports contain a discussion of what happened during the year and some consideration of future prospects. Most firms also publish a *quarterly financial report* that includes a brief income statement for this interim period and, sometimes, a balance sheet. Both of these reports can be obtained directly from the company. To find an address for a company one should consult *Standard & Poor's Register of Corporations, Directors, and Executives.* The Register is published in three volumes of which the most useful for the specified purpose is volume one, which contains an alphabetical listing, by business name, of approximately 37,000 corporations.

Security Prospectus

When a firm wants to sell some securities (bonds, preferred stock, or common stock) in the primary market to raise new capital, the Securities and Exchange Commission (SEC) requires that it file a registration statement describing the securities being offered and containing information on the company. The financial information is more extensive than that required in an annual report and there is also a substantial amount of nonfinancial information on the firm's operations and personnel. A condensed version of the registration statement, referred to as a *prospectus*, is published by the underwriting firm, and contains most of the relevant information. Copies of a prospectus for a current offering can be obtained from the underwriter or from the company.

Required SEC Reports [5]

In addition to registration statements, the SEC requires three *periodic* statements from publicly held firms. The 8–K form is a report which firms registered with the SEC are required to file each month. In this report, any action that affects the debt, equity, amount of capital assets, voting right, or other changes that would be expected to have a significant impact on the stock is indicated.

---

[5] For a further discussion of these reports, see Carl W. Schneider, "SEC Filings—Their Use to the Professional," *Financial Analysts Journal,* Vol. 21, No. 1 (January–February, 1965), pp. 33–38.

The 9–K form is an unaudited report that must be filed every six months, containing revenues, expenses, gross sales, and special items. This is typically more extensive than the quarterly statements are.

The 10–K form is an annual version of the 9–K but is even more complete. Recently, the SEC required that firms indicate in their annual reports that a copy of their 10–K is available from the company upon request without charge.

Commercial Publications

There are numerous firms that sell advisory services supplying information on the aggregate market and individual stocks. Therefore, the following is only a partial discussion of what is available.

Standard & Poor's Corporation Records This is currently a set of seven volumes, the first six of which contain basic information on corporations arranged alphabetically and not according to industry type. The volumes are in binders and are updated throughout the year. The seventh volume is a daily news volume that contains recent data on all companies listed in all the volumes.

Standard & Poor's Stock Reports are comprehensive two-page reports on numerous companies with stocks listed on the NYSE, ASE, and traded OTC. They include the near term sales and earnings outlook, recent developments, key income statement and balance sheet items, and a chart of stock price movements, and are in bound volumes by exchange. These reports are revised at least once every three to four months. A sample page is shown in Figure 6–1.

Standard & Poor's Stock Guide is a monthly publication that contains, in compact form, pertinent financial data on more than 5,100 common and preferred stocks. A separate section covers over 380 mutual fund issues. For each stock, the guide contains information on price ranges (historical and recent), dividends, earnings, financial position, institutional holdings, and ranking for earning and dividend stability. It is a very useful quick reference for almost all actively traded stocks, as is shown by the example in Figure 6–2.

Standard & Poor's Bond Guide is likewise published monthly. It contains the most pertinent comparative financial and statistical information on a broad list of bonds including domestic and foreign bonds (about 3,900 issues), 200 foreign government bonds, and about 650 convertible bonds.

The Outlook is a weekly publication of Standard & Poor's Corporation. It contains advice regarding the general market environment and also has features on specific groups of stocks or industries (e.g., high dividend stocks, stocks with low price to earnings ratios, high yielding bonds, stocks likely to increase their dividends, etc.). It also contains weekly figures for 88 industry groups and other market statistics.

Moody's Industrial Manual is similar to the S&P service. It is currently published once a year in two bound volumes. It covers industrial companies listed on the NYSE and ASE, as well as companies listed on regional exchanges. There is also a section on international industrial firms and an Industrial News Reports section that contains items occurring after publication of the basic manual.

Moody's OTC Industrial Manual is similar to the *Moody's Industrial Manual* of listed firms, but is limited to stocks traded on the OTC market. Supplementary volumes containing information on recent developments are also published.

Moody's Public Utility Manual provides information on public utilities including electric and gas, gas transmission, telephone, and water companies. It also contains a news report section.

Moody's Transportation Manual covers the transportation industry including railroads, airlines, steamship companies, electric railway, bus and truck lines, oil pipe lines, bridge companies, and automobile and truck leasing companies. A supplementary Transportation News Report is also published.

Moody's Bank and Finance Manual is published in two volumes and covers the field of finance represented by banks, savings and loan associations, credit agencies of the United States Government, all phases of the insurance industry, investment companies, real estate firms, real estate investment trusts, and miscellaneous financial enterprises.

Moody's Municipal and Government Manual is published in two volumes and contains data on the U.S. Government, all the states, state agencies, municipalities (over 13,500), foreign governments, and international organizations.

The Value Line Investment Survey is published in two parts. Part one contains basic historic information on about 1700 companies, as well as a number of analytical measures of earnings stability, growth rates, and a common stock safety factor. It also includes extensive two-year *projections* for the given firms and three year *estimates* of performance. In early 1980, it will include a projection for 1980, 1981, and 1983–1985. The second volume includes a weekly service that provides general investment advice and also recommends individual stocks for purchase or sale. An example of a company report is shown in Figure 6–3.

Figure 6–1 **Sample Page from *S&P Stock Reports***

IBM[1]
Options on CBOE

Int'l Business Machines
1210

Stock— CAPITAL	Price Nov. 29'78	*P-E Ratio	Dividend	Yield
	265½	13	[2]$11.52	[2]4.3%

SUMMARY: IBM is the largest manufacturer of business machines and produces over half of the world's computer hardware. Earnings have grown at about a 15% compounded rate over the last 10 years. Aided by higher unit purchases of data processing equipment, share earnings could rise approximately 15% in 1979, following the 11% gain expected for 1978. Several antitrust suits, including a U.S. Department of Justice suit, remain in progress. The dividend could be increased in late 1978 or early 1979.

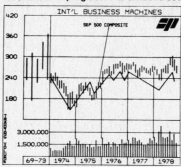

PROSPECTS

Near Term— Total revenues for 1978 are placed in the vicinity of $20.3 billion, up approximately 12% from the $18.1 billion of the prior year. Earnings could be in the area of $20.30 a share, compared with $18.30 in 1977.

For 1979, total revenues should rise about 13%. Sales could be up 18%, reflecting continued heavy outright purchases of business equipment. Rental and services revenues may increase 10%, owing to further moderate net additions to the company's rental and service base and to moderately higher rates.

Margins could widen slightly, reflecting a diminution of new product start-up and introduction costs. Lower interest income may be offset by a slightly lower effective tax rate. Share earnings for 1979 could rise to $23.25. The $2.88 quarterly dividend could be increased to $3.25 in late 1978 or early 1979.

Long Term— Antitrust suits could affect the present dominant market position.

GROSS INCOME (Million $)

Quarter:	1978	1977	1976	1975	1974
March	4,432	4,090	3,815	3,272	3,002
June	4,921	4,419	4,013	3,497	3,260
Sept.	5,284	4,586	3,957	3,600	3,125
Dec.		5,038	4,519	4,068	3,288

Total revenues for the nine months ended September 30, 1978 rose 11.8% from those of the corresponding year-earlier period. Sales were up 13.8%, aided by heavier outright purchases of data processing equipment. Rental and services revenues gained 10.6%, reflecting a greater number of machines in the rental and service base. Margins were narrowed by production start-up costs of the company's new family of mainframe computers and the impact of continued inflationary pressures. The gain in operating income was limited to 9.1%. Significantly heavier interest expense and lower interest income outweighed proportionately lower depreciation charges and pared the increase in pretax income to 7.8%. After taxes at 46.3%, against 46.9%, net income was up 9.1%. On slightly fewer shares outstanding, share earnings equaled $14.34, compared with $12.92.

RECENT DEVELOPMENTS

A Federal Judge in San Francisco declared a mistrial in July, 1978 in an antitrust suit brought against IBM by Memorex Corp.

At year-end 1977 IBM's backlog for data processing machines had a net monthly rental value of about $285 million, up 86% from $153 million a year-earlier.

In August, 1978, a U. S. Court of Appeals overturned an FCC decision that would have allowed Satellite Business Systems (a partnership of units of IBM, Communications Satellite Corp. and Aetna Life and Casualty Co.) to provide domestic satellite communications services. Pending further developments, the companies are proceeding with plans to launch two satellites.

DIVIDEND DATA

A dividend reinvestment plan is available.

CAPITAL SHARE EARNINGS ($)

Quarter:	1978	1977	1976	1975	1974
March	4.01	3.82	3.63	2.95	2.94
June	4.73	4.44	3.94	3.14	3.28
Sept.	5.60	4.66	3.90	3.32	3.23
Dec.		5.38	4.47	3.94	3.02

Amt. of Divd. $	Date Decl.	Ex-divd. Date	Stock of Record	Payment Date
2.88...	Dec. 20	Feb. 3	Feb. 9	Mar.10'78
2.88...	Apr. 24	May 4	May 10	Jun. 10'78
2.88...	Jul. 25	Aug. 3	Aug. 9	Sep. 9'78
2.88...	Oct. 24	Nov. 1	Nov. 8	Dec. 9'78

[1]Listed N.Y.S.E.; also listed Midwest & Pacific S.Es. and traded Boston & Philadelphia S.Es.   [2]Indicated rate.   *Based on latest 12 mos. earns.

STANDARD N.Y.S.E. STOCK REPORTS   **STANDARD & POOR'S CORP.**

© Copyright 1978 Standard & Poor's Corp.

Published at Ephrata, Pa.   Editorial & Executive Offices, 345 Hudson St., New York, N.Y. 10014

Vol. 45, No. 233   Tuesday, December 5, 1978   Sec. 16

Source: *Standard & Poor's Stock Reports* (New York: Standard & Poor's Corp., 1977). Reprinted by permission.

Figure 6–1 continued

1210 INTERNATIONAL BUSINESS MACHINES CORPORATION

[1]INCOME STATISTICS (Million $) AND PER SHARE ($) DATA

Year Ended Dec. 31	Gross Income	% Oper. Inc. of Gross Inc.	Oper. Inc.	Deprec.	Net bef. Taxes	Net Income	[2]Capital Share ($) Data: Earns.	*Funds Generated	Divs. Paid	Price Range	Price-Earns. Ratios HI LO
1978--	------	---	------	-----	-----	-----	----	----	11.52	304½-234¾	-----
1977--	18,133.2	35.6	6,463.5	1,806.0	5,092.4	2,719.4	18.30	35.49	10.00	286¼-244½	16-13
1976--	16,304.3	35.5	5,786.6	1,717.0	4,519.1	2,398.1	15.94	30.82	8.00	288½-223⅜	18-14
1975--	14,436.5	35.3	5,103.0	1,680.0	3,720.9	1,989.9	13.35	27.17	6.50	227⅜-157¼	17-12
1974--	12,675.3	37.4	4,737.9	1,575.0	3,434.6	1,837.6	12.47	25.12	5.56	254 -150½	20-12
1973--	10,993.2	38.5	4,234.2	1,460.8	2,946.5	1,575.5	10.79	22.44	4.48	365¼-235⅛	34-22
1972--	9,532.6	37.9	3,609.0	1,296.6	2,425.3	1,279.3	8.83	19.32	4.32	341⅛-265⅜	39-30
1971--	8,273.6	37.6	3,114.8	1,140.7	2,055.8	1,078.8	7.50	17.03	4.16	292⅝-226⅝	39-30
1970--	7,504.0	39.3	2,947.7	1,066.3	2,011.5	1,017.5	7.14	15.54	3.84	309⅝-175	43-25
1969--	7,197.3	40.7	2,927.4	1,008.6	1,978.9	933.9	6.57	14.62	2.88	295 -233⅜	45-36
1968--	6,888.5	41.0	2,822.4	975.2	1,864.5	871.5	6.17	14.52	2.08	300 -224	49-36

[1]PERTINENT BALANCE SHEET STATISTICS (Million $)

Dec. 31	[3]Gross Prop.	[3]Capital Expend.	Cash Items	Inventories	Receivables	Current Assets	Current Liabs.	Net Workg. Cap.	Cur. Ratio	Long Term Debt	Sharehldrs. Equity	[2]($) Bk. Val. Cap. Sh.
1977--	17,071	3,395	5,407	994	3,104	10,073	5,209	4,864	1.9-1	256	12,618	86.16
1976--	16,054	2,518	6,156	770	2,626	9,920	4,082	5,838	2.4-1	275	12,749	85.02
1975--	15,037	2,439	4,768	741	2,300	8,115	3,363	4,752	2.4-1	295	11,416	76.48
1974--	14,017	2,913	3,805	688	2,083	7,010	3,210	3,800	2.2-1	336	10,110	68.44
1973--	12,264	2,186	3,322	518	1,845	5,830	2,555	3,275	2.3-1	652	8,812	60.28
1972--	11,094	1,728	2,577	441	1,679	4,822	2,259	2,562	2.1-1	773	7,566	52.19
1971--	10,492	1,882	1,875	406	1,578	3,949	2,088	1,861	1.9-1	676	6,642	45.99
1970--	9,558	2,160	1,339	374	1,597	3,389	1,877	1,512	1.8-1	573	5,947	41.52
1969--	8,032	1,647	1,371	268	1,551	3,250	1,436	1,814	2.3-1	555	5,277	37.12
1968--	6,997	1,157	1,826	226	1,201	3,301	1.531	1,770	2.2-1	545	4,569	32.36

[1] Data for 1973 & thereafter as originally reported: data for each yr. prior to 1973 as taken from subsequent yr's. Annual Report; incl. all domestic & foreign subsids. [2]Adj. for stk. splits of 5-for-4 in 1973 & 2-for-1 in 1968. [3]Incl. plant, rental machines & other property.

*As computed by Standard & Poor's

Fundamental Position

International Business Machines is primarily involved in the field of information-handling systems, equipment and services. Data processing equipment accounted for some 81% of gross income and $4.4 billion (94%) of operating income in 1977, office products for 16% and $267 million (6%), Federal systems for 2.7% and $27 million, and other businesses for 0.3% and $8 million. Of some $13.8 billion in assets identified to business segments, about $11.0 billion (80%) were identified to data processing, $2.5 billion (18%) to office products, $286 million (2%) to Federal systems and $33 million to other products.

Some 39% ($7.1 billion) of gross income in 1977 was derived from sales and 61% ($11.0 billion) from rental and service revenues. Data processing equipment accounted for 25% of sales and 45% of rental and service revenues; data processing services, program products and supplies contributed 3% and 8%, respectively

The Data Processing division consists of data processing machines and systems, computer programming, systems engineering, education, and related services and supplies.

Office products include electric typewriters, magnetic media typewriters and systems, information processors, document printers, copiers and related supplies.

The company's Federal Systems division offers specialized information-handling products and primarily services U. S. space, defense and other agencies.

IBM's other products consist of educational, training and testing materials and services for school, home and industrial use.

Foreign operations are conducted through two operating units, IBM World Trade Europe/Middle East/Africa and IBM World Trade Americas/Far East. Europe/Middle East/Africa contributed approximately 35% of gross income in 1977, 33% of net income, and 35% of $18.98 billion in total assets at the end of 1978. Americas/Far East contributed 15%, 16%, and 14%, respectively. European operations accounted for about 95% of gross income in the Europe/Middle East/-Africa area.

Dividends, paid continuously since 1916, averaged 49% of earnings in 1973-77.

Employees: 301,155. Shareholders: 582, 360.

LITIGATION

Trial in the U. S. Justice Department antitrust suit began in May, 1975. A Greyhound Corp. suit has been granted a new trial. Suits by California Computer Products, Transamerica Computer Co., Hudson General Corp., Memorex Corp. Forro Precision, Inc. (on appeal) and DPF Inc. seek damages, after trebling, of $4.2 billion and remain in progress. Xerox and IBM have filed suits charging each other with patent infringement.

Institutional Holdings

Institutions: 1,375. Shares: 47,165,000 (32% of the total outstanding).

CAPITALIZATION

LONG TERM DEBT: $255,244,000.
CAPITAL STOCK: 145,778,258 shs. ($5 par).

Incorporated in N.Y. in 1911. **Office**—Armonk, New York 10504. **Tel**—(914) 765-1900. **Stockholder Relations Dept**—717 Fifth Ave., NYC 10022. **Tel**—(212) 223-4400. **Pres**—J. R. Opel. **Secy**—J. H. Grady. **Treas**—B. H. Witham. **Dirs**—F. T. Cary (Chrmn), S. D. Bechtel, Jr., G. B. Beitzel, W. T. Coleman, Jr., J. M. Fox, G. K. Funston, C. A. Hills, A. Houghton, Jr., J. N. Irwin II, N. deB. Katzenbach, G. Kirk, T. V. Learson, M. McK. Moller, W. H. Moore, J. R. Opel, P. J. Rizzo, W. W. Scranton, I. S. Shapiro, T. J. Watson, Jr., A. L. Williams. **Transfer Agents**—Company's NYC & Chicago offices; Wells Fargo Bank, San Francisco. **Registrars**—Morgan Guaranty Trust Co., NYC; First National Bank of Chicago; Crocker National Bank, San Francisco.

W.C.H.

Figure 6–2 **Example from *S&P Stock Guide***

214 Ten-Tha **STANDARD & POOR'S CORPORATION**

Index	Ticker Symbol	Stocks Name of Issue (Call Price of Pfd. Stocks)	Market	Com Rank & Pfd. Rating	Par Val.	Inst. Hold Cos	Shs. (000)	Principal Business	Price Range 1960-76 High	1960-76 Low	1977 High	1977 Low	1978 High	1978 Low	May Sales in 100s	May, 1978 Last Sale Or Bid High	Low	Last	% Div. Yield	P-E Ratio
1	TGT	Tenneco, Inc	NYS,Bo,Ci,MW,Ph,PS,TS	A—	5	337	24214	Natural gas pipeline:oil/gas	37⅜	15⅜	37¼	28½	33¾	28	10920	33¾	31⅛	31¾	6.3	7
2	WS	Wrrt (Purch 1.07 com at $32)	ASE,MW	...	....	1	53	explor, chemicals, land,	11	2¼	8½	2¾	4½	2¼	1857	4½	3⅜	3⅝	...	..
3	Pr	$5.50 cm Cv Pref ([55]110)vtg	NYS,Ph,PS	BB	No	21	21	shipbldg,pkg,auto comp	139⅛	62¾	138	108½	123	104	38	123	116½	117½	4.7	..
4	Pr B	$7.40 cm Pref([56]101)vtg	NYS	BB	No	20	181	life insurance	....	....	....	....	88⅛	82⅞	1819	84⅞	82⅞	83	8.9	..
5	TOFF	Tenneco Offshore	OTC	NR	1	17	470	Gas & oil offshore Texas,La	10	3	8⅜	2¾	4½	3¼	3631	4½	3¼	4½B	...	..
6	TENN	Tennessee Natl Gas Ln	OTC	B+	1	5	187	Nat'l gas P.L.: subsid dstr	14⅜	6¼	13	9⅞	11	9¾	172	11	10⅜	10⅜B	8.9	9
7	TVBC	Tennessee Valley Banc	OTC	...	6.66	7	406	Bk hldg: Commerce Union	34	10	16¼	12⅝	15½	12⅛	249	15½	14¾	15½B	5.2	9
8	TNY	Tenney Engineering	ASE	B—	10¢	...	...	Environmental test eq	16⅞	⅝	4⅜	1⅜	4¾	2¾	243	4¾	4	4⅝B	...	10
9	TEN	Tensor Corp	ASE	C	10¢	...	...	Hi-intensity lamps:tennis eq	18⅜	¾	1⅞	1	1⅞	1⅛	96	1⅞	1½	1¾B	...	d
10	TER	Teradyne Inc	ASE	B	12½¢	13	733	Instr for test'g electr comp	34¼	5	19⅞	11¼	27⅝	15	5559	27⅝	22¾	25½	...	15
11	TERM	Terminal Data	OTC	NR	1	...	...	Micrographics systems	11⅜	½	4⅝	2⅞	7¾	3⅝	1207	7¾	5⅜	7⅝B	...	11
12	TCI	Terra Chemicals Int'l	ASE,MW	NR	1	5	77	Chemical fertilizers	17⅝	6½	13⅜	9¼	10⅞	9	1154	10	9	9½	8.4	11
13	TDSC	Tesdata Systems	OTC	NR	1¢	9	142	Computer perf measure sys	....	....	19½	12¾	19	13	2355	19	16¼	17¼B	...	11
14	TSO	Tesoro Petroleum	NYS,Bo,Ph,PS	B	16⅔¢	32	606	Integrated oil company	28 15/16	2⅝	17½	7⅜	12⅜	7⅝	11002	12⅜	9½	11½	...	d
15	Pr	$2.16 cm Cv Pfd([57]27½)vtg	NYS	NR	1	15	262	Trinidad, Indonesia, U.S.	31⅜	25	31	18¾	25⅝	19¼	1866	25⅝	21⅝	23⅞	9.0	..
16	TT	Tetra Tech	ASE	NR	50¢	1	10	Underwater TV sys,instr:eng'g	....	....	17	8	16	13⅛	722	15⅜	13⅛	14¾	...	12
17	TXC	Texaco Canada Ltd[58]	TS,MS	A	No	32	226	Large factor in Canadian oil	71⅞	13⅞	41⅝	24¼	43	34	756	40	36	37½	4.2	9
18	TX	Texaco,Inc	NYS,Bo,Ci,MW,PS,TS	A	6¼	592	58115	Third lgs't domestic/world oil	45 1/16	15	30⅝	25¾	27⅝	24⅛	47911	26	24⅛	24⅝	8.1	7
19	TABS	Texas Amer'n Bancshares	OTC	...	5	12	631	Multiple bank hldg:Ft Worth	36¼	11½	23⅞	19¼	28½	21½	416	28½	26½	27B	s3.4	7
20	TOIL	Texas American Oil	OTC	NR	10¢	1	21	Oil & gas prod'n:refinery	12⅝	⅛	6¾	2⅞	6	5⅛	2275	6	5½	5⅞B	s...	8
21	TCB	Texas Commerce Bkshr	NYS	...	4	78	4053	Multiple bank hldg:Houston	50¾	10½	39¼	31⅝	40	34¼	2563	40	39	39⅛	3.1	9
22	TET	Texas East'n Corp	[1]NYS,Bo,Ci,MW,Ph,PS	A	3½	134	7412	Gas P.L. sys:petrol mkt/dstr	61⅝	13⅛	46⅞	36¾	47	37⅜	2393	47	43⅝	46⅜	4.5	8
23	TET Pr	Texas East Tr $2.875 cm [60]Pfd[61]	NYS	BBB	1	4	20	Natural gas pipeline	31	25	32⅜	29⅛	30⅞	28⅛	236	29¼	28⅛	29	9.9	..
24	Pr B	$2.40 cm Pfd([62]27.16 SF25)	NYS	BBB	1	5	111	Texas to New York	28⅝	24¾	29¼	26½	28	25⅜	2466	26½	25⅜	25½	9.4	..
25	TFMR	Texas First Mtge REIT SBI	OTC	...	1	4	106	Real estate investment trust	22¼	¾	3¼	1⅝	3¼	2½	165	2⅞	2⅝	2¾B	...	d
26	TXG	Texas Gas Transmis	NYS,Bo,Ci,MW,Ph,PS	A—	5	87	2742	National gas pipeline,barge	48	19⅝	49	41¾	48⅜	38¾	3303	48⅜	42	47⅝	5.5	7
27	Pr	$1.50 cm Cv Pref (30)vtg	NYS	BB	5	8	5	trucking,oil & gas explor	47⅝	20⅛	49	42	47¾	39	11	47¾	42⅛	47¼	3.2	..
28	TXI	Texas Indus	NYS,Bo,Ph	B+	1	9	382	Concrete products: steel	29¼	2¾	22	13⅜	26⅛	19¼	479	26⅛	24⅜	25⅜	s3.9	7
29	TXN	Texas Instruments	NYS,Bo,Ci,MW,Ph,PS	A—	1	212	10892	Semiconductors:el'tronic eqp	138⅞	9 11/16	102¼	68⅝	81⅝	61⅜	12156	81⅝	73⅜	78⅝	2.1	14
30	TEX	Texas Intl Airlines	ASE	B—	1¢	4	93	Regional air carrier	29¼	1	8	2⅞	13	7½	7369	13	10	12¼	1.3	8
31	TEI	Texas Int'l Co	NYS,PS,TS	B	10¢	11	138	Oil/gas:drill eq:well sv	16¾	2½	12⅜	7¾	11⅛	9	8445	11⅛	9⅜	9⅞	...	13
32	TXO	Texas Oil & Gas	NYS,Bo	A—	50¢	97	5346	Gas gathering:oil & gas	35⅝	1⅜	35	25⅛	34	28⅞	6202	33⅝	30¾	32⅛	0.9	8
33	TPL	Texas Pac Land Tr Sub	NYS,Bo,Ph	B+	50¢	4	23	Holds surface rights:royalties	30¾	6 9/16	40	28¼	49½	38½	332	49½	45½	49	0.8	18
34	TXP Pr	Texas P&L$4.56Pfd(112)	ASE([25])	AA	No	2	2	Elec sv:subsid of Texas Util	102	47	59	54	61¼	52	9	55	52	54B	8.4	..
35	TXU	Texas Utilities	NYS,Bo,Ci,MW,Ph,PS	A+	No	376	31117	Electric utility holding co.	36	15¼	23⅜	18⅞	22⅛	19¼	22708	20¾	19¼	20	7.6	8
36	TG	Texasgulf Inc	NYS,Bo,Ci,MW,Ph,PS,MS,TS	B	No	103	3840	Metal producer: sulphur	53¼	3¾	31⅞	17⅛	22	15⅛	3300	22	18⅜	21⅞	5.5	14
37	Pr	3.00 cm Cv A Pfd ([65]53)	NYS,MS,TS	A	1	24	549	agri/ind'l chems: oil/gas	50	50	55¼	38⅜	41	36¼	563	41	37½	40½	7.4	..
38	TXF	Texfi Indus	NYS	C	1	4	198	Knitted apparel fabrics	67½	2⅝	5⅜	2¼	4¼	2¼	807	4⅛	3⅝	4	...	d
39	TEXT	Textiles Inc	OTC	A—	1	5	135	Combed cotton yarns: threads	21⅝	6⅛	20	14	25¾	18¾	196	25¾	24	25¾B	7.3	5
40	TXT	Textron, Inc	NYS,Bo,Ci,MW,Ph,PS	A—	25¢	88	7690	Consumer,metal,ind'l prod	57⅞	4⅝	29⅞	24	30	22⅛	4807	29¾	27½	29	5.5	7
41	WS	Wrrt (purch 1 com at $10)	ASE,MW,PS	...	....	1	1	aerospace (Bell Helicopter)	49½	1⅞	19⅛	14¾	19½	13¾	47	19¼	17½	19	...	..
42	Pr A	$2.08 cm Cv A Pfd (50)vtg	NYS,Bo	BBB	No	23	375	bearings,castings,zippers	68⅞	19	34⅜	28¼	33¼	28⅛	418	33¼	31⅛	32½	6.4	..
43	Pr B	$1.40 cm Cv B Pfd (45)vtg	NYS,Bo	BB	No	29	918	investment company	50½	14	26¾	21¾	26¼	20¼	792	26¼	24¾	26	5.4	..
44	TFI	TFI Co's	ASE	B	67¢	1	2	Food,beverage:bldg mtl sup	30⅝	⅞	2⅜	1⅜	4⅝	1½	2367	4⅝	1⅝	3⅞	...	13
45	THAL	Thalhimer Bros	OTC	A—	1⅔	5	726	Department stores: Va,NCar	11½	1⅝	9	7¼	15¼	9	1647	15¼	11½	14½B	4.1	11

Uniform Footnote Explanations—See Page 1. Other: [1]TS. [51]®$3.43,'74. [52]®$3.63,'75. [53]®$3.78,'76. [54]®$4.11,'77. [55]To 6-30-78, scale to $100 in'87. [56]Non callable to 1988,scale to $100 in'03. [57]From 1-1-80:scale to $25 in'84. [58]Propose name change to Texaco Canada Inc. [59]Subsid Stk in M$. [60]Callable at $27.444 to 5-31-79. [61]Scale to $25 in'96. [62]To 5-31-79,scale to $25 in'97. [63]F.C.& Pfd divds, Times Earned. [64]Subsid Pfd in M$. [65]To 12-14-78, scale to $50 in'86. [66]■$2.40,'77.

COMMON AND PREFERRED STOCKS **Ten—Tha 215**

Index	Cash Divs. Ea. Yr. Since	Dividends: Latest Payment Per $	Date	Ex. Div.	$ So Far 1978	Total Ind. Rate	$ Paid 1977	Financial Position Mil-$: Cash & Equiv.	Curr. Assets	Curr. Liabs.	Balance Sheet Date	Capitalization: Long Term Debt Mil-$	Shs. 000: Pfd.	Com.	End	$ Per Shr—Earnings—$ Per Shr: 1974	1975	1976	1977	1978	Last 12 Mos.	Interim Earnings or Remarks: Period	$—Per Share—$ 1977	1978	Index
1	1948	Q0.50	6-13-78	5-8	1.00	2.00	1.94	83.7	2779	2194	3-31-78	★2686	p4763	95008	Dc	[51]3.98	[52]4.15	[53]4.15	[54]4.38	E®4.55	4.38	3 Mo Mar	1.10	1.10	1
2	.....	Terms&trad. basis should be checked in detail						Cash or 6% Debs 1979				....	...	2675	Exercise price $30.07 per shr							Warrants expire 4-1-79			2
3	1968	Q1.37½	6-30-78	5-8	2.75	5.50	5.50	Conv into 3.73 shrs common				....	691	...	Dc	114.1	180.8	393.2	595.5	....	....				3
4	1978	Q1.85	6-30-78	5-8	2.466	7.40	....	...	...	...		....	1940	...	Dc	....	....	....	....	....	....				4
5	.....	None Since Public			....	Nil	....	0.58	4.02	3.44	12-31-77	195.	...	4751	Dc	d0.17	d0.17	d0.17	△•Nil	....	Nil				5
6	1950	Q0.23	6-2-78	5-16	0.69	0.92	0.92	4.22	15.0	15.0	12-31-77	26.1	2	1274	Dc	1.21	1.64	1.94	1.40	....	1.17	3 Mo Mar	2.05	1.82	6
7	1925	Q0.20	7-3-78	6-19	0.60	0.80	0.80	Book Value $20.91			3-31-78	37.4	...	3923	Dc	□1.90	□1.97	△2.03	△1.80	....	1.75	3 Mo Mar	△0.52	□0.47	7
8◆	.....	None Paid			....	Nil	....	0.60	3.02	1.15	12-31-77	0.80	...	803	Dc	•0.07	•□0.11	•0.07	•0.38	....	0.46	3 Mo Mar	•0.06	0.14	8
9	.....	None Paid			....	Nil	....	0.05	1.79	0.71	12-31-77	0.06	...	457	Dc	d0.70	0.01	△d0.51	d0.53	....	d0.40	3 Mo Mar	d0.07	△0.06	9
10	.....	None Paid			....	Nil	....	1.89	33.5	13.3	4-1-78	0.18	...	3203	Dc	1.38	0.12	0.71	1.50	....	1.72	3 Mo Mar	0.29	0.51	10
11◆	.....	None Since Public			....	Nil	....	0.02	3.19	1.18	12-31-77	1.85	...	773	Sp	d0.29	•0.15	•0.47	•0.62	....	0.67	6 Mo Mar	•0.25	0.30	11
12	1974	Q0.20	5-22-78	5-2	0.40	0.80	0.80	n/a	101.	50.9	3-31-78	33.7	169	5303	Dc	•3.90	3.25	2.03	1.27	....	0.87	3 Mo Mar	0.12	□d0.28	12
13	.....	None Since Public			....	Nil	....	0.99	9.96	4.04	3-31-78	0.04	...	1225	Dc	0.09	0.41	1.46	1.64	....	1.59	3 Mo Mar	0.38	0.33	13
14◆	1973	0.25	10-3-77	9-13	....	Nil	1.00	36.7	222.	158.	12-31-77	225.	4385	12327	Sp	•6.12	4.04	1.78	d5.52	....	d3.98	6 Mo Mar	d0.41	1.13	14
15	1976	Q0.54	6-15-78	5-24	1.08	2.16	2.16	Cv into 1.7241 shr com:$14.50				....	4367	...	Sp	....	....	....	....	....	....				15
16	.....	None Since Public			....	Nil	....	0.08	15.9	10.8	1-29-78	0.49	...	1095	Jl	0.62	1.17	1.23	1.32	....	1.21	6 Mo Jan	0.65	0.54	16
17	1944	gQ0.39	5-31-78	5-8	g0.78	1.56	g1.56	1.45	378.	263.	j12-31-77	304.	38	9715	Dc	5.65	5.25	2.97	3.76	E4.00	3.43	3 Mo Mar	0.98	0.65	17
18	1903	Q0.50	6-9-78	5-3	1.00	2.00	2.00	636.	7195	5066	12-31-77	2559	...	271467	Dc	5.68	3.06	3.20	3.43	E3.75	3.23	3 Mo Mar	0.89	0.69	18
19◆	1934	Q0.23	7-5-78	6-12	s0.66	0.92	0.761	Book Value $27.65			12-31-77	59.4	...	4299	Dc	□2.78	△2.72	△3.00	△3.45	E4.00	3.67	3 Mo Mar	△0.74	□0.96	19
20◆	.....	5%Stk	1-9-78	12-9	5%Stk	Stk	5%Stk	2.17	12.2	10.2	3-31-78	13.0	...	5233	Dc	•0.32	□0.18	0.19	0.69	....	0.75	3 Mo Mar	0.17	0.23	20
21	1920	Q0.30½	7-1-78	6-5	0.91½	1.22	1.10	Book Value $24.84			12-31-77	50.0	110	±13030	Dc	△2.64	□3.05	□3.33	△3.85	E4.40	4.08	3 Mo Mar	△0.87	△1.10	21
22	1950	Q0.52½	6-1-78	5-1	1.05	2.10	1.97½	69.0	496.	499.	12-31-77	932.	[59]221	24867	Dc	3.71	4.06	4.40	5.02	E5.75	5.28	12 Mo Mar	4.41	5.28	22
23	1975	Q0.71⅞	6-1-78	5-1	1.43¾	2.87½	2.87½	Red restr(11½%)to5-31-85				★1089±	5502	1000	Dc	117.1	33.39	21.97	25.61	....	....	SF fr'81, 120,000 at$25			23
24	1976	Q0.60	6-1-78	5-1	1.20	2.40	2.40	Red restr (9.60%) to 5-31-86				....	2400	...	Dc	[63]1.87	[63]2.03	[63]1.99	[63]2.17	....	....	SF fr'82,120,000 at $25			24
25	.....	0.20	6-27-75	5-23	....	Nil	....	Equity per shr $7.93			12-31-77	....	...	1055	Je	1.82	d8.41	d2.49	△d0.25	....	d0.23	6 Mo Dec△	△d0.05	△d0.03	25
26	1952	Q0.66	6-15-78	5-22	1.26	2.64	2.30	19.0	203.	177.	3-31-78	359.	557	9844	Dc	4.45	4.43	5.72	5.37	E6.50	5.42	12 Mo Mar	5.57	5.42	26
27	1968	Q0.37½	6-15-78	5-22	0.75	1.50	1.50	Conv into common shr for shr				....	452	...	Dc	55.96	66.99	112.1	122.1	....	....				27
28◆	1962	s0.240	5-31-78	5-1	s0.480	1.00	s0.942	6.49	45.0	18.6	2-28-78	53.7	19	3174	My	1.16	1.12	1.22	2.20	....	3.89	12 Mo Feb	0.96	△3.89	28
29	1962	Q0.42	4-24-78	3-31	0.84	1.68	1.32	253.	826.	483.	3-31-78	30.3	...	22815	Dc	3.92	2.71	4.25	5.11	E5.80	5.26	3 Mo Mar	1.20	1.35	29
30	1978	Q0.04	6-9-78	3-9	0.04	0.16	....	13.1	36.4	38.4	3-31-78	★49.6	2253	★2398	Dc	•0.05	d3.58	•0.50	•1.28	....	1.54	3 Mo Mar	0.08	•0.34	30
31	.....	None Paid			....	Nil	....	10.3	69.4	39.7	12-31-77	141.	...	7808	Dc	1.32	0.93	0.64	0.88	....	0.76	3 Mo Mar	0.22	0.10	31
32◆	1965	Q0.07	4-14-78	4-4	0.14	0.28	0.24	3.35	152.	143.	2-28-78	275.	...	19614	Au	1.32	2.05	2.46	3.40	E4.00	3.71	6 Mo Feb	1.57	1.88	32
33◆	1962	A0.40	3-10-78	2-21	0.40	0.40	0.35	1.79	11.1	0.32	12-31-77	....	...	±1757	Dc	0.95	1.12	1.61	2.43	....	2.71	3 Mo Mar	0.62	0.90	33
34	1950	Q1.14	8-1-78	7-3	3.42	4.56	4.56	4.83	90.2	139.	3-31-78	819.	±2274	30750	Dc	48.25	39.09	41.80	46.33	....	....	12 Mo Mar	39.08	46.12	34
35	1917	Q0.38	7-3-78	6-5	1.11	1.52	1.38	22.6	249.	455.	3-31-78	1865	[64]477	★80000	Dc	2.18	2.02	2.29	2.40	E2.65	2.38	12 Mo Apr	2.40	2.38	35
36	1921	Q0.30	6-15-78	5-9	0.60	1.20	1.20	17.0	383.	149.	3-31-78	364.	3000	30841	Dc	4.83	3.37	1.98	1.21	E1.55	1.06	3 Mo Mar	0.42	0.27	36
37	1977	Q0.75	6-15-78	5-9	1.50	3.00	3.00	Cv into 1.5936 shr com $31.375				....	3000	...	Dc	....	....	20.28	15.43	....	....				37
38	.....	None Paid			....	Nil	....	1.21	45.6	18.6	1-27-78	62.6	...	3417	Oc	d0.14	d2.45	d1.63	[66]■d3.79	....	d3.67	6 Mo Apr	d0.88	d0.76	38
39	1941	Q0.47	6-10-78	5-15	0.87	1.88	1.40	9.10	64.5	12.1	12-31-77	20.2	85	2656	Sp	2.08	1.63	4.30	4.90	....	5.64	6 Mo Mar	2.28	3.02	39
40	1942	Q0.40	7-1-78	6-9	1.15	1.60	1.35	202.	1222	488.	12-31-77	299.	7316	30061	Dc	2.62	2.58	3.23	3.65	E4.25	3.96	3 Mo Mar	0.75	1.06	40
41	.....	Terms&trad. basis should be checked in detail						Warrants expire May 1, 1984				....	...	139	Price increases $1¼ May 1,1979										41
42	1968	Q0.52	7-1-78	6-9	1.56	2.08	2.08	Conv into 1.1 shrs common				....	2998	...	Dc	32.66	31.92	40.27	45.65	....	....				42
43	1968	Q0.35	7-1-78	6-9	1.05	1.40	1.40	Conv into 0.9 shrs common				....	4318	...	Dc	21.01	20.51	26.25	33.14	....	....				43
44	.....	None Paid			....	Nil	....	1.88	53.3	35.1	1-31-78	9.70	7	3692	Ja	0.47	d0.24	0.28	0.30	....	0.30				44
45◆	1935	Q0.15	4-28-78	4-4	0.30	0.60	0.505	7.02	62.9	17.8	1-28-78	22.8	5	3874	Ja	0.83	1.10	0.95	1.35	....	1.28	3 Mo Apr	0.04	d0.03	45

◆ **Stock Splits & Divs By Line Reference Index** [8]10%,'78. [11]10%,'78. [14]2-for-1,'74. [19]Adj to 5%,'78. [20]Adj to 5%,'78(ex'77). [28]Adj to 4%,'78. [32]10%,'75. [33]2-for-1,'75. [45]10%,'74,'75,'76,'78:3-for-2,'77.

Source: *Standard & Poor's Stock Guide* (New York: Standard & Poor's Corp., 1978). Reprinted by permission.

Figure 6–3 Sample Listing from Value Line

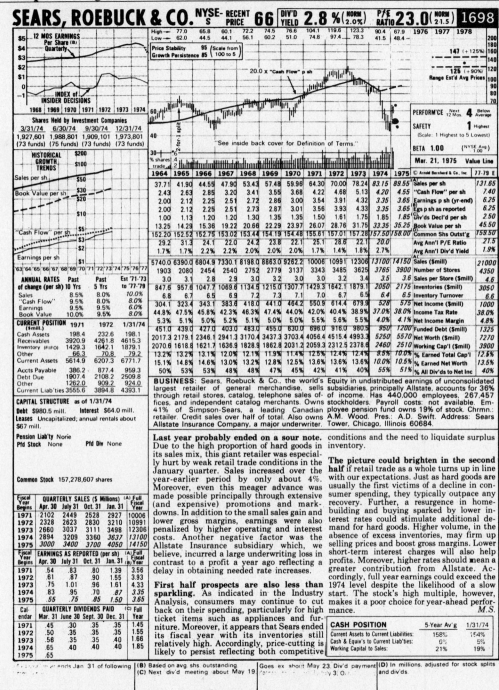

Source: *The Value Line Investment Survey* (New York: Arnold Bernhard & Co.). Reprinted by permission.

The Value Line OTC Special Situations Service is published 24 times a year for the experienced investor who is willing to accept high risk in the hope of realizing exceptional capital gains. In each issue, past recommendations are discussed and eight to ten new stocks are presented for consideration.

Daily Stock Price Records are published by Standard & Poor's. The bound volumes are published quarterly with individual volumes for the NYSE, the ASE, and the OTC market. Each quarterly book is divided into two parts. Part one, "Major Technical Indicators of the Stock Market," is devoted to market indicators widely followed as technical guides to the stock market and includes price indicator series, volume series, and data on odd-lots and short sales.

Part two, "Daily and Weekly Stock Action," gives daily high, low, close, and volume information and data on short interest for the stock, insider trading information, a 200 day moving average of prices, and a weekly relative strength series. The books for the NYSE and ASE are available from 1962 on; the OTC books begin in 1968.

Brokerage Firm Reports
Many brokerage firms prepare reports on individual firms. In some cases, these are rather objective and only contain basic information, while some contain specific recommendations—usually regarding purchase.

Investment Magazines
Forbes is published twice monthly and contains 12–14 articles on individual companies and industries. Several regular columnists who discuss the economy, the aggregate money and stock markets, and the commodity market are also published regularly.

Financial World is likewise published twice a month and generally contains about six articles on companies, industries, and the overall market, and a large number of regular features on taxes, options, and a section containing market data.

OTC Review is a monthly publication devoted to the analysis and discussion of stocks traded on the OTC market. It usually contains an analysis of an industry with numerous OTC companies and a discussion of three or four individual firms. In addition, extended earnings reports on OTC firms, name changes, stock exchange listings, and statistics on OTC trading (prices and volume) are published in the Review.

Academic Journals
The material in academic journals differs from that in investment magazines in timeliness and general orientation. Investment magazines are

concerned with the *current* investment environment and with providing advice for current action. They are generally nonquantitative. The articles in academic journals are longer, more theoretical and quantitative in approach, and typically not expected to be immediately useful. They deal with long-run implications for investments.

Journal of Finance is a quarterly published by the American Finance Association. The articles are almost all by academicians and rather theoretical and empirical. The typical issue will include 15 articles, notes and comments, and book reviews.

Journal of Financial and Quantitative Analysis is a quarterly published by the Western Finance Association and the University of Washington. It is very similar to the *Journal of Finance* in that almost all articles are by academicians. It differs in that it contains fewer articles in the area of monetary economics.

Journal of Financial Economics is a relatively new journal first published in May, 1974 by North Holland Publishing Company in collaboration with the Graduate School of Management of the University of Rochester, New York. The intent of the quarterly is to publish academic research in the following areas: consumption and investment decisions under uncertainty, portfolio analysis, efficient markets, and the normative theory of financial management.

Financial Analysts Journal is published six times a year by the Financial Analysts Federation. An issue contains six or seven articles of interest to practicing financial analysts and/or portfolio managers, a regular feature on securities regulation, and book reviews.

Institutional Investor is published monthly by Institutional Investors Systems, and is aimed at professional investors and portfolio managers with emphasis on what is happening to the investment industry. It is written by a professional staff.

Journal of Portfolio Management is likewise published by Institutional Investors Systems. It is published quarterly with the avowed intent of being a forum for academic research of use to the practicing portfolio manager. Over half the articles are written by academicians, but written to be read by the practitioner.

Financial Management is published quarterly by the Financial Management Association. It is intended for executives and academicians interested in the financial management of a firm, but also contains investment-related articles on such topics as stock splits, dividend policy, mergers, and stock listings.

The Financial Review is currently published twice a year by the Eastern Finance Association. It is a general financial journal directed to the academic community with about half the articles concerned with investments and portfolio management.

The C.F.A. Digest is published quarterly by the Institute of Chartered Financial Analysts. Its purpose is to provide, as a service to members of the investment community, abstracts of published articles considered to be of interest to financial analysts and portfolio managers.

Other General Business Journals

There are a number of general business and economics journals that include articles on finance and some specifically on investments. One of the foremost is the *Journal of Business* published by the University of Chicago which has contained some outstanding articles in the area of investments by members of the U of C faculty (Fisher, Lorie, Fama, and Miller). Other journals to consider include: *Quarterly Review of Economics and Business* (University of Illinois); *Review of Business and Economic Research* (University of New Orleans); *Journal of Business Research* (Elsenier North-Holland); *American Economic Review* (American Economic Association); *Journal of Political Economy* (University of Chicago); *Bell Journal of Economics* (American Telephone and Telegraph).

Summary

The intent of this chapter is to introduce the reader to the major sources of information on the economy, the aggregate securities markets, alternative industries, and individual firms. It should be recognized that this is *only a beginning*. It is virtually impossible to discuss all sources without writing a separate book. The reader is advised to use this as a starting point and attempt to spend some time in a university library examining the many other sources available.

Questions

1. Assume that you want information on the Gross National Product for the past 10 years. Name at least *three* sources for such information.

2. Name two sources for information on rates of exchange with major foreign countries.

3. Assume you are interested in the steel and auto industry and want to compare production for these two industries to overall industrial production for the economy. How would you do it? What data would you use and where would you get the data? Be specific.

4. You are told that there is a relationship between growth in the money supply and stock price movements. Where would you go to get the data to verify this relationship?

5. You are an analyst for Hot Stock Investment Company and the head of research tells you he just got a tip on the Baron Corporation, a stock that is traded on the OTC. He wants you to gather some data on the company's sales, earnings, and recent stock price movements. Where would you go for this information? Name several sources because the company may not be big enough to be included in some of them.

Sources of Investment Information

American Stock Exchange, 86 Trinity Place, New York, New York 10006.

Business Statistics may be obtained from Superintendent of Documents, U.S. Government Printing Office, Washington, D.C. 20402. Approximate price, $5.50.

Dow-Jones & Co., publishers of the *Wall Street Journal* and *Barron's*. Subscriptions office: 200 Burnett Rd., Chicopee, Massachusetts 01021.

Dow-Jones Handbooks. Each of the handbooks is published annually and can be obtained from Dow-Jones Books, P.O. Box 455, Chicopee, Massachusetts 01021. Approximate cost is $5.00 a book.

Economic Indicators. Available from the Superintendent of Documents (address as above). Approximate price, $10/year.

Economic Report of the President may be obtained from Superintendent of Documents, (address as above). Approximate price, $3.00.

Federal Reserve Bulletin may be obtained from the Division of Administrative Services, Board of Governors of the Federal Reserve System, Washington, D.C. 20551. Approximate cost $20.00 a year.

Moody's Investor's Services, Inc., 99 Church Street, New York, New York 10007. (212) 267-8800.

New York Stock Exchange, 11 Wall Street, New York, New York 10005.

Quarterly Financial Report. Available from Superintendent of Documents (address as above). Approximate cost is $10.00 a year.

Standard & Poor's Corporation, 345 Hudson Street, New York, New York 10014.

Statistical Abstract of the United States may be obtained from the Superintendent of Documents. Approximate cost, $10.50 (cloth); $7.00 (paper).

Statistical Bulletin may be subscribed to through the Superintendent of Documents. Approximate cost, $15.00 a year.

Survey of Current Business may be obtained from Superintendent of Documents.

Value Line Services. These are published by Arnold Bernhard and Company, Inc., 5 East 44th Street, New York, New York 10017.

Part 2

Modern Developments in Investment Theory

Introduction to Part 2

Before any analytical study can be attempted, a theoretical framework must be established. This is as true for the analysis of investments as it is for any other academic discipline. In the area of investments, several major theories that affected the way in which the entire subject is approached have been developed in the last 20 years. It is with these theories that Part Two is concerned.

In the late 1950's the "random walk hypothesis" was developed. Most of the research done using this theory dealt with price changes over time, reaching the general conclusion that stock price changes were similar to a random series. This early work eventually became part of a much larger theory known as the efficient market hypothesis that considered not only stock price changes alone, but also these changes as they related to different sets of information. Studies related to the efficient market hypothesis (EMH) are important because of what they can tell us about our financial markets. Therefore, in Chapter 7 we will examine the EMH and discuss numerous studies that produced findings in support of various forms of the hypothesis, as well as some studies that have *not* supported it. We will also consider the implications of the hypothesis for various segments of the investment industry. These implications tend to be misunderstood, so the reader is urged to read the section carefully and keep an open mind.

The second major development in investment theory, which also affected financial management, was the basic portfolio model, developed by Harry Markowitz in 1954. Markowitz indicated the importance of diversification in terms of reducing the overall risk of a portfolio and derived a risk measure for individual securities. In 1964, William Sharpe extended the basic portfolio model into a general equilibrium model that generated an alternative risk measure for all risky assets. Chapter 8 is a nontechnical discussion of these developments and an explanation of the relevant risk measure implied by the Sharpe model, generally referred to as the Capital Asset Pricing Model (CAPM). We have introduced the CAPM at this early stage because the risk measure it generates is subsequently used in all analysis.

Chapter 7   *Efficient Capital Markets*

Efficient capital markets are considered at this point for two reasons. First, since we have already discussed capital markets, it seems natural to consider how efficiently they operate. Second, several *very important implications* for security valuation and portfolio management are derived from the existence of efficient capital markets. Some of these are not very pleasant to accept; so it is crucial for the reader to become aware of them early and avoid "future shock." Also, this knowledge is useful in the subsequent chapters on analysis.

There are four major sections in this chapter. The initial section contains a discussion of why capital markets should be efficient. In the second section we will consider the alternative efficient market hypotheses and the tests of the hypotheses. The results for a number of the studies on this topic are presented and discussed in the third section. The final section deals with the implications of the results for technicians, fundamental security analysts, and portfolio managers.

Rationale of the Efficient Capital Markets Theory

While the definition of an efficient capital market is relatively straight-forward, we often fail to consider *why* capital markets should be expected to be efficient. What conditions do we assume exist in order to have an efficient capital market?

An initial, and very important, premise of an efficient market is that there are a large number of profit maximizing participants concerned with the analysis and valuation of securities and operating independently of each other. A second assumption is that *new information regarding securities comes to the market in a random fashion* and the announcements over time are generally independent from one another. The third assumption of an efficient market is especially crucial. *Investors adjust security prices rapidly to reflect the effect of new information.* While the price adjustment made is not always perfect, it is unbiased (i.e., sometimes there is an overadjustment or an underadjustment, but you don't know which it will be). It is contended that the attempt to adjust the security price takes place rapidly because the number of profit maximizing investors is large. The combined effect of (1) information coming in a random, independent fashion, and (2) numerous investors who adjust stock prices rapidly to reflect this new information is that *price changes are independent and random.*

Finally, because security prices adjust to all new information and, therefore, supposedly reflect all public information at any point in time, *the security prices that prevail at any point in time should be an unbiased reflection of all currently available information.* The price of a security at any point in time is an unbiased estimate of the true intrinsic value of the security at that point in time given all the information available. Based upon the foregoing discussion *an efficient market is one in which security prices adjust rapidly to the infusion of new information, and current stock prices fully reflect all available information including the risk involved.* Therefore, the returns implicit in the price reflect the risk involved, so *the expected return is consistent with risk.*

Alternative Efficient Market Hypotheses and Tests

A great deal of the early work in the area of efficient markets was done under the random walk hypothesis and contained extensive empirical analysis without much theory behind it. The first real attempt to synthesize theory and organize the numerous empirical studies was made by Professor Eugene Fama in a 1970 *Journal of Finance* article,[1] which was the initial presentation of the efficient market theory in terms of the "fair game" model.

Expected Return or "Fair Game" Model[2]

Unlike work done under the random walk hypothesis, which dealt with price movement over time, the fair game model deals with price at a specified period. It assumes that the price of a security fully reflects all available information at that period. The model requires that the price formation process be specified in enough detail so that it is possible to indicate what is meant by "fully reflect." Most of the available models of equilibrium prices formulate prices in terms of rates of return that are

---

[1] Eugene F. Fama, "Efficient Capital Markets: A Review of Theory and Empirical Work," *Journal of Finance,* Vol. 25, No. 2 (May, 1970), pp. 383–417.

[2] This section is drawn heavily from Fama, ibid.

dependent on alternative definitions of risk. All such expected return theories of price formation can be described notationally as follows:

7–1
$$E(\tilde{p}_{j,t+1}|\phi_t) = [1 + E(\tilde{r}_{j,t+1}|\phi_t)]p_{j,t}$$

where:

E — expected value operator
$p_{j,t}$ — price of security j at time t
$p_{j,t+1}$ — price of security j at time t + 1
$r_{j,t+1}$ — the one period percent rate of return for security j during period t + 1
ϕ_t — represents the set of information that is assumed to be "fully reflected" in the security price at time t.

Equation 7–1 indicates that the expected price of security j, given the full set of information available at time t (ϕ_t), is equal to the current price times one plus the expected return on security j given the set of available information. This expected future return should reflect the set of information available at t, which includes the state of the world at time t, including all current and past values of *any relevant variables* such as earnings, the GNP, etc. In addition, it is assumed that this information set includes knowledge of *all the relevant relationships among variables*—i.e., how alternative economic series relate to each other and how they relate to security prices.

If equilibrium market prices can be stated in terms of expected returns that "fully reflect" the information set ϕ_t, this implies that it is *not possible* to derive trading systems or investment strategies based on this current information set and experience returns beyond what should be expected on the basis of risk. Thus, let us define $x_{j,t+1}$ as the difference between the actual price in t + 1 and the expected price in t + 1:

7–2
$$x_{j,t+1} = p_{j,t+1} - E(p_{j,t+1}|\phi_t)$$

Equation 7–2 can be described as a definition of excess market value for security j because it is the difference between the actual price and the expected price projected at t on the basis of the information set ϕ_t. In an efficient market:

7–3
$$E(\tilde{x}_{j,t+1}|\phi_t) = 0$$

This equation indicates that the market reflects a "fair game" with respect to the information set ϕ. In such a "fair game" market, investors can acquire the securities at current prices and be confident that these prices "fully reflect" all available information and are consistent with the risk involved. Fama divided the overall hypothesis and empirical tests into three categories depending upon the information set involved.

Weak Form Efficient Market Hypothesis

The weak form efficient market hypothesis assumes that current stock prices fully reflect all *stock market* information including the historical sequence of prices, price changes, and any volume information. Because current prices already reflect all past price changes and any other stock market information, this implies that there should be no relationship between past price changes and future price changes: i.e., price changes are independent and any trading rule (i.e., the conditions under which an investor will buy or sell stock) that depends upon past price changes or past market data to predict future price changes should be of little value.

There have been two groups of tests for the weak form efficient market hypothesis. The first category involves statistical tests of independence between stock price changes. The second group entails specific testing of trading rules that attempt to generate investment decisions on the basis of past market information as opposed to a simple buy-and-hold policy (i.e. simply buying stock at the beginning of a test period and holding it to the end).

Statistical Tests of Independence As discussed earlier, stock price changes over time should be independent because new information comes to the market in a random, independent fashion, and stock prices adjust rapidly to this new information. Therefore, in an efficient capital market, stock price changes should be independent and random.

Two major statistical tests have been employed to verify this. First were the autocorrelation tests which correlated price changes over time to see if there was independence; i.e., was there significant positive or negative correlation in price changes over time? Is the percent of price change on day t correlated with the percent of price change on day $t-1$, $t-2$, or $t-3$?[3] Those who support the theory of efficient capital markets would expect insignificant correlations between all such combinations.

The second statistical test of independence included "runs" tests. Given a series of price changes, each price change is designated a "plus" ($+$) if it is an increase, or a "minus" ($-$) if it is a decrease. The result is a set of pluses and minuses as follows: $+++-+--++--++$. A run occurs when there is no difference between two changes; two or three *consecutive* positive or consecutive negative price changes is one run. When the price change is to a different sign (e.g., a negative price change followed by a positive price change), the "run" is ended and a new run begins.[4] Even in a series of purely random numbers, one would expect some instances of runs of two, three, or four changes. Therefore, one should not expect the number of runs to equal the number of observations. In fact, the expected number of runs for a

---

[3] For a discussion of tests of independence see Ya-lun Chou, *Statistical Analysis,* 2nd ed. (New York: Holt Rinehart and Winston, 1975), pp. 540–542.

[4] For the details of a runs test see ibid., pp. 537–539.

random series is $1/3(2n - 1)$, where n is the number of observations.[5] If there are too many or too few runs for a given series (the actual number deviates significantly from the expected number noted above), it is probably not a random series because there is too much correlation in the signs. To test for independence, one calculates the number of runs for a given series and compares this with a table that provides the limits above and below the expected number for a random series of that size.

Tests of Trading Rules The second group of tests of the weak form hypothesis were prompted by the assertion of technical analysts that the statistical tests described above were too rigid to pinpoint the very intricate price patterns examined by technical analysts. Supposedly analysts do not believe it is a mechanical number of positive or negative price changes that signal a move to a new equilibrium, but a general consistency in trend over time that might include both positive and negative changes. Technical analysts felt their trading rules were too sophisticated and complicated to be simulated by a rigid statistical test. Therefore, investigators attempted to specifically examine alternative technical trading rules through simulation. Advocates of an efficient market hypothesized that investors using any technical trading rule that asserted that stock prices moved in trends could not derive above average profits (i.e., rates of return greater than returns from a buy-and-hold policy) *if the trading rule depended solely on past market information* whether it be price data, volume data, or what have you.

Semi-Strong Form Efficient Market Hypothesis

The semi-strong form efficient market hypothesis asserts that *security prices adjust rapidly to the release of all new public information;* i.e., stock prices "fully reflect" *all* public information. Obviously the semi-strong hypothesis encompasses the weak form hypothesis because all public information includes all market information (stock prices, trading volume, etc.), plus all nonmarket information such as earnings, stock splits, economic news, political news. A direct implication of this hypothesis is that investors acting on important new information *after* it is public cannot derive above average profits from the transaction, considering the cost of trading, because the security price already reflects the effect of the new public information.

Given the statement of the hypothesis and the direct implication, studies attempting to test the semi-strong form of the EMH have done one or both of the following:

(1) Examined price movements around the time of an important announcement and attempted to see when the expected price adjustment

---

[5] Chou, *Statistical Analysis.*

took place: did security prices adjust *before* the announcement was made; did prices adjust *during* the announcement period, or did prices appear to adjust *after* the announcement? The efficient market hypothesis would imply a price adjustment either *before* the announcement, because of news leaks or other sources of the information, or *during* the period of announcement.

(2) Examined the potential for above average profit assuming an investor acted after the information was public. Assume an investor acquired the security after an announcement was made public and determine whether he enjoyed above average profits compared to buy-and-hold after taking into account transactions costs.

Strong Form Efficient Market Hypothesis

The strong form efficient market hypothesis contends that stock prices "fully reflect" *all* information (public and otherwise). Hence, it implies that no group of investors has a monopolistic access to information relevant to the formation of prices. Therefore, *no group of investors should be able to consistently derive above average profits.* The strong form hypothesis encompasses *both* the weak and semi-strong forms. Further, the strong form hypothesis requires not only efficient markets (where prices adjust rapidly to the release of new public information), but also requires *perfect* markets in which *all information is available to everyone at the same time.* This form of the EMH contends that because all information is immediately available to everyone and is rapidly discounted by everyone, no group has monopolistic access to important new information and, therefore, nobody can derive above average profits.

The tests of this hypothesis involve the analysis of returns over time for alternative identifiable investment groups to determine whether any group consistently received above average returns on a risk-adjusted basis. If any group did consistently receive such returns, this would indicate that either they had monopolistic access to important information or they had the ability to consistently act on public information before other investors could, so the market was not adjusting stock prices to *all* new information rapidly.

Results of Efficient Market Tests

Weak Form Hypothesis Test Results

Recall that the tests of the weak form hypothesis included two sets of statistical tests of independence (serial correlation tests and "runs" tests), and the analyses of results for simulations of trading rules that used past market information to project future price changes.

Statistical Test Results

Analysis of the serial correlations between stock price changes has been done by various authors for several different intervals including one day, four days, nine days, and 16 days.[6] The results consistently indicated *insignificant* correlation in stock price changes over time. The typical range of correlation coefficients was from $+.10$ to $-.10$, but the correlations were typically not statistically significant. Individual stocks had a tendency towards slight negative correlation in stock price changes. In contrast, price changes for aggregate market indicator series tended to have a slight positive correlation. Professor Lawrence Fisher of the University of Chicago has shown that this difference is probably caused by the fact that the numerous stocks in the market indicator series close at different points in time during a day. Therefore, stocks that close early have some lag in price adjustment to late news that is picked up the following day. In any case, the empirical evidence from serial correlation tests consistently indicated that *stock price changes over time are in general statistically independent.* These results imply that one *cannot* use past price changes alone to project future price changes.

Tests of stock price "runs" likewise indicated independence in stock price changes over time. While positive price changes were occasionally followed by positive price changes and vice versa, a number of such cases can be explained by a random model in which you would expect some positive and negative runs. The actual number of runs for stock price series consistently fell into the range expected for a random series. Therefore, these statistical tests likewise supported the notion that stock price changes over time are independent. These statistical tests for independence were repeated on the OTC market and the results likewise supported the EMH.[7]

While the evidence of daily, weekly, and monthly data consistently supported the weak form EMH, the evidence of individual transaction price changes is not supportive. A well-known study by Niederhoffer and Osborn examined price changes in terms of individual transactions on the NYSE and found significant serial correlation.[8] These correlation results were

---

[6] Sidney S. Alexander, "Price Movements in Speculative Markets: Trends or Random Walks," *Industrial Management Review,* Vol. 2, No. 2 (May, 1961), pp. 7–26; Eugene F. Fama, "The Behavior of Stock Market Prices," *Journal of Business,* Vol. 38, No. 1 (January, 1965), pp. 34–105; Maurice G. Kendall, "The Analysis of Economic Time Series," *Journal of the Royal Statistical Society,* Vol. 96 (1953), pp. 11–25; Arnold Moore, "A Statistical Analysis of Common Stock Prices," unpublished Ph.d. dissertation, Graduate School of Business, University of Chicago (1962).

[7] Robert L. Hagerman and Richard D. Richmond, "Random Walks, Martingales and the OTC," *Journal of Finance,* Vol. 28, No. 4 (September, 1973), pp. 897–909.

[8] Victor Niederhoffer and M. F. Osborn, "Market-Making and Reversal on the Stock Exchange," *Journal of American Statistical Association,* Vol. 61, No. 316 (December, 1966), pp. 897–916.

confirmed in a study by Ken Carey.[9] Note that none of the authors attempted to show that the dependence in price movements could be used to derive above average risk-adjusted returns. Therefore, apparently there is some significant correlation among individual transactions caused by the market-making activities of the specialist but it is highly unlikely that this small imperfection could be used by an investor to derive excess profits after transactions costs.

Trading Rule Simulation Results

Simulation studies were conducted to satisfy technicians who contended that their "unique" trading rules could not be analyzed employing rigid statistical tests. Therefore, the intent was to simulate the conditions under which a specific technical system was used to make decisions based on public market information and to compare the investment results derived from such a simulation, including commission costs, to the results from a simple buy-and-hold policy. The reader should be made aware of three major pitfalls that can negate the results of such studies: (1) *only use data that is publicly available* in the decision rule, e.g., the earnings for a firm as of December 31, may not be *publicly* available until April 1; (2) when determining the returns from a trading rule be sure to *include all transactions costs* involved in implementing the trading strategy. This is important because most trading rules involve many more transactions than a simple buy-and-hold policy does; (3) *be sure that the final results are risk-adjusted.* It is possible the trading rule simply helps in the selection of high-risk securities that should experience higher returns.

Two operational problems have been encountered in these tests. First, it is often difficult, if not impossible, to specify a technical trading rule in a manner that makes it possible to mechanically simulate the technique because the trading rules require a fair amount of personal interpretation. In many cases two technical analysts looking at the same set of data might differ on the projection. Therefore, *it is not possible to test some technical rules.* The second problem is that *there is an almost infinite number of potential trading rules* and, therefore, it is not possible to test all of them. As a result, what has been done is to examine a number of the better known technical trading rules that could be specified in a manner conducive to simulation. The tests may be somewhat biased because the studies have concentrated on the simple trading rules which many technicians contend are rather naive. In addition, the authors almost always employ readily available data from the NYSE which means the sample is biased toward well-known, heavily traded stocks that *should* enjoy efficient markets.

The most popular trading technique has been to use filter rules (indi-

---

[9] Kenneth Carey, "A Model of Individual Transactions Stock Prices," unpublished Ph.D. dissertation, University of Kansas (1971).

viduals set filters for a given stock and trade when a stock price change exceeds the filter specified). One might set up a 5 percent filter for a stock based upon past movements. When the stock had risen 5 percent from some base, it is hypothesized by the technical analyst that this movement indicates a "break out" and that stock prices will continue to rise. Therefore, technical traders using this filter would acquire the stock expecting to participate in the continued rise. If the stock declined 5 percent from some peak price, technicians would expect the price to continue to decline and, therefore, would sell the stock acquired previously and possibly sell it short, based upon the expectation of a further price decline.

Studies of this trading rule have used a range of filters from very small (one-half percent) to very large (50 percent), and have generated consistent results which indicated that using *small* filters and *not* taking account of trading commission, one *can* derive above-average profits. Such results are consistent with the small correlation in price changes discussed earlier although the use of small filters resulted in numerous trades and substantial commissions. Therefore, when trading commissions were considered, all the trading *profits* turned to *losses*. These conclusions were true for the Alexander studies, and also the Fama and Blume studies.[10]

Trading techniques have been simulated using past market data other than stock prices. Trading rules have been devised that used odd-lot figures, advanced-decline ratios, and short sales or short positions. In a few cases there were slight profits, but generally the simulations using these trading rules did *not* outperform a buy-and-hold policy after taking account of commissions. An article by George Pinches reviewed a number of these studies.[11] Based upon this review Pinches concluded:

While the results of mechanical trading rules that simulate technical trading rules are not entirely consistent, it appears that these findings could support a very narrow interpretation of the random-walk hypothesis. If mechanical trading rules could be devised that consistently outperformed a random buy-and-hold policy, then substantial proof would exist that the random-walk hypothesis is incorrect. However, with some exceptions, the studies of mechanical trading rules do not indicate that profits can be generated by these rules.[12]

Therefore, it is probably safe to say that the great bulk of the evidence generated by simulating mechanical trading rules supports the weak form of the efficient market hypothesis.

---

[10] Alexander, "Price Movements in Speculative Markets;" Sidney S. Alexander, "Price Movements in Speculative Markets: Trends or Random Walks, Number 2," *Industrial Management Review,* Vol. 5 (Spring, 1964), pp. 25–46; Eugene F. Fama and Marshall Blume, "Filter Rules and Stock Market Trading Profits," *Journal of Business,* Vol. 39, No. 1 (January, 1966 Supplement), pp. 226–241.

[11] George Pinches, "The Random Walk Hypothesis and Technical Analysis," *Financial Analysts Journal,* Vol. 26, No. 2 (March–April, 1970), pp. 104–110.

[12] Ibid., p. 108.

Semi-Strong Form Hypothesis Test Results

Semi-strong tests of the efficient market hypothesis examine *how fast stock prices adjust to all new public information.* Another test considers *whether investors can generate above average profits by trading on the basis of any publicly available information.* This latter test is implied because the efficient market hypothesis contends that stock prices adjust rapidly to available information and, therefore, an investor using *any* publicly available information should *not* be able to derive above average profits, i.e., risk-adjusted returns above those available from a simple buy-and-hold policy.

The first study that one can identify as a test of the semi-strong hypothesis is the well-known one done by Fama, Fisher, Jensen, and Roll (FFJR).[13] The FFJR study is noteworthy because it made a contribution in three areas. First, it is a very well-regarded and extensive study of the long-run effect of stock splits on returns to stockholders. Second, in dealing with stock splits, the authors provided important evidence on the semi-strong efficient market hypothesis because they were concerned with how rapidly stock prices adjusted to this important economic event. Finally, the authors employed a technique to adjust for "market effects" that was based on advances in capital market theory. The market adjustment technique differed substantially from prior methods and has been used extensively since the original study.

Returning to the study itself, it was hypothesized that stock splits alone do not cause higher rates of return because they add nothing to the value of a firm. Therefore, there should be no significant price change following a split. In addition, one would hypothesize that, in an efficient market, investors would adjust for the forthcoming stock split *prior* to the announcement because any relevant information that caused the split has already been discounted. It is contended that the stock price increase that leads a company to split its stock is caused by increases in earnings or other important successes and these bits of information are known and adjusted for prior to the split announcement.

Another reason for expecting a price increase is that companies typically raise their dividends when they split their stock. It is contended that the dividend change has an information effect because it indicates that management is confident that it will have a new, higher level of earnings in the future which will justify a higher level of dividends. Therefore, the price increase that accompanies a dividend increase is *not* caused by the dividend itself, but by the information transmitted by the increase.

Adjustment for Market Effects Prior to the FFJR study, numerous authors had examined the effect of different events on stock prices and realized that it is necessary to adjust returns on an individual stock for market returns

---

[13] E.F. Fama, L. Fisher, M. Jensen, and R. Roll, "The Adjustment of Stock Prices to New Information," *International Economic Review,* Vol. 10, No. 1 (February, 1969), pp. 1–21.

during the same period. The difference is that *prior authors implicitly assumed that all stocks moved the same as the aggregate market* because generally the adjustment process was simply a matter of subtracting the market return from the stock return and any difference was assumed to be the abnormal return. Based upon work in capital market theory, it was contended by FFJR that the adjustment process should recognize that each individual security has a "unique" relationship with the market. A given stock will tend to rise or decline more or less than the market.[14] This "unique" relationship between a stock and the market was derived by computing a regression of stock returns and market returns for a period prior to and subsequent to a split as follows:

$$R_{it} = a_i + B_i R_{mt} + \epsilon$$

R_{it} — the rate of return on security i during period t
a_i — the intercept or constant for security i in the regression
B_i — the regression slope coefficient for security i equal to cov_{im}/σ_m^2
R_{mt} — the rate of return on a market index during period t
ϵ — a random error term that sums to zero

Given that the deviations from the regression line are random, one would expect them to sum to zero over long periods of time. This regression was run for all the stocks in the study using observations from the period 1926–1960 except for the 15 month period before and after the split. It was hypothesized that if there was any abnormal information to be derived from the split it would show up in the residuals (deviations from the regression line). These residuals were considered "abnormal price changes." If there were positive residuals surrounding splits, this would indicate the presence of good information and vice versa. The purpose was to determine *when* the positive effects took place, before or after the split. The authors cumulated the residuals for individual stocks and for all the stocks in the sample over time. To examine the differential effect of dividend increases, the total sample was divided into two groups—stocks that split and also experienced an increase in their dividend rate, and stocks that split but did *not* increase their dividend rate.

The results indicated that both groups of stocks experienced positive abnormal price changes *prior* to the split. Stocks that split but did *not* increase their dividend experienced abnormal price *declines* following the split. In fact, within 12 months the no dividend increase stocks lost all their accumulated abnormal gains.

---

[14] For a discussion of why they should be different and the relevance of the difference see William F. Sharpe, "Capital Asset Prices: A Theory of Market Equilibrium Under Conditions of Risk," *Journal of Finance*, Vol. 19, No. 3 (September, 1964), pp. 425–442. For subsequent analysis of beta coefficient, see Marshall E. Blume, "On the Assessment of Risk," *Journal of Finance*, Vol. 26, No. 1 (March, 1971), pp. 1–10.

In contrast, stocks that split and also increased their dividend experienced no change in their abnormal return pattern after the split; i.e., the abnormal price pattern flattened. This indicated that the full impact of the price changes took place *prior* to the stock split. After the split, stocks with dividend increases were able to maintain their positive abnormal price increase, while stocks that did not increase their dividend, and thereby did not confirm the expectations regarding their favorable outlook, returned to their status prior to the split announcement.

These results were considered substantial evidence that stock splits alone do not result in higher rates of return for stockholders. They also support the semi-strong efficient market hypothesis because they indicate that the price adjustment occurred *prior* to a split.

The authors also considered whether investors could gain from the information on the split after the public announcement. It was argued that investors could *not* have gained by acquiring the stock *after* the split announcement. Although the aggregate results indicated that stocks in general rose prior to the actual split but after the announcement, it was contended that this rising price pattern was due to the aggregation of the returns. The analysis of individual stocks indicated that it would have been impossible to gain from acquiring individual stocks after the stock split was announced. This conclusion regarding market efficiency surrounding a stock split was confirmed in a subsequent study by Hausman, West, and Largay which specifically examined the profit opportunity question.[15]

New Issue Studies During the 1960's a number of closely held companies decided to "go public" by selling some of their common stock. The determination of the appropriate price for a stock that does not have a public market is a difficult task. Because of uncertainty about the price and the risk involved in underwriting such issues, it was hypothesized by some authors that the underwriters would tend to underprice the new issues.[16] The authors therefore hypothesized that investors who acquired the new issues *at the offering price* would tend to receive abnormal profits. There was also a question regarding how fast the market would adjust to the underpricing. To examine the efficiency of the market, the typical test considered the returns to an investor who acquired the new issue *in the after-market* (the public price after the offering) and held it for various periods.[17] The results

---

[15] W. H. Hausman, R. R. West, and J.A. Largay, "Stock Splits, Price Changes, and Trading Profits: A Synthesis," *Journal of Business,* Vol. 44, No. 1 (January, 1971), pp. 69–77.

[16] For a discussion of these reasons see Frank K. Reilly and Kenneth Hatfield, "Investor Experience with New Stock Issues," *Financial Analysts Journal,* Vol. 25, No. 5 (September–October, 1969), pp. 73–80.

[17] Besides the Reilly–Hatfield study, the studies include: Roger G. Ibbotson, "Price Performance of Common Stock New Issues," *Journal of Financial Economics,* Vol. 2, No. 3 (September, 1975), pp. 235–272; Dennis E. Logue, "On the Pricing of Unseasoned New

on the two questions of interest (underpricing and market efficiency), were quite consistent. *All* the studies indicated that, on average, new issues yield abnormally positive short-run returns assuming a purchase *at the offering price*. Most authors attribute these excess returns to underpricing by the underwriters. The results also tended to support the semi-strong efficient market hypothesis because it appears *the market adjusted the prices almost immediately for the underpricing*. The returns from acquiring the new issue shortly after the offering and holding it for various periods either yielded returns consistent with the added risk involved in these new issues, or the returns were actually below expectations. The evidence of rapid price adjustment is most evident in the recent Reilly study in which it is shown that prices adjust by the week following the offering.[18]

Exchange Listing Another economic event that is expected to have a significant impact on a firm and its stock is the decision to become listed on a national exchange or, specifically, to become listed on the NYSE because it is the largest and most prestigious exchange. It is reasoned that such a listing will increase the market liquidity of the stock and, possibly, add to the prestige of the firm. There are two questions of interest. First, does listing on a major exchange cause a permanent change in the value of the firm? Second, given the change in expectations or perceptions surrounding the listing, is it possible to derive abnormal returns from investing in the newly listed stock around the time of the listing? A study by Furst examined the effect of listing on price using a multiple regression model that included all the variables that normally influence price (dividends, growth, retention rate, earnings stability, leverage, and corporate size) plus a dummy variable for listing.[19] The results generally indicated that the dummy variable was not statistically significant, which led the author to conclude that listing did not have an impact on price. A study by Van Horne considered price effects and also the ability to profit from these

---

Issues, 1965–1969," *Journal of Financial and Quantitative Analysis,* Vol. 8, No. 1 (January, 1973), pp. 91–103; J. G. McDonald and A. K. Fisher, "New-Issue Stock Price Behavior," *Journal of Finance,* Vol. 27, No. 1 (March, 1972) pp. 97–102; Brian M. Neuberger and Carl T. Hammond, "A Study of Underwriters' Experience with Unseasoned New Issues," *Journal of Financial and Quantitative Analysis,* Vol. 9, No. 2 (March, 1974), pp. 165–177; Frank K. Reilly, "Further Evidence on Short-Run Results for New Issue Investors," *Journal of Financial and Quantitative Analysis,* Vol. 8, No. 1 (January, 1973), pp. 83–90; Frank K. Reilly, "New Issues Revisited," *Financial Management,* Vol. 6, No. 4 (Winter, 1977), pp. 28–42; Hans R. Stoll and Anthony J. Curley, "Small Business and the New Issues Market for Equities," *Journal of Financial and Quantitative Analysis,* Vol. 5, No. 3 (September, 1970), pp. 309–322.

[18] Reilly, "New Issues Revisited."

[19] Richard W. Furst, "Does Listing Increase the Market Price of Common Stock?" *Journal of Business,* Vol. 43, No. 2 (April, 1970), pp. 174–180.

effects.[20] The analysis compared price movements for stocks listed on the NYSE and ASE and similar movements on the S&P 500 Index. The results indicated positive abnormal price changes for the period between four and two months before listing, but, after taking account of transactions costs and certain biases, the average price change after the listing adjusted for industry price movements was not significant. It is concluded:

On the basis of the studies undertaken, support cannot be marshalled for the hypothesis that market participants can "profit" from buying a stock upon the announcement to list and selling it at the time of listing, nor for the idea that listing is a thing of value.[21]

A study by Goulet considered not only price changes but also the effect on shares outstanding, sales of stock, and the number of stockholders.[22] Typically, there was an increase in the latter variables (shares outstanding and stockholders), but a decrease in stock price after the listing. It is not clear whether an investor could profit from this price change.

There is some contrary evidence in a paper by Ying that examined price movements surrounding the listing and used the FFJR technique to adjust for market movements.[23] The results indicated that the stocks generally experienced positive residuals before listing, with the largest positive values during the two months immediately prior to listing. Following the listing, however, the average residuals were *negative* for eight consecutive months. It is contended that the consistent negative residuals are evidence against the semi-strong EMH because someone could supposedly derive excess profits by selling the stock short when it is listed. Unfortunately, the specific test was not carried out.

In summary, it appears that most of the evidence with regard to profit opportunities related to listings supports the semi-strong EMH although there is some evidence to the contrary.

Stock Prices and World Events A study by Reilly and Drzycimski was related to the semi-strong EMH because it examined the adjustment of stock prices to significant world events.[24] In an efficient market, stock prices should adjust rapidly to the new information contained in the

---

[20] James C. Van Horne, "New Listings and Their Price Behavior," *Journal of Finance,* Vol. 25, No. 4 (September, 1970), pp. 783–794.

[21] Ibid., p. 794.

[22] Waldemar M. Goulet, "Price Changes, Managerial Actions and Insider Trading at the Time of Listing," *Financial Management,* Vol. 3, No. 1 (Spring, 1974), pp. 30–36.

[23] Louis Ying, "Stock Exchange Listings and Securities Returns," Paper presented at Financial Management Association Meeting, October, 1975.

[24] Frank K. Reilly and Eugene F. Drzycimski, "Tests of Stock Market Efficiency Following Major World Events," *Journal of Business Research,* Vol. 1, No. 1 (Summer, 1973), pp. 57–72.

announcement of a world event. Therefore, investors should *not* be able to profit from the information once it is publicly available. The analysis covered the announcement of seven unexpected world events. Several stock price series were analyzed prior to the announcement, at the market opening after the announcement, and during the two days following. The results consistently indicated that the major adjustment in stock prices took place during the time interval between the close before the announcement and the open after the announcement. The major stock price change occurred *before* the market opened after the announcement. While there were some large stock price changes after the opening stock price that followed the announcement, the direction of these changes was not consistent.

On the question of whether investors could have made a profit from investing in stocks at the opening following the announcement, the results consistently indicated that this would not have been possible. There were 245 opportunities for investing, considering different series at the time of the events, and only about 6 percent of these would have generated a profit in excess of commission costs. In fact, there were no profit opportunities related to any stock price series after five of the seven events. Therefore, these tests generally supported the notion that the stock market was semi-strong efficient.

Announcements of Accounting Changes Numerous studies have analyzed the impact of announcements of accounting changes on stock prices. These studies, which implicitly contend that the capital markets are relatively efficient, have implications for the semi-strong EMH. If markets are efficient, and accounting procedures or announcements of accounting changes are important, one should be able to substantiate this by examining what happens to stock prices during the time period surrounding the announcement of an accounting change. It is also possible to determine the effect investors expect the accounting change to have, if any. If the announcement is of a change in accounting technique that will affect the economic value of the firm, a rapid change in stock prices to reflect this would be expected. If the accounting change only affects *reported* earnings but has no economic significance (e.g., a change in the technique used to compute depreciation for bookkeeping purposes), an advocate of an efficient capital market would not expect the announcement to have an impact on stock prices.

Impact of Annual Earnings Reports A study by Brown and Ball examined the differential stock price movements for companies that had experienced "good" earnings reports, and stock price movement of companies that had experienced "poor" earnings reports.[25] They used the FFJR technique to

---

[25] Philip Brown and Ray Ball, "An Empirical Evaluation of Accounting Income Numbers," *Journal of Accounting Research,* Vol. 6 (Autumn, 1963), pp. 159–178.

derive the abnormal price performance of individual stocks relative to the aggregate market. They related these abnormal stock price movements to abnormal earnings changes for the companies, and derived abnormal earnings by examining what the company should have done based upon its past relationship with overall earnings. They derived the historical relationship between the earnings for a company and aggregate earnings. Then, given what happens to aggregate earnings in a specific year, it is possible to determine from the historical regression what investors would expect for a specified company. If a company experienced earnings above expectations, Ball and Brown considered this an abnormally good earnings report and hypothesized that the firm's stock should experience positive abnormal price movements. The opposite was hypothesized for poor earnings reports (earnings below expectations). They divided the sample into companies with good and bad earnings reports, and examined the abnormal stock price returns for the two samples during the year prior to the earnings report.

The results generally confirmed expectations that companies with abnormally good earnings reports also experienced positive abnormal stock price performance. However, most of the stock price adjustment (about 85 percent) took place prior to the end of the year and prior to the release of the annual report. This indicated that stock prices adjust rapidly to the new information. In fact, it appears that prices adjust *prior* to the new information. One might speculate that some of the new information was probably derived from prior quarterly reports.

Effect of Depreciation Changes Archibald examined the market reaction to a change in the depreciation accounting method from a form of accelerated depreciation to a form of straight-line depreciation for financial statement purposes.[26] Because of the change for reporting purposes, all of the 65 firms in the sample experienced an increase in their reported profits over what they otherwise would have reported. Such a change *has no true economic impact.* Therefore, an advocate of an efficient market would hypothesize that no abnormal price changes would accompany the announcement. Those who believe that investors are naive regarding income figures would hypothesize positive abnormal stock price changes consistent with higher reported earnings. The results indicated that the majority of abnormal returns before the accounting change were negative, while abnormal price changes during the 24 months after the change were mixed, with the initial five months after the announcement negative. The author interpreted these results as supporting the efficient markets hypothesis because the stock prices definitely did not move in the direction expected by those who assume investors are naive, but appeared to be reacting to poor earnings performance by these firms.

---

[26] T. Ross Archibald, "Stock Market Reaction to the Depreciation Switch-Back," *Accounting Review,* Vol. 47, No. 1 (January, 1972), pp. 22–30.

Kaplan and Roll examined investor reaction to two accounting changes:[27] (1) the switch in 1964 to the flow-through method of reporting investment credit, and (2) the switch back from reporting accelerated depreciation to reporting straight-line depreciation. Both changes affected only financial statements and had no effect on taxes, cash, or any real economic asset or liability. Using the FFJR market model technique, they examined abnormal stock price movements for the 60 weeks surrounding the announcements. The abnormal price movements were generally negative except for those occurring in the few weeks surrounding the announcements. The authors felt that this indicates that firms making accounting changes are typically performing poorly, as shown by the negative abnormal price changes many weeks prior to the announcement. There apparently is some temporary benefit in the change in accounting technique and the resulting higher reported earnings, as shown during the few weeks around the time of announcement. However, the benefit is temporary and the average negative price changes resumed shortly thereafter and continued to the end of the test period. It appears that such practices are *unsuccessful in permanently affecting stock prices,* which is what one should expect in an efficient capital market.

Effect of Inventory Changes Two studies have examined the effect on stock prices of changes in inventory valuation methods from FIFO (first-in, first-out) to LIFO (last-in, first-out) or vice versa during periods of significant inflation. An extensive study by Shyam Sunder examined 126 firms that changed to LIFO and 29 firms that changed to FIFO during the 21 year period 1946–1966.[28] Two alternative hypotheses were suggested regarding what should happen to stock prices in the period surrounding the announcement of the changes. The naive investor view is that investors rely on reported earnings and, because a change to LIFO will result in a decrease in earnings, stock prices should *decline.* In contrast, if one believes that investors rely on the economic value of the firm, stock prices should *increase* after the change because such a change causes an increase in cash flow (i.e., lower reported earnings cause a reduction in taxes payable, and, therefore, higher cash flow). The expectations were opposite for firms that changed to the FIFO method.

The abnormal price change results derived from a market model that allowed for changes in firm risk over time indicated that the price changes were generally positive for the period prior to the announcement of a change from FIFO to LIFO, and slightly negative for the period after the announcement. The abnormal price changes for the total period were consis-

---

[27] Robert S. Kaplan and Richard Roll, "Investor Evaluation of Accounting Information: Some Empirical Evidence," *Journal of Business,* Vol. 45, No. 2 (April, 1972), pp. 225–257.

[28] Shyam Sunder, "Stock Price and Risk Related to Accounting Changes in Inventory Valuation," *The Accounting Review,* Vol. 50, No. 2 (April, 1975), pp. 305–315.

tently positive. Price changes for firms that changed from LIFO to FIFO were very close to zero. The author felt that these results supported the hypotheses that changes in stock prices are associated with changes in the economic value of the firms rather than with changes in reported earnings.

A study by Reilly, Smith, and Hurt tested the same hypotheses for a sample of 32 firms that changed from FIFO to LIFO during the period 1972–1974.[29] The averages of the abnormal stock price changes for each of the six months prior to the announcements were *always positive*. The averages of the abnormal price changes during the announcement month and the two subsequent months were positive. The results for the following months were generally small negative values. It was concluded that the results supported the efficient market hypothesis because positive price changes are consistent with increases in economic value. In contrast, there is almost no support for the naive reported income hypothesis of negative abnormal price changes.

Stock Prices and Quarterly Earnings Reports A major area of study that does not support the semi-strong efficient market hypothesis relates to the usefulness of quarterly earnings reports. Most studies in this area have been done by Professor H. A. Latané and associates and deal with the usefulness of stock selection models that employed available quarterly data.[30] Although all of these studies suggested that the market is not completely semi-strong efficient as related to quarterly earnings announcements, each of them has a small shortcoming which has been overcome by the most recent study by Joy, Litzenberger, and McEnally (JLM).[31] Therefore, the subsequent discussion concentrates on the latest study by JLM.

Prior studies on the price adjustment to quarterly earnings announcements had typically simply ranked stocks on the basis of their earnings to price ratio (E/P) where E was the latest quarterly earnings and P was the stock price two months after the quarter ended. It was assumed that an investor acquired the stocks with the highest E/P ratio and sold the stocks with the lowest E/P ratio. Analysis of stock price movements over the

---

[29] Frank K. Reilly, Ralph E. Smith, and Ron Hurt, "Stock Market Reaction to Changes in Inventory Valuation Methods," Financial Management Association Meeting, Kansas City, Missouri (October, 1975).

[30] Representative studies in the area are H. A. Latané, D. L. Tuttle, and C. P. Jones, "Quarterly Data: E/P Ratios vs. Changes in Earnings in Forecasting Future Price Changes," *Financial Analysts Journal,* Vol. 25, No. 1 (January–February, 1969), pp. 117–120, 123; H. A. Latané, O. Maurice Joy, and Charles P. Jones, "Quarterly Data, Sort-Rank Routines, and Security Evaluation," *Journal of Business,* Vol. 43, No. 4 (October, 1970), pp. 427–438; C. Jones and R. Litzenberger, "Quarterly Earnings Reports and Intermediate Stock Price Trends," *Journal of Finance,* Vol. 25, No. 1 (March, 1970), pp. 143–148.

[31] O. Maurice Joy, Robert H. Litzenberger, and Richard W. McEnally, "The Adjustment of Stock Prices to Announcements of Unanticipated Changes in Quarterly Earnings," *Journal of Accounting Research,* Vol. 15, No. 2 (Autumn, 1977), pp. 207–225.

subsequent six months typically indicated the high E/P portfolio did better than the market, while the low E/P portfolio experienced inferior performance. Most of these studies did not adjust the results for possible risk differences.

In the study by JLM, the authors selected firms that experience unanticipated changes in quarterly earnings similar to those Ball and Brown used in their annual earnings study, but they also considered different degrees of good and bad earnings. They had two earnings models: (1) the current quarter relative to the same quarter one year earlier, and (2) the current quarter relative to the same quarter a year earlier, assuming earnings growth equal to that attained the prior three quarters. Three categories were established depending on the deviation from expectations. The first is any deviation from expectations (i.e., if actual earnings are above or below expectations it is good or bad irrespective of the deviation). The second category requires the deviation to be plus or minus 20 percent, while the third category requires a 40 percent deviation (earnings must be 40 percent above expectations to be considered "good"). Once the earnings categories were established, the abnormal price changes for the period from 13 weeks prior to the announcement to 26 weeks following it, were analyzed using the FFJR technique to adjust for differential risk relative to the market. The market adjustment procedure differed because the authors adjusted the beta using the Bayesian procedure suggested by Vasicek. Given the adjusted FFJR model, they examined the API (Abnormal Performance Index) for the six groups of stocks (two earnings models, three categories) during the period before and after the announcement.

The results for the two income models and the zero category (any deviation is considered either good or bad), indicated that the abnormal price movement for the good earnings companies was about 1–2 percent during the period. When this is compared to transactions costs of 2–3 percent it indicates that no trading profits are available.

The models with the 20 and 40 percent deviation requirement generated much better results. For the 20 percent above expectations category the postannouncement gain was about 4 percent, compared to 5–6 percent gains for the sample that experienced earnings increases 40 percent above expectations. These abnormal returns would be adequate without information and distribution costs. The price adjustment to unfavorable earnings performance was more rapid and no abnormal returns were possible, irrespective of the category.

An analysis of the cumulative abnormal price index indicated that the postannouncement change was statistically significant for the four models using 20 and 40 percent deviations. Such results suggest that favorable information contained in quarterly earnings reports are not instantaneously reflected in stock prices. Finally, the authors examined whether there is a significant relationship between the size of the unexpected earnings performance and the postannouncement stock price change. The results supported the notion that the price change is influenced by the size of the favorable earnings change.

Price-Earnings Ratios and Returns A study by Basu tested the EMH by examining the relationship between the price-earnings ratios for stocks and the returns on the stocks.[32] Some observers contend that stocks with low price-earnings ratios (p/e ratios) will tend to outperform stocks with high p/e ratios. Apparently there is no well developed reasoning behind this hypothesis, but a belief that growth companies enjoy high p/e's consistent with that growth and possibly the market *overestimates* growth potential and, therefore, *overvalues* the stocks. One might speculate that the market has a tendency to *undervalue* low growth firms that have low p/e ratios. The purpose of the Basu study was to empirically examine whether the investment performance of common stocks is related to their p/e ratios. If there is a definite relationship between the *historical* p/e of a stock and its *subsequent* market performance, this would constitute evidence against the semi-strong efficient market hypothesis because it would imply that one could use available public information (historical p/e's) to generate abnormal returns.

The general methodology was to rank stocks on the basis of their historical p/e ratios and determine the risk and return for portfolios containing high p/e stocks compared to those with low p/e stocks. The p/e ratio for each stock was computed using the market value as of December 31 each year divided by the earnings during the previous year. Although the actual earnings would not be available on December 31, it was contended that by December 31 most analysts are quite certain of the actual earnings. Once a stock is placed into one of five p/e classes it is assumed that an equal amount of each stock *is purchased as of April 1* and held for 12 months with the returns computed for each month.

To evaluate the performance of each of the five portfolios, the author computed average annual returns and alternative measures of risk. The results indicated a significant difference in the level of the p/e for the various portfolios: from about 36 for the high p/e group to less than 10 for the low p/e portfolio. The average annual rates of return were likewise substantially different. The average for the high p/e portfolio was about 9 percent, while the average for the low p/e portfolio exceeded 16 percent and the increase was relatively monotonic. In contrast to what would be expected under capital market theory, *the higher returns on the low p/e portfolios were not associated*

---

[32] S. Basu, "Investment Performance of Common Stocks in Relation to Their Price-Earnings Ratios: A Test of the Efficient Market Hypothesis," *Journal of Finance,* Vol. 32, No. 3 (June, 1977), pp. 663–682. There is a companion article: S. Basu, "The Information Content of Price-Earnings Ratios," *Financial Management,* Vol. 4, No. 2 (Summer, 1975), pp. 53–64.

with higher levels of systematic risk. In fact, the low p/e portfolios had lower risk. When the author employed several composite performance measures that consider return and risk (i.e., the Treynor, Sharpe, and Jensen measures),[33] all the results indicated that the low p/e portfolios experienced *superior* performance relative to the market, while the performance of the high p/e portfolios was significantly *inferior* to the market. The results were tested during the first and second half (1956–1962; 1963–1969) and were found to be consistent. The same tests were carried out assuming realistic taxes. The after-tax results for the low p/e portfolios were reduced slightly, but still indicated consistently superior risk-adjusted returns for the low p/e portfolios.

An analysis of the composite performance measures relative to risk indicated a bias in favor of low risk portfolios.[34] To avoid this apparent bias of the composite performance measures, a number of random portfolios with risk equal to the p/e portfolios were derived. With these equal risk portfolios it is possible to concentrate on the differences in the rates of return. The results indicated that the returns from the high p/e portfolios were consistently *below* the returns from the equal risk random portfolio, while the low p/e portfolio returns were consistently *above* the returns from the equal risk random portfolio (the lowest p/e portfolio return was significantly higher than the return on the random portfolio).

The final analysis considered the potential for investors to derive abnormal profits from this relationship between p/e ratios and rates of return after adjusting for transaction and search costs. Again, there was a comparison of the p/e portfolio and a random portfolio of equal risk. Four classes of investors were considered: (1) tax exempt reallocator, (2) tax paying reallocator, (3) tax exempt trader, and (4) tax paying trader. The difference between the reallocator and trader was that the trader adjusted his total portfolio each year while the reallocator did much less trading. The reallocators who invested in low p/e stocks consistently experienced returns that were 2½–3½ percent above the returns on the random portfolios and the difference was significant. The traders who invested in low p/e stocks also had higher returns, but the returns were not significantly higher.

It appears that publicly available p/e ratios possess information content and should be considered by investors. The fact that the results indicate the ability to use this publicly available information to derive abnormal returns would likewise be considered evidence against the semi-strong efficient market hypothesis.

The great majority of the evidence has supported the semi-strong efficient market hypothesis because the results have indicated that stock prices

---

[33] These portfolio performance measures are discussed in detail in Chapter 22.

[34] This bias is similar to that discussed in Irwin Friend and Marshall Blume, "Measurement of Portfolio Performance Under Uncertainty," *American Economic Review,* Vol. 60, No. 4 (September, 1970), pp. 561–575.

adjust rapidly to the announcement of new information and/or investors are typically not able to derive above average returns from acting on important new information once it is available. The support is *not* unanimous. In several accounting studies, the short-run results were not consistent with expectations although the expected results eventually prevailed. Further, the quarterly earnings results have consistently provided evidence against the hypothesis and the analysis of returns for low p/e stocks likewise did not support it. Finally, some studies that are basically concerned with the strong form hypothesis have results that reflect adversely on the semi-strong form hypothesis. While the *majority* of the evidence supports the hypothesis, more studies should, and obviously will, be conducted in this area.

Strong Form Hypothesis Test Results

The strong form efficient market hypothesis contends that stock prices "fully reflect" *all* information (public and private). Therefore, no group of investors possess information such that they could consistently generate above average profits. As stated, this hypothesis is extremely rigid and requires not only that stock prices must adjust rapidly to new public information, but *also* that no group has monopoly access to specific information. The strong form hypothesis requires that the market adjusts rapidly to new information, but also implies that *all* information is readily available to *all* investors *at the same time*.

The tests of this hypothesis have examined the performance of alternative groups of investors to determine whether an identifiable group has consistently experienced above average risk-adjusted returns. There have been three major groups of investors examined in this regard. First, several studies have analyzed the returns of those possessing inside information by examining the returns experienced by *corporate insiders* in their stock trading. Another group of studies analyzed the returns available to *stock exchange specialists*. The third group of tests examined the overall performance of *professional money managers* with the emphasis on returns generated by mutual funds because of the availability of data.

Corporate Insider Trading Securities laws require that individuals defined as "corporate insiders" report their transactions (purchases or sales) in the stock of the firm for which they are insiders to the SEC each month. Insiders are typically defined as major corporate officers, members of the board of directors, and major stockholders of the firm. About six weeks after the reporting period, this insider trading information is made public by the SEC. Given this information, it has been possible to identify how corporate insiders traded over a period of time and determine whether their transactions were generally profitable; i.e., did they buy on balance before abnormally good price movements and sell on balance prior to poor market periods for their stock? The results of these studies have generally indicated that *corporate insiders consistently enjoyed profits significantly above average.*[35] Corporate insiders consistently had inside information and were able to use this information to derive above average returns on investments in their companies' stocks. These results would be considered evidence against the strong form efficient market hypothesis, which requires that all investors have equal access to information. It appears that corporate insiders have access to valuable information and are able to use it to generate above average profits. The only justification for this finding is that the strong form hypothesis requires more than an efficient market; it requires a *perfect* market in which all participants have equal access to all information. Therefore, this hypothesis requires a perfect *information generating process* and a perfect *information processing* market. In the case of corporate insiders, one would say that insiders have access to valuable information before the public does and, when they act upon this information, they are able to generate above average profits. This is as one would expect in a competitive environment.

In addition to these findings, there is evidence that public investors who consistently traded with the insiders based upon announced insider transactions would have enjoyed returns (after commissions) in excess of those from a simple buy-and-hold policy. This is shown in the Pratt–DeVere study (cited above) in which the authors show results assuming a purchase one, two, three, and four months after the period in which insiders bought or sold. In all cases the returns were superior to market returns. These results are noteworthy because they constitute evidence against the semi-strong efficient market hypothesis. They imply that investors should be able to derive above average returns by simply trading on the basis of available public information (insider transactions).

Stock Exchange Specialists Several studies have examined the function of the stock exchange specialist and determined that specialists have monopolistic access to certain very important information about unfilled limit orders. Therefore, one would expect specialists to derive above average returns from this information. An SEC study found that typically the specialist sells above his last purchase on 83 percent of all his sales, and

---

[35] The major studies on this topic are: James H. Lorie and Victor Niederhoffer, "Predictive and Statistical Properties of Insider Trading," *Journal of Law and Economics,* Vol. 11 (April, 1968), pp. 35–53; Shannon P. Pratt and Charles W. DeVere, "Relationship Between Insider Trading and Rates of Return for NYSE Common Stocks, 1960–1966," included in James Lorie and Richard Brealey, eds., *Modern Developments in Investment Management* (New York: Praeger Publishers, 1972), pp. 268–279; Jeffrey Jaffe, "Special Information and Insider Trading," *Journal of Business,* Vol. 47, No. 3 (July, 1974), pp. 410–428; Joseph E. Finnerty, "Insiders and Market Efficiency," *Journal of Finance,* Vol. 31, No. 4 (September, 1976), pp. 1141–1148; Joseph E. Finnerty, "Insiders Activity and Inside Information: A Multivariate Analysis," *Journal of Financial and Quantitative Analysis,* Vol. 11, No. 2 (June, 1976), pp. 205–215.

buys below his last sale on 81 percent of all his purchases.[36] One would expect such activity to provide above average returns. Niederhoffer and Osborn conducted an extensive analysis of individual transaction data on the NYSE and pointed out that specialists apparently use their access to information about unfilled limit orders to generate excess profits.[37] Further, the extensive Institutional Investor Study (IIS) likewise indicated that the returns derived by specialists were substantially above what one should expect based upon the risk involved.[38] The study indicated that the average return on capital exceeded 100 percent. A study by Reilly and Drzycimski indicated that, following major unexpected world announcements, the typical stock exchange specialist acting *as he is directed,* would have consistently made profits on the trades following such announcements.[39] Assume a specialist bought stocks at the opening following an unfavorable announcement, which would cause most investors to sell, and subsequently sold this accumulation. The specialist consistently would have made a profit on these purchases. He likewise would have made money when he sold stock following favorable announcements.

A study by Reilly and Nielson analyzed the probable experience of specialists with block trades.[40] Assuming a specialist acquired part of a block sale and sold this accumulation during the same day or on the following day, on average, he would have derived a profit. He also would have made a profit, on average, by selling part of a block purchase and reacquiring the stock later. Therefore, while specialists constantly voice concern over being involved in block transactions, it appears that their overall experience in this high risk business is profitable.

Performance of Professional Money Managers The tests of the strong form efficient market hypothesis discussed thus far have been concerned with two small, unique groups of investors who have been able to consistently derive above average returns *because they have monopolistic access to important information and take advantage of it.* The studies dealing with the third group,

---

[36] *Report of the Special Study of the Security Markets* (Washington, D.C.: Securities and Exchange Commission, 1963), Part 2, p. 54.

[37] Victor Niederhoffer and M. F. M. Osborne, "Market-Making and Reversal on the Stock Exchange," *Journal of American Statistical Association,* Vol. 61, No. 316 (December, 1966), pp. 897–916.

[38] U.S. Securities and Exchange Commission, *Institutional Investor Study Report,* 92nd Congress, 1st Session, House Document No. 92–64 (Washington, D.C.: U.S. Government Printing Office, 1971).

[39] Frank K. Reilly and Eugene F. Drzycimski, "The Stock Exchange Specialist and the Market Impact of Major World Events," *Financial Analysts Journal,* Vol. 31, No. 4 (July–August, 1975), pp. 27–32.

[40] Frank K. Reilly and James F. Nielsen, "The Specialist and Large Block Trades on the NYSE," Paper presented at the Southern Finance Association Meeting, Atlanta, Georgia (November, 1974).

professional money managers, are more realistic because one would not expect these investors to have monopolistic access to important new information on a consistent basis. The reasoning behind these studies is that there are highly trained professionals who work full time at investment management and, if any "normal" investors should be able to derive above average profits without inside information, it should be this group. Also, one might speculate that if any noninsider should be able to derive inside information, this is the group that should because professional money managers do extensive management interviews.

While investigators would ideally like to examine the performance of a wide range of money managers, most of the studies have been limited to those involved with mutual funds because data is readily available. It has generally not been possible to analyze performance in other areas, such as bank trust departments, insurance companies, and among investment advisors. Apparently more such data is being made available, but currently it is necessary to extrapolate based upon the performance of mutual funds.

Several studies have examined the performance of a number of mutual funds over extended periods.[41] The results indicated that the majority of the funds were *not* able to match the performance of a buy-and-hold policy. When a large sample of mutual funds was examined in terms of their risk-adjusted rates of return without considering commission costs, slightly more than half did better than the overall market. When commission costs, load fees, and management costs were considered, approximately two-thirds of the mutual funds generally did *not* match the performance of the overall market. In addition, it was found that funds were *not* consistent in their performance. A fund that did well one year could do well the next year, but it was just as likely to be a poor performer. A fund that did better than average two years in a row was no more likely to do well three years in a row than one would expect on the basis of a random chance model. Assuming a .50 probability of doing better than the market, one should expect 25 percent of the funds to outperform the market two years in a row ($.50 \times .50$), and .125 of the funds to do better three years in a row ($.50^3$), etc. This progression is similar to actual findings. A study by Klemkosky examined the consistency in the risk-adjusted performance of a sample of 158 mutual funds at two and four year intervals during the eight year period 1968–1975.[42] Following his analysis he concluded:

---

[41] Notable studies in this area include: William F. Sharpe, "Mutual Fund Performance," *Journal of Business,* Vol. 39, No. 1 (January, 1966 Supplement), pp. 119–139; Michael Jensen, "The Performance of Mutual Funds in the Period 1945–1964," *Journal of Finance,* Vol. 23, No. 2 (May, 1968), pp. 389–416; Jack L. Treynor, "How to Rate Management of Investment Funds," *Harvard Business Review,* Vol. 43, No. 1 (January–February, 1965), pp. 63–75. There is a review of the results of these studies in Chapter 25.

[42] Robert C. Klemkosky, "How Consistently Do Managers Manage?" *Journal of Portfolio Management,* Vol. 3, No. 2 (Winter, 1977), pp. 11–15.

The results of this study indicate that investors should exercise caution in using past relative risk-adjusted performance to predict future relative performance. This is true whether performance was measured relative to other funds or the market. As the evaluation period was expanded, risk-adjusted performance became more consistent. However, the relationships were still not strong enough to make relative predictions with a high degree of certainty.[43]

Therefore, the performance of mutual fund managers supported the strong form efficient market hypothesis. The results indicated that most mutual fund managers, using publicly available information (and anything else available), could not consistently outperform a buy-and-hold policy.

Recently some companies have been collecting performance figures for other institutional investors and the results have been quite consistent with the mutual fund results. A series of articles by Charles Elia in the *Wall Street Journal* has reported the results for various institutions as established by firms that specialize in performance measurement. One article by Elia gave findings compiled by the Frank Russell Co., a Tacoma, Washington firm that analyzes the results for institutions.[44] Judging the findings against the Standard & Poor's 500 stock index showed that the S&P 500 series, adjusted for dividends, was up 38.1 percent in the year ended September 30, 1975. Given 354 investment pools monitored by the firm, only 102 of them could match or exceed the one year performance of the index. The long-run results are shown in Table 7–1 and indicate that none of the groups

Table 7–1
Annual Rates of Return During Periods Ending September 30, 1975

	1 Year	4 Years	8 Years
Bank Equity Pooled Funds	+ 30.3%	− 3.5%	− 0.2%
Insurance Equity Accounts	+ 33.9	− 3.9	− 0.6
Investment Advisors	+ 30.0	− 0.4	a
Bank Special Equity Funds	+ 35.0	− 9.6	a
Growth Mutual Funds	+ 38.8	− 6.0	− 2.5
Balanced and Income Mutual Funds	+ 33.0	− 0.3	+ 2.0
S&P 500	+ 38.1	− 0.3	+ 1.7

a = Not available

outperformed the market during the four year period and only one group did better for the eight year period. Unfortunately, none of the returns are risk-adjusted, which could make some difference. One would expect growth mutual funds and bank special equity funds to be somewhat higher

[43] Ibid., p. 14.

[44] Charles J. Elia, "Institutions Find It Tough to Outperform Index Regardless of Market's Direction," *Wall Street Journal*, November 14, 1975, p. 37.

risk than the S&P 500, while the balanced and income mutual funds would likely be less risky.

In a subsequent article, Elia reported on results obtained by Rogers, Casey, and Barksdale of Stamford, Connecticut for 141 pooled equity funds managed by banks and insurance companies.[45] The median results contained in Table 7–2 indicate clearly that more than half of the funds underperformed the two market series during the four time periods examined because, by definition, results from half the funds are below the median.

Table 7–2
Annual Compound Rate of Return Over Selected Periods (Including Dividends)

	1969–76	1973–76	1975–76	1976
S&P 500	4.1%	1.6%	30.4%	23.8%
DJIA	5.0	4.2	33.5	22.9
Pooled Funds—Median	2.1	−1.2	23.5	19.0

Source: Charles J. Elia, "Most Professionals Lagged Market Average in Past Two Years, Study of Pooled Funds Finds," *Wall Street Journal,* February 28, 1977, p. 1. Reprinted by permission of The Wall Street Journal, © Dow Jones & Company, Inc., 1977. All rights reserved.

As shown, the results tend to indicate that other institutions perform the same as mutual funds, which would lead one to expect their results to be similar to those of the mutual funds, about average or below average with little likelihood of their consistently outperforming the market.

The tests of the strong form efficient market hypothesis generated mixed results, but the bulk of relevant evidence supported the strong form hypothesis. The results for two unique groups of investors (corporate insiders and stock exchange specialists) definitely did not support the hypothesis because both groups apparently have monopolistic access to important information and they use it to derive above average returns. Analysis of performance by professional money managers definitely *supported* the strong form hypothesis. Numerous studies have indicated that these highly-trained, full-time investors could not consistently outperform a simple buy-and-hold policy on a risk-adjusted basis. Because this last group is similar to the bulk of investors who do not have consistent access to inside information, their results are considered most relevant to the hypothesis. Therefore, it is concluded that there is substantial support for the strong form hypothesis as applied to most investors.

Implications of Efficient Capital Markets

Overall, it is safe to conclude that the equity market is generally efficient for the great majority of investors. Because of the substantial and consistent empirical results indicating an efficient market, one who assumes otherwise

---

[45] Charles J. Elia, "Most Professionals Lagged Market Averages in Past Two Years, Study of Pooled Funds Finds," *Wall Street Journal,* February 28, 1977, p. 1.

does so at great risk. This evidence supporting the existence of an efficient equity market makes it important to consider the implication of such a market for those most affected by this efficiency—investment analysts and portfolio managers.

Efficient Markets and Technical Analysis

It is widely recognized that a belief in technical analysis and the notion of efficient markets are directly opposed. A basic premise of technical analysis is that *stock prices move in trends that persist.*[46] Expectations for such a pattern of price movements is based upon the belief that when new information comes to the market, it is *not* immediately available to everyone. Instead, those who advocate technical analysis contend that new information is typically disseminated from the informed professional to the aggressive investing public and then to the great bulk of investors. Also, it is felt that analysis of the information and subsequent action by the various groups is *not* immediate but is spread over time. Given this gradual dissemination of information, and gradual analysis and action, it is hypothesized that the movement of stock prices to a new equilibrium following the release of new information does not occur rapidly, but takes place *over a period of time.* As a result, there are *trends in stock price movements that persist for a period of time.* Technical analysts feel that nimble traders can develop "systems" that help them to detect the beginning of a movement to a new equilibrium. Given some signal indicating the beginning of a movement to a new equilibrium (a "break out"), the technical analyst attempts to buy or sell the stock immediately and thereby take advantage of the remaining price adjustment.

The belief in such a pattern of events is in direct contrast to the efficient market hypothesis which contends that the information dissemination process is quite rapid and, therefore, most interested investors receive new information at about the same time. Advocates of an efficient market contend that the adjustment of security prices to the new information is *very rapid.* It is *not,* however, contended that the price adjustment is perfect. In some cases there will be an overadjustment and in some an underadjustment. Still, because there is nothing certain about whether the market will over or underadjust, it is not possible to consistently derive abnormal profits from the adjustment process.

If the capital market is efficient and prices "fully reflect" all relevant information, any technical trading system that depends only upon past

---

[46] There is an extensive discussion of technical analysis in Chapter 15. The reader is also referred to E. W. Tabell and A. W. Tabell, "The Case for Technical Analysis," *Financial Analysts Journal,* Vol. 20, No. 2 (March–April, 1964), pp. 67–76; and Robert A. Levy "Conceptual Foundations of Technical Analysis," *Financial Analysts Journal,* Vol. 22, No. 4 (July–August, 1966), pp. 83–89.

trading data cannot be of any value because, by the time the information is public, the price adjustment has taken place. Therefore, a purchase or sale using a technical trading rule after information becomes public and after the rapid adjustment in stock prices takes place should not generate above average returns after taking account of commissions.

Efficient Markets and Fundamental Analysis

Advocates of fundamental analysis believe that, at any point in time, there is a basic intrinsic value for the aggregate stock market, and for alternative industries or individual securities, and that this value depends upon underlying economic values. The way to determine the intrinsic value at a point in time is to examine the variables that are supposed to determine value (i.e., current and future earnings and risk variables) and, based upon these variables, derive an estimate of intrinsic value for the aggregate stock market, an industry, or a company. If the prevailing market price differs substantially from intrinsic value (enough to cover transactions cost), appropriate action should be taken—buy if the market price is substantially below the intrinsic value and vice versa. Advocates of fundamental analysis believe that there are instances in which the market price and intrinsic value differ, but they also believe that eventually the market will recognize the discrepancy and correct it. Therefore, if an analyst can do a superior job of estimating intrinsic value, he can consistently acquire undervalued securities and derive above average returns. The following sections deal with the implications of efficient markets on various subcategories of fundamental analysis: aggregate market analysis, industry analysis, company analysis, and portfolio management.

Efficient Markets and Economic Market Analysis

Based upon the work done by Benjamin King and others, it is possible to make a fairly strong case that intrinsic value analysis should begin with a consideration of aggregate market analysis.[47] At the same time, the efficient markets hypothesis implies that if analysis is limited to individual past economic events, it is unlikely the analyst will be able to beat a buy-and-hold policy. This is supported by the findings of the Reilly–Drzycimski study on world events which indicated that the market adjusts very rapidly to individual world events.[48] Still, there is evidence that stock

---

[47] Benjamin F. King, "Market and Industry Factors in Stock Price Behavior," *Journal of Business,* Vol. 39, No. 1 (January, 1966 Supplement), pp. 139–190. Such an approach is also advocated in Frank K. Reilly, "Our Misdirected Emphasis in Security Valuation," *Financial Analysts Journal,* Vol. 29, No. 1 (January–February, 1973), pp. 54–57. There is a detailed discussion of this approach in Chapter 9.

[48] Frank K. Reilly and Eugene F. Drzycimski, "Tests of Stock Market Efficiency."

prices experience long-run movements over time.[49] The fact that these trends exist makes any attempt to project them worthwhile. The efficient market hypothesis indicates that the projection cannot depend only upon past data; there must be a *projection* of the variables that influence the overall economy and the aggregate stock market. An investment based upon a model using only available economic data should not do better than a buy-and-hold policy.

Hence aggregate market analysis is important and can be financially rewarding, but *it is not easy.* Successful market projections require knowledge of the important variables that affect market movements, and a superior *projection* of movements of the crucial variables.

Efficient Markets and Industry and Security Analysis

An examination of alternative industry returns, or returns on individual stocks, indicates a wide distribution. Therefore, industry and stock analysis should be of value because it is important to separate industries and stocks that are in the upper portion of the distribution of returns from those in the lower segment.[50] Again, though, the EMH implies that is it necessary to understand the variables that determine stock prices, but it is also mandatory to project movements in these valuation variables. A study by Malkiel and Cragg developed a model that did an excellent job of explaining past stock price movements for individual stocks employing past company data.[51] However, when they attempted to employ this model to project future stock price changes, still using past company data, the results were consistently inferior to results from a buy-and-hold policy. This implies that, even with a properly specified valuation model, it is not possible to select stocks using only past data.

Another bit of evidence regarding the necessity for accurately projecting future earnings is derived from a study by Niederhoffer and Regan.[52] They showed that the crucial difference between the stocks that enjoyed the best price performance during a given year and the stocks that experienced the worst price performance was the relationship between *estimated* earnings and *actual* earnings. The stock with the best price performance had actual

---

[49] Julius Shiskin, "Systematic Aspects of Stock Price Fluctuations," James Lorie and Richard Brealey, eds., *Modern Developments in Investment Management* (New York: Praeger Publishers, 1972), pp. 670–688.

[50] A study that examines the distribution of industry returns and reviews past studies is Frank K. Reilly and Eugene F. Drzycimski, "Alternative Industry Performance and Risk," *Journal of Financial and Quantitative Analysis,* Vol. 9, No. 3 (June, 1974), pp. 423–446.

[51] Burton G. Malkiel and John G. Cragg, "Expectations and the Structure of Share Prices," *American Economic Review,* Vol. 60, No. 4 (September, 1970), pp. 601–617.

[52] Victor Niederhoffer and Patrick J. Regan, "Earnings Changes, Analysts Forecast, and Stock Prices," *Financial Analysts Journal,* Vol. 28, No. 3 (May–June, 1972), pp. 65–71.

earnings results substantially above the estimated earnings while the stocks with the worst price performance were companies for which the earnings estimates were substantially above actual earnings. Therefore, if an analyst can do a superior job of projecting earnings, he can likely achieve a superior stock selection record. Hence, this study indicates that an important factor is the ability to estimate earnings and also to estimate future changes in the stock's earnings multiple.

Theory and evidence both indicate that is is not impossible to be a superior analyst, but it is very difficult to be consistently superior.[53] An analyst must understand what variables are relevant for changes in valuation and must be able to consistently estimate future values for these variables to be consistently superior. Most analysts can recognize the relevant variables for an individual stock, and most can estimate future values for *some* of these variables for *some* stocks *some* of the time. The difficulty comes in doing this consistently for a number of different stocks. These requirements led Fama to suggest a system for evaluating the performance of analysts.[54]

Evaluating the Performance of Analysts

A survey of practicing security analysts would probably indicate that about 98 percent of them feel that they are "superior," while the other 2 percent feel they are about average. Not everyone can be superior, as the empirical results for professional money managers discussed earlier show. To determine who the superior analysts are, the following relatively simple evaluation system was suggested. Examine the performance of numerous buy and sell recommendations made by an analyst over time relative to the performance of randomly selected stocks *of the same risk class*. The test is whether an analyst can consistently outperform random selection. If the analyst produces results that are *consistently* better than those produced by random selection, he is a superior analyst. The consistency requirement is crucial because one would expect securities chosen by random selection to outperform the market about half the time.

A text on security valuation can indicate the relevant variables to analyze, why these variables are relevant, and point out the important techniques to consider when attempting to project the relevant valuation variables, but the task of deriving the actual estimate is as much an art as it is a science. If the estimates of valuation variables were mechanical, it

---

[53] A much harder line in this regard is taken in Fischer Black, "Implications of the Random Walk Hypothesis for Portfolio Management," *Financial Analysts Journal*, Vol. 27, No. 2 (March–April, 1971), pp. 16–22. Professor Black basically contends that it is virtually impossible to consistently do better than buy-and-hold, especially if one considers the cost of research.

[54] Eugene F. Fama, "Random Walks in Stock Market Prices," *Financial Analysts Journal*, Vol. 21, No. 5 (September–October, 1965), pp. 55–58.

would be possible to program a computer to carry out the function and there would be no need for analysts. Therefore, the superior analyst must understand what is important and have the ability to *estimate* these variables.

Efficient Markets and Portfolio Analysis

Prior studies have consistently indicated that the performance of professional money managers does not consistently exceed a simple buy-and-hold policy on a risk-adjusted basis. One explanation of this is that there are no superior analysts and the cost of research produces these inferior results. Another explanation (favored by the author with no empirical support) is that institutions employ superior and inferior analysts and the average, or inferior, performance is caused by the fact that recommendations of the few superior analysts are offset by the costs and recommendations of the inferior analysts.

Portfolio Management Without Superior Analysts

Recent work in the area of portfolio management has shown that there are ways of increasing profits within a given portfolio even though a manager is dependent upon nonsuperior analysts. The area of portfolio analysis has experienced several significant advances over the past decade that have been heavily dependent upon the existence of efficient capital markets. Work by Markowitz indicated that, in terms of risk, an individual stock's covariance with all other stocks in a portfolio was of crucial importance.[55] It was shown by Sharpe and others that, assuming a risk-free asset and the existence of a market portfolio of risky assets, the relevant risk measure was the stock's systematic risk with the market portfolio.[56] A study by Blume indicated that systematic risk measures were fairly stable over time which would indicate that they could be of value in portfolio construction.[57] Sharpe and Cooper confirmed the Blume results, especially for portfolios of stocks and also indicated that there was a relatively good relationship between the returns for a portfolio of stocks in period t, and risk measures in the previous period.[58] These findings indicate that it is possible to build a portfolio of stocks that will conform to the risk preferences of a portfolio manager's clientele *using available historical risk information.* In addition, one should expect to receive a rate of return that is fairly consistent with the risk

---

[55] Harry Markowitz, *Portfolio Selection: Efficient Diversification of Investments* (New York: John Wiley and Sons, Inc., 1959).

[56] William F. Sharpe, "Capital Asset Prices: Theory of Market Equilibrium Under Conditions of Risk," *Journal of Finance,* Vol. 19, No. 3 (September, 1964), pp. 425–442.

[57] Marshall E. Blume, "On the Assessment of Risk," *Journal of Finance,* Vol. 26, No. 1 (March, 1971), pp. 1–10.

[58] William F. Sharpe and Guy M. Cooper, "Risk-Return Classes of New York Stock Exchange Common Stocks, 1931–1967," *Financial Analysts Journal,* Vol. 28, No. 2 (March–April, 1972), pp. 46–54, 81.

level specified. This selection process does not appear to require extensive research efforts. Therefore, assuming that a portfolio manager recognized that he did not have any superior analysts, one can conceive of how the portfolio should be managed in a world with efficient capital markets to provide maximum risk-adjusted returns for the client.

The major points of this process have been outlined by Lorie and Hamilton.[59] First, the major efforts of the portfolio manager should be directed toward determining, and attempting to measure, the risk preferences of his clientele. Managers tend to transmit their risk preferences to the clients without recognizing that the existence of other investments by the client may influence the client's preferences for a particular portfolio. Therefore, subjective discussions of risk must be transformed into useful quantitative measures which can be used to determine a client's risk preference in terms of the capital asset pricing model (i.e. a model used to measure the risk of an asset based on its covariance with the market portfolio of risky assets).

Once the client's risk preferences are quantified, the second function is to derive a given risk portfolio by investing a certain proportion of the wealth available into a well diversified portfolio of risky assets and the rest into a risk-free asset.[60] Therefore, the second task of the portfolio manager is to construct a portfolio that conforms to the client's quantified risk preferences by combining a portfolio of risk-free assets with a diversified portfolio of risky assets.

The third task is to ensure that the risky asset portfolio is *completely diversified* so that it moves consistently with the aggregate market. The need for complete diversification has been emphasized in an article by Lorie that points out the uncertainty present when there is only 90–95 percent diversification.[61]

If one assumes that the portfolio manager is not capable of predicting future market movements, the fourth task is to *maintain the specified risk level* rather than attempting to change the risk of the portfolio based upon market expectations, i.e., shift to a high risk portfolio during a period when a bull market is projected or change to a defensive portfolio if a bear market is expected. Because of changing market values there will be some change in the risk of a portfolio, so it is necessary to occasionally trade to return to the desired balance.

Finally, it is important to *minimize transaction costs*. Assuming that the portfolio is completely diversified and that past relations between risk and return hold over the long-run, a major deterrent to the client receiving the

---

[59] James Lorie and Mary T. Hamilton, *The Stock Market* (Homewood, Illinois: Richard D. Irwin, Inc., 1973), pp. 105–108.

[60] There will be a detailed discussion of this in Chapters 8 and 19.

[61] James H. Lorie, "Diversification: Old and New," *The Journal of Portfolio Management*, Vol. 1, No. 2 (Winter, 1975), pp. 25–28.

expected return would be excessive transactions costs that do not generate added returns. There are three factors involved in minimizing total transaction costs.[62] One is *minimizing taxes* for the client. How this is accomplished will vary, but it should be given prime consideration when carrying out transactions. The second factor seems rather obvious, *reduce trading turnover to the level necessitated by liquidity needs and risk control* (trades needed to maintain a given risk level). Finally, when trades are made, the portfolio manager should attempt to *minimize the liquidity costs of the trade.* There will typically be a number of stocks available that will accomplish the goal. The stocks used should be those that have low trading costs, but that are also relatively *liquid* so that the trade will have little effect on the price of the stock. To accomplish this, orders to buy or sell several stocks should be submitted at net prices that approximate the specialist's quote (i.e., limit order to buy at bid or sell at ask). The stock that is bought or sold first is the one that meets your criteria and all other orders are withdrawn.

If a portfolio manager does not have any superior analysts he should do the following:

1. Determine the risk preferences of his client and quantify these preferences to be consistent with the capital asset pricing model.

2. Given the risk preferences of the client, divide the total portfolio between a portfolio of risk-free assets and one of risky assets.

3. Be sure the portfolio of risky assets is completely diversified so that returns are closely related to returns for a market portfolio of risky assets.

4. Maintain the specified risk level rather than attempting to shift the risk to conform to expected market movements.

5. Minimize total transactions costs by:
   a. minimizing taxes
   b. reducing turnover; only trade for liquidity and to maintain the desired risk level
   c. minimizing liquidity costs by buying and selling currently liquid stocks as determined by the market.

Index Funds

The discussion above indicates that, if one assumes that there are efficient capital markets and only a limited number of truly superior analysts, a large amount of money should be managed so that the performance simply matches that achieved by the aggregate market and costs are minimized so as not to drop below the market. In response to such an apparent need, three institutions instigated "market funds," also referred to as "index funds,"

---

[62] These factors are discussed in Fischer Black, "Can Portfolio Managers Outrun the Random Walkers?" *Journal of Portfolio Management,* Vol. 1, No. 1 (Fall, 1974), pp. 32–36.

during the early 1970's. Index funds are security portfolios specially designed to duplicate the performance of the overall security market as represented by some selected market index series. Three major funds were started in the early 1970's: (1) American National Bank and Trust Company of Chicago, (2) Batterymarch Financial Management Corporation of Boston, and (3) Wells Fargo Investment Advisors, a division of Wells Fargo Bank in San Francisco. In all cases, these equity portfolios were designed to match the performance of the S&P 500 Index.

The initial history of the funds (1973–1976) was rather quiet but was accompanied by slow growth. A 1976 article in *Fortune* clearly spelled out the reasoning behind index funds and the justification for their existence.[63] An article by Langbein and Posner described in detail the reasoning behind the funds and indicated the legal justification for trust accounts investing in, or establishing, index funds.[64] As a result of these and similar articles, client demand grew and a number of financial institutions that had previously ignored or made adverse comments about index funds established their own. By the end of 1976, index funds were well established and it was almost necessary to justify why a money manager was not in an index fund with at least part of a client's total portfolio.[65]

The reason these funds became popular was a growing belief in efficient capital markets and a recognition that most portfolio managers had not consistently done as well as the aggregate market. Consequently, the intent of index funds was basically to carry out the suggestions made for portfolio management without superior analysts: match returns and minimize research and transactions costs.[66] The ability of the three major index funds to match the market can be seen from the figures in Table 7–3. These quarterly figures for the period 1974–1977 indicate that the correlation among quarterly rates of returns generally exceeded .99. Therefore, it appears that the funds generally are able to fulfill their stated goal of matching market performance.

Portfolio Management with Superior Analysts
If a portfolio manager has superior security analysts with unique insights and analytical ability, they should obviously be utilized. The problem is recognizing the superior analysts and utilizing them, while being able to

---

[63] A. F. Ehrbar, "Index Funds—An Idea Whose Time is Coming," *Fortune* (June, 1976), pp. 145–148.

[64] John H. Langbein and Richard A. Posner, "Market Funds and Trust-Investment Law," *American Bar Foundation Research Journal,* Vol. 1976, No. 1, pp. 1–34.

[65] Charles J. Elia, "Wall Street's New Fad Has People Watching Stock Market Scales," *Wall Street Journal,* March 21, 1977, p. 1.

[66] For further discussion of the advantages and some experiences see "Money Management: Wall Street Goes Slow," *Business Week,* October 11, 1976, pp. 100–104; "Why Money Managers Like the Index Funds," *Business Week,* December 20, 1976, pp. 54–55; and "Fidelities Experiment with Index Funds," *Business Week,* February 14, 1977, p. 107.

Table 7-3
Quarterly Returns for Index Funds and S&P 500: 1974-1977

Qtr./yr.	American National Bank	Battery-march Financial	Wells Fargo	S&P 500
1/74	− 2.80		− 2.92	− 2.81
2/74	− 7.43		− 7.90	− 7.54
3/74	−25.62		−25.11	−25.05
4/74	9.04		9.13	9.41
Year	−27.02		−26.93	−26.03
1/75	23.40	21.3	22.56	22.90
2/75	15.67	14.9	15.24	15.31
3/75	−11.12	−11.0	−10.95	−10.93
4/75	8.64	8.7	8.76	8.64
Year	37.65	34.8	36.36	36.92
1/76	14.89	14.8	14.82	14.96
2/76	2.67	2.8	2.53	2.44
3/76	2.06	1.8	1.71	1.89
4/76	2.11	2.2	3.24	3.18
Year	22.93	22.8	23.63	23.64
1/77	− 8.16	− 7.4	− 7.50	− 7.44
2/77	3.07	3.2	3.31	3.28
3/77	− 2.88	2.8	− 2.77	− 2.80
4/77	− 0.09	− 0.3	− 0.11	− 0.13
Year	− 8.15	− 7.4	− 7.19	− 7.17

Source: Standard & Poor's. Reprinted by permission.

avoid the costs entailed by using inferior analysts. The system suggested earlier should be utilized to determine the truly superior analysts and updated to ensure that they are continuing to be superior. Assuming that several superior analysts are present, the portfolio manager would allow each of them to make investment recommendations for a certain proportion of the portfolio, ensuring that their recommendations are implemented in a way that would maintain the risk preferences of the client. It is also recommended that superior analysts be encouraged to *concentrate their efforts in the second tier of stocks.* Recall that, in the chapter on changes in the capital markets, there was reference to a three tier market created by the need of institutions for large liquid securities. In the article by Reilly it was suggested that the tiered market could be divided into three tiers as follows:[67]

---

[67] Frank K. Reilly, "A Three Tier Stock Market and Corporate Finance," *Financial Management,* Vol. 4, No. 3 (Autumn, 1975), pp. 7-15.

1. Top Tier—companies large enough to accomodate *all* institutions wishing to establish a meaningful position and yet retain liquidity. Assuming it was necessary to have a market value of 400 million dollars or more to be in this tier, approximately 400 firms would meet this criterion.

2. Middle Tier—companies large enough to be acquired by most institutions and large investors, although probably *not* the largest 25–30 institutions. It was reasoned that this tier required a market value of 200 million dollars and an additional 300 companies were estimated to be in this tier.

3. Bottom Tier—all remaining companies not large enough to be considered by insitutions. The total number of public companies in this tier is at least 5,000, and could be over 8,000.

Analysts should be encouraged to concentrate their analytical skills on middle tier firms because these stocks probably possess the required liquidity, but they do not receive the attention given the top tier stocks, so the markets may not be as efficient. Recall that, in the initial discussion of why one should expect markets to be efficient, it was contended that prices would "fully reflect" all information because many investors were receiving the news and analyzing the effect of the new information on security values. If there is a difference in the number of analysts following a stock, one could conceive of differences in the efficiency of the markets. In the case of top tier stocks, it is well recognized that all new information regarding the stock is well publicized and numerous analysts evaluate the effect. Therefore, one should expect the price to adjust rapidly and fully reflect the information. News about middle tier firms is not as well publicized and few analysts follow some of these firms. Therefore, prices may not adjust as rapidly to new information and it would be worthwhile to concentrate analytical skills on these stocks for which the probabilities of finding a temporarily undervalued security are greater. This lack of attention paid to small firms is *increasing* as the number of analysts on Wall Street declines. An article in *The Wall Street Journal* that discussed mergers on Wall Street and the resulting layoff of analysts noted that this decline in analysts affected the number of companies followed.[68] With fewer analysts, fewer companies can be followed and the ones eliminated are small firms that are of limited interest to large institutional customers.

The remainder of the portfolio (probably the majority) would be similar to that created by a portfolio manager without superior analysts. The resulting overall performance of the portfolio should be superior to the average market performance, assuming the superior analysts were not paid

---

[68] Tom Herman, "For Highly Qualified, Wall Street Job Market is Increasingly Gloomy," *Wall Street Journal,* April 20, 1978, p. 1.

too much; i.e., their pay should not exceed the value of their recommendations.

Summary

Efficient capital markets were considered at this point because there are several very important implications that one can derive from the existence of efficient capital markets which have a direct bearing on security analysis and portfolio management.

One should expect capital markets to be efficient mainly because there are a large number of rational profit maximizing investors who react quickly to the release of new information. Because investors adjust prices rapidly to reflect new information, stock prices at any point in time are an unbiased estimate of their true intrinsic value. Therefore, in an efficient capital market, stock prices "fully reflect" all relevant information and are an unbiased estimate of the true equilibrium value for the security. Hence, there is a consistent relationship between return and risk.

Because of the voluminous research on the EMH, the overall hypothesis has been divided into three segments and each has been tested separately. The weak form efficient market hypothesis states that stock prices fully reflect all market information. Any trading rule that uses past market data to predict future returns should not be of value in this context. The tests employed were pure statistical tests of independence (serial correlation tests and "runs" tests) and specific tests of technical trading rules that compared market data to buy-and-hold policies. The results consistently supported the weak form EMH.

The semi-strong efficient market hypothesis asserts that security prices adjust rapidly to the release of all public information and, therefore, price fully reflects all such information. The tests involved the detailed examination of abnormal price movements surrounding the announcement of important new information and an analysis of whether investors could derive above average returns from trading on the basis of the information. Although the majority of the results supported the hypothesis, they were not unanimous. Some of the price adjustments to accounting changes were questionable and several studies have indicated that the adjustment to quarterly earnings reports is certainly not instantaneous. A study of low p/e stocks versus high p/e stocks indicated that there was an opportunity to derive abnormal returns from investing in low p/e stocks. Finally, several studies that examined the investment performance of corporate insiders indicated that the insiders enjoy above average returns, but also indicate that other investors could likewise benefit from information on these transactions when it becomes public.

The strong form efficient markets hypothesis states that security prices reflect all information. Therefore, no group of investors has monopolistic access to important information, and, therefore, no group should be able to consistently derive above average returns. The analysis of returns to corporate insiders and stock exchange specialists did not support the strong form hypothesis. Apparently, both groups possess inside information and make use of it. In contrast, an analysis of results achieved by professional money managers supported the hypothesis because their performance was typically inferior to that achieved with buy-and-hold policies.

The implications for a number of major participants in the equity market, including technical analysts, fundamentalists, and portfolio managers were discussed. Support for the efficient markets hypothesis indicates that technical analysis alone or used in conjunction with intrinsic value analysis should be of no value. Although aggregate market analysis is important and useful, it is also difficult to perform because it requires the ability to *estimate future values* for relevant economic variables.

The results imply that it is possible to be a superior analyst, but it is also very difficult because one must be able to predict future values for relevant variables. Again, stock selection models that employ only historical data should not do better than the results achieved from buy-and-hold because market prices adjust rapidly to available information. Superior analysts must consistently make superior selection, adjusted for risk differences.

Finally, portfolio managers without superior analysts should develop portfolios that are consistent with the risk preferences of their clients, develop a completely diversified risky asset portfolio, and attempt to minimize total transactions costs. During the last several years index funds have been developed that fulfill these requirements. If the portfolio manager is fortunate enough to employ truly superior analysts, his objective should be to manage most of the portfolio so as to attain a position above average market performance. The superior analysts, in order to gain some slight superiority with a portion of the portfolio, should analyze securities in the middle tier where the probability of finding misvalued stocks is higher.

There is some good news and some bad news. The good news is that the practice of security analysis and portfolio management is not an art that has been lost to the great computer in the sky. These are still viable professions for those willing to extend the effort and able to accept the pressures.

The bad news is that, because of the existence of many bright, hard-working people with extensive resources, the game is not easy. In fact, the aforementioned competitors have created a very efficient capital market in which it is very difficult to be superior.

Hopefully, forewarned is forearmed!

Questions

1. Discuss the rationale for expecting the existence of an efficient capital market.

2. Define and discuss the weak form efficient market hypothesis (EMH).

3. Describe the two sets of tests used to examine the weak form efficient market hypothesis.

4. Define and discuss the semi-strong efficient market hypothesis.

5. Describe the two general tests used to examine the semi-strong EMH. Would you expect the results from the two different tests to be consistent? Why?

6. Describe the results of a study that supported the semi-strong EMH and specifically discuss why the results supported the hypothesis.

7. Describe the results of a study that did not support the semi-strong EMH and specifically discuss why the results did not support the hypothesis.

8. Define and discuss the strong form EMH. Why do some observers contend that the strong form hypothesis really requires a perfect market in addition to efficient markets. Be specific.

9. Discuss in general terms how one would go about testing the strong form EMH. Consider why these tests are relevant. Give a brief example.

10. Describe the results of a study that does not support the strong form EMH. Discuss specifically why these results do not support the hypothesis.

11. Describe the results of a study that indicates support for the strong form EMH. Discuss specifically why these results support the hypothesis.

12. What are the implications of the EMH for the use of technical analysis?

13. What are the implications of the EMH for fundamental analysis? Be specific and discuss what the EMH does imply and what it does not imply.

14. In a world with efficient capital markets, what is required in order to be a superior analyst? Be specific.

15. How would you determine whether an analyst was truly superior? Be very specific in discussing the test.

16. What are the implications of an efficient market for a portfolio manager without any superior analysts? Specifically, what should he do; how should he run his portfolio?

17. What are the implications of an efficient market for a portfolio manager with two superior analysts and four "average" analysts? What should he do with his portfolio? Be specific.

18. Do you think the development of a tiered market has any implications for the discussion of efficient capital markets? If so, what are they?

19. When testing the EMH by using alternative trading rules versus a buy-and-hold policy, there are three common mistakes that can bias the results against the EMH. Discuss each individually and explain why it would cause a bias.

20. It is contended by some observers that index funds are the ultimate answer in a world with efficient capital markets. Discuss the purpose of index funds and what they do that is correct in a world with ECM's.

References

Alexander, Sidney S. "Price Movements in Speculative Markets: Trends or Random Walks." *Industrial Management Review,* Vol. 2, No. 2 (May, 1961).

Alexander, Sidney S. "Price Movements in Speculative Markets: Trends or Random Walks, Number 2." *Industrial Management Review,* Vol. 5 (Spring, 1964).

Archibald, T. Ross. "Stock Market Reaction to the Depreciation Switch-Back." *Accounting Review,* Vol. 47, No. 1 (January, 1972).

Ball, Ray. "Changes in Accounting Techniques and Stock Prices." *Empirical Research in Accounting* (Supplement to *Journal of Accounting Research*, Vol. 10, 1972).

Ball, Ray. "Risk, Return, and Disequilibrium—An Application to Changes in Accounting Techniques." *Journal of Finance,* Vol. 27, No. 2 (May, 1972).

Basu, S. "The Information Content of Price-Earnings Ratios." *Financial Management,* Vol. 4, No. 2 (Summer, 1975).

Basu, S. "Investment Performance of Common Stocks in Relation to Their Price-Earnings Ratios: A Test of the Efficient Market Hypothesis." *Journal of Finance,* Vol. 32, No. 3 (June, 1977).

Black, Fisher. "Can Portfolio Managers Outrun the Random Walkers?" *Journal of Portfolio Management,* Vol. 1, No. 1 (Fall, 1974).

Black, Fisher. "Implications of the Random Walk Hypothesis for Portfolio Management." *Financial Analysts Journal,* Vol. 27, No. 2 (March–April, 1971).

Brown, Phillip and Ball, Ray. "An Empirical Evaluation of Accounting Income Numbers." *Journal of Accounting Research,* Vol. 6 (Autumn, 1963).

Brown, Stewart L. "Earnings Changes, Stock Prices, and Market Efficiency." *Journal of Finance,* Vol. 33, No. 1 (March, 1978).

Carey, Kenneth. "A Model of Individual Transactions Stock Prices." Unpublished Ph.D. dissertation, University of Kansas, 1971.

Ehrbar, A. F. "Index Funds—An Idea Whose Timing is Coming." *Fortune* (June, 1976).

Elia, Charles J. "Institutions Find It Tough to Outperform Index Regardless of Market's Direction." *Wall Street Journal,* November 14, 1975.

Elia, Charles J. "Most Professionals Lagged Market Averages in Past Two Years, Study of Pooled Funds." *Wall Street Journal,* February 28, 1977.

Elia, Charles J. "Wall Street's New Fad Has People Watching Stock Market Scales," March 21, 1977.

Fama, Eugene F. "The Behavior of Stock Prices." *Journal of Business,* Vol. 38, No. 1 (January, 1965).

Fama, Eugene F. "Efficient Capital Markets: A Review of Theory and Empirical Work." *Journal of Finance,* Vol. 25, No. 2 (May, 1970).

Fama, Eugene F. "Random Walks in Stock Market Prices." *Financial Analysts Journal,* Vol. 21, No. 5 (September–October, 1965).

Fama, Eugene F. and Blume, Marshall. "Filter Rules and Stock Market Trading Profits." *Journal of Business,* Vol. 39, No. 1 (January, 1966 Supplement).

Fama, Eugene F., Fisher, L., Jensen, M., and Roll, R. "The Adjustment of Stock Prices to New Information." *International Economic Review,* Vol. 10, No. 1 (February, 1969).

"Fidelities Experiment with Index Funds." *Business Week,* February 14, 1977.

Finnerty, Joseph E. "Insiders Activity and Inside Information: A Multivariate Analysis." *Journal of Financial and Quantitative Analysis,* Vol. 11, No. 2 (June, 1976).

Finnerty, Joseph E. "Insiders and Market Efficiency." *Journal of Finance,* Vol. 31, No. 4 (September, 1976).

Firth, Michael. "The Impact of Earnings Announcements on the Share Price Behavior of Similar Type Firms." *The Economic Journal* (June, 1976).

Foster, G. "Stock Market Reaction to Estimates of Earnings Per Share by Company Officials." *Journal of Accounting Research,* Vol. 11, No. 1 (Spring, 1973).

Furst, Richard W. "Does Listing Increase the Market Price of Common Stocks?" *Journal of Business,* Vol. 43, No. 2 (April, 1970).

Goulet, Waldemar M. "Price Changes, Managerial Actions and Insider Trading at the Time of Listing." *Financial Management,* Vol. 3, No. 1 (Spring, 1974).

Hagerman, Robert L. and Richmond, Richard D. "Random Walk Martingales and the OTC." *Journal of Finance,* Vol. 28, No. 4 (September, 1973).

Hausman, W. H., West, R. R., and Largay, J. A. "Stock Splits, Price Changes, and Trading Profits: A Synthesis." *Journal of Business,* Vol. 44, No. 1 (January, 1971).

Herman, Tom. "For Highly Qualified, Wall Street Job Market is Increasingly Gloomy." *Wall Street Journal,* April 20, 1978.

Ibbotson, Roger G. "Price Performance of Common Stock New Issues." *Journal of Financial Economics,* Vol. 2, No. 3 (September, 1975).

Jaffe, Jeffrey. "Special Information and Insider Trading." *Journal of Business,* Vol. 47, No. 3 (July, 1974).

Jensen, Michael. "The Performance of Mutual Funds in the Period 1945–64." *Journal of Finance,* Vol. 23, No. 2 (May, 1968).

Jones, C. and Litzenberger, R. "Quarterly Earnings Reports and Intermediate Stock Price Trends." *Journal of Finance,* Vol. 25, No. 1 (March, 1970).

Jordan, Ronald J. "An Empirical Investigation of the Adjustment of Stock Prices to New Quarterly Earnings Information." *Journal of Financial and Quantitative Analysis,* Vol. 8, No. 4 (September, 1973).

Joy, O. Maurice, Litzenberger, Robert H., and McEnally, Richard W. "The Adjustment of Stock Prices to the Announcements of Unanticipated Changes in Quarterly Earnings." *Journal of Accounting Research,* Vol. 15, No. 2 (Autumn, 1977).

Kaplan, Robert S. and Roll, Richard. "Investor Evaluation of Accounting Information: Some Empirical Evidence." *Journal of Business,* Vol. 45, No. 2 (April, 1972).

Kendall, Maurice G. "The Analysis of Economic Time Series." *Journal of the Royal Statistical Society,* Vol. 96 (1953).

Kiger, J. E. "An Empirical Investigation of NYSE Volume and Price Reactions to the Announcement of Quarterly Earnings." *Journal of Accounting Research,* Vol. 10, No. 1 (Spring, 1972).

Langbein, John H. and Posner, Richard A. "Market Funds and Trust-Investment Law." *American Bar Foundation Research Journal,* Vol. 1976, No. 1.

Latane, H. A., Joy, O. Maurice, and Jones, Charles P. "Quarterly Data Sort-Rank Routines, and Security Evaluation." *Journal of Business,* Vol. 43, No. 4 (October, 1970).

Latane, H. A., Tuttle, D. L., and Jones, C. P. "Quarterly Data: E/P Ratios vs. Changes in Earnings in Forecasting Future Price Changes." *Financial Analysts Journal,* Vol. 25, No. 1 (January–February, 1969).

Levy, Robert A. "Conceptual Foundations of Technical Analysis," *Financial Analysts Journal,* Vol. 22, No. 4 (July–August, 1966).

Loque, Dennis E. "On the Pricing of Unseasoned New Issues, 1965–1969." *Journal of Financial and Quantitative Analysis,* Vol. 8, No. 1 (January, 1973).

Lorie, James H. and Niederhoffer, Victor. "Predictive and Statistical Properties of Insider Trading." *Journal of Law and Economics,* Vol. 11 (April, 1968).

McDonald, J. G. and Fisher, A. K. "New Issue Stock Price Behavior." *Journal of Finance,* Vol. 27, No. 1 (March, 1972).

Moore, Arnold. "A Statistical Analysis of Common Stock Prices." Unpublished Ph.D. dissertation, Graduate School of Business, University of Chicago, 1962.

Neuberger, Brian M. and Hammond, Carl T. "A Study of Underwriters' Experience with Unseasoned New Issues." *Journal of Financial and Quantitative Analysis,* Vol. 9, No. 2 (March, 1974).

Niederhoffer, Victor and Osborne, M. F. M. "Market Making and Reversal on the Stock Exchange." *Journal of American Statistical Association,* Vol. 61, No. 316 (December, 1966).

Pettit, R. Richardson. "Dividend Announcements, Security Performance, and Capital Market Efficiency." *Journal of Finance,* Vol. 27, No. 5 (December, 1972).

Pinches, George. "The Random Walk Hypothesis and Technical Analysis." *Financial Analysts Journal,* Vol. 26, No. 2 (March–April, 1970).

Pinches, George and Singleton, J. Clay. "The Adjustment of Stock Prices to Bond Rating Changes." *Journal of Finance,* Vol. 33, No. 1 (March, 1978).

Pratt, Shannon P. and DeVere, Charles W. "Relationship Between Insider Trading and Rates of Return on NYSE Common Stocks, 1960–66." In James Lorie and Robert Brealey, eds. *Modern Developments in Investment Management.* New York: Praeger Publishers, 1972.

Reilly, Frank K. "Further Evidence on Short-Run Results for New Issue Investors." *Journal of Financial and Quantitative Analysis,* Vol. 8, No. 1 (January, 1973).

Reilly, Frank K. "New Issues Revisited." *Financial Management,* Vol. 6, No. 4 (Winter, 1977).

Reilly, Frank K. and Drzycimski, Eugene F. "The Stock Exchange Specialist and the Market Impact of Major World Events." *Financial Analysts Journal,* Vol. 31, No. 4 (July–August, 1975).

Reilly, Frank K. and Drzycimski, Eugene F. "Tests of Stock Market Efficiency

Following Major World Events." *Journal of Business Research,* Vol. 1, No. 1 (Summer, 1973).

Reilly, Frank K. and Hatfield, Kenneth. "Investor Experience with New Stock Issues." *Financial Analysts Journal,* Vol. 25, No. 5 (September–October, 1969).

Reilly, Frank K. and Nielsen, James F. "The Specialist and Large Block Trades on the NYSE," Paper presented at the Southern Finance Association Meeting, Atlanta, Georgia, November, 1974.

Reilly, Frank K., Smith, Ralph E., and Hurt, Ron. "Stock Market Reaction to Changes in Inventory Valuation Methods." Financial Management Association Meeting, Kansas City, Missouri, October, 1975.

Samuelson, Paul A. "Challenge to Judgement." *Journal of Portfolio Management,* Vol. 1, No. 1 (Fall, 1974).

Samuelson, Paul A. "Proof That Properly Anticipated Prices Fluctuate Randomly." *Industrial Management Review,* Vol. 6 (1965).

Sharpe, William F. "Mutual Fund Performance." *Journal of Business,* Vol. 39, No. 1 (January, 1966 Supplement).

Stoll, Hans R. and Curley, Anthony J. "Small Business and the New Issues Market for Equities." *Journal of Financial and Quantitative Analysis,* Vol. 5, No. 3 (September, 1970).

Sunder, Shyam. "Stock Price and Risk Related to Accounting Changes in Inventory Valuation." *The Accounting Review,* Vol. 50, No. 2 (April, 1975).

U.S. Congress, Securities and Exchange Commission, *Institutional Investor Study Report,* 92nd Congress, 1st Session, Howe Document No. 92–64. Washington, D.C.: U.S. Government Printing Office, 1971.

"Why Money Managers Like the Index Funds," *Business Week,* December 20, 1976.

Ying, Louis. "Stock Exchange Listings and Securities Returns." Paper presented at Financial Management Association Meeting, October, 1975.

Chapter 8

An Introduction to Portfolio Management and Capital Market Theory

The study of portfolio theory and capital market theory is generally placed near the end of a text on investments because it is considered necessary to deal with the analysis of individual securities before you consider how to combine these securities into a portfolio. Unfortunately, such a sequence creates a problem in analyzing individual industries and stocks because capital market theory has generated a risk variable that is very important for such an analysis. Work done in these areas has indicated an important measure of risk for an individual asset in a world in which investors attempt to derive optimum returns from their portfolios. In other words, there is a general principle of risk derived from portfolio theory which must be understood before any attempt to deal with individual securities is made. Therefore, this chapter is a brief introduction to the basic concepts of portfolio theory and capital market theory with an emphasis on the risk measures for individual assets.

An Optimum Portfolio

One basic assumption of portfolio theory is that any investor wishes to maximize the returns from his investments. In order to adequately deal with such an assumption, certain ground rules must be laid. The first of these is that the portfolio being considered by an individual should include all of his assets and liabilities, not only stocks or even only marketable securities, but also such items as the investor's car, house, and other less marketable assets like coins, stamps, antiques, furniture, etc. The full spectrum of assets must be considered because the returns from all of these assets interact and *this interaction is important*. Hence a good portfolio is not simply a collection of individually good assets.

An Assumption—Risk Aversion

It is also assumed that *investors are basically risk averse,* which simply means that, given a choice between two assets with equal rates of return, an investor will select the asset with the lower level of risk. Evidence that most investors are risk averse is provided by the fact that they purchase various types of insurance including life insurance, car insurance, and hospital and accident insurance. Insurance is basically a current certain outlay of a given amount to guard against an uncertain possibly larger outlay in the future. People who purchase insurance are willing to pay to avoid the uncertainty of the future regarding these items. In other words, they want to avoid the risk of a potentially large future loss. Further evidence of risk aversion is the difference in promised yield for different grades of bonds that are supposedly of different risk classes—i.e., the required rate of return (promised yield) increases as you go from AAA (the lowest risk class) to AA to A, etc. This means that investors require a higher rate of return in order to accept higher risk.

The foregoing does not imply that everybody is risk averse, or that investors are completely risk averse regarding all financial commitments. Not everybody buys insurance for everything and there are some people who have no insurance against anything, either by choice or because they can't afford it. In addition, some individuals buy insurance and also gamble at race tracks or in Las Vegas where it is known that the expected returns are negative which means that participants are willing to pay for the excitement of the risk involved. This combination of risk preference and risk aversion can be explained by a utility function that is not completely concave or convex, but is a combination of the two that depends upon the amount of money involved. Friedman and Savage speculate that such is the case for people who like to gamble for small amounts (in lotteries or nickel slot machines), but insure themselves against large losses like fire or accidents.[1]

However, most investors committing large sums of money to developing a portfolio of earning assets are risk averse. This means that there should be a positive relationship between expected return and expected risk.

Definition of Risk

While there is a difference in the specific definitions of risk and uncertainty, for our purposes, and in most financial literature, the two terms are used interchangeably. In fact, one way to define risk is as *the uncertainty of future outcomes.* An alternative definition might be as *the probability of an adverse outcome.*

---

[1] Milton Friedman and Leonard J. Savage, "The Utility Analysis of Choices Involving Risk," *Journal of Political Economy,* Vol. 56, No. 3 (August, 1948), pp. 279–304.

Measures of Risk

There are numerous measures of risk. In the 1950's and early '60's a large segment of the investment community talked about risk, but there was no measurable specification for the term. One of the contributions of the development of the portfolio model is that it required investors to quantify their risk variable. The basic portfolio model was developed at the University of Chicago by Harry Markowitz as part of his Ph.D. dissertation.[2] The purpose of this model is to derive the expected rate of return for a portfolio of assets and an expected risk measure. Markowitz showed that the variance of the rate of return was a meaningful measure of risk under a reasonable set of assumptions and derived the formulas for computing the variance of the portfolio. This portfolio variance formulation indicated the importance of diversification for reducing risk, and showed how to properly diversify.

In fact, one of the best known measures of risk is the *variance or standard deviation of expected returns*. It is a statistical measure of the dispersion of returns around the expected value, i.e., a larger value indicates greater dispersion, all other factors being equal. The idea is that the more disperse the returns, the greater the uncertainty of those returns in any future period. Another measure of risk is the *range of returns* based upon the assumption that a larger range of returns, from the lowest to the highest, means greater uncertainty regarding future expected returns.

In contrast to using measures that analyze any deviation from expectations, some feel that the investor should only be concerned with *returns below expectations*—deviations below the mean value. A measure that only considers such adverse deviations is the semi-variance. An extension of this measure would be *deviations below zero* or negative returns. Both measures implicitly assume that investors want to minimize their regret from below average returns. It is implicit that investors would welcome positive returns or returns above expectations, so these are not considered when measuring risk. Similarly, Zinbarg proposed the use of *negative opportunity returns* as a measure of risk. Negative opportunity returns are returns below the risk-free rate of return.[3]

Although there are numerous potential measures of risk, we begin with the variance or standard deviation of returns because this measure is somewhat intuitive and it is a correct risk measure for most investors.

Portfolio Return

The expected rate of return for a portfolio of assets is simply the weighted average of the expected rates of return for the individual assets in the

---

[2] Harry Markowitz, "Portfolio Selection," *Journal of Finance,* Vol. 7, No. 1 (March, 1952), pp. 77–91; and *Portfolio Selection–Efficient Diversification of Investments* (New Haven, Conn.: Yale University Press, 1959).

[3] Edward D. Zinbarg, "Modern Approach to Investment Risk," *Financial Executive,* Vol. 41, No. 2 (February, 1973), pp. 44–48.

portfolio. The weights are the proportion of total value for the asset. The expected return for a hypothetical individual asset is computed as shown in Table 8–1.

Table 8–1
Computation of Expected Return for Individual Risky Asset

Probability	Potential Return (%)	Expected Return (%)
.25	.08	.0200
.25	.10	.0250
.25	.12	.0300
.25	.14	.0350
		$E(R) = .1100$

The expected return for an individual asset with the set of potential returns and probabilities used in the example would be 11 percent. The expected return for a hypothetical four asset portfolio is shown in Table 8–2.

Table 8–2
Computation of the Expected Return for a Portfolio of Risky Assets

Weight (W_i) (% of Portfolio)	Expected Security Return (%) R_i	Expected Portfolio Return (%)
.20	.10	.0200
.30	.11	.0330
.30	.12	.0360
.20	.13	.0260
		$E(Rport) = .1150$

The expected return for the total portfolio would be 11.5 percent. The effect of adding or dropping any security from the portfolio would be easy to determine, given the new weights, based on value and the expected returns for each of the assets. This computation can be generalized as follows:

$$E(Rport) = \sum_{i=1}^{n} W_i R_i$$

Standard Deviation of Portfolio

A major contribution made by Markowitz was the detailed derivation of the standard deviation for a portfolio of assets under a number of potential assumptions. The most important part was the derivation of the general formulation as follows:[4]

$$\sigma port = \sqrt{\sum W^2_i \sigma^2_i + 2\sum\sum W_i W_j Cov_{ij}}$$

---

[4] Markowitz, "Portfolio Selection;" and *Portfolio Selection–Efficient Diversification of Investments.*

where

σport = standard deviation of the portfolio and

W_i = the weights for each asset i in the portfolio where the weight is the proportion of value.

σ^2_i = the variance for each of the individual assets in the portfolio.

Cov_{ij} = the covariance between the returns for asset i and asset j where the covariance equals $R_{ij}\sigma_i\sigma_j$ (R_{ij} equals the correlation of returns between asset i and j).

This formula is very important to the analysis of risk because it shows that the risk for the portfolio is not simply a weighted average of the risk for the individual assets in the portfolio. Without this calculation, most investors would assume that the standard deviation is a valid measure of risk for a portfolio of earning assets and would intuitively expect the standard deviation for the portfolio to be a weighted average of individual standard deviations; i.e., the expected return for the portfolio is a weighted average.

According to Markowitz, the standard deviation for the portfolio is the square root of the sum of two sets of terms. The first set of terms is the weighted average of individual variances with the weights squared. The second set of terms is the sum of the covariances between all assets in the portfolio. It was proven by Markowitz, and it can be seen upon close analysis, that in a portfolio with a large number of stocks, the weights for the individual variances will become quite small and, as the number of stocks approaches infinity, this individual variance will go to zero. In contrast, the second set of terms concerned with covariances continues to grow and eventually *the variance of the portfolio will become the average covariance between all assets in the portfolio.* In a portfolio the relevant risk measure for an individual asset is not its total variance, but *its covariance with all other assets in the portfolio!* To repeat this very important point, if an investor is contemplating adding a new asset to his portfolio, *he should be mainly concerned with the covariance between the returns for this new asset and the returns on all other assets already in this portfolio.*

The extreme effects of two alternatives can be seen if one considers a two asset portfolio with equal amounts of money invested in each asset. In the one case it can be assumed that both assets are perfectly positively correlated (i.e., they move together perfectly in the same proportion.) Therefore, if one asset experiences a return of 10 percent, the other experiences the same return. In such a case of perfect positive correlation, there is *no benefit from diversification* and the risk of the portfolio is a weighted average of the two standard deviations. When two assets are perfectly positively correlated, for purposes of the portfolio it is as if *they were the same asset.*

In contrast, consider the case in which there is perfect *negative* correlation between two securities (i.e., they move exactly opposite to each other in the same proportion). When one asset has a return 5 percent above its mean return, the other asset will have a return 5 percent below its mean return. Under such conditions, the investor derives the maximum benefits from diversification. In this case the returns would be exactly opposite to each other over time as shown in Figure 8–1.

Figure 8–1
Time Pattern of Returns for Two Assets with Perfect Negative Correlation

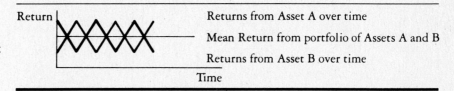

Returns from Asset A over time

Mean Return from portfolio of Assets A and B

Returns from Asset B over time

The result of perfect negative correlation is that the mean return for the two securities combined over time is equal to the mean for each of them and there is no variability of returns for the portfolio. Returns above and below the mean for each of the assets are *completely offset* by the return for the other asset so there is no variability in total returns for the portfolio; it is a riskless portfolio because there is no uncertainty of returns. The combination of two assets that are completely negatively correlated provides the maximum benefits of diversification—it eliminates risk.

The Markowitz Efficient Frontier

Given the formula for the expected return and variance or standard deviation of the return from a portfolio, the next step is to derive all potential portfolios from the set of potential risky assets. While one could possibly consider all available risky earning assets in the universe, it is likely that most portfolio managers would have a subset of several hundred earning assets that they consider appropriate for their clientele. To simplify the discussion, it is assumed that all the earning assets are common stocks. The intent would be to derive and examine all potential portfolios that could be created from this subset. The inputs required by the program would be:

(1) expected rate of return for each stock

(2) the expected variance of return for each stock

(3) the expected covariance of return for each stock with every other potential stock.

In most cases, past results were used as a proxy for expectations. A major practical problem is deriving the numerous covariances. This computational problem was alleviated,[5] but for now we can assume that we will have no problems in deriving the results for our potential portfolios. The derived

---

[5] William F. Sharpe, "A Simplified Model for Portfolio Analysis," *Management Science,* Vol. 10, No. 1 (January, 1963), pp. 227–293.

results on a risk-return graph would appear as shown in Figure 8–2 where each point is either a stock or a portfolio:

Figure 8–2
Scatter Plot of Risk and Return for Potential Alternative Portfolios

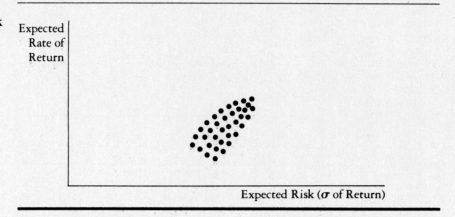

Given all the potential portfolios, the computer determines *for each alternative rate of return the portfolio with minimum risk, or for each alternative level of risk the portfolio with the maximum rate of return.* The set of all portfolios that fulfill either of these constraints is the *efficient frontier.* The efficient frontier is the set of portfolios on the dark line drawn along the left outer edge of the set of potential portfolios shown in Figure 8–3.

Figure 8–3
Efficient Frontier for Alternative Portfolios

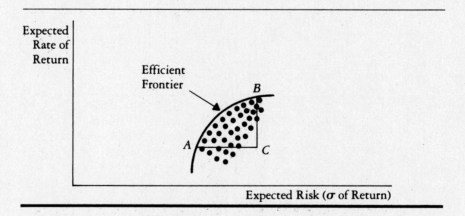

The portfolios or individual stocks that lie to the right or below the efficient frontier are dominated by a portfolio on the efficient frontier that has either a higher return for equal risk, or lower risk for equal return. As an example, portfolio A dominates portfolio C because it has an equal return but substantially less risk. Portfolio B dominates portfolio C because it has equal risk but a higher expected rate of return. Because of the benefits of diversification among assets that are not perfectly correlated, we would expect the efficient frontier to be made up of *portfolios,* with the possible exception of the two end points (i.e., the highest return asset and the lowest risk asset).

It was postulated that investors would determine where they wanted to be along the frontier based upon their utility function and attitude toward risk. They would select some portfolio on the efficient frontier based upon their risk preferences. No portfolio on the efficient frontier is dominated by any other portfolio on the efficient frontier. They all have different return and risk measures and returns increase with risk.

Risk-Free Asset Following the development of the Markowitz portfolio model, several authors considered the effect of the existence of a risk-free asset that, by definition, would have zero variance. It can be shown that such an asset would also have zero correlation with all other risky assets. Such an asset would yield the risk-free rate of return (RFR) and be on the vertical axis of a portfolio graph.

Capital Asset Pricing

Given the existence of a risk-free asset, it was shown by William Sharpe that it is possible to combine this asset with alternative risky asset portfolios and any such combination would lie somewhere along a straight line between the two.[6] The result of combining the risk-free asset with alternative risky asset portfolios on the efficient frontier is a number of possible portfolio lines as shown in Figure 8–4, which provide the investor with a superior set of alternatives.

It is possible for an investor to attain a point anywhere along the lines RFR-A, RFR-B, or RFR-M by combining a portfolio of risk-free assets (i.e., lending money to a riskless borrower such as the U.S. Government) and buying some amount of risky asset portfolio A, B, or M.

Examining the three lines (any number of lines could be drawn to any point on the efficient frontier), one can observe that line RFR-B *dominates* line RFR-A because for all the points along RFR-A you can derive a point on line RFR-B that has equal risk but a higher expected rate of return. This continues as you move up the efficient frontier until you reach a point of tangency with the efficient frontier at point M. Above point M, there are no feasible risky asset portfolios. Therefore, *line RFR-M becomes the new efficient frontier because the portfolios on this line dominate all the portfolios below it on the initial Markowitz efficient frontier.*

An investor can develop a portfolio anywhere along the line RFR-M by

---

[6] William F. Sharpe, "Capital Asset Prices: A Theory of Market Equilibrium Under Conditions of Risk," *Journal of Finance,* Vol. 19, No. 4 (September, 1964), pp. 425–442. The proof for this is given in Chapter 19.

Figure 8–4
Graph of Portfolio Possibilities from Combining a Risk-Free Asset with Risky Asset Portfolios on the Efficient Frontier

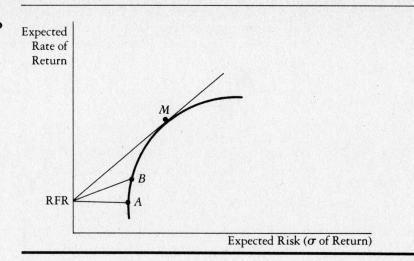

combining an investment in a risk-free asset and an investment in a portfolio of risky assets (M). If the investor wants only risky assets, he will put all his wealth into the risky asset portfolio at point M.

One may ask whether it is possible to develop portfolios along the straight line extending beyond M or will this cause a reversion to the upper portion of the Markowitz efficient frontier? It has been shown that, if one assumes that the investor can borrow money at the RFR and invest that money in the risky asset portfolio M, he can derive portfolios with higher risk and higher return along the extension of line RFR-M.[7] Therefore, the new efficient frontier, referred to as the Capital Market Line (CML), appears as shown in Figure 8–5.

Figure 8–5
Derivation of Capital Market Line Assuming Lending or Borrowing at the Risk-Free Rate

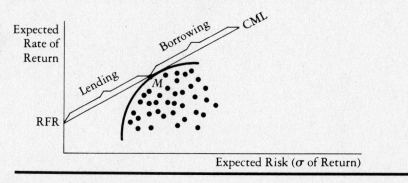

---

[7] The proof of this is presented in Chapter 19.

Because this line CML is the efficient frontier, one would expect all investors to attempt to develop portfolios somewhere along the CML that are consistent with their risk-return preferences. All investors should invest part of their wealth in the risky asset portfolio M and borrow or lend at the risk-free rate to attain some point along the CML that is consistent with their risk preferences.

The M Portfolio

Assuming that all investors want to be on the CML, they will want to invest part of their wealth in the M portfolio. Regarding what risky assets are in the M portfolio, the answer is all of them. Because portfolio M is the optimum risky asset portfolio that all investors want to acquire, all risky assets *have* to be in this portfolio or there would not be any demand for these particular risky assets. Therefore, the M portfolio (hereinafter called the market portfolio) contains all risky assets (not only stocks but bonds, warrants, options, stamps, coins, antiques, etc.) in proportion to their market value. Because the market portfolio contains all risky assets it is *a perfectly diversified portfolio.*

Risk in a CML Environment

In the derivation of the Markowitz efficient frontier, the formula for the standard deviation of return for the portfolio included the individual variances and the average covariance for all securities in the portfolio. If one assumed that there were a fairly large number of securities in the portfolio, the weights for the individual variances would approach zero and, therefore, *the relevant risk variable for an individual security in a portfolio was its average covariance with all other risky assets in the portfolio.* In a capital asset pricing environment, the idea is the same except that with the CML there is only one portfolio of concern, the market portfolio. Therefore, given the CML, *the relevant risk measure for an individual risky asset is its average covariance with all other risky assets or, more specifically, its covariance with the market portfolio of risky assets.* An asset's total variance is *not* the relevant risk variable, but *only* the variance of return that is related to the market portfolio. This variance related to the market portfolio is referred to as "systematic risk." The variance of return not related to the market is referred to as "unique" or "unsystematic" risk. This "unique" variance is not considered relevant because it will be diversified away in a portfolio with a large number of earning assets; i.e., its unique variability is offset by the unique variability of other risky assets. In a perfectly diversified market portfolio, an asset's unique risk is eliminated and all that remains is the systematic market risk or the asset's covariance with the market portfolio. Therefore, *the relevant risk measure for a risky asset is its systematic risk* (its covariance of returns with the market portfolio of risky assets).

Normalized Systematic Risk

Because the covariance measure is an absolute measure of association or risk, it is useful to normalize it relative to risk for the aggregate market. The covariance of an asset with itself is the variance of the asset. Therefore, the systematic risk of the market is its variance of return. Dividing the absolute systematic risk of the individual risky asset (its covariance with the market portfolio) by the systematic risk of the market portfolio (the market variance), one derives a *normalized* measure of systematic risk for an individual risky asset as follows:

$$\text{Normalized Systematic Risk} = \text{Cov}_{im}/\text{Cov}_{mm}$$
$$= \text{Cov}_{im}/\sigma^2_m$$

An earning asset whose covariance with the market is equal to the market variance has a normalized systematic risk value of 1.0; its systematic risk is equal to the market risk. Therefore, the return on this risky asset should equal the market rate of return. An earning asset with market covariance below the market's variance will have a systematic risk value less than one and would be considered lower risk than the aggregate market portfolio. It should therefore receive a return below the market return. An asset with a normalized systematic risk value above one should receive a return above the market rate of return. This normalized measure of systematic risk is referred to as *beta,* because it is the slope coefficient for a regression that relates the returns for an individual asset over time to the returns for the aggregate market portfolio. The form of the regression is as follows:

$$R_{it} = \alpha_i + B_i R_{mt} + \mu$$

where:

R_{it} — rate of return on asset i during period t
α_i — the intercept of the regression
B_i — the slope coefficient of the regression equal to $\text{Cov}_{im}/\sigma^2_m$
R_{mt} — rate of return on the market portfolio during period t
μ — a random error term

This regression equation is referred to as the "characteristic line" for the risky asset. It describes the asset's characteristics relative to the market portfolio. Because beta is the slope coefficient for this regression, it indicates how responsive returns for the individual earning asset are to returns for the market portfolio. Assume that the risky asset's characteristic line has an alpha close to zero and a beta equal to 1.50. This means that, if the market portfolio experiences a rate of return of 10 percent during a given period, on average this asset will experience a 15 percent rate of return. If the market declines by 8 percent, this asset will on average experience a decline of about 12 percent. Therefore, the returns for this asset are approximately 50 percent more volatile than returns on the market portfolio.

Consider the scatter plot of rates of return during some past period as shown in Figure 8–6. The regression line of best fit through these points indicates the alpha and beta for the asset's characteristic line. As stated, the slope of this line is the estimated beta for the asset (an estimate of the asset's normalized systematic risk).

Figure 8–6
Scatter Plot of Rates of Return

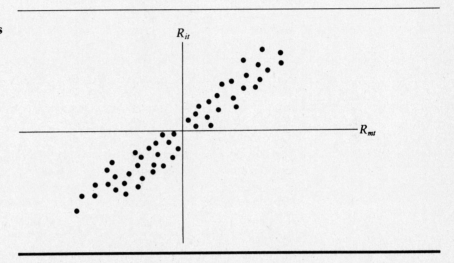

In a capital asset pricing world we assume that all rational, profit maximizing investors will attempt to be somewhere along the CML which means that all investors will attempt to put some portion of their wealth in the market portfolio (M) of all risky assets. Because the market portfolio is the only relevant portfolio of risky assets *the relevant risk measure for an individual asset is its covariance with the market portfolio of risky assets.* When this market covariance (systematic risk) is normalized we derive the beta coefficient which relates the stock's covariance to the market's total variance.[8]

The Security Market Line

Because an asset's systematic risk with the market is the relevant risk measure for an individual asset, one can derive the expected relationship between return and risk. The expected linear relationship is referred to as the Security Market Line (SML) and is shown in Figure 8–7.

---

[8] For a further discussion of beta, including some misinterpretations, see Mary Lindahl-Stevens, "Some Popular Uses and Abuses of Beta," *Journal of Portfolio Management,* Vol. 4, No. 2 (Winter, 1978), pp. 13–17.

Figure 8–7
**Derivation of the
Security Market
Line Based Upon
the CML**

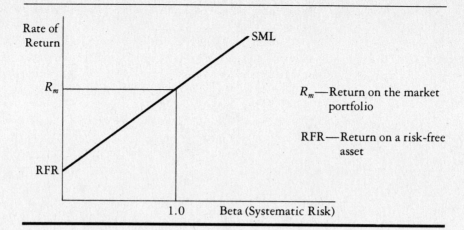

The slope of the SML is the required return to risk for the market and is equal to $\dfrac{R_m - RFR}{Beta}$. All individual assets should fall along the SML depending upon their systematic risk (beta). Given the SML, the expected return on a risky asset is equal to:

$$E(R_i) = RFR + B_i(R_m - RFR)$$

where:

$E(R_i)$ — the expected rate of return for asset i
RFR — the expected risk-free rate
B_i — the measure of normalized systematic risk (Beta) for asset i
R_m — the expected return on the market portfolio

Summary

Introductory material on portfolio theory and capital market theory is presented at this point in the text because these theories have generated new measures of risk for individual risky assets that are important to our subsequent discussion. It is assumed throughout that investors are generally risk averse since, all other things being equal, they would prefer less uncertainty. Risk was defined as uncertainty regarding future rates of return for an earning asset. While there are numerous measures of risk, the measure we used is the variance or standard deviation of returns for the total portfolio.

A major contribution by Markowitz was the derivation of the formula for computing the standard deviation of a portfolio. It was shown that the variance of a portfolio is not simply the weighted average of individual variances of securities within the portfolio, but a combination of the individual variances and the average covariance of these securities. Further, in a portfolio with a large number of securities, it can be shown that the individual variances become unimportant and, hence, the relevant risk variable for an asset is its average covariance with all other assets in the portfolio. Given this formulation, one can derive the efficient frontier which is defined as the set of portfolios with the maximum return for a given level of risk, or minimum risk for each given rate of return.

Building upon the efficient frontier developed by Markowitz, Sharpe assumed the existence of a risk-free asset and demonstrated how investors could derive a set of portfolios that combined the risk-free asset with portfolios of risky assets on the efficient frontier and thereby derive a superior set of alternatives. The result was a new efficient frontier that extended from the risk-free rate to a point of tangency on the efficient frontier. The risky asset portfolio at the point of tangency was shown to be the market portfolio which contains all available risky assets in proportion to their market values. This new efficient frontier was entitled the capital market line, and one would expect all investors to attempt to derive portfolios that will place them somewhere on the CML line by either lending or borrowing at the risk-free rate and buying a portion of the market portfolio. Because the market portfolio of all risky assets is the only relevant portfolio in the capital asset pricing model, the relevant risk variable for an individual asset is its covariance with the market portfolio (systematic risk). A normalized measure of systematic risk is the beta coefficient. Finally, then, one would expect all individual assets to lie somewhere along the security market line (SML) that relates the expected return for an individual earning asset to the risky asset's systematic risk (beta). This risk measure is relevant for all risky assets whether common stocks, bonds, coins, or antiques and is used in all subsequent analysis of industries or stocks.

Questions

1. Draw a properly labeled graph of the Markowitz efficient frontier. Describe in exact terms what the efficient frontier is.

2. Assuming you want to run a computer program to derive the efficient frontier for your feasible set of stocks, what information must you provide for the program, i.e., what are your inputs?

3. In the Markowitz portfolio model, what is your measure of risk for the total portfolio; what risk variable do you want to minimize?

4. Given the formula for deriving the Markowitz risk variable, what is the relevant risk variable for an individual security assuming there are a fairly large number of securities in your portfolio? Why?

5. What happens to the Markowitz efficient frontier when you assume the

existence of a risk-free asset and combine this with alternative risky asset portfolios on the Markowitz efficient frontier? Draw a graph to show what happens and explain it.

6. It has been shown that the Sharpe Capital Market Line (CML) is tangent to one portfolio on the Markowitz efficient frontier. This is referred to as portfolio M. What stocks are in this portfolio and why are they in it? Be precise in your discussion.

7. Given the Sharpe Capital Market Line, what is the relevant measure of risk for an individual security? Why is this the relevant risk measure? Be very precise and complete in your discussion.

8. It is contended that the total variance of returns for a security can be broken down into "systematic" variance and unsystematic or "unique" variance. Describe what is meant by each of these terms.

9. In a capital asset pricing model (CAPM) there is systematic and unsystematic risk for an individual security. Which is the relevant risk variable in a CAPM framework and why is it relevant? Why is the other risk variable not relevant?

10. Draw a properly labeled graph of the Security Market Line (SML) and explain it. How does the SML differ from the CML?

References

Blume, Marshall E. "On the Assessment of Risk." *Journal of Finance,* Vol. 26, No. 1 (March, 1971).

Brigham, Eugene F. *Financial Management.* Hinsdale, Illinois: The Dryden Press, 1977, Chapter 5.

Fama, Eugene F. "Risk, Return and Equilibrium." *Journal of Political Economy,* Vol. 79, No. 1 (January–February, 1971).

Friedman, Milton and Savage, Leonard J. "The Utility Analysis of Choices Involving Risk." *Journal of Political Economy,* Vol. 56, No. 3 (August, 1948).

Jensen, Michael C. "Capital Markets: Theory and Practice." *Bell Journal of Economics and Management Science,* Vol. 3 (Autumn, 1972).

Lindahl-Stevens, Mary. "Some Popular Uses and Abuses of Beta." *Journal of Portfolio Management,* Vol. 4, No. 2 (Winter, 1978).

Mao, James C. T. "Security Pricing in an Imperfect Capital Market." *Journal of Financial and Quantitative Analysis,* Vol. 6, No. 4 (September, 1971).

Markowitz, Harry M. "Portfolio Selection." *Journal of Finance,* Vol. 7, No. 1 (March, 1952).

Markowitz, Harry M. *Portfolio Selection—Efficient Diversification of Investments.* New Haven, Conn.: Yale University Press, 1959.

Modigliani, Franco and Pogue, Gerald A. "An Introduction to Risk and Return." *Financial Analysts Journal,* Vol. 30, No. 2 (March–April, 1974) and Vol. 30, No. 3 (May–June, 1974).

Robichek, Alexander A. "Risk and the Value of Securities." *Journal of Financial and Quantitative Analysis,* Vol. 4, No. 4 (December 1969).

Sharpe, William F. "Capital Asset Prices: A Theory of Market Equilibrium Under Conditions of Risk." *Journal of Finance,* Vol. 19, No. 4 (September, 1964).

Sharpe, William F. "A Simplified Model for Portfolio Analysis," *Management Science,* Vol. 10, No. 1 (January, 1963).

Van Horne, James C. "Portfolio Theory and Efficient Market Considerations." *Financial Management and Policy,* 4th ed. Englewood Cliffs, N.J.: Prentice-Hall Inc., 1977, Chapter 3.

Part 3   *Analysis and Valuation of Equity Securities*

Introduction to Part 3

In order to properly evaluate an investment vehicle, several analyses must be carried out, beginning with a valuation of the aggregate market and progressing through examination of various industries, to a consideration of an individual company and its stock. The techniques used for such valuations are dealt with in this section. Chapter 9 contains a discussion of why our initial and major analysis is of the aggregate stock market, and the next two chapters present techniques for analyzing the aggregate market. Chapter 11 contains a long and detailed discussion of the relevant factors for market analysis.

The chapter on industry analysis employs the same general technique used in the chapter on markets, but it is applied to a specific industry. The company analysis chapter likewise uses the same general approach to valuation and applies it to one company in the industry analyzed in Chapter 12. Chapter 14 is a separate discussion of the analysis of growth companies. This is done because the technique employed in Chapters 10-13 is not applicable to true growth companies given their high current growth rate that cannot be sustained for a long period. Therefore, it is necessary to employ different valuation models to allow for this. Several models are presented and applied to growth company examples.

Throughout this section, we make constant reference to the semistrong efficient market hypothesis. The reader must realize, however, that while many studies have supported this hypothesis, not all have. Therefore, the idea is to present a valuation technique that is consistent and justifiable, but the reader is always reminded that the output of the valuation models is only as good as the *estimated* inputs, and the superior analyst is the one who provides the best *estimates*.

The final chapter in this section deals with technical analysis, an alternative to the fundamental analysis we have discussed thus far. Rather than attempting to estimate value based upon numerous external variables, the technical analyst contends that the market is its own best estimator. Therefore, it is possible to project future stock price movements based upon past stock price changes or other stock market data. A number of techniques used by technical analysts are discussed and demonstrated.

Chapter 9

An Overview of the Valuation Process

Approaching the valuation process is much like the problem of the chicken and the egg. Do you first deal with individual securities and gradually build up to an analysis of the entire economy or vice versa? It is our contention that the discussion should first center on the analysis of the aggregate economy and the overall securities markets. Only afterwards should one consider alternative industries. Finally, following the industry analysis, one should consider the securities issued by various firms within the better industries. Therefore, the analytical process should proceed as shown below. This is referred to as a three step process.

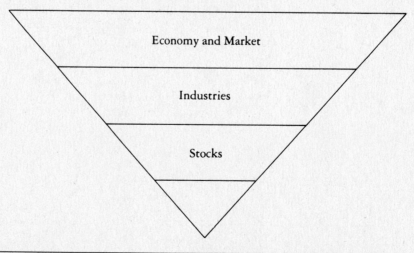

General Economic Influences

It is well recognized that various agencies of the federal government have a major impact on the aggregate economy because they control monetary and fiscal policy. These basic economic forces exert an influence on all industries and all companies in the economy. Fiscal policy can do such things as encourage spending (through investment credits) or discourage spending (through taxes on gasoline). Increases or decreases in spending on defense, unemployment, or highways also influence the general economic picture. All such changes have a major impact on those directly affected by the changes, but there is also a *multiplier* effect on those who supply goods and services to those directly affected.

The same overall impact can result from a significant change in monetary policy. A restrictive monetary policy that produces a decline in the growth rate of the money supply reduces the supply of funds available to all businesses for working capital and expansion, and of funds available to individuals for acquiring goods and services. Monetary policy affects all segments of the economy.

Another overall economic variable that must be considered is *inflation* because it has a major impact on interest rates and on how consumers and corporations save and spend their money.

In addition to domestic monetary and fiscal actions, other occurrences such as war, political upheavals in foreign countries, or international monetary devaluations influence the aggregate economy. Therefore, it is difficult to conceive of any industry or company that will not be affected in some way by macroeconomic developments that affect the total economy.

Because events influencing the aggregate economy also have such a profound effect on all industries and all companies within these industries, *these macroeconomic factors must be considered before industries can be analyzed.* If the economic outlook indicates a recession that will have an impact on all industries and all companies, it must be expected that all security prices will also be affected. Under such economic conditions, an analyst will probably be extremely apprehensive about recommending any industry. The best recommendation would probably be high portfolio liquidity. In contrast, assume that the economic and stock market outlook is bullish. Under such conditions, the analyst would look for an outstanding industry. This would be accomplished through economic analysis because, typically, the future performance of an industry depends upon the economic outlook and the particular industry's expected relationship to the economy.

Industry Influences

Because of the importance of the general economic outlook, one should only consider investing in alternative industries *after* it has been decided that the general outlook is favorable. Assuming that it is, the question then becomes one of deciding on the industry or industries to be considered. The industry outlook is determined by the general economic outlook and special industry factors that are generally national in scope, but have their greatest influence on one or several industries. Examples of industry influence are an industry-wide strike, import or export quotas or taxes, or government imposed regulations.

In addition, industries feel the influence of an economic change at different points in the business cycle. Construction typically lags the business cycle and, therefore, this industry is only affected toward the end of a cycle. Finally, different industries respond differently to the business cycle. As an example, cyclical industries (e.g., steel, autos) typically do much better than the aggregate economy during expansions, but suffer more during contractions. Because of this differential performance it is important to analyze the industry *before* analyzing individual companies within the industry. It is unusual for a company to perform well in a poor industry (even the best company in a poor industry will suffer).

Because of the significance and pervasiveness of industry influences, *an industry evaluation should be conducted prior to analyzing any individual firm.* If the industry outlook is negative, an analyst should not spend a great deal of time on individual firms in the industry. If the industry outlook is good, the prior industry analysis would be useful because a major component of firm analysis is a comparison of individual firms to the entire industry in terms of relevant financial ratios. In fact, many of the ratios employed in security analysis are only valid when viewed in terms of the entire industry.

Empirical Support for the Three Step Process

While the foregoing discussion may appear logical, one may ask whether the implied importance of economic and industry analysis is empirically supported. Is there a relationship between the *earnings* of the aggregate economy, alternative industries, and individual firms? Is there a relationship among the *rates of return* for the aggregate stock market, the stocks in alternative industries, and individual stocks that would indicate that there is value in market and industry analysis?

Association Among Corporate Earnings

It was just such a relationship that was examined by Philip Brown and Ray Ball. The authors dealt with the degree of association between the earnings of an individual firm, the earnings of other firms in the industry, and the earnings of all firms in the economy.[1] Brown and Ball examined the earnings of 316 firms for the 19 year period 1947–1965 using six alterna-

---

[1] Philip Brown and Ray Ball, "Some Preliminary Findings on the Association Between the Earnings of a Firm, Its Industry, and the Economy," *Empirical Research in Accounting, Selected Studies, 1967,* Supplement to Vol. 5, *Journal of Accounting Research,* pp. 55–77.

tive measures of earnings. Employing a linear correlation model, the earnings for individual firms during the period were related to the earnings of all firms except the individual firm being examined. In addition, they related individual firm earnings to the earnings of all other firms in the particular industry.

The results indicated that on average, approximately 30–40 percent of the variability of a firm's annual earnings were associated with the variability of earnings averaged for all firms. Also on average, an additional 10–15 percent of the firm's earnings were associated with the earnings for the industry. Further tests on industry relations indicated that the industries were reasonably well defined and that the firms were well classified by industry.

These results indicate that approximately 45–55 percent of a firm's total variability in annual earnings can be explained by the overall economy and a firm's industry with the economic factor being of greater importance.

While these average results clearly confirm the importance of economic and industry analysis, *there is variation among firms*. On the one hand, a highly diversified industrial firm could have earnings that are more closely related to the economy than these results imply; i.e., earnings might be almost perfectly related to the total economy because, in terms of composition the firm may be an image of the economy. In contrast, only a small portion of the earnings of many small firms with a unique product and clientele can be explained by the behavior of the economy or the firm's industry.

Systematic Stock Price Fluctuations

To justify aggregate market analysis it is necessary to determine whether there is a cyclical pattern in stock prices. A detailed analysis of market movements by Julius Shiskin used the techniques employed by the National Bureau of Economic Research to break the stock price series down into several components: seasonal, irregular, and trend-cycle.[2] For short-run intervals, the irregular component was dominant. *As the interval was increased to three months or longer the cyclical component became dominant.* An analysis of the duration of monthly runs indicated that the average duration of run for monthly and quarterly stock prices was clearly more than expected for a random series. Diffusion indexes for stock prices using 80 industries indicated the proportion of industries that were rising at a point in time. Using a short time span, the diffusion indexes acted like a random series. *As the span of comparison was extended to 9 or 12 months, a clear cyclical pattern emerged and the diffusion indexes definitely led the stock price series.* Finally Shiskin examined the relationship between the stock price series and a number of other economic series (employment, income, production). The

---

[2] Julius Shiskin, "Systematic Aspects of Stock Price Fluctuations," reprinted in James Lorie and Richard Brealey, *Modern Developments in Investment Management,* 2nd ed. (Hinsdale, Illinois: The Dryden Press, 1978), pp. 640–658.

results indicated that stock prices consistently conform to economic expansions and contractions, but *stock prices clearly lead the general economy.* Regarding prediction of these stock price fluctuations, some suggestions were made, but it was acknowledged that it would be difficult because the fluctuations vary in amplitude, pattern, and duration. Therefore, there *is* a cycle in stock prices and it may be useful to predict the cycle if it can be shown to relate to individual stock price returns.

Market and Industry Effect

A study by Benjamin King examined the relationship between market returns, industry returns, and the returns on individual stocks.[3] The object of the study was to determine how much of the total price movement for a given stock over time was attributable to overall market factors, how much was due to industry influences, and how much could be ascribed to a stock's "unique" component. To do this, King examined the price behavior of 63 securities listed on the New York Stock Exchange over a total period of 403 months from June, 1927 through December, 1960, and over four subperiods within this time frame. The variable examined was monthly percentages of change in price. The 63 securities were from the following six industries (number of companies in the industry shown in parentheses): tobacco products (11), petroleum products (11), metals (ferrous and nonferrous) (11), railroads (10), utilities (10), and retail stores (10).

King employed factor analysis which breaks down the variability of each security's price change into that part attributable to common factors ("communality") and the part due to a stock's unique factor. The total communality is the percentage of the stock's total price variance attributable to all the other 62 securities, i.e., an overall market factor, and/or an industry factor. The mean communality for the overall time period was 0.72 which indicates that the "unique" component, on the average, was only 0.28 for the full time period. However, the total communality appeared to weaken over time as indicated by the trend of the communality measure during the four subperiods.

King attempted to determine how much of the variability was attributable to overall market movement, and how much could be traced to industry factors. For the overall period, the mean proportion of price variance explained was 52 percent. King concluded that *about half the variance* in the typical stock for the time period considered was explained by the whole market.[4]

An analysis of the net price changes after the market effect was removed indicated that *almost all of the large positive correlations among individual stocks corresponded to industry groupings* and that all large negative correlations were

---

[3] Benjamin F. King, "Market and Industry Factors in Stock Price Behavior," *Journal of Business,* Vol. 39, No. 1, Part 2 (January, 1960), pp. 139–190.

[4] King, "Market and Industry Factors," p. 251.

with stocks in other industries.[5] King employed cluster analysis to group stocks with the highest correlation in a step-by-step procedure until all the stocks were combined. The results supported an industry influence since the comovement of price changes, after removing the market effect, corresponded to the typical industry classifications. The application of multiple factor analysis and a modified principal components analysis confirmed these results.

These tests indicated that, on an average for the total period, in excess of 10 percent of the total variation in the stock's price could be attributed to the industry influence. It appears that for King's sample and time period, the bulk of the security price changes, 62 percent, were explained by a combination of market and industry components.

Again, the importance of the market factor tended to decline over time and there was also a clear difference in the importance of the market factor for alternative stocks. For some stocks, the market factor explained over 70 percent of the variance, while in other instances the proportion was less than 25 percent.

More on the Market and Industry Factor

A study by Meyers confirmed King's findings regarding market influence, but questioned some of his results in the area of the importance of the industry factor.[6] Meyers selected a sample similar to King's and added a second sample of 5 stocks from each of 12 industries (a total of 60). Principal components analysis was performed on samples for the same periods studied by King and for the seven year period from Janaury, 1961 through December, 1967. The results for both samples were consistent with those reported earlier by King. *The percent of variance explained by the market factor declined from more than 55 percent prior to 1944 to less than 35 percent for the period 1952–1967.* Meyers analyzed the importance of the industry factors using a cluster analysis similar to that employed by King and a somewhat different principal components analysis. The cluster analysis results for the same six industries and time period used by King gave quite similar results. However, the figures for the same industries for the period *after* 1952 indicated a weakening of the industry affiliation. Analysis of the 12 new industries confirmed the expectation that *industry clustering was less dominant for a sample that included less homogeneous and distinct industry groups.* The principal components analysis provided considerably less convincing evidence of an industry relationship than had King's analysis.

Therefore, these results confirm the prior conclusions regarding the importance of market analysis even with the decline in explanatory power over time. They also confirm the importance of industry analysis, but

---

[5] Ibid., p. 153.

[6] Stephen L. Meyers, "A Re-Examination of Market and Industry Factors in Stock Price Behavior," *Journal of Finance,* Vol. 28, No. 3 (June, 1973), pp. 695–705.

indicate quite clearly that *the importance of the industry component varies across industries.*

Market Risk Estimates

A widely read study by Marshall Blume likewise contains evidence of the relative importance of the market factor.[7] Following a discussion that justified the use of beta as a measure of risk, Blume derived the beta coefficient for all stocks on the NYSE that had adequate data for several subperiods from July, 1926 through June, 1968. A summary of some relevant results for the current discussion is contained in Table 9–1. These results document the importance of the market factor since they indicate that, even after a decline, aggregate market behavior explains almost 30 percent of the variance for individual securities.

Table 9–1
Descriptive Statistics

Time Period	Number of Companies	Mean Beta	Coefficient of Determination (R^2)
7/26–6/33	415	1.051	0.51
7/33–6/40	604	1.036	0.49
7/40–6/47	731	0.990	0.36
7/47–6/54	870	1.010	0.32
7/54–6/61	890	0.998	0.25
7/61–6/68	847	0.962	0.28

Source: Adapted from Marshall E. Blume, "On the Assessment of Risk," *Journal of Finance,* Vol. 26, No. 1 (March, 1971), pp. 1–10. Reprinted by permission.

The discussion of empirical studies points toward the following generalizations:

1. The market factor was very important prior to 1940 and has declined so that it currently accounts for about 25–30 percent of individual stock price variance.

2. Even after the decline, the market still accounts for a significant part of the variance in individual securities such that market analysis is important.

3. The importance of the market factor in explaining individual price variance fluctuates among securities, ranging from over 50 percent to below 5 percent.

4. When using time intervals exceeding three months there definitely are cycles in stock price movements which means it is feasible and practical to project market movements (i.e., over longer intervals the market

---

[7] Marshall E. Blume, "On the Assessment of Risk," *Journal of Finance,* Vol. 26, No. 1 (March, 1971), pp. 1–10.

is *not* a random walk). Therefore, market analysis is not only justified but also feasible because of the existence of cycles.

These generalizations confirm the statement made at the beginning—the most important decision is the first decision: *whether to be in common stocks at all!*

An Alternative View

An article by Sharpe questioned the value of attempting to predict market movements and generally argues against the practice.[8] Sharpe's conclusions rebut the assumption that analysis should begin with a view of the entire economy.

The Sharpe Study

Sharpe pointed out that, if one assumes the existence of an efficient market, it is difficult to consistently select undervalued stocks and experience superior returns. He contended that one should not expect to be able to derive superior results from engaging in aggregate market predictions and investing in stocks during good market periods and T-bills during poor market periods. He pointed out that, because T-bills yield less than stocks, if you miss a few turns, you will be at a disadvantage and this loss along with transactions costs will yield a return below that from a buy-and-hold policy.

Sharpe analyzed results that could be produced by predicting market returns under three assumptions. First, the differential average annual capital growth from a buy-and-hold policy was compared to the growth derived from perfect foresight (timing) regarding annual peaks and troughs. Second, he assumed that, for each calendar year, a prediction is made as to whether the year will be a "good" market year (returns on stocks above the returns on cash equivalent T-bills) or a "bad" market year (return on cash equivalents above return on stocks). The returns from perfect foresight regarding good and bad market years and a buy-and-hold stock policy were compared in this context. It was assumed that, with perfect foresight, the investor will invest in T-bills during bad market years, and in stocks during good market years. Third, a comparison was made between returns from a buy-and-hold policy and returns with less than perfect timing. The first two comparisons were done for three time periods: 1929–1972; 1934–1972; and 1946–1972. The final analysis considered only 1934–1972.

Perfect Timing of Peaks and Troughs The results of this comparison indicate the benefits of market timing, although the returns do not include

---

[8] William F. Sharpe, "Likely Gains from Market Timing," *Financial Analysts Journal,* Vol. 31, No. 2 (March–April, 1975), pp. 60–69.

either the dividends on the stocks or the returns from T-bills during market declines. The results, summarized in Table 9–2, indicate substantial returns from the ability to project the peaks and troughs in the market. Clearly, it is not very realistic to expect such ability on a consistent basis.

Table 9–2
Capital Growth in Common Stocks From a Buy-And-Hold Policy Compared to Investing with Perfect Timing

		Annual Rate of Capital Growth	
From	To	Buy-and-Hold	Perfect Timing
1929	1972	3.8%/Year	19.9%/year
1934	1972	6.6	17.3
1946	1972	7.1	15.7

Source: William F. Sharpe, "Likely Gains from Market Timing," *Financial Analysts Journal*, Vol. 31, No. 2 (March–April, 1975), p. 61. Reprinted by permission.

Perfect Timing of "Good" and "Bad" Years This analysis compared the returns from perfect timing of good and bad years, to the returns from a buy-and-hold policy, and to the returns from always investing in cash equivalents (T-bills). The standard deviation of annual returns and the geometric mean returns were also computed. The results for the three time periods are shown in Table 9–3 and assume a 2 percent commission on all switches from stocks to T-bills or vice versa.

Again, the ability to predict good and bad market years obviously has substantial value because it results in higher rates of return and lower risk as measured by the standard deviation of returns. Sharpe points out that the differential return (not adjusted for the risk difference) during the most recent period (1946–1972) was only about 2 percent. A comparison of the average annual return from perfect timing and the return for a mixture of stocks and cash equivalents that had the same standard deviation indicated *differential* returns of 6.76 percent during 1929–1975; 5.01 percent during 1934–1972; and 3.78 percent during 1946–1972.

Less Than Perfect Timing The final analysis derives the returns from alternative decisions and then applies these returns assuming the investor predicts correctly from 50 percent of the time to 100 percent of the time (perfect foresight). Assuming only a 50 percent record, the differential returns for equal risk were negative compared to those for buy-and-hold. As predictive ability increases, the differential returns improve until the returns become positive at 74 percent. This means that if you had predicted the market years correctly 74 percent of the time, you would enjoy higher returns than you would from a simple buy-and-hold policy. Sharpe's overall conclusion from these results is as follows:

Attempts to time the market are not likely to produce incremental returns of more than four percent per year over the long run. Moreover, unless a manager can predict whether the market will be good or bad each year with considerable

Table 9–3 **Overall Performance:**
Cash Equivalents, Stocks, and a Policy with Perfect Timing

	1929 to 1972			
	Cash Equivalents	Stocks	Perfect Timing	Buy-and-Hold versus Perfect Timing
Average Return	2.38%	10.64%	14.86%	4.26
Standard Deviation of Annual Returns	1.96	21.06	14.58	—
Geometric Mean Return	2.36	8.49	13.99	5.50
	1934 to 1972			
	Cash Equivalents	Stocks	Perfect Timing	Buy-and-Hold versus Perfect Timing
Average Return	2.40%	12.76%	15.25%	2.49
Standard Deviation of Annual Returns	2.00	18.17	13.75	—
Geometric Mean Return	2.38	11.23	14.46	3.23
	1946 to 1972			
	Cash Equivalents	Stocks	Perfect Timing	Buy-and-Hold versus Perfect Timing
Average Return	3.27%	12.79%	14.63%	1.84
Standard Deviation of Annual Returns	1.83	15.64	12.46	—
Geometric Mean Return	3.25	11.73	13.99	2.26

Source: William F. Sharpe, "Likely Gains from Market Timing," *Financial Analysts Journal,*
Vol. 31, No. 2 (March–April, 1975), p. 62. Reprinted by permission.

accuracy (e.g., be right at least seven times out of ten), he should probably avoid attempts to time the market altogether.[9]

Comments on the Sharpe Study

The tests and results presented by Sharpe are both interesting and informative in terms of a topic of importance to portfolio managers concerned with justifying their existence. The results are useful because they cover a range of conditions from perfect foresight about peaks and troughs which should result in maximum returns, to a set of results assuming only 50 percent accuracy, which is comparable to no forecasting ability. Sharpe's assumptions and methodology (with one exception) are not questioned, but his interpretation and discussion of the implications are.

---

[9] Sharpe, "Likely Gains," p. 67.

Transactions Costs Sharpe assumes a 2 percent transactions cost for every shift from stocks to T-bills or vice-versa. This charge only affects the results for the various trading cases and is considered excessive because it is generally not necessary to pay a commission on the purchase or sale of T-bills. If one assumes that, at the beginning of a new calendar year, it is going to be a bad market year and further assumes the portfolio is currently in stock, Sharpe apparently charges one percent to sell the stock and one percent to buy T-bills. In fact, it is possible to purchase one year T-bills at the average offering price without paying a commission, or buy 90 day T-bills and turn them over four times during the year. Likewise, at the end of a bad year, if a good year is projected, one need only allow the T-bills to mature (there is no commission paid when the cash is collected) and use the cash to buy stocks. Therefore, there is no reason to charge 2 percent since the only commission is on stocks. Further, even the one percent commission may be somewhat excessive in a world of negotiated rates where discounts are typically in excess of 40 percent from commissions listed on the NYSE on May 1, 1975.

Time Period of Study The study ended with 1972, probably because the latest data available at the start of the study was for this year. Even so, it is important to recognize that this time frame excludes the major bear market of 1973 and 1974 when the market declined 14.5 percent (1973) and 26.0 percent (1974). It also excludes 1975, when the market increased about 37 percent. The inclusion of these figures certainly would have implications for a portfolio manager who could have foreseen these major swings.

Effect of Differential Return Sharpe contends that about all that can be expected from perfect foresight is a 4 percent differential in the rate of return over a long period. Before one speaks disparagingly of "only 4 percent," consider the effect of some of these return differences on the wealth position of a potential investor. Assuming an investor began with a wealth position of 10,000 dollars in either 1929, 1934, or 1946 and then derived the returns shown in Table 9–3, his ending wealth positions would be as shown in Table 9–4.

The point is that it only requires a small differential in the long-run rate of return to cause a major difference in an investor's ending wealth position. However, none of these differential rates of return adjust for risk. Increasing the risk-adjusted rates of return would have provided more dramatic results. "Only 4 percent" is a very important difference in the long-run and is certainly worth some effort.

Requirements for Superiority Sharpe's final consideration was with what happens with less than perfect foresight. He concluded that the manager must be correct seven out of ten times. One can look at these results as an indication of what it takes to be superior. While the manager must do better than five out of ten, it is useful to know that *the point of superiority is at*

Table 9–4 **Ending Wealth Positions Under Different Return Assumptions**	
1929–1972	
$10,000 at 10.64% a year (Buy-and-Hold)—	$ 870,000
$10,000 at 14.86% a year (Perfect Foresight)—	$4,476,000
1934–1972	
$10,000 at 12.76% a year (Buy-and-Hold)—	$1,092,000
$10,000 at 15.25% a year (Perfect Foresight)—	$2,563,000
1946–1972	
$10,000 at 12.79% a year (Buy-and-Hold)—	$ 259,000
$10,000 at 14.63% a year (Perfect Foresight)—	$ 402,000

about three out of four correct projections. This required proportion would decline if one were to include the last several years and also reduce the cost of transactions. Still, these results indicate what it takes to be a superior market analyst. As with security analysis, it is not impossible to be superior, but it is not easy either. But, as shown, the rewards in terms of superior ending wealth can be substantial.

Summary

In this chapter we discussed why market analysis and industry analysis should be considered prior to company and stock analysis. Because aggregate economic changes affect all industries and all companies they should be considered first. There is substantial empirical support for such a sequence. An alternative view indicated that market analysis would not be useful, although the results substantiating this position were affected by the inclusion of an excessive commission charge and by the time period considered. Also, the differentials were more important than implied for an investor's final wealth position. This study found that, to be superior, it was necessary to be correct seven out of ten times. Such a conclusion confirms the contention made in the efficient markets chapter: in an efficient market it is not easy to be superior but it is possible. Given the potential rewards, it is important and clearly worth the effort.

Questions

1. Discuss why it is contended that market analysis and industry analysis should come before individual security analysis.

2. Discuss briefly the empirical evidence given by King that supports the contention above.

3. Would you expect all industries to have a similar relationship to the economy? Why or why not? Give an example.

4. What has happened to the relationship between individual stocks and the aggregate stock market over time? Can you think of any reasons for this change?

5. Would you expect all individual stocks to have a similar relationship to the aggregate stock market? What factors would contribute to the differences?

6. What "batting average" is required to be superior in terms of predicting market turns? Does it seem to be worthwhile to spend time attempting to predict these turns? Discuss.

7. Given an efficient stock market, what do you feel is necessary to make such predictions? Of what value is past information regarding market performance? Discuss.

References

Ahearn, Daniel S. "Investment Management and Economic Research." *Financial Analysts Journal,* Vol. 20, No. 1 (January–February 1964).

Blume, Marshall E. "On the Assessment of Risk." *Journal of Finance,* Vol. 26, No. 1 (March, 1971).

Brown, Philip and Ball, Ray. "Some Preliminary Findings on the Association Between the Earnings of a Firm, Its Industry, and the Economy." *Empirical Research in Accounting: Selected Studies 1967,* supplement to Vol. 5, *Journal of Accounting Research.*

Farretti, Andrew P. "The Economist Role in the Stock Market." *Business Economics,* Vol. 4, No. 1 (January, 1969).

Friedman, Milton and Schwartz, Anna J. "Money in Business Cycles." *The Review of Economics and Statistics,* supplement, Vol. 45, No. 1, Part II (February, 1968).

Keran, Michael W. "Monetary and Fiscal Influences on Economic Activity—The Historical Evidence." Federal Reserve Bank of St. Louis *Review,* Vol. 51, No. 11 (November, 1969).

King, Benjamin F. "Market and Industry Factors in Stock Price Behavior." *Journal of Business,* Vol. 39, No. 1, Part II (January, 1966).

Mennis, Edmund A. "Economics and Investment Management." *Financial Analysts Journal,* Vol. 22, No. 6 (November–December 1966).

Meyers, Stephen L. "A Re-Examination of Market and Industry Factors in Stock Price Behavior." *Journal of Finance,* Vol. 28, No. 3 (June, 1973).

Reilly, Frank K. "The Misdirected Emphasis in Security Valuation." *Financial Analysts Journal,* Vol. 29, No. 1 (January–February, 1973).

Sharpe, William F. "Likely Gains from Market Timing." *Financial Analysts Journal,* Vol. 31, No. 2 (March–April, 1975).

Shiskin, Julius. "Systematic Aspects of Stock Price Fluctuations." Reprinted in Lorie, James and Brealey, Richard, *Modern Developments in Investment Management,* 2nd ed. Hinsdale, Illinois: The Dryden Press, 1978.

Chapter 10
Aggregate Market Analysis: Using Macroeconomic Tools

Our previous discussion indicated the importance of attempting to estimate future aggregate stock market values, and, thereby, future market returns. Therefore, investors should become familiar with the major techniques available for estimating future market values or changes. These are basically three in number: the first is a *macroeconomic* approach based upon the underlying relationship between the aggregate economy and the securities markets. The second is the *present value of dividends* approach that follows directly from valuation theory, using basic valuation techniques to analyze the market. The third is the *technical analysis* approach which assumes that the best way to determine *future* changes in stock market values is to examine *past* movements in security prices. In this chapter, we will begin with macroeconomic analysis of the securities markets.

The Stock Market and the Economy

It is widely accepted that there is a strong relationship between the aggregate economy and the stock market. This is not surprising if you consider the fact that the price of a given stock reflects investor expectations as to how the issuing firm will perform, and that performance is, in turn, affected by the overall performance of the economy. There is substantial empirical support for the existence of this relationship, most of it derived by the National Bureau of Economic Research (NBER) in connection with the bureau's work on business cycles. Based on the relationship of alternative series to the behavior of the entire economy, the NBER has classified numerous economic series into three groups: leading, coincident, and lagging. Based upon extensive analysis, it has been shown that stock prices are one of the "better" leading series in terms of consistency and stability.

Reasons for Lead-Lag Relationship

The evidence clearly indicates not only a relationship between stock prices and the economy, but also that stock prices consistently turn *before* the economy does. Such a leading relationship may appear odd because the logic of the relation is that the stock market reflects the earnings of the companies involved; i.e., stock prices are influenced by corporate earnings and dividends and these variables are affected by the general state of the economy. Since the direction of causation is *from* the economy *to* the stock market, one may ask why stocks turn prior to the economy. There are two probable reasons.

The first is that stock prices reflect *expectations* of earnings and dividends and react to investor perceptions of *future* earnings and dividends. Investors attempt to estimate future earnings, so stock prices are based upon future economic activity, not current activity. If investors are adept at projecting future trends in the economy, they will be able to project earnings and dividends and adjust stock prices accordingly. Under such conditions stock prices should turn before the economy. This line of reasoning is also consistent with the efficient market hypothesis which pointed out that, in order to be a superior analyst, it is necessary to predict the relevant variables.

The second possible reason is that the stock market reacts to various economic series, but the relevant economic series are *leading indicators* of the economy. In this regard the series mentioned most often are corporate earnings, profit margins, and the money supply. The concern with corporate earnings is understandable, but it should be recognized that the earnings series itself tends to turn *before* the aggregate economy, as represented by the GNP or industrial production, does. Another series that is closely watched by analysts is corporate profit margins. This series is likewise a leading series and typically turns even earlier than do corporate earnings. Finally, a series that is watched very closely by many analysts and portfolio managers is the growth rate of the money supply. The fact that monetary growth leads the economy is one of the best documented relationships in economics because of the extensive work done on it by Friedman and Schwartz.[1] Therefore, because analysts and portfolio managers analyze economic series that lead the economy and adjust stock prices rapidly to changes in these relevant economic series, stock prices likewise become a leading series.

Because stock prices turn before the aggregate economy does, it is difficult to use economic behavior in predicting fluctuations in prices, although there are ways of doing so:

---

[1] Milton Friedman and Anna J. Schwartz, "Money and Business Cycles," *Review of Economics and Statistics,* Supplement, Vol. 45, No. 1, Part 2 (February, 1963), pp. 32–78, reprinted in Milton Friedman, *The Optimum Quantity of Money and Other Essays* (Chicago: Aldine Publishing Co., 1969), pp. 189–235.

1. Estimate aggregate economic activity *very far* into the future. Assuming the average lead of stock prices is about nine months, this would indicate that it is necessary to be able to project changes in the aggregate economy close to one year in advance.

2. Analyze other economic series that also lead the economy. The ideal would be to find a series that leads the economy by *more* than stock prices do, i.e., a series that typically leads by more than nine months.

3. Attempt to project the behavior of economic series that do not lead the economy by as much as stock prices do. An example would be a series that leads the economy by six months. The analyst would project fluctuations in this leading series for four or more months ahead which should be easier than attempting to project ups and downs in the aggregate economy for 12 months.

Given these alternatives, our subsequent discussion will concentrate on the leading indicator approach and the use of the money supply series to predict market behavior.

Cyclical Indicator Approach

The cyclical indicator approach to economic forecasting is based on the belief that the economy experiences discernible periods of expansion and contraction. This view has been investigated by the National Bureau of Economic Research (NBER), a nonprofit organization that attempts to ascertain and to present important economic facts and interpret them in a scientific and impartial manner. The NBER explains the business cycle as follows:

The "business cycle" concept has been developed from the sequence of events discerned in the historical study of the movements of economic activity. Though there are many cross-currents and variations in the pace of business activity, periods of business expansion appear to cumulate to peaks. As they cumulate, contrary forces tend to gain strength bringing about a reversal in business activity and the onset of a recession. As a recession continues, forces making for expansion gradually emerge until they become dominant and a recovery begins. . . .[2]

This explanation emphasizes the *cumulative* aspects of the process and indicates that there are certain events that regularly take place during the various phases of the business cycle.

Based upon an examination of the behavior of hundreds of economic time series in relation to past business cycles, the NBER grouped various

---

[2] Julius Shiskin, "Business Cycle Indicators: The Known and the Unknown," *Review of the International Statistical Institute,* Vol. 31, No. 3 (1963), pp. 361–383.

Table 10–1 Economic Series in NBER Leading Indicator Group

Series	Median Lead (−) or Lag (+) in months Peaks	Troughs	All Turns	Scores Economic Significance	Statistical Adequacy	Tim-ing	Con-formity	Smooth-ness	Cur-rency	Total
1. Average Work Week of Prod. Worker-Mfg.	−12	−2	−5	70	80	81	60	60	80	73
2. Index of New Business Formations	−11	−2	−3	80	61	78	59	80	80	73
3. Index of Stock Prices: 500 Common Stocks	− 9	−4	−5½	80	85	89	51	80	100	80
4. Index of New Building Permits	−13	−8	−9½	90	70	80	55	80	80	76
5. Layoff Rate-Manufacturing	−11	−1	−6½	70	80	79	80	60	80	76
6. New Orders-Consumer Goods (1967 Dollars)	− 6	−1	−4½	80	75	76	70	60	80	74
7. Contracts & Orders for Plant & Equipment (1967 Dollars)	− 9	−2	−5½	90	50	87	72	40	80	72
8. Net Change in Inven-tory (1967 Dollars)	− 5	−4	−4½	90	53	83	60	80	40	71
9. Net Change in Sensitive Prices	−15	−5	−5½	70	80	82	60	60	66	72
10. Vendor Performance	− 6	−5	−6	70	75	79	46	60	80	69
11. Money Balance (Ml)-1967	−10	−8	−9	90	85	80	41	100	80	79
12. Percent Change in Total Liquid Assets	− 6½	−6	−6	90	81	84	41	80	66	75

Source: Victor Zarnowitz and Charlotte Boschan, "Cyclical Indicators: An Evaluation and New Leading Indexes," *Business Conditions Digest* (May, 1975), pp. V–XXII.

economic series into three major categories in terms of this relationship. The initial list was compiled in 1938 and it has undergone numerous revisions over the years. The most recent revision was completed in May, 1975 and November, 1975 by Zarnowitz and Boschan.[3]

Indicator Categories

The first category is the *leading indicators* and includes those economic time series that have usually reached peaks or troughs before the corresponding points in aggregate economic activity were reached. The group currently includes the 12 series shown in Table 10–1. One of the 12 is "common stock

---

[3] Victor Zarnowitz and C. Boschan, "Cyclical Indicators: An Evaluation and New Leading Index," *Business Conditions Digest* (May, 1975), pp. V–XXII, and "New Composite Indexes of Coincident and Lagging Indicators," *Business Conditions Digest* (November, 1975), pp. V–XXIV.

prices" which has a median lead of 9 months at peaks and 4 months at troughs. Another leading series is the money supply in constant dollars which has a median lead of 10 months at peaks and 8 months at troughs.

The second category is *coincident indicators* which consist of those economic time series in which the peaks and troughs of the series roughly coincide with the peaks and troughs in the business cycle. Many of the economic time series in this category are employed by the bureau to help define the alternative phases of the cycle.

The third category is *lagging indicators* which includes series that have experienced their peaks and troughs after peaks and troughs occur in the aggregate economy. Timing and scores for the coincident and lagging series are contained in Table 10–2.

Table 10–2 **Economic Series in NBER Coincident and Lagging Indicator Group**

Series Coincident	Median Lead (−) or Lag (+) in months			Scores						
	Peaks	Troughs	All Turns	Economic Significance	Statistical Adequacy	Tim- ing	Con- formity	Smooth- ness	Cur- rency	Total
1. Number of Employees on nonagricultural payrolls	−2	0	0	100	78	89	80	100	80	88
2. Index of Industrial Production	−3	0	− ½	90	72	90	85	100	80	86
3. Personal Income, less transfers (deflated by PEE)	0	− 1	− ½	90	70	74	64	100	80	78
4. Manufacturing & trade sales, deflated	−3	0	− ½	90	65	90	75	80	53	78
Lagging										
1. Average duration of employment	+1	+ 8	+ 3½	90	78	89	95	80	80	86
2. Manufacturing & trade inventories (1967 dollars)	+2½	+ 3	+ 3	90	70	89	64	100	53	80
3. Labor cost per unit output, manufacturing	+8½	+11	+10	80	55	87	51	80	80	73
4. Commercial & industrial loans outstanding, weekly rep. banks	+1½	+ 5	+ 3½	80	60	86	81	100	100	83
5. Ratio of consumer installment debt to personal income	+6½	+ 7	+ 7	80	70	87	44	100	53	74
6. Average prime rate charged by banks	+3½	+14	+ 4	90	95	85	62	100	100	87

Source: Victor Zarnowitz and Charlotte Boschan, "New Composite Indexes of Coincident and Lagging Indicators," *Business Conditions Digest* (November, 1975), pp. V–XXIV.

A final category is entitled, "other selected series," and includes series that are expected to influence aggregate economic activity, but that cannot be neatly categorized in one of the three main groups. This includes such series as U.S. balance of payments, federal surplus or deficit, and military contract awards.

Selection Criteria Employed

The bureau has always employed certain criteria in the selection of indicators, but the process was admittedly rather subjective. One of the principal changes made during a 1966 revision was an attempt to specify the selection criteria in a more rigorous manner and explicitly score each candidate series for each of six criteria as follows:

1) economic significance
2) statistical adequacy
3) historical conformity to business cycles
4) cyclical timing record
5) smoothness
6) promptness of publication.

A high score for a series indicates that the series should be very useful in the analysis of cyclical movements.

Analytical Measures

When examining a given economic series for predictive purposes, it is important to consider more than simply the behavior of the series overall. The NBER has devised certain analytical measures for dealing with behavior within a series.

Diffusion Indexes As the name implies, these indexes indicate how pervasive a given movement is in a series. They are used to specify *the percent of reporting units in a series indicating a given result.* If there are 100 companies that constitute the sample reporting new orders for equipment, the diffusion index for this series would indicate what proportion of the 100 companies were reporting higher orders during an expansion. In addition to knowing that aggregate new orders are increasing, it is helpful to know whether 55 percent of the companies in the sample are reporting higher orders or whether 95 percent are. Such information helps the analyst project the future length and strength of an expansion. It is also helpful to know past diffusion index values to determine whether a trend exists. The existence of a trend is important since it has been shown that *the diffusion indexes for a series almost always reach their peak or trough before the peak or trough in the corresponding aggregate series.*

Rates of Change Somewhat similar to the diffusion index is the rate of change measure for the series. It is one thing to know that there has been an increase in a series, but quite another to know that it is a 10 percent increase as compared to a 7 percent increase the previous month. Like the diffusion index, the rate of change values for a series reach a peak or trough prior to the peak or trough in the aggregate series.

Direction of Change These tables show at a glance which series went up or down (plus or minus) during the period and how long the movement in this direction has persisted.

Comparison with Previous Cycles These tables show the movements of individual series over previous business cycles. Current movements are then compared to previous cycles from the peak or the trough for the same economic series. This comparison indicates how this series is acting in the current expansion or contractions: is it slower or faster, stronger or weaker than it was during the last cycle? This information can be useful because typically movements in the *initial* months of an expansion or contraction indicate the *ultimate* length and strength of the expansion or contraction.

Summary Measures

The NBER has recognized that the cyclical indicator approach alone is not sufficient for economic analysis. Further, it is dangerous to concentrate attention on a single series or several series in a timing category. To forestall such a practice, the bureau has devised several measures that summarize the action of different series.

Amplitude Adjusted General Indexes This involves standardizing results for individual series by deriving the average month-to-month percentage of change for each series using this as the base percentage of change, set equal to one. Subsequent percentage changes are then compared to this base figure to determine whether the series is increasing faster than standard (a value greater than one) or slower than usual (a value less than one). This adjustment makes it possible to combine various series and consider the composite trend for some group of indicators (e.g., all leading indicators) in order to determine the current strength of the expansion or contraction.

Comprehensive Diffusion Indexes As noted, it is possible to derive a diffusion index for an individual series to determine how pervasive is a given movement up or down. Likewise, it is possible to construct a diffusion index for a given class of indicators. The diffusion concept is popularly used with the leading indicator group to determine the percentage of the 12 leading indicators that is increasing at a given point in time. Those who use the diffusion concept contend that when more than 50 percent of the leading indicators decline for more than three months, it signals the end of an expansion.

Timing Distributions This method is used to determine the number of individual series in a category reaching new highs during each of the recent months of an expansion, or new lows during periods of business contraction.[4]

Limitations of the Indicator Approach

The NBER has consistently attempted to improve the usefulness of the indicator approach while acknowledging some very definite limitations. The most obvious limitation is "false signals," i.e., past patterns suggest that the indicators are currently signalling a contraction, but they turn up again and nullify previous signals.

A similar problem occurs when the indicators do not point toward a definite change in direction, but experience a period of hesitancy which is difficult to interpret. These problems are likewise caused by another limitation, the *variability* of the leads and lags. While a given economic series may *on the average* lead the peak or trough in the business cycle by five or six months, the range of leads over the years may have varied from one to ten months. This variability means that the analyst is not able to act with complete confidence based upon short-run signals.

There are also problems both gathering the data (getting the original data as soon as possible) and revising it. Also, many of the series are seasonally adjusted and there may be subsequent adjustments to the seasonal adjustment factors. Finally, the NBER points out that there are numerous political or international developments which significantly influence the economy, but which cannot be encompassed in a statistical system.

Leading Indicators and Stock Prices

Because of the relationship between leading indicators and the economy, some authors have suggested that one might be able to use leading indicators to predict stock prices. A study by Heathcotte and Apilado examined this relationship using the " 1966 short list" of leading economic series and a stock price series (the S&P 500).[5] On the average all the other series on the

---

[4] Monthly presentations of all the series and analytical measures are contained in U.S. Department of Commerce, *Business Conditions Digest* (Washington, D.C.: U.S. Government Printing Office).

[5] Bryan Heathcotte and Vincent P. Apilado, "The Predictive Content of Some Leading Economic Indicators for Future Stock Prices," *Journal of Financial and Quantitative Analysis,* Vol. 9, No. 2 (March, 1974), pp. 247–258.

list led the business cycle at peaks by more than the stock price series did, and two series led by more than stock prices at troughs. Taking into account the publication lag for the various series, with one exception, all series led at peaks but none had a true lead at troughs.

Although the series tended to lead stock prices *on average,* none of the series were consistent for all cycles, so the authors constructed a diffusion index of these leading series which indicated the *overall* direction for the group of series. Because of the volatility of this diffusion series, they computed a three-month moving average of the diffusion index. They proposed to use these diffusion indexes with alternative filter rules to construct an investment policy. (A filter indicates how much a series must increase or decrease before action is taken. A 5 percent filter would mean that, if the series increased by 5 percent from its low, you would take some appropriate action. If the series declined 5 percent from its peak, you would take the opposite action.) Heathcotte and Apilado determined that when the diffusion index of leading indicators increased Y percent, they would buy and hold common stocks until it decreased X percent from a peak at which time they would sell the portfolio and sell short. Different filters were applied at peaks and troughs.

The usefulness of the leading indicator series was tested by examining the difference in investment results using different filters versus a buy-and-hold policy (B&H) that considered commissions, but ignored dividends. Monthly data were considered for the period November, 1959 to November, 1971. The diffusion index for each month included *only* publicly available information. Filters, ranging from one-half of one percent to 100 percent, were applied to the one-month diffusion index (D1) and the three-month moving average index (D3).

The results indicated that some filters were never used and so functioned like a buy-and-hold policy. The results for the two series D1 and D3 were similar. Assuming *perfect foresight* regarding the best filter to use, the trading strategy using D1 outperformed B&H in two of four periods, while the tests using D3 outperformed B&H in all four periods. The geometric annual returns with D1 were 11.3 percent and with D3 they were 14.6 percent, while B&H experienced returns of about 4 percent. Although the trading rules were superior, these results required considerable foresight regarding the best filter to use and it would be difficult to have such foresight because the "best" filter was *not stable* over time. Also the exclusion of dividends biased the results in favor of the trading rule.

The authors considered the trading rule without hindsight by assuming that an investor used the best filter for the *previous* period when making his current investment decision. These results were inconclusive because the D1 index was superior in one period, the same as B&H in another, and inferior in two periods. The trading rules with the D3 index were equal to B&H in one period, inferior in one, and superior in two periods. Adjusting for dividends did not make any difference.

It appears that several of the leading series do lead stock prices and a diffusion index of these series could be useful if one could determine an appropriate filter. Without such foresight these series do not appear to be able to beat a buy-and-hold policy when one takes commissions into account.

Monetary Variables and Stock Prices

One of the economic factors assumed to be most closely related to stock prices is monetary policy. The best known monetary variable in this regard is the money supply. In actuality, the influence of the money supply on stock prices is an offshoot of its influence on the aggregate economy. Milton Friedman and Anna J. Schwartz have thoroughly documented the historical record of the empirical relationship that exists between changes in the growth rate of the stock of money and subsequent changes in aggregate economic activity.[6] Their research indicated that, during the period 1867–1960, declines in the rate of growth of the money supply preceded business contraction by an average of 20 months.[7] Expansions in the growth rate of the money supply, on average, preceded expansions in business activity by about eight months. The timing of the relationship was highly variable but its existence was consistent: every major contraction or expansion during the period 1867–1960 was preceded by a contraction or expansion in the growth rate of the money supply. In addition, Friedman specified the transmission mechanism through which changes in the growth rate of the money supply affect the aggregate economy. The work done by Friedman and Schwartz has led several authors to specifically examine the relationship between alternative monetary variables (typically the M1 money supply) and stock prices.

Money and the Economy

The basic economic principle operating in the quantity theory of money is that money is considered an asset by consumers and businesses, and the demand for money is similar to the demand for other assets. Therefore, spending units allocate their wealth among all assets, including money, by comparing the benefits accruing to them in the form of service and income from each asset and the current price of the asset.[8] Discrepancies between actual and desired holdings of assets will be eliminated through portfolio

---

[6] Milton Friedman and Anna J. Schwartz, "Money and Business Cycles."

[7] In the Friedman-Schwartz study money supply was defined as bank demand deposits and time deposits plus currency in the hands of the public (M2). Business cycle expansions and contractions were used as defined by the National Bureau of Economic Research.

[8] Leonall C. Anderson and Jerry L. Jordan, "Money in a Modern Quantity Theory Framework," Federal Reserve Bank of St. Louis, *Review*, Vol. 49, No. 12 (December, 1967), pp. 4–5.

adjustments, that is, through sales and/or purchases. It is postulated that changes in the growth rate of the money supply cause discrepancies between desired and actual holdings of money and this imbalance initiates a series of portfolio adjustments that eventually influences economic activity and asset prices.

The demand for money by an economic unit generally depends upon: 1) the real wealth of the unit; 2) current and expected interest rates; 3) expectations regarding future prices of goods and services; and 4) other assets in the portfolio. However, changes in the economy's *supply* of money are for the most part *independent* of the factors which determine the *demand* for money by economic units.[9] In general, the size and growth rate of the nominal money stock is controlled by the monetary authorities via the rate at which reserves and currency are supplied to the economy by open-market transactions of the Federal Reserve Board. Thus, these transactions are a potential source of discrepancy between actual and desired money balances.

The Transmission Mechanism

Friedman and Schwartz sketched the effects of an unexpected rise in the growth rate of the money supply caused by an increase in the rate of open-market purchases of government bonds by the Federal Reserve.[10] The initial sellers of the securities will *temporarily* add the proceeds to their asset portfolios. If the seller was a commercial bank, then reserves will be increased accordingly. If the seller was an individual, he will generally deposit the new cash balances in a commercial bank, and thus add to bank reserves. In either case, commercial banks become more liquid. While the seller willingly sold the security for the price offered, the sale has caused an imbalance in his portfolio—too much cash, not enough securities. Both the nonbank seller and/or the commercial bank will attempt to readjust their asset portfolios. In the process, the banks will create money, thereby transmitting the increase in reserves to the total money stock. The nonbank seller and the bank will initially turn to securities comparable to those sold, i.e., fixed-interest coupon, low-risk obligations. As they acquire these securities, prices will be bid up, yields will decline relative to other potential assets and the banks will begin expanding their loans, while nonbank units will turn to other asset categories: higher risk, fixed-coupon securities; equities; real property; etc. As noted by Friedman and Schwartz:

. . . one should expect it to have its first impact on the financial markets, and there, first on bonds, and only later on equities, and only still later on actual

---

[9] It is acknowledged that there is some feedback from the economy to the money supply. The important point is that the *initial* and most important influence runs from changes in the growth rate of the money supply to the economy. For elaboration and empirical proof of this point, see Friedman and Schwartz, "Money and Business Cycles," pp. 211, 213–215.

[10] Ibid., pp. 229–234.

flows of payments for real resources. This is, of course, the actual pattern. The financial markets tend to revive well before the trough.[11]

In turn, as yields on financial assets decline, the demand for nonfinancial assets will increase. As nonfinancial assets become more expensive, demand for newly constructed nonfinancial assets increases. The process continues until the initial impact of the Federal Reserve's increase in bank reserves is diffused throughout the economy.

A similar process of portfolio adjustment operates when liquidity is decreased, i.e., when open-market sales cause a decline in reserves and a reduction in the growth rate of the money supply.

The discussion above provides a plausible explanation of the empirical relationship between changes in the growth rate of the money supply and changes in economic activity. *The hypothesized initial impact of monetary changes is on the bond market, then on the stock market, and finally on the aggregate economy.*

Money Supply–Stock Price Studies

Based upon the transmission mechanism described above, one would expect a relationship between changes in the growth rate of the money supply and changes in the level of stock prices. Several studies have empirically examined this relationship.

Sprinkel Studies

Some of the earliest and most widely read work on this was done by Beryl W. Sprinkel.[12] On the basis of the Friedman–Schwartz findings, Sprinkel hypothesized that changes in the growth rate of the money supply would precede changes in stock prices, and tested this by examining movements in a six month moving average of the growth rate of the seasonally adjusted money supply series relative to a stock price series (the Standard & Poor's Index of 425 Industrials). The initial study examined the period 1918–1963, and was later up-dated through 1970.[13]

The analysis involved an examination of time series plots of money supply growth, stock prices, and the business cycle. A visual analysis indicated that a reduction in the growth rate of the money stock usually preceded stock price declines by 9 months on average; while an increase in the growth rate of money preceded stock price recoveries by two months. After extensive graphic analysis, Sprinkel concluded:

Although we can be reasonably confident that major bull markets cannot develop without expanding monetary growth, and that major bear markets cannot

[11] Ibid., p. 231.

[12] The original work is contained in Beryl W. Sprinkel, *Money and Stock Prices* (Homewood, Illinois: Richard D. Irwin, 1964).

[13] Beryl W. Sprinkel, *Money and Markets: A Monetarist View* (Homewood, Illinois: Richard D. Irwin, 1971).

occur without contracting monetary growth, we cannot be nearly so certain about the length of monetary change prior to major market movements. The lead of expanding monetary growth before bull markets has inevitably been short, usually 1 to 3 months; the lead before bear markets has been much more erratic, ranging from zero in 1912 and 1966 to a typical lead of 12 to 15 months. Clearly, changing monetary growth is not the only factor influencing stock price changes. Equally obvious is the fact that fluctuating liquidity changes appear to have a major impact on equity prices and should not be ignored in making equity investment decisions that require an explicit or implicit forecast of the future.[14]

Palmer Study

A study by Michael Palmer examined the relationship between changes in the growth rate of money and a moving average of *percentage of change* in stock prices for the period 1959–1969.[15] The relationship was quite close except for a period in 1964 and 1965. The turning points in the two series were similar and where a lead relationship existed, the money supply generally led by a few months, except in the first quarter of 1967 when the stock market led the money supply. It was not possible, however, to determine a specific lead period and there was no indicated difference in the leads at peaks and troughs. Some correlation results for coincident time periods were very poor during 1964–1965 and much better for the periods 1959–1963 and 1966–1969.

Keran Study

A study by Keran discussed the factors that determine the level of stock prices and examined each of the individual factors separately.[16] He used a combined regression model to relate the level of quarterly stock prices to money supply growth, economic growth, expected price changes, and expected corporate earnings. The overall results were quite good in explaining the *level* of long-run stock prices. The implied influence of monetary growth was statistically significant but appeared to be minor (i.e., a one percent acceleration in the growth of real money would lead to a 1.31 increase in the stock price index).[17]

Homa–Jaffee Study

Homa and Jaffee (H–J) employed a regression model that used the level of money supply and the rate of growth of the money supply to predict the

---

[14] Ibid., pp. 225–226.

[15] Michael Palmer, "Money Supply, Portfolio Adjustments and Stock Prices," *Financial Analysts Journal*, Vol. 26, No. 4 (July–August, 1970), pp. 19–22.

[16] Michael W. Keran, "Expectations, Money and the Stock Market," Federal Reserve Bank of St. Louis *Review*, Vol. 53, No. 1 (January, 1971), pp. 16–31.

[17] Ibid., p. 26.

level of stock prices.[18] The test model related the current level of stock prices to the current *level* of the money supply, the current *growth rate* of the money supply (as a proxy for expectations), and the growth of the money supply, lagged one quarter.

Because the current level of the money supply and the current growth rate of the money supply were used, the accuracy of stock market predictions depended on the investor's ability to predict the money supply. H–J considered three methods for predicting the level and growth rate: (1) perfect foresight, (2) naive extrapolation of past period values, and (3) regression analysis.

The results indicated a significant correlation between monetary variables and the stock market index although there was significant serial correlation in the residuals. When perfect foresight regarding the money supply was assumed, the investor simulations consistently out-performed the buy-and-hold strategy. The naive extrapolation results were inferior to those from buy-and-hold, while the simulations employing a separate regression model to predict the money supply were superior to results from buy-and-hold. The perfect foresight results were not surprising because one would expect superior results from investors with foresight about *any* relevant variable. The results with naive extrapolation support the efficient market hypothesis that stock prices adjust almost instantaneously to all available information and, therefore, past information alone is not very useful.[19] The superior results with the regression model are difficult to explain.

Hamburger–Kochin Study

Hamburger and Kochin tested the hypothesis that the money supply has a direct effect on the stock market, and examined the problem of measuring common stock risk.[20] They utilized the liquidity effect and the earnings effect to explain how the money supply affects common stocks. They also hypothesized that the risk premium on common stocks is influenced by changes in the money supply; variations in the money supply cause increased variations in the economy and stock prices and the risk premium on stocks will increase as the volatility of the money supply increases.

Hamburger and Kochin tested the "total effect" of the money supply on stock prices by using the following regression equation:

$$\Delta X_t = a + b_1 \Delta M_t + b_2 \Delta M_{t-1} + \ldots + b_{n+1} \Delta M_{t-n}$$

[18] Kenneth E. Homa and Dwight M. Jaffee, "The Study of Money and Common Stock Prices," *Journal of Finance*, Vol. 26, No. 5 (December, 1971), pp. 1045–1066.

[19] See Eugene F. Fama, "Efficient Capital Markets: A Review of Theory and Empirical Work," *Journal of Finance*, Vol. 25, No. 2 (May, 1970), pp. 383–417.

[20] Michael J. Hamburger and Levis A. Kochin, "Money and Stock Prices: The Channels of Influence," *Journal of Finance*, Vol. 27, No. 2 (May, 1972), pp. 231–249.

where M_t is the growth rate of the money supply and X_t represents one of four security market variables: the market yield on three-month treasury bills, the corporate Aaa bond rate, Standard & Poor's composite stock price index, and the Standard & Poor's dividend-price ratio.

The treasury bills coefficients indicated a short-run negative effect of money supply growth on short-term interest rates. In time, though, the growth rate of income, and hence the increase in the demand for money, pushed interest rates back up to their former levels and beyond. In the case of the dividend yield (and stock prices) the initial negative (positive) effect lasted longer and the dependent variable never reached its former level. Changes in monetary growth showed a stronger short-run effect on the stock market than they did on the bond market, suggesting that *changes in the money supply have a direct effect on stock prices.*

The test of the effect of changes in the risk premium on the stock market used data back to 1871 and related the rate of change of the money supply to the rate of change of stock prices. The results showed that higher levels of past economic variability were correlated with lower equity prices, which supported their hypothesis that increased volatility in the money supply had an adverse effect on stock prices.

Miller Comment

The studies by Keran and by Hamburger and Kochin were criticized by Merton Miller because in both there was significant serial correlation in the residuals which could seriously limit their statements about statistical significance and might indicate that the authors had misspecified the variables used in the models.[21] Miller questioned their use of levels and called attention to the number of degrees of freedom used up by the long lags and numerous constraints. Finally Miller contended that the separation of the direct and indirect effects of the money supply on the level of stock prices was somewhat arbitrary.

Pesando Analysis

James Pesando likewise examined several previous studies in terms of the abnormally good forecasts achieved by the models.[22] He extended the Keran, Hamburger-Kochin (H-K), and Homa-Jaffee (H-J) models. Following a discussion of the three alternative models, he considered some potential empirical problems.

Because of these problems, Pesando re-estimated the Keran and H-K models and examined their structural stability. The results with the change

---

[21] Merton H. Miller, "Discussion of Hamburger and Kochin, 'Money and Stock Prices. . . ,' " *Journal of Finance,* Vol. 27, No. 2 (May, 1972), pp. 294–298.

[22] James E. Pesando, "The Supply of Money and Common Stock Prices: Further Observations on the Econometric Evidence," *Journal of Finance,* Vol. 29, No. 3 (June, 1974), pp. 909–921.

in the structure of the model indicated serious deterioration in the coefficients which casts doubt on the stability of the model. An analysis of the models using Canadian data generated mixed results. The basic models were inferior, but the predictions were better. The author also tested the forecasting ability of the H–J model and contended that, even with continual updating, the results were not impressive because the models did not outperform the naive no-change extrapolation. Finally, the models did not specify major turning points. Based upon the foregoing tests, the author concluded:

Finally, the inability of these models to generate accurate *ex post* forecasts of stock prices provides *de facto* evidence of their failure to capture a stable structural relationship. This result, in turn, suggests that one should not place undue confidence in the quantitative estimates of the impact of fluctuations in the money supply on common stock prices.[23]

Cooper Study

In the same issue of the *Journal of Finance*, Richard Cooper examined the relationship between money supply and stock prices in terms of the efficient market hypothesis.[24] He discussed the simple quantity theory of money concept (SQ) and the efficient market hypothesis (EM) that contends one should not be able to use past data to forecast price changes. His combined theory (SQ–EM) states that money supply may influence the market rate of return, but that, because of the existence of aggressive investors who attempt to forecast important variables, market returns may actually *lead* money changes.

His initial tests examined the relationship between percentage of change in M1 money supply and the S&P 500 for the period 1947–1970 using regression analysis. The analysis using monthly data generated very poor results. In contrast, using annual data, the results were quite good ($R^2 = .625$) and indicated a relationship in the long-run.

Tests using spectral analysis indicated that the relationship between the money supply and stock returns was statistically significant for cycles of six months or more. Subsequent tests confirmed a strong relationship for longer periods, but little relationship for short intervals (e.g., one month) and also indicated that money supply fluctuations were amplified several times in terms of fluctuations in stock returns. An analysis of the lead/lag relationship for alternative intervals indicated a relatively constant lag whereby *money seems to lag stock returns by about one to three months.* For short intervals money supply changes led stock returns by a very short period but the relationship was very weak.

---

[23] Ibid., pp. 920–921.

[24] Richard V. L. Cooper, "Efficient Capital Markets and the Quantity Theory of Money," *Journal of Finance,* Vol. 29, No. 3 (June, 1974), pp. 887–908.

Because the SQ–EM model employed predictions of the behavior of the money supply, it also included an analysis of two proxy variables: forecasts of the money supply using past observations of its behavior; and forecasts from current and past monetary base observations. Using a time series model, it was found that money supply changes can be forecast one, two, or three periods ahead with reasonable accuracy. These results are interesting because this forecast period coincides with the lead of securities' returns over money. The results show that money lags stock returns by about one to three months, and that future money changes can be forecast one to three months ahead. This consistency in forecasting lends further support to the SQ–EM model.

Finally, Cooper analyzed the relation between monetary base changes and stock returns. The relationship is not as strong as that between stocks and the money supply, but there are several statistically significant peaks using long interval data. Also, the inclusion of the monetary base helps to account for some of the lead of returns over money.

The author concluded that money supply changes appear to have an important effect on stock returns, but the evidence indicates that stock returns *lead* money supply changes.

Auerbach Study

A study by Auerbach likewise questioned the Keran and Homa–Jaffee findings for statistical reasons.[25] He noted that it is necessary to take account of common long-run trends and cycles in variables that are related, and demonstrated that this could have been a problem with prior studies. He also discussed the efficient market hypothesis which implies that stock behavior should *not* be related to past monetary changes and discussed the regression analysis section of the Cooper study in which the hypothesized relationship is quite weak.

Auerbach removed the trend and cyclical components of the money and stock price series and correlated the adjusted series. The results indicated that past changes in the M1 money supply were *not* related to future stock price changes, but that stock returns *were* related to current and *future* changes in M1, although the relationship was weak. He concluded that his results are consistent with the efficient market hypothesis which contends that historical information is not of value in predicting future stock prices.

Rozeff Studies

Two studies by Rozeff also raised doubts about the usefulness of the money supply in predicting stock price changes. His arguments were based upon

---

[25] Robert D. Auerbach, "Money and Stock Prices," *Monthly Review, Federal Reserve Bank of Kansas City* (September–October, 1976), pp. 3–11.

the existence of efficient capital markets.[26] The author re-examined the returns from Sprinkel's trading rule reported in his first book, and dealt with the relationship using a regression model. In the test of the trading rule, it was noted that Sprinkel apparently sold stock when monetary growth had declined for 15 months and acquired stock after money growth had increased for 2 months after a trough. Based on this trading rule, Sprinkel reported returns exceeding those from a buy-and-hold policy. When Rozeff attempted to replicate the rule, the returns were below those from buy-and-hold. The difference is that Rozeff bought and sold in *all* instances when monetary growth changed, while Sprinkel *only* followed the rule when monetary growth changed before a peak or trough in the economy. This means that, to apply Sprinkel's test, it is necessary to predict peaks and troughs in the economy that are not reported until several months after they occur.

In contrast to Sprinkel's graphic analysis, the author used a three-step regression analysis assuming that money supply changes: *before* stock prices change; *concurrent* with stock prices; and *after* stock prices change. The results with money supply only leading were quite poor; the explanatory power was negligible (1 to 4 percent). He also used the relationship in a trading rule. When commissions were excluded, the returns from the trading rule were similar to those from buy-and-hold; including commissions, the returns from the trading rule were clearly inferior to those from buy-and-hold.

When contemporaneous changes in money supply were added to the regression model, the explanatory power of the model increased to between 4 and 10 percent. It is contended that such a strong link with *current* money supply changes is *not* inconsistent with an efficient market because this data cannot be used to predict stock prices. Finally, when *future* changes in the growth of money supply are included, there is a substantial increase in explanatory power to 15–20 percent. The lead of stock prices over money supply is one to two months. This strong leading relationship is taken as evidence of an efficient stock market for which *money appears to matter,* although the timing of the relationship is contrary to expectations. To further substantiate the importance of future money supply changes, a trading rule was devised that used *future* money supply growth and the returns generally exceeded the buy-and-hold returns even after allowance was made for commissions.

Numerous investigators have examined the empirical relationship between money supply and stock prices. The early work done by Sprinkel indicated that, on average, there was a lead of money over stock prices, but

---

[26] M. S. Rozeff, "Money and Stock Prices: Market Efficiency and the Lag Effect of Monetary Policy," *Journal of Financial Economics,* Vol. 1, No. 3 (September, 1974), pp. 245–302; M. S. Rozeff, "The Money Supply and the Stock Market," *Financial Analysts Journal,* Vol. 31, No. 5 (September–October, 1975), pp. 18–26.

the relationship was variable and the lead declined during the 1960's. This was generally confirmed in studies by Palmer, Keran, Homa–Jaffee, and Hamburger–Kochin, although Miller and Pesando questioned some of the methodology.

Studies by Cooper, Rozeff, and Auerbach contended that, with efficient capital markets, one should not expect changes in monetary growth to precede stock price changes. The recent empirical results have generally supported the efficient market hypothesis. All of these studies have basically concluded that, although there *is* a relationship between money supply growth and stock prices, it is not possible to use the relationship to derive above average returns because the stock market *anticipates* changes in monetary growth.

Summary

This discussion of aggregate market analysis using macroeconomic variables contains some encouraging news and some discouraging information. On the one hand, there is ample evidence of a strong and consistent relationship between activity in the overall economy and in the stock market. At the same time, it has been shown that stock prices consistently turn from four to nine months *before* the economy does. Because of this timing factor, it is necessary to either forecast economic activity 12 months ahead, examine leading indicator series that lead the economy by more than stock prices do, or forecast economic series that lead the economy by less than stock prices do, but forecast them well ahead. The subsequent discussion examined two sets of series that have been suggested as possibly leading the economy by more than stock prices do, the NBER leading indicator series and money supply.

Following description of the leading indicator approach and the specific series available, there was a discussion of a study that attempted to use the leading indicators to time investment decisions. The results indicated that, if the investigator had *perfect foresight* regarding the appropriate filter to use with a diffusion index of leading series, the investment results would clearly be superior to those achieved with a buy-and-hold policy. If the investor attempted to invest using *past* filters as a guide, the results were mixed, and were not consistently superior.

There was an extensive discussion of the expected relationship between the money supply and stock prices which is an outgrowth of the quantity theory of money. Because of the expected relationship between monetary variables and stock prices implied by the theory, there have been numerous empirical studies of the topic. Interestingly, the empirical results have changed over time. The early work indicated that money supply was important and that it could be used in making investment decisions. Contrary evidence began to appear in 1974 with further support provided in 1975. However, all of the studies acknowledge that *there is a significant relationship between money supply and stock prices*. Unfortunately for those looking for a mechanical trading device, recent rigorous research indicates that *monetary growth and stock prices generally turn at about the same point in time or that stock prices turn before the money supply does*. Therefore, it is *not* possible to use the monetary series to develop a mechanical trading rule that will outperform a buy-and-hold policy because the market reacts very quickly to relevant information.

The good news is that there is a relationship between economic variables and the stock market that should be useful in forecasting aggregate stock market movements. The bad news is that the capital markets are quite efficient since it is apparently *not* possible to use past information regarding the economy to develop a mechanical trading rule that will be superior to a simple buy-and-hold policy. It appears that it is necessary to either forecast the aggregate economy far into the future or forecast leading economic series by several months.

Questions

1. Why would you expect there to be a relationship between economic activity and stock price movements?

2. While at a social gathering you discuss the reason for the relationship between the economy and the stock market, but one of the listeners points out that stock prices typically turn *before* the economy. How would you explain this phenomenon?

3. Given that stock prices *lead* the economy, how can you use economic variables to *predict* stock market movements?

4. Define leading, lagging, and coincident indicators. Give an example of each and discuss why you think it is classified as such—i.e., the economic reason for a relationship between this series and the economy.

5. Discuss a diffusion index of leading series and consider why you might expect it to be useful in predicting stock market movements.

6. Briefly describe the results of the Heathcotte–Apilado study and discuss the implications of the results for investors who want to use the leading indicators.

7. Briefly describe the transmission mechanism from a *decline* in the growth rate of the money supply to the economy. Specifically discuss how such a change in monetary policy works its way through the economy.

8. Assuming that changes in monetary growth *should* effect stock price movements, what argument would an advocate of the efficient market hypothesis set forth regarding the ability to use the monetary series to predict stock price changes?

9. Is it a contradiction to say that there is a strong, consistent relationship between money supply changes and stock prices and yet also say that money supply changes cannot be used to predict stock price movements?

10. Discuss the implications of the results of the empirical studies on money and stock prices for an investor attempting to project stock price movements. Do these results support the EMH? Why or why not?

References

Andersen, Leonall C. and Jordan, Jerry L. "Money in a Modern Quantity Theory Framework." Federal Reserve Bank of St. Louis *Review*, Vol. 49, No. 12 (December, 1967).

Auerbach, Robert D. "Money and Stock Prices." *Monthly Review, Federal Reserve Bank of Kansas City* (September–October, 1976).

Bolton, A. H. *Money and Investment Profits.* Homewood, Ill., Dow Jones–Irwin, Inc., 1967.

Cooper, Richard V. L. "Efficient Capital Markets and the Quantity Theory of Money." *Journal of Finance,* Vol. 29, No. 3 (June, 1974).

Friedman, Milton J. *The Optimum Quantity of Money and Other Essays.* Chicago: Aldine Publishing Co., 1969.

Friedman, Milton J. and Schwartz, Anna J. "Money and Business Cycles." *Review of Economics and Statistics,* Vol. 45, No. 1 (February, 1963), Supplement.

Hamburger, Michael J. and Kochin, Levis A. "Money and Stock Prices: The Channels of Influence." *Journal of Finance,* Vol. 27, No. 2 (May, 1972).

Heathcotte, Bryan and Apilado, Vincent P. "The Predictive Content of Some Leading Economic Indicators for Future Stock Prices." *Journal of Financial and Quantitative Analysis,* Vol. 9, No. 2 (March, 1974).

Homa, Kenneth E. and Jaffee, Dwight M. "The Supply of Money and Common Stock Prices." *Journal of Finance,* Vol. 26, No. 5 (December, 1971).

Keran, Michael W. "Expectations, Money and the Stock Market." Federal Reserve Bank of St. Louis *Review,* Vol. 53, No. 1 (January, 1971).

Meigs, A. James. *Money Matters.* New York: Harper & Row Publishers, 1972.

Miller, Merton H. "Money and Stock Prices: The Channels of Influence, Discussion." *Journal of Finance,* Vol. 27, No. 2 (May, 1972).

Moore, Geoffrey H. (ed.) *Business Cycle Indicators.* Princeton, N.J.: Princeton University Press, National Bureau of Economic Research, 1961.

Moore, Geoffrey H. and Shiskin, Julius. "Indicators of Business Expansions and Contractions." Occasional Paper 103, New York: National Bureau of Economic Research, 1967.

Palmer, Michael. "Money Supply, Portfolio Adjustments and Stock Prices." *Financial Analysts Journal,* Vol. 26, No. 4 (July–August, 1970).

Pesando, James E. "The Supply of Money and Common Stock Prices: Further Observations on the Econometric Evidence." *Journal of Finance,* Vol. 29, No. 3 (June, 1974).

Reilly, Frank K. "Aggregate Monetary Variables and Stock Price Movements." University of Wyoming, Working Paper No. 67 (February, 1975).

Rozeff, M. S. "Money and Stock Prices: Market Efficiency and the Lag Effect of Monetary Policy." *Journal of Financial Economics,* Vol. 1, No. 3 (September, 1974).

Rozeff, M. S. "The Money Supply and the Stock Market." *Financial Analysts Journal,* Vol. 31, No. 5 (September–October, 1975).

Shiskin, Julius. "Business Cycle Indicators: The Known and the Unknown," *Review of the International Statistical Institute,* Vol. 31, No. 3.

Sprinkel, Beryl W. *Money and Markets: A Monetarist View.* Homewood, Illinois: Richard D. Irwin, 1971.

Sprinkel, Beryl W. *Money and Stock Prices.* Homewood, Illinois: Richard D. Irwin, 1964.

Zarnowitz, Victor and Boschan, C. "Cyclical Indicators: An Evaluation and New Leading Index." *Business Conditions Digest* (May, 1975).

Zarnowitz, Victor and Boschan, C. "New Composite Indexes of Coincident and Lagging Indicators." *Business Conditions Digest* (November, 1975).

Chapter 11

Aggregate Market Analysis: Micro Techniques

The determination of the future value of the aggregate stock market employing micro techniques is simply the application of basic valuation theory to the aggregate stock market. Therefore, our initial section discusses what is involved in the valuation of common stock and the derivation of a valuation model. Given the model, it will be shown that the valuation process can be divided into two main parts. The rest of the chapter is concerned with a detailed application of the process to the valuation of the S&P 400 index.

Principles of Valuation

Determinants of Value

The reader will recall from courses in accounting and economics that *the value of an asset is the present value of the expected returns from the asset during the holding period.* An investment will provide a stream of returns during the period that it is held, and it is necessary to discount this stream of returns at an appropriate rate to determine the value of an asset.

In order to derive the value of an investment it is necessary to estimate the following:

1. The expected stream of returns, including the size and the form of these returns which can be earnings, dividends, interest, or a multitude of other flows. It has been shown that all approaches are basically equivalent if the assumptions are consistent.[1]

---

[1] Merton H. Miller and Franco Modigliani, "Dividend Policy, Growth and the Valuation of Shares," *Journal of Business,* Vol. 34, No. 4 (October, 1961), pp. 411–433.

2. The time pattern of expected returns. Because money has a time value, it is necessary to consider alternative time streams and discount these streams to the present using an appropriate discount rate.

3. The required rate of return on the investment based upon the systematic uncertainty of returns. Given the security market line prevailing at a point in time, and the estimate of the investment's beta with the market portfolio of risky assets, it is possible to derive the average return that should be required for the investment.

The application of these steps to the valuation of an asset involves various gradients of difficulty. It is easier to compute the value of some assets than of others because some of the estimates are simpler to make. It is relatively easy to derive the value of a bond, assuming that the investor intends to hold the bond until maturity. In such a case, the analyst knows *what* the stream of returns will be (the interest payments and the principal payment at maturity), and *when* the payments will be made (every six months and at maturity). The only unknown is the required rate of return on the bond, which depends on the prevailing risk-free rate (RFR) plus a risk premium that should be a function of the systematic risk of the bond.

Valuation of Common Stocks

The valuation of common stocks is definitely more difficult than that of bonds because almost all the required inputs are unknown. In the case of a bond, the only unknown is the discount rate. In the case of common stock, an investor is uncertain about the size of the returns, the time pattern of returns, and the required return. In addition, some observers ask which stream of returns should be discounted (earnings or dividends). Because it has been shown by Miller and Modigliani that the two approaches are equivalent if comparable assumptions are made, which cash flows are used becomes a matter of choice. Some prefer earnings because they are the source of dividends and some contend that investors discount that which they receive—dividends. We will use the dividend model because it is intuitively appealing and it has been used extensively by others so the reader may be familiar with the reduced form that will be employed later in the chapter. Basically, the dividend model contends that a share of common stock is the present value of all future dividends as follows:

(11–1)
$$P_i = \frac{D_1}{(1 + k)} + \frac{D_2}{(1 + k)^2} + \frac{D_3}{(1 + k)^3} + \cdots + \frac{D_n}{(1 + k)^n}$$

where:

P_i = price of the common stock i
D_i = dividend during period i
k_i = required rate of return on stock i.

Potential Dividend Streams

One can envision three general types of dividend streams: (1) constant (no growth), (2) erratic, and (3) constant growth.

Constant No Growth If the dividend payments are a *constant* stream that never varies, they can be treated like an *annuity* and all that is necessary is to derive the present value of an annuity for the expected period. If the time period is infinite, the annuity factor becomes 1/k, the reciprocal of the required rate of return. The present value of an infinite annuity discounted at 5 percent is 20 (1/.05). The assumption of a *constant, no growth* stream of dividends to infinity obviously simplifies the computations. Unfortunately, it is also *very unrealistic* because it is unlikely that a firm will never change its dividend payments when the earnings stream is growing, or even if the earnings stream is declining. In any case, under such conditions (no growth for an infinite period) the value of the firm is:

$$P_i = \frac{D_i}{k_i} \text{ (constant, no growth stream of dividends)}$$

Erratic Growth The second alternative is that the expected stream of dividends is very erratic or moves in different step functions as shown below.

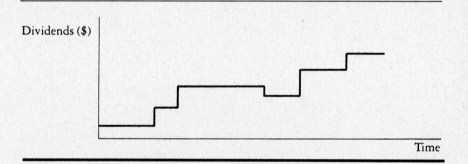

Dividends ($)

Time

Under such conditions, it is necessary to attempt to estimate each increase (or decrease) and how long each rate will last. It is generally necessary to discount each expected dividend payment as follows:

(11–2)
$$P_i = \frac{D_i}{(1+k_i)} + \frac{D_2}{(1+k_i)^2} + \frac{D_3}{(1+k_i)^3} + \cdots \frac{D_\infty}{(1+k_i)^\infty}$$

$$= \sum_{i=1}^{\infty} \frac{D_i}{(1+k_i)^i}$$

If it is assumed that the stream will not continue for an infinite period, the analyst must determine the residual value of the asset at the end of the investment horizon; i.e., it is necessary to determine the sales value of the asset (SP) at the end of the holding period. In such a case the value of the stock is computed as follows:

$$(11\text{--}3) \qquad P_i = \frac{D_i}{(1 + k_i)} + \frac{D_2}{(1 + k_i)^2} + \frac{D_3}{(1 + k_i)^3} + \cdots \frac{D_n}{(1 + k_i)^n} + \frac{SP_n}{(1 + k_i)^n}$$

$$= \sum_{i=1}^{n} \frac{D_i}{(1 + k_i)^i} + \frac{SP_n}{(1 + k_i)^n}$$

In this case, it is necessary to estimate the erratic stream of dividends during the period until n, and also estimate the residual (sales) value (SP) at point n. The value derived from formula (11–2) or (11–3) should be the same since the residual value (SP) should equal the discounted value of all dividends from time n to infinity.

Constant Growth The final alternative is to assume that dividends grow at a *constant rate* for an *infinite time period.* Under these assumptions, it is possible to derive a valuation formula that is quite simple. The formula is probably familiar to the reader because it is widely used in financial management to estimate a firm's cost of equity capital.[2] It is important for the reader to be fully aware of the *unrealistic assumptions* made in this formulation. First, it is hard to conceive of companies that have a constant growth rate for any number of years. All firms have good and bad years simply because of changes in the economic environment and changes in their industry. The best that can be hoped for is a relatively constant *average* growth rate for short periods. Several studies have examined the time series properties of income streams and generally agreed that these series are best described as a random walk.[3] Second, it is even more difficult to imagine that any company can continue to grow at some constant rate for an *infinite* time period. This assumption is even more unrealistic for firms with high growth rates (over 10 percent a year). The only instance in which constant growth over a very long period might be conceivable is when discussing the value of some relatively mature industries or the aggregate economy. Even in these instances, one should look for constant average growth.

The derivation of the reduced form model is presented in an appendix to

[2] For example, see Eugene F. Brigham, *Financial Management* (Hinsdale, Ill.: The Dryden Press, 1977), Chapter 18; James C. Van Horne, *Financial Management and Policy* (4th edition) (Englewood Cliffs, N.J.: Prentice–Hall, Inc., 1977), Chapter 8; O. Maurice Joy, *Introduction to Financial Management* (Homewood, Ill.: Richard D. Irwin, 1977), Chapter 8.

[3] Little, I.M.D., "Higgledy Piggledy Growth," *Institute of Statistics,* Oxford, Vol. 24, No. 4 (November, 1962); John Lintner and Robert Glouber, "Higgledy Piggledy Growth in America," in James Lorie and Richard Brealey (eds.), *Modern Developments in Investment Management* (New York: Praeger Publishers, 1972), pp. 645–662.

this chapter. The reader should examine it and become familiar with the model because it is used extensively in all subsequent analysis. The familiar reduced form of the dividend valuation model is:

(11–4)
$$P_i = \frac{D_1}{(K_i - g_i)}$$

where:

P_i = current price of common stock i

D_1 = expected dividend in period 1

K_i = required rate of return on stock i

g_i = expected constant growth rate of dividends for stock i.

Because of the unrealistic assumptions involved, it is difficult to employ this model to derive an exact value for an *individual* security. The model could be applied to an industry or to the aggregate market, because there is a greater probability that an industry or the aggregate market will maintain a constant or relatively stable growth pattern over a long period. Under such conditions, one might be able to derive something close to an expected value for the industry or the market using this model.

This valuation formula can also be used to determine *the direction of change.* Assuming some expectations of a major change in one of the relevant variables (K or g), it is possible to determine the direction of change in P that will accompany the change in K or g. There are two ways to use the dividend model to determine a specific future value or to determine the direction of change. The next section briefly discusses one of them and includes a detailed discussion of the other.

Alternative Forms of the Dividend Model

Dividend Multiple
The most obvious form of the model is to break the right side of the equation into a dividend component and a dividend multiplier as follows:

$$P = \frac{D_1}{K - g} = D_1 \times \frac{1}{K - g}$$

In this form it is necessary to estimate the dividend in period one and the dividend multiplier, based upon the relationship between K and g.

Earnings Multiple
The more intuitive and clearly more popular approach to valuation is the earnings multiple approach in which investors estimate earnings for some

near term period and apply an earnings multiple to this expected earnings figure to arrive at an expected value. The popularity of the earnings multiple approach is supported by the fact that *The Wall Street Journal* currently carries the price-earnings ratio for all stocks on a daily basis. The procedure is to estimate near term *expected* earnings and a *future* earnings multiple based upon expectations regarding the variables that influence the earnings multiple. To determine what factors should be considered, it is possible to use the dividend model as follows:

$$P = \frac{D_1}{K-g}$$

If we divide both sides by E:

$$P/E = \frac{D_1/E}{K-g}$$

Therefore, it is possible to determine the factors that influence the earnings multiple in a manner similar to that used to ascertain what affects the dividend multiplier.

Estimating Market Returns Using the Earnings Multiple Approach

We will be using the earnings multiple version to generate a market estimate for several reasons: it is more commonly used in practice; it is the more extensive model; and once the earnings multiple model is grasped, understanding the dividend model becomes rather straightforward. Finally, before one can derive a future dividend figure or dividend growth estimate, it is necessary to determine the growth of earnings.

Overall Procedure

The overall procedure is to attempt to estimate the future market value for some major market series, such as the DJIA or the S&P 400, by *estimating* the *future earnings value* and then *estimating* a *future earnings multiple* for the series.[4] In several studies, earnings estimation procedures were analyzed, but the tendency has been to ignore potential changes in the earnings multiple which implies that the authors assumed that the earnings multiple series is quite stable over time. The fallacy of such an incomplete procedure is obvious when one examines what transpired during the period since 1960 as shown in Table 11–1.

---

[4] In line with the efficient market hypothesis, our emphasis will be on estimating future values. The intent is to show the relevant variables and provide a procedural framework. The final estimate depends upon the ability of the analyst.

Table 11–1 **Annual Changes in Corporate Earnings, the Earnings Multiple, and Stock Prices: The S&P 400, 1960–1977**

Year	Earnings Per Share	Percent Change	Year-End Earnings Multiple	Percent Change	Year-End Stock Prices	Percent Change
1960	3.40	—	18.09	—	61.49	—
1961	3.37	− 0.9	22.49	24.4	75.72	23.11
1962	3.83	13.6	17.23	−23.4	66.0	−12.8
1963	4.24	10.7	18.69	8.5	79.25	20.1
1964	4.85	14.4	18.48	− 1.1	89.62	13.1
1965	5.50	13.4	17.90	− 3.1	98.47	9.9
1966	5.87	6.7	14.52	−18.9	85.24	−13.4
1967	5.62	− 4.3	18.70	28.8	105.11	23.3
1968	6.16	9.6	18.35	− 1.9	113.02	7.5
1969	6.13	− 0.5	16.56	− 9.8	101.49	−10.2
1970	5.41	−11.7	18.65	12.6	100.90	− 0.6
1971	5.97	10.4	18.88	1.2	112.72	11.7
1972	6.83	13.9	19.31	2.3	131.87	17.0
1973	8.89	30.9	12.28	−36.4	109.14	−17.2
1974	9.61	8.9	7.96	−35.2	76.47	−29.9
1975	8.58	−10.7	11.62	46.0	100.88	31.9
1976	10.64	24.0	11.23	− 3.4	119.46	18.4
1977	11.74 (est.)	10.3	8.92	−20.6	104.71	−12.4
Mean	—	11.5	—	16.3	—	16.1
Standard Deviation		7.175		13.406		7.661
Coefficient of Variability		0.624		0.822		0.476

Source: Reprinted by permission of Standard & Poor's.

Examples would include figures for 1973 when aggregate profits *rose* by about 30 percent, while stock prices *declined* steadily by about 17 percent. Again, in 1974, earnings *increased* by about 9 percent and stock prices *dropped* by almost 30 percent. The earnings multiple was not stable but declined drastically. The reverse occurred in 1975 when earnings *declined* by 10 percent and stock prices *rose* by over 30 percent. The consistency of large changes in the multiple can be seen from the summary figures at the bottom of Table 11–1 and from the time series plot in Figure 11–1. The mean percentage of change for the multiple is much larger than the mean change in earnings. Therefore, we will initially estimate aggregate earnings, and then become involved in an extensive consideration of the procedure for estimating the aggregate earnings multiple. We will initially attempt to derive an estimate of expected earnings for the market series for the coming

Figure 11–1 **Time Series Plot of Year End Earnings Multiples**
Standard & Poor's 400 Industrial Index 1960–1977

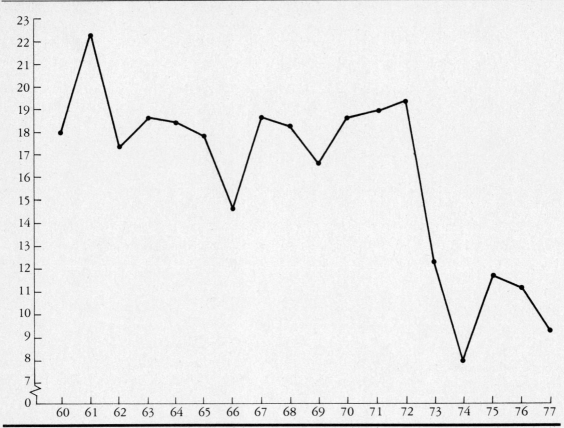

Source: Reprinted by permission of Standard & Poor's.

year based upon the outlook for the aggregate economy and for the corporate sector. The second major step is deriving an expected earnings multiple for the stock market series based upon the current earnings multiple and projected changes in the variables that affect the earnings multiple.

Estimate of Expected Earnings
The Gross National Product (GNP) is basically a measure of aggregate sales in the economy. Therefore, one would expect aggregate corporate sales to be related to the GNP. Hence, an earnings projection begins with an estimate of nominal GNP which can often be obtained from one of several banks or financial services that regularly publish such estimates for public distribution.[5] Assuming an analyst wants to "go it alone," the procedure should

---

[5] This would include, "Business and Money," Harris Trust and Savings Bank, 111 West Monroe Street, Chicago, Illinois 60690, and projections by Standard & Poor's appearing late in the year in *The Outlook*.

include an estimate of "real" increases in output for each of the major sectors of the GNP: (1) personal consumption expenditures, (2) gross private domestic investment, (3) net exports of goods and services, and (4) government purchases of goods and services.[6]

Given the expected outlook for each sector in real terms, the expected rate of price changes (i.e., the expected rate of inflation during the period) becomes a major question. In the recent environment, even though real output has been limited to about 3 percent increase, the generally high rate of inflation has resulted in fairly large *nominal* increases.

After the analyst has derived a reasonable estimate of nominal GNP from one or several public sources, the next step is to estimate corporate sales relative to aggregate economic sales (GNP).

Corporate Sales Relative to GNP

To derive an estimate of earnings for an aggregate stock market series, it is best to use sales figures for such a series if they are available. Fortunately, there is a sales series for the S&P 400 Industrial series on a per share basis.[7] The S&P sales and nominal GNP figures for the recent period are contained in Table 11–2 and a scatter plot for the figures is contained in Figure 11–2. The plot indicates a very close relationship between the two series with only a few years (most notably 1974) in which the difference was more than 2 percent. The equation for the least square regression line relating annual percent changes (%Δ) in the two series for the period 1960–1976 is:

$$\%\Delta\text{S\&P 400 Sales}_t = -2.230 + 1.333(\%\Delta\text{Nom. GNP})_t$$
$$R^2 = .477 \qquad \text{SEE} = 4.176 \qquad F(1,15) = 13.71$$

These results indicate that about 48 percent of the variance in percentage changes in S&P 400 sales can be explained by percentage changes in the nominal GNP. Given the linear regression model results and an estimate of the expected percentage of change in the nominal GNP for the forthcoming year, it should be possible to derive a fairly good estimate of the percentage of change in sales for the S&P 400 series and, therefore, an estimate of the dollar value for sales per share. Assume that the most likely estimate of

---

[6] For an extended discussion of the GNP and its components, the reader is referred to any one of the several macroeconomics texts available including: Thomas F. Dernburg and Duncan M. McDougall, *Macroeconomics* (4th edition) (New York: McGraw–Hill Book Co., 1973); Edward Shapiro, *Macroeconomic Analysis* (2nd edition) (New York: Harcourt, Brace and World, Inc., 1970); Gardner Ackley, *Macroeconomic Theory* (New York: The Macmillan Co., 1961).

[7] The figures are available back to 1945 in Standard & Poor's *Analysts Handbook* (New York: Standard & Poor's Corporation). The book is updated annually and some series are updated quarterly as part of a monthly supplement.

Year	Nominal GNP (billions of dollars)	Percent Change	S&P 400 Sales (dollar sales per share)	Percent Change
1960	506.0	—	59.47	—
1961	523.3	3.4	59.51	0.1
1962	563.8	7.7	64.63	8.6
1963	594.7	5.5	68.50	6.0
1964	635.7	6.9	73.19	6.8
1965	688.1	8.2	80.69	10.2
1966	753.0	9.4	88.46	9.6
1967	796.3	5.8	91.86	3.8
1968	868.5	9.1	101.49	10.5
1969	935.5	7.7	108.53	6.9
1970	982.4	5.0	109.85	1.2
1971	1,063.4	8.2	118.23	7.6
1972	1,171.1	10.1	128.79	8.9
1973	1,306.6	11.6	149.22	15.9
1974	1,413.2	8.2	182.10	22.0
1975	1,516.3	7.3	186.52	2.4
1976	1,691.7	11.6	202.00	8.3
Average:	—	7.9	—	8.0

Table 11–2
Nominal GNP and S&P Industrial Sales per Share: 1960–1976

Source: Reprinted by permission of Standard & Poor's.

nominal GNP for the next year is a 9 percent increase (3 percent "real" plus 6 percent inflation). Given the regression results this implies the following:

$$\%\Delta\text{S\&P } 400 \text{ Sales} = -2.230 + 1.333(9.0)$$
$$= -2.230 + 12.0 \quad = 9.77$$

Alternative Estimates of Corporate Net Profits

Once sales per share for the market series have been estimated, the difficult estimate is that of after-tax profits as a percent of sales, i.e., the net profit margin, for industrial corporations. There are three procedures suggested, all of which are similar but depend upon further aggregation.

The first is the direct estimation of the *net* profit margin based upon recent trends. As shown in Table 11–3 and in the time series plot in Figure 11–3, this net income margin series has been quite volatile over time because of the effect of changes in depreciation as a percent of sales, and of changes in the tax rate over time. Obviously going directly to the bottom line is the most uncertain approach, but should be attempted as a check on other techniques.

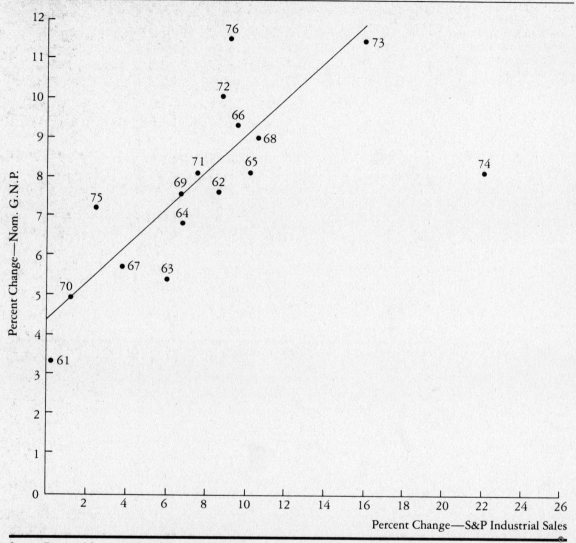

Source: Reprinted by permission of Standard & Poor's.

The second estimate is derived from a separate analysis of the net before tax (NBT) profit margin and an estimate of the expected tax rate. The NBT profit margin is less volatile than the net profit margin is because it is not affected by changes in the tax rate over time. As such the NBT margin should be easier to estimate. Once this is derived, a separate estimate of the tax rate is obtained, based upon recent rates and current government tax pronouncements.

The third method begins with an estimate of the *gross* profit margin (i.e., income before taxes and depreciation as a percent of sales). Because the cash

Year	Net Income	Percent of Sales	NBT	Percent of Sales	Depre-ciation	NBT + Depre-ciation	Percent of Sales
1960	3.40	5.72	6.27	10.54	2.56	8.83	14.85
1961	3.37	5.66	6.17	10.37	2.66	8.83	14.84
1962	3.83	5.93	6.99	10.82	2.89	9.88	15.29
1963	4.24	6.19	7.75	11.31	3.04	10.79	15.75
1964	4.85	6.63	8.55	11.68	3.24	11.79	16.11
1965	5.50	6.82	9.64	11.95	3.52	13.16	16.31
1966	5.87	6.64	10.22	11.55	3.87	14.09	15.93
1967	5.62	6.12	9.73	10.59	4.25	13.98	15.22
1968	6.16	6.07	11.30	11.13	4.56	15.86	15.63
1969	6.13	5.65	11.27	10.38	4.87	16.14	14.87
1970	5.41	4.92	9.64	8.78	5.17	14.81	13.48
1971	5.97	5.04	10.95	9.26	5.45	16.40	13.87
1972	6.83	5.30	12.71	9.87	5.76	18.47	14.34
1973	8.89	5.96	16.48	11.04	6.25	22.73	15.23
1974	9.61	5.28	19.83	10.89	6.86	16.69	14.66
1975	8.68	4.65	18.11	9.71	7.36	25.47	13.66
1976	10.64	5.27	20.80	10.30	7.54	28.34	14.03

Table 11–3
Profit Margins for S&P Industrial Index: Net Income; Net Before Tax; and Net Before Taxes and Depreciation, 1960–1976

Source: Reprinted by permission of Standard & Poor's.

flow as a percent of sales is not influenced by changes in depreciation allowances or tax rates, it should be a relatively stable value over time. This stability can be seen from the data in Table 11–3 and the time series plot of margins in Figure 11–3. It is clear that the gross profit margin series is the least volatile series in terms of relative variability. The following figures on means, standard deviations, and coefficients of variation likewise make this point. As shown, the coefficient of variation, which is a *relative* measure of variability, indicates that the net profit margin is the most volatile series.

Summary Data: 1960–1976 S&P 400

	Mean	Standard Deviation	Coeff. Var.[a]
Net Profit Margin	5.758	0.606	.105
NBT Margin	10.623	0.824	.077
NBT & Depreciation Margin	14.979	0.808	.054

[a] Coefficient of variation = Std. Dev/Mean
Source: Reprinted by permission of Standard & Poor's.

In the next section, we will discuss the factors influencing the gross profit margin. For the time being, once the analyst has derived an estimate

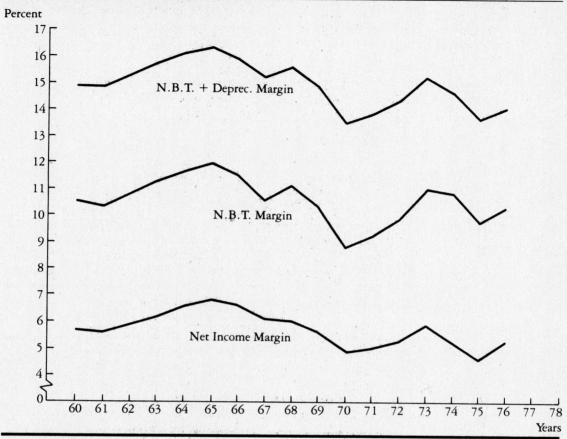

Percent

Source: Reprinted by permission of Standard & Poor's.

of this gross profit margin, he will multiply this by the estimate of sales to derive *a dollar value of earnings before depreciation and taxes (EBDT)*. The second step is to derive a separate estimate of *aggregate depreciation* for the year. This depreciation estimate is then subtracted from the EBDT figure to arrive at earnings before taxes (EBT). Finally, there should be a separate estimate of the expected tax rate based upon the recent trend and current government policy. The estimated tax rate applied to the earnings before tax (EBT) figure indicates the estimated taxes. Subtracting estimated taxes from the NBT figure gives the net income estimate for the coming year.

Hopefully the three estimates will generally confirm one another and thereby allow a consensus estimate of corporate profits. The following sections discuss the details of estimating the earnings per share figure, beginning with the gross profit margin.

Determinants of Aggregate Gross Profit Margin

As pointed out in a study by Finkel and Tuttle, there has been a great deal of analysis of factors that influence the profit margins of individual firms, but limited analysis of what determines the aggregate profit margin.[8] The variables suggested and tested by Finkel and Tuttle to obtain this aggregate were:

1. utilization rate of existing industrial capacity (proportion of capacity being used)
2. unit labor costs of production
3. the rate of inflation
4. the level of foreign competition
5. the unemployment rate.

Utilization Rate The relationship between the utilization rate and the profit margin is quite straightforward. If production increases as a proportion of total capacity, there is a decrease in the fixed production costs per unit of output because more units are being produced in the given plant capacity. In addition, fixed *financial* costs per unit decline. Therefore, one should expect a *positive* relationship between the aggregate utilization rate and the aggregate profit margin. The relationship may not be completely linear at very high rates of utilization because operating diseconomies are introduced as firms are forced to employ marginal labor and/or use older plant and equipment to reach the higher capacity. The figures in Table 11–4 indicate that capacity utilization reached a peak of over 91 percent in 1966 and a low point of less than 74 percent during the recession of 1975.

Unit Labor Cost The change in unit labor costs is really a compound effect of two individual factors: (1) changes in wages per hour, and (2) changes in worker productivity. Wage costs per hour typically increase every year by varying amounts depending upon the economic environment. The figures in Table 11–4 indicate that the annual percent of increase in wages varied from 3.4 percent to about 9.6 percent. If workers did not become more productive, this increase in per hour wage costs would be the increase in per unit labor cost. Fortunately, because of advances in technology and greater mechanization, the units of output produced by the individual laborer per hour have increased over time—the laborer has become *more productive*. If wages per hour increase by 5 percent and labor productivity increases by 5 percent, there would be *no* increase in unit labor costs because the workers would *offset* the wage increase by producing more. Therefore, the increase in *per unit labor cost* is a function of the percent of change in hourly wages minus the increase in productivity during the period. The actual relationship is

---

[8] Sidney R. Finkel and Donald L. Tuttle, "Determinants of the Aggregate Profits Margin," *Journal of Finance,* Vol. 26, No. 5 (December, 1971), pp. 1067–1075.

Table 11–4 **Variables that Affect the Aggregate Profit Margin: Utilization Rate, Compensation, Productivity and Unit Labor Cost: 1960–1977**

Year	Utilization Rate	Compensation/Work Hours[a]		Output/Work Hours[a]		Unit Labor Cost[a]	
		Index	Percent Change	Index	Percent Change	Index	Percent Change
1960	80.1	73.7	4.3	80.3	1.0	91.7	3.3
1961	77.3	76.2	3.5	82.6	2.8	92.3	0.6
1962	81.4	79.4	4.1	86.2	4.4	92.0	− 0.3
1963	83.5	82.3	3.7	89.3	3.5	92.2	0.1
1964	85.7	86.2	4.8	92.6	3.7	93.1	1.0
1965	89.5	89.1	3.4	95.7	3.3	93.2	0.1
1966	91.1	94.5	6.1	98.1	2.5	96.4	3.4
1967	86.9	100.0	5.8	100.0	1.9	100.0	3.8
1968	87.0	107.3	7.3	103.2	3.2	103.9	3.9
1969	86.2	114.2	6.5	103.1	−0.2	110.9	6.6
1970	79.2	121.9	6.7	103.2	0.2	118.1	6.5
1971	78.0	129.9	6.6	106.3	2.9	122.2	3.5
1972	83.1	137.4	5.8	109.5	3.0	125.5	2.7
1973	87.5	148.1	7.8	111.4	1.7	133.0	6.0
1974	84.2	162.0	9.4	108.1	−2.9	149.8	12.7
1975	73.6	177.6	9.6	109.9	1.6	161.7	7.9
1976	80.2	193.1	8.7	114.3	4.1	168.9	4.5
1977	82.4(p)	209.6(p)	8.5	116.7(p)	2.0	179.7(p)	6.4

(p)-preliminary

Source: Federal Reserve Board Series, "Total Manufacturing," contained in *Economic Report of the President,* 1978 (Washington, D.C.: U.S. Government Printing Office).

[a] Private nonfarm business, 1967 = 100: Source: Department of Labor, Bureau of Labor Statistics.

typically not this exact because of measurement problems, but it is quite close as indicated by the figures in Table 11–4. As shown, there is only one instance (1962) in which productivity increased by more than the hourly compensation did, and the result was a decline in unit labor cost. In 1974, wage rates increased by 9.4 percent, productivity actually *declined* by 2.9 percent because of the recession and, therefore, unit labor costs increased by over 12 percent. The rate of increase in unit labor cost declined during 1975 and 1976, but increased again in 1977. Because unit labor is the major variable cost of a firm, one would expect a *negative* relationship between the aggregate profit margin and percentage changes in unit labor cost.

Inflation The precise effect of inflation on the aggregate profit margin is unresolved. In the Finkel–Tuttle article it was hypothesized that there is a positive relationship between inflation and the aggregate profit margin for several reasons. First, it was contended that an increase in the level of inflation increases the ability of firms to pass increasing service costs on to the consumer and thereby increase their profit margin.[9] Second, if the inflation were the classical demand-pull type, the increase would indicate an increase in general economic activity and would be encouraging. Finally, an increase in the rate of inflation might stimulate consumption as individuals attempt to shift their holdings from financial assets to real assets.

The alternative effect of inflation on profit margins is supported by those who doubt the ability of all businesses to consistently increase prices in line with rising costs. Assume a 5 percent increase in the rate of inflation and also assume that the costs of labor and material generally increase by this rate. The question is whether all firms are able to *completely* pass these cost increases along to their customers. If a firm is able to pass cost increases along *completely* in terms of selling price, the result will be a *constant* profit margin, *not* an increase. *Only* if a firm can increase prices by *more* than the increase in costs can the firm increase its margin. Many firms will probably not be able to raise prices in line with increased costs because of the elasticity of demand for their products.[10] In these cases, the profit margin will *decline*. Given the three alternatives, it is hard to imagine most firms increasing their profit margins or even holding them constant. Many firms will suffer declines in their profit margins during periods of inflation which means that the *aggregate* profit margin will be constant or probably decline with an increase in the rate of inflation. Therefore, there are alternative arguments regarding the relationship and only empirical proof will show how inflation has tended to affect the aggregate margin.

Foreign Competition Some observers contend that export markets are more competitive than domestic markets are and, therefore, export sales are made at a lower margin.[11] Therefore, a reduction in the trade surplus, due to a reduction in exports by the United States, would have a positive effect on profit margins because a lower proportion of sales would be made at the lower margin. This line of reasoning was challenged by H. Peter Gray who contended that undue emphasis was placed on the fact that exports increased less than imports did.[12] Gray felt that only exports made at arm's length (i.e., by two independent firms) should be considered and then they

---

[9] This assumes either that there is a wage lag or that the demand curve facing the firm is inelastic so that it can raise prices.

[10] An extreme example of this inability is regulated industries that may not be able to raise prices at all until after a lengthy hearing before a regulatory agency and even then the increase may still not match the cost increases.

[11] This is the reasoning by Finkel–Tuttle, "Determinants," p. 1071.

[12] H. Peter Gray, "Determinants of the Aggregate Profit Margin: A Comment," *Journal of Finance,* Vol. 31, No. 1 (March, 1976), pp. 163–165.

should be examined relative to total output exported. Further, he contended that imports could have an important negative impact on the margin because they influence the selling price of all competing domestic products. Therefore, one may likewise question the ultimate effect of the trade surplus variable and examine the empirical results for support of the alternative views.

The Unemployment Rate This variable is of potential interest but, as with the others, a case can be made for either a positive or negative relationship. On the one hand, a high rate of unemployment would indicate the existence of excess labor and should cause a low rate of increase in unit labor cost and, therefore, a higher profit margin, all other factors being equal. Thus, a positive relation would result. In contrast, one might argue that a high unemployment rate would be related to a period of economic recession and low utilization of capacity, and therefore, would result in a low profit margin. This line of reasoning would indicate a negative relationship.

Empirical Evidence of Determinants of Profit Margins

The study by Finkel–Tuttle (F–T) indicated the following relationships between variables and the profit margin:[13]

trade surplus—negative and significant at .01 level

inflation—positive and significant at .05 level

utilization rate—positive and significant at .10 level

unit labor cost—negative and significant at .01 level

unemployment rate—not significant.

These results were derived using quarterly data for the period 1955–1967. They also attempted to use the model to estimate the aggregate margin during the period from 1968 to the second quarter of 1970. The difference between the estimates and actual results was not significant.

In his comment, Gray attempted to replicate the F–T results with special emphasis on the trade surplus.[14] The results indicated a negative coefficient for the trade surplus variable, but it was not statistically significant. Also, there was a very high correlation between the GNP deflator (the measure of inflation) and the unit labor cost variable.

Some recent work by this author using annual data for the period 1947–1974 confirmed the importance of the utilization rate and unit labor cost. The relationship between the profit margin and the utilization rate was always significant and positive. In contrast, the relationship between unit labor cost and the profit margin was always negative and significant.

---

[13] Finkel–Tuttle, "Determinants."

[14] Gray, "Determinants."

Finally, the inflation rate was never significant in the multiple regression. Further, the simple correlations between the profit margin and inflation were consistently *negative*.

There is consistent strong support for a positive relationship between profit margins and the utilization rate and also for a negative relation between the margin and unit labor cost. Unfortunately, it is not possible to derive an independent effect for inflation, but the simple correlation indicates a *negative* relationship. Finally, the effect of a trade surplus is unresolved at this point. Therefore, when attempting to estimate the gross profit margin, you should pay particular attention to estimates of changes in the utilization rate for the economy and the rate of change in unit labor cost. When the utilization rate is expected to increase by several percentage points, and only small increases are expected in unit labor costs, one might expect a healthy increase in the profit margin. One should also be aware of changes in the rate of inflation and the foreign trade environment, but these variables should receive less emphasis because of the mixed empirical evidence concerning their effect.

After estimating the gross profit margin, one can derive the dollar value of earnings before depreciation and taxes (EBDT) by applying this gross margin estimate to the previously estimated sales figure. The next step is to estimate aggregate depreciation.

Estimating Depreciation

As shown in Table 11–5, the depreciation series has not experienced a decline since 1960 (actually it has not declined since 1946). This is not too surprising because depreciation expense is by definition a fixed cost related to the total amount of fixed assets in the economy which increases over time. Therefore, the relevant question for an analyst estimating depreciation is *not* whether it will increase or decrease, but by *how much will depreciation expense increase?*

One can use the recent *absolute* change, or the recent *percent* of change as a guide to the future increase. Probably the biggest factor that could influence the series is recent capital expenditures, i.e., expenditures during year t–1 and t–2, because, with accelerated depreciation, these recent expenditures become dominant. The data in Table 11–5 indicate that the average percent of increase in depreciation expense has been about 7 percent, with most years falling in the 5 to 9 percent range.

After the analyst has estimated depreciation, the figure obtained is subtracted from the gross profit estimate. The result is a net earnings before taxes estimate.

Expected Tax Rate

The annual tax rates are contained in Table 11–5. The tax rate series was steady during the initial years, declined during 1964–1967, and then returned to the 45–46 percent range in the early 1970's. In 1974, the rate increased sharply to over 50 percent and has subsequently remained at that

Table 11–5
Percentage Changes in Depreciation and Tax Rate for S&P Industrial Index, 1960–1976

Year	Depreciation	Percent of Change	NBT[a]	Income Taxes	Tax Rate
1960	2.56	—	6.27	2.87	45.8
1961	2.66	3.9	6.17	2.80	45.4
1962	2.89	8.6	6.99	3.16	45.2
1963	3.04	5.2	7.75	3.51	45.3
1964	3.24	6.6	8.55	3.70	43.3
1965	3.52	8.6	9.64	4.14	42.9
1966	3.87	9.9	10.22	4.35	42.6
1967	4.25	9.8	9.73	4.11	42.2
1968	4.56	7.3	11.30	5.14	45.5
1969	4.87	6.8	11.27	5.14	45.6
1970	5.17	6.2	9.64	4.23	43.9
1971	5.45	5.4	10.95	4.98	45.5
1972	5.76	5.7	12.71	5.90	46.4
1973	6.25	8.5	16.48	7.59	46.1
1974	6.86	9.8	19.83	10.22	51.5
1975	7.36	7.3	18.11	9.43	52.1
1976	7.54	2.4	20.80	10.60	51.0
Average	—	7.0	—	—	45.9

[a] NBT = net before tax

Source: Reprinted by permission of Standard & Poor's.

level. An obvious concern has to be with whether this rate will remain at about 50 percent or more, or return to its long-run average rate of about 46 percent.

Estimating the future tax rate is difficult because it is heavily influenced by political action. Therefore, it is necessary to consider the current tax rate, but also to evaluate recent tax legislation affecting business firms (e.g., tax credits, etc.).

Given an estimate of the tax rate, the figure is multiplied by the net before tax earnings estimate to derive the estimated net income for industrial corporations which is subsequently used with an earnings multiplier to arrive at an estimate of the future value for the aggregate market.

A Sample Estimate

This attempt at estimating earnings per share for the year is best described as casual since it is meant as an example of the procedure followed. The reader is welcome to check the figures for accuracy as an exercise in data gathering. The major steps are as follows:

1. estimate the nominal GNP for 1978

2. estimate sales for the S&P 400 Index based upon the GNP estimate

3. estimate the gross profit margin for the S&P series, i.e., the profit margin before taxes and depreciation. This is based upon estimates of:

   a. utilization rate in 1978 versus 1977

   b. percent of change in unit labor cost

    c. change in the rate of inflation in 1978 over 1977

    d. foreign trade as a percent of GNP

4. estimate of depreciation for 1978

5. estimate of the average corporate tax rate for 1978.

Nominal GNP for 1978 is based upon an estimate for 1977 of approximately $1,860 billion. Although the economy will be in its fourth year of expansion during 1978, most economists expect the real GNP to increase by about 3 percent and the economy to experience a rate of inflation of approximately 6 percent. Therefore, nominal GNP is estimated as increasing by about 9 *percent* in 1978, to $2,027 billion.

Corporate Sales have consistently followed nominal GNP as shown in Figure 11–1. During 1977, when nominal GNP increased by 10 percent, S&P sales rose by about 12 percent to $227 per share. In 1978, with GNP rising 9 percent, one might estimate an increase in corporate sales of about 10 percent to *$250 per share.* [15]

The Gross Profit Margin increased to about 14.50 percent in 1977, compared to 14.03 percent in 1976. This increase was a function of an increase in the utilization rate from 80.1 in 1976 to almost 83 percent during 1977, a lower rate of increase in unit labor cost (6.5 percent in 1977 versus 7.0 percent during 1976); and a constant rate of inflation of about 6 percent. For 1978, the outlook is for a decline in the gross profit margin. There should be a further increase in the utilization rate to about 85 percent, which is encouraging. Unfortunately, the outlook for the unit labor cost is not good. Compensation per hour will definitely increase, but gains in productivity are expected to be much lower this late in the business expansion. Therefore, the outlook for unit labor cost is for an increase in excess of 7 percent. Finally, the average rate of inflation will probably increase from the 1977 rate on a continual basis throughout the year. Therefore, the overall outlook is for a decline in the gross profit margin from 14.5 percent to 13.5 percent in 1978. Applying a 13.5 percent gross profit margin to the per share sales figure results in a net before taxes and depreciation of *$33.75* (.135 × $250).

Depreciation during 1977 was approximately $8.50 per share. Because the utilization rate continues to increase, the outlook is for an increase in capital expenditures of about 10 percent during 1978 and, therefore, a further increase in depreciation of 8 percent to *$9.18.* Thus the estimated net before taxes is *$24.57* ($33.75 − $9.18).

---

[15] The reader will recall that, using the regression model, the estimate was 9.77 percent. The 10 percent figure is used for ease of computation.

The Corporate Tax Rate during 1977 was apparently slightly lower than it was during 1976. Because no major corporate tax legislation is pending, the outlook for 1978 is for a 50 percent tax rate. Applying a 50 percent rate to the NBT figure of $24.57 indicates that net income will be approximately $12.29 during 1978. Because the estimating procedure is admittedly casual, the figure used in future discussions is $12.50 a share.

Estimating the Earnings Multiple for the Aggregate Stock Market

Many analysts, when attempting to estimate the future value of the aggregate stock market, concentrate their efforts on the earnings estimate, thereby implicitly assuming that the value of the market will move with the earnings changes (the aggregate earnings multiple is constant over time). Reilly and Drzycimski contended that it is incorrect to assume that the multiple is stable because there has been *more volatility* in the *earnings multiple series* over time than in the earnings series.[16] The evidence also indicates that the multiple series turned *before* the earnings series did. Therefore, it is obviously important to consider the variables that influence the earnings multiple and attempt to project them.

Determinants of the Market Earnings Multiple

The factors that influence the earnings multiple depend upon the earnings figure used. If the earnings multiple is being applied to the true *expected* earnings figure that takes into account *all future earnings growth,* then the earnings multiple is only a function of the required rate of return on the investment. In the more typical real world situation, investors apply an earnings multiple to near term future earnings (earnings for the following year). In the latter case, it is necessary to adjust the earnings multiple to take into account long-run future growth expectations.

Multiple Determinants Without Growth

Assume that no growth opportunities exist or that all future growth expectations have been included in the expected earnings figure. The earnings multiple, given an infinite time horizon, becomes 1/K, where K is the total required return on the investment. The multiple is inversely related to the required rate of return; the higher the required rate of return an investor wants, the less he will pay for current and future earnings. An investor's required rate of return is determined by: (1) the economy's risk-free rate (RFR); (2) a risk premium (RP); and (3) the expected rate of inflation (I) during the period of investment.

---

[16] Frank K. Reilly and Eugene F. Drzycimski, "Aggregate Market Earnings Multiples Over Stock Market Cycles and Business Cycles," *Mississippi Valley Journal of Business and Economics,* Vol. 10, No. 2 (Winter, 1974/75), pp. 14–36. Recent evidence of this greater volatility is contained in Table 11–1.

The Nominal Risk-Free Rate The RFR is a general economic variable that is consistent for all firms and investments, and is influenced, during a business cycle, by changes in liquidity (i.e., supply and demand for capital), and the level of real growth in the economy.[17] Liquidity is inversely related to the RFR. In contrast, we would expect a positive relationship between real growth and the RFR, because an increase in real growth means that the marginal returns to all capital will rise and the opportunity costs of all risk-free capital increase.[18]

There is also a positive relationship between the expected rate of inflation (I) and the nominal required rate of return on investments, because investors require compensation for their loss of purchasing power during the period of investment.[19] As is true for the RFR, changes in I are universal in their effect on all classes of investments. Therefore, an increase in I will cause an increase in K and a decrease in the earnings multiple.

Risk Premium An increase in the risk premium (RP) for common stocks causes an increase in the required return and a decline in the earnings multiple. On a macro-economic level, the risk premium on all risky investments is influenced by uncertainty regarding the business outlook, the political environment, or the international situation. On a day-to-day basis, the principal variables affecting the business outlook and, therefore, the risk premiums on common stock are unique to a company and to its stock. What is seen on a macro level is the collection of such individual changes. An individual stock's risk premium was traditionally considered to be determined by the business risk (BR) and financial risk (FR) of the firm and the external market liquidity of the stock (LR). An excellent discussion of business risk is contained in Solomon:

The quality of the expected stream of net operating earnings depends on a complex of factors which we refer to as business uncertainty. These factors include general expectations with respect to overall economic and political trends, specific expectations about the particular regions and markets within which the company acquires resources and sells its products, and the speed and flexibility

---

[17] The relationship between the RFR, liquidity, and productivity is discussed and tested in Michael W. Keran, "Expectations, Money and the Stock Market," Federal Reserve Bank of St. Louis *Review*, Vol. 53, No. 1 (January, 1971), pp. 16–31. The relationship is accepted and tested further in Michael J. Hamburger and Lewis A. Kochin, "Money and Stock Prices: The Channels of Influence," *Journal of Finance,* Vol. 27, No. 2 (May, 1972), pp. 231–249.

[18] Keran, op. cit., pp. 21–22.

[19] The specific effects of inflation on stock prices have been discussed and empirically tested in Keran, op. cit., and also discussed in Daniel Seligman, "A Bad New Era for Common Stocks," *Fortune* (April, 1972). Specific tests of returns to common stockholders during periods of significant inflation are discussed in detail in Frank K. Reilly, "Companies and Common Stocks as Inflation Hedges," New York University Graduate School of Business Administration, Center for the Study of Financial Institutions, *Bulletin* 1975–2 (April, 1975). This relationship is also discussed in Appendix B to this chapter.

with which the company can lower its total operating costs when total revenues decline. All three factors interact, and their combined effect determines the level of uncertainty or quality which is attached to anticipation about the future flow of net operating earnings.[20]

One potential measure of a firm's business risk is the coefficient of variation (CV) of the firm's operating income (EBIT).[21]

Financial risk is determined by the financing decisions of the firm, or more specifically, by the amount of leverage employed,[22] and represents the probability of loss by an investor when a firm cannot meet its fixed obligations. In an all-equity firm there is no financial risk because there is no fixed debt obligation and, hence, no chance of bankruptcy. As the firm increases the proportion of debt in its financial structure, its fixed obligations increase relative to the amount of earnings available to meet these obligations which raises the level of probability that the firm will not be able to meet these obligations and will suffer bankruptcy.

The most common measure of financial risk is the debt/equity ratio that indicates the proportion of capital derived from fixed obligations. Another measure is the fixed charge coverage ratio which relates earnings available for debt service to the firm's fixed obligations; i.e., the greater the fixed debt coverage, the less risk of bankruptcy. Finally, a proposed measure is the CV of earnings available for the common stockholder after the payment of fixed obligations.[23]

In addition to internal variables, investors are concerned with the ability to buy or sell their stock quickly without major price changes. The ability to do this is referred to as market liquidity. The possibility that an investor will *not* be able to buy or sell a position in a stock quickly without a major price change is known as liquidity risk (LR). The greater the uncertainty regarding this ability, the larger the LR and the greater the required rate of return.

---

[20] Ezra Solomon, *The Theory of Financial Management* (New York: Columbia University Press, 1963), p. 71.

[21] This measure is explained in James C. Van Horne, *Financial Management and Policy* (4th edition) (Englewood Cliffs, N.J.: Prentice–Hall, Inc., 1977), p. 118. It is also referred to in Eugene F. Brigham, *Financial Management* (Hinsdale, Ill.: The Dryden Press, 1977), pp. 555–557 and in Ezra Solomon and John J. Pringle, *An Introduction to Financial Management* (Santa Monica, Cal.: Goodyear Publishing Co., 1977), p. 353.

[22] This concept is discussed in almost all financial management texts including Van Horne, op. cit., pp. 725–730; Brigham, op. cit., pp. 561–571; Solomon and Pringle, op. cit., pp. 441–464; O. Maurice Joy, *Introduction to Financial Management* (Homewood, Ill.: Richard D. Irwin, 1977), pp. 234–244.

[23] These measures, or slight variations of them, have been used in Lawrence Fisher, "Determinants of Risk Premiums on Corporate Bonds," *Journal of Political Economy,* Vol. 67, No. 3 (June 3, 1959), pp. 217–237; Fred D. Arditti, "Risk and the Required Return on Equity," *Journal of Finance,* Vol. 22, No. 1 (March, 1967), pp. 19–36; and Burton G. Malkiel and John G. Cragg, "Expectations and the Structure of Share Prices," *American Economic Review,* Vol. 60, No. 4 (September, 1970), pp. 601–617.

Investors have always been aware of liquidity risk, but it has generally not been considered of prime concern for common stocks because they are thought of as one of the most liquid of all investment assets. This attitude changed in the late 1960's and early 1970's when many institutions could not sell their shares in some small growth companies without making large price concessions.[24] Therefore, major financial institutions became very much aware of the great difference in the market liquidity for alternative stocks. Because of the interest, the Amivest Corporation devised a measure of market liquidity for individual stocks that related the dollar volume of trading in a stock to the percent of price change for the stock as follows:

$$\text{Amivest \$ Index} = \frac{\Sigma PiVi}{\Sigma \left| \%\Delta Pi \right|}$$

where

Pi = daily closing price for stock i

Vi = daily share volume for stock i

$\Sigma \left| \%\Delta Pi \right|$ = the sum of the absolute percent of price changes for stock i

The index is meant to represent *the dollar amount of trading possible for a one percent price change.* The more trading that can be accomplished per one percent price change, the more liquid the stock.[25] The Amivest Corporation publishes a monthly booklet that gives the liquidity indexes for all stocks listed on the NYSE and ASE.[26] The figures in the report clearly show the significant difference in market liquidity between individual stocks ranging from IBM (the most liquid stock on the NYSE) to those of small firms. The ratio of difference is easily *50 times*; i.e., it is possible to sell 50 times more IBM stock for a one percent price change than it is to sell some small inactive stock.

Beyond the liquidity measures for individual stocks, it is possible to derive a similar measure for the aggregate stock market. Amivest derives such a measure by computing an average of liquidity ratios for all individual stocks. This aggregate measure has been used by Fouse to explain some

---

[24] See John F. Lyons, "What Happens When Liquidity Disappears?" *Institutional Investor,* Vol. 3, No. 11 (November, 1969), pp. 29–36; David McClintick, "Illiquid Stocks—Lack of Ready Buyers and Sellers Imperils the Stock Market," *Wall Street Journal,* December 10, 1971.

[25] The index is explained and uses for it are discussed in Michael D. Hirsch, "Liquidity Filters: Tools for Better Performance," *Journal of Portfolio Management,* Vol. 2, No. 1 (Fall, 1975), pp. 46–50.

[26] *The Liquidity Report,* published by Amivest Corporation, 505 Park Avenue, New York, New York 10022.

major stock market changes during the early 1970's.[27] It was shown that the liquidity for the aggregate stock market changed over time and influenced total market movements. Reilly and Wright derived a proxy for the Amivest Index that extended back to 1960 (the Amivest series began in 1972).[28] An analysis of the series indicated substantial variability in the liquidity series over time and a strong negative relationship between aggregate market liquidity and stock price volatility.

Recently, the Securities and Exchange Commission derived a market liquidity measure similar to the Amivest measure that is reported monthly in the SEC *Statistical Bulletin*.[29] It was shown in the Reilly–Wright paper that the Amivest series and the SEC series are correlated about .94. Therefore it appears that aggregate market liquidity changes over time and that these liquidity changes influence the required market returns and market movements.

Alternative Market Risk Measures

Because of the development of the Capital Asset Pricing Model (CAPM), an alternative view of investment risk has emerged. In an economy in which investors are risk averse and hold well-diversified portfolios, all investors will hold a combination of a risk-free asset and the market portfolio of risky assets. Because this market portfolio of risky assets is, by definition, completely diversified, there is only systematic (market) risk remaining. Under such conditions, the only *relevant* risk for an individual risky asset is its systematic risk; i.e., its covariance with the market portfolio of risky assets.

This market risk measure must be modified when considering the required return on *all* common stocks, because common stocks constitute a large segment of the risky asset portfolio. Assume that there is a proxy for the true "market portfolio" of all risky assets. In order to estimate the market risk measure (systematic risk) for common stocks, it would be necessary to derive the covariance for the portfolio of all common stocks with this "market portfolio." Because common stocks constitute a large proportion of all risky assets, the covariance would probably be quite high. Unfortunately, it is currently *not possible* to derive such a relationship because *there is no generally acceptable market portfolio that contains all risky assets* or even a good proportion of them. The most widely used proxy for the

---

[27] William L. Fouse, "Risk and Liquidity: The Keys to Stock Price Behavior," *Financial Analysts Journal*, Vol. 32, No. 3 (May–June, 1976), pp. 35–45.

[28] Frank K. Reilly and David Wright, "An Analysis of Aggregate Stock Market Liquidity." Paper presented at the Eastern Finance Association Meeting, Boston, Massachussetts (April, 1977).

[29] Peter Martin, "Analysis of the Impact of Competitive Rates on the Liquidity of NYSE Stocks," Economic Staff Paper 75–No. 3, Office of Economic Research, Securities and Exchange Commission (July, 1975).

market portfolio is the Standard & Poor's Composite Index of 500 common stocks. In this case, the correlation between the S&P 500 and the S&P 400 series which we are attempting to estimate is extremely high, approximately .95. Therefore, the market measure of risk for the aggregate stock market is not its covariance with the market portfolio, but its *own variance of returns or standard deviation of returns over time.*

In summary, it is possible to derive market measures of risk that are consistent with the CAPM. Rather than measuring business risk, financial risk, and liquidity risk, one can employ a market measure: systematic risk of common stock with the market portfolio of risky assets. When attempting to apply this concept to the aggregate stock market, it is not possible to implement the measure because there is no acceptable market portfolio. Therefore, the market measure of risk for common stocks becomes the standard deviation of stock market returns and, when aggregate stock market volatility changes, investors should change their required return on common stocks. An increase in stock market volatility should cause an increase in the required return on common stock.

The required return on common stocks can therefore be stated as:

$$K_{cs} = f(RFR, I, BR, FR, LR)$$

or

$$K_{cs} = f(RFR, I, \sigma_m^2)$$

where

K_{cs} = the required return on common stocks

RFR = the economy's risk-free rate of return

I = the expected rate of inflation

BR = aggregate corporate business risk

FR = aggregate corporate financial risk

LR = aggregate stock market liquidity risk

σ_m^2 = market risk for common stocks measured as the variance of returns.

Multiple Determinants With Growth

In the more realistic situation in which the earning and dividend streams are growing, and/or investors do not fully adjust the expected earnings figure for all future growth, the earnings multiple must take into account the expected growth rate ($\bar{g}$) for the common stock earnings stream.[30]

---

[30] The reader will recognize that the g in the valuation model is the expected growth rate for dividends. In most of the current discussion it is assumed that there is a relatively constant

There is a positive relationship between the earnings multiple and the rate of growth, i.e., the higher the expected growth rate, the higher the multiple. In the extreme case of a constant growth rate over an infinite time period, the multiple will become: D/E/K−g. In the real world earnings are not expected to grow this way and the multiple is determined as being somewhere between:

$$P/E = \frac{D/E}{K} \text{ (no growth for an infinite period)}$$

and

$$P/E = \frac{D/E}{K-g} \text{ (constant rate of growth for an infinite period)}$$

Because the aggregate economy is more consistent with the assumptions of the constant growth model, it is important, when attempting to estimate an earnings multiple for the aggregate market, to consider the expected rate of growth during the investment horizon period and estimate any *changes* in the rate. Such changes will indicate a change in the relationship between K and g and have a profound effect on market value.

A firm's growth rate has been shown to be a function of: (1) the proportion of earnings retained and reinvested by the firm, and (2) the rate of return earned on investments.[31] In fact, assuming an all equity firm, it can be shown that the expected growth rate (g) is equal to the product of the retention rate in percent (b), times the rate of return on investments (r). The multiple should be positively related to both of these variables because an increase in either or both of them causes an increase in the growth rate and an increase in the multiple. Therefore, the growth rate can be stated as:

$$g = f(b, r)$$

where

g = expected growth rate

b = the expected retention rate equal to $1 - \dfrac{D}{E}$

r = the expected return on equity investments.

---

dividend payout ratio (dividend/earnings) so the growth of dividends is dependent on the growth in earnings and the growth rates are approximately equal.

[31] For an excellent discussion of alternative growth models, see Ezra Solomon, *The Theory of Financial Management* (New York: Columbia University Press, 1963), pp. 55–68. A further discussion of growth models, with consideration of outside financing, is contained in Merton Miller and Franco Modigliani, "Dividend Policy, Growth, and the Valuation of Shares," *Journal of Business*, Vol. 34, No. 4 (October, 1966), pp. 411–433.

Since the multiplier (M) is a function of K and g, this discussion can be summarized as:

$$(11-5) \qquad M = f(RFR, I, BR, FR, LR, b, r)$$

or

$$(11-6) \qquad M = f(RFR, I, \sigma_m^2, b, r)$$

Empirical Analysis of Determinants

A study by Reilly and Griggs specified empirical proxies for the several variables in Equation (11–4) and analyzed the relationship during the period 1940–1972.[32] The earnings multiple series employed was the price-earnings ratio for the S&P 400 series. The P/E ratio was obtained by dividing the end of the period stock price index by the seasonally adjusted annual rate of earnings for the corresponding quarter.

The RFR used was the Moody's average yield on Aaa corporate bonds. The rate of inflation proxy was the CPI (all items) with 1969 equaling 100. There was no operating earnings series available for the 1930's, so the seasonally adjusted net income figure for the S&P 400 series was used. A 20 quarter moving coefficient of variation series was derived as a measure of business risk. On a macro-economic basis there are no debt/equity ratios, debt/total cost ratios, or interest coverage figures. There were two financial risk proxies available. The first was a current ratio series from the *Federal Reserve Bulletin*. The second was the failure rate per 10,000 U.S. firms.

Rather than examining the components of growth (b and r), a direct measure of actual growth in earnings per share during alternative past periods was employed similar to the variables used in several previous studies of individual firm P/E ratios.[33] The earnings per share figure employed was the S&P 400 Index (seasonally adjusted quarterly figures) for 1935–1972. For each year, an average of the four quarters was derived and the percent of change computed. Average growth rates were derived for one, three, and five-year periods by computing the average percent of change for each such period on a moving basis.

The model included *percentages of change for all variables* since the major questions of interest were what changes occurred in the earnings multiple,

---

[32] Frank K. Reilly and Frank T. Griggs, "An Analysis of the Determinants of the Aggregate Stock Market Earnings Multiple," University of Wyoming Research Paper No. 32 (April, 1974).

[33] Malkiel and Cragg, "Expectations and the Structure of Share Prices"; and V. S. Whitbeck and M. Kisor, "A New Tool in Investment Decision-Making," *Financial Analysts Journal*, Vol. 19, No. 3 (May–June, 1963), pp. 55–62.

and what variables are most responsible for these changes. The form of the model was as follows:

$$M_t = a_i + b_1 GR_t + b_2 RFR_t + b_3 I_t + b_4 CVE_t + b_5 CR_t + b_6 FLR_t + u_t$$

where

M_t = price-earnings ratio during period t

a_i = intercept

GR_t = the average growth rate in earnings per share for alternative one, 3, and 5 year periods ending during year t

RFR_t = the average risk-free rate during period t

I_t = the rate of inflation during period t

CVE_t = the coefficient of variation in quarterly earnings per share (seasonally adjusted) for the most recent 20 quarters ending in year t

CR_t = the current ratio during period t

FLR_t = the failure rate during period t.

The results were reported in four sections. The first contained the *coincident* variables; the second analyzed the use of *future* explanatory variables; the third considered an attempt to *predict changes* in the earnings multiple by using alternative combinations of past explanatory variables; while the fourth was the results when the model was used as an investment decision tool.

The results with coincident variables, shown in Table 11–6, were quite encouraging. The best model regression had an R^2 of .59 and four of the variables had significant coefficients. Therefore, *the model appeared to explain a substantial amount of the variation in earnings multiple changes over time on the basis of several clearly specified aggregate economic variables.* The four significant variables were: (1) the corporate failure rate, (2) the risk-free interest rate, (3) the five year growth rate of earnings, and (4) the variability of earnings. The inflation rate was not important. This could be partially attributable to the correlation of inflation with the RFR, but was also due to the lag in adjustment to inflation as shown in tests by Reilly and Griggs. This lag in the adjustment to inflation has also been shown in several other studies on the relationship between inflation and interest rates.[34] The very strong

---

[34] Empirical evidence of the lagged adjustment is contained in: W. P. Yohe and D. S. Karnosky, "Interest Rates and Price Level Changes, 1952–1969," Federal Reserve Bank of

results with the failure rate were apparently caused by the fact that the failure rate not only reflects financial risk involved, but also the general state of the economy.

Because of the belief that investors anticipate economic changes, the authors tested the relationship between current changes in the multiple and *future* changes in the explanatory variables. The results indicated clearly that this model was inferior to the tests with the coincident period variables. Only one coefficient approached statistical significance, and most of the coefficients had the wrong sign.

The model was later used to forecast changes in the multiplier on the basis of past changes in the relevant economic variables. The base model was developed using the period 1951–1961, and the multiple was predicted for the period 1961–1972. The coefficients were changed over time depending upon relationships. The results with the regression model were compared to actual results and to a naive model that assumed no change in the multiple from the previous quarter. The correlation between the actual and estimated changes was .21 which was statistically significant. The estimating model was superior to the naive model, but the differences were not statistically significant.

An alternative test of the model used it as an investment tool. Assuming that earnings are relatively stable on a quarter-to-quarter basis, the major factor determining market movements would be changes in the market multiple. Therefore, one should invest in stocks during quarters in which an increase in the multiple is projected, and invest in T-bills during quarters in which the model projects a decline in the multiple. The test only required the model to project the *direction* of the change and also was realistic in the sense that the model used available data. Assuming no commissions were paid, a buy-and-hold portfolio would have experienced a compound annual rate of return of 5.52 percent during the period. In sharp contrast, the test portfolio employing the multiple model had an average compound rate of return of 13 percent. In addition, the standard deviation of quarterly rates of return for the test portfolio was substantially *lower* than that of the buy-and-hold example. Assuming commissions were paid, the buy-and-hold portfolio had a compound rate of growth of 5.36 percent, while the test portfolio experienced a compound rate of growth of 11.68 percent.

In summary, the volatility of the market earnings multiple indicates the need for analyzing this series. The results for coincident changes suggest that the market portfolio is affected by known aggregate economic variables and the relationships were in the expected direction. The results using past

St. Louis *Review*, Vol. 51, No. 12 (December, 1969), pp. 18–38; W. E. Gibson, "Price Expectations Effects on Interest Rates," *Journal of Finance,* Vol. 25, No. 1 (March, 1970), pp. 19–34; and W. E. Gibson, "Interest Rates and Inflationary Expectations: New Evidence," *American Economic Review,* Vol. 62, No. 5 (December, 1972), pp. 854–865.

Table 11–6 Aggregate Earnings Multiples and Explanatory Variables Yearly Data, 1940–1972

(All independent variables were for period t)

(t-values without signs are in parentheses)

	Interc.	1 Yr. GR.	3 Yr. GR.	5 Yr. GR.	RFR	I	CVE	CR	FLR	R²	SEE
Mult (t) =	8.467	+0.004			−0.706	a	−0.194	a	−0.248	.543	14.5
(t)		(1.38)			(1.84)		(2.14)		(3.43)		
Mult (t) =	7.736		+0.003		−0.860	a	−0.192	−0.327	−0.249	.526	15.0
(t)			(0.91)		(2.01)		(2.01)	(0.41)	(3.30)		
Mult (t) =	9.258			+0.020	−0.885	+0.001	−0.188	+0.099	−0.192	.585	14.3
(t)				(2.12)	(2.16)	(0.10)	(2.06)	(0.14)	(2.54)		

a—variable did not enter regression with F-level set at .001.

SEE—standard error of estimate.

Source: Frank K. Reilly and Frank T. Griggs, "An Analysis of the Determinants of the Aggregate Stock Market Earnings Multiple," University of Wyoming Research Paper No. 32 (April, 1974). Reprinted by permission.

values indicated that it is *not* possible to mechanically forecast future changes in the market earnings multiple. Such predictions require *estimating future values* for the relevant variables. Finally, the results using the model for investment purposes confirm the relative importance of the series and its practical usefulness.

Estimating Changes in the Growth Rate

When attempting to estimate changes in the growth rate, it is necessary to examine the basic factors that determine this rate. Recall that the growth rate (g) was a function of the retention rate (b), and the return on equity (r): $g = f(b,r)$. Therefore, you must first estimate changes in the aggregate retention rate. The figures in Table 11–7 indicate that this series was relatively constant in the 45–50 percent range prior to an increase in 1972–1974 that accompanied large earnings increases. Because the valuation model is a long-run model, it is important to consider only changes that are relatively permanent, although short-run changes can affect expectations.

Table 11–7
Factors Influencing Aggregate Growth Rate of Corporate Earnings Per Share Standard & Poor's 400 Index 1960–1976

Year	Dividend Per Share	Percent of Change	Retention Rate	Equity Turnover	Net Profit Margin	Return on Equity
1960	2.00	—	41.2	1.76	5.72	10.08
1961	2.07	3.5	38.6	1.71	5.66	9.67
1962	2.20	6.2	42.6	1.78	5.93	10.53
1963	2.36	7.2	44.3	1.79	6.19	11.11
1964	2.58	9.3	46.8	1.82	6.63	12.06
1965	2.82	9.3	48.7	1.85	6.82	12.64
1966	2.95	4.6	49.7	1.94	6.64	12.88
1967	2.97	0.7	47.1	1.92	6.12	11.76
1968	3.16	6.4	48.7	2.02	6.07	12.27
1969	3.25	2.8	47.0	2.10	5.65	11.86
1970	3.20	−1.5	41.8	2.09	4.92	10.28
1971	3.16	−1.2	47.1	2.14	5.04	10.80
1972	3.22	1.9	52.9	2.21	5.30	11.71
1973	3.46	7.5	61.1	2.37	5.96	14.15
1974	3.71	7.2	61.4	2.69	5.28	14.17
1975	3.72	0.1	56.6	2.61	4.63	12.11
1976	4.20	12.2	60.5	2.66	5.27	14.02
Average:	—	4.5	49.2	2.09	5.75	11.89

Source: Reprinted by permission of Standard & Poor's.

The second variable of interest is changes in the return on equity defined as:

$$r = \frac{\text{Net Inc}}{\text{Equity}}$$

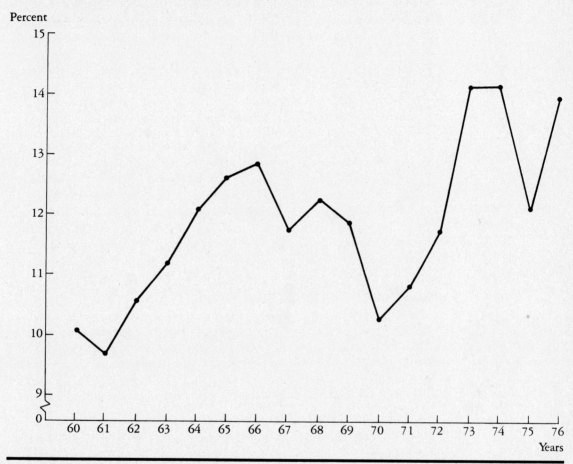

Source: Reprinted by permission of Standard & Poor's.

This return can be broken down into components as follows:

$$\frac{\text{Net Inc}}{\text{Equity}} = \frac{\text{Sales}}{\text{Equity}} \times \frac{\text{Net Inc}}{\text{Sales}} = \left(\begin{array}{c}\text{Equity}\\\text{Turnover}\end{array}\right) \times \left(\begin{array}{c}\text{Net Profit}\\\text{Margin}\end{array}\right)$$

This identity indicates that the two factors affecting the return on equity
are the *equity turnover* and the *net profit margin* on sales. A firm, or the
aggregate economy, can improve its return on equity and, thereby, its
growth rate by *either* increasing its equity turnover or increasing its net
profit margin. The figures in Table 11–7 and the time series plots in Figure
11–4 indicate that the aggregate return on equity for the S&P 400 Index has
increased from about 10 percent to the 12–14 percent range. The increase is

completely attributable to the increase in the equity turnover from about 1.7 to over 2.6, which more than offset the *decline* in the net profit margin during this period. One must ask what caused such increases in equity turnover and whether they can continue. Apparently they were the result of *an increase in debt financing.* One can increase equity turnover by increasing the total asset turnover with a constant proportion of debt and equity. Alternatively, if you increase the proportion of debt financing, the equity turnover will increase simply because the proportion of assets financed by equity has declined. Unfortunately, an increase in the proportion of debt financing increases financial leverage and the financial risk of corporations. Such increases in the proportion of debt financing cannot be continued indefinitely, so further increases in the return on equity will require increases in the net profit margin.

It is possible, therefore, to conceive of two approaches to estimating an aggregate stock market earnings multiple: (1) a macro approach using the variables suggested in the Reilly–Griggs study, or (2) a micro approach in which you consider the specific variables that influence k and g and attempt to estimate whether the spread between k and g will increase or decline in the future.

A Sample Estimate of the Multiple

The idea is to begin with the current multiple and estimate the *direction* and extent of the change based on expectations for either the macro variables or the micro variables that influence the aggregate k and g. The direction of the change is probably more important than the extent of the change is.

The Macro Approach The major variables that must be estimated are:

1. changes in the failure rate of U.S. corporations
2. changes in the risk-free interest rate as represented by a high-grade bond index
3. changes in the five year growth rate of earnings
4. changes in the variability of earnings
5. changes in the rate of inflation.

Assuming that the economy will be in its fifth year of expansion, most of the changes will be adverse. There will likely be an increase in the failure rate for corporations as the expansion either slows down or prepares to turn down. Toward the end of an expansion the rate of inflation typically increases, and this will cause an increase in the interest rate on high-grade bonds. Finally, one should expect a *decrease* in the rate of growth of earnings, but this will be accompanied by a decline in the variability of earnings caused by the slowdown. Therefore, one would probably expect a decline in the multiple relative to what it had been at the end of the previous year. The multiple at the end of 1977 was about 9.0. One might expect it to be about 8.75 at the end of 1978.

The Micro Approach The major variables that must be estimated are:

1. changes in the RFR
2. changes in the market risk premium
3. changes in the rate of inflation
4. changes in the retention rate
5. changes in the return on equity.

The first three are related to k and generally point toward a higher rate. Although there is no reason to expect a change in the real growth rate of the economy, it is likely that there will be some tightness in the money markets at this point in the expansion. Therefore, the tendency is for an increase in the RFR. The outlook for the risk premium is probably neutral since earnings growth will be relatively stable, there is a small tendency for increased debt, and market liquidity looks quite good based upon the heavy trading volume. Therefore, the risk premium will be constant. Finally, the outlook for inflation is for a constantly higher rate throughout the year; in other words, an increase in k during 1978.

The last two variables are the determinants of the expected growth rate. Again, the outlook is pessimistic because the retention rate (60 percent) will probably not increase very much. It will be difficult to continue to increase the return on equity by further increasing financial leverage. This means that it will be necessary to increase the profit margin, and the reader will recall that the outlook is for a decline in the profit margin during 1978. Therefore, the tendency is for a small decline in the expected growth rate.

Based upon an expectation of an increase in k during 1978 and a tendency for a small decline in g, this analysis would likewise project a decline in the earnings multiple.

Putting It Together

Previously we estimated earnings per share for 1978 of $12.50. This earnings figure times 8.75 equals 109.38 which is a point estimate for the value of the S&P 400 at the end of the year. The example was given to aid in understanding of the procedure. The estimation of the relevant variables was very casual and certainly not as extensive as one would like in practice. In addition, this was a point estimate rather than a range of estimates (pessimistic, optimistic, most likely) which would be preferable in this instance. The important point is to derive an understanding of *what the relevant variables are* and *how these variables relate to either corporate earnings or the earnings multiple.*

Summary

The material in this chapter is best summarized by outlining the steps used to arrive at an estimate of the future market value using the earnings multiple approach.

Outline of Earnings Multiple Approach to Projecting Aggregate Stock Market Values

I. **Estimate Expected Earnings**

A. Estimate Nominal GNP for Year
   1. estimate real GNP
   2. estimate inflation rate

B. Estimate Corporate Sales Based Upon Relationship to GNP

C. Estimate Aggregate Operating Profit Margin (NBDT/Sales)
   1. utilization rate
   2. unit labor cost
      a. wage/hour increases
      b. productivity changes
   3. inflation
   4. trade surplus

D. Estimate Net Profits
   1. compute operating profits (operating profit margin times sales)
   2. subtract estimated depreciation
   3. estimate taxes (tax rate times NBT)
   4. subtract taxes

II. **Estimate the Expected Earnings Multiple**

A. Estimate Changes in the Required Return (K)
   1. changes in the risk-free rate (ΔRFR)
   2. changes in the risk premium (ΔRP)
      a. changes in business risk
      b. changes in financial risk
      c. changes in liquidity risk, or
      d. changes in stock price volatility
   3. changes in the expected rate of inflation ($\Delta \hat{I}$)

B. Estimate Changes in the Expected Growth Rate (Δg)
   1. changes in the aggregate earnings retention rate
   2. changes in the return on equity
      a. changes in equity turnover
      b. changes in profit margin

C. Estimate Changes in the Spread Between K and g

III. **Estimate Market Value**

A. Estimated Earnings times Estimated Earnings Multiple

After examining the outline, one will recognize that the process is not easy because of the need to *estimate* numerous variables and then relate these estimates to each other. It is not easy, but it is clearly a useful exercise based upon the discussion in Chapter 10 which indicated the importance of market analysis for the total investment selection process. It can be shown that, on many occasions, the first decision is the most important decision and that first decision is: "Should I invest in stocks during the forthcoming period?" The previous discussion should help an analyst or portfolio manager make that important decision. Under such conditions—it is worth the effort!

Questions

1. At a social gathering you are talking to another investor who contends that the stock market will experience a substantial increase next year because it is estimated that corporate earnings are going to rise by at least 12 percent. Would you agree or disagree? Why?

2. It is shown that there is a relationship between the GNP and corporate sales. How would you explain the existence of such a relationship to a friend who is a music major, i.e., has no knowledge of economics or finance?

3. Go to the library and find at least *three sources* of *historical* information on the nominal and real GNP. Attempt to find two sources that provide an *estimate* of nominal GNP for the coming year or that gave one for the previous year.

4. Prepare a table for the last ten years showing the percent of change each year for: (a) consumer price index—all items, (b) nominal GNP, (c) real GNP (in constant dollars), (d) the GNP deflator. Discuss the proportion of nominal growth that was due to "real" growth and to inflation. Is the outlook for the coming year any different from developments last year? Discuss.

5. Assume you are told that the nominal GNP will increase by about 8 percent next year. Using Figure 11–2, what would you estimate as the "most likely" increase in corporate sales? What would your most optimistic estimate be? Most pessimistic estimate?

6. Since you eventually want to arrive at the *net profit margin,* why do you spend time estimating the gross margin and working down?

7. The long-run trend for all the margins plotted in Figure 11–3 is downward. How would you explain this? What factors might account for the trend?

8. Compute the ratio of depreciation as a percent of sales. What has been the trend in this series? What does this tell you about fixed costs per unit?

9. Compare the utilization rate to the depreciation/sales ratio. Would you expect these variables to be related? What is the empirical relationship?

10. There are contrary arguments regarding the expected relationship between inflation and the aggregate profit margin. Briefly discuss these alternative arguments.

11. You are told that the level of *exports* is going to increase next year. How does this affect your estimate of the aggregate profit margin? Why?

12. You are told that the level of *imports* is going to decline next year. How does this affect your estimate of the aggregate profit margin? Explain your reasoning.

13. There are well regarded estimates that hourly wage rates will increase by about 6 percent next year. How does this affect your estimate of the aggregate profit margin? Is there any other information you need? What is it and why do you need it?

14. It is estimated that hourly wage rates will increase by 7 percent and that productivity will increase by 5 percent. What would you expect to happen to unit labor cost as a result? Given this estimate, how would this influence your estimate of the aggregate profit margin? Discuss.

15. There has generally been a strong cyclical pattern to productivity changes. Following a cyclical trough, the gains in productivity are substantial, while immediately following a peak the productivity gains are very slight or in some instances there are declines. Discuss this phenomenon and why it occurs.

16. The long-run pattern in depreciation expenses is one reason that the NBT margin declines so drastically during an economic recession. Explain this statement.

17. For 1976, assume the tax rate was 49 percent rather than 51.0 percent. What would have been the difference in earnings per share? What would have happened with a tax rate of 48 percent?

18. It is stated that, "The factors influencing the earnings multiple depend upon the earnings figure used." What is meant by this statement?

19. Assuming no growth in earnings, or that the earnings figure is for long-run expected earnings, what factors influence the multiple? Discuss each of the variables and indicate *how* and *why* they influence the multiple.

20. Define external market liquidity risk. Compute the Amivest Dollar Index for a recent three-day period for IBM, McDonald's, and Anheuser Busch. Which do you think is most liquid? Least liquid?

21. In a CAPM world, a risky asset's *systematic* risk is supposed to be the relevant risk variable. How does this apply to the aggregate stock market? What should the measure be? Because of the measurement problems, what is the most likely measure?

22. Assuming a growing earnings stream, what additional variables must be considered to determine changes in the earnings multiple? Discuss each of them.

23. Assume that each of the following changes is independent and, except for this change, all else remains the same. In each case indicate *what* will happen to the earnings multiplier and discuss *why* it will happen:

    A. the Amivest Index for the market increases 15 percent

    B. there is an increase in the return on equity

    C. there is an increase in stock price volatility

    D. the aggregate debt/equity ratio increases

    E. the overall productivity of capital increases

    *F. the rate of inflation goes from 4 percent to 7 percent

    *G. the aggregate dividend payout ratio increases from 45 percent to 55 percent.

References

Arditti, Fred D. "Risk and the Required Return on Equity." *Journal of Finance,* Vol. 22, No. 1 (March, 1967).

Business and Money. Chicago: Harris Trust and Savings Bank, 1978.

Dernberg, Thomas F. and McDougall, Duncan M. *Macroeconomics.* (4th edition.) New York: McGraw–Hill Book Co., 1973.

Finkel, Sidney R. and Tuttle, Donald L. "Determinants of the Aggregate Profits Margin." *Journal of Finance,* Vol. 26, No. 5 (December, 1971).

Fisher, Lawrence. "Determinants of Risk Premiums on Corporate Bonds." *Journal of Political Economy,* Vol. 67, No. 3 (June, 1959).

Fouse, William L. "Risk and Liquidity: The Keys to Stock Price Behavior." *Financial Analysts Journal,* Vol. 32, No. 3 (May–June, 1976).

Gibson, W. E. "Interest Rates and Inflationary Expectations: New Evidence." *American Economic Review,* Vol. 62, No. 5 (December, 1972).

Gibson, W. E. "Price-Expectations Effects on Interest Rates." *Journal of Finance,* Vol. 25, No. 1 (March, 1970).

Gray, H. Peter. "Determinants of the Aggregate Profit Margin: Comment." *Journal of Finance,* Vol. 31, No. 1 (March, 1976).

Hamburger, Michael J. and Kochin, Lewis A. "Money and Stock Prices: The Channels of Influence." *Journal of Finance,* Vol. 27, No. 2 (May, 1972).

Hirsch, Michael D. "Liquidity Filters: Tools for Better Performance." *Journal of Portfolio Management,* Vol. 2, No. 1 (Fall, 1975).

Keran, Michael W. "Expectations, Money and the Stock Market," Federal Reserve Bank of St. Louis *Review*, Vol. 53, No. 1 (January, 1971).

The Liquidity Report. New York: Amivest Corporation.

Malkiel, Burton G. and Cragg, John G. "Expectations and the Structure of Share Prices." *American Economic Review,* Vol. 60, No. 4 (September, 1970).

---

*These could affect the multiplier in either direction. Both effects, and the assumptions they are based on, should be discussed.

Martin, Peter. "Analysis of the Impact of Competitive Rates on the Liquidity of NYSE Stocks." Economic Staff Paper 75—No. 3, Office of Economic Research, Securities and Exchange Commission (July, 1975).

Miller, Merton and Modigliani, Franco. "Dividend Policy, Growth, and the Valuation of Shares." *Journal of Business,* Vol. 34, No. 4 (October, 1966).

Reilly, Frank K. "Companies and Common Stocks as Inflation Hedges." New York University Graduate School of Business, Center for the Study of Financial Institutions, *Bulletin* (April, 1975).

Reilly, Frank K. and Drzycimski, Eugene F. "Aggregate Market Earnings Multiples Over Stock Market Cycles and Business Cycles." *Mississippi Valley Journal of Business and Economics,* Vol. 10, No. 2 (Winter, 1974–1975).

Reilly, Frank K. and Griggs, Frank T. "An Analysis of the Determinants of the Aggregate Stock Market Earnings Multiple." University of Wyoming Research Paper No. 32 (April, 1974).

Reilly, Frank K. and Wright, David. "An Analysis of Aggregate Stock Market Liquidity." Paper presented at the Eastern Finance Association Meeting, Boston, Massachusetts (April, 1977).

Seligman, Daniel. "A Bad New Era for Common Stocks." *Fortune* (October, 1971).

Solomon, Ezra. *The Theory of Financial Management.* New York: Columbia University Press, 1963.

Standard & Poor's. *Analysts Handbook.* New York: Standard & Poor's Corporation.

Whitbeck, V. S. and Kisor, M. "A New Tool In Investment Decision-Making." *Financial Analysts Journal,* Vol. 19, No. 3 (May–June, 1963).

Yohe, W. P. and Karnosky, D. S. "Interest Rates and Price Level Changes, 1952–1969." Federal Reserve Bank of St. Louis *Review,* Vol. 51, No. 12 (December, 1969).

Appendix 11-A
Derivation of Constant Growth Dividend Model

The basic model is:

$$P_o = \frac{D_1}{(1+K_j)^1} + \frac{D_2}{(1+K_j)^2} + \frac{D_3}{(1+K_j)^3} + \cdots \frac{D_n}{(1+K_j)^n}$$

where:

P_o = Current price.

D_i = Expected dividend in period i.

K_j = Required rate of return on asset j.

If growth rate (g) is constant:

$$P_o = \frac{D_o(1+g)^1}{(1+K)^1} + \frac{D_o(1+g)^2}{(1+K)^2} + \cdots \frac{D_o(1+g)^n}{(1+K)^n}$$

This can be written:

(11A-1)
$$P_o = D_o \left[\frac{1+g}{1+K} + \frac{(1+g)^2}{(1+K)^2} + \frac{(1+g)^3}{(1+K)^3} + \cdots \frac{(1+g)^n}{(1+K)^n} \right]$$

Multiply both sides of Equation (11A-1) by $\frac{1+K}{1+g}$:

$$(11A-2) \quad \left[\frac{(1+K)}{(1+g)}\right] P_0 = D_0 \left[1 + \frac{(1+g)}{(1+K)} + \frac{(1+g)^2}{(1+K)^2} + \cdots \frac{(1+g)^{n-1}}{(1+K)^{n-1}}\right]$$

Subtract Equation (11A–1) from Equation (11A–2):

$$\left[\frac{(1+K)}{(1+g)} - 1\right] P_0 = D_0 \left[1 - \frac{(1+g)^n}{(1+K)^n}\right]$$

$$\left[\frac{(1+K) - (1+g)}{(1+g)}\right] P_0 = D_0 \left[1 - \frac{(1+g)^n}{(1+K)^n}\right]$$

Assuming $K>g$, as $N \rightarrow \infty$ the term in brackets on the right side of the equation goes to 1 leaving

$$\left[\frac{(1+K) - (1+g)}{(1+g)}\right] P_0 = D_0$$

This simplifies to:

$$\left[\frac{1 + K - 1 - g}{(1+g)}\right] P_0 = D_0$$

which equals:

$$\left[\frac{K - g}{(1+g)}\right] P_0 = D_0$$

This equals:

$$(K - g)P_0 = D_0(1+g) \text{ but } D_0(1+g) = D_1$$

so:

$$(K - g)P_0 = D_1$$

$$P_0 = \frac{D_1}{K - g}$$

Remember this model assumes:

a constant growth rate

an infinite time period

that the required return on the investment (K) is greater than the expected growth rate (g).

Appendix 11–B
Common Stocks as an Inflation Hedge

One of the most pervasive bits of folklore on Wall Street prior to the 1970's was that common stocks were a good hedge against inflation. This assumption was called into question during the 1970's when very consistent empirical evidence indicated that common stocks had done very poorly during the periods of high inflation since 1966. In addition, several studies examined the long-run evidence and generally indicated that recent experience was not unique and that common stocks have consistently *not* been good hedges. The purpose of this appendix is to explain under what conditions one might expect common stocks to be an inflation hedge, and to analyze the variables that determine whether stocks should be a hedge. Finally, we will briefly review some of the studies that examined the performance of common stocks as hedges during periods of significant inflation.

The Dividend Valuation Model and Inflation

The reader is aware of the dividend valuation model which is as follows:

$$P_i = \frac{D_1}{K_i - g_i}$$

where:

P_i — price of stock i

D_1 — expected dividend in period 1

K_i — the required rate of return on stock i

g_i — the expected growth rate of dividends for stock i

Using this simplified version of the model, it is possible to consider what will happen as a result of a change in expectations regarding inflation and what must happen in order for common stocks to be a complete hedge against inflation.

Complete Inflation Hedge Defined

A hedge is a transaction intended to safeguard against loss on another investment. A hedge against inflation then, is the acquisition of an asset that would be a safeguard against an increase in the general price level. It is an asset that generates a return equal to the increase in the general price level. Unfortunately, the traditional definition of an inflation hedge is incomplete when applied to common stock investments because it overlooks the *normal* required rate of return on an investment in common stocks *regardless* of the current rate of inflation.

Investors normally require a rate of return in line with the economy's risk-free rate of interest, as well as a return commensurate with the business and financial risks involved, or an added return for the stock's systematic market risk. The "normal" required rate does not take inflation into account; it is an inflation-free rate of return. Therefore, *in order for a stock to be a complete inflation hedge, its "real" rate of return must be greater than its normal required rate of return.* This can be represented as follows:

$$r' \geq k$$

where:

$r' =$ "real" rate of return. The "real" rate of return is the nominal rate of return during a period (r), adjusted for the rate of inflation during the period (I). Specifically:

$$= \frac{1 + \text{nominal rate of return}}{1 + \text{rate of inflation}} - 1$$

$$= \frac{1 + r}{1 + I} - 1$$

$k =$ normal rate of return for the risk class of stock assuming a zero rate of inflation

Assume that investors in common stock have a normal required return of 8 percent ($k = .08$); that the general price level is increasing at 4 percent ($I = .04$); and the nominal return from common stocks is 10 percent ($r = .10$). Under these conditions the "real" rate of return is 5.8 percent

$$(r' = \frac{1.10}{1.04} - 1 = .058).$$

When the real rate of return (.058) is compared to the normal required rate of return (.08) it is seen that the real rate is *below* the required rate and therefore, common stocks were *not* a complete inflation hedge during the period. If the nominal return had been 14.0 percent, the real return would have been 9.6 percent which, compared to the 8 percent normally required, would indicate that common stocks were a complete inflation hedge.

Therefore, when there is a change in the expected rate of inflation, *k will increase by this amount.* Given a change in the required return, the crucial question becomes *what will happen to the value of the asset* so that the investor will receive his required return? One possibility is that *nothing else will change* and the stock price will decline so that k will increase as follows:

$$\text{If } P = \frac{D_1}{k-g}$$

then,

$$k = \frac{D_1}{P} + g.$$

If nothing else changes, then *P must decline* until there is an increase in the D_1/P term to compensate for the increase in the required return. Clearly, during this period of adjustment the stockholder will experience negative returns.

Another possibility is that *the growth rate of dividends (g) will increase by the rate of inflation.* If this occurs, the stock price will not change because *the spread between k and g will not change.* K is still equal to:

$$k = \frac{D_1}{P} + g$$

The difference is that the dividend yield does *not* change because P does not change, but the growth rate has increased. Therefore, the return (k) has increased and the stock will be a complete inflation hedge. *G must increase by the change in the rate of inflation if the stock is to be a complete inflation hedge without the stock price declining.* This is the implicit assumption made by many who contend that common stocks will be an inflation hedge. An example is found in an article by Jahnke that employs the dividend model to explain changes in stock prices based upon changes in the spread between k and g.[1] He states, "Thus common stocks should serve as a hedge against inflation to the extent that changes in the rate of inflation are mirrored in the dividend growth rate."[2] The question then becomes, under what conditions will the growth rate increase in line with the rate of inflation?

---

[1] William W. Jahnke, "What's Behind Stock Prices?" *Financial Analysts Journal,* Vol. 31, No. 5 (September–October, 1975), pp. 69–76.

[2] Ibid., p. 71.

Inflation and the Growth Rate

A firm's dividend growth rate is a function of the retention rate (RR) and the return on equity (ROE). In turn, the ROE is a function of the equity turnover rate and the profit margin. Therefore, the growth rate will increase if there is an appropriate increase in one or several of the following variables:

(1) the retention rate

(2) the equity turnover

(3) the net profit margin.

One probably should not expect a major impact from changes in the retention rate because an analysis of the historical series indicates that this rate changes slowly over time and does not change in response to inflation. It can be shown that it would require a significant change to have the desired impact. Therefore, although one might hope for some increase in the retention rate, it is clear that the major impact on growth must come from an increase in the ROE.

The ROE is determined by the equity turnover and the net profit margin. Equity turnover could increase during a period of inflation if the firm is able to increase its sales by the rate of inflation. In additon, it is necessary to *at least* maintain its net profit margin during this period. If sales increase by the rate of inflation and the profit margin is constant, net earnings growth will increase by the rate of inflation; e.g., during a period of 4 percent inflation earnings will increase by 10 percent rather than by only 6 percent. Therefore, during a period of inflation, in order for firms in general to be an inflation hedge it is necessary that the rate of growth of sales increase by the rate of inflation *and* that the net profit margin remain constant.

In order to increase sales by the rate of inflation, it is necessary to raise prices by the rate of inflation. In turn, the ability to raise prices in line with the change in the rate of inflation depends on the elasticity of demand for the product involved and on the amount of regulation of the product's industry. If the demand for the product is very inelastic it may be possible to implement the increase with minor effects on volume. If most companies face elastic demand because of strong domestic or foreign competition (e.g., the steel industry), it may not be possible to increase prices in line with the rate of inflation without reducing physical volume. Assuming it is possible to increase prices *somewhat* in line with the rate of inflation, the crucial consideration is *the ability to maintain or increase profit margins during periods of inflation.*

Profit Margins and Inflation

Most literature dealing with the ability of corporations to hedge against inflation has considered the factors that influence the profit margin. There are three hypotheses offered to explain why given firms might be able to gain during periods of inflation: (1) the wage-lag hypothesis, (2) the net debtor hypothesis, and (3) fixed operating assets or raw materials.

The wage lag hypothesis contends that sales prices can be raised immediately in response to an increase in the rate of inflation while wage rate increases lag because they are generally negotiated at yearly intervals. During the lag period, there is a shift in wealth from wage earners to firms, i.e., profit margins increase at the expense of labor. This effect should be relatively short-term because, eventually, the wage earners should gain during negotiations.

A second possibility is the net debtor-creditor hypothesis which contends that, during periods of inflation, there is a transfer of wealth from creditors to debtors because the money received by a creditor is reduced in value while a debtor pays off his obligation in lower valued money. Given the fixed nature of the obligations, the net debtor firm (i.e., monetary liabilities exceed monetary assets) will enjoy lower capital costs during the period of inflation. Assuming that the prices of products increase in line with the inflation, and that costs other than capital costs increase in line with inflation, the firm's average costs (including capital costs), will *not* increase in line with inflation. Hence, there will be *an increase in the firm's profit margin,* and the company's nominal earnings will increase by more than the rate of inflation.

Finally, one would expect an increase in relative profits when firms have significant operating assets or raw materials acquired prior to the period of inflation that will last throughout the period. Examples could be drawn from capital intensive firms or natural resource firms (e.g., coal, lumber, oil). In these cases, if the prices of products increase in line with inflation, and major material costs are constant, *the firm's profit margin will increase* and nominal earnings will rise at a rate in *excess* of the rate of inflation. In all cases in which a firm gains during a period of inflation this shows up as an *increase in the profit margin during the period.*

Empirical Evidence Regarding Wage-Lag Hypothesis Kessel and Alchian reviewed past studies of this hypothesis and provided new evidence on the topic.[3] They disagreed with most evidence that supported the hypothesis because: (1) the authors did not consider factors other than wages and prices; (2) the data was possibly inadequate; or (3) the beginning and ending points of the study caused biases. They tested the hypothesis by examining the proposition that firms with large annual wage bills would experience a greater increase in profits and stock prices than would firms with smaller wage bills, using data from the total period 1939–1952. The results did not support the hypothesis because they indicated that the

---

[3] Reuben A. Kessel and Armen A. Alchian, "The Meaning and Validity of the Inflation-Induced Lag of Wages Behind Prices," *American Economic Review,* Vol. 50, No. 1 (March, 1960), pp. 43–66.

average increase in equity was greater for firms with lower wage ratios. A multiple correlation analysis including the net debtor position also did not support the wage-lag hypothesis.

Cargill examined numerous wage and price series using spectral analysis to determine whether there was a consistent lead-lag relationship in the United States and England.[4] For the United States there was no particular wage-price relationship. In England the long-run intervals indicated evidence of a wage lag, while there was no relationship, for short-run intervals.

A study by Reilly that examined earnings and prices during the period 1947–1973 hypothesized that the wage-lag would be short-run because labor would eventually require compensation.[5] The analysis indicated that, with one exception, at peaks and troughs *the price series either turned ahead of or coincidentally with the wage series.* It was concluded that prices tended to turn before wages, but the wage-lag was generally short-lived.

Empirical Evidence Regarding Net Debtor Hypothesis Kessel pointed out that net debtor firms would gain during a period of unanticipated inflation relative to creditor firms and that *large* debtors should gain more than small debtors should, while large creditors would lose more than small creditors would.[6] An analysis of bank shares and randomly selected industrial firms consistently supported the hypothesis that, during periods of significant inflation, the stocks of debtor firms gained, while the stocks of creditor firms gained during periods of significant deflation.

DeAlessi employed five independent tests to determine whether net debtor firms in the United Kingdom gained during periods of unanticipated inflation during the years 1948–1957.[7] The results differed somewhat depending upon the sample and the definitions used for wealth and a firm's monetary position. Still, the overall test results *consistently supported the debtor-creditor hypothesis* during the years of significant inflation (i.e., 1949–1952 and 1956–1957).

Before one can judge the impact of the net debtor hypothesis on the aggregate market, it is necessary to determine the number of net debtor firms. DeAlessi examined the proportion of such firms in the U.S. and the U.K.[8] For the U.S., the data indicated that, from the mid-1930's through

---

[4] Thomas F. Cargill, "An Empirical Investigation of the Wage-Lag Hypothesis." *American Economic Review,* Vol. 59, No. 5 (December, 1969), pp. 806–816.

[5] Frank K. Reilly, "Companies and Common Stocks as Inflation Hedges," New York University Graduate School of Business, Center for the Study of Financial Institutions, *Bulletin* (April, 1975).

[6] Reuben A. Kessel, "Inflation-Caused Wealth Redistribution: A Test of a Hypothesis," *American Economic Review,* Vol. 46, No. 1 (March, 1956), pp. 128–141.

[7] Louis DeAlessi, "The Redistribution of Wealth by Inflation: An Empirical Test with United Kingdom Data," *The Southern Economic Journal,* Vol. 30, No. 4 (October, 1963), pp. 113–127.

[8] Louis DeAlessi, "Do Business Firms Gain from Inflation?" *Journal of Business,* Vol. 37, No. 2 (April, 1964), pp. 162–166.

the mid-1950's, the proportion of net debtor firms was about 55 percent. Broussalian found a 50–50 split during the period 1948–1956.[9]

The studies supported the net debtor hypothesis during periods of significant unanticipated inflation but because only about half of U.S. firms are net debtors, the overall impact is probably minimal.

Empirical Evidence on Profit Margins During Inflation

Table 11B–1 contains the net profit margin for the S&P 400 Stock Price Indicator Series for each year from 1946 through 1976 along with a designation of years of significant inflation (defined as an annual rate of 3 percent or more). The figures for the early part of the period (1946–1948) indicated a positive relationship between inflation and profit margins. During the 1950–1951 period, the margin increased the first year and then declined sharply. During 1956–1957 the margin declined slightly both years. Finally, during the inflation that has prevailed since 1966, the margin has consistently declined.

Table 11B–1
Annual Net Profit Margin for S&P 400 Industrial Index

Year	Net Profit Margin	Year	Net Profit Margin	Year	Net Profit Margin
*1946	6.35	1958	5.52	*1970	4.92
*1947	6.75	1959	6.00	*1971	5.04
*1948	7.24	1960	5.72	*1972	5.30
1949	6.61	1961	5.66	*1973	5.96
*1950	7.56	1962	5.93	*1974	5.28
*1951	5.84	1963	6.19	*1975	4.63
1952	5.33	1964	6.63	*1976	5.27
1953	5.19	1965	6.82	*1977	5.13
1954	5.82	*1966	6.64		
1955	6.61	*1967	6.12		
*1956	6.40	*1968	6.07		
*1957	6.33	*1969	5.65		

*Indicates year of significant inflation (over 3 percent annual rate).
Source: Reprinted by permission of Standard & Poor's.

Therefore, recent experience does *not* support the myth that there is a positive relationship between inflation and the aggregate profit margin. This is not too surprising because the two major hypotheses suggested are not very pervasive. The wage-lag effect is short-run and probably would not have a positive impact beyond the first year and the net debtor effect will probably be minimal for the U.S. economy because only about half the firms are net debtors.

---

[9] J. V. Broussalian, "Unanticipated Inflation: A Test of the Debtor-Creditor Hypothesis," Ph.D. dissertation, University of California, Los Angeles, 1961.

Analyzing common stocks in terms of their use as an inflation hedge presents several problems in terms of methodology, as previous studies have shown. Before we attempt our own analysis, we would be well advised to examine some of them.

Problems in Inflation Hedge Analysis

The first problem is the fact that common stocks have been examined over extremely long time periods which include significant inflation, deflation, and relative price stability. This is a mistake because one would expect investors to periodically review their portfolio based upon new expectations so they are only interested in whether an investment is an inflation hedge during periods of significant inflation. They should not care about how common stocks perform as an inflation hedge during periods of price stability or price deflation. When one examines stock performance over an extended period, one finds that common stock prices increase faster than consumer prices during the *total* period. An analysis of common stocks during periods of *differential* price change indicates that common stocks do quite well during periods of price stability and this admirable performance offsets their very poor performance during most periods of significant inflation. However, *it is only the performance of common stocks during periods of significant inflation that is important to the investor looking for an inflation hedge.*

The second problem is that *an investor's normal required rate of return during a period of noninflation has generally been ignored.* Previous analyses implicitly assumed that returns on common stock only had to exceed the rate of inflation to be considered a good hedge. However, investors have a "normal" required rate of return on common stocks. Therefore, when inflation occurs, investors increase their required return by the rate of inflation. To determine whether common stocks have been a complete inflation hedge during a period of significant inflation, it is necessary to compare the "real" return on the stock (r') to the investor's normal required return (K). A good proxy for the long-run required return on common stocks is provided in Lawrence Fisher's analysis which indicates that the median annual return on New York Stock Exchange stocks was 9.8 percent during the period 1926–1960.[10] When this nominal return is adjusted for the 1.5 percent rate of inflation during this period, the estimated "real" normal rate of return was 8.2 percent.

RJS Studies

Several studies by Reilly, Johnson, and Smith (RJS) considered whether common stocks have been complete inflation hedges during periods of

---

[10] Lawrence Fisher, "Outcomes for 'Random' Investments in Common Stocks Listed on the New York Stock Exchange," *Journal of Business,* Vol. 38, No. 2 (April, 1965), pp. 149–161.

significant inflation (annual rate above 3 percent).[11] They divided the total time period into periods of significant inflation, relative noninflation, and deflation and determined what happened to stock prices during the periods of significant inflation. The results for several well-known stock price series during the period 1937–1973 are contained in Table 11B–2. The nominal return is the annual rate of return for the indicator series (including dividends) during the period of inflation. The real return is the nominal return adjusted for the rate of inflation during the period. The net return is the "real" return minus some estimate of a "normal" return. If the net return is positive for a given normal return, common stocks were a complete inflation hedge during the period.

The results in Table 11B–2 indicate that, during most of the periods of significant inflation, *real rates of return were negative* even before allowing for a normal rate of return. Except for the S&P 425 series, all the weighted average real returns were negative. Based upon these results and subsequent analysis, the authors concluded that common stocks have generally *not* been a complete inflation hedge. A later study considered the tax effects and confirmed the prior results.[12] An analysis of total "real" rates of return on common stocks indicated that the worst results were derived during periods of significant inflation, while encouraging results were experienced during periods of price stability.[13] In addition, the authors examined the performance of a sample of individual stocks and the results were very consistent with the aggregate market results.[14]

Further Studies

A study by Oudet indicated that, during the total period 1953–1970, the rates of return on common stock were highest during the periods of least inflation and lowest during periods of high inflation.[15] As a crude confirma-

---

[11] The results reported are from Frank K. Reilly, "Companies and Common Stock," p. 45. These were updated from Frank K. Reilly, Glenn L. Johnson, and Ralph E. Smith, "Inflation, Inflation Hedges and Common Stock," *Financial Analysts Journal*, Vol. 26, No. 1 (January–February, 1970), pp. 104–110.

[12] Frank K. Reilly, Glenn L. Johnson, and Ralph E. Smith, "A Note on Common Stocks as Inflation Hedges—the After Tax Case," *Southern Journal of Business*, Vol. 7, No. 4 (November, 1972), pp. 101–106.

[13] Ralph E. Smith, Glenn L. Johnson, and Frank K. Reilly, "A Year-by-Year Analysis of 'Real' Rates of Return on Common Stocks," *Quarterly Review of Economics and Business*, Vol. 14, No. 1 (Spring, 1974), pp. 79–88.

[14] G. L. Johnson, F. K. Reilly, and R. E. Smith, "Individual Common Stocks as Inflation Hedges," *Journal of Financial and Quantitative Analysis*, Vol. 6, No. 3 (June, 1971), pp. 1015–1024; Frank K. Reilly, Glenn L. Johnson, and Ralph E. Smith, "A Correction and Update Regarding Individual Common Stocks as Inflation Hedges," *Journal of Financial and Quantitative Analysis*, Vol. 10, No. 5 (December, 1975), pp. 871–880.

[15] Bruno A. Oudet, "The Variation of the Return on Stocks in Periods of Inflation," *Journal of Financial and Quantitative Analysis*, Vol. 8, No. 2 (March, 1973), pp. 247–258.

Table 11B–2
Market Indicators as Inflation Hedges During Periods of Inflation September 30, 1937 to December 31, 1973

Market Indicators	Nominal Return (r)	Real Return (r')	Net Return or Real Return Minus Alternative Normal Returns (k)		
			(3%)	(6%)	(9%)
3/31/41 to 6/30/43					
D-J Industrials	12.8	2.7	−0.3	−3.3	−6.3
S&P 425 Industrials	17.6	7.1	4.1	1.1	−1.9
S&P Utilities	6.5	−3.1	−6.1	−9.1	−12.1
S&P Rails	21.3	10.5	7.5	4.5	1.5
S&P 500 Stocks	16.6	6.2	3.2	0.2	−2.8
3/31/46 to 9/30/48					
D-J Industrials	0.2	−11.0	−14.0	−17.0	−20.0
S&P 425 Industrials	−0.7	−11.7	−14.7	−17.7	−20.7
S&P Utilities	−5.8	−16.3	−19.3	−22.3	−25.3
S&P Rails	−6.0	−16.4	−19.4	−22.4	−25.4
S&P 500 Stocks	−1.5	−12.5	−15.5	−18.5	−21.5
3/31/50 to 12/31/51					
D-J Industrials	24.9	16.9	13.9	10.9	7.9
S&P 425 Industrials	31.5	23.1	20.1	17.1	14.1
S&P Utilities	8.5	1.5	−1.5	−4.5	−7.5
S&P Rails	30.1	21.8	18.8	15.8	12.8
S&P 500 Stocks	28.4	20.2	17.2	14.2	11.2
3/31/56 to 3/31/58					
D-J Industrials	−2.1	−5.6	−8.6	−11.6	−14.6
S&P 425 Industrials	−6.2	−9.5	−12.5	−15.5	−18.5
S&P Utilities	7.2	3.4	0.4	−2.6	−5.6
S&P Rails	−16.0	−19.0	−22.0	−25.0	−28.0
S&P 500 Stocks	−3.1	−6.5	−9.5	−12.5	−15.5
12/31/65 to 12/31/73					
D-J Industrials	1.9	−2.8	−5.8	−8.8	−11.8
S&P 425 Industrials	4.4	−0.4	−3.4	−6.4	−9.4
S&P Utilities	−0.8	−5.3	−8.3	−11.3	−14.3
S&P Rails	2.9	−1.8	−4.8	−7.8	−10.8
S&P 500 Stocks	4.0	−0.8	−3.8	−6.8	−9.8
Weighted Average[a]					
D-J Industrials	5.1	−1.6	−4.6	−7.6	−10.6
S&P 425 Industrials	7.0	0.3	−2.7	−5.7	−8.7
S&P Utilities	1.4	−4.9	−7.9	−10.9	−13.9
S&P Rails	4.7	−1.9	−4.9	−7.9	−10.9
S&P 500 Stocks	6.6	−0.1	−3.1	−6.1	−9.1

[a] Weights are equal to number of months in each inflationary period.

Source: Updated results as reported in Frank K. Reilly, Glenn L. Johnson, and Ralph E. Smith, "Inflation, Inflation Hedges and Common Stock," *Financial Analysts Journal,* Vol. 26, No. 1 (January–February, 1970), pp. 104–110. Reprinted by permission.

tion of this phenomenon, the current author divided all years from 1916 to 1974 into years of significant inflation (over 3 percent increase in prices), years of deflation (over one percent decrease in prices), and years of relative price stability (between 3 percent increase and one percent decrease). The average of the annual changes in the S&P 500 during periods of significant inflation was −0.25 percent; the average change during years of price stability was + 12.31 percent, while the average change during years of deflation was −0.34 percent.

Some studies examined international stock price series as inflation hedges. Branch examined stock price indexes, inflation rates, and industrial production rates for 22 industrialized countries for the total period 1953–1969 and concluded that stocks were a partial inflation hedge.[16] Unfortunately, during most of this period there was price stability, which means the results are not indicative of performance during significant inflation. Further, if one eliminates Chile (which had very inconsistent results) and divides the rest of the countries into those with low inflation (under 3 percent) and high inflation (over 3 percent), the results indicate that the average rate of stock price increase was 1.96 percent for the high inflation countries, and 7.16 percent for the low inflation countries. Apparently, investors were better off investing in low inflation countries.

A study by Cagan dealt with long-run returns from stocks for alternative countries.[17] He considered a combination of price change periods and, assuming that investors held common stocks through all periods, concluded that common stocks were a good inflation hedge in the long-run. A careful reading of the results indicates that stocks apparently did not do well during the periods of inflation, but eventually made up for the loss after the inflation was over.

Finally, Townsend analyzed the performance of stocks from 15 industries and 474 companies during the period 1965–1974.[18] He concluded that his results provided overwhelming evidence of the inability of all the selected industries and most of the individual companies (95 percent) to protect against declining purchasing power during the period 1965–1974.

It appears, then, that common stocks have *not* been complete inflation hedges. They have generally been rather *poor investments* during periods of significant inflation. Apparently this poor performance for common stocks is caused by the fact that the growth rate in dividends has *not* kept up with the increases in the required rate of return due to the increases in the rate of

---

[16] Ben Branch, "Common Stock Performance and Inflation: An International Comparison," *Journal of Business,* Vol. 47, No. 1 (January, 1974), pp. 48–52.

[17] Phillip Cagan, "Common Stock Values and Inflation—The Historical Record of Many Countries," *National Bureau Report Supplement* (New York: National Bureau of Economic Research, Inc., March 1974).

[18] James E. Townsend, "Relative Strengths of Common Stocks of Various Industries to Serve as Inflation Hedges," paper presented at Southwestern Finance Association Meeting, Houston, Texas, (March, 1975).

inflation. In turn, the growth rate has not increased because profit margins have declined.

Effect on Industries and Companies

The foregoing has emphasized the necessity of examining the factors that should cause stocks to be inflation hedges. This is especially important when analyzing individual industries and companies because, although common stocks *in the aggregate* are not good inflation hedges, this does *not* mean that some individual industries or stocks cannot be. The analyst must examine alternative industries and companies within the industry to determine how the industry or company growth rate will be affected by inflation. Inflation will have different effects due to differences in the elasticity of demand, the wage component, the net debtor position, and the cost components of the industry or company.

Chapter 12   *Industry Analysis*

Ask an analyst what he does and he will typically reply that he is an oil analyst, a retail analyst, or a business machine analyst. Portfolio managers talk about being in or out of the oils, the autos, or the utilities. This is because most practitioners in the securities markets are extremely conscious of alternative industries and organize their analyses and portfolio decisions according to industry groups. In contrast, the results of academic research have been mixed in terms of indicating the usefulness of industry analysis. There have been several studies that have important implications for industry analysis, and we will begin our discussion with these studies of industry performance and risk. Subsequently, we will discuss what should be considered when analyzing alternative industries and how industries should be analyzed.

Previous Studies of Industry Analysis

Cross Sectional Return Performance

Several studies have examined the performance of alternative industries during a specific period of time; e.g., how did different industries perform during 1978? Such studies have major implications for industry analysis because, if there is complete consistency over time for different industries, it would indicate that industry analysis is not necessary once a market analysis has been completed. Assume that, during 1978, the aggregate market rose by 10 percent and *all* industry returns were bunched between 9 and 11 percent. Under these conditions, one might ask how much it would be worth to find an industry that will return 11 percent when random selection would provide about 10 percent (the average return).

One of the first studies of industry performance was done by Latané and Tuttle, who examined the long-run price performance of 59 industries listed in the Standard & Poor's *Analysts Handbook* for the years 1950 and 1958 and for the month of October, 1967.[1] The results indicated that, between 1950 and 1967, the aggregate market had increased by a factor greater than five times, but that *the difference between alternative industries was substantial,* ranging from a decline for one industry (brewing) to an increase of almost 40 times (office and business equipment). They also found that the wide dispersion between industries did not decline over time even with the growth of conglomerates.

These findings were confirmed in a study done by Brigham and Pappas of rates of return for 658 industrial and utility firms during the period 1946–1965.[2] After dividing the sample into 103 standard industrial classifications and examining the difference between industries they concluded that, "an aggregate rate of return is by no means representative of all industries in the sample."[3]

Reilly and Drzycimski examined the performance of the 30 *Barron's* Industry Averages for the total period 1958–1970 and during selected subperiods.[4] The authors concluded that there was substantial divergence in relative performance among industries during any given time period.

There is consistent empirical evidence that industries do *not* perform in the same way over a long time period or over selected shorter subperiods.[5] This would imply that *industry analysis is a very necessary part of the valuation and portfolio management process.* It is clearly worthwhile to attempt to determine the differences in performance that can be expected for various industries.

Time Series Return Performance

This discussion naturally leads to our next question, whether industry performance is consistent over time. Do industries that perform well in one time period continue to perform well or at least continue to outperform the aggregate market? Latané and Tuttle examined the performance of individual industries and found *almost no association in industry performance over*

---

[1] Henry A. Latané and Donald L. Tuttle, "Framework for Forming Probability Beliefs," *Financial Analysts Journal,* Vol. 24, No. 4 (July–August, 1968), pp. 51–61.

[2] Eugene F. Brigham and James L. Pappas, "Rates of Return on Common Stock," *Journal of Business,* Vol. 42, No. 3 (July, 1969), pp. 302–316.

[3] Ibid., p. 311.

[4] Frank K. Reilly and Eugene Drzycimski, "Alternative Industry Performance and Risk," *Journal of Financial and Quantitative Analysis,* Vol. 9, No. 3 (June, 1974), pp. 423–446.

[5] Various financial services provide graphs of *annual* rates of return for alternative industries. Again, these indicate the substantial variance between industries.

time.[6] These results are confirmed in the Reilly–Drzycimski study that analyzed the relative performance of alternative industries for different types of market periods and concluded that there was a *very low correlation* in industry performance over sequential rising or falling markets, or over sequential periods irrespective of market behavior.[7] Tysseland examined the performance of 40 major industries over the period 1949–1966 inclusive.[8] Rank correlations were used to test for the consistency of industry returns over successive time periods (one, three, six, and nine year periods). He found significant and positive results for short-run periods, but negative results (with few exceptions) for longer periods of time.

These studies imply that it is not possible to use past performance to project future performance for an industry. Although this conclusion is consistent with the weak form efficient market hypothesis, it does not negate the usefulness of industry analysis. Such findings mean that it is not possible to simply extrapolate past performance and, therefore, it is necessary to *project* future industry performance on the basis of *future estimates* of the relevant variables.

Performance within Industries

The final relevant question with regard to industry performance is whether there is consistency *within* an industry. Do the firms within an industry experience similar performance during a specified time period? If the distribution of returns was consistent within an industry, it would reduce the need for company analysis since, once the industry analysis was complete, one could expect all the firms in the industry to perform similarly.

A detailed discussion of 14 firms in the paper industry, done by Brigham and Pappas, indicated *a wide range of returns* for alternative firms, leading the authors to state: "A further examination of the data revealed that the volatility found in the paper industry is not atypical."[9]

Tysseland also contends that there is variability *within* industries, but there are no figures supporting his contention.[10] A study by Cheney examined percent of price changes during 1964 and 1965 for a sample of eight industries and 227 stocks.[11] He examined both growth and non-

---

[6] Latané and Tuttle, "Framework for Forming Probability Beliefs."

[7] Reilly and Drzycimski, "Alternative Industry Performance."

[8] Milford S. Tysseland, "Further Tests of the Validity of the Industry Approach to Investment Analysis," *Journal of Financial and Quantitative Analysis,* Vol. 6, No. 2 (March, 1971), pp. 835–847.

[9] Brigham and Pappas, "Rates of Return," p. 311.

[10] Tysseland, "Further Tests," p. 840.

[11] Harlan L. Cheney, "The Value of Industry Forecasting as an Aid to Portfolio Management," *Appalachian Financial Review,* Vol. 1, No. 5 (Spring, 1970), pp. 331–339.

growth industries to determine the amount of cohesion within these two types of industry. He found a definite central tendency for the food industry, "some" central tendency for the building, paper, and steel industries, and no central tendency for the growth industries. It was concluded:

This study of industry cohesiveness does little to reassure the investor that he can expect individual stocks to follow the industry trend, as exposed by the industry index, over the short and intermediate term.[12]

Several other studies have implicitly considered the relationship between a company and its industry by examining the relationship of returns over time for a group of stocks relative to the aggregate market and other stocks. The best known study was done by Benjamin King.[13] The reader will recall that King found, on average, about 52 percent of the variance of individual stocks was attributable to the market and an additional 10 percent was related to the industry component. King clearly felt that there was an industry influence after taking account of the market.

Gaumnitz used cluster analysis to detect the impact of the industry component on stock price movements.[14] The Gaumnitz sample was selected on the basis of size and included 140 stocks from every industrial classification except the air transport industry. He concluded that there was a clustering of *some* stocks along industry lines, but for the majority of stocks the clusters had little correspondence to the initial industrial classifications.

Meyers modified King's statistical techniques, looked at an expanded sample of industries over a longer period, including the years 1961–1967, and came to conclusions similar to those reached by Gaumnitz.[15] The results for the overlapping industries and periods were consistent with King's, but showed some weakening in the relationship after 1960. The results for six new industries that were not as homogeneous as King's indicated that industry clustering was not as dominant as it was in the original six, especially during the most recent period, 1961–1967.

The studies done by Gaumnitz and Meyers indicate that there is a strong comovement for companies within some industries, but the pattern is clearly not universal. For most industries, there is not a strong relationship between returns for different companies within the industry.

Livingston analyzed the industry effect after removing the market effect

---

[12] Ibid., p. 335.

[13] Benjamin F. King, "Market and Industry Factors in Stock Price Behavior," *Journal of Business,* Vol. 39, No. 1, Part 2 (January, 1966), pp. 139–190.

[14] Jack E. Gaumnitz, "Influence of Industry Factors in Stock Price Movements," paper presented at Southern Finance Association Meeting, October, 1970. Subsequently released at University of Kansas, School of Business Working Paper No. 42 (June, 1971).

[15] Stephen L. Meyers, "A Re-Examination of Market and Industry Factors in Stock Price Behavior," *Journal of Finance,* Vol. 28, No. 3 (June, 1973), pp. 695–705.

using regression analysis rather than factor analysis.[16] The author compared 734 companies from over 100 industries of varying size to a broad market index. Each security's monthly rate of return was regressed against the S&P Composite Index for the period January, 1966 through June, 1970. The purpose was to analyze the residuals from this market regression to determine the market correlation between the residuals of different companies in a specified industry (within industry effect) and for different companies in different industries (the cross industry effect). It was concluded that there is very strong evidence of positive within industry comovement after the market effect is removed. Also, while the *average* within industry correlation was significant, it was definitely *not* universal for all industries.

Livingston suggested that *each industry be examined to determine the importance of residual industry comovement.* He estimated the proportion of total variance explained by the industry effect to be about 18 percent. A table that listed the values indicated a wide range from .15 to .75. Those industries that had the lowest correlations with the aggregate market had the strongest industry factors. Examples of cohesive industries are gold mining, agricultural machinery, department stores, meat packers, and vegetable oil companies. The author concluded that the results supported the concept of industry analysis and also implied that alternative industries should be considered when diversifying one's portfolio.

Implications of Intraindustry Dispersion

Some observers have contended that, because all firms in an industry do not move together, industry analysis is useless. Such a contention is wrong because it requires too much from industry analysis. It would be desirable if all firms in an industry were tightly bunched around some mean value because then, after analyzing the industry, it would not be necessary to do a company analysis. Dispersion may be caused by the fact that different companies have different industry betas; i.e., they have a different relationship to the industry in the same way that they have a different relationship to the market. Assuming that a firm does have a different industry beta, if the relationship (industry beta) is stable, it would be a valuable piece of information. For industries in which there is a strong, consistent industry component, such as gold, steel, tobacco, railroads, etc., one can possibly reduce the emphasis on company analysis once the industry analysis is complete. For most industries in which the industry component is not so strong, *the analyst's job is not as easy as it might be, because company analysis is necessary.* Even for the nonhomogeneous industries, industry analysis is valuable because it is much easier to select a superior company from a good industry than to find a good company in an industry expected to experience

---

[16] Miles Livingston, "Industry Movements of Common Stocks," *Journal of Finance,* Vol. 32, No. 2 (June, 1977), pp. 861–874.

inferior performance. It seems likely that one of the *worst* companies in a *good* industry will outperform the *better* companies in one of the *poor* industries. Therefore, after completing the industry analysis, you have a *substantially higher probability* of selecting a high return stock. Once you have selected the best stock or stocks within an industry with good expectations, the chances are *substantially less* that your good company analysis will be negated by poor industry performance.

Analysis of Differential Industry Risk

In contrast to studies done on industry return performance, there have been few done on industry *risk* measures. The Reilly–Drzycimski study (R&D) referred to earlier contained an analysis of industry risk in terms of the beta coefficient derived from the CAPM.[17] The authors derived the systematic risk for the 30 *Barron's* industry groups using weekly data for the period January, 1958 through December, 1970, and for several subperiods that conformed to alternative market periods.

There were two questions of interest: (1) what was the difference in risk for alternative industries during a given time period; and (2) how stable was the industry risk measure over time?

The analysis of the beta coefficients during specified time periods indicated *a wide range of systematic risk*. As shown in Table 12–1, the systematic risk for the total period ranged from 1.426 (air transportation) to −0.002 for gold mining. If gold mining is eliminated, the low value was 0.662 for grocery chains. The range between industries was typically larger for successive rising and falling markets, indicating that it is important to consider the differences in risk for the various industries.

The authors examined the persistence of the risk measures by correlating the beta values for the first seven years with those for the last six years, during the nine sequential subperiods, and between alternative periods of rising and falling stock prices. The correlations contained in Table 12–2 indicated a *reasonably stable relationship* between the beta coefficients for alternate periods. There was stability during the last ten years, with the best results derived during the final five years. The correlation coefficient between the betas for the sixth and seventh alternative periods was +0.657; the coefficient for the seventh and eighth periods was +0.731; and for the eighth and ninth periods, +0.732. The results indicated a large measure of correspondence and agree substantially with those obtained by Blume and Levy for portfolios of stocks, which is what an industry can be considered.[18]

---

[17] Reilly-Drzycimski, "Alternative Industry Performance."

[18] Marshall E. Blume, "On the Assessment of Risk, *Journal of Finance,* Vol. 26, No. 1 (March, 1971), pp. 1–10; Robert A. Levy, "On the Short-Term Stationarity of Beta Coefficients," *Financial Analysts Journal,* Vol. 27, No. 6 (November–December, 1971), pp. 55–62.

Table 12–1 Industry Beta Values for All Periods Examined

	1958 to 1970	1958 to 1964	1965 to 1970	1/2/58 to 5/28/59 (R)	5/28/59 to 10/27/60 (F)	10/27/60 to 12/14/61 (R)	12/14/61 to 6/28/62 (F)	6/28/62 to 2/10/66 (R)	2/10/66 to 10/6/66 (F)	10/6/66 to 12/5/68 (R)	12/5/68 to 5/28/70 (F)	5/28/70 to 12/30/70 (R)
Number of Weeks	679			74	74	59	28	189	34	113	77	31
Aircraft Mfg.	1.192	.754	1.557	.472	.717	1.227	.719	.761	2.273	1.232	1.147	2.141
Air Transp.	1.426	1.149	1.657	1.095	1.014	1.181	.838	1.385	2.368	1.776	1.257	1.803
Autos	1.259	1.164	1.330	1.134	1.238	1.053	1.004	1.340	1.113	1.553	1.301	1.296
Auto Equipment	.922	.921	.924	1.042	1.071	.632	.827	.961	.847	1.110	.737	.928
Banks	.751	.624	.858	.548	.304	.397	.833	.758	.865	.676	1.063	.715
Bldg. Materials	.983	.850	1.017	.720	.793	1.032	.815	.911	.815	1.041	1.101	.883
Chemicals	1.085	1.134	1.040	1.358	1.332	1.084	.910	1.069	.722	1.379	.977	.904
Drugs	1.103	1.156	1.059	.985	1.006	1.387	1.335	1.203	.787	1.092	1.187	.942
Electrical Equip.	1.037	1.174	.923	1.046	1.262	1.163	1.165	1.240	1.127	1.079	.819	.437
Farm Equipment	.970	.948	.978	.893	.883	.648	.872	1.106	1.144	.951	.863	.994
Food & Beverages	.756	.742	.767	.579	.674	.505	.842	.780	.417	1.033	.866	.559
Gold Mining	-.002	.363	-.304	.714	.452	.911	.144	-.089	.022	-.874	-.138	-.634
Grocery Chains	.662	.751	.585	.719	.616	.617	.699	.827	.524	.340	.954	.140
Installment Fin.	.799	.748	.845	.434	.340	.802	1.340	.654	.396	.920	.928	.981
Insurance	.887	.672	1.061	.591	.441	.299	.885	.825	.899	.773	1.361	1.139
Liquor	.633	.637	.626	.626	.648	.674	.647	.650	.666	.728	.569	.380
Machine Tools	.861	.814	.904	.280	.663	.487	.952	.849	.933	1.143	.569	.968
Heavy Machinery	1.101	1.026	1.167	.886	1.053	1.103	1.082	.942	.837	1.182	1.256	1.319
Motion Pictures	1.161	1.024	1.285	.500	.765	1.169	.936	1.304	1.353	1.175	1.266	1.522
Office Equipment	1.266	1.321	1.225	1.099	.956	.801	1.635	1.512	1.183	1.190	1.145	1.552
Oil	.949	1.005	.902	1.227	1.279	1.127	.911	.839	.813	.813	.965	.971
Packing	.988	1.219	.808	1.127	1.339	.855	1.324	1.246	.723	.813	.616	.639
Paper	.863	.707	1.007	.648	.678	.719	.705	.732	.824	1.104	1.190	.854
Railroad Equip.	1.040	.977	1.092	.816	1.003	.784	1.148	1.039	1.264	1.064	1.051	.868
Retail Merch.	.867	.863	.867	.609	.751	.554	.984	1.016	.485	.963	1.020	.763
Rubber	1.156	1.269	1.068	1.124	1.133	1.520	1.035	1.446	1.022	1.193	1.151	.732
Steel and Iron	1.038	1.163	.935	1.423	1.253	1.298	1.014	1.012	.727	1.199	.904	.792
Television	1.422	1.343	1.484	.673	.950	1.248	1.786	1.616	1.853	1.521	1.144	1.512
Textiles	1.066	1.080	1.047	.742	1.322	.881	1.023	1.218	1.090	1.016	.860	.980
Tobacco	.707	.806	.625	.268	.628	.593	1.137	.956	.342	.572	.681	.718

Source: Frank K. Reilly and Eugene Drzycimski, "Alternative Industry Performance and Risk," *Journal of Financial and Quantitative Analysis*, Vol. 9, No. 3 (June, 1974), p. 442. Reprinted by permission. © June, 1974.

Table 12-2 Correlation of the Industry Beta Values During Various Time Periods

Number of Weeks	1958 to 1964	1965 to 1970	1/2/58 to 5/28/59 (R) 74	5/28/59 to 10/27/60 (F) 74	10/27/60 to 12/14/61 (R) 59	12/14/61 to 6/28/62 (F) 28	6/28/62 to 2/10/66 (R) 189	2/10/66 to 10/6/66 (F) 34	10/6/66 to 12/5/68 (R) 113	12/5/68 to 5/28/70 (F) 77
1965 to 1970	.618									
1958 to 1959 (R)	.641	.175								
1959 to 1960 (F)	.807	.355	.800							
1960 to 1961 (R)	.543	.350	.333	.495						
1961 to 1962 (F)	.736	.496	.149	.334	.219					
1962 to 1966 (R)	.916	.739	.392	.606	.357	.740				
1966 to 1966 (F)	.445	.841	.101	.254	.394	.247	.555			
1966 to 1968 (R)	.691	.915	.287	.480	.383	.530	.767	.654		
1968 to 1970 (F)	.439	.832	.136	.150	.101	.402	.594	.525	.731	
1970 to 1970 (R)	.465	.932	.220	.198	.288	.443	.579	.800	.790	.732

Source: Frank K. Reilly and Eugene Drzycimski, "Alternative Industry Performance and Risk," *Journal of Financial and Quantitative Analysis*, Vol. 9, No. 3 (June, 1974), p. 444. Reprinted by permission. © March, 1970.

Therefore, regarding industry risk, there is some bad news and some good news. The bad news is that there is a substantial amount of dispersion in the risk for alternative industries which means that this risk must be considered in analyzing industries. The good news is that there is a fair amount of stability in the risk measure over time, which means that the past risk analysis for alternative industries can be of some benefit in analyzing future risk.

Estimating Industry Returns

The Overall Procedure

The procedure for estimating the expected returns for alternative industries is similar to that employed in aggregate market analysis. It is a two step process in which the initial phase involves estimating the expected earnings per share for an industry and then estimating the future industry earnings multiple.

Estimating Earnings Per Share

This involves several phases, the first of which is deriving an estimate of sales per share based upon an analysis of the relationship between sales of the given industry and aggregate sales for some relevant economic series; e.g., automobile sales are influenced by aggregate GNP or national income, but are typically more closely related to disposable personal income. Having derived a relationship to some economic variables, the next step is to estimate the future performance of these independent variables for the next year and thereby derive an estimate of sales per share for the industry.

If this analysis is meant to generate a long-run estimate of the sales outlook rather than a one year projection, input-output analysis should be used to indicate the long-run relationship between industries. Such an analysis indicates which other industries supply the inputs for the industry of interest and who gets the output. Knowing this, it is a matter of determining the long-run outlook for both your suppliers and major customers. For an explanation of input-output analysis, the reader is referred to an article by Hodes.[19]

The second step is deriving an estimate of the profit margin for the industry. As before, one can consider the gross margin (net before taxes and depreciation), the net before tax margin (NBT), or the net margin. The gross margin is preferred because it should be relatively less volatile. The depreciation and tax rate figures must then be estimated to derive a net income estimate.

An Industry Example

To demonstrate the analysis procedure, we will use the information in Standard & Poor's Composite Retail Store Index. This composite index

---

[19] D. A. Hodes, "Input-Output Analysis: An Illustrative Example," *Business Economics,* Vol. 1 (Summer, 1965), pp. 35–37.

contains four subindustries: (1) department stores, (2) retail stores (drugs), (3) food chains, and (4) general merchandise chains. The reader is probably familiar with a number of the companies included in these categories. The department store group includes eight companies:

Allied Stores
Carter Howley Hales Stores
Federated Department Stores
Marshall Field & Co.

Associated Dry Goods
Dayton Hudson
R. H. Macy
May Department Stores

The retail drug stores index was only started in 1970 and includes:

Eckerd (Jack)
Rite Aid

Revco D. S. Incorporated

The retail food chain group includes:

American Stores
Food Fair Stores
Great Atlantic and Pacific
Jewel Company

Kroger Company
Lucky Stores
Safeway Stores
Winn-Dixie Stores

Finally, the general merchandise chains index was started in 1970 and includes:

S. S. Kresge Company
J. C. Penney Company

Sears Roebuck & Company
F. W. Woolworth Company

Given the companies involved and the wide spectrum of stores, this industry group involves a fairly diversified portfolio.

Sales Forecast

The sales forecast for the retail store industry involves an analysis of the relationship between sales for the industry and some aggregate economic series that is related to the goods and services produced by the industry. The products of the retail store industry range from a basic necessity (food) to general merchandise such as that sold by Sears, Roebuck, to an equally varied range of products sold in department stores like R. H. Macy. Therefore, the economic series should be fairly broad to reflect the demand for these products. The primary economic series considered are disposable personal income (DPI), and personal consumption expenditures (PCE). Table 12–3 contains the aggregate and the per capita values for the two series.

The scatter plot of retail sales versus the two economic series contained in Figure 12–1 indicates *a strong linear relationship between retail sales per share and these economic series*. Retail sales appear to be strongly related to either disposable personal income or personal consumption expenditures. Therefore, if one can do a good job of estimating changes in either of these series,

Table 12–3 **S&P Composite Retail Store Sales and Various Economic Series 1960–1977**

Year	Composite Retail Stores	Disposable Personal Income	Personal Consumption Expenditures	Per Capita Disposable Personal Income	Personal Consumption Expenditures
1960	122.65	349.4	324.9	1,934	1,798
1961	127.04	362.9	335.0	1,976	1,824
1962	134.34	383.9	355.2	2,058	1,904
1963	140.75	402.8	374.6	2,128	1,979
1964	147.58	437.0	400.4	2,278	2,087
1965	156.75	472.2	430.2	2,430	2,214
1966	169.68	510.4	464.8	2,597	2,365
1967	179.15	544.5	490.4	2,740	2,468
1968	198.39	588.1	535.9	2,930	2,670
1969	214.75	630.4	579.7	3,111	2,860
1970	224.38	685.9	618.8	3,348	3,020
1971	239.11	742.8	668.2	3,588	3,227
1972	263.04	801.3	733.0	3,837	3,510
1973	284.72	901.7	809.9	4,285	3,849
1974	311.56	982.9	887.5	4,639	4,188
1975	315.80	1,080.9	973.2	5,062	4,558
1976(p)[a]	342.98	1,181.8	1,078.6	5,494	5,014
1977(e)[b]	375.00	1,303.5	1,189.7	6,016	5,490

[a] (p) preliminary

[b] (e) estimate

Source: *Analysts Handbook* (New York: Standard & Poor's Corp., 1977). *Economic Report of the President* (Washington, D.C.: U.S. Government Printing Office, 1977).
Reprinted by permission of Standard & Poor's.

one should derive a good estimate of expected changes in sales per share for a composite of retail stores. This close relationship with an aggregate economic series is not too surprising given the number of retail stores involved and the diverse nature of these stores, which means they would be a good reflection of aggregate retail sales. If the intent is to project sales for one of the component groups, such as food chains, it would be preferable to consider a subset of consumer expenditures such as expenditures for nondurables. *As the industry becomes more specialized and unique, it is necessary to find a more unique economic series that reflects the demand for the industry's product.*

One might also consider *per capita* disposable personal income. Although aggregate DPI increases each year, there is also an increase in the aggregate population, so the increase in the DPI per capita (the average DPI for each adult and child) will typically be less than the increase in the aggregate series. During 1976 aggregate DPI increased about 9.3 percent, but per

Figure 12–1 **Scatter Plot of Retail Store Sales and Disposable Personal Income and Retail Store Sales and Personal Consumption Expenditures 1960–1977**

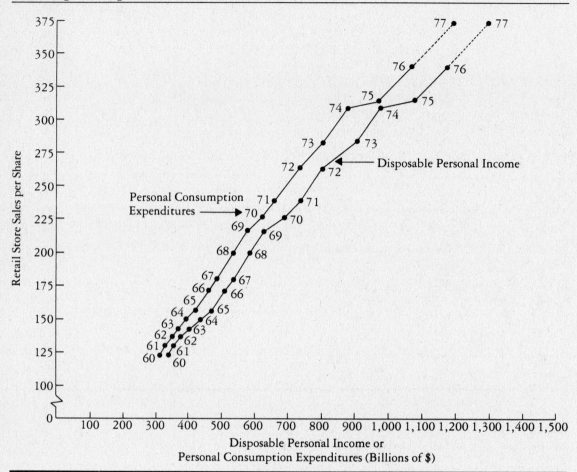

capita DPI only increased 8.5 percent. Because the per capita series may have a closer relationship to the retail sales series in some instances it should be considered. Finally, it is often useful to analyze the relationship between *changes* in the economic variable and changes in industry sales. Such an analysis will indicate how the two series move together, but will also highlight any changes in the relationship. Using percentage of changes, it is possible to derive the following regression model:

$$\%\Delta\text{Industry Sales} = \alpha_i + \beta_i \, (\%\Delta \text{ in Economic Series})$$

The size of the β_i coefficient should indicate how closely the two series move together. Assuming the intercept (α_i) is close to zero, a slope (β_i) value of

1.00 would indicate relatively equal percentage of change (e.g. a 10 percent increase in DPI is typically related to a 10 percent increase in industry sales). A β_i of less than unity would imply that industry sales are not growing as fast as the economy is. This analysis would help the analyst find the series that most closely reflects the demand for the industry's products *and* would indicate the form of the relationship.

Table 12–4 contains the results for several of the regressions discussed. The regressions that relate the level of sales to the level of DPI and PCE

Table 12–4 **Results for Regressions Relating Retail Store Sales to Aggregate Economic Series (DPI and PCE) 1960–1977**

Variable		α	β	R^2	S.E.	F.	D.W.
Dependent	Independent	(t)	(t)				
Industry Sales	DPI (Levels)	31.577 (6.278)	.2745 (38.105)	.990	7.528	1451.99	0.89
Industry Sales ($\%\Delta$)	DPI ($\%\Delta$)	.041 (1.550)	.3210 (.987)	.065	.026	0.97	2.40
Industry Sales	PCE (Levels)	28.941 (5.429)	.3062 (36.411)	.989	7.874	1325.79	0.64
Industry Sales ($\%\Delta$)	PCE ($\%\Delta$)	.013 (.624)	.6814 (2.548)	.317	.022	6.49	2.18
Industry Sales	DPI per capita (Levels)	5.915 (1.003)	.0638 (36.579)	.989	7.839	1338.06	0.84
Industry Sales ($\%\Delta$)	DPI per capita ($\%\Delta$)	.045 (2.171)	.3273 (1.135)	.084	.025	1.29	2.43
Industry Sales	PCE per capita (Levels)	2.326 (0.366)	.0713 (34.496)	.988	8.307	1189.94	0.58
Industry Sales ($\%\Delta$)	PCE per capita ($\%\Delta$)	.027 (1.603)	.5965 (2.487)	.306	.022	6.18	2.20

confirm the close relationship, but these results also indicate that the long-run trend in the alternative series is a strong factor. The more sensitive percent of change regressions (whether absolute or per capita) indicate that percentages of change in retail sales are more closely related to percentages of change in the PCE than they are to percentages of change in the DPI. The slope coefficients (B_i) are less than one, which indicates that retail sales are less volatile than the aggregate economy is. Consider the percent of change regression relating industry sales to PCE. The equation is as follows:

$$\%\Delta \text{Industry Sales}_t = .013 + .6814(\%\Delta\text{PCE})$$

Because the intercept (.013) is not considered significant, it should not be included in the estimate. Assuming that economists estimate that the PCE will increase by 11 percent next year, the analyst using this regression will estimate that retail store sales would increase by 7.5 percent (.6814 × 11.0). Because the slope is less than one, sales will not increase as much as the economy will during expansions, but also will not decline as much as the economy will during recessions.

Industry Profit Margin Forecast

The next step is to estimate the profit margin that will apply to this sales figure. Although it is possible to consider the *gross* profit margin (earnings before taxes and depreciation), the net before tax profit margin, or the net profit margin, the net profit margin is the most volatile and the hardest to estimate directly. An alternative is to begin with the gross profit margin and progress to an estimate of depreciation and the tax rate. Therefore, the initial step involves an estimate of the gross profit margin for the industry.

Estimating the Industry's Gross Profit Margin It is natural to expect that the estimate of the industry gross profit margin will be done in a manner similar to that used in market analysis. Recall that the market analysis specified the factors that should influence the economy's margin, including capacity utilization, unit labor cost, inflation, and net exports and then analyzed the relative effect of each. The most important variables were capacity utilization and unit labor cost. It is not possible to conduct such an analysis for individual industries because the relevant variables are not available on an industry basis, except in rare cases.

Although it is not possible to derive these figures, one might assume that movements in these variables affecting the industry profit margin are related to movements in similar variables for the aggregate economy. As an example, when there is an increase in capacity utilization for the aggregate economy, there is probably a comparable increase in utilization for the auto industry or the chemical industry. The same could be true for unit labor cost and exports. *If there is some generally stable relationship between these variables for the industry and the economy, one should expect a relationship to exist between the profit margin for the industry and the profit margin for the economy.* It is not necessary that the relationship be completely linear with a slope of one. The most important characteristic is a generally stable relationship.

To demonstrate such a comparison, the gross profit margin for the S&P 400 Industrial Index and the S&P Composite Retail Store Index is contained in Table 12–5 and a scatter plot is contained in Figure 12–2. As shown in the plot, except for 1974, the relationship was quite consistent. One could derive a more detailed estimate of the relation by computing a regression line for the plot. It is wise to exclude 1974 since the inclusion of figures for this year would cause a major change in the coefficients and the figures apparently represent a random event that probably will not be repeated.

One might also consider analyzing *percentages of change* in the profit margins for each year to determine how sensitive the industry is to aggre-

Table 12–5 **Profit Margins for S&P 400 Industrial Index and S&P Composite Retail Store Index 1960–1976**

| Year | Gross Profit Margin | | Depreciation | | NBT Margin | | Tax Rate | | Net Profit Margin | |
	S&P 400	S&P Composite Retail Store	S&P 400	Composite Retail Store	S&P 400	Composite Retail Store	S&P 400	Composite Retail Store	S&P 400	Composite Retail Store
1960	14.85	5.52	2.56	1.30	10.54	4.46	45.8	49.9	5.72	2.23
1961	14.84	5.57	2.66	1.38	10.37	4.48	45.4	49.4	5.66	2.27
1962	15.29	5.52	2.89	1.51	10.82	4.40	45.2	49.4	5.93	2.23
1963	15.75	5.43	3.04	1.61	11.31	4.28	45.3	47.4	6.19	2.25
1964	16.11	5.85	3.24	1.71	11.68	4.69	43.3	45.5	6.63	2.55
1965	16.31	5.96	3.52	1.83	11.95	4.79	42.9	44.6	6.82	2.65
1966	15.93	5.76	3.87	2.04	11.55	4.56	42.6	44.4	6.64	2.53
1967	15.22	5.75	4.25	2.21	10.59	4.52	42.2	44.3	6.12	2.52
1968	15.63	6.15	4.56	2.57	11.13	4.85	45.5	49.1	6.07	2.47
1969	14.87	5.92	4.87	2.52	10.38	4.75	45.6	49.1	5.65	2.42
1970	13.48	5.58	5.17	2.62	8.78	4.41	43.9	47.0	4.92	2.34
1971	13.87	5.60	5.45	2.82	9.26	4.42	45.5	45.1	5.04	2.43
1972	14.34	5.25	5.76	3.05	9.87	4.09	46.4	43.2	5.30	2.32
1973	15.23	5.43	6.25	3.24	11.04	4.30	46.1	44.0	5.96	2.41
1974	14.66	3.89	6.86	3.58	10.89	2.74	51.5	47.6	5.28	1.43
1975	13.66	5.35	7.36	3.71	9.71	4.18	52.1	46.5	4.65	2.24
1976	14.03	5.31	7.54	3.79	10.29	4.20	48.8	43.8	5.27	2.36

Gross Profit Margin = Net Before Tax and Depreciation/Sales.
Source: *Analysts Handbook* (New York: Standard & Poor's Corp., 1977). Reprinted by permission of Standard & Poor's.

gate changes. Again, in the current case one would probably ignore 1974. The form of the regression would be:

$$\%\Delta\text{Industry Profit Margin} = \alpha + \beta_i\,(\%\Delta\text{Aggregate Profit Margin})$$

The slope coefficient (β_i) indicates how sensitive the industry's profit margin is to economic changes. If the industry is relatively stable (as retail stores are) one would expect this slope coefficient to be less than one, which would indicate that the industry profit margin does not increase or decrease as much as the economy's profit margin does.

Table 12–6 contains the results for several regressions that related the GPM for the retail store industry and the GPM for the S&P 400 Index. Note that the exclusion of 1974 has a significant positive impact on both the levels regressions. Again, the most useful regression is the percent of change model, excluding 1974 figures. The intercept is close to zero, but

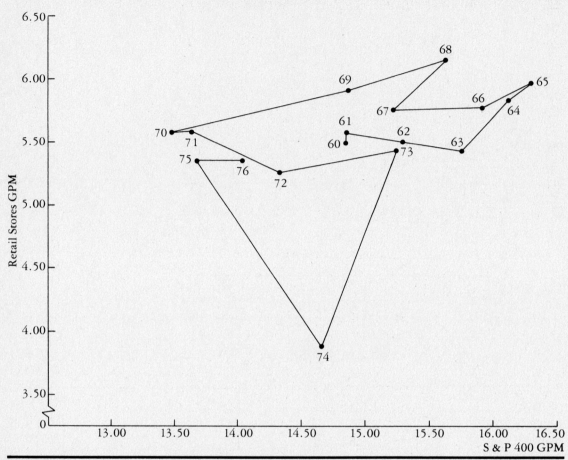

Source: Reprinted by permission of Standard & Poor's.

the slope coefficient indicates that the retail store margin is only about .37 as volatile as the aggregate market GPM is. If the market analyst estimated a small decline in the GPM for the aggregate market, you would expect a smaller decline in the GPM for retail stores. Assume a market GPM of 15 percent, a retail stores GPM of 5 percent, and an estimate of a 5 percent decline in the market GPM (from 15 percent to 14.25). Given the coefficient of .3684 you would estimate a decline in the retail store margin of 1.84 percent (.3684 × 5.0). Therefore, the retail store margin would decline from 5.00 to 4.91 (5.0 × .9816).

This analysis can be a very useful tool, but the technique should not be applied mechanically. The analyst should be aware of any unique factors affecting the specific industry such as price wars, contract negotiations, or building plans. These "unique" events should be considered as adjustment

Table 12-6 **Results for Regressions Relating the Gross Profit Margin for the Retail Store Industry to the GPM for the S&P 400 Industrial Index 1960–1976**

Variables		α	β	R^2	S.E.	F	D-W
Dependent	Independent	(t)	(t)				
Industry GPM	S&P GPM (Levels)	2.432 (1.193)	.2066 (1.517)	.133	0.469	2.30	1.62
Industry GPM	S&P 400 GPM (w/o '74) (Levels)	5.137 (3.321)	.1661 (2.635)	.332	0.216	6.95	0.88
Industry GPM (%Δ)	S&P 400 GPM (%Δ)	.0046 (.140)	−.1266 (−.164)	.002	.132	0.03	3.02
Industry GPM (%Δ)	S&P 400 GPM (w/o '74) (%Δ)	−.0009 (−.090)	.3684 (1.818)	.203	.037	3.30	2.13

Source: Reprinted by permission of Standard & Poor's.

factors when estimating the final gross profit margin or used in estimating a range of profit margins (optimistic, pessimistic, most likely) for the industry.

Estimating Industry Depreciation After estimating the industry's gross profit margin, the next step is to estimate industry depreciation. This is typically easier to estimate than other variables are because the series generally is always increasing; the only question is by how much. As shown in Table 12–5, except for 1969, the depreciation series for retail stores has increased every year since 1960. During recent years, the typical increase has been between .10 and .20 per share. The regressions in Table 12–7 relate industry depreciation to depreciation for the S&P 400 Index. The results indicate a strong relationship between levels, with the retail store depreciation consistently at about 50 percent of that for the aggregate market. This is true for the total period and for most individual years. Apparently, in recent years, retail store depreciation has not increased quite as fast as total market depreciation has, as indicated by the percent of change coefficient of .829. These regressions, along with estimates of market depreciation, should provide realistic estimates of depreciation for the retail store industry.

When the estimated depreciation is subtracted from the gross profit figure, the result is the net before tax (NBT) figure. The final step is estimating the tax rate for the industry and, therefore, the net income profit margin for the industry.

Estimating the Industry Tax Rate Although different industries have different tax factors to contend with, one would generally assume that most tax changes influence all industries in a comparable manner. Therefore, one

Table 12–7 **Results of Regressions Relating Depreciation and Taxes for the Retail Store Industry and the S&P 400 Industrial 1960–1975**

Variable							
Dependent	Independent	α (t)	β (t)	R^2	S.E.	F	D.W.
Industry Depreciation	S&P 400 Depreciation (Levels)	.077 (1.512)	.5031 (48.668)	.994	0.068	2368.56	1.71
Industry Depreciation	S&P 400 Depreciation (%Δ)	.012 (.355)	.8291 (1.822)	.192	0.038	3.32	2.73
Industry Tax Rate	S&P 400 Tax Rate (Levels)	41.728 (4.308)	.1040 (.492)	.016	2.353	0.24	0.68
Industry Tax Rate	S&P 400 Tax Rate (%Δ)	−.011 (−1.481)	.7988 (4.587)	.600	0.030	21.04	1.63

Source: Reprinted by permission of Standard & Poor's.

would expect a relationship to exist between changes in the aggregate tax rate and changes in the tax rate for various industries.

The composite retail store industry's tax rate has generally moved with the economy's tax rate. However, because of a few unique years, the tax rate for the industry has changed in its relationship to the economy. During the early years of the period in question, the industry tax rate was *above* the economy's rate and the tax rates almost always moved in the same direction. In 1971 and 1972, the economy's tax rate increased and the industry tax rate declined. As a result, the industry tax rate is now *below* the economy's. This is also reflected in the regressions in Table 12–7 that relate the industry and the market tax rates. The percent of change results indicate that the industry tax rate has not been as volatile as the market rate has been. Again, given some estimate of a change in the market tax rate, it should be possible to estimate a tax rate for the retail store industry.

Example of Earnings Estimate

To help the reader understand the procedure discussed, the following is a "rough" estimate of the net income for the retail store industry based upon the estimates for the economy set forth in Chapter 11 and the relationship between the industry and market derived in this chapter. It should be remembered that a practicing analyst would use these as an initial estimate that would be modified based upon his knowledge of the industry and of current events.

Based upon the regression analysis contained in Table 12–4, the best relationship was between percentages of change in retail sales and percentages of change in PCE. The outlook for PCE during 1978 is for a 10.2

percent increase.[20] This estimate indicates an increase in retail sales of approximately 6.95 percent (.6814 × 10.2). Therefore, given that retail sales were estimated at $375.00 in 1977, the 1978 estimate is *$401.06* (1.0695 × 375.00).

The GPM for retail stores was 5.31 in 1976. During 1977 aggregate margins increased by 3 percent, and retail store margins probably increased less, to about 5.40. The aggregate GPM was expected to decline by 7 percent during 1978 (13.50 vs. 14.50) because of higher unit labor costs. Based upon the regression results in Table 12–6, this would indicate that retail store margins should decline by about 2.6 percent (.3684 × 7.0) to 5.26 (5.40 × .974). This indicates that the gross profit per share for the retail store industry should be *$21.10* (5.26 × $401.06).

Aggregate depreciation for the S&P 400 series during 1978 was estimated to be $9.18. Assuming the retail store industry will maintain its 50 percent ratio, this would imply an estimate of $4.59 for retail stores and a net before tax earnings of *$16.51* (21.10 − 4.59).

The tax rate for the retail store industry has been lower than the aggregate, which was estimated at 50 percent during 1978. Therefore, a rate of about 45.5 percent seems appropriate for the retail store industry. This implies that taxes should be 7.51 (16.51 × .455) during 1978 and net income would be *$9.00 per share,* indicating a net profit margin of 2.24 percent (9.00/401.06) which is consistent with recent experience.

Therefore, at this point, the analyst has derived an estimate of the industry's net income per share. The next step is to estimate the likely earnings multiple for this industry in the period ahead.

Industry Earnings Multiples

There are two approaches to estimating a multiple for an industry. One is similar to the technique used for estimating the market multiple, i.e., examining the specific variables that influence the earnings multiple—the dividend payout ratio, the required rate of return (K), and the expected growth rate of earnings and dividends (g). This technique will be referred to as the *micro* approach. On the other hand, one can conceive of a *macro* approach in which the relationship between the industry multiple and the aggregate market multiple is analyzed.

Macro Analysis of Industry Multiples

The macro approach is based on the assumption that several of the major variables influencing the industry multiple are related to similar variables

---

[20] Herbert E. Neil, Jr., "Review and Outlook, 1978," *Business and Money* (Chicago: Harris Trust and Savings Bank, November, 1977).

for the aggregate market. It is hypothesized that there is a relationship between changes in K and g for specific industries and comparable changes in K and g for the aggregate market. If these relevant variables are related in their movements (even though they are not the same values), then there will be a relationship between *changes* in the industry multiple and *changes* in the market multiple.

A study by Reilly and Zeller contained an extensive analysis of the relationship between the p/e ratios for 71 Standard & Poor's industries and the p/e for the S&P 400 Index during the period 1946–1971.[21] The study examined both levels and percentages of change, but the current discussion will be limited to the percent of change results. The analysis considered four partially overlapping 21 year periods. The slope coefficients varied from about 0.10 to 3.00, and the r^2 averaged about .36. About 76 percent of the slope coefficients were statistically significant, which led the authors to contend that, "there was a statistically significant positive relationship between percent changes in earnings multiples for the majority of industries examined."[22] An analysis of the predictive ability of the percent of change model compared to a naive model that assumed no change indicated that the predictive model was superior during three of the four periods analyzed. Finally, there appeared to be a difference between industries in terms of performance. Therefore, the industries were judged on the basis of the stability of the slope coefficient and the size of the percent errors when predicting. Nineteen industries were superior in all the tests, roughly another 20 were superior in one of the tests, and three were seriously inferior in all tests. It was concluded that the results supported the general expectation of a relationship between the earnings multiples for alternative industries and the market, but that the significant relationship is not universal. Therefore, it is necessary to examine the quality of the relationship between an industry and the market before using this technique.

The results of an analysis of the relationship for the retail store industry during the period 1960–1976 are contained in Table 12–8. They are encouraging since they indicate that most of the coefficients are significant. The best results relate the levels of the p/e during the most recent period, excluding 1974. The percent of change regressions for the total period are significant and indicate that the industry p/e is less volatile than the market p/e ratios. Unfortunately, the percent of change relationship was *not* stable in terms of the coefficient, i.e., it was .695 during 1960–1968 and 1.198 during 1969–1976. Therefore, this technique should be considered, but it certainly will be necessary to use the micro approach and analyze the multiple on the basis of the variables that determine it.

---

[21] Frank K. Reilly and Thomas Zeller, "An Analysis of Relative Industry Price-Earnings Ratios," *The Financial Review* (1974), pp. 17–33.

[22] Ibid., p. 23.

	α (t)	β (t)	R^2	S.E.	F.	D.W.
Levels: 1960–1976 w/o 1974	5.7426 (1.643)	.7860 (3.708)	.496	2.171	13.75	1.74
Levels: 1960–1968	8.5752 (1.010)	.6176 (1.266)	.186	1.875	1.60	1.27
Levels: 1969–1976 w/o 1974	4.8726 (.920)	.8519 (2.453)	.546	2.845	6.02	2.02
Percent of Change: 1960–1976 w/o 1974	.0227 (.532)	.9093 (2.418)	.310	.161	5.85	2.43
Percent of Change: 1960–1968	.0067 (.324)	.6951 (2.448)	.315	.079	5.99	2.04
Percent of Change: 1969–1976 w/o 1974	.0586 (.493)	1.1981 (1.398)	.328	.245	1.95	2.54

Source: Reprinted by permission of Standard & Poor's.

Micro Analysis of Industry Multiple

The micro analysis examines the three major variables affecting the earnings multiple and compares the industry values to the comparable market values in order to determine how the industry multiple should relate to the market multiple—should it be above, below, or about equal to the market's multiple during the next period. Initially, one should examine the long-run relationship between the industry and market multiple and then look for factors that would cause differences over time.

Industry vs. Market Multiple

The mean of the high and low multiple for the aggregate market and the composite retail store industry is contained in Table 12–9. The figures indicate that the multiple for retail stores has almost always been above the aggregate market multiple. The only exceptions were during 1967 and 1971. This observation is also supported by the average multiples for the period (16.29 for the market compared to 18.53 for the composite retail store index). *Why do the multiples differ over time?* Why are investors consistently willing to pay more for a dollar of earnings from retail stores than they are for a dollar of earnings from the aggregate market? An analysis of the factors that determine the earnings multiple should indicate the cause for this difference.

Dividend Payout As shown in Table 12–9, the retention rates have typically been quite similar, usually within 2 percentage points of each other. On balance, the payout for the S&P 400 has been slightly higher, 51.6 percent for the aggregate market and 48.4 percent for the composite retail store index. This small differential would not be a major factor in explaining the difference in the multiple. Still, the difference that does exist would indicate a higher multiple for the S&P 400 series.

Table 12–9 **Earnings Multiple for the S&P 400 Index and the Composite Retail Store Index with Variables that Influence Earnings Multiples 1960–1976**

Year	Mean Earnings Multiple		Retention Rate		Return on Equity		Equity Turnover		Net Profit Margin	
	S&P 400	Composite Retail Store	S&P 400	Composite Retail Store	S&P 400	Composite Retail Store	S&P 400	Composite Retail Store	S&P 400	Composite Retail Store
1960	17.70	17.47	41.2	41.2	10.08	9.18	1.76	4.11	5.72	2.23
1961	20.41	21.21	38.6	43.1	9.67	9.46	1.71	4.17	5.66	2.27
1962	16.98	19.82	42.6	40.8	10.53	9.55	1.78	4.29	5.93	2.23
1963	17.07	19.67	44.3	43.2	11.11	9.45	1.79	4.20	6.19	2.25
1964	17.63	20.89	46.8	49.3	12.06	11.18	1.82	4.38	6.63	2.55
1965	16.82	22.05	48.7	50.0	12.64	11.74	1.85	4.42	6.82	2.65
1966	15.20	17.37	49.7	48.6	12.88	11.66	1.94	4.60	6.64	2.53
1967	17.04	16.21	47.1	50.1	11.76	11.13	1.92	4.42	6.12	2.52
1968	17.30	18.66	48.7	51.8	12.27	10.98	2.02	4.44	6.07	2.47
1969	17.46	19.23	47.0	52.8	11.86	11.96	2.10	4.95	5.65	2.42
1970	16.49	17.72	41.8	52.6	10.28	11.33	2.09	4.84	4.92	2.34
1971	18.02	16.66	47.1	54.8	10.80	11.61	2.14	4.79	5.04	2.43
1972	17.95	24.11	52.9	57.3	11.71	11.39	2.21	4.90	5.30	2.32
1973	13.38	19.24	61.1	61.2	14.15	12.11	2.37	5.03	5.96	2.41
1974	9.43	20.63	61.4	38.3	14.17	7.75	2.69	5.40	5.28	1.43
1975	10.79	12.83	56.6	62.0	12.11	11.72	2.36	5.24	4.63	2.24
1976	10.45	13.38	60.5	66.3	14.02	12.50	2.65	5.29	5.27	2.36
Mean[a]	16.29	18.53	48.4	51.6	11.75	11.06	2.03	4.65	5.87	2.39

[a] 1974 not included
Source: Reprinted by permission of Standard & Poor's.

Required Return The required rate of return on *all* investments is influenced by the risk-free rate and the inflation rate, so the *differentiating factor is the risk premium*. The difference in the required return on the aggregate stock market and the required return for composite retail stores is caused by a difference in the risk premium for the two indexes. The risk premium is a function of business risk (BR), financial risk (FR), and liquidity risk (LR). In an environment with the Capital Asset Pricing Model, the risk premium is a function of the systematic risk of the asset, i.e., its covariance with the market portfolio of risky assets. Therefore, an analyst could measure the BR, FR, and LR for the industry and compare these directly to comparable variables for the aggregate market. The other alternative is to compute the systematic risk for the industry and determine whether the beta is above or below unity.

The business risk for the retail store industry is clearly below average. Business risk is typically considered to be a function of relative sales volatility and operating leverage. Analysis of the percentage of change in retail sales compared to aggregate sales (Table 12–4) indicated that industry sales were only about 70 percent as volatile as overall economy sales were. Analysis of the gross profit margin likewise indicated that the GPM for retail stores was also much less volatile than the aggregate market GPM was (the percent of change coefficient in Table 12–6 was .3684). Therefore, since both sales and the GPM were less volatile, it implies that operating profits are substantially less volatile and *business risk for the retail store industry is below average.*

The financial risk for this industry is difficult to judge because leases on buildings are extensive. Based upon reported liabilities prior to 1977, these firms had low debt/equity ratios and high coverage ratios. When the firms were required to capitalize their lease obligations, the ratios changed drastically. In most cases the debt and interest figures increased by a factor of four or five. If one considers the capitalized leases, the firms in this industry generally have *above average financial risk.*

Based upon an analysis of the Amivest liquidity ratios for a number of companies in the retail store industry, there is substantial variation among the firms which range from Safeway and Sears, Roebuck, *very* liquid, to American Stores, quite illiquid.[23] Generally, most of the stocks are slightly below average in liquidity. Therefore, retail stores probably have *slightly above average liquidity risk.*

Business risk is definitely below average, financial risk is above average, and liquidity risk is slightly above average for retail stores. Assuming that business risk is the most significant variable, the consensus is that *overall risk is about even with the market or slightly below average* on the basis of internal characteristics.

The systematic risk for the composite retail store industry is computed using the market model as follows:

$$\%\Delta CRS_t = \alpha_i + \beta_i\ (\%\Delta\ S\&P\ 400_t)$$

$\%\Delta CRS_t$ = percent price change in composite retail store (CRS) index during month t

---

[23] Amivest Corporation, *The Liquidity Report,* Vol. 8, No. 4 (February, 1978).

α_i = regression intercept for CRS industry

β_i = systematic risk measure for CRS Industry equal to $Cov_{i,m}/\sigma_m^2$

$\%\Delta$ S&P 400_t = percent price change in S&P 400 Index during month t.

To derive an estimate in the current case, the model specified was run with monthly data for the five year period 1972–1977 (excluding 1974). The results for this regression are as follows:

$$\alpha_i = -.0059 \qquad R^2 = .560$$

$$\beta_i = +1.019 \qquad S.E. = .039$$

$$\text{t-value} = 8.59 \qquad F = 73.83$$

The systematic risk for the retail store industry is slightly above unity indicating an average risk industry (i.e., risk equal to the markets). Those results are generally consistent with the evaluation based upon micro internal variables (business risk, financial risk, and liquidity risk). It was generally concluded that the industry risk was slightly *below* average because of the dominant effect of lower business risk.

Translating this systematic risk into a required return figure calls for using the security market line which is specified as follows:

$$K_i = RFR + \beta_i (R_m - RFR)$$

Assuming a nominal risk-free rate during this period of 6 percent (.06), a market return (R_m) of 12 percent, and a beta for the industry of 1.019 yields the following:

$$K_i = .06 + 1.019 (.12 - .06)$$

$$= .06 + .0611$$

$$= .1211$$

Based upon a micro estimate of risk slightly *below* average and a market risk estimate slightly *above* average, one should probably assume a consensus risk *equal* to the market risk (B = 1.0). This would imply an earnings multiple for this industry equal to the market multiple, all other factors being equal.

Expected Growth

The prime determinants of earnings growth are the retention rate and the return on equity investments; i.e., how much is put back into investments and what is the return on these investments:

$$g = f(\text{retention rate; return on equity})$$

Return on equity can be broken down into equity turnover and net profit margin as follows:

$$\text{Net Income/Equity} = \frac{\text{Sales}}{\text{Equity}} \times \frac{\text{Net Income}}{\text{Sales}}$$

Therefore, it is necessary to examine each of these variables to determine whether there is any factor that would imply a difference in expected growth for the composite retail trade as compared to expected growth for the aggregate market. The data for the series involved are contained in Table 12–9.

Retention Rate The retention rate is simply one minus the payout rate discussed earlier. The two series were quite similar, with the S&P 400 series having a slightly higher payout rate which means that the composite retail store industry has a slightly higher retention rate (51.6 percent versus 48.4 percent). The small difference indicates a higher growth rate for the composite retail store industry.

Return on Equity Because the return on equity is a function of the equity turnover and profit margin, these two variables are examined individually.

A comparison of the equity turnover indicates that both series experienced a substantial increase over time and that the CRS series has consistently been higher. The S&P 400 series turnover increased from 1.76 in 1960 to 2.65 in 1976, a 50 percent increase. Concurrently, the CRS industry turnover went from 4.11 to 5.29, a 29 percent increase. The average for the period was 2.03 for the S&P 400 versus 4.65 for CRS. Therefore, *the average equity turnover for the CRS industry was more than double that for the aggregate market.*

A comparison of the net profit margin tells a different story. *The profit margin for the S&P 400 was consistently higher than the margin for the CRS industry, typically more than double.* Both series were relatively stable during the total period; the S&P 400 series declined a little, while the CRS series increased slightly. The higher profit margin for the market offset the higher turnover in the CRS industry. This is a prime example of what can be done to generate high returns on investment. One can either have a low turnover but a high profit margin, or accept a lower profit margin but have rapid turnover of inventory.

Combining the two factors, the return on equity for the two groups is reasonably close, with the S&P 400 being higher for almost every individual year and on average (11.75 percent versus 11.06 percent). These average percentages are quite consistent with what would be derived from multiplying the components as follows:

	Turnover × Profit Margin	= Return on Equity
S & P 400:	2.03 × 5.87	= 11.92
CRS:	4.65 × 2.39	= 11.11

Estimating Growth The growth rate is a function of the retention rate times the return on equity. The CRS industry has a slightly higher retention rate (51.6 vs. 48.4), while the S&P 400 has a slightly higher return on equity (11.75 vs. 11.06). When these are combined the estimated long-run growth rate is as follows:

$$\text{S\&P 400: } 48.4 \times 11.75 = 5.69 \text{ percent}$$

$$\text{CRS: } \quad 51.6 \times 11.06 = 5.71 \text{ percent}$$

Clearly, *the expected growth rates for the two series based upon the historical values are almost identical.* Therefore, the difference in past earnings multiples probably cannot be explained on the basis of a difference in the growth rates.

Why the Difference?

Based upon the dividend growth model, it was noted that the earnings multiple was a function of (1) the dividend payout ratio, (2) the required rate of return, and (3) the expected growth rate. Any differences in earning multiples should likewise be explained in terms of differences in one or several of these variables.

Our initial analysis indicated that the earnings multiple for the combined retail store industry was consistently higher than the multiple for the S&P 400. The question then became: why should the CRS industry have this premium in terms of its multiple? There was almost no difference in the payout ratio for the two series and the difference that did exist would favor the S&P 400 series. The analysis of risk in terms of internal characteristics and a market measure of risk concluded that the best estimate was that the industry risk was about equal to the market risk.

Finally, an analysis of the growth characteristics of the two series indicated very significant differences in equity turnover and profit margin, but relatively similiar return on equity figures. When the return on equity figures was combined with offsetting retention rates, the implied growth rates were almost identical.

Therefore, although the historical record indicated that the CRS multiple was consistently higher, an analysis of historical values for the relevant variables does not support this relationship. Almost all the variables were identical, which would indicate that the earnings multiple for the CRS industry should be quite similar to the market multiple. The only reason for the higher multiple is that investors *perceived* lower risk for the CRS industry.

Estimating the Future

The purpose of our discussion up to this point was to demonstrate a technique and to indicate the relationships that should exist between an industry and the market so that the reader will be aware of the variables that are important to the analysis. At the same time, it should never be forgotten that *the past alone is of little value in projecting the future* because past relationships may not hold in the future, *especially in the short-run*. For the analyst attempting to *project* the earnings multiple for the CRS industry, it is necessary to have an estimate of the market multiple and then to determine whether the CRS multiple will be above or below the market multiple based upon estimates of the expected relevant variables. Our previous discussion indicated the relevant variables to consider and how these variables are related to each other and to the multiple. The function of the analyst is to determine the future values for these relevant variables based upon his unique knowledge of the industry. The analyst who does a better job of estimating the payout, risk, and growth for the industry will derive a better estimate of the industry earnings multiple relative to the market multiple and a better estimate of returns for the industry.

Example of Multiple Estimate

Ideally one would like to apply both techniques (macro and micro) to estimate the earnings multiple and produce estimates that are reasonably consistent. In the current case, the macro approach was supported by the significance of the relationship, but the results were discouraging because the percent of change coefficients were not stable. The full period results indicate that the retail store p/e is slightly *less* volatile than the market p/e is, but results for the recent period indicate that the retail store p/e is more volatile. Overall, it was decided to assume that the retail store multiple is slightly more volatile $(1.05 - 1.10)$. In Chapter 11 it was estimated that the market multiple would decline slightly in 1978 from about 8.92 to 8.75 (about 2 percent). Therefore, one would expect a comparable decline for the retail store industry. Using available data from 1976, the average market multiple has declined 16 percent during the two year period (10.45 to 8.75), so one would expect a decline of about 18 percent for retail stores (from 13.38 to 10.97).

The analysis of individual components generally indicated that there should be little difference in the multiple for the market and the retail store industry because almost all of the components were very similar. The only difference was the risk factor for retail stores was perceived to be lower. Assuming the existence of a slight premium for retail stores would imply a multiple of about 9.0 for the retail stores versus a multiple of 8.75 for the market.

At this point which of these multiples to use, 10.97 or 9.0, would be a somewhat subjective decision. The personal preference of the author is for the lower figure because the micro variables were quite consistent and there was concern with the coefficients in the macro approach.

The Total Estimate

The net earnings estimate was for nine dollars a share during 1978. This, coupled with a multiple estimate of 9.0, implied an index value estimate of 81.0 at the end of 1978.

Summary

This chapter had two major parts. In the first, a number of studies dealing with cross section industry performance and risk and time series measures of industry performance were dealt with. The studies generally showed that there was a wide dispersion in the performance of alternative industries during specified time periods which implies that industry analysis would be of value. It was also shown that the performance of specific industries over time was *not* consistent, which means past performance is not of value in projecting future performance. Also, performance within industries is not very consistent for many industries, which means that individual companies must be analyzed after an industry analysis is done. The analysis of industry *risk* indicated wide dispersion between industries, but a fair amount of consistency over time for individual industries. This implies that risk analysis is important, but also that past values may be of some use.

The second section discussed the procedure for analyzing an industry using the dividend growth model. This procedure involves estimating sales based upon the relationship of the industry to some economic variables. Then the net profit margin was derived based upon an estimate of the gross profit margin, depreciation, and the industry tax rate. The second half of the procedure involves estimating the earnings multiple for the industry using either a macro or micro approach.

Because of the dispersion of industry performance and its volatility over time, it seems clear that industry analysis is both necessary and can be very lucrative. The function of a good analyst is to estimate the relevant variables. As always, the superior analyst will be the one who does the best job of *estimating* based upon knowledge of the industry and insights regarding relevant information.

Questions

1. Several studies have examined differences in the performance of alternative industries over specific time periods. Briefly describe the results of these studies and discuss their implications for industry analysis.

2. A number of studies have considered the time series of industry performance. Briefly describe the empirical results of these studies and discuss their implications for those who are involved in industry analysis. Do they make industry analysis easier or harder?

3. Assuming you are told that all the firms in a particular industry have consistently experienced rates of return *very similar* to the results for the aggregate industry, what does this imply regarding the importance of industry analysis for this industry? What does it imply regarding the importance of individual company analysis for this industry? Discuss.

4. Some authors contend that, because there is a great deal of dispersion in the performance of different firms in an industry, industry analysis is of little value. Would you agree or disagree with this contention? Why?

5. What are some factors that might cause different companies in a given industry to experience some similarity in their operating results? Discuss several of these briefly.

6. Would you expect there to be a difference in the industry influence for companies in different industries? What is the empirical evidence on this question? Describe it briefly.

7. There has been an analysis of the difference in the risk for alternative industries during a specified time period. Describe the results of this analysis briefly and discuss their implications for the practice of industry analysis.

8. What were the results when the risk for alternative industries was examined during successive time periods? Describe the results and discuss the implications for those involved in industry analysis.

9. Select three industries from the S&P *Analyst's Handbook* with different characteristics in terms of demand and indicate what economic time series you would use in the analysis of the sales growth for each industry. What is the source of the economic time series? *Why* is this series relevant for this industry?

10. Do a scatter plot of industry sales and economic values over the last ten years using information available in the *Analyst's Handbook* for one of the three industries selected in question nine. Discuss the results of the scatter plot; do you think the economic series was very closely related to industry sales?

11. If you could derive the data, what would you examine to determine future values of the gross profit margin for an industry?

12. Why is it contended that one should expect a relationship between the profit margin for a given industry and the aggregate profit margin?

13. Prepare a scatter plot of the profit margin for a selected industry and the aggregate profit margin for the S&P 400 Index for the most recent ten years. How close is the relationship? What factors would make this industry's margin different?

14. Prepare a time series plot of the annual mean price-earnings ratio (highest ratio + lowest ratio/2) for your industry and the S&P 400 for the most recent ten years available. Has the relationship between the two series been consistent over time?

15. Prepare a table that contains the relevant variables that influence the earnings multiple for your industry and the S&P 400 series for the most recent ten years.
A. Does the average payout differ and how should this influence the difference between the multiples?
B. Would you expect the systematic risk for this industry to differ from that for the market? In what direction and why? What effect will this have on the industry multiple relative to the market multiple?

C. Analyze the different components of growth (retention rate, equity turnover, and profit margin) for your industry and the S&P 400 during the most recent ten years and discuss each of the components. On the basis of this discussion, would you expect the growth rate for your industry to be above or below the growth rate for the S&P 400? How would this difference affect the difference between the multiples?

D. Given the conclusions reached in A, B, and C above, is the difference in the industry multiple found in question 14 logical and justified?

References

Brigham, Eugene F. and Pappas, James L. "Rates of Return on Common Stock." *Journal of Business,* Vol. 42, No. 3 (July, 1969).

Cheney, Harlan L. "The Value of Industry Forecasting as an Aid to Portfolio Management." *Appalachian Financial Review,* Vol. 1, No. 5 (Spring, 1970).

Gaumnitz, Jack E. "The Influence of Industry Factors in Stock Price Movements." Paper presented at Southern Finance Association Meeting, October, 1970. Subsequently released as University of Kansas School of Business Working Paper No. 42 (June, 1971).

King, Benjamin F. "Market and Industry Factors in Stock Price Behavior." *Journal of Business,* Vol 39, No. 1, Part 2 (January, 1966).

Latané, Henry A. and Tuttle, Donald L. "Framework for Forming Probability Beliefs." *Financial Analysts Journal,* Vol. 24, No. 4 (July–August, 1968).

Levy, Robert A. "On the Short-Term Stationarity of Beta Coefficients." *Financial Analysts Journal,* Vol. 27, No. 6 (November–December, 1971).

Livingston, Miles. "Industry Movements of Common Stocks." *Journal of Finance,* Vol. 32, No. 3 (June, 1977).

Meyers, Stephen L. "A Re-Examination of Market and Industry Factors in Stock Price Behavior." *Journal of Finance,* Vol. 32, No. 3 (June, 1973).

Reilly, Frank K., and Drzycimski, Eugene. "Alternative Industry Performance and Risk." *Journal of Financial and Quantitative Analysis,* Vol. 9, No. 3 (June, 1974).

Reilly, Frank K., and Zeller, Thomas. "An Analysis of Relative Industry Price-Earnings Ratios." *The Financial Review,* 1974.

Tysseland, Milford S. "Further Tests of the Validity of the Industry Approach to Investment Analysis." *Journal of Financial and Quantitative Analysis,* Vol. 6, No. 2 (March, 1971).

Chapter 13

Company Analysis

At this point it is assumed that you have made two decisions. First, after an extensive analysis of the economy and aggregate stock market, you have decided that some portion of your portfolio should be in common stocks. Second, after an extensive analysis of a number of industries you determined that certain industries will experience above average risk-adjusted performance over the relevant investment horizon. The question you now face is, *which companies within these desirable industries are best?* In this chapter we will discuss the procedure for analyzing all the companies in an industry. Although in the discussion we will only consider one firm, *the same procedure should be applied for all firms in the industry to derive a ranking of firms.* Our ultimate objective is to select the best firms in the better industries and invest in them.

But before we discuss company analysis, we must consider the differences between companies and types of stocks.

Types of Companies and Types of Stock [1]

The label given to a company is principally determined *internally* by the investment decisions of the firm (what assets they own) and by the operating and financial philosophy of the firm's management. When a company invests in assets (whether human or physical), it thereby determines its characteristics and accepts the accompanying risks and opportunities. At

---

[1] The discussion in this section draws heavily on Frank K. Reilly, "A Differentiation Between Types of Companies and Types of Stock," *Mississippi Valley Journal of Business and Economics,* Vol. 7, No. 1 (Fall, 1971), pp. 35–43.

the same time, two different sets of management personnel can obtain substantially different results with the same set of assets. Management's operating and financial decisions can influence not only the expected flow of earnings, but also the *risk* inherent in it. Therefore, it is necessary to consider the assets of the firm, what the corporate management is capable of doing with these assets, and what they intend to do with them. Finally, these company factors should be compared to similar factors for all other companies to determine the firm's *relative* position in the universe of all companies. The type of stock is determined by comparing the expected returns and the uncertainty of the returns for a particular stock relative to these same measures for all other available stocks.

Growth Companies and Stocks

Growth companies have historically been defined in terms of results, rather than causes. They are companies that consistently experience above average growth in sales and earnings. Unfortunately, such a definition means that many firms qualify on the basis of results that are not internally generated but are the consequence of certain accounting procedures introduced in the course of mergers, or other factors not indicative of superior markets or superior managements.

Currently, as a result of the writings of Solomon, Miller and Modigliani, and others, it has become generally accepted that *a true growth company is a firm with the management ability and the opportunities to invest in projects that yield returns greater than the firm's required rate of return* (i.e., its average cost of capital).[2] A growth company would be one that has the ability to acquire capital at an average cost of, say, 10 percent and yet has the management ability and the opportunity to invest those funds (whether internally generated or externally acquired) at rates of return in excess of 10 percent. As a result, the firm enjoys profits and earnings growth greater than that experienced by other firms in a similar risk category.

The result of being a true growth company (above average investment opportunities) is that the firm should, and typically does, retain a large portion of its earnings to invest in above average investment alternatives. Sales and earnings of the true growth firm grow faster than they do for average firms or for the overall economy. Given these expected results, the search for growth firms *ex post* typically involves examining a large cross section of firms to find companies that retain a substantial portion of earnings and also have consistently experienced above average increases in earnings. This method allows growth companies to be identified by *results,* in contrast to the suggested definition that concentrates on *causes.* Searching for results means that the growth firm can be identified only after the

---

[2] Ezra Solomon, *The Theory of Financial Management* (New York: Columbia University Press, 1963), pp. 55–68; M. Miller and F. Modigliani, "Dividend Policy, Growth, and the Valuation of Shares," *Journal of Business,* Vol. 34, No. 4 (October, 1961), pp. 411–433.

fact. Examining firms in terms of causes may make it possible to identify a firm *before* it has exhibited superior growth, or at least *while* it is in the early stages of growth.

A growth stock is a stock possessing superior return capabilities when compared to other stocks in the market with similar risk characteristics. This superior return potential is due to the fact that the stock is undervalued at a given point in time relative to other stocks in the market. In a strong form efficient market with perfect information, all firms would generate rates of return consistent with the systematic risk involved and there would never be any growth stocks.[3] While the stock market is relatively efficient in adjusting stock prices to new information, it is also very likely that the information is not perfect or complete.[4] This means that, at any point in time, owing to imperfect information or the lack of information a given stock may be undervalued or overvalued.[5] If it is undervalued, the stock price should increase to reflect its value when the correct information becomes available. During the period in which the stock changes from an undervalued security to a properly valued security, the returns will exceed the market average, and the stock will be considered a growth stock.

A future growth stock is basically a currently undervalued stock that has a high probability of being properly valued in the near term. This means that *growth stocks are not necessarily limited to growth companies.* If investors recognize a growth firm and discount the future earnings stream properly, the current market price will reflect the future growing earnings stream. The investor who acquires the stock at this "correct" market price will receive only the market rate of return, even when the superior earnings growth is attained. If investors *overprice* the stock of a growth company and an investor pays the inflated price, his returns will be below the risk-adjusted normal return. A future growth stock can be issued by any type of company; it is only necessary that the stock has not been properly valued by the market at a given point in time.

As with a growth company, the search for a growth stock after the fact is relatively easy since it is necessary only to examine past returns. The search for *future* growth stocks is the function of a securities analyst. The ability to *consistently* uncover such stocks is, by definition, the description of a superior analyst.[6]

---

[3] For a discussion of the relationship and a summary of some empirical evidence on the subject see Richard A. Brealey, *An Introduction to Risk and Return from Common Stocks* (Cambridge, Mass.: The MIT Press, 1969), pp. 47–54.

[4] For a discussion of price adjustment to new information see Eugene F. Fama, "Efficient Capital Markets: Review of Theory and Empirical Work," *Journal of Finance*, Vol. 25, No. 2 (May, 1970), pp. 383–417. For a discussion of recent evidence, see Chapter 7.

[5] As noted in Chapter 7, an analyst is more likely to find such stocks outside the top tier of companies that is already being scrutinized by numerous analysts.

[6] See Eugene F. Fama, "Random Walks in Stock-Market Prices," *Financial Analysts Journal*, Vol. 21, No. 5 (September-October, 1965), pp. 55–58.

Defensive Companies and Stocks

A defensive company possesses assets and management such that there is a high probability that future earnings will withstand an economic downturn. Typical examples of defensive firms are public utilities or grocery chains; they supply basic consumer necessities and, therefore, should not suffer a decline in sales and earnings during a period of reduced economic activity.

There are two concepts of a defensive stock; the first is consistent with the specification of a defensive company, while the second is derived from the statistical portfolio model. The first definition states that a defensive stock *is a stock that is not expected to experience a reduced rate of return during an overall market decline or that will experience significantly better performance than the market will during market declines.*

In contrast to a definition that is concerned only with the stock's rate of return during overall market *declines*, the second definition considers all price performance. In the discussion of portfolio theory it was noted that, in a state of equilibrium, the relevant risk measure for any risky asset is its covariance with the market portfolio of risky assets, i.e., its systematic risk. A stock with *low systematic risk* (a small beta) would be considered defensive according to this theory. Because there are two definitions, it will be necessary, in the search for a defensive stock, to specify the definition being employed.

Cyclical Companies and Stocks

A cyclical company is one whose future earnings will be heavily influenced by aggregate business activity. In turn, this volatile net earnings pattern is a function of the firm's business risk and financial risk.

A cyclical stock is expected to experience changes in rates of return as great as or greater than changes in overall market rates of return. As was true of the growth company–growth stock relationship, the stock of a cyclical company is not necessarily cyclical. If investors recognize a company as cyclical and discount future earnings accordingly, it is possible that the rates of return on the stock of a cyclical company may hold up substantially better than aggregate market rates of return during a market decline. A cyclical stock could be the stock of a cyclical company or the stock of any company the price of which is more volatile than overall market prices.[7] In terms of the CAPM, these stocks would have high beta values.

Speculative Companies and Stocks

A speculative company is one whose assets involve great risk; it offers a relatively large chance for a loss and a small chance for a large gain. The returns from the assets of

---

[7] For a discussion of why the stocks of growth companies will decline more during periods of declining markets, see Burton Malkiel, "Equity Yields, Growth, and the Structure of Share Prices," *American Economic Review,* Vol. 53, No. 5 (December, 1963), pp. 1004–1031.

a speculative firm have a great risk connected with them. There is a high probability that the returns to the firm will be either very low, nonexistent, or negative. Typically, there is also a small probability of very substantial returns. A good example of a speculative firm is one involved in oil exploration.

A speculative stock is one that possesses a high probability of low or negative rates of return during a given period and a low probability of normal or high rates of return. There are two types of speculative stocks. The first is closely akin to the speculative company and is typified by the penny mining stock. There is a high probability that there will be no return on the stock during a given period and eventually a complete loss. At the same time, there is some small probability of very substantial gains.

The second type of speculative stock is almost the opposite of a growth stock. A growth stock is undervalued at the present time. In contrast, the second type of speculative stock is overpriced; therefore, there is a high probability that, in the future, when the market adjusts the stock price to its true value, there will be either very low or possibly negative rates of return on it. This might be the case for an excellent growth company whose stock is selling at an extremely high price-earnings ratio. In such a case the current stock price is reflecting a belief that outstanding growth will continue for a substantial period in the future.[8] If there is any reduction in the growth pattern, or any disruption in growth, this price-earnings ratio can drop rapidly and substantially. The level of the current price-earnings ratio indicates that there is a very strong likelihood of a substantial decline if everything does not conform to the most optimistic expectations. Therefore, an overpriced stock is considered speculative.

Company Analysis Procedure

Analyzing an individual firm involves examining the internal characteristics of the firm and its relationship to its industry and to the economy. Based upon such an examination, an analyst should have some very strong convictions regarding the firm in terms of the time pattern of its earnings stream and its financial characteristics. This includes knowing something about the firm's sales volatility and operating leverage and, therefore, its *business risk.* Based upon an analysis of the firm's capital structure, it is possible to derive some estimates of its *financial risk.* The analyst should have an opinion about the *type of company* he is dealing with—is it a cyclical company, a defensive company, a speculative company, or a growth company?

After analyzing the company, it is necessary to consider the char-

---

[8] For a method of measuring the implied period of growth see Charles C. Holt, "The Influence of Growth Duration on Share Prices," *Journal of Finance,* Vol. 17, No. 3 (September, 1962), pp. 465–475.

acteristics of the firm's common stock. *The type of company and the type of stock may not necessarily be the same!* As mentioned, the stock of a cyclical company may not be cyclical.

An Example

To demonstrate the procedure, we will analyze Safeway Stores, one of the firms in the retail food chain industry. For purposes of comparison with the industry analysis, using a firm within the composite retail store group seemed appropriate. Unfortunately, it was not possible to examine any companies in the retail drug or the general merchandise group because the industry indexes for both of these were only started in 1970 and we wanted specific industry data available since 1960 to allow reasonable historical analysis.

Safeway Stores is the largest grocery store chain in the United States. As of January, 1978, the firm operated over 2,400 stores: about 2,100 in the U.S., the remainder in Canada, the United Kingdom, Australia, and West Germany. Of the stores in the U.S., the vast majority (about 90 percent) are located west of the Mississippi River.

It is assumed that you have decided to invest in equities and also that you predict that the retail food chain industry should experience above average performance during the relevant investment horizon. Therefore, your company analysis involves examining all of the firms in the retail food chain industry to determine which stocks should experience the best performance within the industry. The objective is to estimate the expected return and risk for all the individual firms over the investment horizon. These values are then used by the portfolio manager as inputs into the portfolio model.

Estimating Expected Return

The analyst estimates the expected return for the investment by estimating the future value for the security which indicates the expected capital gain or loss and, when combined with the expected dividend yield, indicates the expected return. The future value of the security is estimated using the dividend growth model to predict expected earnings, and the expected earnings multiple for the stock. In turn, expected earnings is a function of the sales forecast and the estimated profit margin for the firm.

Sales Forecast

The sales forecast includes an analysis of the relationship of company sales to various economic series that should influence the demand for the firm's products and a comparison of the firm's sales to the sales for the company's industry. Such an analysis is supported by the sales forecast derived in the industry analysis. This company—industry analysis indicates how the company is performing in relation to its most immediate competition.

Table 13–1 contains data on sales for Safeway Stores, sales per share for

Table 13–1 **Sales for Safeway Stores, the Retail Food Store Industry, and Various Economic Series, 1960–1977**

Year	Safeway Stores (Millions of $)	Retail Stores Food Industry (Sales per Share)	Personal Consumption Expenditures (PCE) (Billions of $)	PCE per Capita ($)	PCE– Food (Billions of $)	PCE: Food/Total %
1960	2,469.0	293.76	324.9	1,798	81.1	25.0
1961	2,538.0	302.82	335.0	1,824	83.2	24.8
1962	2,509.6	311.17	355.2	1,904	85.5	24.1
1963	2,649.7	318.81	374.6	1,979	87.8	23.4
1964	2,817.6	331.89	400.4	2,087	92.7	23.2
1965	2,939.0	339.20	430.2	2,214	98.9	23.0
1966	3,345.2	367.21	464.8	2,365	106.6	22.9
1967	3,360.9	377.07	490.4	2,468	109.6	22.3
1968	3,685.7	399.19	535.9	2,670	118.3	22.1
1969	4,099.6	439.97	579.7	2,860	126.1	21.8
1970	4,860.2	464.40	618.8	3,020	136.3	22.0
1971	5,358.8	482.38	668.2	3,227	140.6	21.0
1972	6,057.6	526.29	733.0	3,510	150.4	20.5
1973	6,773.7	563.16	809.9	3,849	168.1	20.8
1974	8,185.2	588.26	889.6	4,197	189.9	21.3
1975	9,716.9	637.67	980.4	4,591	209.5	21.4
1976	10,442.5	619.18	1,094.0	5,084	225.5	20.6
1977(p)[a]	11,249.3	660.00(e)[b]	1,210.1	5,580	246.3	20.4

[a](p)—preliminary   [b](e)—estimate
Source: Reprinted by permission of Standard & Poor's

the retail food store industry, and several personal consumption expenditure (PCE) series. The most relevant is the personal consumption expenditure for food (PCE–Food), which has comprised between 20 and 25 percent of total PCE. The scatter plot of Safeway sales and the PCE–Food expenditures contained in Figure 13–1 indicates a good linear relationship, and also indicates that Safeway sales have been growing at a faster rate than the PCE for food has. During the period 1960–1977 Safeway sales increased by about 356 percent, compared to an increase in PCE–Food of 204 percent. In addition, Safeway sales grew from about 3.0 percent of the total PCE for food to over 4.6 percent. The first two regressions in Table 13–2 that relate Safeway sales to PCE–Food support the relationship of levels and percentages of change. The percent of change results reflect a significant relationship and also indicate that Safeway sales are more volatile than the PCE is because they are growing faster than the PCE for food is.

The figures in the last column of Table 13–1 indicate that, during this period, the proportion of PCE allocated to food went from 25 percent in

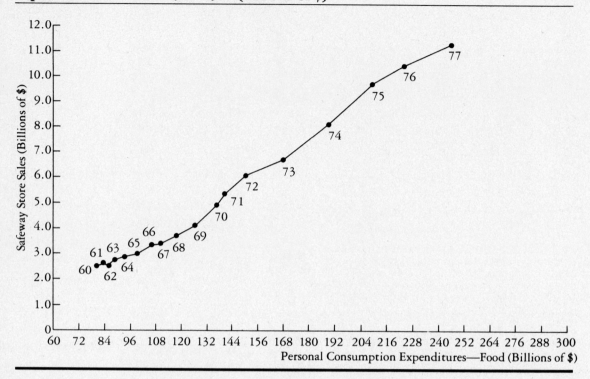

1960 to only 20.4 percent in 1977. Therefore, Safeway derived an increasing share of these expenditures. The declining proportion of PCE spent on food, especially at retail food chains, apparently is a function of the changing life style of consumers. An increasing proportion of meals are consumed outside the home, so a larger percentage of income is spent at restaurants and fast-food outlets.

Regarding the relationship between Safeway sales and the total PCE, Safeway grew faster than the total, 356 percent for Safeway versus 272 percent for total PCE. Most of Safeway's growth has been internal since the number of common shares outstanding during this period has only gone from 24,866,580 (adjusted for a split) in 1960 to 25,985,006 at the end of 1976. In turn, internal growth has been a function of a small increase in the number of stores, from 2,207 in 1960 to 2,428 in 1977. *The more important change has been a major increase in the annual sales per store because of the upgrading of stores.* The net number of stores has increased by about 200, which includes the construction of a number of new, large stores and the closing of many smaller stores in declining areas.

The regressions in Table 13–2 confirm that there is a significant relationship between sales and total PCE. Notably, the relationship is not as strong

Table 13-2 **Results for Regressions Between
Safeway Sales and Various Economic and Industry Series**

Dependent Variable	Independent Variable	α (t-value)	β (t-value)	R^2	S.E.	F	D.W.
Safeway Sales (Levels)	PCE–Food (Levels)	−2575.07 (−11.124)	56.8491 (33.681)	.987	305.10	1134.42	0.41
Safeway Sales (%△)	PCE–Food (%△)	−.0090 (−.388)	1.5889 (5.003)	.641	.040	25.03	1.79
Safeway Sales (Levels)	PCE (Levels)	−1646.7 (−5.895)	10.9146 (24.766)	.976	412.65	613.36	0.47
Safeway Sales (%△)	PCE (%△)	−.0454 (−.851)	1.8131 (2.739)	.349	.054	7.50	2.04
Safeway Sales (Levels)	PCE–Per Capita (Levels)	−2608.97 (−8.701)	2.5469 (26.097)	.978	392.07	681.05	0.52
Safeway Sales (%△)	PCE–Per Capita (%△)	−.0152 (−.375)	1.6754 (2.905)	.376	.053	8.44	2.08
Safeway Sales (Levels)	Retail Food Stores Sales (Levels)	−4401.90 (−6.898)	21.2769 (14.932)	.937	670.53	222.98	0.41
Safeway Sales (%△)	Retail Food Stores Sales (%△)	.0450 (1.755)	1.0602 (2.388)	.289	.056	5.70	1.22

as the one with PCE–Food, and the coefficients that are greater than one indicate the large percentages of change in Safeway sales relative to the PCE series.

The relationship between sales for Safeway Stores and sales per share for the retail food store industry is not as consistent as the prior economic analysis but is even more impressive in terms of the performance by Safeway. Again, for the total period, Safeway sales increased by 356 percent compared to an increase for the industry of only 124 percent. Because industry figures are sales per share, this could make some difference, but would have little effect on Safeway because total outstanding shares have only increased by about 4 percent during the 16 years being considered.

This performance by Safeway is not very surprising given the previous analysis. Safeway sales grew faster than the total PCE, and the total PCE has grown faster than the PCE for food. Finally, the sales growth for the retail food store index has been smaller than the growth in the PCE for food. The industry index grew 124 percent during the period 1960–1977 as compared to PCE–Food growth of 204 percent.

The last two regressions in Table 13–2 confirm that there is a relationship between Safeway sales and retail food industry sales but, again, the relationship is not as strong as the one with the aggregate series is. The slope of the percent of change regression is not as large as one might expect, but the intercept, at about 4 percent, is significant. This would indicate an average long-term growth of 4 percent in Safeway sales *in addition to* the growth in aggregate retail sales.

Sample Estimate of Safeway Sales

Based on this, an analyst would likely concentrate on the regressions that relate Safeway sales to PCE–Food. To estimate PCE–Food it would be preferable to initially estimate total PCE and then estimate the food component. Economists were generally forecasting an increase in PCE of 10.2 percent during 1978. Given a 1977 preliminary figure of $1,210.1 billion, this implies a 1978 figure of $1,333.5 billion (1.102 × 1,210.1). Regarding how much of this will be spent on food, the data indicate a consistent decline to 20.4 percent in 1977. Assuming a further decline to 20.2 percent, this indicates an estimate of PCE–Food of $269.4 billion in 1978 (.202 × 1,333.5) which is a 9.4 percent increase from 1977 (269.4/ 246.3). Using the second regression in Table 13–2, which has a coefficient of 1.5889, this implies a 14.9 percent increase in Safeway sales (1.5889 × 9.4). Admittedly, this appears to be a very generous estimate following two years with increases of less than 8 percent.

Because other estimates with the regressions would generally confirm this estimate, they are not considered. An alternative estimate can be derived using company data on stores, square footage, sales per store, and sales per square foot. The figures are contained in Table 13–3. The data

Table 13–3
Data on Number of Stores, Store Area and Sales for Safeway: 1967–1977

Year	Number of Stores	Sales Per Store	Store Area (1000 sq ft)	Sales Per 1000 sq ft
1977	2,428	4,633,195	55,184	203,853
1976	2,438	4,283,237	53,223	196,203
1975	2,451	3,964,459	51,854	187,398
1974	2,426	3,373,945	50,159	163,185
1973	2,364	2,865,350	46,480	145,733
1972	2,331	2,258,727	44,844	135,082
1971	2,283	2,347,279	42,752	125,347
1970	2,297	2,115,876	41,769	116,358
1969	2,260	1,784,783	40,169	102,060
1968	2,241	1,644,663	39,033	94,425
1967	2,237	1,502,405	37,850	88,795

confirm the earlier discussion in which it was noted that Safeway had experienced substantial increases in sales with a relatively small increase in the net number of stores. In general, the company has closed smaller stores and built a number of very large stores that sell a variety of higher priced items. The result has been a consistent increase in total store area *and* an increase in sales per 1,000 square feet. The store area has generally increased by 2,000,000 square feet per year. Assuming such an increase in 1978, total area would be about 57,200,000 square feet. Sales per square feet have likewise increased and, assuming a further increase to $210,000, this would imply a sales forecast of $12,012.0 million for 1978 which is a 6.8 percent increase over 1977.

Given the two estimates, the preference is for the lower figure with a small upward adjustment to 7 percent. Therefore the final sales forecast for 1978 is *$12,036.7 million.*

The next step is to derive an estimate of the net profit margin for the firm.

Estimating the Profit Margin

Analysis of the firm's profit margin should consider two general areas: the firm's internal performance and any changes that have occurred; and the firm's relationship to its industry. The initial analysis should indicate general trends for the firm and point out areas of concern. When company performance is related to the industry, the analysis should indicate whether the company's performance (good or bad) is attributable to the industry or is unique to the firm. Profit margin figures for Safeway and the retail food industry are in Table 13–4. The figures on the net before tax margin for Safeway and the retail food industry indicate a relatively steady decline for both series. This indicates that Safeway experienced a decline in its profit margin over the past 16 years and that part of this decline is related to a similar phenomenon in the total industry. Moreover, the change in the margin for Safeway during 1976 was inferior to that for the industry because Safeway declined during 1976 while the industry was constant after a recovery in 1975. The analyst should understand the reason for the industry decline, and also what added factors contributed to Safeway's performance.

Industry Factors

The major factors influencing the decline in industry profit margins over the past two decades have been the increased cost of advertising and other promotional drives, and, more important, a number of price wars among the large chains.[9] Because of some overbuilding of stores during the 1950's, the chains engaged in heavy promotion and advertising during the 1960's in an attempt to hold their share of the market or even to increase it. In the early 1970's there were numerous price wars as A&P (The Great Atlantic and Pacific Tea Company), owing to its decline in volume, introduced price cuts to become competitive. These price wars continued sporadically for several years and seriously affected profit margins for several of the chains. The outlook is for generally more stability in prices and some improvement in the industry margins.

---

[9] For a more complete discussion see *Standard and Poor's Industry Surveys,* "Retailing—Food" (New York: Standard & Poor's Corp., 1977).

Table 13-4 **Profit Margins for Safeway Stores and the Retail Food Industry 1960–1976**

	Safeway Stores						Retail Food Store Index[b]		
Year	Earnings After Costs & Expenses[a] (Millions of $)	Percent Sales	Income Before Taxes (Millions of $)	Percent Sales	Net Income	Percent Sales	Operating Profit Margin	NBT Margin	Net Profit Margin
1960	76.9	3.11	75.2	3.05	34.8	1.41	3.61	2.70	1.29
1961	81.1	3.20	78.6	3.10	36.6	1.44	3.54	2.59	1.25
1962	85.7	3.41	83.3	3.32	39.3	1.57	3.58	2.56	1.23
1963	95.9	3.62	94.7	3.57	44.8	1.69	3.41	2.40	1.19
1964	101.9	3.62	97.9	3.47	50.0	1.77	3.45	2.39	1.24
1965	99.1	3.37	95.1	3.24	48.2	1.64	3.33	2.28	1.23
1966	121.2	3.62	117.8	3.52	59.7	1.78	3.28	2.22	1.20
1967	103.4	3.08	100.2	2.98	50.9	1.51	3.08	2.07	1.10
1968	118.5	3.21	115.5	3.13	55.1	1.49	3.19	2.11	1.07
1969	112.9	2.75	108.9	2.66	51.3	1.25	3.18	2.13	1.07
1970	146.1	3.01	140.7	2.89	68.9	1.41	3.19	2.14	1.10
1971	158.4	2.96	155.3	2.90	80.2	1.50	2.77	1.69	0.92
1972	176.3	2.91	168.6	2.78	91.1	1.50	1.90	0.86	0.53
1973	166.6	2.46	157.5	2.33	86.3	1.27	2.48	1.35	0.78
1974	156.2	1.91	140.8	1.72	79.2	0.97	2.58	0.85	0.27
1975	287.9	2.96	275.3	2.83	148.6	1.53	2.53	1.59	0.90
1976	196.9	1.89	191.3	1.83	105.6	1.01	2.53	1.59	0.87

[a] Costs and expenses include "cost of sales" and selling, general and administrative expenses.
[b] Source: Standard & Poor's, *Analysts Handbook* (New York: Standard & Poor's Corp., 1977). Reprinted by permission.

Company Factors

The major factor that affected Safeway's profit margin during the last several years has been the sporadic outbreak of price wars. The effect on Safeway was more intense during 1976 because the conflict was especially heavy in California where Safeway is highly concentrated. The general outlook for profit margins is good because of the continued building of larger stores that contain more nonfood items and high margin facilities such as delicatessens.

Two disruptive factors increase the problem of predicting the firm's profit margin. The first is ascertaining foreign gains and losses because the firm has heavy exposure in the overseas market. As of 1976, there were 276 stores in Canada, 83 stores in the United Kingdom, 57 in Australia and 24 in Germany. As a result, there was a $0.15 per share gain during 1976 and a loss from foreign exchange of about \$0.25 per share during 1977. The second factor is relatively widespread in the retail store industry—leasing. Retail store firms (food and otherwise) typically do not build their own stores but generally specify the building requirements and then enter into a long-term lease with the builder. A forthcoming pronouncement by the American Institute of Certified Public Accountants (AICPA) will require that long-term (financial) leases be capitalized and there will be a change in the expense treatment. According to estimates by *Value Line,* 1976 earnings would have been \$0.25 less per share if this procedure had been in effect. Once the change is made, this should have a relatively constant effect.

Specific estimates for Safeway should probably begin with an analysis of the relationship between the firm's margin and the food chain industry margin as specified by the following linear correlation model:[10]

$$\text{Safeway Net Profit Margin}_t = a_i + b_i \text{ (Retail Food Chain Net Profit Margin}_t)$$

The results of such a model for the period 1960–1976 indicated the following:

$$a_i = 0.930 \qquad b_i = 0.518 \qquad R^2 = .401$$
$$(t) = 3.17 \qquad F = 10.06$$

These correlation results, along with the estimate of the food chain profit margin for the subsequent year, would imply one estimate. As always, it would be necessary to consider any unique factors that would cause this long-run relationship to deviate from expectations this coming year: e.g., foreign exchange charges; an abnormal number of store openings; any expectations regarding price wars that would affect Safeway more or less than the average.

One might want to consider the relationship between percentages of change $(\%\Delta)$ in the profit margins as follows:

$$\%\Delta \text{ Safeway Net Profit Marg}_t = a_i + b_i \text{ (}\%\Delta \text{ Food Chain Industry Net Profit Marg}_t)$$

$$a_i = -0.022 \qquad b_i = 0.233 \qquad R^2 = .538$$
$$(t) = 4.04 \qquad F = 16.31$$

Again, following the industry analysis one would have an estimate of the percentage of change in the industry margin. Using this long-run relationship, it would be possible to derive another estimate for Safeway that could be adjusted for any unique expectations.

---

[10] Both the operating margin and the net before tax margin were analyzed but the results indicated that the net profit margins yielded the best relationships.

Table 13–5 **Common Size Income Statement for Safeway Stores: 1971–1977**

	1977		1976		1975	
	$ ('000)	%	$ ('000)	%	$ ('000)	%
Sales	11,249,398	100.0	10,442,531	100.0	9,716,889	100.0
Cost of Goods Sold	8,916,719	19.3	8,363,555	80.1	7,750,304	79.8
Gross Profit	2,332,679	20.7	2,078,976	19.9	1,966,585	20.2
Operating & Administrative Expense	2,082,246	18.5	1,838,045	17.6	1,632,824	16.8
Interest Expense	70,104	0.6	63,254	0.6	68,816	0.7
Other Income—Net	(3,918)		(6,218)		(5,397)	
Net Before Taxes	184,247	1.6	183,895	1.8	270,342	2.8
Income Taxes	81,942	0.7	83,052	0.8	124,088	1.3
Net Income	102,305	0.9	100,843	1.0	146,254	1.5
Tax Rate	44.5%		45.2%		45.9%	

Source: Safeway *Annual Report, 1977*, Safeway Stores, Inc.

In addition, the investor should analyze the firm's income statement for a number of years on the basis of a 100 percent breakdown (also referred to as a common size statement). The extent of the breakdown depends upon the consistent detail provided by the firm. As an example, Table 13–5 contains a common size statement for the period 1971–1977. The main items of interest would be "cost of goods sold" and "operating and administrative expense." An analysis of these items for Safeway is both encouraging and discouraging. The cost of goods figure has been under control and was at its lowest point in 1977. In contrast, the firm's operating and administrative expense (O&A) has grown steadily over time and, during the last three years, it has increased by more than sales have. As a result, the O&A expense has grown steadily from 16.4 percent in 1974 to 18.5 percent in 1977 and more than offset the gains in cost of goods sold. The firm's interest expense has also increased as the firm added new store leases, but this expense has been consistent with growth because the percentage has declined slightly. The impact of the rising O&A expense can be seen from the net before tax margin that went from 2.8 percent to 1.6 percent in 1977. Even with a relatively low tax rate, the net income margin is 0.9 percent.

Net Margin Estimate

The overall outlook for the industry is encouraging because of a decline in price wars and generally more stable prices. Also, there has been an increase in mechanization within the industry and a continuing tendency to broaden product lines to include high profit items like drugs and cosmetics. Therefore, the industry margin should increase during 1978 and, given the relationship of Safeway to the industry, the firm should likewise show an increase. In addition, it is felt that Safeway should be able to reduce the rate

1974		1973		1972		1971	
$ ('000)	%	$ ('000)	%	$ ('000)	%	$ ('000)	%
8,185,190	100.0	6,773,687	100.0	6,057,633	100.0	5,358,837	100.0
6,647,799	81.2	5,447,736	80.4	4,837,185	79.9	4,263,937	79.6
1,537,391	18.8	1,325,951	19.6	1,220,448	20.1	1,094,900	20.4
1,339,075	16.4	1,121,580	16.6	1,007,661	16.6	902,869	16.8
66,683	0.8	55,326	0.8	51,638	0.9	44,182	0.8
(4,739)		(4,616)		(3,616)		(3,967)	
136,372	1.7	153,661	2.3	164,765	2.7	151,816	2.8
59,271	0.7	69,204	1.0	75,495	1.2	73,280	1.4
77,101	1.0	84,457	1.3	89,270	1.5	78,536	1.4
43.5%		45.0%		45.8%		48.3%	

of increase in the O&A expense and any improvement in this area will be reflected in the margin. Therefore, the estimate for Safeway's net margin in 1978 is 0.95 percent.

This margin estimate combined with the prior sales estimate of $12,036.7 million indicates net income of *$114.35 million*. Assuming about 26 million common shares outstanding, this implies earnings of *$4.40 per share* for 1978. This constitutes an increase of about 12 percent over the earnings of $3.93 per share in 1977. The next step is to estimate the earnings multiple for Safeway.

Estimating the Earnings Multiple

Similar to the procedure for the industry multiple, this analysis involves the macro relationships between the company multiple and the industry and market multiples and a micro analysis of the individual variables that affect a firm's multiple.

Macro Analysis of Earnings Multiple

Table 13–6 contains the mean earnings multiple for the company, the retail food store industry, and the aggregate market for each year from 1960–1976. In general, the earnings multiple for Safeway has been lower than the multiple for either the retail food industry or the aggregate market. This is true for almost all the individual years and on average. The regression relationship of Safeway's multiple to its industry and the market is shown in Table 13–7. All the regressions indicate that the relationships are significant and the levels results confirm that the Safeway multiple has been smaller than the industry or market multiple. Further, the percent of

Table 13–6
Average Earnings Multiple for Safeway, the Retail Food Store Industry, and the S&P 400 1960–1976

	Safeway					Retail Food Stores			S&P 400
Year	EPS[a]	High	Price[a] Low	Mean	Mean P/E	EPS	Mean Price	Mean P/E	Mean P/E
1960	1.36	20.25	16.25	18.25	13.42	3.78	55.45	14.67	17.70
1961	1.42	31.87	18.33	25.11	17.68	3.78	74.09	19.60	20.41
1962	1.53	30.18	18.12	24.15	15.79	3.83	67.33	17.58	16.98
1963	1.75	32.37	22.68	27.53	15.73	3.79	64.73	17.08	17.07
1964	1.94	37.75	28.00	32.88	16.95	4.13	68.81	16.66	17.63
1965	1.89	42.25	30.12	36.19	19.15	4.16	73.51	17.67	16.82
1966	2.35	31.50	23.67	27.38	11.65	4.39	59.31	13.51	15.20
1967	2.00	28.12	21.37	24.75	12.38	4.13	53.44	12.94	17.04
1968	2.16	31.25	23.25	27.25	12.62	4.29	61.52	14.34	17.30
1969	2.01	30.25	23.50	26.88	13.37	4.76	61.66	13.12	17.46
1970	2.70	34.37	22.12	28.25	10.46	5.09	49.50	11.69	16.49
1971	3.15	40.25	32.12	36.19	11.49	4.44	69.18	15.58	18.02
1972	3.55	44.25	34.00	39.13	11.02	2.80	61.63	22.01	17.95
1973	3.34	44.12	27.25	35.69	10.69	4.37	55.67	12.74	13.38
1974	3.06	43.87	29.62	36.75	12.01	1.61	50.18	31.17	9.43
1975	5.73	52.62	34.12	43.37	7.57	5.71	52.19	9.14	10.79
1976	4.06	50.25	39.25	44.75	11.02	5.41	57.40	10.61	10.45
Mean[b]	2.56	25.26	25.32	30.29	13.74	4.30	62.21	14.93	16.96

[a] Adjusted for 2-for-1 split in 1964.
[b] Excluding 1974.
Source: Reprinted by permission of Standard & Poor's.

change regression indicates that Safeway's multiple is less volatile than the industry multiple (.455) and about equal in volatility to the market multiple. The better relationship in terms of explanatory power (R^2) was with the market multiple.

Micro Analysis of Earnings Multiple

The variables that should influence the multiple are the dividend payout ratio, the risk for the security, and the expected growth rate for the firm which, in turn, is a function of the retention rate and the return on equity. The historical data for these series are contained in Table 13–8. The relevant questions are: why has the Safeway multiple been consistently below the market multiple, and would we expect this relationship to persist based upon the relationship of the relevant variables?

Dividend Payout The dividend payout ratio for Safeway compared to its industry indicates that the payout for Safeway has consistently been lower than that of its industry, and this is reflected in the average for the period

Table 13–7
**Results of
Regressions
Between Safeway
Multiple and
Multiple for the
Industry and the
Market 1960–1976**

Dependent Variable	Independent Variable	α	β	R^2	S.E.	F	D.W.
Safeway P/E (w/o '74) (Levels)	Ret Food St P/E (w/o '74) (Levels)	4.5156 (1.560)	.5807 (3.066)	.402	2.481	9.40	1.09
Safeway P/E (w/o '74) (%Δ)	Ret. Food St P/E (w/o '74) (%Δ)	−.0201 (−.494)	.4549 (2.597)	.360	.152	6.75	2.69
Safeway P/E (w/o '74) (Levels)	S&P 400 P/E (w/o '74) (Levels)	1.4931 (.3656)	.7177 (2.898)	.375	2.536	8.40	0.93
Safeway P/E (w/o '74) (%Δ)	S&P 400 P/E (w/o '74) (%Δ)	.0056 (.142)	1.0197 (3.052)	.437	.143	9.32	2.32

(47.12 vs. 54.61). The relationship between the Safeway payout and the market payout is less consistent; there were six years in which the Safeway payout was higher. Even so, the overall relationship is for Safeway to have a slightly lower payout. Taken by themselves, these results would indicate that the Safeway multiple should be *below* the multiple for the industry or the aggregate market.

Required Rate of Return (K) This analysis should consider the firm's internal risk characteristics (BR, FR, LR), and the stock's systematic market risk (beta). One would expect Safeway to have relatively low business risk because of its sales growth which has been more stable than that of both its industry and the aggregate economy (in terms of food expenditure). Unfortunately, over the long-run the firm has experienced a relatively high level of operating leverage because of the price wars discussed earlier. As a result, the operating profit figures for Safeway have been quite volatile. In fact, the firm's coefficient of variation (CV) of operating earnings during the last five and ten year periods has been substantially above comparable figures for the industry and for the S&P 400. As shown in Table 13–9, the firm's five year CV was almost double that for the S&P 400, and the ten year comparison was even more detrimental. Because the ten year figure could have been influenced by growth,[11] the analysis was

---

[11] The standard deviation is adversely affected by a strong growth trend because the deviations are computed from the overall mean. Therefore, high growth firms will have a higher standard deviation just because of growth.

Table 13–8 **Variables That Influence the Earnings Multiple for Safeway, Retail Food Chains, and the S&P 400 1960–1976**

Year	Safeway				Retail Food Chains				S&P 400			
	Div. Earn	Equity Turnover	Profit Margin	ROE	Div. Earn	Equity Turnover	Profit Margin	ROE	Div. Earn	Equity Turnover	Profit Margin	ROE
1960	50.77	10.63	1.41	15.00	48.94	10.02	1.29	12.89	58.82	1.76	5.72	10.08
1961	52.03	10.11	1.44	14.58	52.12	9.67	1.25	12.07	61.42	1.71	5.66	9.67
1962	51.06	9.29	1.57	14.54	59.27	9.45	1.23	11.63	57.44	1.78	5.93	10.53
1963	46.24	9.00	1.69	15.22	59.37	9.30	1.19	11.06	55.66	1.79	6.19	11.11
1964	46.75	8.74	1.77	15.51	57.14	9.15	1.24	11.39	53.20	1.82	6.63	12.06
1965	52.66	8.49	1.64	13.92	58.89	9.06	1.23	11.11	51.27	1.85	6.82	12.64
1966	43.58	8.74	1.78	15.60	57.63	9.28	1.20	11.10	50.26	1.94	6.64	12.88
1967	54.97	8.34	1.51	12.63	63.20	9.18	1.10	10.05	52.85	1.92	6.12	11.76
1968	50.92	8.58	1.49	12.82	58.04	9.27	1.07	9.96	51.30	2.02	6.07	12.27
1969	54.65	8.99	1.25	11.25	54.04	9.54	1.07	10.19	53.02	2.10	5.65	11.86
1970	42.55	9.78	1.41	13.86	50.29	9.67	1.10	10.60	59.15	2.09	4.92	10.28
1971	41.41	9.79	1.50	14.64	59.91	9.63	0.92	8.86	52.93	2.14	5.04	10.80
1972	38.04	9.94	1.50	14.94	75.36	10.44	0.53	5.55	47.14	2.21	5.30	11.71
1973	44.79	10.25	1.27	13.06	41.88	10.75	0.78	8.34	38.92	2.37	5.96	14.15
1974	55.46	11.75	0.97	11.37	133.54	12.27	0.27	3.36	38.61	2.69	5.28	14.17
1975	33.14	12.28	1.53	18.78	36.43	12.60	0.90	11.28	43.36	2.63	4.63	12.11
1976	50.39	12.30	1.01	12.43	41.22	12.87	0.87	11.25	39.47	2.65	5.27	14.02
Mean[a]	47.12	9.71	1.49	14.31	54.61	11.53	1.06	10.46	51.64	2.05	5.78	11.75

[a] Excluding 1974.

Source: Reprinted by permission of Standard & Poor's.

repeated computing the deviation from a trend line that adjusted for growth. The result was a smaller CV for Safeway, but it still exceeded the CV for the industry and the market. Therefore, one would have to conclude that Safeway has experienced *higher business risk* than its industry or the market has experienced.

The firm's financial risk is comparable to that of its industry and somewhat above that of the aggregate market, after considering the effect of capitalizing leases. When they were not required to capitalize leases, retail firms had only minimal debt on their balance sheet. After capitalizing leases and adjusting the interest charges, Safeway had an interest coverage ratio of 3.6 and a debt to total capital ratio of about 50 percent. These ratios are about equal to those for other retail firms after capitalizing leases. The interest coverage ratio is a little below the aggregate market average of about 4.0, and the debt/total capital ratio is above the overall average of approximately 40 percent. Therefore, one would probably conclude that Safeway's *financial risk is somewhat above average.*

Table 13–9
Coefficient of Variation of Operating Earnings: Safeway; Retail Food Stores; S&P 400

	Safeway	Retail Food Store	S&P 400
5 Year (1972–1976)	.241	.156	.138
10 Year (1967–1976)	.983	.131	.260
10 Year Around Trend	.185	.096	.116

Source: Reprinted by permission of Standard & Poor's.

The firm's external market *liquidity risk* is quite low compared to that for its industry and substantially below the figure for the average firm in the aggregate. The factors generally indicating market liquidity are: (1) the number of stockholders, (2) the number of shares outstanding, (3) the number of shares traded, and (4) institutional interest in the stock as indicated by the number of institutions that own the stock and the proportion of stock owned by institutions. As of January 1, 1977, the firm had 57,619 holders of common stock compared to the NYSE requirement of only 2,000 round lot owners (i.e., owners of 100 shares or more). In terms of its ranking among all firms on the NYSE, it is almost certain that this number would place Safeway in the top 150 or better. As of the end of 1977, there were almost 26,000,000 common shares outstanding with a market value of *over one billion dollars*. Clearly Safeway would qualify as an investment for those institutions that require firms with large market value (recall that the limit was set at between 200 and 400 million dollars to be in the top tier). The percent of shares traded averages about 2 percent per month, which would indicate monthly volume of over 500,000 and annual turnover of 24 percent, somewhat above the NYSE average of 20–21 percent. All of these characteristics are apparently appreciated by financial institutions since they own about seven million shares of Safeway, constituting about 27 percent of the outstanding shares. Finally, if one considers the *Amivest Liquidity Ratio* a useful measure of market liquidity, as of February, 1978 the three month average ratio for Safeway was 903 which ranked it 153 among all stocks on the NYSE and ASE. This compares to an Amivest value of 124 for A&P ranked 724 and 157 for Jewel which was ranked 662. In fact, the food store chain closest to Safeway was Kroger with an Amivest Ratio of 790 and a rank of 185. The overall average for 35 food chains was 101. Therefore, based upon almost any measure of external market liquidity, *Safeway has the lowest liquidity risk in its industry.* The firm's liquidity relative to the aggregate market is also quite good as indicated by its rank of 153 on the NYSE. This is further confirmed by comparing Safeway's Amivest ratio of 903 to an average for all NYSE stocks of 427, which indicates that Safeway has about twice as much liquidity as the average stock on the exchange has. Therefore, Safeway has *much lower liquidity risk* than the aggregate market does.

It appears, then, that Safeway has above average business risk and somewhat above average financial risk. It is clear that Safeway's common stock has a below average liquidity risk. Because of the overriding importance of business and financial risk, one would probably conclude that the overall risk for Safeway is above the average for the market.

The systematic risk for Safeway is derived using the linear regression model that relates rates of return for Safeway to comparable rates of return for the S&P 500 series. According to a December, 1977 *Value Line* report on Safeway, the firm's historical beta was .90 which would indicate a below average market risk.

The overall consensus probably indicates risk about equal to that of the aggregate market with a tendency toward above average risk. This would suggest a multiple equal to or slightly below the market multiple.

Expected Growth Rate (g)

The expected growth rate of dividends is dependent on the expected growth rate of earnings, which is a function of the retention rate and the return on equity (ROE). Based upon our discussion of the dividend payout, we know that, generally, Safeway has had a lower payout than either the industry or the aggregate market had, which implies a slightly higher retention rate.

We know that the firm's ROE is a function of the equity turnover and the profit margin. The figures in Table 13–8 indicate that the equity turnover for Safeway has been consistently *lower* than it has been for the overall industry, although *the difference is not very large* as shown by the average values (9.71 vs. 9.99). The yearly and average turnover for Safeway is substantially larger than that for the aggregate market, as one would expect given the nature of the retail industry. This comparison would indicate that the industry should grow at a higher rate than Safeway will.

The profit margin results indicate that Safeway does better than the industry overall. The profit margin for Safeway is *always* larger than that for the industry, usually by a substantial amount. The average margin for Safeway is more than 40 percent larger than the industry margin (1.49 vs. 1.06). Again, as expected, the Safeway margin is always lower than the aggregate margin.

The combined effect of turnover and profit margin indicates an ROE for Safeway that is substantially higher than the industry figure (14.31 vs. 10.46) and also higher than the aggregate market figure (14.31 vs. 11.75). The computed ROE figures implied by the turnovers and margin figures are very close to the long-run average figures, as one would expect.

	Equity Turnover	Profit Margin	Expected ROE	Average ROE
Safeway	9.71	1.49	14.47	14.31
Industry	9.99	1.06	10.59	10.46
S&P 400	2.05	5.78	11.85	11.75

Source: Reprinted by permission of Standard & Poor's.

These results for ROE combined with the results for the retention rate imply a much higher growth rate for Safeway than will be experienced by the industry or the economy. The derived figures are shown below.

	Retention Rate	ROE	Expected Growth Rate
Safeway	.529	14.31	7.57
Retail Food Chain Industry	.454	10.46	4.75
S&P 400	.484	11.75	5.69

Source: Reprinted by permission of Standard & Poor's.

These results indicate a higher growth rate for Safeway and, other things being equal, a higher multiple.

The Combined Effect The overall effect of the three variables indicates that the earnings multiple for Safeway should be about equal to, or slightly above, that for its industry and the market. The payout indicates a lower multiple and the risk likewise indicates a lower multiple for Safeway. In contrast, the growth rate for Safeway has been clearly above that of the industry and the market. On balance it is felt that the higher growth rate outweighs the other factors slightly.

An Example of a Multiple Estimate

The macro analysis indicated that Safeway's multiple was below that of the industry and less volatile. Alternatively, it indicated percentages of change comparable to those occurring in the market. The micro analysis indicated a multiple comparable to the market's or slightly above it. It was estimated that the market multiple would be about 8.75 and the retail store multiple would be about 9.0. Based upon the foregoing, the multiple for Safeway should be at least 9.0 and could go to 9.5.

Price Estimate In the earnings section, we estimated earnings for Safeway of $4.40 per share. Assuming a multiple of 9.0 implies a year end price of about *$39.50* (9.0 × $4.40). Using a multiple of 9.5 implies a price of about *$42.00* (9.5 × $4.40).

Alternative Earnings Multiple Models

In contrast to the approach in which individual components of the multiple are examined in relation to the industry and market, several authors have analyzed a large cross-section of stocks using regression analysis. The best known study was done by Whitbeck and Kisor and examined the estimated earnings multiple for a cross-section of stocks for which the multiple was computed as the current price for the stock divided by the "normalized" earnings for the company as estimated by the analysts at a New York bank.[12] The estimated multiple was regressed against three variables that intuitively seemed related to the multiple. Although there was no formal model used, the variables selected were quite consistent with those derived from the dividend growth model: the dividend payout ratio, an earnings variability measure to reflect business risk, and an earnings growth variable.

The results indicated that all the variables had the expected sign and apparently were significant (although no standard errors were reported). The empirical regression results were as follows for the historical period:

$$\text{Theoretical P/E Ratio} = 8.2 + 1.5 \text{ (growth rate)} + 6.7 \text{ (payout)} - 0.2 \text{ (standard deviation)}$$

The authors then tested the usefulness of the model in stock selection. For each of the 135 stocks in their sample, they computed the "theoretical p/e" based upon their *projected* payout, earnings variability, and growth, and compared this theoretical p/e value to the prevailing value. Stocks that had an actual p/e 15 percent below their theoretical p/e were considered undervalued, while stocks with a p/e 15 percent above the theoretical value were considered overvalued. An analysis of the two groups indicated that the undervalued group consistently outperformed the S&P 500 on the basis of rate of return during the four individual quarters. The overvalued group consistently underperformed the S&P 500.

While these results are quite encouraging, it should be recognized that they contain a great deal of nonhistorical information. The p/e ratio is not historical but is equal to price over earnings "normalized" by an analyst. Further, all the explanatory variables are estimates generated using historical data adjusted by an analyst to take account of current and projected events.

Numerous papers on the same general topic followed, but one of the most complete and informative for practical purposes was done by Malkiel and Cragg.[13] After developing a dividend growth valuation model, the authors employed the following empirical variables: the dividend/payout ratio, the variance of earnings, a systematic risk variable (beta), a financial risk variable, and (long-term and short-term) growth variables. The model was tested using *historical* financial measures and *expected* values for each of the variables (including normalized earnings) as estimated by analysts at 17 investment firms.

The initial results considered regressions using historical variables for growth, instability, and payout, and comparable regressions using expecta-

---

[12] V. Whitbeck and M. Kisor, "A New Tool in Investment Decision Making," *Financial Analysts Journal*, Vol. 19, No. 3 (May–June, 1963), pp. 55–62.

[13] Burton G. Malkiel and John G. Cragg, "Expectations and the Structure of Share Prices," *American Economic Review*, Vol. 60, No. 4 (September, 1970), pp. 601–617.

tional variables. The regression results using expectational data were clearly superior to the historical data results (r^2 was approximately .50 with historical data versus .75 with expectations data). Using beta as the risk measure gave superior results in some instances, but not in all. Regressions that employed a combination of expectations and historic data generated results that were quite good (r^2 from .78 to .85), the growth variables were most important and the financial risk variable was also significant. The dominance of the growth variable was apparent in additional regressions with only expectations variables.

The authors also dealt with changes in the valuation relationship over time, a point that is very important for the long-run use of the models to estimate the intrinsic value of securities. If the variable coefficients change each year, the usefulness of the coefficients in estimating future earnings multiple values is reduced substantially. The authors state:

An inspection . . . indicates that the coefficients of our equation change considerably from year to year and in a manner that is consistent with the changing standards of value in vogue at the time.[14]

Finally, they considered whether the models could be used to select securities by comparing the actual market p/e ratios to the normal p/e ratio predicted by the valuation equation. As did Whitbeck and Kisor, the authors assumed that, if the actual p/e was below the normal p/e, the stock was underpriced and vice versa. Malkiel and Cragg did not limit their discussion to those stocks 15 percent above or below their theoretical p/e, but included all stocks. The test related the percentage of under or over pricing to the return on the stock; i.e., a stock that is heavily underpriced should have a large positive return during the subsequent year. Based upon the results for five individual years, it was stated:

. . . in only three of the five years for which this experiment was performed was the relationship negative, and the degree of association was extremely low. In the other two years, there was either a positive or zero relationship.[15]

Discussion of the reasons for the poor results with the predictive model indicated that better results were derived assuming perfect foresight rather than only using historical data, and even better results could be derived assuming knowledge of future expectations. Therefore, although the models were quite good in explaining past variance in price-earnings ratios, the analysis was not successful in isolating underpriced securities.

This lack of success appears to have been caused by a lack of stability in the variable coefficients. Therefore, although it is possible to explain past results with these models, it is not possible to use them to select stocks if

---

[14] Ibid., p. 613. This instability of coefficients was evident in *all* tables in the article.

[15] Ibid., p. 615.

only historical information is taken into account. Such results are obviously consistent with the semi-strong efficient market hypothesis.

Summary

This chapter dealt with the procedure for evaluating individual common stocks using the dividend growth model. It was initially pointed out that the analyst should be aware of the fact that there are several different types of companies and of common stocks and that there is a high probability that the two are not the same; i.e., a growth company may not issue a growth stock. The procedure for the analysis was demonstrated using Safeway Stores as an example. The earnings estimate was derived based upon an analysis of the sales performance of Safeway in relation to the performance of its industry and of an aggregate economic series. The profit margin estimate considered the firm's relationship to its industry and any unique features.

The comparison of the earnings multiple for Safeway to the figure for its industry and the market indicated that the Safeway multiple was consistently below the others. Each of the components that influence the multiple was analyzed indicating that, on balance, the Safeway multiple should have been about equal to that for the industry or the market based upon these historical results.

The final section discussed two studies dealing with the cross-sectional analysis of earnings multiples and internal corporate variables. Such models are helpful in explaining past multiples, but they are not useful in selecting underpriced securities.

Questions

1. Define a growth company and a speculative stock.

2. Give an example of a growth *company* and discuss why you would expect it to be considered a growth company. Be specific.

3. Give an example of a cyclical *stock* and discuss why you have designated it as such a stock. Is it also issued by a cyclical company?

4. Select a company outside the retail store industry and indicate what economic series you would use for a sales projection. Discuss why this is a relevant series.

5. Select a company outside the retail store industry and indicate what *industry* series you would use in an industry analysis (try to use one of the industry groups designated by Standard & Poor's). Discuss why this is most appropriate and whether there were several possible alternatives.

6. Taking the company and industry selected in Question 5, examine the operating profit margin for the company as it relates to the operating margin for the industry. Discuss the annual results in terms of levels and changes and the long-run averages for the latest 10 year period.

7. Compute the average earnings multiple for a company for each of the last ten years and relate this to a comparable multiple for the market (consider using the High + Low/2, in which case the market figures are included in Table 13–6). Discuss the short-run and long-run differences.

8. Compare your average company multiple to a similar industry multiple for the last ten years. Discuss the short-run and long-run differences.

9. Assume that there is some difference between your company and its industry. What are the three major variables that could account for this difference? Discuss each individually and indicate what difference in each (holding everything else constant) would explain it, e.g., the company multiple is higher because variable A is lower and this influences the multiple in the following way.

10. *Case Project*—Collect the data for your company and your industry and analyze all the variables that should affect the multiple to determine whether the historical differences are consistent with the historical relationship between the multiples; i.e., can you explain why the average company multiple is higher or lower than the industry multiple?

References

Arditti, Fred D. "Risk and the Required Return on Equity." *Journal of Finance,* Vol. 22, No. 1 (March, 1967).

Benishay, Haskell. "Variability in Earnings-Price Ratios of Corporate Equities." *American Economic Review,* Vol. 51, No. 1 (March, 1961).

Bower, Richard S. and Bower, D. H. "Risk and the Valuation of Common Stock." *Journal of Political Economy,* Vol. 77, No. 3 (May–June, 1969).

Cragg, John G. and Malkiel, Burton G. "The Consensus and Accuracy of Some Predictions of the Growth of Corporate Earnings." *Journal of Finance,* Vol. 23, No. 1 (March, 1968).

Friend, Irwin and Puckett, M. "Dividends and Stock Prices." *American Economic Review,* Vol. 54, No. 4 (September, 1964).

Gordon, Myron J. *The Investment, Financing, and Valuation of the Corporation.* Homewood, Illinois: Richard D. Irwin, 1962.

Graham, Benjamin, Dodd, D. L., and Cottle, S. *Security Analysis, Principles and Techniques* (4th edition). New York: McGraw–Hill Book Co., Inc., 1962.

Lintner, John. "The Valuation of Risk Assets and the Selection of Risky Investments in Stock Portfolios and Capital Budgets." *Review of Economics and Statistics,* Vol. 47, No. 1 (February, 1965).

Lintner, John and Glauber, Robert. "Higgledy Piggledy Growth in America." Lorie, James and Brealey, Richard, eds., *Modern Developments in Investment Management.* New York: Praeger Publishers, Inc., 1972.

Malkiel, Burton G. and Cragg, John. "Expectations and the Structure of Share Prices." *American Economic Review,* Vol. 60, No. 4 (September, 1970).

Mossin, Jan. "Equilibrium in a Capital Asset Market." *Econometrics,* Vol. 34, No. 4 (October, 1966).

Niederhoffer, Victor and Regan, Patrick J. "Earnings Changes, Analysts' Forecasts, and Stock Prices." *Financial Analysts Journal,* Vol. 28, No. 3 (May–June, 1972).

Pratt, J. W. "Risk Aversion in the Small and in the Large." *Econometrics,* Vol. 32, No. 1 (January–February, 1964).

Whitbeck, V. and Kisor, M. "A New Tool in Investment Decision Making." *Financial Analysts Journal,* Vol. 19, No. 3 (May–June, 1963).

Chapter 14   *Analysis of Growth Companies*

Investment literature contains numerous accounts of the rapid rise of growth companies such as IBM, Xerox, and Polaroid and stories about investors who became wealthy because of timely acquisitions of these stocks. Given such increases in value, it is clear that the proper valuation of true growth companies can be extremely rewarding. At the same time, for every IBM or Xerox that became successful, there are numerous firms that did not survive. Further, there are instances in which the stock price of a true growth company became overvalued and the subsequent returns were clearly below expectations. As stated—the common stock of a growth company is *not* always a growth stock!

By now, the reader should be aware of the dividend valuation model, of the important factors in valuation, and of the basic assumption of the model, i.e., that dividends are expected to grow at a *constant rate for an infinite time period.* As noted, these assumptions are reasonable when evaluating the aggregate market and some large industries, but they become more tenuous when analyzing individual securities. The point of this chapter is that *these assumptions are extremely questionable for a growth company.*

Definition

A growth company is defined as a firm that has the opportunities and ability to invest capital in projects that generate returns greater than the firm's cost of capital. Such a condition is considered to be *clearly temporary.* In a competitive economy, all firms are expected to produce at the point where marginal revenue equals marginal cost and, under such conditions, the returns to the producer will exactly compensate for the risks involved. If the returns are below what is expected for the risk involved, the producer will leave the industry. In contrast, if the investment returns for a given industry exceed the returns expected based upon the risk involved, other investors will enter the industry, increase the supply, and drive the prices down until the returns *are* consistent with the inherent risk, resulting in a state of equilibrium.

Actual Returns Above Expected Returns

The notion of consistently earning returns above the expected rate requires elaboration. Firms are engaged in business ventures that offer opportunities for investment of corporate capital, and these investments entail some uncertainty or risk. Investors determine their required return for owning this firm based upon the risk of the investments made by the firm compared to the risk of other firms. Take a firm that is involved in producing and selling medical equipment and assume perfect capital markets. There is some uncertainty about the sales of this equipment, and about the ultimate profit that will be derived from these sales. Comparing this composite uncertainty to the uncertainty involved in other investments, and the rates of returns expected from these others, one can estimate the return investors should require from an investment in the production and sale of medical equipment. Based upon the CAPM, one would expect the difference in the required rate of return to be a function of the difference in the systematic risk for the firm's investments which affect the stock's systematic risk. Investors derive a required return for investing in a firm based upon the systematic risk of the investments made by the firm. *This required rate of return is referred to as the firm's cost of capital.* In a perfect market in a state of equilibrium, one would expect *these two rates of return to be equal.* The return derived from risky investments by the firm would equal the return required by investors. Any returns earned by the firm above those required for the systematic risk involved are referred to as "pure profits." One of the costs of production is the cost of the capital employed. Therefore, in a purely competitive environment, marginal revenue should equal marginal costs (including capital costs) and there are no excess returns or "pure profits".[1] Such excess profits are only possible in a noncompetitive environment. Assume that the medical equipment firm is able to earn 20 percent on its capital, while investors only require 15 percent on such investments, given the systematic risk involved. The extra 5 percent is defined as pure profit. In a totally competitive environment, numerous companies would enter the medical equipment field in order to enjoy the excess profits available. These competitors would increase the supply of equipment and reduce price until the marginal returns equaled the marginal costs.

The fact that a number of firms have been able to derive excess profits for a number of years indicates that these excess returns are probably not due to

---

[1] For a further discussion of "profits," see George J. Stigler, *The Theory of Price* (revised ed.) (New York: The Macmillan Co., 1952), pp. 180–182.

a temporary disequilibrium, but are due to some noncompetitive factors that are allowed to exist in our capitalistic economy, such as patent or copyright laws that provide a firm or person with monopoly rights to a process or a manuscript for a specified period of time. During this period of protection from competition, the firm has the ability to derive above normal returns without fear of competition. Also one can conceive of a firm possessing special management skills that provide added profits (e.g., a unique marketing technique or other organizational characteristic). Finally, in some instances the capital required to enter an industry can be a barrier (e.g., the auto industry).

In a purely competitive economy with no frictions there should be no such thing as a true growth company because competition would negate such growth. As it is, our economy is not a perfect competitive model (although this is probably the best model to use in most cases), and there are a number of real world frictions that restrict competition. Therefore, it is possible to envision the *temporary* existence of true growth companies in our economy. The question is—how long can they last?

Growth Companies and Growth Stocks

In many instances the characteristics of a company and those of its stock are distinct. At this point it is appropriate to briefly recall the definitions of a growth company and a growth stock to ensure that the reader does not assume that the two are synonymous.

A growth *company* has the opportunities and ability to consistently invest capital in projects that generate rates of return greater than the firm's cost of capital. A growth *stock* is a security that is expected to experience above average risk-adjusted rates of return during some future period. This definition of a growth stock means that *any* stock that is currently undervalued can be a growth stock *irrespective* of the type of company issuing it. The securities of growth *companies* that have become temporarily overvalued could be speculative stocks because the probability of deriving below normal returns from them would be very high. A major intent of this analysis of growth companies is to present models that will help the analyst evaluate the *unique* earnings stream of the growth company and thereby devise a "better" estimate of the value of the growth firm and its stock. The result should be superior judgement regarding whether the stock of the growth company is: (1) a growth stock, (2) simply a properly valued stock, or (3) a speculative stock.

Growth Companies and the Dividend Model

The dividend model assumes a *constant rate of growth for an infinite time period.* It should be clear that it is *impossible* for a true growth firm to exist in a purely competitive economy. Further, even in a competitive economy with some noncompetitive factors, a true growth firm cannot exist for very long.

Patents and copyrights run out, unusual management practices can eventually be copied, and large amounts of capital can be accumulated. Therefore, the dividend growth model is *not* appropriate for the valuation of growth companies, and it is necessary to consider special valuation models that allow for finite periods of abnormal growth and for the possibility of different rates of growth. The rest of the chapter deals with models that can be used in the valuation of growth companies.

Alternative Growth Models[2]

In this section we will consider the full range of growth models, from no growth and negative growth to dynamic true growth. Knowledge of the full range will help the reader understand why the dividend growth model used extensively in financial literature is unrealistic and not applicable to true growth firms. This background will also be useful in understanding growth company valuation models. Each model assumes that the company is an all-equity firm in order to simplify the computations.

No Growth Firm

The no growth firm is that mythical company that is established with a specified portfolio of investments that generate a constant stream of earnings equal to r times the value of assets. Earnings are calculated after allowing for depreciation to maintain the assets at their original value. Therefore:

$$E = r \cdot \text{Assets}$$

It is also assumed that *all earnings of the firm are paid out in dividends*; i.e., if b is the rate of retention, b = 0. Hence:

$$E = r \cdot \text{Assets} = \text{Dividends}$$

Under these assumptions, the value of the firm is the discounted value of the perpetual stream of earnings (E). The discount rate (the required rate of return) is specified as Ke. In this case, it is assumed that r = Ke. The firm's *rate of earnings on assets is exactly equal to the required rate of return*. The value of the firm is:

$$V = \frac{E}{Ke} = \frac{(1-b)E}{Ke}$$

---

[2] The discussion in this section is drawn to a great extent from Ezra Solomon, *The Theory of Financial Management* (New York: Columbia University Press, 1963), pp. 55–63. Another article in which the value for true growth companies is derived is M. Miller and F. Modigliani, "Dividend Policy, Growth, and the Valuation of Shares," *Journal of Business,* Vol. 34, No. 4 (October, 1961), pp. 411–433. This latter article is heavily involved in discussing the importance of dividends in valuation.

In the no growth case, the earnings stream never changes because the asset base never changes and the rate of return on the assets never changes. Therefore, the value of the firm never changes and investors continue to receive Ke on their investment:

$$Ke = E/V.$$

Long-Run Growth Models

These models differ from the models for a no growth firm because *they assume some of the earnings are reinvested.* We will begin with the case in which a firm retains a *constant dollar amount of earnings* and reinvests these retained earnings in assets that obtain a return above the required rate.

In all cases it is postulated that the market value (V) of an all-equity firm is the capitalized value of three component forms of returns discounted at the rate Ke:

E = the level of (constant) net earnings expected from existing assets, without further net investments

G = the gross present value of capital gains expected from reinvested funds. The return on reinvested funds is equal to r which equals mKe. If m is equal to one, then r = Ke, if m is greater than one, then these are considered true growth investments (r > Ke), and if m is less than one, the investments are generating returns (r) below the cost of capital (r < Ke).

R = the reinvestment of net earnings is equal to bE, where b is a percent between zero (no reinvestment) and unity (total reinvestment; no dividends).

Simple Growth Model

It is assumed that the firm has investment opportunities that provide rates of return equal to r, where r is greater than Ke (m is above one). Further, it is assumed that these opportunities allow the firm to invest R dollars a year at these rates and that R = bE; R is a *constant dollar amount* because E is the constant earnings at the beginning of the period.

The value of G, the capital gain component, is computed as follows: the first investment of bE dollars yields a stream of earnings equal to bEr dollars, and this is repeated every year. Each of these earnings streams has a present value, as of the year it begins, of bEr/Ke which is the present value of a constant perpetual stream discounted at a rate consistent with the risk involved. Assuming the firm does this every year, it has a *series* of investments, each of which has a present value of bEr/Ke. The present value of *all* these series is (bEr/Ke)/Ke which equals bEr/Ke^2. But because $r = mKe$, this becomes:

(14–1)
$$\frac{bEmKe}{Ke^2} = \frac{bEm}{Ke}$$ (Gross present value of growth investments)

In order to derive these flows, it was necessary to invest bE dollars each year. The present value of these annual investments is equal to bE/Ke. Therefore, the *net* present value of growth investments is equal to:

(14–2)
$$\frac{bEm}{Ke} - \frac{bE}{Ke}$$ (Net present value of growth investments)

The important variable is the value of m which indicates the relationship of r to Ke. Combining this growth component with the capitalized value of the constant earnings stream indicates the value of the firm is:

(14–3)
$$V = \frac{E}{Ke} + \frac{bEm}{Ke} - \frac{bE}{Ke}$$

This equation indicates that the value of the firm is equal to the constant earnings stream plus a growth component equal to the *net* present value of reinvestment in growth projects. By combining the first and third terms in Equation (14–3) this becomes:

(14–4)
$$V = \frac{E(1-b)}{Ke} + \frac{bEm}{Ke}$$

Because E(1–b) is the dividend, this model becomes:

(14–5)
$$V = \frac{D}{Ke} + \frac{bEm}{Ke}$$ (Present value of constant dividend plus the present value of growth investments)

It can be stated as earnings only by rearranging Equation (14–3).

(14–6)
$$V = \frac{E}{Ke} + \frac{bE(m-1)}{Ke}$$ (Present value of constant earnings plus present value of excess earnings from growth investments)

Expansion Model

The expansion model assumes a firm retains earnings to reinvest, but only gets a rate of return equal to the cost of capital (m = 1, so r = Ke). The effect of such a change can be seen in Equation (14–2) where the net present value of growth investments would be zero and, therefore, Equation (14–3) would become:

(14–7)
$$V = \frac{E}{Ke}$$

It would still be possible to have equations comparable to (14–4), but it would become:

(14–8)
$$V = \frac{E(1-b)}{Ke} + \frac{bE}{Ke} = \frac{E}{Ke}$$

Equation (14–5) is still valid, but the present value of the growth investment component would be smaller because m would be equal to one. Finally, the last term in Equation (14–6) would disappear.

This indicates that, simply because a firm retains earnings and reinvests them, it is not necessarily of benefit to the stockholder unless the reinvestment rate is above the required rate (r > Ke). Otherwise, the investor would be as well off with all earnings paid out in dividends.

Negative Growth Model
The negative growth model applies to a firm that retains earnings (b > 0), and reinvests these funds in projects that generate rates of return *below* the firm's cost of capital (r < Ke or m < 1). The effect of such a practice on the value of the firm can be seen from an examination of Equation (14–2) which indicates that with m < 1, the net present value of the growth investments would be *negative*. This implies that the value of the firm in Equation (14–3) would be *less* than the value of a no growth firm or an expansion firm. This can also be seen by examining the effect of m < 1 in Equation (14–6). The firm is withholding funds from the investor and investing them in projects that generate returns less than those available from comparable risk investments.

Such poor performance may be difficult to uncover because the asset base of the firm and the earnings of the firm *will increase* if it earns *any positive rate of return* on the new assets. The earnings will not grow by as much as they should, so the value of the firm will decline when investors discount this reinvestment stream.

What Determines Capital Gain Component?
These equations highlight the factors that influence the capital gain component. All the equations beginning with (14–1) suggest that the gross present value of the growth investments is equal to:

$$bEm/Ke$$

This indicates that three factors are important to the size of this term. The first is the size of b, *the percentage of earnings retained for reinvestment.* The greater the proportion of earnings retained, the larger the capital gain component. The second is the value of *m which indicates the relationship between the firm's return on investments and the firm's required return (i.e., its cost of capital).* A value of one indicates that the firm is only earning its required return. A firm with an m greater than one is a true growth company and the important question is, how much greater than one is the return? The final factor of importance is *the time period for the superior investments.* This is easily overlooked because, throughout the discussion, we assume an infinite horizon to simplify the computations. However, when analyzing growth companies, the length of time a firm can continue to invest large amounts of funds at superior rates in a relatively competitive environment is clearly a major consideration. The three factors that influence the capital gain component are:

1. the amount of capital invested in growth investments

2. the rate of return earned on the funds retained relative to the required return

3. the time horizon in which these growth investments will be available.

Dynamic True Growth Model

This model applies to a firm that invests a constant *percentage* of current earnings in projects that generate rates of return above the firm's required rate (r > Ke, m > 1). The effect of this is that the firm's earnings and dividends will grow at a *constant rate* that is equal to br (the percentage of earnings retained times the return on investments). In the current model, this would equal bmKe, where m is greater than one. Given these assumptions, the dynamic growth model for an infinite time period would be the dividend valuation model derived in the Appendix to Chapter 11:

$$V = \frac{D}{Ke-g}$$

This model applied to the true growth company means that earnings and dividends are growing at a constant rate and *the firm is investing larger and larger dollar amounts in projects that generate returns greater than Ke.* Moreover, it is implicitly assumed that the firm can continue to do this for an infinite time period. If the growth rate (g) is greater than Ke, the model blows up and indicates that the firm should have an infinite value. Because of this possibility, Durand basically concluded that, although many firms had current growth rates above the normal required rates of return, very few of their stocks were selling for infinite values.[3] He felt that the best explana-

---

[3] David Durand, "Growth Stocks and the Petersburg Paradox," *Journal of Finance,* Vol. 12, No. 3 (September, 1957), pp. 348–363.

tion for this phenomenon was the expectation that the reinvestment rate would decline or that the investment opportunities would not be available for an infinite time period.

Table 14–1
Summary of Company Descriptions

	Retention	Return on Investments
No Growth Company	b = 0	r = Ke
Long-Run Growth (assumes reinvestment)		
Negative Growth	b > 0	r < Ke
Expansion	b > 0	r = Ke
Simple Long-Run Growth	b > 0 (Constant $)	r > Ke
Dynamic Long-Run Growth	b > 0 (Constant %)	r > Ke

The Real World

All of these models are simplified to allow the development of a range of alternatives. As a result, several of the models are extremely unrealistic. *The real world is composed of companies that are a combination of these models.* Unfortunately, most firms have made some investments where r < Ke and many firms invest in projects that generate returns about equal to the cost of capital. Finally, almost all firms have the opportunity to invest in some projects that provide rates of return above the firm's cost of capital (r > Ke). How much is invested in these growth projects and how long these opportunities last are crucial considerations.

In the remainder of this chapter we will discuss various models that concentrate on these questions to help the analyst derive better estimates of the value of the growth company.

Growth Duration

The earnings multiple for a stock (the p/e multiple) is a function of, (1) the firm's expected rate of growth in terms of earnings per share, (2) the required rate of return on the security based upon its systematic risk, and (3) the firm's dividend payout ratio. If one assumes that the risk for different firms is similar, and also assumes no significant difference in the payout ratio for different firms, then the principal variable affecting the earnings multiple is the difference in the growth estimate. Further, the growth estimate must be considered in terms of the *rate* and *duration* of expected growth. No company can continue to grow indefinitely at a rate substantially above normal. IBM cannot continue to grow at 20 percent a year for an extended period or it will eventually become the entire economy. IBM or any similar growth firm will run out of high profit investment projects. Continued growth at a sustained rate requires that larger and larger amounts of money be invested in high return projects. Eventually competition will encroach upon these high return investments and the firm's growth rate will decline to a rate consistent with the rate for the overall economy. Ascertaining the duration of the growth period therefore becomes significant.

Computation of Growth Duration

The growth duration concept was originally derived by Charles Holt,[4] who showed that, if risk between a given security and a "market" security (he used the Dow-Jones Industrial Average as the market security) is assumed to be constant, it is possible to examine the differential past growth rates for the market and for the growth firm. Then, given the alternative p/e ratios, one can compute the market's implied growth duration for the growth firm. If $E'(0)$ is the firm's current earnings, then $E'(t)$ is earnings in period t according to the expression:

$$(14\text{–}9) \qquad E'(t) = E'(0) (1+G)^t$$

where G is the annual percent of growth rate for earnings. To adjust for dividend payments, it was assumed that all such payments are used to purchase further shares of the stock. This means the number of shares (N) will grow at the dividend rate (D). Therefore:

$$(14\text{–}10) \qquad N(t) = N(0) (1+D)^t$$

To derive the total earnings for a firm $E(t)$, the growth rate in per share earnings and the growth in shares are combined as follows:

$$(14\text{–}11) \qquad E(t) = E'(t) \, N(t) = E'(0) \, [(1+G) \, (1+D)]^t$$

Because G and D are small, this expression can be approximated by:

$$(14\text{–}12) \qquad E(t) \cong E'(0) \, (1+G+D)^t$$

Assuming that the general characteristics of the growth stock (g) and the nongrowth stock (a) are the same (similar risk and payout), one would expect the market to value the shares of the two stocks in direct proportion to their earnings in year T, when T is the investor's horizon. In other words, *current prices should be in direct proportion to the expected future earnings ratio in year T.* This can be stated:

---

[4] Charles C. Holt, "The Influence of Growth Duration on Share Prices," *Journal of Finance,* Vol. 17, No. 3 (September, 1962), pp. 465–475. The discussion in this section draws on the original article. A subsequent article that "rediscovered" the concept is Robert M. Baylis and Suresh L. Bhirud, "Growth Stock Analysis: A New Approach," *Financial Analysts Journal,* Vol. 29, No. 4 (July–August, 1973), pp. 63–70.

$$(14\text{–}13) \qquad \left(\frac{Pg\ (0)}{Pa\ (0)}\right) \cong \left(\frac{Eg\ (0)\ (1+Gg+Dg)^T}{Ea\ (0)\ (1+G_a+D_a)^T}\right)$$

or

$$(14\text{–}14) \qquad \left(\frac{Pg(0)/Eg(0)}{P_a(0)/E_a(0)}\right) \cong \left(\frac{1+Gg+Dg}{1+G_a+D_a}\right)^T$$

The result is that *the p/e ratios of the two stocks are in direct proportion to the ratio of composite growth rates raised to the Tth power.* It is possible to solve for T by taking the log of both sides as follows:

$$(14\text{–}15) \qquad \ln\left(\frac{Pg(0)/Eg(0)}{P_a(0)/E_a(0)}\right) \cong T \ln\left(\frac{1+Gg+Dg}{1+G_a+D_a}\right)$$

The growth duration model answers the question: "How long must the earnings of the growth stock grow at the past rate, relative to the nongrowth stock, to justify its current premium in p/e ratio relative to the nongrowth stock?" It is the function of the analyst to determine whether the *implied* duration estimate is reasonable in terms of his analysis of the company's potential.

Consider the following example. The stock of a well-known growth company is currently selling for 63 dollars a share with expected per share earnings of $3.50 (earnings multiple is 18). The firm's average growth rate in earnings per share during the past five and ten year periods has been 15 percent a year, and the dividend yield has averaged 3 percent. In contrast, the S&P 400 Industrial Index has a current p/e of 10, an average dividend yield of 5 percent, and an average growth rate of 6 percent. Therefore, the comparison looks as follows:

	S&P 400	Growth Company
P/E ratios (Current Price ÷ Expected Earnings)	10.00	18.00
Average growth rate	.0600	.1500
Dividend yield	.0500	.0300

Inserting these values into Equation (14–15):

$$\ln\left(\frac{18.00}{10.00}\right) \cong T \ln\left(\frac{1+.1500+.0300}{1+.0600+.0500}\right)$$

$$\ln(1.800) \cong T \ln\left(\frac{1.1800}{1.1100}\right)$$

$$\ln(1.800) \cong T \ln(1.063)$$

$$T = \ln(1.800)/\ln(1.063)$$

$$= .255273/.026533 \text{ (log base 10)}$$

$$= 9.62 \text{ years}$$

These results indicate that the market is implicitly assuming that the growth company can continue to grow at this composite rate (18 percent) for almost 10 more years, after which it is assumed that the growth company will grow at the same rate as the aggregate market, as represented by the S&P 400, will. The question the analyst must ask at this point is, "Can this growth rate be sustained for at least this period?" If the implied growth duration is greater than the analyst feels is reasonable, he will likely discourage purchase of the stock. If it is below his expectations, he will likely recommend the purchase.

Intra-Industry Analysis

Besides using it to compare a company to some market base, it is possible to use this technique for a direct comparison of two firms. When doing an inter-company analysis, it is best to consider firms in the same industry because then it is likely that one of the assumptions of the growth duration technique—equal risk—is valid.

Consider the following example from the cosmetics industry:

	Company A	Company B
P/E ratios	21.00	15.00
Average annual growth rate	.1700	.1200
Dividend Yield	.0250	.0300
Growth rate plus dividend yield	.1950	.1500
Estimate of T^a		8.79 years

^{a} The reader should check to see that he gets the same answer.

These results imply that the market expects Company A to grow at a total rate of almost 20 percent for about 9 years followed by a decrease to the same rate of growth as Company B will experience. The analyst must decide whether he agrees with this implicit market valuation. If he feels the implied duration is too long he will prefer Company B; if he feels it is reasonable or low, he will recommend Company A.

An Alternative Use of T

Instead of solving for T and then deciding whether the figure derived is reasonable, it is also possible to use this formulation to derive a "reasonable" earnings multiple for a security relative to the aggregate market (or another stock) if the implicit assumptions are reasonable for the stock involved. Assume that you have been analyzing a growth company and you estimate that its composite growth will be about 20 percent a year compared to the market growth of 11 percent. Further, you feel that this firm can maintain such superiority for about seven years. Using Equation (14–15), this becomes:

$$\ln (X) = 7 \cdot \ln \frac{1.20}{1.11}$$

$$= 7 \cdot \ln (1.081)$$

$$= 7 \cdot (.033826)$$

$$= .236782$$

To determine what the p/e ratio should be, it is necessary to derive the antilog of .236782, which is approximately 1.725. Therefore, assuming the market multiple is 10.00, the earnings multiple for this growth company should be about 1.725 times the market p/e or 17.25.

Factors to Consider

When employing this tool, the following major factors should be recognized. First, the technique assumes *equal risk* between the securities compared. Although this assumption may be acceptable when comparing two large, well-established firms (e.g., General Motors and Standard Oil), it is very likely *not* true when comparing a small firm to the aggregate market.

Another problem is deciding *which growth estimate to use.* In the typical case, historical growth rates used are for five and ten year periods. Which time interval is most relevant? Which does the market employ? What about using the expected rate of growth?

Third, *the technique assumes that the stock with the higher p/e ratio has the higher growth rate.* In numerous instances, the stock with the higher p/e ratio did not have a higher historical growth rate. In these cases, the formulation generates a negative growth duration value which is of no use to the analyst. Inconsistency between growth and the p/e ratio could be attributed to one of four factors:

1. A major difference in the risk involved

2. Inaccurate growth rate estimates. Possibly the firm with the higher p/e ratio is expected to grow at a higher rate in the future than it did in the past. It is important to consider the growth rate figures employed and whether any changes in the rate are expected.

3. An undervaluation of a stock with a low p/e ratio relative to its growth rate. (Before this is accepted, the first two alternatives should be considered.)

4. An overvaluation of a stock with a high p/e ratio and low growth rate. (Before this is accepted, consider alternative 2 above.)

The growth duration concept is valid, *given the assumptions made,* and can be useful in evaluating investments. It is by no means universally valid because it generates an answer that is only as good as the data inputs (relative growth rates) and the applicability of the assumptions. The answer must be evaluated on the basis of the analyst's knowledge. The technique is probably most useful for spotting clearly overvalued growth stocks when the multiple exceeds 50 or 60. In such a case, this technique will indicate that it is necessary for the company to continue to grow at some very high rate for an extended period of time (e.g., 25–30 years) to justify such a multiple. Also, it is very helpful in deciding between two growth companies in the same industry.

A Flexible Growth Stock Valuation Model

Several years ago, Professor James Mao developed an investment opportunities growth model that incorporated some of the previous work on growth stock valuation.[5] Mao noted that the earlier studies done by Solomon, and Miller and Modigliani had recognized the true nature of a growth firm; i.e., one that had opportunities to consistently invest funds at rates of return greater than the firm's required rate of return. However, in order to simplify the exposition, these authors assumed the existence of infinite growth horizons which do not exist in a competitive environment. Therefore, their presentations have been extremely useful in developing an understanding of valuation, but the models have not been applicable to practical problems because their assumptions concerning the growth period are unrealistic.[6] To alleviate this problem, Mao developed a three-stage model of valuation that applied the investment opportunities approach of Solomon, and Miller and Modigliani and also recognized the finite growth pattern of firms. The Mao model took into account: (1) *a dynamic growth period* during which it is assumed that the firm invests a constant percentage of current earnings in growth projects, (2) *a simple growth period* during which it is assumed that the firm invests a constant dollar amount in growth opportunities, and finally, (3) *a declining growth period* during which the amount in growth investments declines to zero. The result was a theoretically correct and realistic model, but, unfortunately, it was rather difficult to use because of the computations required. In addition, the model was somewhat rigid in its assumptions about the parameters b (the retention rate), r (the return on growth investments), and K (the required rate of return on the stock). Because of these problems, the model has not been applied as widely as one might expect. In this section we will discuss the basics of the flexible growth model more thoroughly, apply it to a growth company, and discuss the effects of varying the parameters.

---

[5] James C. T. Mao, "The Valuation of Growth Stocks: The Investment Opportunities Approach," *Journal of Finance,* Vol. 21, No. 1 (March, 1966), pp. 95–102.

[6] As noted previously, the Holt "growth duration" model assumed away other facets of the growth model and concentrated on the duration problem. Its shortcoming was that the model ignored risk differences and alternative growth patterns.

The Valuation Model

Mao assumed that the price of the stock is equal to: (1) the present value of current earnings, E, discounted to infinity at the required rate of return, K, (P = E/K) plus (2) the net present value of growth opportunities. The difference between Mao and previous authors is that he allowed for three stages of growth.

The first stage in Mao's three-stage model is a period of dynamic growth that lasts for n_1 years. During this period, it is assumed that each year the firm has opportunities to invest a given percentage of current earnings in projects that generate returns equal to r, and that r is greater than K (r > K). Since b is a constant percentage of current earnings, and current earnings are growing each year, the dollar amount invested in these growth projects is growing at an exponential rate. The value of the dynamic investments is given by:

$$(14\text{-}16) \qquad \left(\frac{r-K}{K}\right) (bE) \sum_{t=1}^{n_1} \frac{(1+br)^{t-1}}{(1+K)^t} \quad \text{(Value of dynamic growth opportunities)}$$

The second stage is a period Solomon referred to as simple growth that lasts for n_2 years. During this period, it is assumed that the firm still has opportunities to invest in growth projects (r > K), but the amount to be invested in these growth projects is a *constant dollar amount* (bE). The value of these projects is given by:

$$(14\text{-}17) \qquad \left(\frac{r-K}{K}\right) (bE) \sum_{t=1}^{n_2} \frac{1}{(1+K)^t} \quad \text{(Value of simple growth opportunities)}$$

During the final period of declining growth (which lasts n_3 years), it is still assumed that the firm has opportunities to invest funds in growth projects, but the dollar amount that can be invested at r > K *declines* steadily from bE to zero. The amount of the decline is steady at $1/n_3$ each year. If bE equals 100,000 dollars and n_3 is 20, then the amount invested in growth projects would decline by 5,000 dollars a year. The value of this component is:

$$(14\text{-}18) \qquad \left(\frac{r-K}{K}\right) (bE) \sum_{t=1}^{n_3} \frac{(n_3 - t + 1)}{n_3 (1+K)^t} \quad \text{(Value of declining growth opportunities)}$$

The complete model is then simply a combination of the no growth component (E/K) plus the three growth factors. If A stands for the final summation term in Equation (14–16), B stands for the summation in Equation (14–17), and C stands for the summation term in Equation (14–18), this formulation can be written as follows:

$$(14\text{-}19) \quad P = \frac{E}{K} + \left(\frac{r - K}{K}\right) (bE) \left[A + \frac{(1 + br)^{n_1 - 1}}{(1 + K)^{n_1}} B + \frac{(1 + br)^{n_1 - 1}}{(1 + K)^{n_1 + n_2}} C \right]$$

Mao provided some tables that contained limited values for A and C (B is the present value of an annuity). Even with the tables and no change in the parameters, the computation of a single value is rather tedious.

Flexible Parameters

In the Mao model, it is assumed that, irrespective of the firm's stage of growth, there is no change in the required rate of return (K); the firm always gets the same rate of return on growth projects (r); and it always retains the same percentage of earnings (b) during different periods of growth. The assumption of constant parameters was probably made to avoid complicating a technique that already involved fairly extensive computations. Also, many analysts may agree with these assumptions. However, there is some work which indicates that investors probably change their required return (K) on stocks during different phases of the firm's life cycle. Malkiel has shown that it is logical to require a higher return on high growth stocks because the stream of returns is such that they are inherently longer duration securities.[7] At the other end of the spectrum, a firm, during its declining years, may be more subject to cyclical variations that would indicate more business risk and, therefore, would bring about an increase in the required rate of return.

Regarding the return on investments (r), it could be considered rather optimistic to assume that, during the period of simple growth, the firm can continue to earn very high rates even on a stable dollar amount. Many analysts would probably prefer to use a large n_2 and assume a somewhat smaller r.

Finally, is it realistic to assume that a firm will retain the same percentage of earnings (b) over its life cycle? It seems more logical to expect a high retention rate during the early years when opportunities for growth investment are abundant and capital is scarce, and a low rate during the later years when growth investment opportunities are limited, the level of earnings is high, and outside capital is available.

In any case, the model should be more useful if flexibility is possible in these parameters. For the analyst not interested in changing them, it is possible to simply repeat the original values.

Application of the Model

Mao applied the investment opportunities technique to a valuation of the Polaroid Corporation using several tables to aid in determining the

---

[7] Burton G. Malkiel, "Equity Yields, Growth, and the Structure of Share Prices," *American Economic Review*, Vol. 53, No. 5 (December, 1963), pp. 1004–1031.

dynamic growth value and declining growth value. The simple growth value was derived using a standard annuity table. Given a computer program, it is only necessary to prepare three computer cards for each case. Because of the ease of application, an analyst should consider several alternative sets of parameters including most pessimistic, most optimistic, most likely, and, in the case of a stock with a very high earnings multiple, determine the alternative sets of estimates that *would be required* to justify the prevailing market price.

In applying this technique to the evaluation of growth companies, the following suggestions might prove useful.

1. The earnings figure (E) is assumed to be the figure for the coming year. It can be crudely estimated as the actual earnings for the most recent year times the long-run growth rate for the past five or ten years.

2. The retention rate (b) can be estimated as the average percent of earnings retained for the last several years, assuming that this is a relatively stable decision by management.

3. The estimate of the return on investment (r) is obviously crucial. One means of deriving it is to ascertain the average return on equity during the recent period. Another is to separately estimate the two factors that should influence this ratio, the equity turnover and the profit margin, and use the product of these two estimates. Finally, Mao suggested using the return on recently retained earnings by computing the *increase* in earnings per share during some period divided by the amount of earnings retained over a comparable period with a one year lag, e.g., the increase in earnings per share for the period 1976–1981, divided by the retained earnings for the period 1975–1980. This computation attempts to estimate what the firm is currently deriving from retained earnings. The typical estimate of return on equity is current net earnings to current equity, which is an average figure that can be heavily influenced by past performance. Also, this latter method uses historical equity, which can become seriously distorted over time. The suggested estimate is current and more in the nature of a marginal return on equity.

4. The required return estimate (K) could be the actual return derived from all common stocks during some recent period or even the return from the specific stock during the recent period. Such an estimating procedure would likely suggest a rate in the range of 9–11 percent for most periods. Because all prior uses have indicated that *the model is extremely sensitive to changes in K,* it is strongly suggested that the analyst consider a full range of alternative K's from *about 6 percent to 16 percent.*

An Example

Assume the following about a firm that you consider to be a true growth company:

| Earnings: | 1980 | $2.50 |
| | 1981 (Estimated) | 2.88 ($2.50 × 1.15) |

Annual Growth Rate in EPS (1976–1980)	.15
Retention Rate (1976–1980)	.65
Average Return on Equity (1976–1980)	.24
Marginal Return on Equity (1976–1980)	.26
Estimated r for Analysis	.25

Given these estimates of the major parameters, it is possible to derive a number of stock price values by simply changing the values for the three n's (n_1, n_2, n_3) and the required returns. It is possible to change the values for each of these parameters for each growth period, but it will simplify the analysis to hold them constant at these historical values. Subsequent estimates should consider alternative parameters.

For the example, the initial estimates of the n's are relatively conservative (5, 5, 10) and are changed to more liberal estimates as follows:

(A) $n_1 = 5$, $n_2 = 5$, $n_3 = 10$

(B) $n_1 = 5$, $n_2 = 10$, $n_3 = 15$

(C) $n_1 = 10$, $n_2 = 10$, $n_3 = 15$

(D) $n_1 = 15$, $n_2 = 15$, $n_3 = 20$

The K's considered ranged from 6 percent to 16 percent in increments of 2 percent (6, 8, 10, 12, 14, 16). The results are contained in Table 14–2.

Table 14–2
Estimated Values for Stock Assuming Alternative Time Periods and Required Rates of Return (E = $2.88; b = .65; r = .25)

N_1	N_2	N_3	.06	.08	.10	.12	.14	.16
5	5	10	183.51	117.91	81.71	59.60	45.14	35.22
5	10	15	204.49	126.33	84.89	60.47	45.00	34.66
10	10	15	299.57	170.08	105.76	70.22	49.06	35.73
15	15	20	497.79	252.06	142.07	86.78	56.54	38.89

These results clearly indicate a wide range of values for the example. The function of the analyst at this point is to select the "best" estimate of the three periods and, most important, *the superior estimate of the required return for this stock* based upon its systematic risk and the expected security market line (SML). Because almost all growth companies have above average systematic risk (i.e., betas above 1.00), the required return will typically exceed the expected market return.

Assume the following estimates regarding the SML: RFR = .08; Rm = .12. Further assume that the company has a beta of 1.5. Then the estimate of required return would be:

$$Ke = RFR + B_i (Rm - RFR)$$

$$Ke = .08 + 1.5 (.12 - .08)$$

$$Ke = .14$$

This would indicate further consideration of the .14 column and possibly the adjoining columns. A comparison of these prices with the prevailing market prices will indicate whether the stock should be considered for inclusion in the portfolio.

It is also possible to draw a graph of the values for the stock for a given set of n values and different K's. If this is done for the several sets of n's, one will derive a set of curves sloping downward to the right as shown in Figure 14–1. Given this graph, there are two ways of examining the results of the model. First, compare the prevailing market price or range of recent prices to the range of computed values. Beyond expecting the prevailing price to be somewhere within the total range, one might also get an indication of relative undervaluation or overvaluation depending upon whether the current market price is toward the upper or lower end of the range. Second, examine the market price in terms of the implied rate of return. This can be done by drawing the current market price horizontally across the valuation curves. Assuming that the valuation curves generally represent the full range of feasible parameters, the intersection of the price line with the curve to the right indicates the highest K that can be expected with the most liberal parameters if you acquire the stock at the current market price. The curve to the left indicates the lowest K possible if you acquire the stock at the price indicated.

Summary

The purpose of this chapter was to demonstrate the impossibility of employing standard valuation models when analyzing true growth companies. The reason is the standard models assume constant growth for long periods of time, and true growth companies, which, by definition, are able to earn above normal profits on their investments, cannot continue to grow abnormally for indefinite periods.

The second section reviewed the full range of growth company models from negative growth to dynamic true growth. The final section discussed two models that should be of help in the valuation of growth companies. The growth duration model should assist the analyst in concentrating on the major question of concern with true growth companies: how long will this superior growth last?

A flexible model by Mao concentrates on the relevant variables that affect growth. The three stage model was presented and explained. Use of the

Figure 14–1
**Plot of Values For
Flexible Growth
Model**

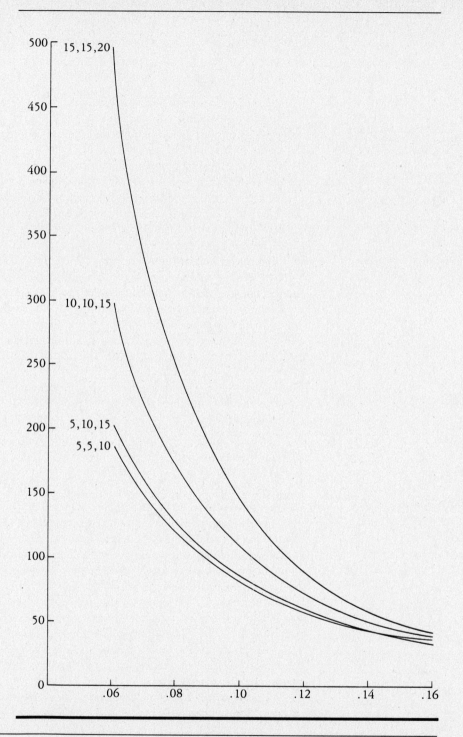

model was demonstrated with an example and it was shown that there are several uses for the set of values derived from the model.

Because of the potential rewards possible from the analysis of growth companies, one should expect strong competition in the valuation process. The models discussed in this chapter and the techniques presented should give the analyst an edge. As always, although models can help deriving a value for a firm, *it is the estimated inputs that are crucial.* The superior analyst will be the one who consistently derives the best estimates.

Questions

1. What are the basic assumptions of the dividend growth model?

2. What is the definition of a true growth company? Be very specific.

3. You are told that a company retains 80 percent of its earnings and its earnings are growing at a rate of about 8 percent a year versus an average of 6 percent for all firms. Is this a growth company?

4. It is contended by some that, in a true competitive economy, there would never be a true growth company. Discuss the line of reasoning behind such a contention.

5. Why is it not feasible to use the dividend growth model in the valuation of true growth companies?

6. Assume a firm has an expected dividend of 2.00 dollars a share, a required return of .10, and a growth rate of .08. What is its value? What is the value if the required return is only .07? Show all computations and discuss your results.

7. What are the major assumptions of the growth duration model? Discuss each of them and why they could present a problem.

8. You are told that a growth company has a p/e of 10 times and a growth rate of 15 percent compared to the market growth rate of 10 percent. The market has a p/e of 11 times. What does this imply regarding the growth company? What else do you need to know to properly compare the growth company to the aggregate market?

9. Define the following:
   A. a negative growth company
   B. an expanding company
   C. a simple growth company
   D. a dynamic growth company

10. Of those listed in Question 9 which label would you give IBM? Why?

11. What label would you give U.S. Steel? Why?

12. When using the flexible growth valuation model, what are the most important variables that must be estimated?

References

Benishay, Haskel. "Variability in Earnings—Price Ratios of Corporate Equities." *American Economic Review,* Vol. 51, No. 1 (March, 1961).

Bernstein, Peter L. "Growth Companies vs. Growth Stocks." *Harvard Business Review,* Vol. 34, No. 5 (September–October, 1956).

Brigham, Eugene F. and Pappas, James L. "Duration of Growth, Change in Growth Rates, and Corporate Share Prices." *Financial Analysts Journal,* Vol. 22, No. 3 (May–June, 1966).

Durand, David. "Growth Stocks and the Petersburg Paradox." *Journal of Finance,* Vol. 12, No. 3 (September, 1957).

Holt, Charles C. "The Influence of Growth Duration on Share Prices." *Journal of Finance,* Vol. 17, No. 3 (September, 1962).

Malkiel, Burton. "Equity Yields, Growth, and the Structure of Share Prices." *American Economic Review,* Vol. 53, No. 5 (December, 1963).

Malkiel, Burton G. and Cragg, John G. "Expectations and the Structure of Share Prices." *American Economic Review,* Vol. 60, No. 4 (September, 1970).

Mao, James C. T. "The Valuation of Growth Stocks: The Investments Opportunity Approach." *Journal of Finance,* Vol. 21, No. 1 (March, 1966).

Miller, Merton and Modigliani, Franco. "Dividend Policy, Growth, and the Valuation of Shares." *Journal of Business,* Vol. 34, No. 4 (October, 1966).

Molodovsky, Nicholas, May, C., and Chottiner, S. "Common Stock Valuation: Theory and Tables." *Financial Analysts Journal,* Vol. 20, No. 2 (March–April, 1965).

Nerlove, Marc. "Factors Affecting Differences Among Rates of Return on Investments in Individual Common Stocks." *Review of Economics and Statistics,* Vol. 50, No. 3 (August, 1968).

Niederhoffer, Victor and Regan, Patrick J. "Earnings Changes, Analysts Forecasts, and Stock Prices." *Financial Analysts Journal,* Vol. 28, No. 3 (May–June, 1972).

Reilly, Frank K. "Differentiation Between Types of Companies and Types of Stocks." *Mississippi Valley Journal of Business and Economics,* Vol. 7, No. 1 (Fall, 1971).

Soldofsky, Robert M. and Murphy, James T. *Growth Yield on Common Stocks: Theory and Tables* (revised ed.). Iowa City: State University of Iowa, Bureau of Business and Economics Research, 1964.

Solomon, Ezra. *The Theory of Financial Management.* New York: Columbia University Press, 1963.

Wendt, Paul F. "Current Growth Stock Valuation Methods." *Financial Analysts Journal,* Vol. 21, No. 2 (March–April, 1965).

Chapter 15   *Technical Analysis*

"The market reacted yesterday to the report of a large increase in the short interest on the NYSE."

"Although the market declined today it was not considered bearish because there was very light volume."

"The market declined today after three days of increases due to profit taking by investors."

These and similar statements appear almost daily in the financial news as commentators attempt to explain stock market changes. All of these statements have as their rationale one of numerous technical trading rules. The purpose of this chapter is to explain the reasoning behind technical analysis and discuss many of the trading rules.

Prior to the development of the efficient market theory, investors were generally divided into two groups—"fundamentalists" and "technicians". Fundamental analysts contend that the price of a security is determined by basic underlying economic factors such as expected return and risk considerations. To arrive at estimates of these return and risk expectations for a security, an analyst should examine the underlying factors from the economy, to the industry, and then to the company. After extensive analysis, the analyst derives an estimate of the "intrinsic value" of the security, which is then compared to its market price. If the "value" exceeds the market price, the security should be acquired and vice versa. The fundamentalist attempts to derive value and compare it to market price and acts based upon the implicit assumption that the market price for the security should approach the "intrinsic value" in the future.

Technicians contend that it is *not* necessary to study economic fundamentals in order to know where the price of a security is going because past price movements will indicate future price movements. In the first section of this chapter, we will examine the basic philosophy underlying all technical approaches to market analysis and the assumptions of these approaches. The next section contains a discussion of the supposed advantages of the technical approach and some problems in this area of analysis. The remaining sections discuss alternative technical trading rules.

Basic Philosophy and Assumptions of Technical Analysis

The basic philosophy and assumptions of technical analysis are well summarized in an article by Robert A. Levy:

1. Market value is determined solely by the interaction of supply and demand.

2. Supply and demand are governed by numerous factors, both rational and irrational. Included in these factors are those relied upon by the fundamentalist, as well as opinions, moods, guesses, and blind necessities. The market weighs all of these factors continually and automatically.

3. Disregarding minor fluctuations in the market, *stock prices tend to move in trends which persist for an appreciable length of time.* (Emphasis added.)

4. Changes in trend are caused by the shifts in supply and demand relationships. These shifts, no matter why they occur, *can be detected sooner or later in the action of the market itself.*[1] (Emphasis added.)

The emphasis is added to highlight those aspects of the technical approach that differ from the belief of fundamentalists and advocates of an efficient market. The two initial statements are almost universally accepted by technicians and nontechnicians alike. Almost anyone who has had a basic course in economics would agree that, at any point in time, the price of a security (or any good or service) should be determined by the interaction of supply and demand. In addition, most observers would acknowledge that supply and demand are governed by a multitude of variables. The only difference might be that some observers would expect the irrational factors to be rather transitory and that, therefore, the rational factors would prevail in the long-run. Finally, everyone would expect the market to weigh and evaluate these factors continuously.

A difference of opinion begins to become apparent in the third statement because it implies something about the *speed of adjustment* of stock prices to changes in supply and demand factors. *Technicians expect stock prices to move in trends which persist for long periods.* This is based upon a belief that new information causing a change in the relationship between supply and demand does *not* come to the market at one point in time, but comes over a period of time because there are alternative sources of information or

[1] Robert A. Levy, "Conceptual Foundations of Technical Analysis," *Financial Analysts Journal,* Vol. 22, No. 4 (July–August, 1966), p. 83.

because certain investors receive the information earlier than others and analyze the effect before others do. As various groups ("insiders", well-informed professionals, the "average" investor) receive the information and invest or disinvest accordingly, the price is *partially* adjusted toward the new equilibrium. Therefore, the price adjustment is *not* abrupt because there is a gradual flow of information from insiders, to high powered analysts, and eventually to the mass of investors. As a result, the pattern of price adjustment involves a *gradual* movement to the new equilibrium price. The following graph shows what technicians contend happens when new information causing a decrease in the equilibrium price for a security begins to enter the market.

Figure 15–1 **Technicians' View of Price Adjustment to New Information**

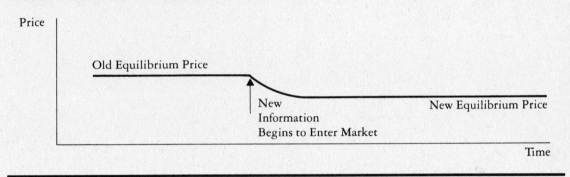

The price adjusts, but the implied adjustment is not very rapid. Therefore, *during the adjustment period,* prices tend to move in one direction (i.e., in a trend) that persists until the stock reaches its new equilibrium. Given this gradual adjustment in price, the point made in the fourth statement follows: *when the change occurs the shift to a new equilibrium can be detected in the market itself.* Therefore, the task of the technical analyst is to derive a system that allows him to detect the *beginning* of a movement from one equilibrium value to a higher or lower equilibrium value in a stock (or in the aggregate market). Technical analysts are not concerned with why the change in equilibrium value occurred, but only with the fact that there is a definite movement and that they can take advantage of this change in equilibrium value to derive above average returns. Technicians emphasize *detecting the start of a change* in the supply-demand relationship. The idea is to get on the bandwagon early and benefit from the ride to a new equilibrium. If the adjustment process was very rapid, the ride would be very short and not worth the effort; i.e., the ride would be over before you could get on the bandwagon.

Advantages of Technical Analysis

Most technical analysts would probably admit that a fundamental analyst with good information and good analytical ability should be able to do better than a technician, but that is a qualified statement. If the analyst can get the new information before other investors can, and if he has the ability to process it correctly and quickly, then he should be able to derive returns above what a technical analyst can expect, because the technician must wait until the movement is underway and so he misses part of the potential return. However, *technical analysts do not believe that it is possible to consistently get good information and process it quickly.* Therefore, our discussion of the advantages of technical analysis will be basically concerned with the limitations of fundamental analysis.

A major advantage claimed for technical analysis is that it is not heavily dependent on financial accounting statements, which are a major source of information about the past performance of a firm or industry. The fundamentalist uses them to evaluate past performance and thereby to project future returns and risk characteristics. The technician is quick to point out several major problems with published financial statements.

1. They do not contain a great deal of the information that is desired by analysts, such as details on sales and general expenses and sales and earnings by product line and customers.

2. There are several ways of reporting expenses, assets, or liabilities that can give vastly different results and all of them are equally acceptable for accounting purposes. As a result, it is difficult to compare two firms in the same industry, much less firms in different industries.

3. Many psychological factors and other nonquantitative variables are not included in the statements. Examples would include employee training and loyalty and customer goodwill.

Technicians are somewhat suspicious of financial statements and consider it an advantage that they generally are not dependent upon them. As our later discussion will show, most of the data used by technicians is derived from the stock market itself.

Once a fundamental analyst has some new information, it is necessary to process this data *correctly* and *very quickly* in order to derive a new value before the competition can. The technician asks how many analysts can do this consistently and remain ahead of the competition. Technicians contend that they do not have to be the first to see the impact, but only be quick to recognize a movement to a new equilibrium *for whatever reason.*

Finally, assume an analyst has determined that a given security is under or overvalued much before the competition has. This can present the problem of determining *when* to make the purchase or sale. Ideally, an investor would like to buy or sell a stock just before the change in market value occurs. Because a technician doesn't invest until the move to the new equilibrium is under way, he is not likely to purchase a stock that must be held for a long period of time before it is revalued.

Disadvantages of Technical Analysis

The major problem with technical analysis stems from the efficient market hypothesis. The problems considered here are in addition to this.

An obvious problem is that the past price patterns may not be repeated in the future. Also, many price patterns may become self-fulfilling prophecies because everyone believes in them. Assume that a stock is selling at 40 dollars a share and it is widely recognized that, if it "breaks out" of a trading channel at 45 dollars, it will be expected to go to 50 dollars or more. If it does get to 45 dollars, a number of technicians will buy and the price will probably go to 50 dollars, which is exactly what was predicted. In fact, some technicians may place a stop buy order at such a "break out" point.

Also, the success of a trading rule will encourage competition which will eventually neutralize the value of the technique. If a large number of investors are using a rule, some of them will eventually attempt to anticipate what will happen and either ruin the "expected" price pattern or take the profits away from most users of the rule. If it becomes known that some technicians who have been investing on the basis of odd lot data have also been enjoying very high rates of return, other technicians will start using these data and affect the stock price pattern following odd lot changes so that the rule that worked previously may no longer work, or will only work for the first few investors who react.

Finally, as will be discussed later, all of the rules or techniques imply a great deal of subjective judgement. In some cases, two technical analysts looking at the same price pattern will arrive at widely different interpretations and investment decisions.

Technical Trading Rules

There are numerous technical rules and a larger number of interpretations for each of them. Most technical analysts use more than one rule and some watch many alternatives. This section contains a discussion of most of the well-known techniques, but certainly does not attempt to be all-inclusive.

Contrary Opinion Rules

One set of technical trading rules contends that the majority of investors are wrong most of the time, or at least they are wrong at peaks and troughs. Therefore, the idea is to determine when the majority is either very bullish or very bearish and trade in the opposite direction.

The Odd Lot Theory contends that the small investor is almost always wrong, especially at the peaks and troughs. To determine what the small investor is doing one should watch the odd lot transactions reported daily in the financial press. In contrast to other trading reports, the figures on odd lots indicate how many shares were purchased and how many were sold, and the two figures obviously do not have to match. Using these figures, technicians develop a ratio of purchases to sales and examine the trend of this ratio, trading when it becomes very bullish or bearish. Historically, the purchase to sales ratio has fluctuated between .60 (very strong sales ratio) to about 1.35 (high proportion of purchases). During the week ended April 28, 1978, odd lot purchases totalled 1,168,000 shares, while odd lot sales were 2,268,000 indicating a purchase/sales ratio of .51. These figures indicate a relatively bullish market (i.e., the very bearish actions of the odd lot trader would be bullish to a believer in contrary opinion). A major problem with this ratio is that individual investors have been net sellers of common stocks (i.e., selling more than they buy) since the late 1960's so the ratio is biased down by this trend effect.

The Odd Lot Short Sales Theory is an extension of the general odd lot theory. The use of short sales is generally considered bearish because it is based upon an expectation of declining stock prices. It is also considered to be a fairly high risk form of investing. Most small investors are optimists and would consider short selling too risky. Therefore, they do not get involved in it except when they feel especially bearish. Hence, the technical rule is to consider a relatively high rate of odd lot short sales as an indication of a very bearish attitude by small investors. Again, contrary opinion would consider this high short sale ratio bullish because the small investor is expected to be wrong at the extremes, in this case at the trough.

Mutual Fund Cash Position is considered a contrary tool by some technical analysts. Mutual funds report the ratio of cash (as a percent of total assets) in their portfolio over time and this ratio typically varies from a low point of less than 5 percent to a high point in excess of 15 percent. The contrary opinion technicians consider the mutual funds the odd lotters of the institutional investor group and contend that mutual funds are usually wrong at the peaks and troughs. They expect mutual funds to have heavy cash positions (a high ratio of cash) near the trough of a market cycle indicating they are very bearish exactly at the time that they should be fully invested to take advantage of the impending market rise. At the peak, they expect mutual funds to be almost fully invested (a low ratio of cash) indicating a bullish outlook at a point where they should have liquidated part of their portfolio. Therefore, these technicians watch for the mutual fund cash position to be at one of the extremes and act contrary to mutual funds behavior; i.e., invest when the cash ratio exceeds 12–13 percent and sell when the cash ratio approaches 5 percent.

Heavy mutual fund cash positions are also considered bullish because they are potential buying power. Whether the cash balances have built up because of the previous sale of stocks in the portfolio, or because of purchases of the fund by investors, technicians feel these funds will eventually be invested and cause an increase in stock prices.

Credit Balances result when investors sell stocks and leave the proceeds with their broker because they expect to reinvest it shortly. These credit balances are reported by the SEC. A high level of credit balances is subject to two interpretations. On the one hand, these funds are considered to be a pool of potential purchasing power which is bullish. On the other, some contrary opinion technicians note that these balances are maintained by small investors and usually increase just before market peaks because of the enthusiasm of this group which is typically wrong.

Follow the Smart Money

An alternative set of rules for technical analysts attempts to determine what smart, sophisticated investors are doing and follow them.

The Confidence Index, published by *Barron's,* is the ratio of Barron's average yield on 10 top grade corporate bonds to the yield on the Dow-Jones average of 40 bonds,[2] indicating the difference in yield spread between high-grade bonds and a large sample of bonds. One would expect the yield on high-grade bonds to be lower than that on a large cross-section of bonds, so the ratio would be below 100 and should never exceed 100.

The theory behind the ratio is that, during periods of high confidence, investors invest more in lower quality bonds for the added yield. This increased demand for lower quality bonds should cause a decrease in the yield on a large cross-section of bonds relative to the yield on high-grade bonds. Therefore, the ratio of yields will increase (the Confidence Index increases). When investors are pessimistic, they avoid the low quality bonds and increase their investments in high-grade bonds, which increases the yield differential between the two groups and the Confidence Index declines.

A major problem with the concept has been that it is basically demand oriented. It assumes that changes in the yield spread are almost wholly caused by changes in investor demand for different quality bonds. There have been several instances in which the yield differences have changed because of an increased *supply* of bonds in one of the groups or in a related group (e.g., government bonds). A large issue of high-grade AT&T bonds could cause a temporary increase in yields on all high-grade bonds which would cause an increase in the Confidence Index although investors' attitudes did not change. In other words, the change was supply oriented. Under such conditions, the series gives a false signal of a change in confidence. Advocates of the index feel that it can be used as an indicator of

---

[2] Historical data for this series is contained in Maurice L. Farrell, ed., *The Dow-Jones Investor's Handbook* (Princeton, N. J.: Dow-Jones Books, 1978).

future stock price movements although one may ask why investors in bonds would change their attitude before equity investors do. Several studies that have examined its usefulness for predicting stock price movements have not been very supportive regarding the predictive ability of the series.

Short Sales by Specialists are regularly reported by the NYSE and the SEC. It will come as no surprise that technicians who want to follow the smart money attempt to determine what the specialist is doing and act accordingly. Specialists regularly engage in short-selling as a part of their market-making function, but they also have some discretion when they feel strongly about major changes. The "normal" ratio of specialists short sales to the total amount of short sales on the exchange is about 55 percent. When this ratio declines much *below 40 percent* it is considered a sign that specialists are generally *bullish* and are attempting to avoid short-selling. When the ratio *exceeds 65 percent,* it is contended that specialists are generally *bearish* and are attempting to do as much short selling as possible. During the week of April 14, 1978, this ratio was 5,400,000/13,832,300 or .39 which would be considered somewhat bullish. Two points should be noted regarding this ratio. First, do not expect it to be a long-run indicator; given the nature the specialists' portfolio, it will probably serve only in the short-run. Second, there is a two week lag in the reporting of this data. The data for the week ending April 14, 1978 was contained in *Barron's* dated May 1, 1978. Even with the lags, an analysis of the graph for the ratio indicates that an investor could have made timely purchase decisions on the basis of the extreme values.

Debit Balances in Brokerage Accounts are considered indicative of the attitude of a sophisticated group of investors because debit balances represent borrowing by individuals from their brokers, i.e., margin purchases. Margin buying is typically done only by sophisticated traders and, therefore, an increase in these balances indicates an increase in purchasing by this group and would be a bullish sign. There can be problems in using this series because it does not include borrowing from other sources (banks, etc.).

Other Techniques

There are several other general techniques available.

Breadth of Market is a measure of the number of issues that have increased each day and the number of issues that have declined. Everyone is aware of the direction of change in composite market indicator series like the DJIA or the S&P 400 Index, but they may not be aware of what caused the change. Most of the popular stock market indicator series are either confined to large popular stocks or are heavily influenced by the stocks of large firms because most indicator series are value-weighted. On occasion the composite series may go up, but the majority of individual issues are not increasing, which is cause for concern. Such a situation can be detected by examining the advance-decline figures along with the composite series.

The advance-decline series is a cumulative series of net advances or net declines. Each day major newspapers publish figures on the number of issues on the NYSE that advanced, the number that declined, and the number that were unchanged. The figures for a five day sample, as reported in *Barron's,* were as follows:

Table 15–1
Daily Advances and Declines on NYSE

Day	1	2	3	4	5
Issues Traded	1,908	1,941	1,959	1,951	1,912
Advances	1,110	1,050	708	1,061	1,125
Declines	409	450	749	433	394
Unchanged	389	441	502	457	393
Changes in DJIA	+10.47	+3.99	−5.15	+4.16	+5.56

Source: Reprinted by permission of the New York Stock Exchange.

One derives a net figure by subtracting declines from advances. The figures for the sample week would be:

$$+701 \qquad +600 \qquad -41 \qquad +628 \qquad +731$$

The cumulative series would be:

$$+1,301 \qquad +1,260 \qquad +1,888 \qquad +2,619$$

These figures, along with the market indicator figures at the bottom of the table, indicate a strong market advance. Not only was the DJIA increasing, but there was a strong net advance figure which indicates that the increase was broadly based, i.e., most individual stocks were increasing. Even the results on Day 3, when the market declined 5 points, were somewhat encouraging because there was a very small net decline figure of 41. The market average was down, but individual stocks were split just about 50-50.

The usefulness of the advance-decline series is supposedly greatest at market peaks and troughs because, at such times, the composite value-weighted average would be moving either up or down, but the advance or decline would *not* be broadly based and the majority of individual stocks might be moving in the opposite direction. Near a peak, the DJIA would be increasing but the net advance-decline ratio would become negative and the cumulative series would begin to decline. The *divergence* between the aggregate series and the cumulative advance-decline series is a signal for a market peak. At the trough, the composite series would be declining, but the advance-decline ratio would become positive and the cumulative series would turn up before the aggregate market series did.

The principle behind the advance-decline ratio is somewhat akin to the notion of a diffusion index used by the National Bureau of Economic Research. A diffusion index for a given economic series, such as new orders for durable goods, indicates how many of the reporting units show an increase in new orders; i.e., a diffusion index of 60 means 60 percent of the sample report an increase in new orders. During a period of rapid expansion, the diffusion index would be high and the composite series would be increasing rapidly. Near the peak of an economic expansion, the diffusion index would turn down (e.g., from 90 to 70), but the composite would continue to increase. Therefore, the diffusion index turns *before* the composite.

Short Interest is the ratio between the number of shares sold short and not covered and average daily volume on the exchange. The interpretation of this ratio by technicians is probably contrary to your initial intuition. Because short sales are made by investors who expect prices to decline, one would expect an increase in the ratio would be bearish. On the contrary, technicians consider a high short interest ratio *bullish,* indicating *potential demand* for stock by those who sold short because they will have to buy the stock in the future to cover their outstanding short position. The ratio has generally fluctuated between 1.00 and 1.75 (i.e., a ratio of 1.00 means that the outstanding short interest on the NYSE is equal to about one day's trading volume). The short interest position is calculated as of the twentieth of each month and reported about two days later in the *Wall Street Journal.* The short interest for the month ended May 20, 1978 was 42,868,973 shares. At that point in time, average daily volume on the NYSE was about 32 million shares, indicating a ratio of about 1.34 which would be about in the middle of the long-run range.

The results for a number of studies on the usefulness of the series as a predictor of stock price movements have been extremely mixed. For every study that supported the technique, another indicated that it should be rejected.[3]

Stock Price and Volume Techniques

Most technicians also use trading rules for the market and individual stocks that are based upon stock price and volume movements. Technicians believe

---

[3] Barton M. Biggs, "The Short Interest—A False Proverb," *Financial Analysts Journal,* Vol. 22, No. 4 (July–August, 1966), pp. 111–116. Joseph J. Seneca, "Short Interest: Bearish or Bullish?" *Journal of Finance,* Vol. 22, No. 1 (March, 1967), pp. 67–70. Thomas H. Mayor, "Short Trading Activities and the Price of Equities: Some Simulation and Regression Results," *Journal of Financial and Quantitative Analysis,* Vol. 3, No. 3 (September, 1968), pp. 283–298. Randall Smith, "Short Interest and Stock Market Prices," *Financial Analysts Journal,* Vol. 24, No. 6 (November–December, 1968), pp. 151–154. Thomas J. Kerrigan, "The Short Interest Ratio and Its Component Parts," *Financial Analysts Journal,* Vol. 32, No. 6 (November–December, 1974), pp. 45–49. William Goff, "Letter to the Editor," *Financial Analysts Journals,* (March–April, 1975), pp. 8–10.

that prices move in trends that persist so it is therefore possible to determine future price trends from an astute analysis of past price and volume trends. Technicians contend that *price alone is somewhat inadequate* and investors should *also examine the volume* of trading that accompanies price changes.

The Dow Theory

Any discussion of technical analysis using price and volume must begin with a consideration of the Dow Theory developed by Charles Dow, publisher of the *Wall Street Journal* during the late 1800's. Dow contended that stock prices moved in trends that were analogous to the movement of water. There were three types that should be analyzed over time: (1) major trends that are like tides in the ocean, (2) intermediate trends that are similar to waves, and (3) short-run movements that are like ripples. The idea is to detect which way the major trend (tide) is going, recognizing that there will be intermediate movements in the opposite direction. An increase does not go straight up, but is accompanied by small price declines as some investors decide to take profits. The typical bullish pattern will be as follows:

Figure 15–2
An Example of a Bullish Price Pattern

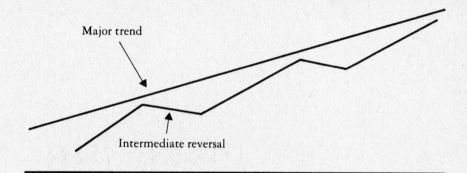

The technicians would look for each recovery to reach a high point above the prior peak with heavy trading volume, while each reversal should have a trough above the prior trough and volume should be relatively light during the reversals. When this no longer happens, the major trend (tide) may be ready for a permanent reversal.

Support and Resistance Levels

A *support level* is the price range at which the analyst would expect a considerable increase in the demand for a stock. Generally, a support level will develop after the price has increased and the stock has begun to experience a reversal because of profit-taking. At some price there are other investors who did not buy during the first rally and have been waiting for a small reversal to get into the stock. When the price reaches the point at which they want to buy, there is an increase in demand and the price begins to increase again.

A *resistance level* is the price range at which the analyst would expect the supply of stock to increase substantially and any price rise to be abruptly reversed. A resistance level tends to develop after a stock has experienced a steady decline from a higher price level. Because of the decline, investors who acquired the stock at a higher price are waiting for an opportunity to sell it and get out at about the break-even point. Therefore, this supply of stock is overhanging the market and, when the price rebounds to the target price set by these investors, the supply increases dramatically and the price trend is reversed.

Importance of Volume

Technicians are clearly not only concerned with price movements, but also watch volume changes as an indicator of changes in supply and demand for a stock or for stocks in general. A price movement in one direction indicates that the *net* effect is in that direction, but does not say anything about how *widespread* the excess demand or supply is at that time. A price increase of a half point on volume of 1,000 shares indicates excess demand, but not much overall interest. In contrast, a one point increase on volume of 20,000 shares indicates a large demand. Therefore, it is not only a price increase, but also heavy volume relative to the stock's normal trading volume that interests the technician. Following the same line of reasoning, a price decline with heavy volume is very bearish because it means strong and widespread desire to sell the stock. A generally bullish pattern is a price increase on heavy volume and a price reversal with light trading volume indicating only limited desire to sell and take profits.

Moving Average Line

Technicians are constantly looking for ways of detecting changes in major price trends for an individual stock or for the aggregate market. One relatively popular tool is constructing a moving average of past stock prices as an indicator of the long-run trend and examining current prices in terms of this trend to see whether they signal a change. The number of days used in computing the moving average is a matter of judgement but *a 200 day moving average* is a relatively popular measure for the aggregate market. If the overall trend has been down, the moving average line would generally be above the individual prices. If prices reverse and break through the moving average line from below on heavy volume, one might speculate that the declining trend had been reversed. In contrast, given a rising trend, the moving average line would be rising and would be below the current prices. If current prices broke through the moving average line from above on heavy volume, this would be a bearish indication of a reversal of the long-run rising trend.

Relative Strength

Technicians believe that, once a trend is initiated, it will continue until some major event causes a change in direction. This is also true of *relative* performance. If a stock is outperforming the market, technicians believe it will continue to outperform the market. To detect this relative performance, technicians compute relative strength ratios for individual stocks in terms of some aggregate market series on a weekly or monthly basis. This is simply a ratio of the stock price to the value for some market series like the DJIA or the S&P 400. If the ratio increases over time, the stock is outperforming the market and it is believed that this will continue for a time. The relative strength ratios work during declining and rising markets (i.e., if the stock does not decline as much as the market does, the relative strength ratio will continue to rise). It is felt that, if the ratio holds up or increases during a bear market, the stock should do very well during the ensuing bull market. These ratios are used for industry analysis as well as for company analysis.[4]

Bar Charting

The basic chart used in technical analysis is one on which the time series of prices for specified time intervals (daily, weekly, monthly) are plotted. For a given interval, the technical analyst will plot the high and low price and connect the two points to form a bar. Typically, he will also draw a small horizontal line across it to indicate the closing price. Finally, almost all bar charts also include the volume of trading at the bottom of the chart so that the analyst can relate the price and volume movements as discussed. An example is given in Figure 15–3 which is the bar chart for the DJIA from *The Wall Street Journal* along with the volume figures for the NYSE.

The technical analyst might also include a 200 day moving average for the series and possible resistance and support levels based upon past patterns. Finally, if it is a bar chart for an individual stock, it could contain a relative strength line. Most technicians include as many price and volume series as is reasonable on one chart and attempt to arrive at a consensus concerning future movement for the stock based upon the performance of several technical indicators.

Point-and-Figure Charts

Another popular device used by technicians is called point-and-figure charting.[5] As is true of all other technical tools, its purpose is to detect

---

[4] For further discussion of this technique by a leading advocate, see Robert A. Levy, "Relative Strength as a Criterion for Investment Selection," *Journal of Finance,* Vol. 23, No. 5 (December, 1967), pp. 595–610; and Robert A. Levy and Spero L. Kripotos, "Sources of Relative Price Strength," *Financial Analysts Journal,* Vol. 25, No. 6 (November–December, 1969), pp. 60, 62, 64.

[5] Daniel Seligman, "The Mystique of Point-and-Figure," *Fortune* (March, 1962), pp. 113–115, ff.

Figure 15–3
A Typical Bar Chart

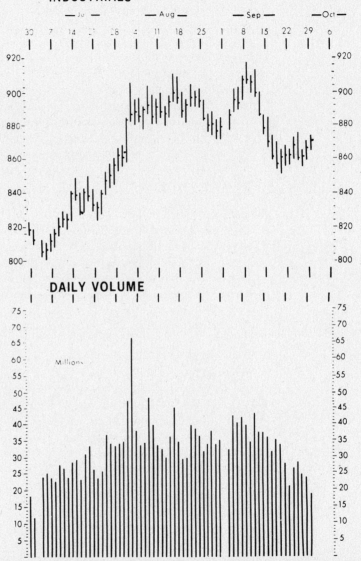

The Dow Jones Averages

INDUSTRIALS

changes in the supply and demand for a particular security. In contrast to
the bar chart that typically includes all ending prices and volume for
purposes of detecting a trend, the point-and-figure chart only includes
"significant" price changes irrespective of the time interval involved. The

analyst determines which significant price changes will be recorded (1 point, 2 points, etc.) and when a price reversal will be recorded. The following example should make this clear. Assume that you want to chart a stock that is currently selling for 40 dollars a share and it is quite volatile (beta of 1.60). Because of its volatility, you feel that anything less than a two point price change is not relevant. Also, you feel that anything less than a four point reversal is quite minor. Therefore, you would set up a chart similar to the one in Figure 15–4 that starts at 40 and progresses in two point increments. If the stock moves to 42, you place an X in that box above 40 and do nothing else until the stock rises to 44 or drops to 38 (a four point reversal from its high of 42). If it drops to 38, you move over a column to the right and begin again at 38 (fill in boxes at 42 and 40). Assume the stock price drops to 34, you enter an X at 36 and another at 34. If the stock then rises to 38 (another four point reversal), you move to the next column and begin at 38 going up (fill in 34 and 36). Assume the stock then goes to 46, you would fill in as shown and wait for further increases or a reversal.

Figure 15–4
Example of a Point-and-Figure Chart

50							
48							
46			X				
44			X				
42	X	X	X				
40	X	X	X				
38		X	X				
36		X	X				
34		X	X				
32							
30							

Depending upon how fast the prices rise and fall, this process may have taken anywhere from two to six months. Given these figures, the analyst would attempt to determine trends in the same manner as he did with the bar chart.

As always, you are looking for "break outs" to either higher or lower price levels. A long sideways movement in which you have many reversals but no major shifts in any direction would be considered a period of "consolidation" as the stock is moving from one group to another with no strong consensus of direction. Once the stock "breaks out" and moves up or down, it is assumed that this is a major move because of the previous trading that set the stage for it. The difference between point-and-figure and bar charts is that with the former you have a compact record of movements because only those price changes considered relevant for the particular stock analyzed are recorded. Therefore, it is easier to work with and to use in visualizing movements.

Summary

The purpose of this chapter was to introduce the reader to *what* technical analysts do, *why* they do it, and *how* they do it. Our initial discussion considered the basic rationale behind technical analysis and how it differed from the practices of those who believe in an efficient stock market. The main differences relate to the information dissemination process (does everybody get the information at about the same time) and to how quickly investors adjust stock prices to reflect this new information. Because technical analysts believe that the information dissemination process is not the same for everyone, and that price adjustment is not instantaneous, they contend that *stock prices move in trends that persist* and, therefore, that one can determine future price trends.

This was followed by a discussion of the advantages and disadvantages of technical analysis. The rest of the chapter discussed specific technical trading rules under four general categories: contrary opinion rules, follow the smart money, other trading rules, and stock price and volume techniques. It was noted that most technicians use several rules at any one point in time and attempt to derive a consensus decision which can be buy, sell, or do nothing. According to many technicians, their conclusion on many occasions is to do nothing.

Questions

1. The basic belief of technical analysts is that it is possible to use past price changes to predict future price changes. What is the principal contention that makes this basic belief possible?

2. Technicians contend that stock prices move in trends that persist for a long time. What is there about the real world that causes those trends? Put another way, what do technicians believe happens in the real world that would cause stock prices to move in trends?

3. Briefly discuss the problems involved with fundamental analysis that are considered to be advantages for technical analysis.

4. What are some of the disadvantages of technical analysis?

5. The odd lot purchase/sales ratio reaches 1.40. What would this indicate to a technician who believed in the notion of contrary opinion? What is the reasoning behind this belief?

6. The mutual fund cash position increases to 13 percent; is this bullish or bearish? Why? Give two reasons for your position.

7. Define the Confidence Index and describe the reasoning behind it. Discuss why the fact that the Confidence Index is demand oriented is a problem.

8. The ratio of specialists' short sales to total short sales increases to 70 percent. As a technician would you consider this bullish or bearish and

why? How would you feel if there was an increase in odd lot short sales? Why?

9. Why is an increase in debit balances considered bullish? What problems are involved with using this series as a technical tool?

10. Describe the Dow tide theory and its three components. Which component is most important?

11. Why is volume important to a technician? Describe a bearish price and volume pattern and discuss why it is bearish.

12. Describe the computation of the breadth index and discuss how it is used to confirm an important peak in stock prices.

13. Describe a support and a resistance level and explain why they are expected to occur.

14. What is the purpose of computing a moving average line for a stock? Describe a bullish pattern using a moving average line and discuss why it is considered bullish.

15. How would you construct a relative strength series for a stock? What do you mean when you say a stock had good relative strength during a bear market?

16. Select a stock on the NYSE and construct a daily high, low, close bar chart for the stock that includes volume for ten trading days.

17. Compute the relative strength ratio for the stock in Question 16 relative to the S&P 500 Index and prepare a table that includes all the data and indicates the computations as follows:

Day	Closing Price		Stock Price/S&P 500
	Stock	S&P 500	

18. Plot the relative strength ratio computed in Question 17 on your bar chart and discuss whether the stock's relative strength is bullish or bearish.

19. Construct a one point interval point-and-figure chart and use a two point reversal rule for a stock selling at 25 dollars a share. Fill in the chart for the following closing prices: 24; 22; 21; 24; 26; 28; 29; 27; 24; 22; 20; 19.

References

Branch, Ben. "The Predictive Power of Stock Market Indicators." *Journal of Financial and Quantitative Analysis,*" Vol. 11, No. 2 (June, 1976).

Crouch, Robert L. "Market Volume and Price Changes." *Financial Analysts Journal,* Vol. 26, No. 4 (July–August, 1970).

Dines, James. *How the Average Investor Can Use Technical Analysis for Stock Profits.* New York: Dines Chart Corporation, 1974.

Drew, Garfield A. *New Methods for Profit in the Stock Market,* 4th edition. Wells, Vermont: Fraser Publishing Co., 1966.

Drew, Garfield A. "A Clarification of the Odd Lot Theory." *Financial Analysts Journal,* Vol. 23, No. 5 (September–October, 1967).

Edwards, R. D. and Magee, John, Jr. *Technical Analysis of Stock Trends.* Springfield, Massachusetts: Stock Trend Service, 1966.

Ehrbar, A. F. "Technical Analysts Refuse to Die." *Fortune* (August, 1975).

Encyclopedia of Stock Market Techniques. Larchmont, New York: Investor's Intelligence.

Gould, Alex and Buchsbaum, Maurice. "A Filter Approach to Stock Selection." *Financial Analysts Journal,* Vol. 25, No. 6 (November–December, 1969).

Jiler, William L. *How Charts Can Help You in the Stock Market.* New York: Commodity Research Publications Corp.

Levy, Robert A. "Conceptual Foundations of Technical Analysis." *Financial Analysts Journal,* Vol. 22, No. 2 (July–August, 1966).

Levy, Robert A. "Random Walks: Reality or Myth." *Financial Analysts Journal,* Vol. 23, No. 6 (November–December, 1967).

Levy, Robert A. "Relative Strength as a Criterion for Investment Selection." *Journal of Finance,* Vol. 22, No. 5 (December, 1967).

Levy, Robert A. and Kripotos, Spero L. "Sources of Relative Price Strength." *Financial Analysts Journal,* Vol. 25, No. 6 (November–December, 1969).

Pinches, George E. "The Random Walk Hypothesis and Technical Analysis." *Financial Analysts Journal,* Vol. 26, No. 2 (March–April, 1970).

Seligman, Daniel. "The Mystique of Point-and-Figure." *Fortune* (March, 1962).

Shaw, Alan R. "Technical Analysis," in Levine, Sumner N. (ed.) *Financial Analysts Handbook,* Vol. 1. Homewood, Illinois: Dow-Jones Irwin, Inc., 1975.

Tabell, Edmund W. and Tabell, Anthony W. "The Case for Technical Analysis." *Financial Analysts Journal,* Vol. 20, No. 2 (March–April, 1964).

Ying, Charles C. "Stock Market Prices and Volume of Sales." *Econometrica,* Vol. 34, No. 3 (July, 1966).

Part 4

Analysis and Management of Bonds

Introduction to Part Four

As an investment vehicle, bonds have undergone a cycle of popularity during the twentieth century. In the early decades, bonds were the major investment instrument. This changed during the "Roaring 20's" when the stock market became the favorite of investors who thought they could become wealthy overnight by investing in common stock purchased on large margins. This dream ended with the stock market crash in 1929. In reaction to the crash there was increased interest in bonds because of the safety involved. During the "Flying Fifties" and "Soaring Sixties" the pendulum again swung in favor of common stocks and it was generally felt that the only investors interested in bonds were those on pensions or those who did not recognize the excitement and advantages of common stock. Toward the end of this period (about 1965), even the large financial institutions drastically changed their portfolio mix toward common stocks. Finally, since the onset of significant inflation in 1966 it has become clear that common stocks have not performed very well and investors are recognizing the fact that common stocks are *not* a good hedge during periods of significant inflation. After about a decade of poor performance by common stocks and reasonably good returns from bonds, beginning in about 1975, the pendulum began swinging back rather strongly toward a renewed interest in bonds. In contrast to past periods, it is felt that the current interest is more balanced and rational and is partially attributable to the recognition that bonds contribute to a well-diversified portfolio. Also, as will be discussed in these chapters, investors realize that superior returns can be derived from a certain amount of trading in bonds.

Because of this renewed interest in bonds, the purpose of the three chapters in this section is to provide the reader with a thorough background in the attributes of bonds, which are generally discussed in Chapter 16. Chapter 17 is concerned with the valuation of bonds and considers the several factors that influence bond value and price movements. Finally, Chapter 18 discusses trading strategies that can be used by bond investors attempting to increase their returns. There is also a consideration of alternative portfolio policies that can be followed and how they are implemented.

Chapter 16   *Bond Fundamentals*

The market for fixed income securities is large and diverse, and represents an exciting and profitable outlet for investment. This chapter is primarily concerned with publicly issued, long-term, nonconvertible, straight-debt obligations of both public and private issuers. In later chapters, we will consider other fixed income securities, such as preferred stock and convertible bonds. An understanding of bonds is helpful in an efficient market because bonds and other forms of fixed income securities increase the universe of investment options necessary for diversification.[1]

In this first of three chapters dealing with bonds, we will discuss bond fundamentals including a review of some basic features of bonds, an extensive examination of the fixed income securities market structure, and a look at alternative fixed income investment vehicles. The chapter ends with a brief review of the data requirements of bond investors and the sources of such information.

Basic Features of a Bond

Essentially, bonds are the long-term, public debt of an issuer that has been marketed in a convenient and affordable denomination. They differ from other forms of debt, such as mortgages and privately placed obligations, because they have been placed in the hands of numerous public investors,

---

[1] William F. Sharpe, "Bonds Versus Stocks: Some Lessons from Capital Market Theory," *Financial Analysts Journal,* Vol. 28, No. 6 (November–December 1973), pp. 73–79.

rather than channeled directly to a single lender. Bond issues are considered fixed income securities because the debt service obligations of the issuer are fixed: the issuer agrees 1) to pay a fixed amount of periodic *interest* to the holder of record, and 2) to repay a fixed amount of *principal* at the date of maturity.

Normally, interest on bonds is paid every six months. Occasionally, however, a bond issue may carry provisions to pay interest in intervals as short as a month or as long as a year. The principal is due at maturity and represents the par value of the issue which is its denomination. The par value on most debt issues is fairly substantial, very rarely less than 1,000 dollars and often more.

Another important dimension of bonds is their term-to-maturity, or the life of issue. The public debt market is often divided into three time segments, defined in terms of an issue's original maturity. The short-term segment is devoted to instruments with maturities of one year or less, and is commonly known as the "money market." The intermediate segment involves issues with maturities in excess of one year but less than seven to ten years. These are known as "notes" and there is a particularly active market for these maturities in the government and agency sectors of the market. Finally, long-term obligations ("bonds") have maturities in excess of seven to ten years. The lives of debt obligations, however, are constantly changing as the issues progress toward maturity. Thus, "seasoned" issues (i.e., those that have been outstanding in the secondary market for any period of time) move from one maturity segment to shorter segments. Such movement is important because the price volatility of a debt obligation is affected by, among other things, the prevailing maturity of the issue. Thus, a three year obligation, other things being equal, will have less price volatility than, say, a 23 year obligation, and the fact that the three year bond was originally a 25 year bond would have absolutely no effect on its *current* price behavior.

Obligations of the Issuer

Bonds are considered fixed income securities because the interest and principal obligations of the issuer, for the most part, do not vary over the life of the issue.

Beyond simply meeting principal and interest payments, the issuer must also live up to the terms of the indenture (the contract stipulating the conditions under which the bond was issued). Every public bond issue contains an indenture. Some of the popular indenture provisions are discussed later, but for now, keep in mind that, from the investor's point of view, such provisions are far more than legal technicalities! Bond provisions stipulate what the issuer can or cannot do, and these provisions can have *dramatic* effects on the yield and price behavior of an issue.

Bond Returns

Sources of return on bonds can be divided between the obvious and the not-so-obvious. It is obvious that two important sources of return to investors are the coupon income (interest) that is generated on a semiannual basis, and the return of principal at maturity. However, there is another important source of returns (or losses) that originates in the market, i.e., bond price variations and the opportunity to generate capital gains or losses from the sale or purchase of bonds. Too often, the uninformed investor thinks that, since bonds represent "fixed income obligations," the returns are also fixed. This is patently untrue! There has been substantial price fluctuation in bonds since the latter '60s, and this segment of the total return has overshadowed coupon and principal as sources of return. The most rewarding source of return on a short-term basis is price volatility and, by emphasizing price action, the more speculatively inclined investor can generate very attractive rates of return.

Bond Price Behavior

The price of a bond is determined by the coupon that the issue carries, the length of its term-to-maturity, and prevailing market interest rates. While the next chapter contains the detailed mathematics of bond price behavior, it is important at this point to gain a basic understanding of this behavior. Given the coupon and maturity of an issue, the price behavior of bonds is intimately related to the behavior of *market interest rates*. This relationship, however, is of an inverse nature, i.e., as market interest rates move up, the price of a bond moves down, and vice versa.

Because bonds are so closely tied to market interest rates, the price of an issue actually depends on its prevailing *yield*. In practice, therefore, the yield of an issue is determined *first,* and then the dollar price of the obligation is derived. The reason for this is that a wide diversity of coupons and maturities exist in the market at any point in time, and the yield-based computation serves as an effective equalizer, allowing market-makers to systematically account for variations in coupon and/or maturity in the pricing of an issue. To appreciate the complexity of trying to directly price issues with different coupons and maturities, all one has to do is quickly glance at the bond quote page of the *Wall Street Journal* or *Barron's* and observe the myriad different combinations of coupons and maturities.

Of course, bond price volatility is directly affected by the magnitude of movement in interest rates. But bond price behavior, unfortunately, is more than a simple function of interest rates, because different bonds react differently to changes in these rates. Price will vary according to the coupon and maturity of the issue, and bonds with longer maturities and/or lower coupons will respond most vigorously to a given change. Other factors likewise cause variations, including the call feature, but they are typically much less important. Even so, to the extent that they affect comparative rates of return, such factors certainly should not be ignored.

Bond Yields

Because the concept of yield is critical to the mechanics of bond pricing, it is important to differentiate among the types of yields. In the simplest sense, there are two: current yield and promised yield to maturity, or what is commonly known as "promised" yield.[2] Current yield is the amount of current income that a bond provides (annual interest) relative to its prevailing market price. It is to a bond what dividend yield is to common stocks and has very little use in the bond valuation process. Promised yield, in contrast, is very important and is the yield upon which all bond prices are based! It encompasses interest income and price appreciation (or depreciation) in the valuation process, and total cash flow received over the life of the issue. Because it entails cash flow timing, the promised yield computation is based on the present value concept. Indeed, it is the same mathematical process as *internal rate of return* considered in the study of basic corporation finance. In discussing yield, the percentage point has been broken into 100 parts with each part being called a "basis point." Thus, a basis point is 1/100th of 1 percent and is a widely used and convenient means of depicting changes in yield or yield comparisons; e.g., a decline in yield from 8.5 percent to 8.0 percent is a 50 basis point decline.

Bond Characteristics

One can characterize a bond in many different ways: each bond has intrinsic features that relate to the issue itself; there are different types of bonds, which differentiate one issue from another; and there are various indenture provisions which can affect the yield and/or price behavior.

Intrinsic Characteristics There are several features that are important in this regard: coupon, maturity, the principal value of the issue, and finally, the type of bond ownership. The coupon indicates the income that the bond investor will receive over the life (or holding period) of the issue, and is known as interest income, coupon income, or nominal yield.

The maturity of an issue specifies the date at which the bond will mature (or expire), and is referred to as term-to-maturity. Two important types of bonds can be distinguished on the basis of maturity, a term bond and a serial issue. A *term bond* has a single maturity date specified in the issue and is the most common type of corporate or government bond. A *serial obligation* is actually made up of a series of maturity dates. Thus, a single 25 year issue, for example, may possess 20 or 25 different maturity dates. Each maturity, though a subset of the total issue, is really a small bond issue in itself with a different maturity and, generally, a different coupon. Municipalities are the biggest issuers of serial bonds.

---

[2] There are actually two other types of yield which exist in either special situations or with regard to holding period returns, both of which will be discussed in subsequent chapters.

The principal or par value of the issue represents the original principal value of the obligation and is generally stated in thousand dollar increments. While 1000 dollars is a popular principal value, there are many issues with denominations that go much higher, to 25,000 dollars or more. Principal value is *not* necessarily the same as market value. It is not uncommon to find issues traded at market values that are substantially above or below their original principal value. Such price behavior is the result of a difference between the coupon of the obligation and the prevailing market rate of interest. When market rates go up, lower coupon issues decline in market value to a market value below par. If the issue carries a coupon comparable to the market rate, its market value will correspond to its original principal value.

The final intrinsic provision is whether the issue is a "bearer bond" or a "registered" issue. With the former type, which is the more common, the holder, or bearer, is the owner. The issuer keeps no account of transfers in ownership, and interest is paid by "clipping coupons" and sending them to the issuer for payment. Such payment is usually handled through local commercial banks in a routine, systematic manner. The issuers of registered bonds keep track of owners of record and, at the time of principal or interest payment, simply pay the owner of record automatically, by check.

Types of Issues As is not true with common stock, a given issuer of bonds can have many different types outstanding at a single point in time. Generally, one type of bond is differentiated from another by the type of collateral behind the issue. Bonds can be distinguished as either senior or junior securities. The former are generally thought of as "secured bonds," that is, they are backed by a legal claim on some specified property of the issuer—for example, "mortgage bonds," which are secured by real assets, and "Equipment Trust Certificates," which are popular with railroads and airlines, and indicate a senior position in the equipment of the railroad or airline.

Unsecured (junior) bonds are issues backed only by the promise of the issuer to pay interest and principal on a timely basis. There are several classes of unsecured bonds. One is a "debenture," which is simply a bond secured by the general credit of the issuer. In addition, there are "subordinated debentures" that represent a claim on income that is subordinated (or secondary) to the claim of another debenture bond. "Income issues" probably represent the most junior type. Such unsecured obligations specify that interest need be paid only to the extent to which income is earned. They entail no legally binding requirement to pay interest on a periodic basis. While they are unusual in the corporate sector, they are a very popular municipal issue, and are referred to as "revenue bonds."

Finally, an issue could be a "refunding" type which means that one bond is prematurely retired by paying off its principal from the proceeds of the sale of another issue. The second issue remains outstanding after the refunding operation. Thus, such terms as "first and refunding" refer to refunding obligations. A refunding bond can take either a junior or senior position, depending upon whether it is secured or not. The type of issue really has only marginal effect on comparative yield and price behavior. This is logical since it is the credibility of the issuer that basically determines the quality of the obligation. In fact, one of the early major studies of corporate bond price behavior found that the collateral of the obligation, or lack of it, did not become important until the issue approached default.[3] Usually, the question of collateral and security is rather insignificant, and only influences yield differentials when such senior/junior positions affect the quality ratings given to a bond by agencies such as Moody's or S&P.

Indenture Provisions The indenture is the contract between the issuer and the bond holder specifying the legal conditions that must be met by the issuer. While the instrument helps in the maintenance of a well-ordered capital market, most of the provisions are of little interest to bond investors because the trustee (i.e., the organization or institution acting in behalf of the bond holders) sees to it that all of the provisions are met, including the timely and orderly distribution of interest and principal.

However, investors should be keenly aware of a few popular indenture provisions, especially the "call features." There are three types of call provisions: 1) the bond can be "freely callable," which means that the issuer can retire the bond at any time within its life given a notification period of, usually, 30 to 60 days; 2) the obligation can be "noncallable," which means that the issuer *cannot* retire the bond prior to its maturity; and 3) it may have a "deferred call" feature, stipulating that the obligation cannot be called for a certain length of time after the date of issue (recently the most popular time period has been between five and ten years). At the end of the deferred call period, the issue becomes freely callable. The investor should also be aware of the "call premium," the added cost the issuer must bear (and which is paid to the bond holder) for prematurely retiring the bond.

In lieu of a call feature, a bond may contain a "refunding" provision which is exactly like the call feature *except that* it only prohibits (or allows) one thing: the retirement of an issue from the proceeds of a lower coupon refunding bond. This means that the obligation can still be called and prematurely retired for any reason other than refunding! If a firm has excess cash, for example, the issue could carry a nonrefunding provision but still be retired prior to maturity. In fact, during 1975, many investors found out the difference between a call feature and a refunding provision the hard way when their supposedly secure issues, which carried only nonrefundng or deferred refunding provisions, were called. The issuers did not refund the obligation but, instead, simply retired these costly high coupon issues early

---

[3] W. Braddock Hickman, *Corporate Bond Quality and Investor Experience* (Princeton, N. J.: Princeton Univeristy Press, 1958).

because they had the cash and viewed the action as a viable investment opportunity.

Another provision that is important to investors is the "sinking fund" feature which specifies how the bond will be amortized (or repaid) over its life. While most issues require some form of sinking fund provisions, a number of industrial obligations and government issues do not. In these cases, all or most of the issue is payable at maturity, and no attempt is made to systematically retire these obligations over their life. Such provisions have an effect on comparative yields at date of issue, but have little or no effect on comparative price behavior over time.

There are many different types of sinking fund provisions. For example, utility issuers often employ provisions actually giving them the right to use the periodic sinking fund to either acquire outstanding bonds *or increase the capital assets of the firm*. This is known as an "improvement" fund and requires an annual sinking fund of at least one percent of the *total* bonds outstanding. The size of the sinking fund can be a percentage of a given issue or of the *total* debt outstanding. Moreover, it can be a fixed or variable sum, stated on a dollar or percentage basis. The amount of the issue that must be repaid before maturity ranges from a nominal sum to 100 percent; and the payments may commence at the end of the first year or be deferred for as long as five to ten years from date of the issue.

Like a call or refunding provision, the sinking fund feature also carries a nominal call premium, perhaps one percent or less. Unlike call or refunding features, however, a sinking fund provision must be carried out regardless of interest rate behavior or other market conditions. Therefore, a potential small risk for investors in a bond with a sinking fund is that the bond issue could be called on a random basis. Basically, that is one way that sinking fund provisions are enforced—the bonds are simply called randomly by lot. Such public calls have been fairly rare since most bonds have been trading at a discount (i.e., at a price below par) and are retired for sinking fund purposes through direct negotiations with institutional holders. Essentially, the issuer or trustee negotiates with a big institutional holder, usually an insurance company or pension fund, to buy back the necessary amount of bonds at a price slightly above the current market price.

An Overview of Bond Market Structure

The market for fixed income securities is gigantic and literally dwarfs the listed equity exchanges (NYSE, ASE, et al.). One reason is that corporations tend to issue bonds rather than common stock. For example, Federal Reserve figures indicate that, during 1977, out of almost 51 billion dollars in new corporate security issues, only about 11 billion (approximately 22 percent) were equity, which included preferred as well as common stock. Corporations do not issue common or preferred stock more frequently because the major source of equity financing for a firm is internally generated funds, which do not fall into the realm of new publicly issued obligations. Also, unlike the equity market, which is strictly corporate derived, the bond market has three substantial noncorporate sectors: the U.S. Treasury, several U.S. government agencies, and state and local governments. Federal Reserve figures reveal that, while recent corporate bond issues have been substantial, such volume has accounted for only 15–18 percent of *total* new bond issues! In 1977 the face value of corporate bonds outstanding was approximately 40 billion dollars, whereas the noncorporate sector added over 200 billion dollars in bonds to the market. Further evidence of the economic dimensions of the bond market can be gleaned from Table 16–1, which lists the dollar volume of par value outstanding for different types of bonds, as well as the annual net changes in new issues each year.

The Participants

There are five different types of issuers: 1) the U.S. Treasury, 2) various agencies of the U.S. government, 3) various state and local political subdivisions (known as municipalities), 4) corporations, and 5) institutional issuers.

U.S. Treasury The market for "treasuries" is the largest and the best known; it includes bonds, notes, and other debt instruments issued as a means of meeting the burgeoning needs of the U.S. government. These different types of debt instruments, along with obligations of several other issuers, will be reviewed in detail in the following section of this chapter.

Government Agencies An important issuer, that has experienced the most rapid increase in size, is the various agencies of the United States Government. These agencies represent political subdivisions of the government, though the securities are *not* direct obligations of the treasury. The agency market is composed of two types of issuers: government sponsored enterprises and federal agencies. Similar to treasuries, these securities are issued under the authority of an act of Congress, and the proceeds are used to finance many of the legislative mandates of that body. A number of these obligations carry guarantees of the U.S. Government and, therefore, effectively represent the full faith and credit of the U.S. Treasury although they are not direct obligations of the government. Moreover, some have unusual interest payment provisions and tax features. But, in general, tax exposure of "agencies" is like that of treasury issues; while they are subject to the usual IRS federal tax provisions on interest and capital gains, the interest income is *free* from state and local levies. This is an important feature to investors since it can obviously increase the net return. Finally, another important feature is that the market yield of such agency obligations is generally above that attainable from treasuries. Therefore, agencies represent a way to increase returns with only marginal differences in risk.

Table 16–1 **Total Amounts Outstanding (in billions of dollars, at year end)**

	1970	1971	1972	1973	1974	1975	1976	1977
U.S. Treasury Obligations:								
Bills	87.90	97.50	103.90	107.80	119.70	157.50	164.00	161.10
Notes	101.20	114.00	121.50	124.60	129.80	167.10	216.70	251.80
Bonds	58.60	50.60	44.10	37.80	33.40	38.60	40.60	47.00
Total—Marketable Issues	247.70	262.10	269.50	270.20	282.90	363.20	421.30	459.90
Total—Nonmarketable Issues[b]	138.70	159.70	176.90	197.60	208.70	212.50	231.20	255.30
Grand Total	386.40	421.70	446.40	467.80	491.60	575.70	652.50	715.20
Corporates:								
Total	180.95	204.67	223.74	236.43	261.52	293.41	323.29	345.92
Municipals:								
Long Terms	123.50	139.90	154.00	167.30	179.20	196.10	213.90	232.90
Agency Issues:								
Federal Agencies[c]	9.3	12.5	11.1	11.55	12.72	19.05	21.90	23.14[a]
Federally Sponsored[d]	8.3	35.7	51.3	60.04	76.66	78.63	81.43	85.90[a]
Federal Financing Bank[e]	NA	NA	NA	NA	4.47	17.15	28.71	36.72[a]
Total	17.6	48.2	62.4	71.59	93.85	114.83	132.04	145.76[a]

[a] October 1977 figures.
[b] Includes: Securities issued to the Rural Electrification Administration and to state and local governments, depositary bonds, retirement plan bonds, and individual retirement bonds.
[c] Includes: Defense Department, Export-Import Bank, FHA, GNMA, Postal Service, TVA, and U.S. Railway Association.
[d] Includes: federal home loan banks, Federal Home Loan Mortgage Corp., FNMA, federal land banks, federal intermediate credit banks, banks for cooperatives, and Student Loan Marketing Association.
[e] The FFB, which began operations in 1974, is authorized to purchase or sell obligations issued, sold, or guaranteed by other federal agencies. Since FFB incurs debt solely for the purpose of lending to other agencies, its debt is not included in the main portion of the table in order to avoid double counting.
Source: *Federal Reserve Bulletin,* various issues.

Corporations The major nongovernmental issuer of debt is, of course, the corporate sector. Corporate bonds represent obligations of firms domiciled in the United States, Canada, and a few foreign countries. The market for corporate bonds is commonly subdivided into several segments: *industrials* (the most heterogeneous of the groups), *public utilities* (the dominant group in terms of volume of new issues), *rails and transportation* bonds, and *financial* issues (including those issued by banks, finance companies, and holding companies). The corporate sector probably provides the greatest diversity in types of issues and is also characterized by a wide variety of quality. In effect, the issuer can range from the highest investment grade firm, such as

American Telephone and Telegraph or IBM, to highly speculative issuers with substantially less attractive track records.

Municipalities are another major sector of the market, but are unlike any of the preceding three. The major difference is that *interest income* on municipal obligations (which includes the issues of states, school districts, cities, or any other type of political subdivision such as a state university) is not subject to federal income tax. In contrast, however, *capital gains* on these issues are subject to normal federal income taxes. Moreover, with the exception of Puerto Rican issues, the obligations enjoy exemption from state and local taxes *when they are issues of the state or locality in which the investor resides.* That is, while a California issue would not be taxed in California, its interest income would be subject to state tax if the investor happens to reside in New York. The interest income of Puerto Rican issues enjoys total federal, state, and local immunity to taxes. Another distinguishing feature of municipal bonds is that the issues typically are serial obligations. Finally, while revenue obligations are rare in other sectors of the market, they are popular with some municipal issuers and account for a substantial portion of the municipal market.

Institutions The final group are institutional obligations which are marketed by a variety of private, nonprofit institutions like schools, hospitals, and churches. These securities represent only a minute segment of the market, although they have some features which many investors would find fairly attractive. Unfortunately, there is a very thin, almost nonexistent, secondary market for these issues since most of the activity in the institutional segment of the market is centered in new issues. Many of the issuers are affiliated with a religious order (Roman Catholic-affiliated organizations have traditionally dominated the market). Likewise, hospital issues have been the preponderant type of obligation. These issues are sometimes referred to as "heart bonds" because of their emotional appeal, and some investors consider these investments charitable activities in support of their church or local hospital. However, because of the substantial yield spreads that such obligations offer, an astute investor might find them much more than charity!

Participating Investors

All sorts of individual and institutional investors, with myriad investment objectives, participate in the fixed income security market because they feel that these securities yield competitive risk-adjusted rates of return. Wealthy individual investors make up a substantial, though still relatively minor, portion of the market. This is probably because sophistication is required to invest wisely in fixed income securities and the minimum denominations of these issues discourage many small individual investors.

Institutional investors dominate the bond market and have traditionally accounted for the vast majority of activity, sometimes 90–95 percent of the trading.[4] Of course, different segments of the market are more institutionalized than others. For example, the agency market is heavily institutional whereas individuals play a significant role in the municipal sector. Institutions have a substantial influence on the behavior of market yields because of the magnitude of their involvement. The size of their transactions is fairly substantial, often millions of dollars. It is not unusual for a few institutions (three or four) to acquire 70–80 percent of a 50–100 million dollar new issue.

A variety of different institutions regularly invest a substantial proportion of their resources in the bond market. *Life insurance companies* are heavy investors in corporate bonds and, to a lesser extent, in treasury and agency securities; *commercial banks* invest substantial sums in the municipal market, as well as in government and agency issues; *property and liability insurance companies* are heavy investors in municipal obligations, as well as in treasuries; *private and governmental retirement and pension funds* are heavily committed to corporates, and also invest in treasuries and agencies. Finally, *mutual funds,* because of their traditional equity orientation, have seldom considered bonds and fixed income securities as an investment outlet, though attitudes are changing as various types of bond mutual funds attract the investing public. As the above review suggests, certain types of institutions tend to favor certain types of issues, although institutional bonds have been almost completely ignored, probably because of their lack of liquidity. There are two factors affecting these preferences: 1) the tax liability of the investing institution, and 2) the nature of the liability that the institution assumes in relation to its depositors or clients. For example, commercial banks are subject to normal taxation and have fairly short-term liability structures. As a result, they favor short to intermediate-term municipals. Life insurance companies and pension funds are virtually tax free institutions with long-term commitments, so they prefer high yielding long-term corporate bonds. Such institutional investment practices affect the supply of loanable funds and interest rate changes over short-run periods.

Investment and Trading Opportunities

Fixed income securities are useful for investors who require current income, although an investor with a more speculative, shorter term investment horizon can also find abundant trading opportunities. An important dimension of recent bond investment has been high interest rates that provide attractive competitive returns, while the volatility of yields presents capital gains opportunities.

In contrast to the equity market, the bond market is primarily a new

---

[4] Sidney Homer, "The Historical Evolution of Today's Bond Market," *Journal of Portfolio Management,* Vol. 1, No. 3 (Spring 1975), pp. 6–11.

issue (primary) market. As a result, the secondary market for seasoned securities is relatively thin and lacking in trading activity. Fortunately, some segments have fairly active secondary markets, including the treasury market, which is large enough so that even a relatively small amount of trading activity provides a liquid secondary market. Likewise, agencies are fairly actively traded in the secondary market, as are public utilities within the corporate market. In contrast, the municipal and institutional bond secondary markets are much less active. In fact, it is almost impossible for individual investors without access to certain specialized institutional publications to keep abreast of the price activity of municipal holdings because quotes do not appear regularly in the popular financial media. The reason for this illiquidity is that most new municipal issues are relatively small, with total par values of less than 15–20 million dollars. In addition, since most municipals are serial obligations, the total issue is actually subdivided into a series of smaller issues, which compounds the size problem.

The trading of bonds is also unlike that followed with equity shares. For example, commercial banks are popular dealers in government, agency, and municipal securities. Moreover, the trust departments of large commercial banks often act as secondary market dealers in the corporate OTC sector. While national and regional brokerage firms are active in marketing new issues, they only trade listed bond issues in the secondary market, and the listed issues only represent a small portion of total activity. Thus, there are few transactions in the secondary bond market because order placement and execution are carried out by specialized investment houses.

Extra care must be exercised by trading oriented investors to ensure that a substantial purchase or sale order can be executed rapidly. An investor who wishes to buy 50 bonds of a particular corporate issue (and this is certainly not a large order) may discover that normal volume in this issue amounts to less than ten bonds a week. Clearly, it would be very time consuming to fill the order and probably equally time consuming to dispose of the position at the end of the investment horizon. During this time lag, substantial changes in yield and price could occur. Because such changes may seriously alter holding period returns, it clearly behooves investors to consider an issue's trading volume before investing in it.

Bond Ratings

Agency ratings are an integral part of the bond market. Most fixed income securities in the corporate, municipal, and institutional markets are regularly evaluated and rated by one agency or more. The exceptions are bonds considered too small to rate and certain industry categories like bank issues (known as "nonrated" bonds). The rating agencies include two well known firms, Moody's and Standard and Poor's, and a third, much smaller agency, Fitch's Rating Service. The two large firms dominate the corporate and municipal sectors, while the major rating service for institutional issues is

Fitch. Occasionally, some agency issues, such as those of the Tennessee Valley Authority (TVA), are rated by one of the "Big Two," although the ratings are always "prime grade" (a rating indicating very little probability of default) and really don't have much influence on investors since they only serve to confirm the obvious.

Bond ratings are a very important service in the market for fixed income securities because they provide the fundamental analysis for thousands of issues.[5] The rating agencies conduct extensive analyses of the intrinsic characteristics of the issuing organization and of the issue to determine the default risk for the investor, and inform the market of their analysis through their ratings. Thus, in contrast to the situation with common stock, with bonds, the rating agencies have performed the fundamental analysis for the investor. Given the large, highly qualified staffs of the rating agencies, the general consensus is that additional analysis would only yield marginal insight regarding the instrinsic value or strength of an issue.

The primary question in bond analysis is not necessarily the growth prospects of the firm, but, rather, the ability of the firm to service a fixed amount of debt over the life of a given issue. Such an emphasis requires less attention be paid to highly uncertain expectations and forecasts, and more concern with available data regarding the historical and current financial position of the company. Fortunately, the agencies have done an admirable job, although rare mistakes happen.[6] If anything, the rating services tend to be overly conservative to the extent that a recent study[7] suggests that risk of default has actually been *over*estimated by the market, resulting in unnecessarily high risk premiums given recent default experience.

Since investors rely so heavily on agency ratings it follows that there should be some concrete evidence to support the relationship between bond ratings and the quality of the issue. The first major study in this regard was done by Horrigan[8] who concluded that the accounting data and financial ratios of the firm were, indeed, imbedded in corporate bond ratings. A subsequent study[9] that attempted to determine which intrinsic characteristics affect an assigned agency rating found that bond ratings possess a high degree of quantitative documentation. They tend to vary directly with profitability, size, and earnings coverage, while they move inversely with

---

[5] Irwin Ross, "Higher Stakes in the Bond-Rating Game," *Fortune* (April 1976), pp. 132–140.

[6] Hickman, *Corporate Bond Quality*.

[7] Gordon Pye, "Gauging the Default Premium," *Financial Analysts Journal,* Vol. 30, No. 1 (January–February, 1974), pp. 49–52.

[8] James O. Horrigan, "The Determination of Long-Term Credit Standing with Financial Ratios," *Empirical Research in Accounting: Selected Studies,* 1966, Supplement to *Journal of Accounting Research,* Vol. 4, pp. 44–62.

[9] Thomas F. Pogue and Robert M. Soldofsky, "What's in a Bond Rating?" *Journal of Financial and Quantitative Analysis,* Vol. 4, No. 2 (June 1969), pp. 201–208.

financial leverage and earnings instability. The results of these and other empirical studies[10] clearly demonstrate that agency ratings are far more than the qualitative judgments of analysts.

The ratings assigned to bonds at the time of issue are important in terms of the marketability and effective interest rate of the issue. Generally, Moody's and S&P will rate bond issues the same. When an issue carries one rating from one service and a different rating from the other, it is known as "split ratings" and is viewed by market participants as merely "shading" the quality of the issue upward or downward, similar to being awarded a grade of B+, rather than B. Seasoned issues are also regularly reviewed to ensure that the assigned rating is still valid. While most issues will carry a given rating for an extended period of time (often over the life of the issue), it is not uncommon for some issues to experience revisions in their assigned ratings. Revisions can be either upward or downward, and are usually done in increments of one rating grade. Finally, although it may appear that the firm is receiving the rating, it is actually the issue that gets the grade. As a result, a firm can have issues outstanding with two different ratings. It is possible for senior securities to carry one rating and junior issues to be assigned one grade lower.

The agencies assign letter ratings, depicting what they view as the risk of default of an obligation. Letter ratings range from AAA to D. Table 16–2 specifies the various ratings that can be assigned to issues by the two major services. Except for the slight variation in designations, the meaning and interpretation is basically the same. The top four ratings are generally considered to be "investment grade" securities. Bonds in these groups are the most interest sensitive (i.e. their prices will be most affected by changes in interest rates) and are most actively traded. The next level of securities is known as "speculatives" and include the BB and B rated obligations. Speculative grade securities are less interest sensitive because the prospects of the firm are the important factor in terms of the price behavior of the issues.[11] The last group is the C and D categories, which are generally either income obligations or revenue bonds, many of which are trading "flat" (they are in arrears with regard to interest payments). In the case of DDD through D rated obligations, the issues are in outright default, with the ratings indicating the bond's relative salvage value. Moody's also identifies the better quality *municipals* within the A and Baa categories as A1 and Baa1, respectively.

---

[10] See for example: Richard R. West, "An Alternative Approach to Predicting Corporate Bond Ratings," *Journal of Accounting Research,* Vol. 8, No. 1 (Spring 1970), pp. 118–125; and George E. Pinches and Kent A. Mingo, "A Multivariate Analysis of Industrial Bond Ratings," *Journal of Finance,* Vol. 28, No. 1 (March, 1973), pp. 1–18.

[11] Michael D. Joehnk and James F. Nielsen, "Return Risk Characteristics of Speculative Grade Bonds," *Quarterly Review of Economics and Business,* Vol. 15, No. 1 (Spring 1975), pp. 35–43.

Table 16–2 **Bond Ratings**

	Moody's	Standard & Poor's	Definition
High Grade	Aaa	AAA	The highest rating assigned to a debt instrument indicating an extremely strong capacity to pay principal and interest. Bonds in this category are often referred to as "gilt edge" securities.
	Aa	AA	High quality bonds by all standards with strong capacity to pay principal and interest. These bonds are rated lower primarily because the margins of protection are not as strong as Aaa and AAA.
Medium Grade	A	A	These bonds possess many favorable investment attributes but elements may be present which suggest a susceptibility to impairment given adverse economic changes.
	Baa	BBB	Bonds regarded as having adequate capacity to pay principal and interest but certain protective elements may be lacking in the event of adverse economic conditions which could lead to a weakened capacity for payment.
Speculative	Ba	BB	Bonds regarded as having only moderate protection of principal and interest payments during both good and bad times.
	B	B	Bonds that generally lack characteristics of other desirable investments. Assurance of interest and principal payments over any long period of time may be small.
Default	Caa	CCC	Poor quality issues that may be in default or in danger of default.
	Ca	CC	Highly speculative issues that are often in default or possessing other marked shortcomings.
	C		The lowest rated class of bonds. These issues can be regarded as extremely poor in investment quality.
		C	Rating given to income bonds on which no interest is being paid.
		D	Issues in default with principal and/or interest payments in arrears.

Adapted from: *Bond Guide* (New York: Standard & Poor's Corporation, monthly); *Bond Record* (New York: Moody's Investor Services, monthly). Reprinted by permission.

Market Rates of Return

Interest rate behavior is probably the most important variable to the investment grade bond investor. Figures 16–1 to 16–3 illustrate different important characteristics of bond market interest rates. The first shows comparative yields in different market sectors and indicates that *there is not a single market rate* applicable to all segments of the bond market. Each segment of the market has its own, somewhat unique, level. Those shown are just four of the many different rates that exist in the market at any given point in time. For example, the corporate rate could be broken down into different segments of the corporate market (such as industrials, public utilities, and rails) and each of these could be further subdivided according

Figure 16–1 **Comparative Bond Yield Behavior**

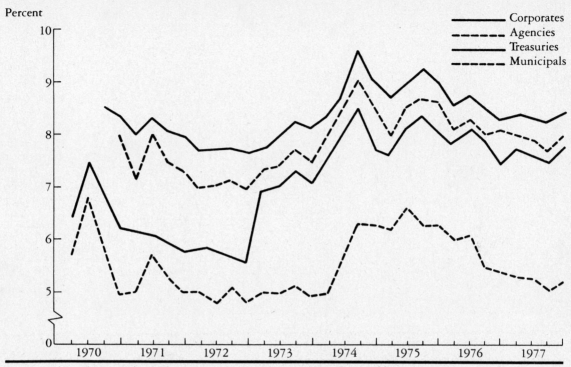

Source: *Bond Record* (New York: Moody's Investors Services, Inc., monthly). Reprinted by permission.

to different quality levels (Aaa through Baa). Observe that, generally, the various market segments tend to move together, a common characteristic in investment grade securities. In fact, a recent study[12] indicated that correlations *within* a wide variety of short, intermediate, and long-term yield series nearly always exceeded 90 percent.

Another dimension of market interest rates is depicted in Figure 16–2, i.e., the differences in yields for new and seasoned issues. Interest rates for new issues generally exceed those on comparable seasoned bonds. Some contend that this is caused by the relatively heavy trading volume in the new issue market, and by the desire of bond underwriters to minimize their inventory of new issues by providing as high a return as possible to investors.[13]

---

[12] Joehnk and Nielsen, "Return Risk Characteristics."

[13] See, for example: Andrew F. Brimmer, "Credit Conditions and Price Determination in the Corporate Bond Market," *Journal of Finance,* Vol. 15, No. 3 (September 1960), pp. 353–370; and Mortimer Kaplan, "Yields on Recently Issued Corporate Bonds: A New Index," *Journal of Finance,* Vol. 17, No. 1 (March 1962), pp. 81–109. An alternative view of the relationship is espoused by John R. Lindvall, "New Issue Corporate Bonds, Seasoned Market Efficiency and Yield Spreads," *Journal of Finance,* Vol. 32, No. 4 (September, 1977), pp. 1057–1067.

Figure 16–2 **Yields on Corporate Bonds: Seasoned vs. New**

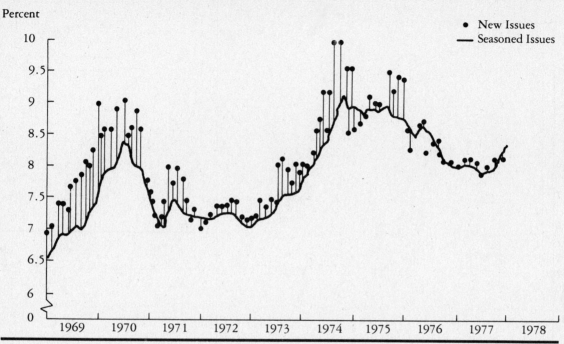

Source: *Bond Record* (New York: Moody's Investors Services, monthly). Reprinted by permission.

Finally, an aspect important to bond investors is how interest rates have performed historically, as shown in Figure 16–3. The data span more than 45 years and include the average behavior of one representative segment of the market: corporate investment grade securities. Behavior in the first half of the period differs significantly from that in the second half and indicates why investors have recently found the bond market to be an attractive investment outlet. Prior to the mid-60s, the bond market was fairly stable and there were few opportunities for aggressive investing. After the mid-'60s interest rates moved to highly competitive levels and substantial swings in interest rates provided opportunities for capital gains-oriented investors.

Bond Investment Risks

The typical bond investor is exposed to the same risk that any other investor faces. The important risks for bond holders include: 1) interest rate, 2) purchasing power, 3) market, 4) liquidity or marketability, and 5) business.

The most important of these is interest rate risk which is a function of the variability of bond returns (prices) caused by changes in the level of interest rates. Because of the relationship between bond prices and interest rates, no segment of the market, except perhaps for the highly speculative issues, is

Figure 16-3 **Corporate Bond Yields by Ratings**

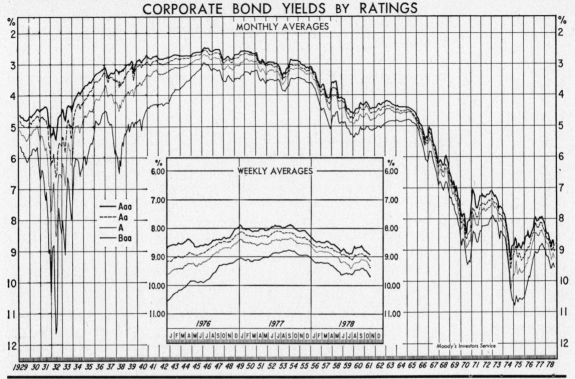

Note: As of December 1976, railroad bonds were removed from the combined Corporate
Averages, retroactive to January 1974. This adjustment was necessary because of a lack of
comparability to the Industrial and Public Utility averages, reflecting the limited
availability of reasonably current coupon railroad bonds.

Source: *Bond Record* (New York: Moody's Investors Services), November, 1978. Reprinted
by permission.

free of this important and powerful force. The price stability of investment
grade securities is mainly a function of interest rate stability and, therefore,
interest rate risk.

Purchasing power and market risks are closely related to interest rate
risk. Purchasing power risk is linked to inflation and the loss of purchasing
power over time; market risk, in contrast, is the effects of the market in
general on the price behavior of securities. In the latter case, since virtually
all segments of the bond market are responsive to interest rates, it follows
that market risk is directly linked to interest rate risk.[14] Also, while
purchasing power may decline over time with a given level of inflation,
what is important to bond investors is the effect of inflation on yields and
prices. While the level of inflation affects the promised yield, changes in

[14] Frank K. Reilly and Michael D. Joehnk, "Association Between Market-Determined
Risk Measures for Bonds and Bond Ratings," *Journal of Finance,* Vol. 31, No. 5 (December,
1976), pp. 1387–1403.

the rate of inflation (or inflation expectations) lead to changes in the level of interest rates and thereby changes in the prices of seasoned issues.

Marketability risk has to do with the liquidity of the obligation and the ease with which an issue can be sold at the prevailing market price. Smaller issues and those with thin secondary markets will often experience marketability difficulties and are, therefore, subjected to such risk. Fisher provided evidence that marketability was important in affecting the yield performance of an obligation.[15] The greater the assumed marketability risk, the greater the required yield.

Finally, business risk is the risk of default entailed by the financial and operating risks of the issuer. Such risks are only relevant for corporate, municipal, and institutional obligations. Fortunately, agency ratings adequately reflect differences in business risk, and the ratings, in turn, influence the promised yields (the lower the default risk, the higher the agency rating and the lower the prevailing yield to maturity). Default risk and marketability risk have an insignificant effect on price behavior because they only affect prevailing *levels* of yields. In contrast, interest rate risk and purchasing power risk can have dramatic effects on the price behavior of an obligation over time.

Alternative Investment Vehicles

Numerous sectors exist within the bond market characterized by fundamentally different issuers, the major categories of which include: the U.S. Treasury and government agencies, municipalities, corporations, and institutions. This section briefly reviews some of the popular issues available in these market sectors.

Treasury and Agency Issues

The dominant fixed income market is that for U.S. Treasury obligations. Acting on behalf of the United States Government, and with the backing of its full faith and credit, the U.S. Treasury issues long-term obligations in one of two forms: government notes, which have maturities of ten years or less; and treasury bonds, with maturities of more than 10 years (current maximum maturities go to about 25 years). A few years ago, government notes were particularly popular with government money managers because Congress established a 4½ percent interest rate ceiling on government bonds making them less desirable investments. When interest rates increased in the latter 60's, this provision effectively cut off the U.S. Treasury as a viable issuer of long-term bonds. Congress recently, however, revised the interest rate limitation statute, authorizing the treasury to issue up to 10 billion dollars in government bonds with *no* interest rate ceiling, hence, there is less reliance on treasury notes.

---

[15] Lawrence Fisher, "Determinants of Risk Premiums on Corporate Bonds," *Journal of Political Economy,* Vol. 67, No. 3 (June 1959), pp. 217–237.

Treasury obligations come in denominations of 1000 and 10,000 dollars, although a few older issues carry 500 dollar par values, and are either in registered or bearer form. The interest income from the U.S. government securities is subject to federal income tax but *exempt* from state and local levies. Such obligations are popular with individual and institutional investors because they possess substantial liquidity. Unlike treasury bills, which are sold at a discount to provide the desired yield (the return is the difference between the purchase price and par at maturity), government notes and bonds carry semiannual coupons, which specify the nominal yield of the obligation.

While government notes and bonds are similar to other straight debt issues in most respects, they do have some unusual features. First, the deferred call feature on treasury issues is unusually long and is generally measured relative to the *maturity* date of the issue, rather than from date of issue. For example, many treasury issues carry a deferment feature that expires five years *prior* to the *final* maturity date.

Also, certain government issues provide a tax break to investors because some U.S. government bonds can be used, at par, to pay federal estate taxes! It is possible, therefore, for an investor to acquire a treasury bond at a substantial discount and, shortly thereafter, for his estate to use the issue at par to pay estate taxes. Such bonds have been given a nickname, "flower bonds." Although *new* flower bonds can no longer be issued, there are still approximately a dozen such issues available in the market. Most of these carry 2¾–4½ percent coupons, and have maturities that range between 1980 and 1998. This is advantageous to the investor since the lower the coupon, the better the price discount, and the more assurance of price appreciation at "time of departure". Recent revisions in estate tax laws that increased the size of estates exempt from taxes, have reduced the demand for such issues.

Agency issues are obligations issued by the U.S. Government through some political subdivisions such as a government agency or government sponsored corporation. While there are only six government sponsored enterprises (Banks for Co-ops, Federal Home Loan Banks, Federal Home Loan Mortgage Corporation, Federal National Mortgage Association, Federal Intermediate Credit Banks, and Federal Land Banks), there are over two dozen federal agencies, the six largest of which are the Export-Import Bank, Farmers Home Administration, Federal Housing Administration, Government National Mortgage Association, TVA, and the U.S. Postal Service. To alleviate some of the marketing problems involved in federal agency securities, in 1974 Congress established the "Federal Financing Bank" as an instrumentality of the U.S. Treasury to consolidate the financing of all federal agencies of the U.S. Government. Such consolidation should reduce borrowing costs for federal agency issuers, and increase the liquidity and secondary market activity of the issues because of increased issue size.

Table 16–3 lists selected characteristics of the more popular government

Table 16–3 Agency Issues: Selected Characteristics

Type of Security		Minimum Denomination	Form	Life of Issue	Tax Status		How Interest is Earned
Government Sponsored:							
Banks for Cooperatives (Co-ops)		$5,000	Bearer	6 months to (currently) 3½ years	Fed.: State: Local:	Taxable Exempt Exempt	Interest bearing; 360-day year
Federal Intermediate Credit Banks (FICB's)		$5,000	Bearer	9 months to 4 years	Fed.: State: Local:	Taxable Exempt Exempt	Interest bearing; 360-day year
Federal Home Loan Bank		$10,000	Bearer	1 to 20 years	Fed.: State: Local:	Taxable Exempt Exempt	Semiannual interest payments
Federal Home Loan— Mortgage backed bonds		$25,000	Registered or Bearer	12 to 25 years	Fed.: State: Local:	Taxable Taxable Taxable	Semiannual interest payments
Mortgage Corporation— Participation certificates (FHLMC)		$100,000	Registered	15 to 30 years	Fed.: State: Local:	Taxable Taxable Taxable	Monthly interest payments
Federal Land Banks (FLB's)		$1,000	Bearer	1 to 10 years	Fed.: State: Local:	Taxable Exempt Exempt	Semiannual interest payments
Federal National Mortgage Association (FNMA)	Discount notes	$5,000[a]	Bearer	30 to 270 days	Fed: State: Local:	Taxable Taxable Taxable	Discounted 360-day year
	Secondary-Market notes and debentures	$10,000	Registered and Bearer	3 to 25 years	Fed.: State: Local:	Taxable Taxable Taxable	Semiannual interest payments

	Minimum Purchase	Form	Maturity	Tax Status		Interest
Federal Agencies:						
Export-Import Bank (Exim Bank)	$5,000	Registered or Bearer	3 to 7 years	Fed.: State: Local:	Taxable Taxable Taxable	Semiannual interest payments
Farmers Home Administration (FHDA) (notes)	$25,000	Registered or Bearer	4 to 15 years	Fed.: State: Local:	Taxable Taxable Taxable	Annual interest payments
Federal Housing Administration (FHA)	$50,000	Registered	1 to 40 years	Fed.: State: Local:	Taxable Taxable Taxable	Semiannual interest payments
Government National Mortgage Association Mortgage backed and participation	$25,000	Registered or Bearer	1 to 25 years	Fed.: State: Local:	Taxable Taxable Taxable	Semiannual interest payments
(GNMA) Modified Pass Through	$25,000	Registered	1 to 25 years (12 year average)	Fed.: State: Local:	Taxable Taxable Taxable	Monthly interest payments
Tennessee Valley Authority (TVA)	$1,000	Registered or Bearer	3 to 25 years	Fed.: State: Local:	Taxable Exempt Exempt	Semiannual interest payments
U.S. Postal Service	$10,000	Registered or Bearer	25 years	Fed.: State: Local:	Taxable Exempt Exempt	Semiannual interest payments
Other						
Federal Financing Bank	$10,000	Registered or Bearer	1 to 20 years	Fed.: State: Local:	Taxable Exempt Exempt	Semiannual interest payments

a Minimum Purchase Requirement of $50,000

Source: Adapted from: David M. Darst, *The Complete Bond Book* (New York: McGraw-Hill, Inc., 1975), pp. 274–283. Copyright © 1975 by McGraw-Hill, Inc. Reprinted by permission.

sponsored and federal agency obligations. It includes recent size of the market, typical minimum denominations, tax features, and the availability of bond quotes. (The issues in the table are only meant to be representative of the wide variety of different obligations available to the investor and not an exhaustive list.) Generally, agency issues are similar to those of other issuers.[16] Interest is usually paid semiannually, principal is due in full at maturity, and the minimum denominations vary between 1000 and 10,000 dollars, although there are exceptions. These obligations are unusual because they are *not* direct issues of the treasury, yet they carry the full faith and credit of the United States Government. Moreover, unlike government obligations, some of the issues are subject to state and local income tax, while some are specifically exempt from such levies.[17]

Except for the fact that they are of high quality and involve special tax provisions, agency obligations are not unique. However, one agency issue offers particularly attractive investment opportunities: GNMA ("Ginnie Mae") pass through certificates, which are obligations of the Government National Mortgage Association.[18] These bonds represent an undivided interest in a pool of federal insured mortgages. The issues are literally "put together" by large mortgage lenders who, in turn, sell the pool of mortgages to Ginnie Mae at a discount; Ginnie Mae then issues securities to the public against these mortgages. The bond holders receive monthly, rather than semiannual, payments from Ginnie Mae and these payments include both principal and interest, since they represent a pass through of the mortgage payments made by the original borrower (the mortgagee) to Ginnie Mae. This is why the bond has come to be known as a pass through obligation.

The pass throughs carry coupons that are somewhat related to the interest charged on the pool of mortgages. Also, since part of the cash flow represents return of capital (i.e., the principal part of payment), that portion is tax free. The interest income is subject to federal, state, and local taxes. The issues are marketed in minimum denominations of $25,000, which eliminates some individual investors from this market. They come with maturities of 25 to 30 years, but generally have an average life of only 12 years because, as pooled mortgages are paid off, payments and prepay-

---

[16] For expository purposes, we will no longer distinguish between federal agency and government sponsored obligations; instead, the term "agency" shall apply to either type of issue.

[17] Federal National Mortgage Association (Fannie Mae) debentures, for example, are subject to state and local income tax, whereas the interest income from Federal Home Loan Bank bonds is exempt. In fact, a few issues are even exempt from *federal* income tax as well, e.g., Public Housing bonds.

[18] For a more extensive discussion of mortgage backed securities, see: "Mortgage Securities Make It Big On Wall Street," *Savings & Loan News,* Vol. 98, No. 12 (December, 1977), pp. 33–35.

ments are passed through to the investor. This also implies, however, that unlike the case with other issues, the monthly payment is *not* fixed.

Another important feature of these securities is that they are "modified" pass throughs since the bonds are the obligation of the issuing body, the Government National Mortgage Association, and *not* the ultimate borrower, who is the home owner making the mortgage payment. Thus, the cash flow to the mortgage pool is quite distinct from the obligation of Ginnie Mae and totally separate from the cash flow to the bond investor. Moreover, the rates of return are relatively attractive compared to those for corporates. Most of the return is tax free, at least in the early life of the obligation. A major disadvantage of GNMA issues, however, is that they tend to be self-depletive. The monthly cash flow represents interest and a return of capital, so the obligation does not have a maturity value in the normal sense of the word.

Municipal Obligations

Municipal bonds are issued by states, counties, cities, and other political subdivisions. Basically, municipalities issue two distinct types of bonds: (1) general obligation bonds, and (2) revenue issues. General obligation bonds (GO's) are essentially backed by the full faith and credit of the issuer and its taxing power. Revenue bonds, in turn, are serviced by the income generated from specific revenue producing projects of the municipality, for example, bridges, toll roads, municipal coliseums, public utility and water works, etc. As might be expected, revenue bonds generally provide higher returns to investors than GO's do, because the default risk inherent in the former obligations is greater. A revenue bond is like a general obligation bond except that, should a municipality fail to generate sufficient income from a project used to secure a revenue bond, it has *no* legal debt service obligation until the income becomes sufficient.

Another feature of municipal bonds, particularly the general obligations, is that they tend to be issued on a serial basis. Most general obligations are set up this way so that the issuer's cash flow requirements will be steady over the life of the obligation. Therefore, the principal portion of the total debt service requirement generally begins at a fairly low level and builds up over the life of the obligation. In contrast, revenue obligations are mostly term issues, so the major portion of the issue's total principal value is not due until the final maturity date or last few dates. In fact, even if a revenue issue is serial, it is generally set up so that the serial portion amortizes a relatively small amount of the bond (perhaps 10–25 percent), with the majority of the obligation due at or near final maturity. As an example, see the 137.3 million dollar State of Florida Pollution Control Bond issue in Figure 16–4.

The most important feature of municipal obligations is, of course, that the interest payments are exempt from federal income tax, as well as taxes in

Figure 16–4
An Example of a Municipal Bond Offering

Interest exempt, in the opinion of Bond Counsel, from present Federal Income Taxes, under existing statutes, court decisions, regulations and rulings. The Bonds and the interest thereon are exempt from all taxation by the State or any county, municipality, political subdivision, agency, or instrumentality of the State, except as otherwise set forth in the Official Statement.

New Issue / June 15, 1978

$137,300,000

State of Florida

Full Faith and Credit

Pollution Control Bonds, Series J
Division of Bond Finance of the Department of General Services

Dated: January 1, 1978 / Due: July 1, as shown below

Principal and interest (July 1 and January 1, first coupon payable January 1, 1979) payable at the principal office of The Chase Manhattan Bank, N.A., New York, New York, as Paying Agent, or, at the option of the holder, at a co-paying agent bank designated by the Division of Bond Finance prior to delivery of the Bonds.

These Bonds are callable in accordance with the provisions set forth in the Official Statement.

AMOUNTS, MATURITIES, COUPON RATES AND YIELDS OR PRICES

Amount	Maturity	Rate	Yield	Amount	Maturity	Rate	Yield	Amount	Maturity	Rate	Price or Yield
$3,965,000	1982	5½%	4.65%	$6,060,000	1989	5.60%	5.10%	$ 8,205,000	1994	5.60%	@100
4,215,000	1983	5½	4.75	6,440,000	1990	5.60	5.20	8,720,000	1995	5.70	@100
4,475,000	1984	5½	4.85	6,845,000	1991	5.60	5.30	9,265,000	1996	5.70	5.75%
4,755,000	1985	5½	4.95	7,270,000	1992	5.60	5.40	9,845,000	1997	5.70	5.80
5,055,000	1986	5.60	5.00	7,725,000	1993	5.60	5.50	10,460,000	1998	5.70	5.90
5,370,000	1987	5.60	5.00					11,115,000	1999	5.70	5.95
5,705,000	1988	5.60	5.05					11,810,000	2000	5.70	6.00

(accrued interest from June 1, 1978 to be added)

These Bonds are offered for delivery when, as and if issued, subject to the approval of Messrs. Bryant, Franson, Miller, Olive and Brant, Bond Approving Counsel, Tallahassee, Florida.

The offering of these Bonds is made only by the Official Statement, copies of which may be obtained in any State from such of the undersigned as may lawfully offer these securities in such State.

Salomon Brothers

Morgan Guaranty Trust Company
of New York

Goldman, Sachs & Co.

Southeast First National Bank
of Miami

United California Bank

John Nuveen & Co. **North Carolina National Bank**
Incorporated

Barnett Bank of Jacksonville, N.A.

Central Bank of Birmingham **The First National Bank**
of Oregon

First National Bank of Commerce **Cowen & Co.**
(New Orleans)

The Boatmen's National Bank
of St. Louis

Donaldson, Lufkin & Jenrette
Securities Corporation

Ehrlich-Bober & Co., Inc.

Wm. E. Pollock & Co., Inc.

Arch W. Roberts & Co.

Park, Ryan, Inc.

First Equity Corporation
of Florida

Source: *Wall Street Journal*, June 16, 1978. Reprinted by permission.

the locality and state in which the obligation was issued. This means that people in different income brackets find municipal bonds to be of varying attractiveness. The investor can convert the *tax free yield* of a municipal to an equivalent *taxable* yield using the following equation:

$$TY = \frac{i}{(1 - t)}$$

where

TY = equivalent taxable yield

i = coupon rate of the municipal obligations

t = marginal tax rate of the investor.

(Note that TY can also be used to find the yield of treasury and/or agency obligations whenever state and local taxes are an issue.) An investor in the 30 percent marginal tax bracket would find that a 5 percent municipal yield is equivalent to a 7.14 percent fully taxable yield according to the following calculations:

$$TY = \frac{.05}{(1 - .3)} = .0714$$

This conversion is essential since the tax free yield is presumed to be the major motive for investing in municipal bonds. As a result, an investor's marginal tax rate is a *primary* concern in determing whether municipals are a viable investment vehicle. As a rough rule of thumb, an investor must be in the 30–35 percent tax bracket before municipal bonds offer yields that are competitive with those from fully taxable bonds because before tax municipal yields are substantially *lower* than returns available from fully taxable issues, such as corporates. However, only the interest is tax free; any capital gains are treated in the normal way.

Pollution Control Revenue Bonds Most issues of municipal bonds are fairly standard and, as a result, seldom offer issue oriented opportunities. One notable exception falls within the revenue category. Specifically, pollution control revenue bonds are actually disguised forms of *corporate* obligations which derive their debt service funds through leases, or other similar payment pledges, made between a municipality and a business firm, such as a public utility. To illustrate, in December 1977, Marshall County, West Virginia issued 50 million dollars of term revenue bonds, due 2007, secured with a long-term payment pledge from the Ohio Power Company. Congress maintained that our environment has to be cleaned up, and this financing vehicle was provided as a means to help corporations meet the gigantic expense, and also to encourage industrial development in smaller communities.[19]

Pollution control issues are very popular in the new issues market because an investor is often able to increase his yield relative to GOs and possibly improve his risk of default, and also such issues enjoy a fairly active secondary market. The substantial volume of new pollution control issues coming to the market each year has affected the availability and cost of funds to municipalities. Therefore, several states are considering ways of reducing or eliminating corporate use of such bonds.

Municipal bond guarantees are another unusual, though widespread, feature of the municipal bond market. They provide the bond holder with the assurance of a third party *other than the issuer* that the principal and interest payments will be promptly made. The third party provides an additional source of collateral. The guarantees are actually a form of insurance placed on the bond at date of issue and are *unrevokable* over the life of the issue. The issuer purchases the insurance for the benefit of the investor and the municipality benefits from lower issue costs.

In 1975, four states and two private organizations provided municipal bond guarantees. The states included: California, which guarantees certain forms of health facilities; New Hampshire, which guarantees school and sewage bonds; Minnesota, which guarantees any general obligations; and Michigan, which guarantees GO school bonds. The two private guarantors provide bond insurance throughout the country, rather than within a particular state. The first is a consortium of four large insurance companies that market their ·product under the name of Municipal Bond Insurance Association (MBIA). The second is a subsidiary of a large Milwaukee based private insurer known as American Municipal Bond Insurance Corporation (AMBAC). Both of the private guarantors will insure either general obligation or revenue bonds issued for any purpose. In order to qualify for private bond insurance, the issue must carry an S&P rating of triple-B or better. Because MBIA enjoys a triple-A rating from Standard & Poor's, it has been able to capture more of the market than AMBAC. A purported effect of the private guarantee is that such issues enjoy a more active secondary market and, therefore, greater liquidity, although such claims have not been documented.

---

[19] These bonds are not to be confused with industrial development revenue bonds, which were popular in the 50's and 60's. In fact, such issues became so popular that federal statutes had to be rewritten to severely restrict and reduce the use of industrial development obligations, particularly the amount of such obligations a community can issue. As might be expected, this almost led to the demise of these issues.

Corporate Bonds

Corporate bonds are one of two categories of *private* issues and represent, by far, the most significant segment.[20] Utilities dominate the corporate market. The other important segments include industrials (which rank second only to utilities and include everything from mining firms to multinational oils to retail concerns), rail and transportation issues, and financial issues. This market includes debentures, first mortgage issues, convertible obligations, bonds with warrants, subordinated debenture bonds, income bonds (similar to municipal revenue bonds), collateral trust bonds (typically backed by financial assets), equipment trust certificates, and mortgage backed bonds.

If we ignore equity related securities, equipment trust certificates, and mortgage backed bonds, the above list of obligations varies essentially according to the type of collateral behind the bond. Most issues have semiannual interest payments, sinking funds, and the issues have a single maturity date. Maturities range from 25 to 40 years, with public utilities generally on the longer end and industrials preferring the 25 to 30 year range. Nearly all corporate bonds carry deferred call provisions that range from five to ten years. The length of the deferment tends to vary directly with the level of the interest rates (i.e., the higher the prevailing interest rate level, the more likely an issue will carry a seven to ten year deferment). On the other hand, "corporate notes," which normally carry maturities of from five to seven years, are generally noncallable. Notes are popular with virtually all issuers, and tend to increase in popularity during periods of higher interest rates because issuers prefer to *avoid* long-term obligations during such periods.

Generally, the average yields for industrial bonds will be the lowest of the three major sectors, followed by utility returns, with yields on rail and transportation bonds generally being the highest. The differential between utilities and industrials is simply a matter of demand for loanable funds. Because utilities dominate the market in terms of the supply of bonds, yields must rise to attract the necessary demand.

Corporate issues are popular with individual and institutional investors because of the availability of such issues and the relatively attractive yields that they offer. *Established* firms have very low default records, leading many investors to consider corporate bonds a means of attaining higher returns without assuming abnormal risk.

Equipment Trust Certificates Several corporate issues contain unusual features. One is the equipment trust certificate issued by railroads (which are the biggest users of these obligations), airlines, and other transportation

---

[20] The other category is institutional bonds issued by hospitals, churches, etc. They will be discussed in the following section.

concerns. The proceeds are used to purchase equipment (freight cars, railroad engines, and airplanes) that serves as collateral for the equipment trust issue. These obligations are usually issued in serial form, but carry a uniform coupon throughout. Different yields are obtained for each of the maturities by pricing the obligation above, equal to, or below par value. Normally, because of the preponderance of upward sloping yield curves, the reoffering yields increase with time. Hence, the early maturities will be issued at a premium, while the longer maturities will be distributed at a discount. However, the spread between the shortest and the longest yield is generally one percentage point or less, so the discount or premium is relatively *small*. Equipment trust issues generally carry maturities that range from one year to a maximum that seldom exceeds 15 to 17 years. The fairly short maximum maturities are popular because of the nature of the collateral. Equipment is subject to substantial wear and tear and tends to deteriorate rapidly.

Equipment trust certificates appeal to investors because of their *attractive yields,* and they have a record of very few defaults. Equipment trust certificates do not enjoy the same visibility and acceptance as other forms of corporate bonds do, but they have active secondary markets and attractive liquidity. Unfortunately, market and price information on these issues is not as easily attainable as it is for other, more popular, forms of corporate debt.

Mortgage Backed Bonds Another unusual form of corporate debt initiated in September, 1977 is the mortgage backed bond. These issues are marketed by commercial banks, savings and loan associations, and mortgage lenders, and are exactly like the GNMA pass through certificates. They are backed by a pool of mortgages which provide the collateral for the bonds. These securities differ because they are *not* backed by the full faith and credit of the U.S. Government but, instead, carry the insurance of a third party, usually a private mortgage insurance company that provides insurance against defaults on the mortgages in the pool. The biggest private mortgage insurer for these bonds is the MGIC Investment Corporation discussed previously.

Mortgage backed bonds also carry relatively large minimum denominations of $25,000, but are highly liquid due to the relatively large size of these issues. For example, Bank of America, which was first to issue such obligations, came to market with a 150 million dollar bond. Home Savings and Loan Association in California offered a two part 200 million dollar mortgage backed bond that was sold out immediately. The issues enjoy relatively attractive yields and provide a monthly cash flow to investors that is partially tax-exempt since it represents a return of principal.

Variable Rate Notes were available in Europe for decades but were not introduced in this country until the summer of 1974. It became popular during the period of high interest rates, but subsequently declined in popularity. Still, a substantial amount of such obligations is outstanding in the secondary market, although no new issues were sold during 1976 and 1977. Currently there are nine of these notes available on the NYSE bond market, representing a combined principal value in excess of 1.5 billion dollars. The typical variable rate note possesses two unique features:

1. After the first 6–18 months of the issue's life, during which a minimum rate is often guaranteed, the coupon "floats," so that every six months it is pegged at a certain amount, usually one percent above a stipulated short-term rate (normally defined as the preceding three weeks average 90 day T-bill rate); and

2. after the first year or two, the notes are redeemable at par, at the *holder's* option, usually on a six months interval.

Thus, such notes represent a long-term commitment on the part of the borrower, yet provide the lender with all the markings of a short-term obligation. All nine of the actively traded variable rate notes are rated by Fitch, with four of them also being rated by either Moody's or Standard & Poor's. All are triple-A rated except one which carries a split rating of Aa by Moody's. Such obligations are available to investors in minimum denominations of 1000 dollars. Because of the unusual features of such obligations, variable rate notes could be attractive to yield conscious, liquidity oriented investors. However, although the six month redemption feature provides liquidity, the variable rates can subject the issue to wide swings in semiannual coupons.

Institutional Bonds

By far the smallest sector of the bond market is that for institutional issues such as hospital bonds. Even though these obligations have a virtually spotless default record, they offer returns of 100–150 basis points above comparably rated corporates because most institutional obligations do *not* enjoy an active secondary market! Offsetting such a handicap are many benefits in addition to the extra returns. For example, the obligations are issued on a serial basis with relatively short maximum maturities (seldom exceeding 15 to 18 years). Unlike most other serial bonds, institutional obligations generally call for *semiannual* maturities within the serial structure. Finally, they typically have deferred call features.

Obtaining Information on Bonds

As might be expected, the data needs of bond investors are considerably different from those of stockholders. For one thing, fundamental intrinsic analysis is far less important because of the widespread reliance on rating agencies for in depth analysis of the risk of default. In fact, except in the case of speculative grade bonds and questionable revenue obligations, most fixed income investors rely on the rating agencies to determine the default risk of an obligation. Some very large institutions employ in-house analysts to confirm assigned agency ratings, or to uncover marginal incremental return opportunities. Given the vast resources that these institutions invest each year, the rewards of only a few more basis points can be substantial and they enjoy economies of scale in research. Finally, because of an increasing demand for an independent appraisal of bond ratings several private firms have established research houses that concentrate on bonds.[21]

So what type of information do bond investors require? In addition to information on risk of default, (1) information on market and economic conditions; and (2) information on intrinsic bond features. Market and economic information allows investors to stay abreast of the general tone of the market, overall interest rate developments, and yield spread behavior between different market sectors. Bond investors also require information on certain bond characteristics such as call features and sinking fund provisions that can affect comparative yield and price behavior.

Where do bond holders find such information? Some is readily available in such popular publications as *The Wall Street Journal, Barron's, Business Week, Fortune,* and *Forbes.* In addition, bond investors are regular users of other publications, many specifically dealing with bonds. We will deal with some of the more representative ones, but *not* with the numerous "financial services" which are available at varying costs. Two popular sources of bond data are the *Federal Reserve Bulletin* and the *Survey of Current Business* that were described in Chapter 6.

Treasury Bulletin includes average yields on long-term treasury, corporate, and municipal bonds as well as graphs of monthly average yields on new double-A corporate bonds, treasury bonds, and municipal bonds. The bulletin is published monthly.

The Standard & Poor's Bond Guide is published monthly and presents a condensed review of pertinent financial and statistical information. This was likewise described in Chapter 6. Moody's has a comparable publication available to investors entitled *Moody's Bond Record.* (Nearly all bond publications produced by Standard & Poor's have counterparts marketed by Moody's.)

Moody's Bond Survey is published weekly and provides information on current conditions in the economy and their possible effects on bond markets. Recent and prospective taxable bond offerings are listed along with information such as assigned agency rating, offering date, amount of

---

[21] Reba White, "Is Credit Analysis a Growth Industry?" *Institutional Investor,* Vol. 10, No. 1 (January, 1976), pp. 57–58; Robert J. Cirino, "Building a Fixed-Income Boutique," *Institutional Investor,* Vol. 12, No. 3 (March, 1978), pp. 35–36.

offer, name and type of issue, call price, re-offering price and yield, and recent bid price and yield. For each of the *major* government, agency, corporate, and municipal obligations coming to the market, *detailed* information is provided on bond features, indenture provisions, and corporate or municipal finances. This is a valuable source of information to bond investors because it provides information on all three categories of bonds.

Moody's Manuals These include the *Municipal and Government Manual, The Bank and Financial Manual, Industrial Manual, OTC Industrial Manual, Transportation Manual,* and *Public Utility Manual.* These publications were described in Chapter 6 and are a primary source of fundamental information pertaining to the risk of default, but also contains data on various features of each outstanding issue.

Investment Dealers Digest provides extensive information on new issues and new issue market activity, sections dealing with reviews of various segments of the bond market, and the market outlook. Detailed new issue information is published weekly including extensive data on the features of bond issues currently in underwriting. The digest also contains the most extensive list of pending and recent issues available, which is helpful in obtaining insight into future demand for loanable funds and the effects of such demand on interest rates.

Sources of Bond Quotes

The above list included sources intended to fill three needs of investors: evaluating risk of default, staying abreast of market and interest rate conditions, and obtaining information on specific bonds. Another important data need is *current* market information, i.e., bond quotes and prices.

As noted earlier, obtaining current market quotes on institutional bonds, municipal bonds, and many corporate issues is a significant problem. However, with the possible exception of institutional bonds, substantial price information is available on a wide array of issues in all segments of the market. Unfortunately, many of these are simply not widely distributed. For example, *Bank and Quotation Record* is a valuable, though not widely circulated, source that provides a summary of price information on a monthly basis for government and agency bonds, a large number of listed and OTC corporate issues, municipals, and many money market instruments. Quotes on municipal bonds are only available through a fairly costly publication, used by many financial institutions, entitled *The Blue List. The Blue List* contains over 100 pages of price quotes for municipal bonds, municipal notes, industrial development, and pollution control revenue bonds. Daily information on all publicly traded treasury issues, most important agency obligations, and many corporate issues is published in *The Wall Street Journal.* Similar data is available on a weekly basis in *Barron's.* While the list is fairly extensive for treasury and agency obligations, corporate bond quotes in *The Wall Street Journal/Barron's* include only listed obligations which represent a minor portion of the total market. In addition to these published sources, major market dealers maintain firm quotes on a variety of issues that are available to clients and/or cooperating institutions.

Interpreting Bond Quotes

Essentially, all bonds are either quoted on the basis of yield or price. When they are quoted on the basis of price, the quote is always interpreted as a *percent of par.* For example, a quote of 98½ is not interpreted as $98.50, but 98½ percent of par. The dollar price can then be derived from the quote, given the par value. If par is 5000 dollars on a particular municipal bond, then the price of an issue quoted at 98½ would be $4925. Actually, the market follows three systems of bond pricing: one system for corporates, another for governments (this includes both treasuries and agency obligations), and a third for municipals.

Figure 16–5 is a listing of corporate bond quotes and NYSE bond quotes which appeared in *The Wall Street Journal* of Friday, June 16, 1978. The data pertain to trading activity on June 15. Several quotes have been circled for illustrative purposes. The first is an AT&T (American Telephone and Telegraph) issue and is representative of most corporate prices. In particular, the "7⅛s03" indicates the coupon and maturity of the obligation; in this case, the AT&T issue carries a 7⅛ percent coupon and matures in 2003. The small "s" between the coupon and maturity is interpreted as "series" and has no real meaning. The next column provides the *current* yield of the obligation and is found by comparing the coupon to the current market price—e.g., a bond with an 8 percent coupon selling for 95 would have an 8.4 percent current yield. The next column is the volume of 1000 dollar par value bonds traded that day. The next columns indicate the high, low, and closing quote, which is followed by the net change in close from the last day the issue was traded. In this case, the issue went up by ½ of a point or $5.00 (since that is ½ of one percent of $1,000). The second circled quote, for the Crt Ad bond, has one unique feature that makes a very significant difference. A small letter "f" follows the maturity date of the obligation; this means that the issue is trading "flat." Simply stated, the issuer is not meeting interest payments on the obligation. Therefore, the coupon of the obligation may be inconsequential. The next two circled bonds are both TVA obligations traded on the NYSE. The first TVA is the 7.4 percent of '97 and is circled because of the small letter "r" which follows the maturity date. This letter specifies a *registered* issue, which is fairly rare. The 7.35 series of 98 is circled because of an unusual aspect of the bond quote, a capital B behind the maturity date which defines the issue series more exactly because there are several 7.35-98's outstanding.

All fixed income obligations, with the exception of preferred stock, are traded on an *accrued interest basis*. The prices pertain to principal value only

Figure 16–5
**Sample Bond
Quotations**

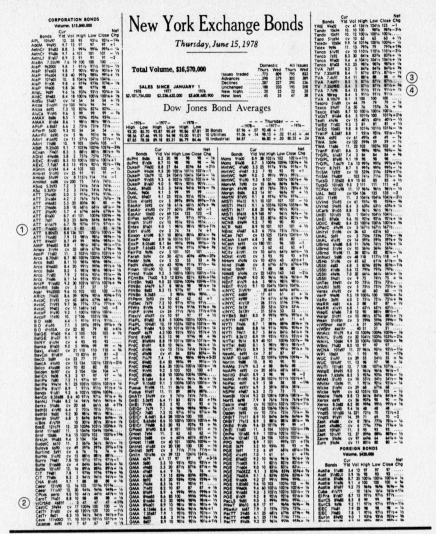

Source: *The Wall Street Journal*, June 16, 1978. Reprinted by permission of The Wall Street Journal, © Dow Jones & Company, Inc., 1978. All rights reserved.

and exclude interest that has accrued to the holder since the last interest payment date. The actual price of the bond will exceed the quote listed because accrued interest must be added. With the AT&T 7⅛ percent issue, if two months have elapsed since interest was paid, then the current holder of the bond is entitled to ²⁄₆ (or ⅓) of the normal semiannual interest payment. More specifically, the 7⅛ percent coupon provides semiannual interest income of $35.625. The investor who held the obligation for two months beyond the last interest payment date is entitled to ⅓ of that $35.625 in the form of accrued interest. There will be added to the price of 850 dollars an accrued interest value of $11.87.

Figure 16–6 illustrates the quote system used with treasury and agency issues. These quotes are like those customarily used for other over-the-counter securities since they contain both bid and ask prices, rather than high, low, and close. Looking first at the U.S. Treasury bond quotes, observe the small "n" behind the maturity date indicating that the obligation in question is actually a treasury *note*. All other obligations in this section are, of course, treasury bonds. The first circled quote is the 7 percent issue. The security identification is slightly different from that used with corporates since it is not necessary to list the issuer. Instead, the usual listing indicates the coupon, the year of maturity, the *month* of maturity, and any information on the call feature of the obligation. For example, the 7 percent issue carries a maturity of 1993–98; this means that the issue has a deferred call feature until 1993 (and is thereafter freely callable), and a (final) maturity date of 1998. The bid/ask figures are then provided and are also stated as a percent of par. The bid represents the current price at which the investor can sell this bond (since it indicates the price the dealer is currently bidding for the obligation), whereas the ask is the price at which the investor can buy the issue, since this represents the price asked by the government bond dealer. Unlike the current yield figure used with corporate issues, yield to maturity or *promised* yield is used with all other issues including treasuries, agencies, and municipals.

The next circled quote is 8⅜ percent obligation of 1995–00 which demonstrates the basic difference in the price system of governments (i.e., treasuries and agencies). The bid quote is 98.29 and the ask is 99.1. Governments are traded in thirty-seconds of a point (rather than eighths) and the figures to the right of the decimal indicate the number of thirty-seconds in the fractional bid or ask. The bid price is actually $98^{29}/_{32}$, and the ask is $99^{1}/_{32}$ percent of par.

The securities listed below the treasury bond section are (with the exception of U.S. Treasury Bills) various agency securities. For example, those of the Federal Home Loan Bank, the World Bank, FNMA, and Federal Land Bank are four of the agency issues regularly quoted in *The Wall Street Journal*. As the third circled quote indicates, these obligations follow the same pricing system used with treasuries; i.e., the coupon, month, and year maturities are provided under each of the several issuers, followed by bid/ask prices in thirty-seconds, and the yield is promised yield to maturity.

The final illustration, Table 16–7, pertains to municipal bond quotes and is drawn from *The Blue List of Current Municipal Offerings* for Monday, May 1, 1978. As the exhibit suggests, *The Blue List* provides daily quotes on municipal bonds ordered according to states and alphabetically within states. The information provided for each issue is: the amount of bonds being offered (in thousands of dollars), the name of the security, the coupon rate, the maturity (which includes month, day, and year), the yield and price, and, finally, the dealer offering the bonds. The first bond circled is $25,000 worth of Highland Park obligations. These are 3.375 percent

Figure 16–6
Sample Quotes for Treasury and Agency Issues

Government, Agency and Miscellaneous Securities

Thursday, June 15, 1978

Over-the-Counter quotations; sources on request.

Decimals in bid-and-asked and bid changes represent 32nds; 101.1 means 101 1/32. a-Plus 1/64. b-Yield to call date. d-Minus 1/64. n-Treasury notes.

Treasury Bonds and Notes

	Rate	Mat.	Date	Bid	Asked	Bid Chg.	Yld.
	6⅞s,	1978	Jun n	99.30	100	.....	6.65
	6⅞s,	1978	Jul n	99.29	99.31	.....	6.96
	7⅝s,	1978	Aug n	99.31	100.1	.....	7.23
	8¾s,	1978	Aug n	100.5	100.7	.....	7.13
	6⅝s,	1978	Aug n	99.25	99.27	.....	7.28
	6¼s,	1978	Sep n	99.18	99.20	.....	7.51
	5⅞s,	1978	Oct n	99.11	99.13	.....	7.49
	6s,	1978	Nov n	99.10	99.12	.....	7.55
	5¾s,	1978	Nov n	99.4	99.6	.....	7.60
	5¼s,	1978	Dec n	98.22	98.24	.....	7.70
	8⅛s,	1978	Dec n	100.5	100.7	.....	7.70
	5⅞s,	1979	Jan n	98.25	98.29	.....	7.72
	7s,	1979	Feb n	99.13	99.17	.....	7.74
	5⅞s,	1979	Feb n	98.18	98.22	.....	7.84
	6⅛s,	1986	Nov	87.14	88.14	.....	8.04
	7⅝s,	1987	Nov n	95	95.4	– .1	8.38
	8¼s,	1988	May n	98.31	99.1	.....	8.40
	3½s,	1990	Feb	74.14	75.14	.....	6.54
	8¼s,	1990	May	98.26	99.10	.....	8.34
	4¼s,	1987-92	Aug	74.22	75.22	.....	6.98
	7¼s,	1992	Aug	90.3	90.11	– .1	8.43
	4s,	1988-93	Feb	75.4	76.4	.....	6.56
	6¾s,	1993	Feb	86.20	87.20	.....	8.22
	7⅞s,	1993	Feb	95.4	95.8	.....	8.45
	7½s,	1988-93	Aug	91.20	92.20	.....	8.37
	4⅛s,	1989-94	May	75.16	76.16	.....	6.52
	3s,	1995	Feb	74.20	75.20	.....	5.21
①	7s,	1993-98	May	86.18	87.18	.....	8.29
	3½s,	1998	Nov	74.18	75.18	.....	5.51
	8½s,	1994-99	May	100.8	100.24	– .2	8.42
	7⅞s,	1995-00	Feb	94.4	94.12	.....	8.45
②	8⅜s,	1995-00	Aug	98.29	99.1	+ .1	8.48
	8s,	1996-01	Aug	95.6	95.14	.....	8.45
	8¼s,	2000-05	May	97.26	98.2	.....	8.43
	7⅝s,	2002-07	Feb	91.8	91.16	.....	8.42
	7⅞s,	2002-07	Nov	93.28	94.4	+ .1	8.41

n– Treasury notes.

U.S. Treas. Bills

Mat	Bid Discount	Ask Discount	Mat	Bid Discount	Ask Discount
6-22	7.48	7.26	10-12	6.92	6.82
6-27	6.87	6.35	10-17	6.98	6.88
6-29	6.87	6.37	10-19	7.00	6.90
7- 6	6.48	6.18	10-26	7.03	6.93
7-13	6.46	6.14	11- 2	7.10	7.02
7-20	6.56	6.32	11- 9	7.12	7.04
7-25	6.66	6.48	11-14	7.16	7.10
7-27	6.64	6.46	11-16	7.13	7.07
8- 3	6.66	6.52	11-24	7.17	7.11
8-10	6.66	6.54	11-30	7.19	7.13
8-17	6.67	6.57	12- 7	7.18	7.12
8-22	6.71	6.59	12-12	7.18	7.08
8-24	6.68	6.58	12-14	7.17	7.15
8-31	6.66	6.56	1- 9	7.18	7.10
9- 7	6.65	6.55	2- 6	7.33	7.27
9-14	6.66	6.64	3- 6	7.38	7.34
9-19	6.80	6.68	4- 3	7.43	7.37
9-21	6.73	6.63	5- 1	7.45	7.42
9-28	6.81	6.71	5-29	7.47	7.45
10- 5	6.87	6.77			

Fed. Home Loan Bank

Rate	Mat	Bid	Asked	Yld
9.10	11-78	100.17	100.25	7.51
8.65	2-79	100.10	100.18	7.76
9.45	2-79	100.28	101.4	7.70
7.50	5-79	99.16	99.20	7.92
8.65	5-79	100.14	100.22	7.86
8.75	5-79	100.18	100.26	7.82

FNMA Issues

Rate	Mat	Bid	Asked	Yld	
7.15	9-78	99.27	99.31	7.15	
7.45	9-78	99.29	100.1	7.17	
6.75	12-78	99.12	99.20	7.55	
8.95	12-78	100.12	100.20	7.58	
7.25	3-79	99.8	99.20	7.76	
7.85	6-79	99.20	100	7.85	
9.80	6-79	101.12	101.24	7.90	
8.10	7-79	99.29	99.31	8.11	
6.40	9-79	97.20	98.4	8.02	
7.80	9-79	99.8	99.24	8.00	
8.50	10-79	100	100.16	8.07	
6.55	12-79	97.12	97.28	8.11	
7.75	12-79	99	99.16	8.11	
6.88	3-80	97.8	98	8.13	
7.25	3-80	98.4	98.20	8.11	
7.38	4-80	98.8	98.24	8.12	
6.70	6-80	96.28	97.12	8.16	
8.50	6-80	100.4	100.20	8.15	
6.88	7-80	97.4	97.20	8.15	
7.50	9-80	98.8	98.24	8.12	
8.75	9-80	100.20	101.4	8.18	
6.60	12-80	95.20	96.20	8.13	
8.00	12-80	99.8	99.24	8.11	③
7.05	3-81	96.28	97.12	8.14	
7.35	3-81	97.20	98.4	8.12	
6.85	4-81	96.8	96.24	8.16	
7.25	6-81	96.20	97.20	8.16	
7.95	6-81	98.28	99.12	8.19	
7.25	9-81	96.12	97.12	8.19	

Source: *The Wall Street Journal,* June 16, 1978. Reprinted by permission of The Wall Street Journal, © Dow Jones & Company, Inc., 1978. All rights reserved.

Figure 16–7
**Quotes for
Municipals**

MICHIGAN—CONTINUED

	Coupon	Maturity		Yield/Price	Dealer
1750(GENESEE COUNTY	4.40	5/ 1/80		4.15)(A.G.BECKER MUN S.,INC.	(HARRIS TRUST & SAVING (FIRST N.B.OF CHICAGO
(DTD 4/1/78 F/C 11/1/78 W.I.					(FIRST PENNCO SEC. (WAUTERLEK&BROWN,INC. (AMER.N.B&T. (CGO) (SMITH,HAGUE & CO.INC
15 GENESEE COUNTY	4.70	5/ 1/92		5.50	E.F.HUTTON & CO.(CGO.
5 GENESEE COUNTY	5	5/ 1/93		5.60	FIRST OF MICHIGAN CRP
5 GLADSTONE AREA PUB.SCHS.	7.20	5/ 1/94	C88	5.85	E.F.HUTTON & CO.(CGO.
(CA @ 103)					
5 GLADSTONE AREA PUB.SC QUAL	7.40	5/ 1/05		6.20	FIRST OF MICHIGAN CRP
25 GRAND RAPIDS BLDG. AU P/C @ 104	6.60	11/ 1/93	C82	4.70	LOEB,RHOADES,HORN(NY)
5 GRAND RAPIDS&KENT CO.JT.BLDG.AU.	5.50	8/ 1/01		5.80	LOEB,RHOADES,HORN(NY)
5 GROSSE ILE TWP. S.D.	5.375	5/ 1/93		5.30	E.F.HUTTON & CO.(CGO.
15 HAZEL PARK	3.75	4/ 1/86		5.70	FIRST OF MICHIGAN CRP
① 25 HIGHLAND PARK	3.375	9/ 1/86		5.25	NEWHARD,COOK & CO.
15 HOLLAND SCHOOL DIST. U.T.Q.	5.75	1/ 1/98	C	5.60	WM.C.RONEY & CO.
15 INGHAM CO.	5.50	11/ 1/00		100	FIRST OF MICHIGAN CRP
10 JACKSON COUNTY	6.75	11/ 1/92	C87	5.45	LOEB,RHOADES,HORN(DET
(CA @ 103)(Y/M 5.60)					
5 KENT COUNTY W/S G.O.	5.95	11/ 1/91		5.40	LOEB,RHOADES,HORN(NY)
+ 100 KENT HOSP.FIN.AU.	5.40	1/ 1/85		5.25	LISS,TENNER&GOLDBERG
+ 400 KENT HOSP.FIN.AU.	5.70	1/ 1/87		5.55	LISS,TENNER&GOLDBERG
+ 100 KENT HOSP.FIN.AU.	6	1/ 1/89		5.80	LISS,TENNER&GOLDBERG
+ 60(KENT HOSP.FIN.AU.	6.15	7/ 1/91		5.80)(D.WITTER REYNOLD(DET)	
((BUTTERWORTH)					)(MANLEY,BENNETT,MCDON
5 LK.SUPERIOR ST.COLL.	7.125	9/15/02		6.75	LOEB,RHOADES,HORN(DET
10 LITCHFIELD C.S.D. QUAL	6.60	5/ 1/95	C86	5.40	LOEB,RHOADES,HORN(DET
(CA @ 103)(Y/M 5.70)					
25 LIVONIA IND.DEV.REV.	6	4/ 1/97		73	LAIDLAW ADAMS&PECK(NY
(ALLIED SUPERMARKETS)					
+ 25 LIVONIA PUB.SCH.DIST. QUAL	3.50	5/ 1/85		5.45	FIRST OF MICHIGAN CRP
15 LUDINGTON S.D.	5.25	11/ 1/98		6.10	FIRST OF MICHIGAN CRP
50 MACKINAC BRIDGE AUTH.	4	1/ 1/94		101 1/2	BARR BROS. & CO.,INC.
25 MACKINAC BRIDGE AUTH.	4	1/ 1/94		101	BONNIWELL & CO., INC.
25 MACKINAC BRIDGE AUTH.	4	1/ 1/94		101	R.E.D.CHASE&PARTNERS
25 MACKINAC BRIDGE AUTH.	4	1/ 1/94		101	F.B. COOPER & CO.,INC
25 MACKINAC BRIDGE AUTH.	4	1/ 1/94		101	DONALDSON,LUFK,JENR.
25 MACKINAC BRIDGE AUTH.	4	1/ 1/94		100 1/2	FIRST OF MICHIGAN CRP
15 MACKINAC BRIDGE AUTH.	4	1/ 1/94		100 1/2	WEEDEN & CO.,INC.
② 3 MACKINAC BRIDGE AUTH.	5.25	1/ 1/94		100	F.B. COOPER & CO.,INC.
10 MACOMB CO.	3.75	5/ 1/88		5.50	A.F. STEPP INVEST.INC
+ 50(MACOMB CO.	3.75	11/ 1/90		6.00)(D.WITTER REYNOLD(DET)	
					)(MANLEY,BENNETT,MCDON
10 MACOMB CO. G.O.	4.85	5/ 1/92		5.60	WM.C.RONEY & CO.
25 MACOMB CO. CA @ 102	5.75	5/ 1/95	C88	100	KIDDER,PEABODY(TOLEDO
25 MARQUETTE WTR/SWR.RV.	5.75	7/ 1/01	C	100	KIDDER,PEABODY(TOLEDO
15 MAYVILLE S.D. QUAL	7.25	5/ 1/96		5.75	LOEB,RHOADES,HORN(DET
5 MONROE SCH. DIST. QUAL	5	5/ 1/88		4.70	FIRST OF MICHIGAN CRP
200 MONROE COUNTY SWR.D.	5.75	11/ 1/84		4.50	ROOSE,WADE (CLEVELAND
700 MONROE CO.POLL.CTL.RV	5.75	6/ 1/03		6.25	MANLEY,BENNETT,MCDON
(DETROIT ED.)					
10 MONROE CO.POLL.CTL.RV CA @ 103	7	3/ 1/05	C87	6.35	LOEB,RHOADES,HORN(DET
(DETROIT ED.)(Y/M 6.05)					
25 MONTABELLA COMM.S.D.	5.75	5/ 1/03		5.80	BECKER & COWNIE, INC.
+ 250(MUNISING P.S.D.	5.95	5/ 1/00		100)(	(FIRST OF MICHIGAN CRP (BLYTH,EASTMAN DILLON
+ 325(DTD 4/1/78 U.T.Q. (85,240)	6	5/ 1/01-02		100-100)(	(THE OHIO COMPANY (PRESCOTT,BALL&TURBEN
+ 250(F/C 11/1/78 W.I.	6	5/ 1/04		6.05)(	LOEB,RHOADES,HORN(DET
+ 140(	6	5/ 1/07		6.10)(	
					(BACHE HALSEY(CGO.TR.) (E.F.HUTTON & CO.(CGO. (PAINE,WEB,JACK,CURT.
20 NORTHVILLE P.S.D. QUAL	5.75	5/ 1/97		5.75	LOEB,RHOADES,HORN(DET
50 NORTHVILLE P.S.D.	5.80	5/ 1/98	C	5.60	FIRST OF MICHIGAN CRP
150 NORTHVILLE P.S.D.	5.80	5/ 1/99		5.70	VAN KAMPEN SAUERMAN
10 NORTHVILLE P.S.D. #2	3.75	5/ 1/86		5.50	LOEB,RHOADES,HORN(DET
25 NOVI G.O.	4.60	10/ 1/85		4.85	BLYTH,EASTMAN(CHICAGO
+ 30 OAKLAND COUNTY	6.25	5/ 1/83		4.70	E.F.HUTTON & CO.(CGO.
15 OAKLAND COUNTY	4.375	5/ 1/84		5.00	FIRST N.B.OF CHICAGO
25 OAKLAND COUNTY	6.25	5/ 1/84		4.95	NATL.BK. OF DETROIT
25 OAKLAND COUNTY	6.50	5/ 1/84		4.70	FOLGER,NOLAN,FLEM,DOU
45 OAKLAND COUNTY	6.50	5/ 1/84		4.75	LOEB,RHOADES,HORN(DET

MONDAY MAY 1, 1978   PAGE 63

Source: *The Blue List of Current Municipal Offerings,* May 1, 1978. The Blue List, Division of Standard & Poor's. Reprinted by permission.

coupon bonds which mature September 1, 1986, and are part of a series of bonds that came out with this particular serial obligation. The $25,000 in bonds are being offered by Newhard, Cook and Co. at a yield of 5.25 percent. Municipals are the only segment of the bond market that regularly trade a major portion of the issues on the basis of *yield to maturity,* rather than percent of par. Indeed, an analysis of the page reveals that most obligations, particularly general obligation bonds are quoted on a yield basis. In order to determine the dollar price of this issue, one would have to compute the present value of a 3.375 percent, 8.33 year bond that is yielding 5.25 percent.

The second issue circled, $3,000 of the Mackinac Bridge Authority 5¼ percent of 94, is highlighted because the quote is stated as a percent of par. This is a customary pricing procedure with *term revenue issues*. Most of these bonds are quoted on a dollar basis, rather than on a yield basis—thus these are called "dollar bonds." Actually, the quote is still listed as a percent of par, rather than a dollar price, although the dollar figure is much easier to obtain for the Mackinac Bridge Authority than for the Highland Park issue.

Summary

The purpose of this chapter was to deal with the fundamental aspects of bonds in order to provide the necessary background for a discussion of bond valuation and investment strategies. We initially looked at the basic features of bonds with respect to interest, principal, and maturity.

Several key relationships were discussed in regard to price behavior. First, price is essentially a function of coupon, maturity, and prevailing market interest rates. Second, bond price volatility depends on coupon and maturity. In general, bonds with longer maturities and/or lower coupons respond most vigorously to a given change in market rates. Finally, other factors, including intrinsic characteristics, type of issue, and indenture provisions, must be considered.

Major benefits to investors included: high returns for nominal risk, potential for capital gains, certain tax advantages, and the opportunity for additional returns based on aggressive trading of bonds. Major concerns for the aggressive bond investor include secondary market activity, investment risks, and interest rate behavior.

Several popular issues available in the various market sectors were reviewed, with consideration given to liquidity, yield spreads, tax implications, and special features unique to each sector. The final section contained a discussion of the information needs of investors. In terms of default risk, most bond investors rely on agency ratings as their source of information. For additional information on market and economic conditions, and information on intrinsic bond features, individual and institutional investors rely on a host of readily available publications. Various examples of typical issue quotes were given with accompanying explanations.

Questions

1. How does a bond differ from other types of debt instruments?
2. Explain the difference between calling a bond and bond refunding.

3. Identify the three most important factors in determining the price of a bond. Describe the effect of each.

4. Define two different types of bond yields.

5. What factors determine whether a bond is "senior" or "junior?" Give examples of each type of bond.

6. What is a bond indenture?

7. Explain the differences in taxation of income from municipal bonds as opposed to U.S. Treasury bonds and corporate bonds.

8. List several types of institutional participants in the bond market and explain why they are likely to purchase bonds.

9. Why should an investor be aware of the trading volume for a particular bond in which he is interested?

10. What part does a bond's rating play in the evaluation of a bond for investment?

11. Demonstrate through an example the effects of interest rate risk on the price of a bond.

12. An investor in the 35 percent tax bracket is trying to decide which of two bonds to purchase. One is a corporate bond, carrying an 8 percent coupon and selling at par. The other is a municipal bond, with a 5½ percent coupon, and it, too, sells at par. Assuming all other relevant factors are equal, which bond should the investor select?

13. Compare and contrast a corporate mortgage backed bond with a Ginnie Mae pass through certificate.

14. In the latter part of this chapter, a large number of sources of information on bonds were described and their contents discussed. Yet the statement was made earlier that ". . . it is almost impossible for individual investors . . . to keep abreast of the price activity of municipal holdings . . ." Discuss this apparent paradox, explaining how such a condition might exist.

15. Using various sources of information as described in the chapter, name at least five bonds, rated B or better, that have split ratings.

16. Using various sources of information, select five bonds from those firms listed on the NYSE. Prepare a brief description of each bond, including such factors as its rating, call features, collateral, if any, interest dates, and refunding provisions.

References

Ahearn, Daniel S. "The Strategic Role of Fixed Income Securities." *The Journal of Portfolio Management,* Vol. 1, No. 3 (Spring, 1975).

Baskin, Elba F. and Crooch, Gary M. "Historical Rates of Return on Investments in Flat Bonds." *Financial Analysts Journal,* Vol. 24, No. 6 (November–December, 1968).

Bierman, Harold and Hass, Jerome. "An Analytical Model of Bond Risk Differentials." *Journal of Financial and Quantitative Analysis,* Vol. 10, No. 5 (December, 1975).

Brimmer, Andrew F. "Credit Conditions and Price Determination in the Corporate Bond Market." *Journal of Finance,* Vol. 15, No. 3 (September, 1960).

Bullington, Robert A. "How Corporate Debt Issues Are Rated." *Financial Executive,* Vol. 42, No. 9 (September, 1974).

Darst, David M. *The Complete Bond Book.* New York: McGraw–Hill Book Company, 1975.

Fisher, Lawrence. "Determinants of Risk Premiums on Corporate Bonds." *Journal of Political Economy,* Vol. 67, No. 3 (June, 1959).

Hickman, W. Braddock. *Corporate Bond Quality and Investor Experience.* Princeton, N.J.: Princeton University Press, 1958.

Homer, Sidney. "The Historical Evolution of Today's Bond Market." *The Journal of Portfolio Management,* Vol. 1, No. 3 (Spring, 1975).

Horrigan, James O. "The Determination of Long-Term Credit Standing with Financial Rates." *Empirical Research in Accounting: Selected Studies, 1966,* Supplement to *Journal of Accounting Research,* Vol. 4.

Joehnk, Michael D. and Nielsen, James F. "Return Risk Characteristics of Speculative Grade Bonds." *Quarterly Review of Economics and Business,* Vol. 15, No. 1 (Spring, 1975).

Kaplan, Mortimer. "Yields on Recently Issued Corporate Bonds: A New Index." *Journal of Finance,* Vol. 17, No. 1 (March, 1962).

Landsea, William F. "Agency Bonds in Liquidity Portfolios." *Mississippi Valley Journal,* Vol. 7, No. 2 (Winter, 1971–72).

Meyer, Kenneth, R. "The Dividends from Active Bond Management." *The Journal of Portfolio Management,* Vol. 1, No. 3 (Spring, 1975).

Pinches, George E. and Mingo, Kent A. "A Multivariate Analysis of Industrial Bond Ratings." *Journal of Finance,* Vol. 28, No. 1 (March, 1973).

Pogue, Thomas F. and Soldofsky, Robert M. "What's in a Bond Rating?" *Journal of Financial and Quantitative Analysis,* Vol. 4, No. 2 (June, 1969).

Pye, Gordon. "Gauging the Default Premium." *Financial Analysts Journal,* Vol. 30, No. 1 (January–February, 1974).

Reilly, Frank K. and Joehnk, Michael D. "Association Between Market-Determined Risk Measures for Bonds and Bond Ratings." *Journal of Finance,* Vol. 31, No. 5 (December, 1976).

Ross, Irwin. "Higher Stakes in the Bond-Rating Game." *Fortune* (April, 1976).

"Say Hello To Tax-Free Bond Funds." *Savings and Loan News,* Vol. 98, No. 2 (February, 1977).

Shakin, Bernard. "Swinging in Bonds." *Barron's,* October 11, 1976.

Sharpe, William F. "Bonds Versus Stocks: Some Lessons from Capital Market Theory." *Financial Analysts Journal,* Vol. 29, No. 6 (November–December, 1973).

Thygerson, Kenneth J. and Parliment, Thomas J. "Mortgage Securities Make It Big On Wall Street." *Savings and Loan News,* Vol. 98, No. 12 (December, 1977).

Van Horne, James C. *Financial Market Rates and Flows.* Englewood Cliffs, N.J.: Prentice-Hall, Inc., 1978.

Weil, Roman. "Realized Interest Rates and Bondholder's Returns." *American Economic Review,* Vol. 60, No. 3 (June, 1970).

West, Richard R. "An Alternative Approach to Predicting Corporate Bond Ratings." *Journal of Accounting Research,* Vol. 8, No. 1 (Spring, 1970).

White, Shelby. "Unwelcome Call: It's on the Way to Holders of High-Coupon Bonds." *Barron's,* October 4, 1976.

Chapter 17   *Principles of Bond Valuation*

Like any long-term investment, fixed income securities are valued on the basis of their future stream of income. Periodic interest income, along with payment of principal at maturity, are the two fundamental sources of return to bond holders. The basic problem of bond valuation revolves about the specification, at desired levels of certainty, of the various components of the future cash flow to be realized by the bond investor, especially the size of capital recovery (i.e., payment of principal).

The purpose of this chapter is to explore the valuation process and to identify the important determinants that affect bond price and yield. It represents an extension of the preceding chapter since it explicitly demonstrates how many of the important variables introduced there can affect promised yield and realized return. Initially there is an overview of the general concepts and fundamental dimensions of the bond valuation process. The arithmetic of bond prices and bond yields will then be examined and the mathematics of tax-exempt issues will be addressed. The role of interest rates in affecting bond yields and prices will then be explored, as will the determinants of interest rates and yield spreads. Finally, there is an analysis of the causes and effects of variations in bond price volatility.

Fundamentals of the Bond Valuation Process

Present Value Model

Basically, the bond valuation process is similar to the procedures used with equity securities since the value of a bond is equal to the present value of expected cash flows. The only real difference is that the cash flow involved is the periodic interest payments and capital recovery. In a theoretical framework, the basic principles of bond valuation can be described in the following present value model:

$$(17\text{–}1) \qquad P = \sum_{t=1}^{n} C_t \frac{1}{(1+i)^t}$$

where:

n = the number of periods in the investment horizon, or what is more popularly known as term-to-maturity

C_t = the cash flow (periodic interest income and principal) received in period t and

i = the rate of discount (or market yield) for the issue.

Essentially, any fixed income security can be valued on the basis of equation (17–1), which provides an indication of what the investor expects to realize by holding the issue over a given investment horizon. In most cases, the holding period is equal to the term to maturity of the obligation and, as a result, the rate of discount represents the *"promised" yield to maturity* that can be earned by purchasing the obligation and holding it to its expiration date. Aggressive bond investors, however, normally do not hold obligations to maturity. Rather, the intent is to buy and sell the security prior to that point. Under such conditions, *"realized" yield* is a more important description of performance, and, in such a case, Equation 17–1 would represent an expected realized yield, rather than promised return.

The present value model is attractive because it incorporates several important aspects of bond yields and prices. Current income is a facet of coupon receipts and is included in C_t. More important, we know that interest rate behavior is a critical aspect of bond yield and bond price performance. The effect of interest rates is incorporated in i, where the discount rate is interpreted as the prevailing bond yield (described as promised yield to maturity) at a given point in time. Another important dimension is changes in interest rates because it affects the level of capital gains (or losses) that would be realized by an investor who buys and sells an issue prior to maturity,[1] and is incorporated into the model within the cash flow component, C_t.

Because the present value model is a valuation procedure applicable to individual securities, another important aspect of defining capital gains in terms of the model is the effect of changes in *yield spreads* over the investment horizon. These spreads are simply differences in yields that exist

---

[1] Indeed, for many aggressive investors, it is *the* major facet because their major objective is attractive capital gains.

between different market sectors or types of issues. Yield spreads account for the subtle differences in performance owing to such aspects as differential call feature, variations in coupons and maturities, etc.

The bond valuation framework rests on an evaluation of interest receipts, interest rates, changes in interest rates, and yield spreads. *The major problem facing the bond analyst is determining the extent of interest rate changes and yield spread behavior.* The definition of coupon income and par value is not a significant problem since it is specified and fixed. The only real concern is determining the risk of default, and much of that is handled by agency ratings. Moreover, if an investor is examining an obligation solely on the basis of promised yield, then prevailing available market rates define i. In contrast, the computation of *realized* yield assumes that the investment horizon is less than term to maturity, and is directly related to the possibility of capital gains or losses. Further, the potential capital gains or losses depend upon interest rate changes and yield spreads.

The investor must not only understand those forces which affect the *level* of interest rates in order to judge current market rates, but also must be able to project future interest rates. Once interest rate levels have been evaluated, and anticipated *changes* in rates have been formulated, attention shifts to the more specific consideration of differential market rates, and that implies examination of yield spreads. That is, an evaluation of the yield spread behavior over the holding period will indicate that certain segments of the market will be more attractive because of their relative yield performance. In effect, yield spread analysis is the application of the general notion of interest rate behavior to specific segments of the market.

Finally, there is a considerable difference in the valuation process when an investor follows a buy-and-hold approach versus a trading strategy. In the latter case, there is considerable risk and uncertainty surrounding future bond prices and expected capital gains opportunities. After the formulation of future price behavior through the evaluation of interest rates and yield spreads, it is necessary to select the appropriate coupon, maturity, call feature, etc. in order to procure the performance that one seeks.

Buy-and-hold investors deal with similar estimates, although their magnitude is *substantially* less than that for the investor with a trading strategy. For example, the buy-and-hold investor must consider the technical dimensions of bond valuation, such as maturity, coupon, and call features, to determine how such features might affect investment objectives. The buy-and-hold investor is working with *known* information and the only uncertainty is whether or not the time is right to buy or sell. His uncertainty over interest rates is nominal compared to that assumed by aggressive capital gains orientated bond investors, because *failure to formulate interest rates correctly* has much *less* impact on the realized gains of the buy-and-hold investor; at the worst, it means not realizing quite as much as hoped. For the aggressive capital gains orientated investors, such errors can mean not only reduced profit, but *substantial losses* as well!

The subsequent discussion of the valuation process pertains to investment grade securities which possess acceptable levels of interest sensitivity. Essentially, speculative grade securities are less sensitive to interest rates and, given the importance of interest rates in the bond valuation process, the framework specified would be inappropriate for bonds that are not interest sensitive.[2]

The Mathematics of Bond Pricing and Yields

Basically there are five types of yields in bond market trading vernacular: nominal yield, current yield, promised yield, yield to call, and realized yield. Nominal yield is the coupon rate a particular issue carries. A bond with an 8 percent coupon would have an 8 percent nominal yield. It has practical significance, only to the extent that it provides a convenient way of describing the coupon characteristics of an issue.

Current yield is to bonds what dividend yield is to stocks, and is computed as:

(17–2)
$$CY = c_t/P_m$$

where:

c_t = the annual coupon payment of the obligation; and

P_m = the current market price of the issue.

This yield indicates the relative level of current income provided by the obligation, and is important to income oriented investors. Unfortunately, it excludes an important component in the bond valuation process, capital recovery.

Promised Yield

Promised yield is *the* most important and widely used bond valuation model! Essentially, promised yield indicates the fully compounded rate of return offered to the investor at prevailing prices, assuming the investor *holds the obligation to maturity*. Also known as *yield to maturity*, it excludes any trading possibilities. The concept simply involves prevailing market prices, periodic coupon income, and par value (which, when related to prevailing market price, accounts for capital appreciation or depreciation).

---

[2] For a more detailed discussion of the determinants of speculative grade bond yields and price behavior, see: Michael D. Joehnk, and James F. Nielsen, "Return and Risk Characteristics of Speculative Grade Bonds," *Quarterly Review of Economics & Business,* Vol. 15, No. 1 (Spring, 1975), pp. 35–43 and Elba F. Baskin and Gary M. Crooch, "Historical Rates of Return on Investments in Flat Bonds," *Financial Analysts Journal,* (November–December, 1968), pp. 95–97.

Then, assuming the investor buys and holds the bond to maturity, the computation indicates the issue's yield to maturity.

Like any present value based computation, promised yield has important reinvestment implications. In particular, the promised yield is the required reinvestment rate that the investor must subsequently earn on each of the interim cash flows (coupon receipts) in order to realize a return equal to, or greater than, promised yield. This is directly related to compound value and is also known as "interest-on-interest."[3] The yield to maturity figure is the return promised so long as the issuer meets all interest and principal obligations on a timely basis *and the investor reinvests coupon income to maturity at an average rate equal to the computed promised yield.* If a bond offers an 8 percent yield to maturity, the investor must reinvest coupon income at a rate equal to 8 percent in order to realize that return. If coupons are not reinvested, or if future investment rates during the life of the issue are less than the promised yield at purchase, then the *realized* yield earned will be *less* than promised yield to maturity.

This important and often overlooked concept is fully developed in an excellent study by Homer and Leibowitz.[4] The importance of interest-on-interest varies directly with coupon and maturity; the higher the coupon and/or the longer the term to maturity, the more important is reinvestment. Figure 17–1 depicts the concept and the impact of interest-on-interest assuming an 8 percent, 25 year bond was bought at par to yield 8 percent. Almost 60 percent of total return is seen to accrue from the successful reinvestment of the coupon income. Moreover, observe the terminal values and yields of the investment at points A and B. When the investor is able to reinvest the coupon income at rates between 0 and 8 percent, he will realize a yield between 4½ and 8 percent. On the other hand, if he can consistently reinvest at rates greater than 8 percent, he will realize a yield in excess of the promised yield. In fact, when rates are extremely high, many uninformed bond investors experience "yield illusions." That is, while the market may offer attractive promised returns, many uninitiated bond investors fail to realize that, to achieve these levels of return over the life of the obligation, *it is necessary to reinvest coupon income at equally high market rates!*

Approximate Promised Yield

Depending upon the accuracy desired, there are several procedures that can be used to compute promised yield. (Although it is currently assumed that the yield computations are executed on interest payment dates, this unrealistic assumption will be relaxed later). It can be computed on the basis of approximate yield, or, for slightly more accuracy, it can be measured on

---

[3] Sidney Homer and Martin L. Leibowitz, *Inside the Yield Book* (Englewood Cliffs, N.J.: Prentice-Hall, 1972), Chapter 1.

[4] Op. cit.

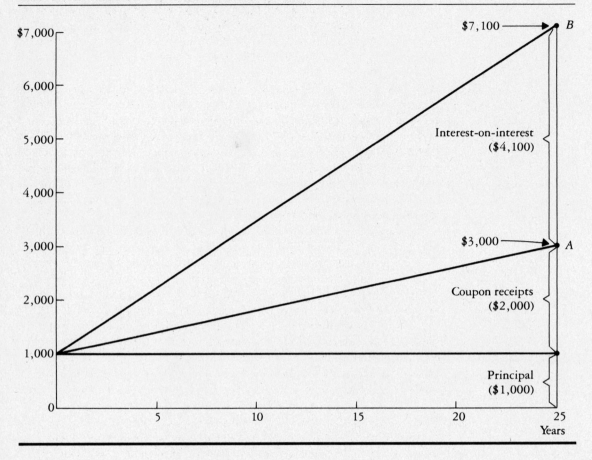

Promised yield at promise 8.00%
Realized yield over the 25 year investment horizon with no coupon reinvestment (pt. A) . 4.50%
Realized yield over the 25 year horizon with coupons reinvested at 8% (pt. B) 8.00%

the basis of present value using annual compounding. Finally, promised yield can be computed in terms of semiannual compounding, which is the most precise procedure and is used in the marketplace.

Looking first at the approximate promised yield (APY), the mechanics of this measure are relatively straightforward as seen in Equation (17–3):

$$(17\text{--}3) \qquad APY = \frac{c_t + \dfrac{P_p - P_m}{n}}{\dfrac{P_p + P_m}{2}}$$

where:

$$P_p = \text{par value of the obligation}$$

$$n = \text{number of years to maturity}$$

$$c_t = \text{the } \textit{annual} \text{ coupon value of the obligation and}$$

$$P_m = \text{the current market price of the issue.}$$

APY is an approximate estimate of the promised yield of an obligation that assumes interest is compounded annually. It is useful because, unlike present value computations, it does not require iteration.

Assume that we want to determine the approximate promised yield of an 8 percent bond, with 20 years remaining to maturity, and a current price of 900 dollars. The approximate yield of this bond is 8.95 percent:

$$APY = \frac{80 + \dfrac{1000 - 900}{20}}{\dfrac{1000 + 900}{2}}$$

$$= 8.95\%.$$

For even more accuracy, promised yield can also be computed using the present value model and annual compounding. Equation (17–4) shows this version of the promised yield valuation model:

(17–4)
$$P_m = \sum_{t=1}^{n} \frac{c_t}{(1 + i)^t} + \frac{P_p}{(1 + i)^n}$$

where all the variables are as described above. This model is more accurate but is also more complex because iteration must be employed to arrive at a solution. It is a variation of internal rate of return and involves the determination of that discount rate, i, which will equate the present value of the stream of coupon receipts (c_t) and principal value (P_p) with the current market price of the obligation (P_m). Using the same illustration as above (the 8 percent, 20 year bond, priced at 900 dollars), we can see that promised yield now amounts to 9.11 percent:

$$900 = 80 \sum_{t=1}^{20} \frac{1}{(1.0911)^t} + 1000 \frac{1}{(1.0911)^{20}}$$

$$= 80 \, (9.0625) + 1000 \, (.1750)$$

$$= 900$$

(Note in the above illustration that the values for $\dfrac{1}{1 + i}$ were obtained from present value interest factor tables.)

A comparison of the results from Equation (17–4) with those obtained from the approximate promised yield computation indicates a variation of 16 basis points in computed promised yield. As a rule, approximate yield tends to *understate* actual promised yield for issues trading at a discount, with the size of the differential varying directly with the length of the holding period, i.e., the greater n is, the bigger the difference will be. Note that, with APY the *ranking* of yields based on Equation (17–3) will generally be identical to the rankings determined by more precise methods.

For maximum accuracy, semiannual, rather than annual, compounding should be used since the cash flow from bonds is semiannual. Even in those situations in which the cash flow occurs over something other than six month intervals (for example, GNMA pass throughs), semiannual compounding is still employed as a basis for yield valuation. Semiannual compounding can be calculated by altering Equation (17–4) as follows:

$$(17\text{--}5) \qquad P_m = \sum_{t=1}^{2n} \frac{c_t/2}{(1 + i/2)^t} + \frac{P_p}{(1 + i/2)^{2n}}$$

where all the variables are as described above. The major adjustments include doubling the number of periods within the investment horizon, since each now covers six months rather than one year. Since coupons are received every six months, the value of c_t is halved. The promised yield with this method amounts to 9.09 percent. The mechanics of the calculation are identical to those in Equation (17–4), so an illustration is unnecessary. The student can, instead, test his skills by using Equation (17–5) to arrive at the indicated yield.

Clearly, the improvement in accuracy (two basis points) is nowhere near as great as it was when we moved from approximate yield to Equation (17–4). Such improved accuracy would be necessary only for large investment sums and large bond portfolios. Notably, Equation (17–5) is the procedure used to determine published bond quotes.

Given prevailing market prices for issues with different coupons and maturities, the investor would use Equations (17–3), (17–4), or (17–5) to select the obligation which provided the most attractive yield opportunities. Determining promised yield and evaluating the return opportunities relative to perceived risk provides an investor with insight into the investment merits and attractiveness of competing obligations.

Yield to Call

While promised yield to maturity is used most often, it is occasionally necessary to establish return on the basis of promised yield to call. Whenever a *premium bond* is quoted at a value equal to or greater than par plus one year's interest, yield to call should be computed in place of yield to maturity, because the marketplace bases its pricing on the most conservative (i.e., lowest) yield measure. Therefore, when bonds are trading at or above a certain dollar value, the "cross-over point" which approximates par plus one year's interest, yield to call will normally provide the lowest yield measure. It assumes that the obligation will *not* remain outstanding to maturity, but instead will be retired at the end of the deferred call period. Thus, it is the promised yield based on an investment horizon extending only to the call date. Yield to call has become a particularly important measure recently because of the many high yielding, high coupon obligations that have been issued which possess substantial levels of call risk.

Yield to call is calculated by using variations of Equations (17–3), (17–4), or (17–5). If the approximate yield to call (AYC) was desired, then the investor would use the following variation of the approximate promised yield computation:

(17–6)
$$AYC = \frac{c_t + \dfrac{P_c - P_m}{nc}}{\dfrac{P_c + P_m}{2}}$$

where:

P_c = the call price of the obligation (as noted above, this is generally equal to par value plus one year's interest) and

nc = the number of years to first call date.

All other variables in the model are as defined above. Observe that this model is comparable to approximate yield to maturity, except that P_c has replaced P_p (in Equation (17–3) and nc has replaced n.

As an illustration, we will return to our 8 percent, 20 year bond, but, in this case, assume that the issue is trading at 115 ($1150) and has five years remaining to first call at a price of 108 ($1080). Using Equation (17–6), we see that:

$$AYC = \frac{80 + \dfrac{1080 - 1150}{5}}{\dfrac{1080 + 1150}{2}} = 5.92\%$$

The approximate yield to call of the obligation is 5.92 percent, and is derived under the assumption that the issue will be prematurely retired after five years at the call price of 108. The student can compute the approximate promised yield to maturity of this issue to confirm that yield to call is the more conservative value. (Promised yield based on Equation (17–3) will equal 6.74 percent).

Similar simple adjustments can be made in present value models (17–4) and (17–5). For the annual compounding approach, yield to call would appear as follows:

(17–7)
$$P_m = \sum_{t=1}^{nc} \frac{c_t}{(1 + i)^t} + \frac{P_c}{(1 + i)^{nc}}$$

where all the variables are described as above. For the semiannual approach to bond valuation, yield to call can be determined using the following model:

(17–8)
$$P_m = \sum_{t=1}^{2nc} \frac{c_t/2}{(1 + i/2)^t} + \frac{P_c}{(1 + i/2)^{2nc}}$$

where all the variables are described as above. The same two changes that were noted with the approximate method are used with the present value methods; i.e., P_p (par value) is replaced with the call price of the issue (P_c), and the remaining life of the obligation is no longer considered term to maturity (n) but, instead, is the number of years or semiannual periods to call (nc).

Finally, note that the return measures determined via the approximate and annual compounding methods are more precise under yield to call situations since they deal with considerably shorter investment horizons. Using the annual compounding procedure (Equation 17–7), the yield to call for our 8 percent, 20 year bond amounts to 5.86 percent. The difference from approximate yield to call (5.92 percent) is only six basis points, though it is in the *opposite* direction than the promised yield comparison; a common relationship with premium bonds. It is normal to expect approximate yield figures to exceed more precise compounding results for *premium* bonds.

Realized Yield

The final measure is realized yield. Rather than assuming that the issue is bought and held to maturity (or first call), realized yield assumes that the investor is taking a trading position and intends to liquidate the bond prior to maturity (or first call) date. In essence the investor has a holding period (hp) which is less than n (or nc). The objective of realized yield is to determine the level of return attainable from trading bonds over relatively short investment horizons. Such information is used to compare realized yield performance in order to select the most promising issue or issues. The evaluation process considers the forecasted value of the bond at date of liquidation, which is, of course, subject to normal levels of uncertainty. (It is also possible to use this procedure to measure *actual* realized yield earned in a completed buy and sell transaction.)

The measure of realized yield is based on the basic promised yield valuation models (17–3), (17–4), and (17–5). The approximate realized yield (ARY) is given in Equation (17–9):

(17–9)
$$ARY = \frac{c_t + \dfrac{P_f - P_m}{hp}}{\dfrac{P_f + P_m}{2}}$$

where:

P_f = the future (selling) price of the issue and

hp = the holding period of the issue, in years.

All other variables are as defined above. Again, the same two variables change: the holding period (hp) is used instead of n and P_f is used in lieu of P_p. Also note that P_f is a *computed value,* rather than a given contractual value. It is calculated through use of promised yield, by defining the years remaining to maturity as n-hp, and by stipulating a forecasted future market yield, i. The computation of future price will be more fully explored in the section below.

Once hp and P_f are determined, approximate realized yield can be calculated. Using our 8 percent, 20 year bond as a basis of illustration, consider a situation in which an investor buys the issue at 750 and anticipates selling it two years later, after interest rates have, hopefully, experienced a substantial decline, at a price of 900. The realized yield of this example would be:

$$ARY = \frac{80 + \dfrac{900 - 750}{2}}{\dfrac{900 + 750}{2}} = 18.79\%$$

The high return is the result of the expected realization of a substantial capital gains in a fairly short period of time.

In a comparable manner, the introduction of P_f and hp into the annual and semiannual compounding versions of yield provides the respective present value versions of realized yield:

(17–10)
$$P_m = \sum_{t=1}^{hp} \frac{c_t}{(1 + i)^t} + \frac{P_f}{(1 + i)^{hp}}$$

and

$$(17\text{--}11) \qquad P_m = \sum_{t=1}^{2hp} \frac{c_t/2}{(1 + i/2)^t} + \frac{P_f}{(1 + i/2)^{2hp}}$$

Because of the usually small number of periods in hp, the added accuracy of these measures is somewhat marginal. In fact, it could be argued that, to the extent that realized yield measures are based on expected price performance, and given the uncertainty inherent in such forecasts, there is ample justification for using either the approximate or annual compounding methods. Surely they would provide more than adequate levels of accuracy under most circumstances. In contrast, if *actual* realized yield is being measured for performance purposes, there is justification for using the more accurate semiannual basis of compounding.

Bond Prices

There are two conditions under which bond dollar prices are important. The first is with regard to realized yield; i.e., the determination of the future price of an issue (P_f). The second condition is when issues are quoted on a (promised) yield basis, as with municipals.

Depending upon the accuracy desired and whether the analyst wishes to work with annual or semiannual compounding, the conversion of a yield based quote to a dollar price can be readily accomplished using Equations (17–4) or (17–5). Using (17–5) as a basis for discussion, it can be seen that the mechanics are simple and no longer involve iteration. Instead, the analyst need only solve the equation for P_m. Coupon (c_t) is given, as is par value (P_p), and market yield (i), which is used as the discount rate. Consider a 5 percent bond with 25 years remaining to maturity that is quoted to yield 6.5 percent. Using the semiannual version of model (17–5) to price this issue:

$$P_m = 50/2 \sum_{t=1}^{50} \frac{1}{\left(1 + \frac{.065}{2}\right)^t} + 1000 \frac{1}{\left(1 + \frac{.065}{2}\right)^{50}}$$

$$= 25 \quad (24.5516) + 1000 \,(.2021) = \$815.90$$

Unlike comparative yield measures, computed price data per se cannot be used alone as a basis for investment decisions since such information really only indicates the amount of capital commitment required to purchase a given security.[5]

In contrast to current market price, anticipated future price (P_f) is computed when bond traders attempt to establish the expected realized

---

[5] Note that if the quoted yield is based on yield to call, then models (17–7) or (17–8) would be used to price the obligation.

yield performance of alternative issues. Portfolio managers with relatively short investment horizons who trade bonds on a regular basis for the capital gains consider expected realized yield, rather than promised yield, to be critical to the investment decision. Again, depending on whether annual or semiannual compounding is desired, P_f can be determined by using the following variations of the realized yield models (17–10) and (17–11):

$$(17-12) \qquad P_f = \sum_{t=1}^{n-hp} \frac{c_t}{(1 + i)^t} + \frac{P_p}{(1 + i)^{n-hp}}$$

and

$$(17-13) \qquad P_f = \sum_{t=1}^{n-2hp} \frac{c_t/2}{(1 + i/2)^t} + \frac{P_p}{(1 + i/2)^{2n-2hp}}$$

where all of the variables are as previously defined.

Observe that Equations (17–12) and (17–13) are simply versions of promised yield: derived measures which, in turn, are based on expected price performance at the *end* of the holding period (hp). Essentially, n-hp defines the remaining term to maturity of the issue at the end of the investor's holding period, i.e., the number of years (or six month periods) remaining at the date the issue is to be sold. The determination of P_f is based on coupon (c_t) and par value (P_p), both of which are given. In contrast, the length of the holding period, and, therefore, the number of years remaining to maturity at date of sale (n-hp), and the expected prevailing market yield at time of sale (i) must be forecast by the analyst. Once this information is obtained/generated, the future price of the obligation can be determined. The real difficulty (and potential source of error) in specifying P_f lies in formulating hp and i.

Consider a 5 percent, 25 year bond, and assume it carries a current price of 816 dollars (which implies a promised yield to maturity of 6.5 percent). Based on extensive evaluation, the market yield for this obligation is expected to decline to 5½ percent in two years. Thus, Equation (17–12) reveals that the P_f will be:

$$P_f = 50 \sum_{t=1}^{25-2} \frac{1}{(1.055)^t} + 1000 \frac{1}{(1.055)^{23}}$$

$$= 50 (12.875) + 1000 (.2919) = \$935.65$$

The mechanics involve determining price two years hence (hp), given the remaining term to maturity and expected interest rates. The computation is identical to that used with promised yield Equations (17–4) and (17–5). Of course, P_f would then be used in either realized yield model (17–10) or (17–11) to compute the expected level of realized return that the issue offers.

Price and Yield Determination on Noninterest Dates

So far, in the bond valuation process we have assumed that the investor buys (or sells) an obligation precisely on the date that interest is due. As a result, the measures are only accurate when issues are traded exactly on coupon payment dates. If approximate yield or the annual compounding version of the present value based model is used, sufficient accuracy is normally obtained by simply employing the computed values, or, perhaps, by roughly extrapolating for transactions that take place on noninterest payment dates. The investor would be dealing with varying degrees of approximation as it is, and certainly a bit more will not upset matters.

However, when the semiannual version of the models is employed, and when high degrees of accuracy are necessary, another version of the price and yield model must be employed for transactions that occur on noninterest payment dates. Fortunately, to do this the basic models presented thus far need be extended only one more step, since, even in practice, the value of an issue that trades X years, Y months, and so many days from maturity is found by extrapolating the bond value (price or yield) for the month before and the month after the day of transaction. Thus, the valuation process involves full months to maturity, rather than years or semiannual periods.[6]

Bond valuation on a noncoupon payment date involves the following simple algorithm:

1. determine the price of the issue via the standard semiannual compounding model for the *next* coupon payment date

2. add the coupon payment to be received at the *next* coupon date (since it is not included in step one)

3. discount this sum, which is equivalent to the value of the bond on the next coupon payment date, to its present value and

4. adjust the computed value for accrued interest.

This can be shown as:

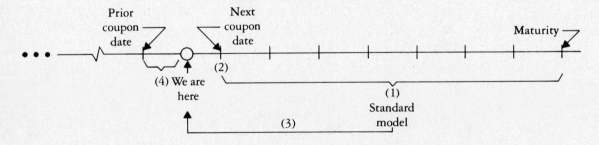

---

[6] Note that for corporate, agency, and municipal markets, a month is described as a 30 day period, regardless of the number of days actually in the month; in contrast, treasury obligations use a 365 (or 366) day calendar and actually count the number of days in the month. For our purposes, we will assume that the standard 30 day month prevails.

Essentially, we find the value of the bond on the next coupon date (step one), add the interest payment to be received on the next coupon date (step two), discount the sum of these back to the present (step three), and finally, net out accrued interest (step four). This can conveniently be put in equation form as follows:

(17–14)

$$P_m = \left[\frac{\sum_{t=1}^{2n} \dfrac{c_t/2}{(1 + i/2)^t} + \dfrac{P_p}{(1 + i/2)^{2n}} + \dfrac{c_t}{2}}{(1 + i/2)^{m/6}} \right] - \frac{c_t}{2}\left(1 - \frac{m}{6}\right)$$

where

m = the number of months to the next coupon payment date and

n = the number of semiannual periods to maturity *after* the next coupon payment date, and all other variables are as defined above.

An examination of Equation (17–14) quickly reveals the four steps in the algorithm. It is a suprisingly simple procedure and does not involve extensive computational complexity. Model (17–14) can be used to determine *yield* by solving for i (through iteration) or, when given a market yield, can also be used to determine *price* by solving for P_m. In addition, with slight variations of this basic (promised yield to maturity) model, yield to call, and expected realized yield can be readily computed.

To demonstrate the application of the model, consider the following example. Assume we want to find the price, on an accrued interest basis, of a 1,000 dollar, 4 percent bond with 12 years and 3 months remaining to maturity that is being traded to yield 3.75 percent. Using Equation (17–14), we can determine its price as follows:

$$P_m = \left[\frac{\sum_{t=1}^{24} \dfrac{40/2}{(1.01875)^t} + \dfrac{1000}{(1.01875)^{24}} + \dfrac{40}{2}}{(1.01875)^{3/6}} \right] - \frac{40}{2}\left(1 - \frac{3}{6}\right)$$

$$= \left[\frac{20\,(19.185) + 1000\,(.6403) + 20}{1.00933} \right] - 20\,(.5)$$

$$= \left[\frac{1044}{1.00933} \right] - 10 = \$1024.35$$

This procedure is universal in finding the price or yield of an obligation that trades on any date other than the interest payment date. For those situations in which the issue trades within the month, (17–14) is used to find the price (or yield) at full monthly intervals on both sides of the purchase date. To find the price of an issue that has 12 years, 3 months, and 15 days to maturity, one would value the obligation (in full monthly increments) on both sides of the 15 days; i.e., find the price with 12 years and 3 months to maturity, and with 12 years and 4 months to maturity. The value at 12 years, 3 months was determined above. What is lacking is the price figure for 12 years, 4 months (which, of course, is also computed via [17–14]). Once the investor has these two values, he would simply use extrapolation to determine the price or yield of the obligation.

Tax-Exempt Issues

Municipal bonds, treasury issues, and many agency obligations possess one common characteristic: their interest income is partially or fully tax-exempt. Recall that treasury and federal agency obligations are exempt from state and local taxation. In fact, some agencies are even free from federal income taxes (HUD project notes, for example). And, of course, the interest income on municipal obligations is exempt from federal and local levies.

Using promised yield as a basis of discussion, the tax status of an issue (including its ordinary income and capital gains tax liability) can be included in the valuation model as follows:

(17–15)
$$P_m = \sum_{t=1}^{2n} \frac{C_{t/2}(1 - \tau)}{(1 + i/2)^t} + \frac{P_p - k(P_p - P_m)}{(1 + i/2)^{2n}}$$

where:

τ = the investor's marginal tax liability on ordinary income

k = the investor's capital gains tax rate,

and the other terms are as defined above. While (17–15) provides a measure of *after tax* promised yield, it follows that, with slight variations, yield to call and realized yield can also be modified to readily accommodate the various tax effects (likewise, to transactions that occur on noninterest payments dates).

In addition, the tax adjusted models can be used when some of the issues are subject to normal taxation and others are totally tax-free. The valuation process itself adjusts for the specific tax liability of the obligation in generating after tax yield (or price) because the specification of τ and k in (17–15) does not define the source or extent of tax liability. As a result, these variables should include appropriate federal, state, and/or local tax rates (depending, of course, on the exposure of the specific issue). For example, τ would equal 0 for a person holding a municipal bond in the state of Texas, since Texas has no state or local income taxes. Likewise, it would be 0 for a California resident holding a California issue. In contrast, however, that same California issue would require a $\tau > 0$ for a person living in New York city, as the issue would not be tax-exempt for residents of New York and residents of that city are subject to state and local income taxes.

Place of residency is, of course, totally irrelevant in the case of capital gains. Since the mechanics of yield and price valuation for the tax adjusted models are no different than those for other approximate yield and present value based models, it is unnecessary to provide a detailed illustration of computational techniques. Instead, if the reader wants to try his hand, he might consider the following example. Assume a resident of Texas (with $\tau = 0$) is considering the purchase of a 5 percent, 25 year municipal obligation that is currently priced at $3,827. (Remember par value with municipals is normally $5,000). The investor has a 20 percent capital gains tax rate and wants to determine the after tax promised yield of the issue.[7]

Undoubtedly the most popular and one of the most often cited measures of performance for municipal issues is the "fully taxable equivalent yield (FTEY)." This is a simple adjustment for computing promised yields for those issues with tax-exempt features. The process involves determining promised yield using any of the variations presented above. The computed promised yield figure is then adjusted to reflect the rate of return that must be earned on fully taxable issues, such as corporates, in order to provide a yield equivalent to the fully or partially tax-exempt obligation. It is measured as:

$$(17\text{--}16) \qquad\qquad FTEY = \frac{i}{1 - T}$$

where:

i = promised yield and

T = the amount and type of tax *exemption* provided by the issue in question, and all other terms are as defined earlier.

A caveat is in order, however. This simple computation is applicable only to par bonds or current coupon obligations, such as new issues. In other words, the measure considers only interest income and, by ignoring capital gains, is inappropriate for issues trading at significant variations from par value. Like τ in the after tax promised yield model (17--15), T in the fully taxable equivalent yield computation includes any applicable federal, state, or local income taxes. Rather than dealing with an issue's tax liability, as was done with (17--15), T is concerned with the extent of tax *exemption* provided by the bond.

Bond value tables, commonly known as "bond books" or "yield books" are available to eliminate much of the mathematics from bond valuation. An illustration of a page from a yield book is provided in Figure 17--2. It is

---

[7] Using (17--15), the answer is 6.91 percent.

Figure 17-2 A Yield Book

A — YEARS and MONTHS — 8%

Yield	14-6	15-0	15-6	16-0	16-6	17-0	17-6	18-0
4.00	143.69	144.79	145.88	146.94	147.98	149.00	150.00	150.98
4.20	140.96	141.97	142.97	143.95	144.91	145.84	146.76	147.66
4.40	138.29	139.23	140.14	141.04	141.92	142.78	143.62	144.44
4.60	135.69	136.55	137.39	138.21	139.01	139.80	140.56	141.31
4.80	133.15	133.94	134.71	135.46	136.19	136.90	137.60	138.28
5.00	130.68	131.40	132.09	132.77	133.44	134.09	134.72	135.33
5.20	128.27	128.92	129.55	130.16	130.76	131.35	131.92	132.47
5.40	125.91	126.50	127.07	127.62	128.16	128.69	129.20	129.70
5.60	123.62	124.14	124.65	125.15	125.63	126.10	126.55	127.00
5.80	121.38	121.84	122.30	122.74	123.16	123.58	123.98	124.38
6.00	119.19	119.60	120.00	120.39	120.77	121.13	121.49	121.83
6.10	118.11	118.50	118.87	119.24	119.59	119.93	120.26	120.59
6.20	117.05	117.41	117.76	118.10	118.43	118.75	119.06	119.36
6.30	116.01	116.34	116.67	116.98	117.29	117.58	117.87	118.15
6.40	114.97	115.28	115.58	115.88	116.16	116.43	116.70	116.96
6.50	113.95	114.24	114.51	114.78	115.05	115.30	115.54	115.78
6.60	112.94	113.20	113.46	113.71	113.95	114.18	114.40	114.62
6.70	111.94	112.18	112.42	112.64	112.86	113.07	113.28	113.48
6.80	110.95	111.17	111.39	111.59	111.79	111.99	112.17	112.35
6.90	109.98	110.18	110.37	110.56	110.74	110.91	111.08	111.24
7.00	109.02	109.20	109.37	109.53	109.70	109.85	110.00	110.15
7.10	108.07	108.22	108.38	108.52	108.67	108.80	108.94	109.07
7.20	107.13	107.27	107.40	107.53	107.65	107.77	107.89	108.00
7.30	106.20	106.32	106.43	106.54	106.65	106.75	106.85	106.95
7.40	105.28	105.38	105.48	105.57	105.66	105.75	105.83	105.92
7.50	104.37	104.46	104.54	104.62	104.69	104.76	104.83	104.90
7.60	103.48	103.54	103.61	103.67	103.73	103.78	103.84	103.89
7.70	102.59	102.64	102.69	102.73	102.78	102.82	102.86	102.90
7.80	101.72	101.75	101.78	101.81	101.84	101.87	101.89	101.92
7.90	100.85	100.87	100.88	100.90	100.91	100.93	100.94	100.95
8.00	100.00	100.00	100.00	100.00	100.00	100.00	100.00	100.00
8.10	99.16	99.14	99.13	99.11	99.10	99.09	99.07	99.06
8.20	98.32	98.29	98.26	98.24	98.21	98.18	98.16	98.14
8.30	97.50	97.45	97.41	97.37	97.33	97.29	97.26	97.22
8.40	96.68	96.62	96.57	96.51	96.46	96.41	96.37	96.32
8.50	95.88	95.81	95.74	95.67	95.61	95.55	95.49	95.43
8.60	95.08	95.00	94.91	94.84	94.76	94.69	94.62	94.56
8.70	94.29	94.20	94.10	94.01	93.93	93.85	93.77	93.69
8.80	93.52	93.41	93.30	93.20	93.10	93.01	92.92	92.84
8.90	92.75	92.63	92.51	92.40	92.29	92.19	92.09	92.00
9.00	91.99	91.86	91.73	91.61	91.49	91.38	91.27	91.17
9.10	91.24	91.09	90.96	90.82	90.70	90.57	90.46	90.34
9.20	90.50	90.34	90.19	90.05	89.91	89.78	89.66	89.54
9.30	89.76	89.60	89.44	89.29	89.14	89.00	88.87	88.74
9.40	89.04	88.86	88.69	88.53	88.38	88.23	88.09	87.96
9.50	88.32	88.13	87.96	87.79	87.62	87.47	87.32	87.18
9.60	87.61	87.42	87.23	87.05	86.88	86.72	86.56	86.42
9.70	86.91	86.71	86.51	86.32	86.15	85.98	85.81	85.66
9.80	86.22	86.01	85.80	85.61	85.42	85.24	85.08	84.91
9.90	85.54	85.31	85.10	84.90	84.70	84.52	84.35	84.18
10.00	84.86	84.63	84.41	84.20	84.00	83.81	83.63	83.45
10.20	83.53	83.28	83.05	82.82	82.61	82.41	82.20	82.04
10.40	82.23	81.97	81.72	81.48	81.25	81.04	80.84	80.64
10.60	80.96	80.68	80.42	80.17	79.93	79.71	79.50	79.29
10.80	79.72	79.43	79.15	78.89	78.64	78.41	78.19	77.98
11.00	78.50	78.20	77.91	77.64	77.39	77.14	76.91	76.70
11.20	77.31	77.00	76.71	76.43	76.16	75.91	75.67	75.45
11.40	76.15	75.83	75.52	75.24	74.96	74.70	74.46	74.23
11.60	75.02	74.68	74.37	74.07	73.79	73.53	73.28	73.04
11.80	73.90	73.56	73.24	72.94	72.65	72.38	72.13	71.89
12.00	72.82	72.47	72.14	71.83	71.54	71.26	71.00	70.76

8% — YEARS and MONTHS — B

Yield	18-6	19-0	19-6	20-0	20-6	21-0	21-6	22-0
4.00	151.94	152.88	153.81	154.71	155.60	156.47	157.32	158.16
4.20	148.54	149.40	150.25	151.08	151.89	152.68	153.46	154.22
4.40	145.24	146.03	146.80	147.56	148.29	149.02	149.72	150.41
4.60	142.05	142.76	143.46	144.15	144.82	145.47	146.11	146.74
4.80	138.95	139.60	140.23	140.85	141.45	142.05	142.62	143.19
5.00	135.94	136.52	137.10	137.65	138.20	138.73	139.25	139.76
5.20	133.02	133.54	134.06	134.56	135.05	135.52	135.99	136.44
5.40	130.18	130.65	131.11	131.56	132.00	132.42	132.84	133.24
5.60	127.43	127.85	128.26	128.66	129.04	129.42	129.79	130.14
5.80	124.76	125.13	125.49	125.84	126.18	126.51	126.84	127.15
6.00	122.17	122.49	122.81	123.11	123.41	123.70	123.98	124.25
6.10	120.90	121.20	121.50	121.78	122.06	122.33	122.59	122.84
6.20	119.65	119.93	120.21	120.47	120.73	120.98	121.22	121.46
6.30	118.42	118.68	118.93	119.18	119.42	119.65	119.87	120.09
6.40	117.21	117.45	117.68	117.91	118.13	118.34	118.55	118.75
6.50	116.01	116.23	116.45	116.66	116.86	117.05	117.24	117.43
6.60	114.83	115.04	115.23	115.43	115.61	115.79	115.96	116.13
6.70	113.67	113.86	114.04	114.21	114.38	114.54	114.70	114.85
6.80	112.53	112.69	112.86	113.01	113.17	113.31	113.46	113.59
6.90	111.40	111.55	111.70	111.84	111.97	112.11	112.23	112.36
7.00	110.29	110.42	110.55	110.68	110.80	110.92	111.03	111.14
7.10	109.19	109.31	109.42	109.54	109.64	109.75	109.85	109.94
7.20	108.11	108.21	108.31	108.40	108.50	108.60	108.68	108.77
7.30	107.04	107.13	107.22	107.30	107.38	107.46	107.54	107.61
7.40	105.99	106.07	106.14	106.21	106.28	106.35	106.41	106.47
7.50	104.96	105.02	105.08	105.14	105.19	105.25	105.30	105.35
7.60	103.94	103.99	104.03	104.08	104.12	104.16	104.20	104.24
7.70	102.93	102.97	103.00	103.04	103.07	103.10	103.13	103.16
7.80	101.94	101.96	101.99	102.01	102.03	102.05	102.07	102.09
7.90	100.96	100.98	100.99	101.00	101.01	101.01	101.02	101.04
8.00	100.00	100.00	100.00	100.00	100.00	100.00	100.00	100.00
8.10	99.05	99.04	99.03	99.02	99.01	99.00	98.99	98.98
8.20	98.11	98.09	98.07	98.05	98.03	98.01	97.99	97.98
8.30	97.19	97.16	97.13	97.10	97.07	97.04	97.01	96.99
8.40	96.28	96.24	96.20	96.16	96.12	96.08	96.05	96.02
8.50	95.38	95.33	95.28	95.23	95.19	95.14	95.10	95.06
8.60	94.49	94.43	94.37	94.32	94.26	94.21	94.16	94.12
8.70	93.62	93.55	93.48	93.42	93.36	93.30	93.24	93.19
8.80	92.76	92.68	92.60	92.53	92.46	92.40	92.34	92.28
8.90	91.91	91.82	91.74	91.66	91.58	91.51	91.44	91.38
9.00	91.07	90.98	90.89	90.80	90.72	90.64	90.56	90.49
9.10	90.24	90.14	90.04	89.95	89.86	89.78	89.70	89.62
9.20	89.43	89.32	89.21	89.11	89.02	88.93	88.84	88.76
9.30	88.62	88.51	88.40	88.29	88.19	88.09	88.00	87.91
9.40	87.83	87.71	87.59	87.48	87.37	87.27	87.17	87.08
9.50	87.05	86.92	86.79	86.68	86.57	86.46	86.36	86.26
9.60	86.27	86.14	86.01	85.89	85.77	85.66	85.55	85.45
9.70	85.51	85.37	85.24	85.11	84.99	84.87	84.76	84.66
9.80	84.76	84.62	84.48	84.34	84.22	84.10	83.98	83.87
9.90	84.02	83.87	83.72	83.59	83.46	83.33	83.21	83.10
10.00	83.29	83.13	82.98	82.84	82.71	82.58	82.45	82.34
10.20	81.86	81.69	81.53	81.38	81.24	81.10	80.97	80.85
10.40	80.46	80.28	80.12	79.96	79.81	79.67	79.53	79.40
10.60	79.10	78.92	78.74	78.58	78.42	78.28	78.13	78.00
10.80	77.78	77.59	77.41	77.24	77.08	76.92	76.78	76.64
11.00	76.49	76.29	76.11	75.93	75.76	75.61	75.46	75.31
11.20	75.23	75.03	74.84	74.66	74.49	74.33	74.17	74.03
11.40	74.01	73.80	73.61	73.42	73.25	73.08	72.93	72.78
11.60	72.82	72.61	72.41	72.22	72.04	71.87	71.71	71.56
11.80	71.66	71.44	71.24	71.05	70.87	70.70	70.53	70.38
12.00	70.53	70.31	70.10	69.91	69.72	69.55	69.39	69.23

Source: Reproduced with permission from Expanded Bond Values Publication #83, pp. 879–880, copyright 1970 Financial Publishing Co., Boston, Mass.

like a present value interest factor table to the extent that a matrix of bond prices is provided relative to a stated coupon rate, various terms to maturity (on the horizontal axis), and promised yields (on the vertical axis). Such a table allows the user to readily determine either promised yield or price. Observe in situation A that a 17½ year, 8 percent bond yielding 10 percent would carry a price of *83.63*. Likewise, in situation B, a 20 year issue which is priced at 109.54 would yield 7.*10 percent*. As might be expected, access to computers via office and portable terminals has substantially reduced the need for and use of yield books. For our purposes though, it is essential that the detailed mechanics and subtleties of the various yield and price models be fully understood in order to appreciate the dimensions of promised yield, yield to call, realized yield, and bond prices.

Determinants of Bond Yields and Yield Spreads

The value of a bond is equal to the present value of its future cash flow stream. An important dimension of the bond valuation model is the rate at which the future cash flows are discounted. In the promised yield version of the model, this rate reflects prevailing market interest rates and indicates the importance of interest rates in the bond valuation process. Because the prices of both new and seasoned issues are closely related to interest behavior, they are stated in terms of economic cost, *bond yields* or *interest rates*. Thus, market interest rates are reflected in bond yields which, in turn, influence the cost of funds to issuers in the new issues market, the return to investors in the new and seasoned issues segments of the market, and the price behavior of obligations in the secondary market. It follows that bond managers must constantly evaluate the current level of market interest rates and expected changes in these rates.

This book takes a practical view of the role of interest rates in the bond investment decision. We maintain that the assessment of interest rates is absolutely essential to the attainment of attractive bond portfolio returns. But the assessment of interest rates, and the development of interest rate formulations, is a complex economic matter which often involves extensive econometric modeling, a task we shall leave to the professional economist. Instead, our goal as bond investors and bond portfolio managers should be to continually monitor current and expected interest rate behavior. This can be done in an informal fashion if attention is paid to the determinants of interest rates. A bond portfolio manager can assess the *major* dimensions of interest rate behavior on his own, and rely on economic service bureaus for more detailed insight into the structure and behavior of market rates. This is precisely the way many bond houses and large bond portfolio management firms operate.

Fundamental Determinants of Interest Rates

According to published market sources, average interest rates for long-term corporate bonds in September of 1975 amounted to a whopping 10.1 percent. Some 15 months later, the same average corporate bond rate had dropped to 7.8 percent. A primary concern to the bond investor is *why* interest rates behave this way. Obviously, bond prices rose dramatically during the period when market interest rates dropped and very attractive returns were obtained by aggressive, knowledgeable bond investors. Although this is only a single case in point, it indicates the need for monitoring interest rates. Essentially, interest rates (r) can be specified according to the following conceptual model:

$$(17-17) \qquad\qquad r = RFR + RP + I$$

where:

$$RFR = \text{the risk-free rate of interest}$$

$$RP = \text{the risk premium and}$$

$$I = \text{expected inflation.}$$

While (17–17) appears deceptively simple, it is a complete statement of the complex nature of interest rate behavior. The difficult part is the specification of *future* behavior with regard to such aspects as inflation, default, and other economic considerations. In this regard, interest rates are not unlike stock prices since they are extremely difficult to forecast with any degree of accuracy.[8]

In essence, interest rates can be viewed as being related to economic and issue characteristics:

$$r = f \text{ (economic forces + issue characteristics)}$$

$$= (RFR + I) + RP$$

This is nothing more than a rearranged version of Equation (17–17), but it facilitates a more thorough discussion of the fundamental determinants of interest rates.[9]

The pure rate of interest (RFR) is the economic cost of money, and represents the opportunity cost necessary to compensate individuals for foregoing consumption. The pure rate of interest is some interest rate level below which investors would be indifferent to holding either cash or a financial asset like bonds. The pure rate is that fairly stable marginal rate of return which must be offered in order to induce individuals to save or invest.

Inflation is the other economic dimension of interest rates. The *level of inflation* (I) is added to the risk-free rate (RFR) in order to specify a general *market based* level of interest. For example, if the RFR is 3 percent, and expected inflation is 5½ percent, then it follows that the market based (nominal) risk-free rate of interest (r) would equal approximately 8½ percent. Given the stability of the RFR, it is clear that *the wide swings in r*

---

[8] Oswald D. Bowlin and John D. Martin, "Extrapolations of Yields Over the Short Run; Forecast or Folly?" *Journal of Monetary Economics,* 1 (1975), pp. 275–488; and Stephen F. Leroy, "Interest Rates and the Inflation Premium," Federal Reserve Bank of Kansas City Monthly *Review* (May, 1973), pp. 11–18.

[9] For an excellent and extensive exploration of interest rates and interest rate behavior, the interested reader is strongly urged to see James C. Van Horne, *Financial Market Rates and Flows* (Englewood Cliffs, N.J.: Prentice-Hall, Inc., 1978).

experienced in the past decade or so can largely be attributable to swings in real or perceived inflation.

Supply and demand for loanable funds are the fundamental variables within the economic dimensions of r. For example, as the supply of loanable funds increases, the level of interest rates declines, other things being equal; the opposite effect, of course, holds when the demand for loanable funds increases. On the *supply side,* the actions of the Federal Reserve Open Market Committee have a definite influence on the cost of funds because they affect the supply of money. In addition, the supply of loanable funds is influenced by institutional investment policies. The technical side of the market, including such things as the unsold inventory of new issues held by underwriters and the new issue calendar, also affects supply.

Affecting demand are the capital and operating needs of the U.S. Government, federal agencies, state and local governments, corporations, and institutions.[10] Essentially, the *net* intensity of demand varies according to requirements in each of the sectors. The taxation and expenditures policy (fiscal policy) of the federal government often leads to deficit budgets and increases demand for loanable funds from the treasury. Likewise, the level of consumer demand, along with the amount of internally generated funds (net of dividend payouts), will help determine corporate needs to raise capital.

An article by Feldstein and Eckstein (F&E)[11] described the fundamental determinants of interest rates using many of the same economic variables noted above. They attempted to define the determinants of yield on seasoned long-term Moody's AAA rated corporate bonds over the 62 quarters from 1954 through 1969. F&E found that bond yields were inversely related to money supply, and directly related to the level of real personal income (used as a proxy for economic activity), the demand for loanable funds (from the treasury), the level of inflation, and changes in short-run interest rate expectations (included as a "psychological" facet of market behavior). The r^2 value of their model was a hefty 99.2 percent. Variable relationships with interest rates were as expected, and many of the economic variables noted above were significant determinants. Such findings imply that because of the importance of interest rates in yield and price behavior, investors should monitor such economic factors as the supply and demand for loanable funds, Federal Reserve policy, fiscal policy, and prices.

Interest rates (r) are also influenced by issue characteristics. The *risk premium* (RP) component of r is directly associated with the characteristics of the issue and issuer. Whereas the economic forces (the risk-free rate and

---

[10] William C. Freund and Edward D. Zinbarg, "Application of Flow of Funds to Interest Rate Forecasting," *The Journal of Finance,* Vol. 13, No. 2 (May, 1963), pp. 231–248; and Edmund A. Mennis, "Aggregate Measures of Corporate Profits," *Financial Analysts Journal,* Vol. 20, No. 1 (January–February, 1964), pp. 30–31.

[11] Martin Feldstein and Otto Eckstein, "The Fundamental Determinants of the Interest Rate," *The Review of Economics and Statistics,* Vol. 52, No. 4 (Nov., 1970), pp. 363–375.

inflation) reflect a market or system wide level of interest rates, issue characteristics are unique to individual securities or market sectors. Thus, the differences in the yields of corporate and treasury issues are *not* caused by economic forces, but by differential issue characteristics, i.e., differences in the risk premium.

There are three major components within the risk premium that should be considered by bond investors and portfolio managers:

1. quality differentials (or risk of default)

2. term to maturity, which can affect rate uncertainty as well as yield and price volatility,

3. indenture provisions (including collateral, call features, and sinking fund provisions).

Of the three, quality and maturity considerations are the most important and dominate the risk premium.

Quality Considerations reflect the risk of default. These are largely captured in agency ratings. The matter of quality is primarily the ability of the issuer to service outstanding debt obligations. The greater the ability of the issuer to service the debt, the lower the risk of default. Quality considerations mean yield differentials will exist not only between differently rated issues, but also between different market segments. For example, AAA rated obligations possess lower risk of default than, say, BBB obligations do and, therefore, provide lower yield.

There is substantial empirical support for the position that quality derived risk premiums are largely dependent upon the intrinsic characteristics of the issuer.[12] Note, however, that quality based yield premiums are, at times, also closely related to prevailing economic conditions. When the economy becomes depressed and activity begins to slacken, the desire for quality increases and higher quality issues are bid up in price as investors abandon low quality obligations to seek the security of higher rated bonds. Except in these times of depressed economic activity (when quality derived yield spreads are abnormally wide), the default risk component of the risk premium is fairly stable and tends to vary inversely with the quality of the issue.

Maturity is also an important determinant of the risk premium because it affects the level of uncertainty assumed by the investor as well as price and yield volatility. While this component will be discussed in the section

---

[12] See for example: Lawrence Fisher, "Determinants of Risk Premiums on Corporate Bonds," *Journal of Political Economy*, Vol. 67, No. 3 (June, 1959), p. 217; Larry K. Hastie, "Determinants of Municipal Bond Yields," *Journal of Financial and Quantitative Analysis*, Vol. 7, No. 3 (June, 1972), pp. 1729–1748; and Joseph J. Horton, Jr., "Statistical Classification of Municipal Bonds," *Journal of Bank Research* (Autumn, 1970), pp. 29–40.

dealing with the term structure, it should be clear that, other things being equal, there is generally a positive relationship between the term to maturity of an issue and the level of interest rates.

Bond Indenture Provisions are the final risk premium determinant. Relevant aspects include the amount of collateral provided, the call feature, and sinking fund provisions. Collateral provides capital protection to the investor on those rare occasions of corporate insolvency and forced liquidation,[13] and is the factor that distinguishes a mortgage bond from a debenture obligation. Because it influences the quality of an issue, collateral is often an aspect of an agency rating. However, differences of several basis points are common for comparably rated issues which differ only in terms of collateral provisions.

The call feature is perhaps the most influential bond indenture provision. Other things being equal, the greater the call risk protection provided, the lower the market yield of the obligation, particularly for new issues and current coupon obligations.[14] Clearly, a ten year deferred call feature provides more call risk protection than, say, a freely callable provision does, and, therefore, should logically result in lower yield. This call protection becomes especially important and valuable during a period of high interest rates.

The final indenture provision affecting the risk premium is the sinking fund feature. This has a fairly nominal effect and its main influence is felt in the new issues market. The sinking fund provision is normally a means of reducing the investor's risk and therefore should result in lower yield for two major reasons. First, a sinking fund reduces default risk by providing for orderly debt service and systematic reduction of outstanding principle. Second, purchases for a sinking fund are viewed as providing support for the bond because of added demand and also a more liquid secondary market because of the increased trading. In fact, Jen and Wert[15] demonstrated that the lower yields on sinking fund issues can be explained in terms of the term structure of interest rates. Since sinking fund provisions result in reduced average maturity, their effect is to reduce the risk premium component of interest rates much like a shorter maturity would reduce yield.

Thus, such issue characteristics as sinking funds, call features, and collateral, along with term to maturity and risk of default, should be

---

[13] Harold G. Fraine and Robert H. Mills, "Effect of Defaults and Credit Determination on Yields of Corporate Bonds," *Journal of Finance*, Vol. 16, No. 3 (September, 1961), pp. 423–434.

[14] Frank C. Jen and James E. Wert, "The Value of the Deferred Call Privilege," *National Banking Review*, Vol. 3, No. 1 (March, 1966), pp. 369–378; and Michael D. Joehnk and James E. Wert, "The Call-Risk Performance of the Discounted Seasoned Issue," *Mississippi Valley Journal of Business and Economics*, Vol. 9, No. 2 (Winter, 1973–1974), pp. 1–15.

[15] Jen and Wert, "The Value of the Deferred Call Privilege."

carefully evaluated in order to fully appreciate current and expected levels of market yield on *competitive* fixed income securities.

Term Structure of Interest Rates

The term structure of interest rates has long intrigued theoreticians, academicians, and practitioners. As a result, this concept has been the subject of considerable theoretical and empirical work.[16] Burton Malkiel notes in one of his works that,

. . . indeed the major reasons for differences in bond yields may be unrelated to the maturity of the securities involved. Nevertheless, one of the most intriguing differences among market interest rates concerns the relationship among the yield of high grade securities that differ only in their term to maturity . . .[17]

The term structure of interest rates (or the "yield curve" as it is more popularly known) is a static function which relates *term* to maturity to *yield* to maturity at *a given point in time.* Thus, it represents a cross section of yields for a category of bonds that *are comparable in all respects but maturity.* The quality of the issues must be held constant, as should coupon, call feature, and perhaps even industry category. One can derive different yield curves for treasury issues, government agencies, prime grade municipals, AAA utilities, and so on.

As an example, consider Figure 17–3 below. The yield curve is constructed for U.S. Treasury obligations that traded on February 23, 1978. Yield to maturity information on a variety of comparable treasury issues was obtained from *The Wall Street Journal.* These promised yields are represented on the graph by the several plotted points. After the yields are plotted, the yield curve itself is drawn.

All yield curves, of course, do not have the same shape as Figure 17–3. Quite the contrary, for, while yield curves per se are static in nature, *their behavior over time is quite fluid!* As a result, the shape of the yield curve can undergo dramatic alterations. In particular, it can follow one of the four patterns shown in Figure 17–4. The ascending curve is the most common and tends to prevail when interest rates are at low or modest levels. The declining yield curve is relatively common and tends to exist when rates are at relatively high levels. The humped yield curve occurs when interest rates

---

[16] See, for example: J. Huston McCulloch, "Measuring the Term Structure of Interest Rates," *Journal of Business,* Vol. 44, No. 1 (January, 1971), pp. 19–31; William T. Carleton and Ian A. Cooper, "Estimation and Uses of the Term Structure of Interest Rates," *Journal of Finance,* Vol. 31, No. 4 (September, 1976), pp. 1067–1084; and Burton G. Malkiel, *The Term Structure of Interest Rates* (Princeton, N.J.: Princeton University Press, 1966).

[17] Burton G. Malkiel, *The Term Structure of Interest Rates: Theory, Empirical Evidence, and Applications* (New York: The McCaleb–Seiler Publishing Company, 1970), p. 12.

Figure 17–3 **Construction of a Yield Curve**

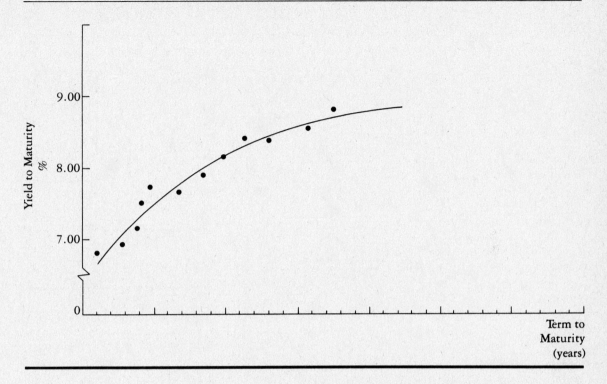

are extremely high and about to retreat to more normal levels. Finally, there is the flat yield curve which rarely exists for any period of time. In all of the yield curve illustrations, the slope of the line tends to level off after 15 years. This is common market behavior. After a point ($\cong$ 15 years), promised yield differentials which exist with longer maturities tend to be rather insignificant, especially relative to the spreads that occur at the shorter end.

While the effects of term to maturity on comparative promised yield (r) are obvious from examining the various shapes of the term structure, it is *not* equally clear why the term structure assumes different shapes. Fortunately, there is an extensive body of theoretical and empirical literature available to help explain the shape of yield curves. Three major theories are available: the expectations hypothesis, the liquidity preference hypothesis, and the segmented market hypothesis.[18]

---

[18] For a more extensive discussion of the alternative theories of the term structure of interest rates, see: Malkiel, *Term Structure of Interest Rates: Theory, Empirical Evidence* and James C. Van Horne, *Financial Markets*.

Figure 17–4 **Types of Yield Curves**

A Rising Yield Curve is formed when the yields on short-term issues are low and rise consistently with longer maturities and flatten out at the extremes.

A Declining Yield Curve is formed when the yields on short-term issues are high and yields on subsequently longer maturities decline consistently.

A Flat Yield Curve has approximately equal yields on short-term and long-term issues.

A Humped Yield Curve is formed when yields on intermediate-term issues are above those on short-term issues, and the rates on long-term issues decline to levels below those for the short-term and then level out.

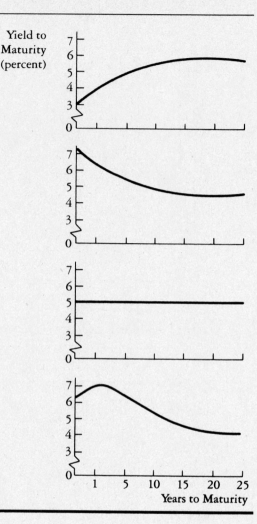

Expectations Hypothesis

According to this theory, the shape of the term structure is explained by the interest rate expectations of market participants. More specifically, *any long-term rate is simply the geometric mean of current and future one year rates expected to prevail over the horizon of the issue.*

In essence, a series of intermediate and long-term rates are part of the term structure, each of which, in turn, is a reflection of the geometric average of current and expected one year rates. Under such conditions, the equilibrium long-term rate is clearly that which the long-term investor would expect to earn through successive investments in short-term securities over an investment horizon equal to the term to maturity of the longer term issue. This relationship can be formalized in a general manner as follows:

(17–18)

$$(1 + {}_tR_N) = [(1 + {}_tR_1)(1 + {}_{t+1}r_1) \ldots (1 + {}_{t+n-1}r_1)]^{1/N}$$

where:

R_N = actual long term rate

N = term to maturity (in years) of long issue

R = current one year rate and

${}_{t+i}r_1$ = expected one year yield during some future period, $t + i$.

As a practical approximation of Equation (17–18), it is, of course, possible to use the *arithmetic* average of one year rates to generate long-term yields.

The expectations theory can account for any shape of yield curve. If short-term rates are expected to rise in the future, then the yield curve will be ascending; if short-term rates are expected to fall, then the long-term rates will lie below the short-term rates and the term structure will descend. Similar explanation can be made for flat and humped yield curves. Consider the following example of how the expectations hypothesis can explain the shape of the term structure of interest rates. Given:

$${}_tR_1 = 5\tfrac{1}{2}\% \qquad {}_{t+1}r_1 = 6\% \qquad {}_{t+2}r_1 = 7\tfrac{1}{2}\% \qquad {}_{t+3}r_1 = 8\tfrac{1}{2}\%$$

and also that:

$${}_tR_1 = 5.50\% \text{ (given)}$$

$${}_tR_2 = (.055 + .06)/2 = 5.75\%$$

$${}_tR_3 = (.055 + .06 + .075)/3 = 6.33\%$$

$${}_tR_4 = (.055 + .06 + .075 + .085)/4 = 6.88\%$$

In the above illustration (which uses the arithmetic average as an approximation of geometric mean), the yield curve is upward sloping because investors currently expect future short-term rates to be above current short-term rates. This is not how the term structure is formally constructed. It is constructed as demonstrated in Figure 17–3 with regard to prevailing promised yields for issues with different maturities. Rather, what the expectations hypothesis attempts to explain is *why* the yield curve is upward sloping, downward sloping, humped, or flat. It attempts to explain the type of expectations implicit in various term structures. The evidence is fairly substantial (and convincing) that the expectations hypothesis is a workable and (somewhat) practical explanation of the term structure.[19]

The implications of the expectations hypothesis are, of course, quite clear. If, for example, lower rates are more likely to occur in the future than high yields are, then the term structure should be descending. This expectation would suggest that long-term bonds may be attractive investments because the investor would want to lock in prevailing higher yields (which should decline in the future) and/or capture the capital gains potential that should accompany a decline in rates. Such expectations based action on the part of investors will only reinforce the descending shape of the yield curve as long maturities are bid up (and yields decline) and short issues are avoided (so yields rise). These shifts between long and short-term maturities will continue until equilibrium occurs or expectations are revised. Similarly, an ascending yield curve indicates that investors expect rates to rise. Under such conditions, investors would prefer shorter maturity securities because the decline would not be as severe when rates rise and the shorter maturities can be "rolled over" (sold) and the proceeds used to invest in higher yielding securities when rates rise. Again, this preference will accentuate the rising curve as investors switch out of long-term securities into short-term securities.

Because of its documentation, relative simplicity, and intuitive appeal, the expectations hypothesis of the term structure of interest rates is widely accepted in both academia and in the market.

Liquidity Preference
This theory holds that long-term securities should provide higher returns than short-term obligations do, since rational investors are willing to pay a price premium (i.e., accept lower yields) on short maturity obligations to avoid the risk of principal volatility which is an intrinsic aspect of the long maturity obligation. The liquidity preference theory is the product of an important criticism leveled at the expectations hypothesis; i.e., one of the important (and questionable) assumptions of the latter hypothesis is that bond investors possess perfect certainty and perfect foresight. Given the uncertainty which exists in the real world, it follows that short-term issues should be more desirable than longer maturities because they can easily be converted into cash should unforeseen events occur. As noted by Malkiel, "the crux of the liquidity preference theory is that long term bonds, because of their greater potential price volatility, ought to offer the investor a larger return than the short term securities."[20]

---

[19] See for example: David Meiselman, *The Term Structure of Interest Rates* (Englewood Cliffs, N.J.: Prentice–Hall, Inc., 1962); and Franco Modigliani and Richard Sutch, "Innovations in Interest Rate Policy," *American Economic Review: Papers and Proceedings,* Vol. 56, No. 2 (May, 1966), pp. 178–197.

[20] Malkiel, *Term Structure of Interest Rates: Theory, Empirical Evidence,* p. 13.

The liquidity preference theory argues that, in the absence of market anomalies, the yield curve should be upward sloping and any other shape should be viewed as a temporary aberration. While this theory is an outgrowth of a major criticism leveled at the expectations hypothesis, it is also an extension of the same hypothesis. In particular, the formal liquidity preference position contends that the liquidity premium inherent in longer yields is formally expressed as an amount to be added to the expected future rate in arriving at long-term yields. Thus, because the liquidity premium (L) is provided to compensate the long-term investor, the general liquidity preference model is simply a variation of Equation (17–18), and may be stated as follows:

(17–19)

$$(1 + {}_tR_N) = [(1 + {}_tR_1)(1 + {}_{t+1}r_1 + L_2) \cdots$$

$$(1 + {}_{t+N-1}r_1 + L_N)]^{1/N}$$

Like the expectations hypothesis, the liquidity preference theory has been subjected to empirical testing and found to possess considerable validity.[21] Available evidence indicates that expectations alone are not the unique determinant of the term structure because the yield curve shows a definite upward bias which implies that a combination of the two theories is probably preferable to either alone.

Segmented Markets Theory

The segmented market theory is a simple, yet interesting, variation of the theory of the term structure of interest rates. Unfortunately, the empirical evidence offered in support of this theory has been meager and rather inconclusive. Nonetheless, it still enjoys wide acceptance among market practitioners. The segmented market theory—also known as preferred habitat, the institutional theory, or the hedging pressure theory—asserts that different groups of institutional investors have different maturity needs, which lead them to confine their security selections to specific maturity segments of the term structure. Thus, it is argued that the term structure is ultimately a function of the investment policies of major financial institutions.

Financial institutions tend to structure their investment policies in line with such things as their tax liability, liability structure, and the level of earnings demanded by savers and depositors. Therefore, because commercial banks, for example, are subject to normal corporate tax rates, and because their liability is generally short to intermediate in length (due to the short-term nature of time and demand deposits), we find commercial

---

[21] See: Reuben A. Kessel, "The Cyclical Behavior of the Term Structure of Interest Rates," Occasional Paper 91, National Bureau of Economic Research, 1965; and Cagan, Phillip, *Essays on Interest Rates* (New York: Columbia University Press for the National Bureau of Economic Research, 1969).

banks consistently invest in short to intermediate-term municipals. In a like manner, because life insurance companies have little tax exposure and long-term obligations/liabilities, they tend to seek out high yielding, long-term corporate bonds. Therefore the segmented market theoretician contends that these forces, along with legal and regulatory limitations, tend to coerce or prompt alternative financial institutions into consistently allocating their resources to particular types and maturity segments of the market. In fact, in its strongest form, the segmented market theory holds that the maturity preferences of different investors and borrowers are so strong that they would *never* purchase securities outside of their preferred maturity range to take advantage of yield differentials. As a result, advocates of this hypothesis argue that the short and long maturity markets are effectively segmented, and yields are determined solely by supply and demand *within* each market maturity segment.

Trading Implications of the Term Structure

Information on maturity behavior can be used to formulate yield expectations by simply observing the shape of the term structure; e.g., if the shape is humped, then historical evidence suggests that the odds are fairly good that interest rates are about to undergo a broad based decline. Ardent expectations theorists would suggest that one need *only* examine the prevailing yield curve to obtain some idea of what interest rates should do in the future.

A more significant use of the term structure is in predicting future movements. In effect, it is essential to formulate predictions of the future shape of the term structure, along with interest rates, in order to assess yield volatility by maturity sector. Such an analysis allows those maturity segments which offer the greatest yield and, therefore, potential price appreciation, to be identified.

A final, albeit less important, use of the term structure is to identify under or overpriced issues. Figure 17–3 contained a yield curve based on observations of individual promised yields prevailing at a given date. Since the issues are supposedly comparable in all respects but maturity, if an issue (whose yield is indicated by one of the plotted points on the graph) offers a promised yield substantially above the yield curve line, such an obligation is apparently providing an unusually high yield and therefore is underpriced. As a result, the issue should be viewed as one which offers a temporary investment opportunity. Likewise, issues that plot substantially below the yield curve provide abnormally low yields, are apparently overpriced, and may be good sell candidates. If the issues in the yield curve are really comparable, then one should assume the chance of issue anomalies is remote and the under or over priced issues are a temporary market phenomenon. Of course, the higher the quality of the obligation, the more faith we can place in such an assumption. However, when dealing with rated obligations, such as corporates and municipals, it should be remembered that this behavior may not necessarily be an aberration so much as a rational market perception of differential quality *within* a rating class.

Yield Spreads

Another important dimension of interest rate behavior is yield spreads. Basically, *a yield spread is a difference in promised yield, which exists at any given point in time, between different bond issues or segments of the market* and which acts in a rather mechanical fashion on the comparative price behavior of bonds. These differences are issue or market specific and, thus, are additive to the rates determined by economic forces (RFR + I). Yield spreads and their behavior are caused by issue orientated risk premium variables. The basic causes of yield spreads are quality differentials, different maturities, and unique call features. These variables were discussed with regard to the risk premium component of the determinant of interest rates, and were shown to lead to different promised yields for different types of securities.

Yield spreads are also caused by differences in coupon and in the tax liability of the obligation. If an issue's interest income is tax exempt as is true with municipals, this will obviously have an effect on promised yield because of the effect such tax provisions have on investors' expected after tax return. In essence, such preferential tax treatment should lead to lower yields until an equilibrium is reached with regard to comparative fully taxable obligations. In an efficient market, any other relationship would cause investors to shift funds from one area to the other until yields moved to an equilibrium point.

Likewise, differential coupons can affect the promised yield offered by alternative investments. Generally, the lower the coupon, the lower the promised yield. As a rule, coupons are generally divided into three categories: premium issues, current coupon issues, and discounted obligations. A premium issue carries a coupon in excess of prevailing new issue rates and, therefore, sells at a price in excess of par value. Current coupon issues, on the other hand, carry coupons that are comparable to prevailing new issue rates, and hence sell at or near par. Finally, discount obligations carry coupons below prevailing new issue nominal yields and, therefore, sell at prices below par. Premium bonds will normally promise returns in excess of those offered by current coupon obligations, with discount obligations providing the lowest promised yield to maturity of all three types of obligations. Such yield spreads are common and tend to behave in a fairly structured and predictable manner over time.

Using the current coupon issue as a bench mark, there is a rational explanation of why premium bonds provide higher returns than current coupons do, and why discount issues provide lower yields. Such differential yield behavior is normally attributable to differential call protection, reinvestment risk, and tax treatment. The higher yields of premium bonds can be traced to higher call risk, higher reinvestment risk, and of course, the tax loss that will accompany the decline in capital position as the bond matures. Given market efficiency, all of these undesirable facets naturally lead to higher promised yield. In contrast, discounted issues provide lower yield to maturity because they have less call risk exposure, fewer reinvestment problems,[22] and enjoy preferential tax treatment with regard to the capital gains that will occur at maturity or sooner. Therefore, the yields on discounted obligations are less than those on current coupons to the extent that expected *realized yields* of the competitive issues are equal.

A yield spread may be either positive or negative, depending upon whether a particular bond provides a promised yield to maturity in excess of (or less than) that offered on an alternative issue. Moreover, *the magnitude or direction of these yield spreads changes over time*. A yield spread "narrows" whenever the differences in yield become smaller, and it "widens" as the difference becomes greater.[23]

Table 17—1 provides average data on a variety of past yield spreads. Yield spreads are common and their size is subject to change. This is due to changing levels of interest rates and variations in investor perceptions of risk. The structure of market rates suggests that four major factors account for the existence of various yield differentials:

1. different *segments* of the bond market (e.g., governments vs. agencies, or governments vs. corporates)

2. different *sectors* of the same market segment (e.g., prime grade municipals vs. good grade municipals, or AA utilities vs. BAA utilities, or AAA industrials vs. AAA public utilities)

3. different *coupons* within a given market segment/sector (e.g., current coupon governments vs. deep discount governments, or new AA industrials vs. seasoned AA industrials) and

4. different *maturities* within a given market segment/sector (e.g., short agencies vs. long agencies, or 3 year prime municipals vs. 25 year prime municipals).

Whether yield spreads are a result of segment, sector, coupon, and/or maturity differences, they exist because there are different market rates associated with different types of bonds. The structure of yield spreads is important to bond price behavior since it can affect comparative yield to maturity performance, leading to yield changes and different price behavior, and therefore, different realized yield opportunities. In effect, yield

---

[22] This is due not only to the obligation's low coupon per se, but also to the fact that the issue sells below par and, therefore, enjoys automatic reinvestment at the promised yield rate within the capital appreciation process.

[23] Michael D. Joehnk, "The Effects of Yield Spreads on Comparative Bond Price Behavior," *The Financial Planner*, Vol. 6, No. 4 (April, 1977), pp. 34–40.

Table 17–1 **Selected Mean Yield Spreads (reported in basis points)**

Comparisons[a]	1969	1970	1971	1972	1973	1974	1975[b]
Short Govts: Long Govts	+56	+70	−4	+10	+23	+22	+75
Short Munies: Long Munies	+77	+150	+192	+157	+95	+100	+166
Long Govts: Long Corps	+119	+162	+173	+172	+75	+132	+131
10 Yr Govts: 10 Yr Agencies	+55	+70	+80	+53	+45	+85	+83
Long Munies: Long Corps	+172	+202	+217	+234	+254	+337	+296
10 Yr Munies: 10 Yr Agencies	+191	+256	+256	+261	+273	+301	+259
Long Prime Munies: Long Good Munies	+20	+15	+20	+10	+10	+10	+10
Long Aa Utils: Long Baa Utils	+112	+75	+93	+53	+79	+191	+354
Long Aa Utils: Long Aa Ind'ls	−26	−48	−44	−28	−29	−50	−49
Long Disc'd Corps: Long Curr. Cpn Corps	+60	+86	+58	+42	+37	+108	+81

The yield spreads are based on average market rates (monthly observations) existing for each of the respective market sectors; the "short" maturities are considered 3–5 years while the "long" maturities are considered 20–25 years; unless otherwise noted, the municipals are rated as prime grade, while the corporates are represented by Aa public utilities.

[a] The yield spreads are reported using the bond sector listed first as the benchmark, e.g., a + yield spread with the "Short Govts: Long Govts" comparison means the latter type of issue is providing the higher average market yield.

[b] The 1975 data include observations through the first six months—January through June.

Source: Michael D. Joehnk, "The Effects of Yield Spreads on Comparative Bond Price Behavior," *Financial Planner,* Vol. 6, No. 4 (April 1977), p. 35. Reprinted by permission.

spreads are the "fine tuning" component of interest rate expectations. Such differentials are issue specific, and, since they can affect comparative investment opportunities, they are especially important to aggressive bond investors. A bond investor should evaluate yield spreads because they influence price behavior and comparative realized yield performance over a given investment horizon. In this regard, *changes* in yield spreads are the more influential and critical variable. A change in the magnitude and/or direction of a yield spread can lead to substantial differences in comparative bond performance because it affects comparative yield over a particular investment horizon. If (in the absence of yield spreads) two issues undergo an identical 150 basis point change in yield over an equal investment horizon, then, other things being equal, there would be nothing to make one preferable to the other as an investment. If the yield spread change over time is greater for one than for the other, then the issue which enjoyed the larger drop in yield would provide the superior realized yield (because of its greater price volatility).

There are three important types of yield spread conditions in the market: 1) a normal beginning yield spread which is expected to become *abnormal* (i.e., the spread is expected to move to an abnormally wide or narrow position); 2) a beginning yield spread that is abnormally wide or narrow but is expected to become *normal*; and 3) a normal beginning yield spread that is expected to change, but remain normal, with an anticipated *major swing* in market interest rates. Economic and market analysis would be necessary in order to arrive at any of these expectations. Each of the conditions possesses one common denominator: *the potential for yield spreads to undergo substantial change.*

Having identified the market conditions which can result in differences in investment returns, let us discuss the types of anticipated yield spread behavior. Since each of the three conditions is based on the premise that a normal or abnormal yield spread exists initially, it is necessary to consider both the initial yield spread and the expected change in the spread, even though the change is far more important. Other things being equal, when a positive (+) beginning yield spread exists and is expected to narrow (−) over time, the *higher* yielding issue would provide the greatest return. If a negative yield spread (−) exists initially and is expected to widen (+), the *lower* yielding bond would be the superior investment. This applies for any of the three market conditions and in any interest rate environment. Actually, having ascertained future market conditions, the investor would know which type of yield spread behavior to anticipate, and, using the procedure discussed could identify the issue with the greatest potential. Assume that a negative yield spread is abnormally narrow but is expected to move to its normal relationship. This implies that the negative (−) spread should widen (+) so the lower yielding bond would be selected.

Such analysis should enable the investor to capitalize on temporary yield spread anomalies and to gain the most from anticipated major swings in market rates.

Bond Price Volatility

Numerous variables can affect yield behavior and are, therefore, important to price conscious bond investors. Price volatility, however, is not linked solely to yield behavior. So what causes the variations in price? Burton Malkiel used the bond valuation model to demonstrate that the market price of a fixed income security is ultimately a function of four factors: 1) the par value of an obligation, 2) the issue's coupon, 3) its years to maturity, and 4) the prevailing market rate.[24] Using these variables in the context of the basic bond valuation model, Malkiel showed (with mathematical proofs) that the following relationships ("theorems") exist between yield changes and bond price behavior:

1. Bond prices move inversely to bond yields.

2. For a given change in market yield, changes in bond prices are greater for longer term maturities; i.e., bond price volatility is *directly* related to term to maturity.

---

[24] Burton G. Malkiel, "Expectations, Bond Prices, and the Term Structure of Interest Rates," *Quarterly Journal of Economics,* Vol. 76, No. 2 (May, 1962), pp. 197–218.

3. The amount of maturity derived price volatility (percentage of price change) increases at a diminishing rate as term to maturity increases.

4. Price movements resulting from equal absolute increases or decreases in yield are not symmetrical since a decrease in yield raises bond prices by more than a corresponding increase in yields lowers prices.

5. The higher the coupon of the issue, the smaller will be the percentage of price fluctuation for a given change in yield; i.e., bond price volatility is *inversely* related to coupon.[25]

Homer and Leibowitz[26] showed that the absolute level of market yields significantly affects bond price volatility, i.e., the higher the level of prevailing yields, the greater the price volatility of bonds. They showed that yield swings are greatest when prevailing interest rates are also greatest (and therefore, so, too, is price volatility).

Thus, price volatility is a function of the percentage of change in yield, the issue's coupon, the term to maturity of the obligation, the level of yields, and the direction of yield change. However, while both the level and direction of change in yields may be interesting variables to consider, they do not provide concrete trading strategies. This is not true of the other variables. Any time price volatility is sought (or avoided), the percentage of change in yield must be of paramount importance. Attention can then shift to the two variables within the selection process over which investors have control, coupon and maturity. As yields change, these two variables have a dramatic effect on comparative bond price volatility.

The Concept of Duration

Given that price volatility varies inversely with coupon but directly with maturity, it follows that serious problems can arise in the bond selection process if price is an important decision variable. A measure which incorporates the dimensions of both coupon and maturity is obviously needed. Fortunately, such a measure was developed over 40 years ago by F. R. Macaulay,[27] and is known as the "duration" of a security. Macaulay showed that duration was a more appropriate measure of the time element of a bond than term to maturity because it takes into account not only the ultimate

---

[25] It should be noted that some empirical evidence demonstrates that the lowest coupon bond does not always provide maximum price volatility when interest rates decline; however, this evidence does not totally negate the *general* implications of theorem 5. See Michael D. Joehnk, H. Russell Fogler, and Charles D. Bradley, "The Price Elasticity of Discounted Bonds: Some Empirical Evidence," *Journal of Financial and Quantitative Analysis*, Vol. 13, No. 3 (September, 1978).

[26] Homer and Leibowitz, *Inside the Yield Book.*

[27] Frederick R. Macaulay, *Some Theoretical Problems Suggested by the Movements of Interest Rates, Bond Yields, and Stock Prices in the United States since 1856* (New York: National Bureau of Economic Research, 1938).

recovery of capital at maturity, but also the size and timing of coupon payments that occur prior to final maturity. *Duration is defined as the weighted average time to full recovery of principal and interest payments.* Using annual compounding, we can define duration (D) as:

(17–20)
$$D = \frac{\sum\limits_{t=1}^{n} \dfrac{C_t\,(t)}{(1+i)^t}}{\sum\limits_{t=1}^{n} \dfrac{C_t}{(1+i)^t}}$$

where:

t = the time period in which the coupon and/or principal payment occurs and is the rating mechanism of the duration concept

C_t = the interest and/or principal payment that occurs in period t, and

i = the market yield on the bond.

The denominator in Equation (17–20) is the price of an issue as determined by the present value model. The numerator is also a present value concept of price, except that all cash flows are weighted according to the length of time to receipt.

Duration, which is a measure of the average life of a debt instrument, has several characteristics which should be understood. First, when the issue is a single payment (zero coupon) bond, duration will always equal the term to maturity of the obligation, since there is no interim cash flow from coupons. Moreover, duration is always less than term to maturity for a bond with coupons because the average time of payments is reduced. Other things being equal, a higher market rate reduces the duration of an obligation because it reduces the present value of future flows. For example, a 6 percent, 20 year bond priced to yield 6 percent will have a duration measure of 11.904, whereas the same obligation priced to yield 8 percent will have a duration measure of 10.922. Most important, it has been shown empirically that bond price movements *will vary proportionally* with duration.[28] *The percentage of change in price is equal to the change in yield times duration.* As an example, if yields decline by one percent (100 basis points),

---

[28] For a more extensive discussion of duration, see: Lawrence Fisher and Roman L. Weil, "Coping with the Risk of Interest Rate Fluctuations: Returns to Bondholders from Naive and Optimal Strategies," *Journal of Business,* Vol. 44, No. 4 (October 1971); Roman L. Weil, "Macaulay's Duration: An Appreciation," *Journal of Business,* Vol. 46, No. 4 (October, 1973), pp. 589–592; James C. Van Horne, *Financial Market Rates and Flows;* and R.W. McEnally, "Duration as a Practical Tool for Bond Management," *Journal of Portfolio Management,* Vol. 3, No. 4 (Summer, 1977), pp. 53–57.

a bond with a duration of ten years will increase in price by 10 percent. Thus, maximum price variation is achieved with the longest duration. These and other characteristics of duration are shown in Table 17–2.

Table 17–2
Bond Duration in Years for Bond Yielding 6 Percent Under Different Terms

Years to maturity	Various coupon rates			
	.02	.04	.06	.08
1	0.995	0.990	0.985	0.981
5	4.756	4.558	4.393	4.254
10	8.891	8.169	7.662	7.286
20	14.981	12.980	11.904	11.232
50	19.452	17.129	16.273	15.829
100	17.567	17.232	17.120	17.064
∞	17.167	17.167	17.167	17.167

Source: L. Fisher and R. L. Weil, "Coping with the Risk of Interest Rate Fluctuations: Returns to Bondholders from Naive and Optimal Strategies," *Journal of Business,* Vol. 44, No. 4 (October 1971), p. 418. Copyright © 1971 by The University of Chicago Press. Reprinted by permission of The University of Chicago Press.

While bond price variation tends to move proportionally with duration, Table 17–2 demonstrates that there is a variety of ways of achieving a given duration measure. Thus, if an investor anticipates a decline in interest rates and he wants to capture maximum capital gains, there are several maturity/coupon combinations that would provide desired price performance under desired risk conditions. The duration concept has become increasingly popular with institutional bond portfolio managers because it is a convenient way of grasping the time element of a security in terms of *both* coupon and term to maturity.

One interesting implication of the duration concept is "immunization."[29] Because of the conflict between price and reinvestment risks, it is maintained that, in order to "immunize" fixed income investments from subsequent changes in market rates, these two risks must be balanced so that they completely offset one another. Balancing occurs only when an investment horizon is equal to a bond's measure of duration. *When duration equals the planning period, risk is minimized.* Thus, an investor with a 15 year horizon should not necessarily seek an issue with 15 years to maturity, but should seek issues with maturity/coupon combinations that provide a duration of approximately 15.0. The duration concept has implications for both aggressive and conservative bond investors. It is an important idea which conveniently encompasses the coupon *and* maturity dimensions of bond price behavior.

---

[29] See for example: Lawrence Fisher and Roman L. Weil, "Coping with the Risk," and G. O. Bierwag and George C. Kaufman, "Coping with the Risk of Interest Rate Fluctuations: A Note," *Journal of Business,* forthcoming.

Summary

The concept of bond valuation is essentially the same as that for equity pricing, i.e., the present value of all future cash flows accruing to the investor. Cash flows for the bond investor include periodic interest payments and capital recovery. The present value model incorporated several important dimensions of bond yields and prices, including coupon receipts, interest rates, interest rate changes, and yield spread changes. *The major problem facing the bond analyst is estimating expected changes in interest rate and yield spread behavior.* Once these factors have been evaluated, the next step is to select the coupon, maturity, call feature, etc. that best capture the performance sought by the investor. Errors in estimating interest rates and yield changes can, however, lead to substantial losses for the aggressive investor and reduced return for the buy-and-hold strategist.

The next part of the chapter reviewed the mathematics of bond pricing and bond yields. We looked at the five basic types of yields including: nominal yield, current yield, promised yield, yield to call, and realized yield. The concept of interest-on-interest, or coupon reinvestment, was discovered to be an extremely important factor in calculating realized yield.

Because an important aspect of bond pricing is the rate at which future cash flows are discounted, we examined the fundamental determinants of interest rates. They were seen to be a function of the risk-free rate, a risk premium, and an inflation premium. Consideration was then given to the term structure of interest rates, i.e., yield curve analysis. The four basic patterns of yield curves were examined with theoretical explanations given for the different shapes of yield curves, based on the expectations hypothesis, the liquidity preference hypothesis, and the segmented markets hypothesis. Trading strategies were developed using yield curve analysis and related changes in the yield curve.

In the final section of the chapter, we saw that bond price volatility was a function of the percentage of change in yield, the coupon of the issue, the term to maturity, the level of yields, and the direction of yield changes. In developing trading strategies based on price volatility, emphasis is placed on the percentage of yield change with consideration given to coupon and maturity. The concept of duration was developed to incorporate the latter.

Questions

(Note: In all bond valuation problems, assume a par value of $1000)

1. Why does the present value equation appear to be more useful for the bond investor than for the common stock investor?

2. What is the most crucial assumption the investor makes when he calculates promised yield? Why is it crucial to the computation?

3. An investor purchases a bond with a nominal yield of 6 percent for 800 dollars. If the bond has 20 years to maturity, find promised yield by
a. the approximation method
b. present value method, assuming annual interest payments
c. present value method, assuming semiannual interest payments

4. A bond is currently quoted at $1100 and has a current yield of 6.36 percent. The remaining life of the bond is 15 years, but it has three years remaining on a deferred call feature.
a. Calculate promised yield using:
(1) approximation method
(2) present value method, assuming annual payments.
b. Calculate yield-to-call, assuming a call premium equal to one year's interest, using:
(1) approximation method
(2) present value method, assuming annual payments.

5. An investor purchases a bond during a period of high yields. He pays 800 dollars for a 7¾ percent bond, expecting rates to drop over the next three years to the point at which the value of the bond would increase to $1050. However, interest rates edge slightly upward, so that when he sells the bond three years later, he actually receives $750 for it.
a. Calculate the realized yield the investor anticipated using the approximation method.
b. Calculate the actual yield he realized, using the present value method, assuming semiannual receipts.

6. A bond with a 7 percent coupon and 10 years to maturity is selling to yield 9 percent. What is its price?

7. A speculator has decided that, because of anticipated declines in interest rates, a given bond should be selling for $950 two years from now. It carries a 10 percent coupon, but because of capital gains, he figures that he could make 15 percent if he could buy it at a certain price. What is the price, assuming semiannual payments?

8. A new 20 year bond with an 8 percent nominal yield and paying an annual coupon is priced to yield 10 percent. An investor purchasing the bond expects that, two years from now, yields on comparable bonds will have declined to 9 percent. Calculate his realized yield if he expects to sell the bond in two years.

9. A bond carrying a 6 percent coupon has eight years and seven months to maturity.
a. What would its price be if similar bonds yield 8 percent? Assume semiannual coupon payments.
b. Find the price if the term to maturity were 8 years, 7 months, and 15 days.

10. **a.** Define the variables included in the following model:

$$r = (RFR, RP, I)$$

b. Comment on the appropriateness of the model, given the information that the firm whose bonds you are considering is not expected to break even this year.

11. The following exercise deals with the problem of differing reinvestment rates. An investor purchases a bond for 900 dollars with a 7 percent coupon, maturing in five years. Find the promised yield, assuming annual payments and that:

a. interest payments are reinvested in more of the same bonds at the same promised yield

b. interest payments are reinvested in a Mexican bank savings account at 12 percent

c. interest payments are not reinvested at all, but are spent as they arrive.

12. Using the most current information available, construct a graph depicting the term structure of interest rates for Aaa-rated corporate bonds. (See Figure 17–3 for example.)

13. Of the three hypotheses mentioned in the text, which one do you feel best explains the reasons for a "yield curve"? Defend your choice.

14. Construct a chart demonstrating current ranges of yields for bonds of various ratings. For example, you might want to randomly select three or four bonds in each rating category and show the average yield on each group, as well as the spread for each group.

15. Demonstrate through an example that Malkiel's second theorem is valid.

16. Compute the duration of a 10 year bond with a 7 percent coupon, and yielding 8 percent. Show all work.

References

Axilrod, Stephen A. and Young, Ralph A. "Interest Rates and Monetary Policy." *Federal Reserve Bulletin,* Vol. 43, No. 3 (September, 1962).

Baskin, Elba F. and Crooch, Gary M. "Historical Rates of Return on Investments in Flat Bonds." *Financial Analysts Journal,* Vol. 24, No. 6 (November–December, 1968).

Bowlin, Oswald D. and Martin, John D. "Extrapolations of Yields Over the Short Run; Forecast or Folly?" *Journal of Monetary Economics,* Vol. 1 (1975).

Burton, John S. and Toth, John R. "Forecasting Secular Trends in Long-Term Interest Rates." *Financial Analysts Journal,* Vol. 30, No. 5 (September–October, 1974).

Cagan, Phillip (ed.). *Essays on Interest Rates* (New York: Columbia University Press for the National Bureau of Economic Research, 1969).

Conard, Joseph W. and Frankena, Mark W. "The Yield Spread Between New and Seasoned Corporate Bonds."*Essays on Interest Rates,* Vol. 1, 1969.

Ederington, Louis H. "The Yield Spread on New Issues of Corporate Bonds." *Journal of Finance,* Vol. 27, No. 5 (December, 1974).

Feldstein, Martin and Eckstein, Otto. "The Fundamental Determinants of the Interest Rate." *The Review of Economics and Statistics,* Vol. 52, No. 4 (November, 1970).

Fisher, Lawrence. "Determinants of Risk Premiums on Corporate Bonds."*Journal of Political Economy,* Vol. 67, No. 3 (June, 1959).

Freund, William C. and Zinbarg, Edward D. "Application of Flow of Fund to Interest Rate Forecasting." *Journal of Finance,* Vol. 13, No. 2 (May, 1963).

Hastie, Larry K. "Determinants of Municipal Bond Yields." *Journal of Financial and Quantitative Analysis,* Vol. 7, No. 3 (June, 1972).

Homer, Sidney "Distortions Within Bond and Money Markets."*Financial Analysts Journal,* Vol. 24, No. 4 (July–August, 1968).

Homer, Sidney and Leibowitz, Martin L. *Inside the Yield Book.* Englewood Cliffs, New Jersey: Prentice–Hall, Inc., 1972.

Jen, Frank C. and Wert, James E. "The Value of the Deferred Call Privilege." *National Banking Review,* Vol. 3, No. 1 (March, 1966).

Joehnk, Michael D. and Nielsen, James F. "Return and Risk Characteristics of Speculative Grade Bonds." *Quarterly Review of Economic & Business,* Vol. 15, No. 1 (Spring, 1975).

Joehnk, Michael D. and Wert, James C. "The Call-Risk Performance of the Discounted Seasoned Issue." *Mississippi Valley Journal of Business and Economics,* Vol. 9, No. 2 (Winter, 1973–1974).

Johannesen, Richard I., Jr. "The Effect of Coupon on Bond Price Fluctuations." *Financial Analysts Journal,* Vol. 24, No. 5 (September–October, 1968).

Johnson, Ramon E. "Term Structure of Corporate Bond Yields As A Function of Risk of Default." *Journal of Finance,* Vol. 22, No. 2, (May, 1967).

Kessel, Reuben A. "The Cyclical Behavior of the Term Structure of Interest Rates." Occasional Paper 91 National Bureau of Economic Research, 1965.

Lindvall, John R. "New Issue Corporate Bonds, Seasoned Market Efficiency and Yield Spreads." *Journal of Finance,* Vol. 32, No. 4 (September, 1977).

Malkiel, Burton G. "Expectations, Bond Prices, and the Term Structure of Interest Rates." *Quarterly Journal of Economics,* Vol. 76, No. 2 (May, 1962).

Malkiel, Burton G. *The Term Structure of Interest Rates: Theory, Empirical Evidence, and Applications.* New York: The McCaleb–Seiler Publishing Company, 1970.

Meiselman, David. *The Term Structure of Interest Rates.* Englewood Cliffs, New Jersey: Prentice–Hall, Inc., 1962.

Modigliani, Franco and Sutch, Richard. "Innovations in Interest Rate Policy," *American Economic Review Papers and Proceedings,* Vol. 56, No. 2 (May, 1966).

Rea, John D. "The Yield Spread Between Newly Issued and Seasoned Corporate Bonds." Federal Reserve Bank of Kansas City *Monthly Review* (June, 1974).

Van Horne, James C. *Financial Market Rates and Flows.* Englewood Cliffs, New Jersey: Prentice–Hall, Inc. 1978.

Weil, Roman L. "Macaulay's Duration: An Appreciation." *Journal of Business,* Vol. 46, No. 4 (October, 1973).

Yohe, William P. and Karnosky, Denis S. "Interest Rates and Price Level Changes, 1952–69," Federal Reserve Bank of St. Louis *Review* (December, 1966).

Chapter 18

Bond Trading Strategies and Portfolio Management

Successful bond investment involves far more than mastering myriad technical aspects. Investors and portfolio managers use such information, in combination with economic and market data, to formulate viable portfolio policies and investment strategies. Technical information is only useful if it can help investors generate higher returns. In this chapter, we shift attention from the technical dimensions to the equally important question of bond trading strategies and portfolio management.

Different bond investors, with different risk profiles, follow one of several basic trading positions ranging from simple buy-and-hold tactics to sophisticated bond swaps, and we will examine several of these. The discussion will lay the foundation for our remarks on portfolio strategies. We will also analyze the effects of alternative investment vehicles on period returns. In other words, can the type of investment vehicle affect returns? We will then consider several distinct portfolio objectives, including high current income, maximizing long-term total income, and, finally, speculation, and short-term trading. The chapter concludes with an analysis of the portfolio implications of capital market theory, bond price behavior in a CAPM framework, and the extent of bond market efficiency. In essence, our final discussion centers on the application of modern capital market and portfolio theory to bonds, and addresses the question of whether or not bonds are viable candidates for inclusion in a portfolio.

Investment Strategies

To understand bond trading strategies and bond portfolio management requires knowledge of various bond investment techniques. Our discussion involves three basic strategies: 1) buy-and-hold; 2) forecasted interest rates; and 3) bond swaps.

Buy-and-Hold

This is the simplest strategy and is obviously not unique to bond investors. It involves finding an issue with desired quality, coupon levels, term to maturity, and important indenture provisions, such as call feature. The buy-and-hold-investor does not consider trading in and out of positions to achieve attractive returns. Rather, because of his risk-return preferences, he seeks modest returns with little risk. Buy-and-hold investors also tend to look for vehicles whose maturities (or duration) approximate their stipulated investment horizon, in order to reduce price and reinvestment risk.

Many successful bond investors and portfolio managers (particularly institutional managers) follow a *modified* version of the buy-and-hold strategy. The approach is similar to strict buy-and-hold in the sense that investment is made in an issue with the intention of holding it until the end of the investment horizon. However, such investors actively look for opportunities to trade into more desirable positions.

Whether the investor follows a strict, or a modified, buy-and-hold approach, the key ingredient is finding investment vehicles that possess attractive features such as maturities and yields. The strategy does not restrict the investor to accepting whatever the market has to offer, nor does it imply that selectivity is unimportant. Attractive and high yielding issues with desirable features and quality standards are actively sought. The buy-and-hold investor is aware that buying agencies will provide him with attractive incremental returns relative to treasuries, with little sacrifice in quality; and that utilities provide higher returns than comparably rated industrials; and that various call features affect not only the risk of an issue, but realized yield as well.

Thus, the successful buy-and-hold investor actively evaluates investment outlets and uses his knowledge of markets and issue characteristics to seek out attractive yields. Aggressive buy-and-hold investors will incorporate timing considerations into their investment decisions. Given their knowledge of market rates and expectations, if they do not like prevailing returns, they can always wait for higher yields by "sitting on the side lines" in cash or very short-term money market investments.

Investment Selection Based on Forecasted Interest Rate Behavior

This approach to bond investment is perhaps the riskiest strategy because it involves relying on uncertain forecasts of future interest rate behavior as a guide to restructuring a bond portfolio. This strategy entails preserving capital when an increase in interest rates is anticipated, and achieving attractive capital gains when interest rates are expected to decline. Such objectives are usually attained by altering the maturity structure of the portfolio, i.e., shortening the maturity (duration) of the bonds in the portfolio when interest rates are expected to increase and lengthening the average maturity when a decline in yields is anticipated.

The risk in such portfolio restructuring is largely a function of maturity alterations. When the portfolio manager shortens his maturities to preserve capital, he could sacrifice substantial income and the opportunity for capital gains. Similarly, when the investor anticipates a decline in rates, his risk is great because the coupon at this point in the interest rate cycle is normally reduced as maturity increases. Therefore, the investor is sacrificing current income (by investing in lower coupon bonds), and exposing the portfolio to substantial price volatility (with an unexpected increase in yields). Comparatively speaking, an anticipated increase in rates involves less risk since it involves less chance of an absolute capital loss. Therefore, the worst that can happen is interest income is reduced and/or capital gains foregone (opportunity cost) by shortening maturities.

Once future (expected) interest rates have been determined, the procedure relies largely on technical matters. Assume that an investor anticipates an increase in interest rates and wants to preserve his capital by reducing maturities as much as possible. Most bond portfolio managers would look for high yielding, short-term obligations such as treasury bills. While a primary goal is preservation of capital, the question of *income* is not totally ignored. Therefore, the investor would look for the best return possible given the maturity constraint. *Liquidity* is also important since an investor who is maintaining this posture involving yield sacrifice would only want to sit on the side lines when rates were drifting upward. When rates were either level or declining, the investor would want to *quickly* shift positions in order to seize the opportunity for higher income and/or capital gains.

One way to shorten maturities is to use a "cushion bond" which is a very high yielding long-term obligation. Such a bond carries a coupon substantially above the current market rate and has a current call feature. Because of its call price ceiling, its actual market price is below what it should be, given current market yields. With the price of the issue being held back because of its call exposure, its yield is higher than normal. Knowledgeable bond investors look for cushion bonds when a *modest* increase in rates is anticipated since such an issue provides attractive current income and protection against capital loss. The issue gives capital loss protection because it is trading at an abnormally high yield so market rates would have to *rise to its level* before its price would react. The investor who anticipates an increase in interest rates therefore has two simple strategies available, either shorten maturities or select an attractive cushion bond. In either case, a very liquid issue is sought.

A totally different posture is assumed by investors anticipating a *decline* in interest rates. Although there are substantial risks involved in restructuring a portfolio to take advantage of a decline, substantial capital gains and holding period returns can be realized. When investors anticipate a decline in interest rates, the basic rule is to *lengthen maturities* (duration) because the longer the duration, the greater the price volatility. *Liquidity* is also important because the investor wants to be able to close out the position *quickly* when the drop in rates has been completed.

Given the constraints of duration and liquidity, the investor attempts to determine the most attractive market segments and issues. The object is to find the market segment which promises the greatest price reaction to the decline in interest rates.

Generally, one would expect investors who anticipate rate declines to look for *long maturities and low coupons* (i.e., long duration). An exception might be when only a *modest* decrease in yields is anticipated. Under such circumstances, a portfolio manager might consider a *current coupon obligation,* since such issues are more interest sensitive than deep discounted bonds are and, therefore, they react to small changes in yield. Of course, long maturity would still be important.

In any investment strategy based on a decline in interest rates, *interest sensitivity* is critical so high grade securities (e.g., Baa through Aaa) should be used. Likewise treasuries and agencies might be attractive since they are also very interest sensitive. In fact, the higher the quality of the obligation, the more sensitive it is to interest rate behavior.

Bond Swaps

This is perhaps the most intriguing of the various investment strategies. *Bond swaps involve liquidating a current position and (simultaneously) buying a different issue in its place.* An investor holds a particular bond in his portfolio and is offered another bond with similar attributes except that it offers the chance for improved return. Many large portfolio managers employ this strategy to attain substantial portfolio returns.

Swaps can be executed to increase current yield, to increase yield to maturity, to take advantage of shifts in interest rates or realignments of yield spreads, to improve the quality of a portfolio, or for tax purposes. Some swaps are highly sophisticated and require a computer to fully comprehend the details. Most, however, are fairly simple transactions, with obvious goals and chances of risk. They go by such names as "profit take outs," "substitutions swaps," "intermarket spread swaps," or "tax swaps." While many of these swaps involve low risk (such as the pure yield pick-up swap), others entail substantial risk (the rate anticipation swap). Regardless of the risk involved, or the swap used, all swaps are employed for one basic reason: *as a means to portfolio improvement.*

Most swaps involve several different types of risk. One obvious risk is that the market will move against the investor while the swap is "outstanding." Interest rates may move up over the holding period and cause the investor to incur a loss. Another risk is that such things as yield spreads may fail to respond in the anticipated fashion, thus offsetting the benefits of the bond swap. The new bond may not, in fact, be a true substitute; even if our expectations and interest rate formulations are correct, the swap may be unsatisfactory because the *wrong* issue was selected. Finally, if the work out time is longer than anticipated, the realized yield might be less than expected, or a loss may result.

These risks will become more obvious as we examine several types of popular bond swaps. Such risk is accepted by the investor in order to realize portfolio improvements through improved yield. Three of the more popular potential bond swaps will be briefly reviewed below.[1]

The Pure Yield Pick-Up Swap

A yield pick-up swap is basically long-term and involves little or no estimation of market rates. An investor swaps out of a low coupon bond into a comparable higher coupon bond to realize an automatic and instantaneous increase in current yield and yield to maturity. The investor's risks are that the market will move against him, and, possibly, that the issue may not be a viable swap candidate. Also, because the portfolio manager is moving to a higher coupon obligation, there is greater call risk.

An example of a pure yield pick-up swap begins with an investor who currently holds a 30 year Aa rated 5 percent issue that is trading at 6.60 percent. Assume that the investor is offered a comparable 30 year Aa rated obligation bearing a 7 percent coupon priced to yield 7 percent. The investor would report (and realize) some book loss if he bought the original issue at par, but he is also able to simultaneously improve current yield and yield to maturity if the new obligation is held to expiration date. An explanation of this swap is contained in Table 18–1.

The investor need not predict rate changes and the swap is not based on any imbalance in yield spread. It is simply a matter of seeking out higher yields through a bond swap. Quality and maturity stay the same, as do all other factors *except coupon*. The major risk is that future reinvestment rates may not be as high as expected and, therefore, the total terminal value of the investment (capital recovery, coupon receipts, and interest-on-interest) may not be as high as expected, or even comparable to that of the original obligation. This reinvestment risk can be evaluated by analyzing the results with a number of rates to determine the minimum reinvestment rate that must prevail before the swap becomes unacceptable.

Substitution Swap

In contrast to our previous illustration, the substitution swap is generally short-term, relies heavily on interest rate expectations, and is subject to considerably more risk. The procedure rests on the existence of a short-term imbalance in yield spreads which is expected to be corrected in the near future. Moreover, it is assumed that the yield spread imbalance exists in issues which are perfect substitutes for each other. The investor might hold a 30 year 6 percent issue that is yielding 6 percent, and be offered comparable 30 year 6 percent bonds that are yielding 6.10 percent. The

---

[1] For additional information on these and other types of bond swaps, the reader is directed to: Sidney Homer and Martin L. Leibowitz, *Inside the Yield Book* (Englewood Cliffs, N.J.: Prentice–Hall, Inc., 1972); and Martin L. Leibowitz, "How Swaps Can Pay Off," *Institutional Investor,* Vol. 7, No. 8 (August, 1973), pp. 49ff.

| | Table 18–1 **A Pure Yield Pick-up Swap** | Pure Yield Pick-up Swap: Bond Swap Involving a Switch from a Low Coupon Bond to a Higher Coupon Bond of Similar Quality and Maturity in Order to Pick Up Higher Current Yield and a Better Yield to Maturity |

Table 18–1
A Pure Yield Pick-up Swap

Pure Yield Pick-up Swap: Bond Swap Involving a Switch from a Low Coupon Bond to a Higher Coupon Bond of Similar Quality and Maturity in Order to Pick Up Higher Current Yield and a Better Yield to Maturity

Example: Currently Hold: 30 yr. 5% coupon priced @ $792.13 to yield 6.60%
　　　　Swap Candidate: 30 yr. Aa 7% coupon priced @ $1000.00 to yield 7.00%

	Current Bond	Candidate Bond
Dollar investment	$792.13	$1,000.00[a]
Coupon	50.00	70.00
i on one coupon (7% for 6 mos.)	.875	1.225
Principal value at year end	794.45	1,000.00
Total $ accrued	845.325	1,071.23
Realized compound yield	6.613%	7.000%

Value of swap: 38.7 basis points in one year (assuming a 7% reinvestment rate).

[a] Obviously the investor can invest $792.13, the amount obtained from the sale of the bond currently held, and still obtain a realized compound yield of 7.00%.

The rewards for a Pure Yield Pick-up Swap are automatic and instantaneous in that both a higher coupon yield and a higher yield to maturity are realized from the swap.

Other advantages include: (1) No specific work out period needed since the investor is assumed to hold the new bond to maturity.
(2) No need for interest rate speculation.
(3) No need to analyze prices for overvaluation or undervaluation.

A major disadvantage of the PYP swap is the book loss involved in the swap. In this example, if the current bond were bought at par the book loss would be ($1000–792.13) $207.87.

Other Risks involved in the Pure Yield Pick-up Swap include:
(1) Increased risk of call in the event interest rates decline.
(2) Reinvestment risk is greater at higher coupon rates.

Swap evaluation procedure is patterned after technique suggested by Sidney Homer and Martin L. Leibowitz. Source: Adapted from the book *Inside the Yield Book* by Sidney Homer and Martin L. Leibowitz, Ph.D. © 1972 by Prentice–Hall, Inc. Published by Prentice–Hall, Inc., Englewood Cliffs, New Jersey 07632.

issue offered will trade at a price less than 1000 dollars. Thus, for every issue sold, the investor can buy more than one of the offered obligations.

The expectation is that the yield spread imbalance will be corrected because the yield on the offering bond will *decline* to the level of the issue that the investor now holds. Thus, the investor will realize capital gains by switching out of his current position into the higher yielding obligation. This swap is described in Table 18–2.

While there are only modest differential rewards in *current* income, it is clear that, as the yield imbalance is corrected, attractive capital gains can be earned causing a handsome differential in *realized* yield. The work out time is important in order to realize as high a differential return as possible. Yet, remember that, even if the yield is not corrected until maturity, 30 years hence, the investor will still attain minor improvement in realized yield (less than 10 basis points). In contrast, if the correction takes place in one year, the differential return is much greater, as shown in the table which assumes this work out time.

At the end of the work out time, the investor has an improved capital position, which can be used for a subsequent swap or investment transactions. Of course, many of the typical risks are present in this swap. In addition to the pressure of work out time, the market could move *against* the investor, the yield spread may *not* be temporary, and the issue may *not* be a viable swap candidate if the spread exists because the issue is of a lower quality.

Tax Swap

The "tax swap" is the most popular swap with individual bond investors. It is a relatively simple procedure that involves no projections and few risks. The concept rests on the existence of tax laws and of *realized capital gains* in some other part of the portfolio. Assume an investor held 100,000 dollars worth of corporate bonds for a period of two years and, at the time of liquidation, sold the securities for 150,000 dollars. As a result, the investor has a capital gain of 50,000 dollars. One way to eliminate the tax liability of that capital gain is to review the portfolio for any issues that may have comparable long-term capital losses.[2] If the investor found another long-term investment of 100,000 dollars that presently has a current market value of 50,000 dollars, he could execute a tax swap to establish the 50,000 dollar capital loss. By offsetting this capital loss and the comparable capital gain, the investor will enjoy *reduced income taxes*.

Municipal bonds are considered particularly attractive tax swap candidates since the investor can *increase his tax-free income* and still use the capital loss (which is subject to normal federal and state taxation) to *reduce capital gains tax liability*. To continue our illustration, assume that the investor owns 100,000 dollars worth of New York City, 20 year, 5 percent bonds which presently have a market value of 50,000 dollars. He, therefore, has the tax loss; now all that is needed is a comparable bond swap candidate. Suppose he is offered (or finds) a New York City bond of comparable

---

[2] While discussion in this part of the book deals with tax swaps that involve bonds, it should be obvious that comparable strategies could be used with other types of investments.

Table 18–2
**A Substitution
Swap**

Substitution Swap: Swap Executed to Take Advantage of Temporary Market
Anomalies in Yield Spreads between Issues That Are Equivalent with Respect to
Coupon, Quality, and Maturity

Example: Currently Hold: 30 yr. Aa 6% coupon priced at $1,000 to yield
6.00%
Swap Candidate: 30 yr. Aa 6% coupon priced at $986.31 to yield
6.10%
Assumed workout period: 1 year
Reinvested @ 6.00%

	Current Bond	Candidate Bond
Dollar investment	$1,000.00	$ 986.31
Coupon	60.00	60.00
i on one coupon @ 6% for 6 mos.	.90	.90
Principal value at year end (@ 6% YTM)	1,000.00	1,000.00
Total $ accrued	1,060.90	1,060.90
Total $ gain	60.90	74.59
Gain per invested $	.0609	.07563
Realized compound yield	6.00%	7.43%

Value of swap: 143 basis points in one year

The rewards for the Substitution Swap are realized in terms of additional basis
point pick-ups for YTM and realized compound yield, and in capital gains that
accrue when the anomaly in yield corrects itself.

In the Substitution Swap, it is important for the investor to realize that any
basis point pick-up (143 points in this example) will be realized only during
the work out period. Thus, in our example, in order to obtain the 143 basis
point increased in realized compound yield, the investor must swap an average
of once each year and pick up an average of 10 basis points in yield to maturity
on each swap.

Potential risks associated with the substitution swap include:
  (1) A yield spread thought to be temporary may, in fact, be permanent,
       thus reducing capital gains advantages.
  (2) The market rate may change adversely.

Swap evaluation procedure is patterned after a technique suggested by Sidney Homer and
Martin L. Leibowitz. Source: Adapted from the book *Inside the Yield Book* by Sidney
Homer and Martin L. Leibowitz, Ph.D. © 1972 by Prentice–Hall, Inc. Published by
Prentice–Hall, Inc., Englewood Cliffs, New Jersey 07632.

maturity which carries a 5.1 percent coupon and also has a market value of
50. By selling his New York 5's and instantaneously reinvesting in a
comparable amount of New York 5.1's, the investor would totally eliminate
any capital gains tax liability from the corporate bond transaction. In effect,
the investor has 50,000 dollars of capital gains "tax free," and is also able to

Table 18–3
A Tax Swap

Tax Swap: A Swap Undertaken in a Situation in Which the Investor Wishes to Offset Capital Gains in Other Securities through the Sale of a Bond Currently Held and Selling at a Discount from the Price Paid at Purchase. By Swapping into a Bond with As Nearly Identical Features As Possible, the Investor Can Use the Capital Loss on the Sale of the Bond for Tax Purposes, and Still Maintain His Current Position in the Market.

Example: Currently Hold: $100,000 worth of Corporate Bonds with a current market value of $150,000 *and* $100,000 in N.Y., 20 year, 5% bonds with a current market value of $50,000.

Swap Candidate: $50,000 in N.Y., 20 year, 5.1% bonds,

A. Corporate bonds sold and long-term capital gains
   profit established $50,000
   Capital gains tax liability—assume investor has
   25% capital gains tax rate ($50,000 × .25) $12,500
B. N.Y. 5's sold and long-term capital *loss* established $50,000
   Reduction in capital gains tax liability
   ($50,000 × .25)   ($12,500)
        Net Capital Gains Tax Liability   0

        Tax *Savings* Realized $12,500

C. Complete tax swap by buying N.Y. 5.1's from
   proceeds of N.Y. 5's sale—therefore, amount
   invested remains largely the *same.* [a]
   Annual Tax Free Interest Income—N.Y. 5's $ 5,000
   Annual Tax Free Interest Income—N.Y. 5.1's $ 5,100

        Net *Increase* in *Annual* Tax Free Interest
        Income $ 100

[a] N.Y. 5.1's will result in substantial capital gains when liquidated at maturity (since they were bought at deep discounts) and therefore will be subject to future capital gains tax liability. The swap is designed to use the capital loss resulting from the swap to offset capital gains from other investments. At the same time, the investor's funds remain in a security almost identical to his previous holding while he receives a slight increase in both current income and YTM.

Since the Tax Swap involves no projections in terms of work out period, interest rate changes, etc., the risks involved are minimal. The investor's major concern should be to avoid potential wash sales.

increase his current tax-free yield. Of course, the money saved by eliminating the tax liability can then be used for investment purposes to increase the yield on the portfolio. This is shown in Table 18–3.

The only caveat is that the investor cannot swap *identical* issues. In other words, he could not sell the New York 5's to establish a loss and then instantaneously buy back the same New York 5's. If it is not a different issue, the IRS considers such a transaction a "wash sale" and does not allow the loss to be claimed. It is easier to avoid wash sales in the bond market than it is in the stock market because every bond issue, even though it might have identical coupons and maturities, is considered distinct. Likewise, it is easier to find comparable issues in the bond market that have only modest differences in coupon, maturity, quality, etc. Such tax swap transactions are common at year end, as investors establish capital losses. Also remember that the capital loss *must* occur in the *same taxable year* as the capital gain does.

This procedure is slightly different from other swap transactions since it does not rest upon temporary market anomalies. Rather, it exists solely because of tax statutes.

Effects of Investment Vehicle Selection on Period Return

When developing alternative investment strategies, it is logical to consider the effect of different investment vehicles on desired investment goals. One of the major themes throughout the bond chapters is the need to recognize the effects of different investment outlets on period returns. There is a wide array of bond instruments that offer a portfolio manager certain investment possibilities and enhance the possibility of achieving various portfolio objectives.

Consider the deep discounted issue. This obligation offers little to the income oriented investor because of the sacrifice in yield that accompanies lower coupons.[3] However, deep discounted issues are attractive to aggressive investors seeking high capital gains during periods when there are substantial declines in interest rates. Discounted issues are also attractive to investors who want to minimize capital reinvestment risk, because they offer an "automatic" reinvestment feature. With any discounted issue, compound reinvestment of principal is implicit as the issue moves toward par at maturity. Therefore, as an issue moves from a discount price to par, it is accumulating capital at the compound rate implicit in promised yield. Also, there is the potential for long-term capital gains, and the special tax treatment for capital gains.

Other *sets* of examples are agency obligations vs. treasuries, public utilities vs. industrials, or revenues vs. general obligations. In all three instances, there is one common denominator; while the issues are generally quite comparable, the first issue is more attractive because it offers a higher yield. Other examples could be given, but the point is the same in all instances; some issues provide better performance under certain conditions so they provide more desirable outlets for certain investment objectives.

Bond Portfolio Construction

Some or all of the various investment strategies discussed are ultimately used in bond portfolio management. The bond portfolio, in effect, reflects the

---

[3] Note that, should an investor seek discounted issues as a means of reducing call risk, we presume that a more moderately discounted/higher coupon obligation would be selected to achieve such an investment goal without unnecessary sacrifice in yield.

investment objectives of the institution or investor.[4] We should expect *portfolio objectives* to remain fairly fixed over time, but *investment strategies* to vary with prevailing conditions in the capital market. The idea is to capture as many of the beneficial attributes of a market as possible by altering the investment strategies while keeping in mind portfolio objectives.

Portfolio options vary from maximizing current income, to speculation and short-term trading. Tactics vary according to the type of income sought. While our discussion is limited to three basic types of portfolios, it is possible to construct a portfolio that falls anywhere along the portfolio objective continuum by emphasizing one strategy over another.

Portfolios vary according to their risk-return objectives and it is possible to alter the risk-return profile by varying investment strategies. The various bond portfolios can be visualized as points along an upward sloping line on which the portfolio that maximizes current income would be at the lowest point because it has low risk and promises the lowest yield. Farther up we would encounter the portfolio that seeks to maximize total income in which the investor strives to maximize *long-term* coupon income and capital gains, and is willing to assume a modest amount of risk. Finally, there is speculation, which, because of the substantial amount of risk involved, offers the highest level of expected return. These portfolio relationships can be seen in Figure 18–1. The portfolio manager can alter his position on the capital line by changing investment tactics and strategies.

Maximizing Current Income

Given this portfolio objective, generating regular and sizable cash flows is of paramount importance. Such might be the objective of a retired couple, or a college endowment fund that requires a high cash flow for operating purposes, or of part of an insurance company or pension fund portfolio that must provide a substantial amount of money to beneficiaries. In all these cases the investor requires *a high level of current cash flow,* safety of principal and certainty of cash flow. These objectives reduce or eliminate the possibility of lowering bond quality to attain higher returns.

The actual construction of a current income portfolio will generally take one of three forms with regard to maturity considerations: maturities might be concentrated in one particular sector; they could follow a laddered approach in which approximately equal amounts of the portfolio are allotted to the various maturity segments, or the portfolio manager may use a barbell tactic, putting part of the capital into *short* maturities and the remainder into long maturity bonds and ignoring everything in between. Although any of the three maturity strategies could be employed with a

---

[4] Of course, when dealing in an institutional framework, the objectives and constraints of the portfolio would be defined by the legal and operating requirements of the institution and/or by the wishes of its clients.

Figure 18–1
**Characteristic
Line: Bond
Portfolios**

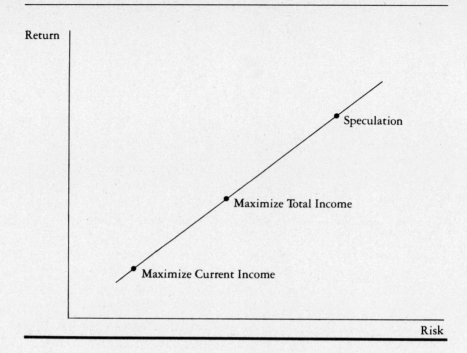

current income portfolio, the most logical approach is the maturity concentration tactic for two reasons. First, in most cases, long-term bonds have higher returns. Second, with a properly defined investment horizon (via duration or some other measure), the maturity concentration approach would reduce trading requirements as well as reinvestment and interest rate risks.

Once maturity questions are resolved, the investor can move to other important dimensions of portfolio construction. Three technical matters would be important here, yield spread considerations, call risk protection, and tax implications. The latter point is obvious. To the extent that income taxes are important, it follows that the return on *tax-free issues* would serve as a *bench mark of minimum return requirements*. Call risk protection is important since one of the major goals of the investor is to *lock in high returns* for a maximum period. Thus, deferred call privileges would be attractive. At the same time, the call risk protection provided by deep discounted issues would be *unattractive* because of the lower yield on such obligations and the favorable tax treatment of the capital gain return.

Finally, the income oriented bond investor must be keenly aware of yield spreads and the incremental return opportunities offered by alternative investment vehicles. Because active trading is generally not desirable, the investor must look for the highest comparative promised yields in the initial investment. Such investors would generally consider utility issues more attractive than industrial obligations. The one constraint when evaluating yield spread is the question of *quality*. Low quality presumably cannot be tolerated in income oriented portfolios since the objective of the portfolio is to generate a high and *consistent* level of coupon income and this objective depends on the quality of the obligation. Careful consideration of the coupon and call features might lead to the selection of premium or cushion bonds, and a few basis points may be added to total returns by selecting issues without sinking funds.

Buy-and-hold would probably be the strategy employed by income oriented investors. Investment selections based on forecasted interest rate behavior would likely be unpopular with such investors who would use such forecasts only in the timing of their investments. However, certain bond swaps may prove very effective and profitable. In particular, the extensive use of substitution swaps, pure yield pick-up swaps, and tax swaps may provide incremental returns over the investment horizon without violating the trading constraints and risk preferences.

Speculation and Short-Term Trading

The objective of the speculator is quite simple, attain substantial capital appreciation in as little time as possible. The means to such an end, however, are far more complex because the rewards and the risks can be equally large. This type of portfolio management requires *extensive knowledge* of interest rate behavior, yield spreads, market characteristics, and issue features. The approach rests on the estimation of interest rates over the short-term. Given interest rate expectations, a speculator uses his extensive knowledge of the markets and alternative investment vehicles to derive maximum capital gains (when rates are expected to fall), or reap maximum returns while preserving capital (when rates move up).

There is only one maturity strategy followed by speculative or trading portfolio managers, maturity concentration. Securities are selected on the basis of forecasted interest rates, and occasional bond swaps (such as rate anticipation or market spread swaps) are made. This portfolio approach would be most appealing to highly aggressive investors, to certain mutual funds or pension funds that seek relatively high yields, and to common trust funds offered in the trust departments of progressive commercial banks. This approach is similar to that found in the equity markets. If anything, it represents the new line of thinking in the bond market; one which enthusiastically embraces the concept of aggressive, and occasionally speculative, portfolio management in the quest for attractive incremental returns.[5]

When interest rates are expected to *fall,* the short-term trader searches for substantial capital gains. Margin trading is often used to magnify

---

[5] Daniel S. Ahearn, "The Strategic Role of Fixed Income Securities," *Journal of Portfolio Management*, Vol. 1, No. 3 (Spring, 1975), pp. 12–16.

available returns by increasing the leverage of the investment. Table 18–4 illustrates the effect of margin trading on average return performance over four selected holding periods. It shows the dramatic effect that various levels of margin trading can have on holding period returns. Of course, the results could have worked *against* the investor. If interest rates had moved up, investor losses would also be magnified! The extent of margin trading used for a given transaction is largely a function of investor confidence in interest rate formulations. The more confident he is regarding interest rate predictions, the greater the margin an investor would use. Margin buying is particularly attractive to aggressive bond traders since *very high* levels of leverage are available with investment grade obligations. For treasury and agency obligations, it is possible to margin as low as *5 percent,* which implies a magnification (leverage) factor of 20 times. With top investment grade corporate bonds, it is possible to margin as low as 10 percent.[6]

One feature of speculating in bonds is somewhat unique in the realm of capital markets. Short-term trading in the quest of substantial capital gains is usually done with *high-grade investment securities.* The securities involved are almost always A rated and above, and are often agency and treasury obligations. Thus, risk of default is *not* a factor in the transaction. Quality obligations are employed because a high degree of interest sensitivity is required in order to take advantage of the price behavior that accompanies swings in interest rates.

However, while quality may be important to short-term traders, matters such as call risk protection, sinking fund provisions, and similar indenture provisions are relatively insignificant. Attention is centered on intermarket yield spread behavior, anticipated yield curves, coupons, and term to maturity (duration). The two former market conditions that determine duration are thoroughly analyzed in order to find the market segments which promise the greatest changes in yield and price volatility. The investor then shifts his attention to issue characteristics and selects a maturity in line with anticipated term structure behavior, and a coupon in line with anticipated swings in interest rates and yield spreads. Generally, lower coupons and longer maturities are sought because they are longer duration and, therefore, have greater price volatility.

After the decline in rates has occurred, the bond speculator takes his profit and moves to the side lines, awaiting the next major swing. Thus, as interest rates *level off,* or begin to *rise,* the trader assumes a more defensive position with short-term securities. On the other hand, he might seek out intermediate-term notes, in order to reap a higher return. (A particularly

---

[6] However, note that margin trading is *not* a viable approach with municipal obligations since the IRS does not recognize interest as a tax deductible expense. In fact, if municipals are even an integral part of a portfolio, the IRS may go so far as to prohibit any interest deductions on margin trading for transactions involving fully taxable obligations, such as corporates. This should be kept in mind when margin trading and, of course, when in doubt about a potential tax ruling, seek competent tax advice.

Table 18-4 **Effects of Margin Trading on Holding Period Return**

June 1970 to March 1971: Interest Rate Movement = 9.1% → 7.5%
(period of 9 months)

	Price Change[a]	Rate of Return[a] with margin of:			
		100%	50%	25%	10%
Average price of long-term	$840 → $960	14.7%	29.4%	58.8%	147.0%
Aa Utility Bonds:	(14.7% pr. chg.)	(19.6%)[b]	(39.2%)[b]	(78.4%)[b]	(196.0%)[a]

August 1971 to December 1971: Interest Rate Movement = 8.2% → 7.3%
(period of 5 months)

	Price Change[a]	Rate of Return[a] with margin of:			
		100%	50%	25%	10%
Average price of long-term	$760 → $830	9.3%	18.6%	37.2%	93.0%
Aa Utility Bonds:	(9.3% pr. chg.)	(22.3%)[b]	(44.6%)[b]	(89.3%)[b]	(223.2%)[b]

August 1973 to October 1973: Interest Rate Movement = 8.5% → 7.7%
(period of 8 *weeks*)

	Price Change[a]	Rate of Return[a] with margin of:			
		100%	50%	25%	10%
Avg. price of long-term	$846 → $928	9.7%	19.4%	38.8%	97.0%
Aa Utility Bonds:	(9.7% pr. chg.)	(58.2%)[b]	(116.4%)[b]	(232.8%)[b]	(582.0%)[b]

September 1976 to December 1976: Interest Rate Movement = 10.10% → 7.8%
(period of 3 months)

	Price Change[a]	Rate of Return[a] with margin of:			
		100%	50%	25%	10%
Average price of long-term	$719 → $912	26.8%	53.6%	107.2%	268.0%
Aa Utility Bonds:	(26.8% pr. chg.)	(107.2%)[b]	(214.4%)[b]	(428.8%)[b]	(1072.0%)[b]

[a] Price change and rate of return figures *exclude* interest income.
[b] Parenthesized figures represent equivalent *annual* rates of return.

Note that in each of the three periods used above an anticipated decline in interest rates was generally widespread and therefore, relatively "easy" to predict; however, for each profitable example such as the ones above, there are one or more examples of substantial price declines which accompanied a rise in interest rates over relatively short periods of time.

attractive issue in this regard might be variable rate notes.) Likewise, a high yielding cushion bond might be attractive if the investor is willing to assume a bit more risk.

Maximizing Total Income

Basically, this middle-of-the-road approach involves a bit of speculation, and a bit of current income optimization. The investment portfolio designed to maximize total income is constructed on the belief that *either* source of return (current coupon income or capital gains) is welcome. Moreover, the portfolio takes a *long-term* outlook and generally involves a fairly aggressive investment posture. As pointed out by Ahearn, fully managed bond portfolios that are dedicated to maximizing total income can offer very attractive competitive returns relative to equity securities.[7]

Total income portfolio managers would probably select securities based on anticipated interest rate behavior, would likely use bond swaps, would often employ modified buy-and-hold approaches, and, when conditions were right, would use short-term trading strategies to improve returns. In effect, these managers actively seek *all* these sources of bond income (coupons, interest-on-interest, and capital gains). The concept of the required reinvestment rate is particularly important to this type of portfolio because it seeks to fully employ capital assets at all times. High yielding obligations are sought for their reinvestment attributes, and bond swaps are frequently used because of the effects they have on incremental returns.

No particular maturity strategy dominates the total income portfolio, just as no specific investment strategy dominates the portfolio. This portfolio approach appeals to both individuals and institutions. It is appealing because it tends to avoid extremes. *Active* bond portfolio management considers the many dimensions of fixed income securities, and attempts to avoid concentration or extremes. Part of the portfolio, therefore, might be aimed at high coupon income through the use of current coupon obligations and some cushion bonds, while another portion might be aimed at potential capital gains through the use of moderately discounted obligations. The total income portfolio approach is very challenging and requires a high degree of investor knowledge and sophistication about the bond market, the effect of alternative issue characteristics, and trading tactics.

Portfolio Implications

The high level of interest rates that has prevailed since the latter part of the 1960's has provided increasingly attractive returns to bond investors, while the wide *swings* in interest rates that have accompanied the high levels of market yield have provided capital gains opportunities for the more aggressive portfolio managers. It might be argued that this recent performance of fixed income securities is not out of the ordinary and, in fact, may be substandard when compared to performance of other investment vehicles, which may raise questions about the place of these securities in a *total* portfolio. An important consideration for portfolio managers, therefore, is the proper role of fixed income securities in an efficient market.

---

[7] Ahearn, "The Strategic Role of Fixed Income Securities."

The widely quoted study by Fisher and Lorie[8] reveals that, over the 40 year period from 1926 to 1965, the average rate of return from common stocks was a hefty 9.3 percent. When these rates of return are contrasted with those available on bonds, the latter appear meager. The Hickman study[9] of bond returns over the 44 year period ending in 1943 shows an annual rate of return of 5.6 percent, whereas Fisher and Weil[10] suggest that only about 3.5 percent was earned on bonds over the period 1926 to 1968. A more recent study by Ibbotson and Sinquefield showed that, while stocks have dominated the investment universe over the long-run, the comparative annual returns since 1969 have *favored* fixed income securities about half the time.[11] This becomes readily apparent when one examines Table 18–5 which contains the year-by-year total returns for several competing investment vehicles. Apparently the lofty and violent yields that have prevailed during the last decade have created a whole new investment environment in which fixed income obligations are competitive with equities for the investor's dollar. Further, aggressive bond management tactics, such as those discussed, are becoming commonplace. As a result, bonds are more fully and aggressively managed, and bond portfolio returns are improving accordingly. This more aggressive posture was reviewed in an article by Daniel Ahearn who showed that, in the first half of the 1970's, fully managed bond portfolios outperformed the S&P 500 by a wide margin.[12]

Bonds in a Total Portfolio Context

A more attractive market environment, along with more aggressive and sophisticated management tactics, has enhanced the investment role of fixed income securities. In fact, when viewed in an efficient market context, the performance of fixed income securities has improved even more than indicated by returns alone because bonds offer substantial diversification benefits in fully managed portfolios. In an efficient market, neither stocks nor bonds should dominate a portfolio. Instead, some combination of

---

[8] Lawrence Fisher and James H. Lorie, "Rates of Return on Investments in Common Stock: The Year-by-Year Record, 1926–65," *Journal of Business,* Vol. 41, No. 3 (July, 1968), pp. 291–316.

[9] W. Braddock Hickman, *Corporate Bond Quality and Investor Experience,* a study by the National Bureau of Economic Research (Princeton, N.J.: Princeton University Press, 1958).

[10] Lawrence Fisher and Roman L. Weil, "Coping with the Risk of Interest-Rate Fluctuations: Returns to Bondholders from Naive and Optimal Strategies," *Journal of Business,* Vol. 44, No. 4 (October, 1971), pp. 408–431.

[11] Roger G. Ibbotson and Rex A. Sinquefield, *Stocks, Bonds, Bills, and Inflation: The Past (1926–1976) and the Future (1977–2000)* (Financial Analysts Research Foundation, 1977).

[12] Ahearn, "The Strategic Role of Fixed Income Securities."

Table 18–5
Year-by-Year Total Returns on Comparative Investments 1926–1976

Year	Common Stocks	Long-Term Government Bonds	Long-Term Corporate Bonds	U.S. Treasury Bills	Consumer Price Index
1926	0.1162	0.0777	0.0737	0.0327	−0.0149
1927	0.3749	0.0893	0.0744	0.0312	−0.0208
1928	0.4361	0.0010	0.0284	0.0324	−0.0097
1929	−0.0842	0.0342	0.0327	0.0475	0.0019
1930	−0.2490	0.0466	0.0798	0.0241	−0.0603
1931	−0.4334	−0.0531	−0.0185	0.0107	−0.0952
1932	−0.0819	0.1684	0.1082	0.0096	−0.1030
1933	0.5399	−0.0008	0.1038	0.0030	0.0051
1934	−0.0144	0.1002	0.1384	0.0016	0.0203
1935	0.4767	0.0498	0.0961	0.0017	0.0299
1936	0.3392	0.0751	0.0674	0.0018	0.0121
1937	−0.3503	0.0023	0.0275	0.0031	0.0310
1938	0.3112	0.0553	0.0613	−0.0002	−0.0278
1939	−0.0041	0.0594	0.0397	0.0002	−0.0048
1940	−0.0978	0.0609	0.0339	0.0000	0.0096
1941	−0.1159	0.0093	0.0273	0.0006	0.0972
1942	0.2034	0.0322	0.0260	0.0027	0.0929
1943	0.2590	0.0208	0.0283	0.0035	0.0316
1944	0.1975	0.0281	0.0473	0.0033	0.0211
1945	0.3644	0.1073	0.0408	0.0033	0.0225
1946	−0.0807	−0.0010	0.0172	0.0035	0.1817
1947	0.0571	−0.0263	−0.0234	0.0050	0.0901
1948	0.0550	0.0340	0.0414	0.0081	0.0271
1949	0.1879	0.0645	0.0331	0.0110	−0.0180
1950	0.3171	0.0006	0.0212	0.0120	0.0579
1951	0.2402	−0.0394	−0.0269	0.0149	0.0587
1952	0.1837	0.0116	0.0352	0.0166	0.0088
1953	−0.0099	0.0363	0.0341	0.0182	0.0062
1954	0.5262	0.0719	0.0539	0.0086	−0.0050
1955	0.3156	−0.0130	0.0048	0.0157	0.0037
1956	0.0656	−0.0559	−0.0681	0.0246	0.0286
1957	−0.1078	0.0745	0.0871	0.0314	0.0302
1958	0.4336	−0.0610	−0.0222	0.0154	0.0176
1959	0.1195	−0.0226	−0.0097	0.0295	0.0150
1960	0.0047	0.1378	0.0907	0.0266	0.0148
1961	0.2689	0.0097	0.0482	0.0213	0.0067

Table 18-5 (cont.)

Year	Common Stocks	Long-Term Government Bonds	Long-Term Corporate Bonds	U.S. Treasury Bills	Consumer Price Index
1962	-0.0873	0.0689	0.0795	0.0273	0.0122
1963	0.2280	0.0121	0.0219	0.0312	0.0165
1964	0.1648	0.0351	0.0477	0.0354	0.0119
1965	0.1245	0.0071	-0.0046	0.0393	0.0192
1966	-0.1006	0.0365	0.0020	0.0476	0.0335
1967	0.2398	-0.0919	-0.0495	0.0421	0.0304
1968	0.1106	-0.0026	0.0257	0.0521	0.0472
1969	-0.0850	-0.0508	-0.0809	0.0658	0.0611
1970	0.0401	0.1210	0.1837	0.0653	0.0549
1971	0.1431	0.1323	0.1101	0.0439	0.0336
1972	0.1898	0.0568	0.0726	0.0384	0.0341
1973	-0.1466	-0.0111	0.0114	0.0693	0.0880
1974	-0.2648	0.0435	-0.0306	0.0800	0.1220
1975	0.3720	0.0919	0.1464	0.0580	0.0701
1976	0.2384	0.1675	0.1865	0.0508	0.0481

Source: Roger G. Ibbotson and Rex A. Sinquefield, *Stocks, Bonds, Bills, and Inflation: The Past (1926–1976) and the Future (1977–2000)* (Financial Analysts Research Foundation, 1977). Reprinted by permission.

stocks and bonds should provide a superior risk-adjusted return compared to one composed solely of either taken alone, assuming low correlation between stocks and bonds. Such was the theme of an article by Sharpe.[13] Sharpe confirmed that stock returns were superior to bond yields over his test period of 1938–1971. However, when bonds were viewed in the context of a financial portfolio, his results showed that, due to the favorable covariance between bonds and equities, the addition of fixed income securities to an equity portfolio vastly improved the return per unit of variability measure. Therefore, the diversification attributes of fixed income securities should be fully appreciated by investors and portfolio managers.

Bonds and Capital Market Theory

Modern capital market theory contends that, when the universe of financial assets is evaluated in terms of risk-return characteristics, an upward sloping market line will occur, i.e., greater return is accompanied by greater risk.

---

[13] William F. Sharpe, "Bonds vs. Stocks: Some Lessons from Capital Market Theory," *Financial Analysts Journal*, Vol. 29, No. 6 (November–December 1973), pp. 74–80.

Financial assets which characteristically exhibit high levels of return logically possess higher levels of risk. Compared to other market vehicles, fixed income securities have traditionally been viewed as low risk and, therefore, the rates of return demanded by investors have been correspondingly modest.

A brief review of historical bond yields will quickly confirm this. In the absence of abnormal inflation (in the late 50's and early 60's), the returns from fixed income securities were low. Since the late 60's, however, when the inflation rate increased, the level of bond yields likewise increased. In periods of high economic uncertainty, such as the recession of 1974, yields on low rated bonds (Baa obligations) moved to levels that *greatly* exceeded those on comparable higher rated obligations; i.e., the risk premiums on bonds increased substantially. This is rather common during periods of economic stress and points out the effect of perceived risk of default on investor returns. Because the risk of default for low rated obligations is naturally felt to increase during economic recessions the yield on such obligations moves up accordingly.[14]

Clearly the risk-return behavior of fixed income securities, in terms of yield for bonds of different quality, is compatible with traditional capital market theory. Capital market theory, however, also relates the risk-return behavior of fixed income securities to *other* types of financial assets. Because fixed income securities are considered to be relatively conservative investments, we would expect long-term bonds to be on the lower end of the capital market line. Numerous tests have been conducted on capital market behavior and one of the earlier studies examined the comparative risk-return characteristics of 14 classes of long-term securities.[15] Government bonds, various grades of corporate bonds, preferred stock, and common stock were compared in terms of their risk premium behavior. Figure 18–2 shows the basic findings of the study, and confirms the a priori expectations since bonds behaved in line with capital market theory. More recent results of a study comparing corporate and government bonds to common stocks and treasury bill obligations were similar. Table 18–6 indicates that the long-run risk-return behavior was as expected. Treasury bills have the least amount of risk and therefore provide the lowest risk-return profile, followed by government bonds, corporates, and finally, the most risky alternative, common stocks.[16]

Of course, such behavior is the reason for the diversification benefits of fixed income securities. Because bonds have risk-return profiles that are

---

[14] For a detailed discussion on this topic that considers several studies on the subject, see James C. Van Horne, *Financial Market Rates and Flows* (Englewood Cliffs, N.J.: Prentice–Hall, Inc., 1978), Chapter 6.

[15] Robert M. Soldofsky and Roger L. Miller, "Risk Premium Curves for Different Classes of Long-term Securities, 1950–1966," *Journal of Finance*, Vol. 24, No. 2 (June, 1969), pp. 429–446.

[16] Ibbotson and Sinquefield, *Stocks, Bonds, and Bills.*

Figure 18–2 **Risk Premium Curve,**[a] **1950–1966**

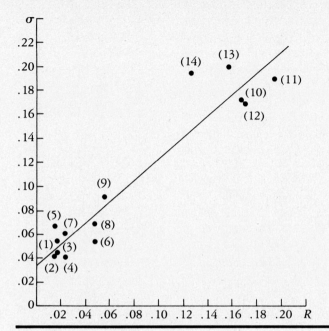

[a] Minimum Term to Maturity on Bonds is 15 Years.

Equation for Least Squares Regression Line is $y = .035 + .8783 x$ $R^2 = .90992$

Source: Robert M. Soldofsky and Roger L. Miller, "Risk Premium Curves for Different Classes of Long-term Securities, 1950–1966," *Journal of Finance*, Vol. 4, No. 2 (June, 1969). Reprinted by permission.

different from those of equity securities, they provide viable diversification opportunities for portfolio managers. As Sharpe noted, while there is some correlation in the return behavior of stocks and bonds, the "amount of such correlation by no means eliminates the advantages to be obtained from holding both types of investments."[17]

Finally, the behavior of bonds in the current decade has been somewhat atypical since bond returns have been very positive while those from common stocks have been low or negative. As a result, the recent (short-run) risk-return profile of bonds has been more attractive to investors than that of equities has been because the risk for fixed income securities remains below that for equities, and compounded returns for fixed incomes have, by some standards, actually exceeded those for common stock. Thus, if the returns on equities have declined to levels closer to those on fixed incomes, and if their risk has not changed, it follows that the capital market line depicted in Figure 18–2 will have much less of a slope. In a recent article

[17] Sharpe, "Bonds vs. Stocks," p. 77. Sharpe's analysis of market behavior also uncovered similar risk-return behavior for stocks vs. bonds as observed in Figure 18–2 and Table 18–6.

Table 18–6 **Basic Series Investment Total Annual Returns 1926–1976**

Series	Geometric Mean	Arithmetic Mean	Standard Deviation	Distribution
Common Stocks	9.2%	11.6%	22.4%	
Long Term Corporate Bonds	4.1%	4.2%	5.6%	
Long Term Government Bonds	3.4%	3.5%	5.8%	
U.S. Treasury Bills	2.4%	2.4%	2.1%	
Inflation	2.3%	2.4%	4.8%	

−50%   0%   +50%

Source: Roger G. Ibbotson and Rex A. Sinquefield, *Stocks, Bonds, Bills, and Inflation: The Past (1926–1976) and the Future (1977–2000)* (Financial Analysts Research Foundation, 1977). Reprinted by permission.

Andrew Carter showed that, between 1970 and 1976, when the S&P 500 produced an overall total return (dividends and capital gains) of 43 percent, the Salomon Brothers "High Grade Corporate Bond Total Rate of Return Index" moved up by 76 percent.[18] Recall that Ahearn showed superior performance on the part of bonds during the first half of the 1970's.[19] Capital market theory, however, is based on *long-term performance* and it remains to be seen whether such comparative behavior is merely temporary.

Bond Price Behavior in a CAPM Framework

The Capital Asset Pricing Model (CAPM) provides an excellent framework for explaining security returns as a function of risk. Typically security returns are defined as *ex post* holding period returns and, therefore, rather than examining promised yield behavior, attention is directed toward *realized* yields.

---

[18] Andrew M. Carter, "Value Judgements in Bond Management," *Bond Analysis and Selection* (The Financial Analysts Research Foundation, 1977), pp. 35–53.

[19] Ahearn, "The Strategic Role of Fixed Income Securities."

When dealing with the CAPM, we are addressing the question of nondiversifiable market risk. It is logical to expect the returns from bonds to be directly linked to risk of default, as well as to interest rate risk. Certainly, interest rate risk should be nondiversifiable, but what about the risk of default? There is some evidence to suggest that default risk is also largely nondiversifiable because default experience is closely related to swings in the business cycle.[20] Thus, the major bond risks are largely nondiversifiable and, therefore, we should be able to define bond returns in the context of CAPM.

Owing to serious problems in obtaining data, relatively few studies have been directed toward bond price behavior in a CAPM framework. One of the early works that addressed this problem only showed a *modest* effect of beta on bond returns.[21] Using a population of 175 bonds, and a bond portfolio as the measure of market return, betas were computed and used to explain realized returns. Beta was found to have a small (the regression coefficient equaled .00983), though significant, effect on return within a multiple regression model. However, when beta was examined as a function of bond and issuer characteristics, it was found that bond betas were more responsive to the intrinsic characteristics of the issue than of the issuer. This is not surprising since it indicates that the price behavior of an issue is intimately linked to such features as coupon, maturity (duration), and other characteristics that are influenced by the market behavior of interest rates.

Similar default risk results were uncovered by a more recent study on bond betas.[22] The study dealt with the relationship between market risk and bond ratings and found that *average betas have no significant and consistent relationships with agency rating.* The explanation offered was that, since the data base involved only investment grade securities, it followed that bond prices were reacting to interest rate movements *across* ratings. Thus, since the study dealt with interest sensitive securities, interest rate risk, which is a market related risk, has an overpowering effect on price performance, and largely negated the effects of differential default risk, which is a company-specific risk, as reflected in comparative agency ratings. This is certainly compatible with our previous discussion because market evidence clearly indicates that the general movement in interest rates represents a far more powerful force than the fine tuning functions of yield spreads and differential bond yields which exist as a result of differential risk of default and agency ratings. Thus, while the Capital Asset Pricing Model provides a

---

[20] Hickman, *Corporate Bond Quality,* and T. R. Atkinson, *Trends in Corporate Bond Quality* (New York: National Bureau of Economic Research, 1967).

[21] John Percival, "Corporate Bonds in a Market Model Context," *Journal of Business Research,* Vol. 2, No. 4 (October, 1974), pp. 461–467.

[22] Frank K. Reilly and Michael D. Joehnk, "The Association Between Market-Determined Risk Measures for Bonds and Bond Ratings," *Journal of Finance,* Vol. 31, No. 5 (December, 1976), pp. 1387–1403.

formal framework for exploring risk-return relationships for the total set of fixed income securities, its application to specific bonds is not without limitations.

Bond Market Efficiency

The efficient capital market hypothesis contends that market prices "fully reflect" all information so that consistently superior performance on the part of investors is largely unattainable. No institution or body of investors can command a superior investment position based on public information and/or timing advantages. Two versions of the efficient market hypothesis are examined in the context of fixed income securities, the weak and the semi-strong theories.

The weak form assumes that security prices fully reflect all market information and maintains that price movements are independent events, and, therefore, *historical* price information is largely useless in predicting *future* price behavior. There has not been an abundance of empirical research on the question of bond market efficiency. However, the studies that considered the weak form of bond market efficiency have provided convincing evidence of price efficiency.

The vehicle for studying the efficiency of bond prices has been the ability of investors to *forecast interest rates.* Such studies are logical because of the effects that interest rates have on price behavior and of the prominent position that interest rate expectations occupy in bond portfolio management. If interest rates can be forecast with a high degree of certainty, so, too, can future price behavior. Several studies[23] reached the same conclusion; interest rate behavior *cannot* be consistently forecast with a high degree of accuracy! In fact, one study goes so far as to suggest that the best forecast is no forecast at all. In these studies, the models developed ranged from the naive approach to fairly sophisticated techniques; some models used historical information and some ignored it. One study incorporated the interest rate expectations of acknowledged experts. The results were always the same since *the most naive model, or no forecast at all, provided the most successful measure of future interest rate behavior.* Thus, it is clear that, if interest rates cannot be forecast, then neither can bond prices using historical prices which supports the weak form efficient market hypothesis.

The semi-strong efficient market hypothesis has only recently been subject to empirical documentation in the bond market. This version of the hypothesis asserts that current prices fully reflect *all public knowledge* and that efforts to obtain and evaluate such information are largely unproduc-

---

[23] See, for example: Michael J. Prell, "How Well Do the Experts Forecast Interest Rates?" Federal Reserve Bank of Kansas City *Monthly Review* (September–October, 1973), pp. 3–13; Oswald D. Bowlin and John D. Martin, "Extrapolations of Yields Over the Short Run: Forecast or Folly? *Journal of Monetary Economics,* Vol. 1 (1975), pp. 275–288; R. Roll, *The Behavior of Interest Rates* (New York: Basic Books, 1970).

tive. Three studies on the information content of *bond ratings* are worth noting in this context.[24] The studies did not question the accuracy of agency ratings in reflecting the financial strength of the issuers, but were directed toward examining the informational value of bond rating *changes*. The contention of the efficient market proponents, of course, is that a rating change should have no effect on bond prices since the information is not new, but is already a factor in the current price of the issue. The results of the semi-strong form of bond market efficiency are mixed but generally *supportive*. Some studies have indicated that the market fully anticipated bond rating changes, while others provide evidence that indicates no anticipation prior to public announcement of reclassification.

It has also been suggested that industrial bonds are more efficient than public utility bonds are in anticipating rating changes. As an aside, the major reason cited for the possible lack of market efficiency is the domination of the bond markets by institutions that are unable to buy and sell large positions and the generally low level of trading in the secondary market. Thus, from a semi-strong perspective, it could well be, as suggested by Pinches and Singleton,[25] that the bond market is, indeed, "less efficient" than the stock market is.

What does documentation of market efficiency imply regarding specific bond market phenomena, such as bond swaps and yield spreads? By their very nature, bond swaps suggest the existence of some degree of market inefficiency. If temporary anomalies exist within or between market segments, then such occurrences afford alert investors the opportunity for extraordinary returns. The widespread use of profitable swap opportunities suggests that underlying price irregularities are neither rare nor random events. An increase in yield through a quality bond swap that results in *reduced* agency rating certainly does *not* imply any market inefficiency since the approach is totally compatible with efficient market theories, i.e., the greater the risk, the greater the return. However, to derive improved return through a swap based on temporary price anomalies, as in a substitution swap, does imply some degree of market inefficiency.

Such opportunities may be caused by the *institutional* nature of the market and the resulting *market segmentation*. In effect, it may be largely artificial constraints, regulations, and statutes that lead to the opportunity to execute profitable bond swaps. An example of this is provided by Andrew Carter.[26] He cited a situation that occurred in 1973 in which Ginnie Mae

---

[24] Steven Katz, "The Price Adjustment Process of Bonds to Rating Reclassifications: A Test of Bond Market Efficiency," *Journal of Finance,* Vol. 29, No. 2 (May, 1974), pp. 551–559; George W. Hettenhouse and William L. Sartoris, "An Analysis of the Informational Value of Bond-Rating Changes," *Quarterly Review of Economics and Business,* Vol. 16, No. 2 (Summer, 1976), pp. 65–78; George E. Pinches and Clay Singleton, "The Adjustment of Stock Prices to Bond Rating Changes," *Journal of Finance,* Vol. 33, No. 1 (March, 1978), pp. 29–44.

[25] Pinches and Singleton, "The Adjustment of Stock Prices."

[26] Carter, "Value Judgements in Bond Management."

obligations were yielding *more* than high rated corporate utilities were. He pointed out that this was due to the shift of savings out of savings institutions in order to acquire higher yielding market securities. This restriction by the major buyers of these securities and the federal government's need to float more Ginnie Mae issues in order to support the housing market caused an increase in GNMA rates. As a result, in the fall of 1973, it was possible to sell high-grade corporate bonds and reinvest the proceeds in *higher* quality Ginnie Mae's, thus realizing an *increase* in both yield and quality. This is obviously irrational and inefficient, and the situation eventually corrected itself, though the process took several months. Such market inefficiency was clearly institutional and a function of artificial forces.

Yield spreads, on the other hand, are indications of high degrees of market efficiency because they reflect equilibrium yield rates that are based on differential standards of risk, quality, and other issue characteristics. In effect, their existence is totally rational. A triple A corporate *should* yield less than an A rated obligation does because it possesses a different risk-return profile. Moreover, the magnitude of such spreads can be traced (theoretically) to comparative equilibrium realized yields and this is additional evidence (or confirmation) of market efficiency. The existence of yield spreads is rational, and the sizes of such spreads are determined in a highly efficient manner.

In light of the foregoing discussion, the logical question is: Are bonds viable portfolio candidates? Based on the evidence and discussion provided in the last several chapters, the answer has to be affirmative. Fixed income securities provide beneficial covariance features, attractive competitive yields, and nominal risk. Moreover, they can be employed in numerous trading strategies to attain a variety of portfolio objectives.

Summary

In the first part of this chapter, we looked at three basic investment strategies available to bond investors: the simple buy-and-hold approach; a strategy using forecasted interest rate behavior; and bond swaps.

The second part of the chapter addressed bond portfolio construction based on risk-return tradeoffs. Three major types of bond portfolios were reviewed as were some popular investment strategies used with each type.

The final section reviewed the role of fixed income securities in an efficient market. Historical returns for equities and fixed income securities were compared, with specific attention given to the returns available from bonds in recent years. We also reviewed the risk-return tradeoff for fixed income securities in the CAPM framework. Finally, the efficiency of the bond market was discussed in terms of weak and semi-strong tests.

Questions

1. Explain the difference between a pure buy-and-hold strategy and a modified buy-and-hold strategy.

2. Using Moody's, Standard and Poor's, etc., find five "cushion bonds." To what level would interest rates have to rise before the price would be affected?

3. Briefly define the following bond swaps: pure yield pick-up swap, substitution swap, and tax swap.

4. What are two primary reasons for investing in deep discounted bonds?

5. What primary investment objective would the purchaser of a "flower bond" have if he is not simply interested in capital gains?

6. Why would an income oriented investor be unlikely to use an investment strategy based on forecast changes in interest rates?

7. Speculating in common stocks often requires the purchase of low quality stocks in anticipation of wide price movements. The same investment objective using bonds requires bonds of the highest qualities. Explain why the latter is true.

8. Choose an investment strategy, i.e., a current income, total income, or speculative strategy, then assemble a portfolio of bonds that meets the objectives of your strategy. Defend your choices.

9. Comment on the efficiency of the bond market with respect to tests of both the weak and semi-strong forms.

10. Explain how bonds could be attractive additions to a portfolio in spite of the higher historical yields of common stock.

11. What is meant by a laddered approach to portfolio construction?

12. An investor is able to purchase 20 year bonds at par with a coupon of 8 percent. Promised yields one year from now on bonds with similar risk are expected to be 7 percent. What would his rate of return be after one year if he can buy on a 10 percent margin?

References

Ahearn, Daniel S. "The Strategic Role of Fixed Income Securities." *Journal of Portfolio Management,* Vol. 1, No. 3 (Spring, 1975).

Bowlin, Oswald D. and Martin, John D. "Extrapolations of Yields Over the Short Run: Forecast or Folly?" *Journal of Monetary Economics,* Vol. 1 (1975).

Carter, Andrew M. "Value Judgements in Bond Management." *Bond Analysis and Selection.* Financial Analysts Research Foundation, 1977.

Fisher, Lawrence and Lorie, James H. "Rates of Return on Investments in Common Stock: The Year-by-Year Record, 1926–65." *Journal of Business,* Vol. 41, No. 3 (July, 1968).

Fisher, Lawrence and Weil, Roman L. "Coping with the Risk of Interest-Rate

Fluctuations: Returns to Bondholders from Naive and Optimal Strategies." *Journal of Business,* Vol. 44, No. 4 (October, 1971).

Hickman, W. Braddock. *Corporate Bond Quality and Investor Experience.* A study by the National Bureau of Economic Research. Princeton, New Jersey: Princeton University Press, 1958.

Homer, Sidney and Leibowitz, Martin L. *Inside the Yield Book.* Englewood Cliffs, New Jersey: Prentice–Hall, Inc., 1972.

Ibbotson, Roger G. and Sinquefield, Rex A. *Stocks, Bonds, Bills and Inflation: The Past (1926–1976) and the Future (1977–2000).* Financial Analysts Research Foundation, 1977.

Katz, Steven. "The Price Adjustment Process of Bonds to Rating Reclassifications: A Test of Bond Market Efficiency." *Journal of Finance,* Vol. 29, No. 2 (May, 1974).

Leibowitz, Martin L. "How Swaps Can Pay Off." *Institutional Investor,* Vol. 7, No. 8 (August, 1973).

Percival, John. "Corporate Bonds in a Market Model Context." *Journal of Business Research,* Vol. 2, No. 4 (October, 1974).

Pinches, George E. and Singleton, Clay. "The Adjustment of Stock Prices to Bond Rating Changes." *Journal of Finance,* Vol. 33, No. 1 (March, 1978).

Prell, Michael J. "How Well Do the Experts Forecast Interest Rates?" Federal Reserve Bank of Kansas City *Monthly Review* (September–October 1973).

Reilly, Frank K. and Joehnk, Michael D. "The Association Between Market-Determined Risk Measures For Bonds and Bond Ratings." *Journal of Finance,* Vol. 31, No. 5 (December, 1976).

Roll, R. *The Behavior of Interest Rates.* New York: Basic Books, 1970.

Sharpe, William F. "Bonds vs. Stocks: Some Lessons from Capital Market Theory." *Financial Analysts Journal,* Vol. 29, No. 6 (November–December 1973).

Soldofsky, Robert M. and Miller, Roger L. "Risk Premium Curves for Different Classes of Long-term Securities, 1950–1966." *Journal of Finance,* Vol. 24, No. 2 (June, 1969).

Portfolio Analysis and Management

Introduction to Part 5

In Chapter 8 the reader was introduced to the areas of portfolio and capital market theory because it was necessary to derive the systematic risk measure to be used in the analysis chapters. In Chapter 19 we return to these areas and examine the theory in a more detailed and rigorous manner. Chapter 20 is an extension of Chapter 19 since the first part considers portfolio work done since the development of the original Markowitz model. The latter half of the chapter considers further extensions of the Capital Asset Pricing Model and briefly discusses some of the problems encountered in subsequent work.

Chapter 21 is concerned with an area in which theory has apparently developed far in advance of possible implementation. The notion of international diversification certainly has intuitive appeal for a U.S. investor attempting to improve his diversification. Further, a review of several studies that have empirically examined the relationship among stocks from different countries *consistently* support the benefits of international diversification. In spite of this, such diversification has seldom been put into practice. The final section discusses some of the problems with implementing this investment strategy. Because of the obvious benefits, the author is convinced that innovative portfolio managers will eventually overcome the current problems.

The final chapter in this section deals with evaluating the performance of portfolio managers using several techniques that allow the investigator to consider risk-adjusted performance. After presenting several techniques, it is suggested that, when evaluating performance, all the techniques be employed because they provide different insights into performance.

Chapter 19

Portfolio Theory and Capital Market Theory Revisited

We normally assume that investors are risk averse and this appears to be a reasonably accurate generalization. Any rational investor would prefer a higher return to a lesser return; unfortunately, a higher return normally involves a higher degree of risk and, as a result, an investor is continually faced with a compromise. He may want to accept an alternative with a very high expected return, but can do so only if he is willing to assume a perhaps unacceptably high degree of expected risk. The investor's utility curves specify precisely which tradeoffs he is willing to make between expected risk and expected return.

One of the primary reasons most investors hold *portfolios* of assets, rather than *individual* assets, is because of the opportunities a portfolio offers for reducing risk. With the exceptions of the extremely risk averse individual (who would likely invest primarily in savings accounts, certificates of deposit, government securities, or similar financial assets), or the very mildly risk averse person (who might prefer a single security or an inadequately diversified portfolio), the vast majority of investors would be expected to seek at least a moderately diversified portfolio. As we shall demonstrate, in the realm of risky assets, a diversified portfolio will nearly always offer a lower expected level of risk for a given level of expected return than a single asset will.[1] Thus, we are especially interested in showing how an investor can reduce expected risk through diversification, why this risk

---

[1] The primary exception to this generalization would be the single security with the highest return. Unless more than one security has the same (highest) expected return, no portfolio could be constructed with the same expected return and lower risk.

reduction results from "proper" diversification, and how the investor may estimate the expected return and expected risk level of a given portfolio of assets.

Markowitz Portfolio Theory

Pre-Markowitz Diversification Theory

Prior to publication of work of Markowitz,[2] it was commonly believed that the way to reduce risk through diversification was to hold a fairly large number of securities in a portfolio, preferably securities from different industries.[3] The rationale behind such an assumption was the belief that companies within the same industry group would be subject to similar economic influences and thus should show strong similarities in performance during a given time period. By choosing securities of firms in different industries, the assets would be subject to different influences and thus (hopefully) poor performance by some of the securities would be offset by the good performance of others, causing total *portfolio* performance to show less variability over time than it would if all the securities were from the same industry.

This would eliminate most of the unsystematic risk of a portfolio, if the number of securities in the portfolio is sufficiently large, but will not reduce portfolio risk below the systematic risk level. Studies by Evans and Archer,[4] and Gaumnitz,[5] for example, found that less than 20 securities appear to be adequate to eliminate the major portion of unsystematic risk for randomly selected portfolios, or for portfolios selected by stratified random sampling from clusters with similar characteristics. Nearly half of the unsystematic risk can be removed, on average, by going from a one security to a two security portfolio. Thus, there appears to be little reason for an investor to invest in more than a dozen or so securities, if the method used is a naive random selection or across industry selection procedure.[6]

---

[2] Harry Markowitz, "Portfolio Selection," *Journal of Finance,* Vol. 3, No. 1 (March, 1952), 77–91, and Harry Markowitz, *Portfolio Selection: Efficient Diversification of Investments* (New York: John Wiley and Sons, Inc., 1959).

[3] Throughout much of the remaining discussion, we will be using examples and directing the discussion toward securities, especially common stocks, rather than using the more general "assets." The discussion could apply equally well to any type, or combination of types, of real or financial assets.

[4] John L. Evans and Stephen H. Archer, "Diversification and the Reduction of Dispersion: An Empirical Analysis," *Journal of Finance,* Vol. 24, No. 1 (December, 1968), pp. 761–769.

[5] Jack E. Gaumnitz, "Maximal Gains from Diversification and Implications for Portfolio Management," *Mississippi Valley Journal of Business and Economics,* Vol. 6, No. 3 (Spring, 1971), pp. 35–43.

[6] It is interesting to note that some brokerage firms and investment advisory services still emphasize the naive "across industry" approach to diversification.

Assumptions of Markowitz Portfolio Model

The Markowitz model is based on several assumptions regarding investor behavior:

1. Investors consider each investment alternative as being represented by a probability distribution of expected returns over some holding period.

2. Investors maximize one period expected utility and possess utility curves which demonstrate diminishing marginal utility of wealth.

3. Individuals estimate risk on the basis of the variability of expected returns.[7]

4. Investors base decisions solely on expected return and risk, i.e., their utility curves are a function of expected return and variance (or standard deviation) of returns only.[8]

5. For a given risk level, investors prefer higher returns to lower returns. Similarly, for a given level of expected return, investors prefer less risk to more risk.

Under these assumptions, *a single asset or portfolio of assets is considered to be "efficient" if no other asset or portfolio of assets offers higher expected return with the same (or lower) risk or lower risk with the same (or higher) expected return.*

In order to derive the set of efficient portfolios, it is necessary to derive the formula for computing the variance of returns for a portfolio which is the measure of risk used. The next section contains a detailed discussion of the concept of covariance and correlation because these terms are so important in defining and measuring the variance of a portfolio.

Covariance of Returns—Discussion and Example

Covariance is a measure of the degree to which two random variables "move together" over time. In portfolio analysis, we usually are concerned with

---

[7] Perhaps it would be more appropriate to state the assumption in terms of *expected* variability, since the model relies on estimated values over the assumed holding period.

[8] Use of variance as a measure of risk obviously assumes that the variance of returns exists. Empirical evidence from various studies of returns on individual common stocks and commodities, the primary return series that have been studied to date, casts some doubt on the assumption that the variance exists. For example, see Benoit Mandelbrot, "New Methods in Statistical Economics," *Journal of Political Economy,* Vol. 71, No. 5 (October, 1963), pp. 421–440; "The Variation of Certain Speculative Prices," *Journal of Business,* Vol. 36, No. 4 (October, 1963), pp. 394–419; and "The Variation of Some Other Speculative Prices," *Journal of Business,* Vol. 40, No. 4 (October, 1967), pp. 393–413. Studies by other authors generally confirm Mandelbrot's results, though arguments could be advanced for the nonnormal behavior of stock returns (arguments which do *not* involve a nonexistent variance).

the covariance of *returns* rather than that of prices or some other variable.[9] If the covariance is positive, this indicates that returns tend to move in the same direction at the same time; if covariance is negative, the returns tend to move in opposite directions. The *magnitude* of the covariance depends upon the variances of the individual return series, as well as on the relationship between them.[10]

For two assets, i and j, the covariance of returns is defined as:

$$Cov_{ij} = E\{[R_i - E(R_i)] [R_j - E(R_j)]\}$$

As an example, Table 19–1 contains data on monthly prices for Avon and IBM common stock during 1976. For simplicity, we have ignored dividends in this example, though they normally would be included. Without looking at the return figures, one might expect them to show a reasonably low covariance because of the difference in product lines. As we shall see shortly, this is *not* the case at all; they had a very high covariance of returns during this time period.[11] Monthly returns were computed by taking

$$R_{it} = \frac{P_{it} - P_{i,t-1}}{P_{i,t-1}}$$

and similarly for R_{jt}. The expected returns were the arithmetic mean of the monthly returns:

$$E(R_i) = \frac{1}{12}\sum_{t=1}^{12} R_{it} \text{ and } E(R_j) = \frac{1}{12}\sum_{t=1}^{12} R_{jt}$$

All figures (except those in the last column) were rounded to the nearest tenth of one percent.

From the table, we can compute the covariance as follows:[12]

$$Cov_{ij} = \frac{1}{12} (300.17) = 25.014$$

Figure 19–1 shows the two return series across time. Interpretation of a number like 25.014 may not be easy (is 25 high or low for a covariance?),

---

[9] Returns, of course, can be measured in a variety of ways, depending upon the type of asset being considered.

[10] It should also be noted that covariance is a measure of a *linear* relationship between returns, thus it may be relatively insensitive to other types of relationships between variables.

[11] Part of the reason for this was that the stock market in general showed a strong performance during 1976. Covariances normally would be expected to be high when the market is showing a strong trend in *either* direction.

[12] In computing covariance (and later, the variances), we are treating the data as a population rather than a sample.

Table 19-1 **Computation of Covariance of Returns for Avon and IBM**

	Closing Prices		Monthly Return (%)				
	Avon	IBM	Avon (R_i)	IBM (R_j)	$R_i - E(R_i)$	$R_j - E(R_j)$	$[R_i - E(R_i)] [R_j - E(R_j)]$
12/75	34⅞	224¼	—	—	—	—	—
1/76	40¼	257¾	16.8	14.9	13.6	12.9	175.44
2/76	39¼	255⅝	−2.5	−0.8	−5.7	−2.8	15.96
3/76	42⅜	262	8.6	2.5	5.4	0.5	2.70
4/76	42	253⅜	−1.5	−3.3	−4.7	−5.3	24.91
5/76	44⅜	256⅝	5.7	1.3	2.5	−0.7	−1.75
6/76	47¼	276¾	6.5	7.8	3.3	5.8	19.14
7/76	45¾	272⅛	−3.2	−1.7	−6.4	−3.7	23.68
8/76	47	273⅝	2.7	0.6	−0.5	−1.4	0.70
9/76	47⅞	281⅜	1.9	2.8	−1.3	0.8	−1.04
10/76	46¼	271¾	−3.4	−3.4	−6.6	−5.4	35.64
11/76	47⅛	271	1.9	−0.3	−1.3	−2.3	2.99
12/76	49½	279⅛	5.0	3.0	1.8	1.0	1.80
		E(R) =	3.2%	2.0%			300.17

but Figure 19-1 demonstrates that there appears to be a reasonably strong relationship between the return series.

Figure 19-2 shows a scatter diagram with paired values of R_{it} and R_{jt} plotted against each other. This demonstrates the linear nature and strength of the relationship.

Covariance and Correlation

Covariance is affected by the variability of the two return series. Therefore, interpreting a number such as the 25.014 computed in the previous section is difficult because, if the two individual series were very volatile, 25 might not indicate a very strong relationship. One easy way to "standardize" the covariance which greatly enhances interpretation, is to make use of the relationship:

$$Cov_{ij} = r_{ij}\sigma_i\sigma_j,$$

where:

r_{ij} = the correlation coefficient of returns

σ_i = the standard deviation of R_{it}

σ_j = the standard deviation of R_{jt}

$\sigma_i^2 = E\{[R_{it} - E(R_i)]^2\}$

$\sigma_j^2 = E\{[R_{jt} - E(R_j)]^2\}$

Figure 19–1
**Returns for Avon
and IBM by
Month—1976**

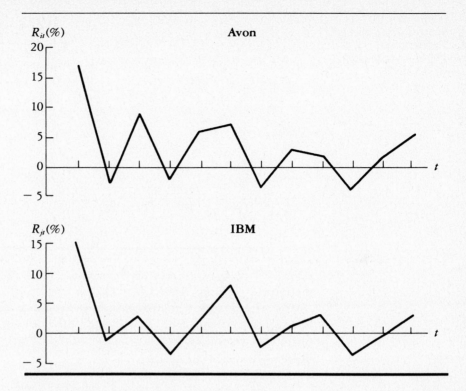

We have values for $R_i - E(R_i)$ and $R_j - E(R_j)$ in Table 19–1. Squaring and summing these values gives:

$$\sigma_i^2 = \frac{1}{12}(377.23) = 31.436, \text{ and}$$

$$\sigma_j^2 = \frac{1}{12}(288.46) = 24.038,$$

from which:

$$\sigma_i = 5.6\%, \text{ and } \sigma_j = 4.9\%$$

Thus, the correlation coefficient is

$$r_{ij} = \frac{\text{Cov}_{ij}}{\sigma_i \sigma_j} = \frac{25.014}{(5.6)(4.9)} = 0.91$$

We know that r_{ij} must be within the range $-1 \leq r_{ij} \leq +1$. A value of $+1$ would indicate a perfect positive linear relationship between R_i and R_j; a

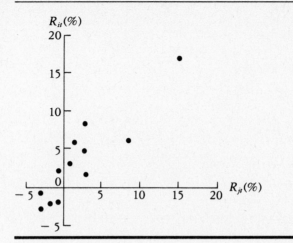

value of -1 would indicate a perfect negative linear relationship. If $r_{ij} = 0$, the returns are uncorrelated.[13]

The value of $r_{ij} = 0.91$ is very high and confirms the impressions given by Figures 19–1 and 19–2. Even though their product lines differ greatly, the returns to stockholders of Avon and IBM during 1976 were very highly correlated.

**Determination
of Portfolio Risk**

In order to estimate the total risk (σ_{port}) of a portfolio of assets, several estimates are needed: the variance of each individual asset under consideration for inclusion in the portfolio (σ_{ii} or σ_i^2), and the covariance, or correlation coefficient, of each asset with each of the other assets (r_{ij} or Cov_{ij} for $i \neq j$). Given these estimates, of which there can be a great many if the number of individual assets is large,[14] we can compute the expected portfolio risk as

$$E(\sigma^2_{port}) = \sum_{i=1}^{n} \sum_{j=1}^{n} W_i W_j Cov_{ij}$$

$$= \sum_{i=1}^{n} \sum_{j=1}^{n} W_i W_j r_{ij} \sigma_i \sigma_j$$

---

[13] A value of zero for r does *not* necessarily mean that the returns are *independent,* just that there is no *linear* relationship. This distinction may not be vital, given the nature of the typical relationship between security returns, but it is important from a statistical viewpoint. Independence implies *no* relationship between returns, while $r_{ij} = 0$ implies *only* the lack of a *linear* relationship.

[14] If there are n individual assets under consideration, estimates will be needed for n variances and $(1/2)(n^2 - n)$ covariances (or correlation coefficients), for a total of $n(n + 1)/2$ estimates. For $n = 10$, a fairly small portfolio, 55 estimates would be needed to compute $E(\sigma_{port})$; for $n = 100$, 5050 estimates would be required.

$$= \sum_{i=1}^{n} W_i^2\sigma_i^2 + 2 \sum_{i=1}^{n} \sum_{j=i+1}^{n} W_iW_j\text{Cov}_{ij}$$

$$= \sum_{i=1}^{n} W_i^2\sigma_i^2 + 2 \sum_{i=1}^{n} \sum_{j=i+1}^{n} W_iW_jr_{ij}\sigma_i\sigma_j$$

All four forms of the equations are equivalent. W_i and W_j are the weights of security i and j, respectively, in the portfolio (i.e., the proportion of the total portfolio value invested in security i and j). The other variables (Cov_{ij}, σ_i, σ_j, σ_i^2, σ_j^2, and r_{ij}) are as previously defined.

The Two Asset Portfolio

Examining the simplest case, in which only two assets are combined to form a portfolio, serves to illustrate the computations involved and to help explain the characteristic shape of the efficient frontier. Since the Markowitz model assumes that any asset, or portfolio of assets, can be described by only two parameters—the expected return and expected standard deviation of returns—the following could be applied to two *individual* assets with the indicated parameters and correlation coefficients, or to two *portfolios* of assets with the same indicated parameters and correlation coefficients.

Equal Risk and Return—Changing Correlations

Consider first the case in which both assets have the same expected return and expected standard deviation of return. As an example, let us assume:

$$E(R_1) = .20 \qquad E(\sigma_1) = .10$$

$$E(R_2) = .20 \qquad E(\sigma_2) = .10$$

If the returns were normally distributed, the distribution of each asset's returns would appear as shown in Figure 19–3. At first glance, it might appear that identical $E(R_i)$ and $E(\sigma_i)$ would imply that

$$E(R_{port}) = .20, \text{ and } E(\sigma_{port}) = .10,$$

regardless of the correlation between the returns of assets 1 and 2. While this *is* true of *expected portfolio return* (as can easily be verified by reference to the equation for computing expected returns), it is *not* true of expected portfolio standard deviation, unless the returns are perfectly positively correlated. Even though the *distribution* of possible returns is identical for the two assets, *individual outcomes* from the probability distribution will *not* be the same in all time periods unless r_{12} (the correlation coefficient) is $+1.0$.

Figure 19–3
**Example of
Distribution if
Returns Are
Normally
Distributed**

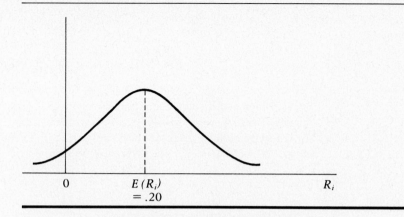

In general, the expected return for a two asset portfolio is:

$$E(R_{port}) = W_1 E(R_1) + W_2 E(R_2)$$

For our example, this becomes:

$$E(R_{port}) = W_1(.20) + W_2(.20)$$

$$= .20(W_1 + W_2)$$

$$= .20(1)$$

$$= .20$$

Since we assume that funds are fully invested, the sum of the weights $(W_1 + W_2)$ *must* equal 1. Thus, $E(R_{port}) = .20$, regardless of the value of r_{12}.

The expected variance (or its square root, the expected standard deviation), on the other hand, *will* be a function of r_{12}, since:

$$E(\sigma^2_{port}) = \sum W_i^2 \sigma_i^2 + 2 \sum \sum W_i W_J Cov_{ij}$$

$$= \sum W_i^2 \sigma_i^2 + 2 \sum \sum W_i W_J r_{ij} \sigma_i \sigma_j$$

For a two asset portfolio, this becomes

$$E(\sigma^2_{port}) = W_1^2 \sigma_1^2 + W_2^2 \sigma_2^2 + 2 W_1 W_2 r_{12} \sigma_1 \sigma_2$$

Substituting values for σ_1 and σ_2, we have

$$E(\sigma^2_{port}) = .01W_1^2 + .01W_2^2 + .02W_1 W_2 r_{12}$$

Suppose $r_{12} = +1$, then

$$E(\sigma^2_{port}) = .01W_1^2 + .01W_2^2 + .02W_1W_2$$
$$= (.1W_1 + .1W_2)^2 = [.1(W_1 + W_2)]^2$$
$$= [.1(1)]^2 = [.1]^2 = .01$$

Thus,

$$E(\sigma_{port}) = \sqrt{E(\sigma^2_{port})} = \sqrt{.01} = .1, \text{ and}$$
$$E(\sigma_{port}) = E(\sigma_i)$$

as expected with $r_{12} = +1$.

If $r_{12} = -1$, then

$$E(\sigma^2_{port}) = .01W_1^2 + .01W_2^2 - .02W_1W_2$$
$$= (.1W_1 - .1W_2)^2 = [.1(W_1 - W_2)]^2$$

From this we can see that $E(\sigma^2_{port})$ can be reduced to *zero* if $W_1 = W_2$. Since $W_1 + W_2 = 1$, this would imply $W_1 = W_2 = .5$ for $E(\sigma^2_{port}) = 0$. Suppose $W_1 = \frac{1}{4}$ and $W_2 = \frac{3}{4}$, then

$$E(\sigma^2_{port}) = [.1(\frac{1}{4} - \frac{3}{4})]^2 = [-.05]^2 = .0025, \text{ and}$$

$$E(\sigma_{port}) = \sqrt{.0025} = .05$$

Since $\sigma \geq 0$, we always use the positive square root.

For other values of r_{12}, different results are obtained from substituting values into the basic equation and assuming different values of W_1 and W_2. The results for several other values are shown in Table 19–2.

Table 19–2
Values of $E(\sigma_{port})$ for Various Combinations of Values of r_{12}, W_1, and W_2

$W_1 =$	0	¼	½	¾	1
$W_2 =$	1	¾	½	¼	0
$r_{12} = +1$	.1000	.1000	.1000	.1000	.1000
$r_{12} = +\frac{1}{2}$	.1000	.0901	.0866	.0901	.1000
$r_{12} = 0$	.1000	.0791	.0707	.0791	.1000
$r_{12} = -\frac{1}{2}$	.1000	.0661	.0500	.0661	.1000
$r_{12} = -1$	.1000	.0500	0	.0500	.1000

Although Table 19–2 shows values of $E(\sigma_{port})$ for a few assumed values of W_1, W_2, and r_{12}, it appears that the *lowest* expected portfolio standard

Figure 19–4 **Values of E(σ_{port}) as Weights and Correlation Vary**

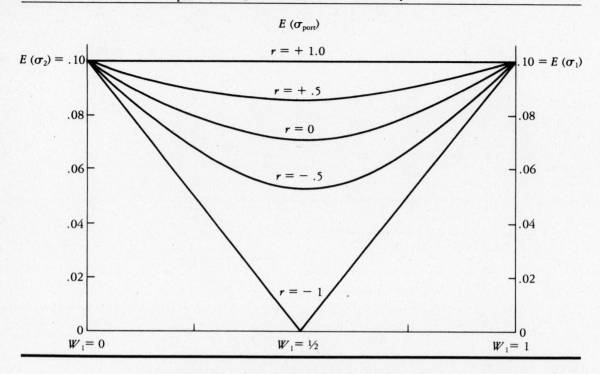

$E(\sigma_{port})$

deviation occurs when $W_1 = W_2 = .5$, regardless of the value of r_{12}. This is true *whenever* $E(\sigma_1) = E(\sigma_2)$, as can be readily proven.[15] Figure 19–4 is a graph of the way the expected portfolio standard deviation varies with the weights and correlations.

The important thing to note in the figure is that expected *portfolio* standard deviation will be reduced below the expected standard deviation of either asset alone, *so long as the two assets are less than perfectly positively correlated.* If they are perfectly *negatively* correlated ($r_{12} = -1$), expected portfolio risk can be totally eliminated by appropriate choice of weights ($W_1 = W_2 = 1/2$). As we shall see shortly, one can always totally eliminate expected portfolio risk in a two asset portfolio by this means if $r_{12} = -1$. The appropriate weights, however, will vary depending upon the expected standard deviations of the individual assets.

Different Risk and Return—Changing Correlations

Consider now a case in which we want to combine two assets with different expected returns and different expected risks in a portfolio. Suppose:

[15] The proof is contained in Appendix 19–A.

$$E(R_1) = .20 \qquad\qquad E(\sigma_1) = .20$$

$$E(R_2) = .10 \qquad\qquad E(\sigma_2) = .10$$

If the returns were normally distributed, the two distributions would appear as shown in Figure 19–5.

Figure 19–5
Example of Distributions if Expected Returns and Expected Risk are Unequal

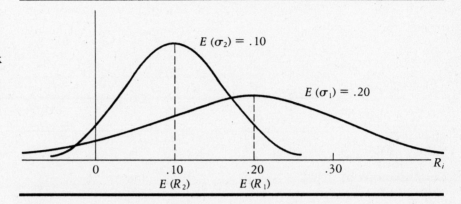

Substituting values for the expected returns of the individual assets into the general expression for a two asset portfolio, we have

$$E(R_{port}) = .20W_1 + .10W_2$$

Since $W_2 = 1 - W_1$, we could rewrite the expression

$$E(R_{port}) = .20W_1 + .10(1 - W_1)$$
$$= .10 + .10W_1$$

This equation is the expression for a straight line increasing from a value of .10 at $W_1 = 0$ to .20 at $W_1 = 1$, and is shown in Figure 19–6.

The expression for expected portfolio variance is not so easily handled, since it depends upon the correlation between the returns of the two assets. Substituting values for expected standard deviations of the two assets, we have:

$$E(\sigma^2_{port}) = W_1^2\sigma_1^2 + W_2^2\sigma_2^2 + 2W_1W_2r_{12}\sigma_1\sigma_2$$

$$E(\sigma^2_{port}) = .04W_1^2 + .01W_2^2 + .04W_1W_2r_{12}$$

We can select different values of r_{12}, W_1, and W_2 to substitute into this expression to solve for $E(\sigma^2_{port})$, then take the (positive) square root to find $E(\sigma_{port})$. Table 19–3 shows the results of these calculations for the same combinations used earlier in Table 19–2.

Figure 19–6
Values of $E(R_{port})$ as Weights Vary

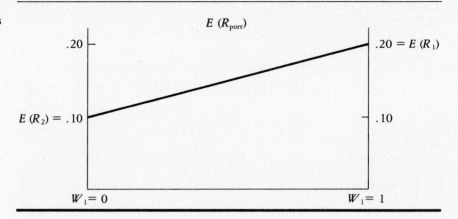

Table 19–3
Values of $E(\sigma_{port})$ for Various Combinations of Values of r_{12}, W_1, and W_2

$W_1 =$	0	¼	½	¾	1
$W_2 =$	1	¾	½	¼	0
$r_{12} = +1$	.100	.125	.150	.175	.200
$r_{12} = +\frac{1}{2}$	.100	.109	.132	.164	.200
$r_{12} = 0$	.100	.090	.112	.152	.200
$r_{12} = -\frac{1}{2}$	.100	.066	.087	.139	.200
$r_{12} = -1$	.100	.025	.050	.125	.200

As was not true in the earlier example, none of the values we chose gave $E(\sigma_{port}) = 0$ when $r_{12} = -1$. However, if we try $W_1 = \frac{1}{3}$, we find

$$E(\sigma_{port}^2) = .04(\frac{1}{9}) + .01(\frac{4}{9}) + .04(\frac{1}{3})(\frac{2}{3})(-1)$$

$$= \frac{1}{9}(.04 + .04 - .08) = 0$$

So it is possible to totally eliminate expected portfolio risk by choosing $W_1 = \frac{1}{3}$, $W_2 = \frac{2}{3}$ in this case. In general, it is easy to show[16] that expected portfolio risk will be zero in a two asset portfolio when $r_{12} = -1$ and the weights are chosen so that

$$W_1 = \frac{\sigma_2}{\sigma_1 + \sigma_2}, \text{ and } W_2 = 1 - W_1 = \frac{\sigma_1}{\sigma_1 + \sigma_2}$$

Figure 19–7 is a graph of the variation in expected portfolio standard deviation as weights and correlation vary.

By combining Figures 19–6 and 19–7, we can see why the efficient frontier must take on its characteristic shape. Point 1 in Figure 19–8 shows

---

[16] This is done in Appendix 19–B.

Figure 19–7 **Values of E(σ_{port}) as Weights and Correlation Vary with Unequal Asset (Eσ_i)**

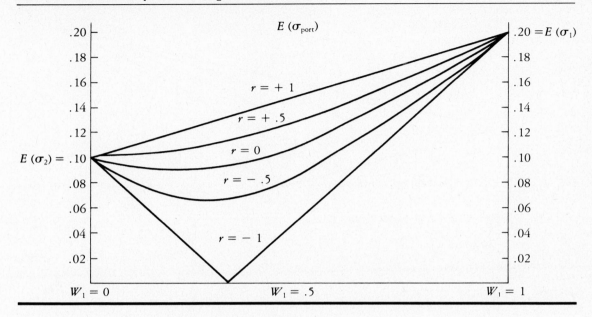

the combination of expected return and expected risk if 100 percent of the available funds are inveted in asset (or portfolio) 1; point 2 shows the combination if 100 percent is invested in asset 2. Suppose we invest 50 percent in each asset; then we know that E(R_{port}) = .15, regardless of r_{12}. We also know that E(σ_{port}) is at least .050 (Table 19–3 when r_{12} = −1). Thus, a 50–50 combination of assets 1 and 2 must lie somewhere along the line AB in Figure 19–8, and the exact position will depend upon r_{12}. Point A corresponds to r_{12} = +1 and point B to r_{12} = −1. By similar reasoning, we can combine the information in Figure 19–7 with the linear relationship of E(R_{port}) to arrive at the set of curves shown in Figure 19–8. Since the returns on most financial assets (at least those of similar types, such as all common stocks or all corporate bonds) are not perfectly positively correlated ($r_{12} \neq$ + 1.0), but are generally positively correlated ($r_{12} > 0$), we tend to see a *slight* curvature, but not the extreme curvatures shown in Figure 19–8 for $r_{12} < 0$. Thus, the efficient set tends to have the general shape shown in Figure 19–9. Except in the area of stocks and bonds, relatively little work has been done on measuring correlations of returns among assets of different types (e.g., real estate investments, commodities, antiques, etc.).[17]

---

[17] One of the few studies on this topic is Alexander A. Robichek, Richard A. Cohn, and John J. Pringle, "Returns on Alternative Investment Media and Implications for Portfolio Construction," *Journal of Business*, Vol. 45, No. 3 (July, 1972), pp. 427–443.

Figure 19–8 Combination of Assets in Return-Risk Space

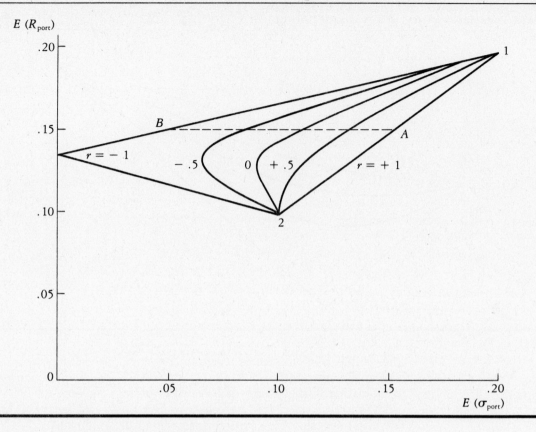

Figure 19–9 Typical Shape of Efficient Frontier for Risky Assets of Similar Type

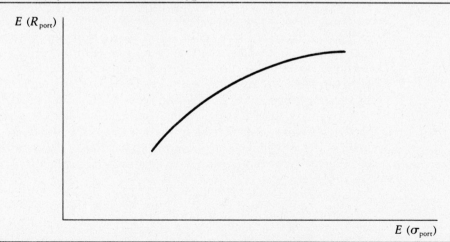

Multi-Asset Portfolio[18]

In dealing with portfolios containing more than two assets, one usually employs quadratic programming[19] or a calculus minimization (or maximization) approach using Lagrangian multipliers and Jacobian matrices.[20] Since we do not assume that the reader is familiar with such optimization techniques, we will instead present a discussion of the derivation of the efficient frontier for a three asset portfolio, primarily through an example.

Derivation of the Efficient Frontier

For three assets, the basic problem can be described in terms of the following equations:

$$E(R_{port}) = W_1E(R_1) + W_2E(R_2) + W_3E(R_3)$$

$$E(\sigma^2_{port}) = W_1{}^2E(\sigma_1)^2 + W_2{}^2E(\sigma_2)^2 + W_3{}^2E(\sigma_3)^2$$

$$+ 2W_1W_2Cov_{12} + 2W_1W_3Cov_{13} + 2W_2W_3Cov_{23}$$

subject to the constraints:

$$W_1 + W_2 + W_3 = 1$$

$$W_1 \geqq 0, \ W_2 \geqq 0, \ W_3 \geqq 0$$

For simplicity in the remainder of the discussion, we will drop the expected value operator on R_i and σ_i. Since we assume the portfolio is fully invested ($W_1 + W_2 + W_3 = 1$), we can substitute

$$W_3 = 1 - W_1 - W_2$$

into the expressions for $E(R_{port})$ and $E(\sigma^2_{port})$ to obtain:

$$E(R_{port}) = W_1(R_1 - R_3) + W_2(R_2 - R_3) + R_3$$

and

$$E(\sigma^2_{port}) = (\sigma_1{}^2 + \sigma_3{}^2 - 2Cov_{13})W_1{}^2$$

$$+ 2(\sigma_3{}^2 + Cov_{12} - Cov_{13} - Cov_{23})W_1W_2$$

---

[18] This section is a detailed presentation of the derivation of the efficient frontier. If the reader is not interested in the specifics, he can skip to the section entitled, "The Efficient Frontier and Investor Utility" with no loss in continuity.

[19] For example, see A. D. Martin, Jr., "Mathematical Programming of Portfolio Selections," *Management Science,* Vol. 1, No. 2 (January, 1955), pp. 152–166.

[20] See Harry Markowitz, "The Optimization of a Quadratic Function Subject to Linear Constraints," *Naval Research Logistics Quarterly,* Vol. 3 (March–June, 1956).

$$+ (\sigma_2{}^2 + \sigma_3{}^2 - 2\text{Cov}_{23})\text{W}_2{}^2$$

$$+ 2(\text{Cov}_{13} - \sigma_3{}^2)\text{W}_1 + 2(\text{Cov}_{23} - \sigma_3{}^2)\text{W}_2 + \sigma_3{}^2$$

By making use of the weight constraint, we have reduced $E(R_{\text{port}})$ to a linear equation in two unknowns (W_1 and W_2) and $E(\sigma^2_{\text{port}})$ to a quadratic in the same two unknowns. We also note that the non-negativity constraints on the W_i's, combined with $\text{W}_1 + \text{W}_2 + \text{W}_3 = 1$ implies that each weight, W_i, is $\leqq 1$. Thus, the "basic problem" implies no leverage or short selling.

A minimum variance portfolio (MVP) can be constructed quite readily from these three assets, as can a maximum return portfolio (MRP). We know that both of these portfolios (MVP and MRP) will be in the efficient set; in fact, they will be the "end points."

Assuming that the three assets have different expected returns ($R_1 \neq R_2 \neq R_3$), the MRP will be the *single* asset with the highest expected return.[21] The MVP can be found by taking partial derivatives of $E(\sigma^2_{\text{port}})$ with respect to W_1 and W_2, setting these equations equal to zero, and solving for the optimal weights, $\text{W}_1{}^*$ and $\text{W}_2{}^*$. Then $E(R_{\text{port}})$ and $E(\sigma^2_{\text{port}})$ can be found for the MVP by substitution of $\text{W}_1{}^*$ and $\text{W}_2{}^*$ into the appropriate expressions.

$$\frac{\partial E(\sigma^2_{\text{port}})}{\partial \text{W}_1} = 2(\sigma_1{}^2 + \sigma_3{}^2 - 2\text{Cov}_{13})\text{W}_1 + 2(\sigma_3{}^2 + \text{Cov}_{12} - \text{Cov}_{13} - \text{Cov}_{23})\text{W}_2$$

$$+ 2(\text{Cov}_{13} - \sigma_3{}^2) = 0$$

$$\frac{\partial E(\sigma^2_{\text{port}})}{\partial \text{W}_2} = 2(\sigma_3{}^2 + \text{Cov}_{12} - \text{Cov}_{13} - \text{Cov}_{23})\text{W}_1$$

$$+ 2(\sigma_2{}^2 + \sigma_3{}^2 - 2\text{Cov}_{23})\text{W}_2 + 2(\text{Cov}_{23} - \sigma_3{}^2) = 0$$

If we divide through both equations by two, we have

$$(\sigma_1{}^2 + \sigma_3{}^2 - 2\text{Cov}_{13})\text{W}_1 + (\sigma_3{}^2 + \text{Cov}_{12} - \text{Cov}_{13} - \text{Cov}_{23})\text{W}_2$$

$$+ (\text{Cov}_{13} - \sigma_3{}^2) = 0$$

$$(\sigma_3{}^2 + \text{Cov}_{12} - \text{Cov}_{13} - \text{Cov}_{23})\text{W}_1 + (\sigma_2{}^2 + \sigma_3{}^2 - 2\text{Cov}_{23})\text{W}_2$$

$$+ (\text{Cov}_{23} - \sigma_3{}^2) = 0$$

Given estimates of $\sigma_i{}^2$ and Cov_{ij} for $i, j = 1, 2, 3$ and $i \neq j$, this system can be solved for $\text{W}_1{}^*$ and $\text{W}_2{}^*$ for the MVP ($\text{W}_3{}^*$ will be $1 - \text{W}_1{}^* - \text{W}_2{}^*$).

---

[21] If two of the assets have the same expected return, the MRP will be the combination of the two with the minimum variance. If all three returns are equal, the same condition holds, but the efficient set would be reduced to a single point.

To illustrate, let us assume

i	R_i	σ_i^2	Cov_{ij}
1	.05	.04	$Cov_{12} = .020$
2	.10	.06	$Cov_{13} = .010$
3	.03	.02	$Cov_{23} = .015$

$$(.04 + .02 - .02)W_1 + (.02 + .02 - .01 - .015)W_2 + (.01 - .02) = 0$$

$$(.02 + .02 - .01 - .015)W_1 + (.06 + .02 - .03)W_2 + (.015 - .02) = 0$$

$$.04W_1 + .015W_2 = .01$$

$$.015W_1 + .05W_2 = .005$$

Or, multiplying both equations by 200:

$$8W_1 + 3W_2 = 2 \qquad \times 3: \qquad 24W_1 + 9W_2 = 6$$

$$3W_1 + 10W_2 = 1 \qquad \times 8: \qquad 24W_1 + 80W_2 = 8$$

Subtracting the first equation from the second gives:

$$71W_2 = 2$$

from which $W_2{}^* = 2/71 = .0282$

$$3W_1 + 10(\frac{2}{71}) = 1$$

$$W_1{}^* = \frac{51}{3(71)} = 17/71 = .2392$$

and

$$W_3{}^* = 1 - W_1{}^* - W_2{}^* = 52/71 = .7324$$

As expected, the MVP contains mostly asset 3 (with the lowest individual variance) and practically none of asset 2 (with the highest variance). If the covariances of the assets had been greatly different, this might not have been the case. Given these weights:

$$E(\sigma_{MVP}^2) = (.04+.02-.02)(\frac{17}{71})^2 + 2(.02+.02-.01-.015)(\frac{17}{71})(\frac{2}{71})$$

$$+ (.06+.02-.03)(\frac{2}{71})^2 + 2(.01-.02)(\frac{17}{71}) + 2(.015-.02)(\frac{2}{71}) + .02$$

$$E(\sigma_{MVP}^2) = \underline{.0174} \text{ and } E(\sigma_{MVP}) = \sqrt{.0174} = \underline{.1319}$$

The expected return of the MVP is

$$E(R_{MVP}) = \frac{17}{71}(.05 - .03) + \frac{2}{71}(.10 - .03) + .03 = \underline{.0368}$$

The maximum return portfolio (MRP) will consist of *only* asset 2, thus $W_1 = 0$, $W_2 = 1$, $W_3 = 0$, and

$$E(R_{MRP}) = E(R_2) = \underline{.10}$$

$$E(\sigma_{MRP}^2) = E(\sigma_2^2) = \underline{.06}$$

$$E(\sigma_{MRP}) = \sqrt{.06} = \underline{.2449}$$

Thus we have the two end points of the efficient set for risky portfolios consisting of combinations of these three assets:

	$E(R_{port})$	$E(\sigma_{port})$
MVP	.0368	.1319
MRP	.1000	.2449

To locate other points on the efficient frontier, we must locate points on what is typically called the *critical line* in W_1, W_2 space. Although the MVP and MRP are end points of this line (for efficient portfolios) as well, however, the line will *not* generally be a straight line connecting them, but will be a "kinked" line which is straight until it hits a boundary of the feasible space ($W_i \leqq 1$, $W_i \geqq 0$ for i = 1, 2, 3) and then will follow one of the boundaries until it reaches the MRP. If the weights are unconstrained, the critical line will be a straight line from the MVP extending indefinitely in the direction of increasing return. Figure 19–10 shows some possible alternatives for the critical line.[22] With the weights constrained, as we have assumed here, the triangle XYZ represents the boundaries of the feasible set. At point X, $W_3 = 1$, $W_1 = W_2 = 0$; at point Y, $W_2 = 1$, $W_1 = W_3 = 0$. At any point along the boundary between X and Y, $W_1 = 0$ and both W_2 and W_3 are > 0. Similar conditions hold along the other boundaries. Point A represents the MVP, and the critical line would be ABY with constrained weights.[23] If the weights are unconstrained, the critical line would be ABD.

The critical line represents points of tangency between an *isomean* line and an *isovariance* ellipse. An isomean line, such as E_1 in Figure 19–10, is a line along which all portfolios have equal $E(R_{port})$. Isovariance curves containing portfolios with equal $E(\sigma_{port})$ are ellipses, similar to the curve V_1

---

[22] The figure is drawn in general; that is, it does *not* represent the situation in the example.

[23] This assumes that expected return increases as you move in the northwest direction, which would generally be the case if $E(R_1) < E(R_3) < E(R_2)$.

Figure 19–10
**Graph of Feasible
Space and the
Critical Line under
Different
Assumptions**

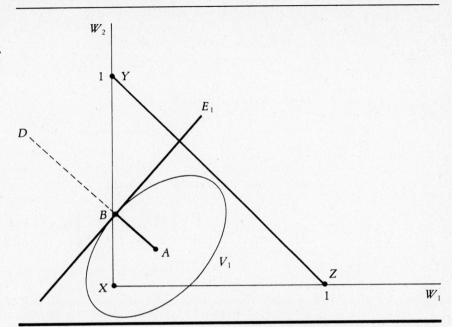

in Figure 19–10. If $E(R_1) \neq E(R_2) \neq E(R_3)$, the isomean lines will be a series of parallel lines. The isovariance curves will be a series of concentric ellipses, centered at the MVP. Because variance increases as we move away from the MVP, we can see why points of tangency between isomeans and isovariances are so important. Since E_1 represents portfolios with the same level of $E(R_{port})$, the point of tangency is *the portfolio with the minimum variance for this level of return.* Any other point along E_1 will represent a portfolio with $E(\sigma_{port}) > V_1$. The isomeans are parallel lines and the isovariance ellipses are concentric, therefore these points of tangency will form a straight line, the *critical line.* Points on the critical line in W_1, W_2 space will be on the efficient frontier in $E(R)$, $E(\sigma)$ space, since they represent the minimum variance portfolios for a given level of return.

We could solve for several points of tangency at various levels of $E(R_{port})$ to arrive at various points on the critical line. However, this is not necessary. We already know one point on the critical line. Thus we only need to determine *one* point of tangency to determine the equation for the critical line. It is really immaterial whether the point of tangency we determine is within the feasible region (line AB in Figure 19–10) or outside (line BD). Once the equation is determined, we know that only points on the line with feasible values of W_1 and W_2 will be on the segment AB.[24]

---

[24] Recall that Figure 19–10 is not representative of our example. The critical line, as we shall see shortly, goes in a different direction in the example.

Returning to our example, we have

$$E(R_{port}) = .02W_1 + .07W_2 + .03$$

$$E(\sigma^2_{port}) = .04W_1^2 + .03W_1W_2 + .05W_2^2 - .02W_1 - .01W_2 + .02$$

From the first equation:

$$W_2 = \frac{1}{7}[100E(R_{port}) - 2W_1 - 3]$$

Substituting this into the second equation and rearranging terms (after multiplying through by 100) yields:

$$\frac{174}{49}W_1^2 + \left[\frac{100E(R_{port}) - 87}{49}\right]W_1 + \frac{50,000}{49}[E(R_{port})]^2$$

$$-\frac{3700}{49}E(R_{port}) - 100E(\sigma^2_{port}) + \frac{66}{49} = 0$$

We can find the point of tangency by taking the derivative[25] with respect to W_1 and solving:

$$\frac{d}{dW_1} = \frac{348}{49}W_1 + \frac{100E(R_{port}) - 87}{49} = 0$$

From which:

$$W_1 = \frac{87 - 100E(R_{port})}{348}$$

This will give us the W_1 coordinate of the point of tangency of an isovariance ellipse with the isomean line and expected return $E(R_{port})$. Substitution of this value of W_1 and the same value of $E(R_{port})$ used to determine W_1 into:

$$W_2 = \frac{1}{7}[100E(R_{port}) - 2W_1 - 3]$$

will give the other coordinate. For example, suppose we choose $E(R_{port}) = .05$, then

$$W_1 = \frac{87 - 5}{348} = \frac{82}{348} = \underline{.2356}$$

$$W_2 = \frac{1}{7}[5 - 2(.2356) - 3] = \underline{.2184}$$

---

[25] For a discussion of this procedure, see Jack C. Francis and Stephen H. Archer, *Portfolio Analysis* (Englewood Cliffs, N.J.: Prentice–Hall, Inc., 1971), p. 247.

We know $E(R_{port}) = .05$ at this point. Substituting these values into the expression for $E(\sigma^2_{port})$ gives:

$$E(\sigma^2_{port}) = .01925 \qquad E(\sigma_{port}) = \sqrt{.01925} = \underline{.1387}$$

Thus, we have another point on the efficient frontier. Also, we can now determine the equation of the critical line, since we have two points on the line. Suppose we represent the coordinates of the MVP as $(W_1{}^0, W_2{}^0) = (.2392, .0282)$ and the point of tangency just located as $(W_1{}^1, W_2{}^1) = (.2356, .2184)$. We know that the equation of the line through these two points is:

$$W_2 - W_2{}^0 = \frac{W_2{}^1 - W_2{}^0}{W_1{}^1 - W_1{}^0}(W_1 - W_1{}^0)$$

Substituting:

$$W_2 - .0282 = \frac{.2184 - .0282}{.2356 - .2392}(W_1 - .2392)$$

from which:

$$W_2 = 12.67 - 52.83W_1$$

This is the equation for the critical line. The line is nearly vertical, but moves slightly to the left of vertical as W_2 increases.

We also can determine where this line intersects the boundary of the feasible set. Since it is nearly vertical (in fact, W_1 only varies from .2398 to .2209 as W_2 varies from 0 to 1), it will intersect the diagonal boundary, where

$$W_3 = 0 = 1 - W_1 - W_2$$

Thus, the point of intersection is at the coordinates (W_1, W_2) which satisfy both

$$W_2 = 12.67 - 52.83W_1 \text{ and } W_2 = 1 - W_1$$

Subtracting:

$$0 = 11.67 - 51.83W_1$$

from which:

$$W_1 = .2252 \text{ and}$$

$$W_2 = 1 - W_1 = .7748$$

At this point:

$$E(R_{port}) = .02(.2252) + .07(.7748) + .03 = \underline{.0887}$$

$$E(\sigma^2_{port}) = .04(.2252)^2 + .03(.2252)\ (.7748) + .05(.7748)^2$$

$$- .02(.2252) - .01(.7748) + .02 = \underline{.04503}$$

$$E(\sigma_{port}) = \sqrt{.04503} = \underline{.2122}$$

Figure 19–11 shows a graph of the critical line with the points we have calculated summarized in Table 19–4. Other points along the portion of the line from the MVP to point B could be obtained by substituting values of

Figure 19–11
Graph of the Critical Line for Example Problem

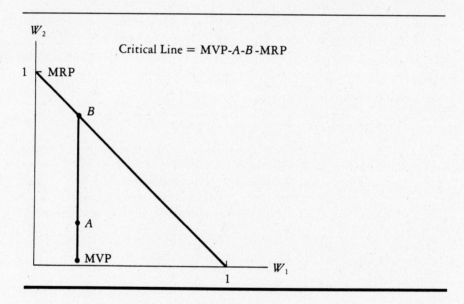

W_1 between .2392 and .2252 into the equation $W_2 = 12.67 - 52.83W_1$; substituting the resulting (W_1, W_2) coordinates into the expressions for $E(R_{port})$ and $E(\sigma^2_{port})$ would yield corresponding points on the E-σ efficient set. Similarly, points on the critical line between point B and the MRP could be found by obtaining (W_1, W_2) coordinates from $W_2 = 1 - W_1$ for $W_1 < .2252$.

Figure 19–12 shows the E-σ efficient set for the example with the points we computed indicated for comparison with Figure 19–17. Note that the scales on the two axes are unequal. The curve would appear "flatter" if the same scale had been used for both $E(R_{port})$ and $E(\sigma_{port})$.

Table 19–4
**Summary of Points
on Critical Line**

Point[a]	W_1	W_2	W_3	$E(R_{port})$	$E(\sigma_{port})$
MVP	.2392	.0282	.7324	.0368	.1319
A	.2356	.2184	.546	.0500	.1387
B	.2252	.7748	0	.0887	.2122
MRP	0	1	0	.1000	.2449

[a] As labeled in Figure 19–11.

The Efficient Frontier and Investor Utility

Once the efficient frontier has been determined for portfolios formed from the securities under consideration, the investor has a choice to make. The efficient frontier will show him the portfolio which offers the highest attainable expected return for each attainable risk level (or the lowest attainable risk for each attainable expected return level). However, as Figure 19–12 shows, the shape of the efficient frontier for risky assets is

Figure 19–12 E-σ Efficient Frontier for Example Problem

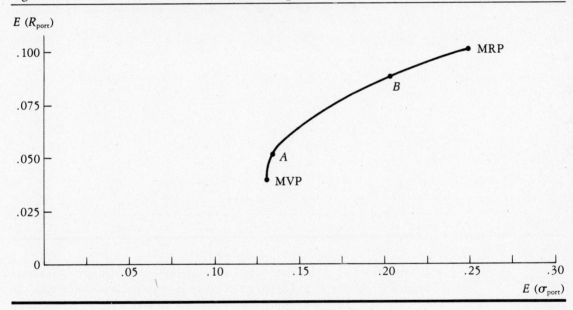

generally such that one has to tolerate more and more risk to achieve higher returns. The slope of the efficient frontier

$$\frac{\Delta E(R_{port})}{\Delta E(\sigma_{port})}$$

decreases steadily as you move from the MVP to the MRP. This implies that taking on the same amount of added risk, as you move up the efficient frontier, will add progressively *less* of an increment in expected return.

The utility curves for an individual specify the tradeoffs he is willing to make between expected return and risk, and are used in conjunction with the efficient frontier to determine which *particular* efficient portfolio is the best, given these risk-return preferences. Two investors will not choose the same portfolio from the efficient set unless their utility curves are identical. In Figure 19–13, two sets of utility curves have been drawn along with the

Figure 19–13 **Choice of the Optimal Risky Portfolio**

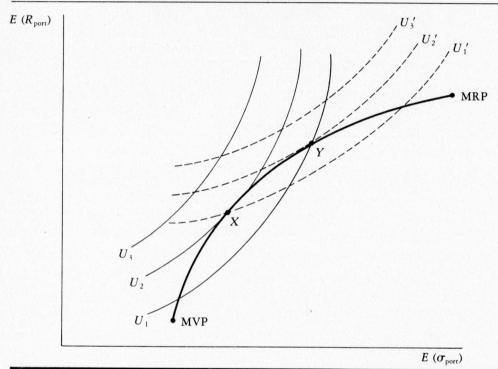

efficient frontier. The curves labelled U_i are for a very risk averse investor (with $U_3 > U_2 > U_1$). These curves are quite "steep," indicating that the investor will not tolerate much additional risk to obtain additional returns. The investor is indifferent to any $E(R), E(\sigma)$ combinations along a specific utility curve (e.g., U_1).

The curves labelled U_i' ($U_3' > U_2' > U_1'$) are for a less risk averse investor. He is willing to tolerate a bit more risk to get a higher expected return, and thus will choose a portfolio with higher risk and expected return than will the investor whose preferences are described by U_1, U_2, and U_3.

The *optimal portfolio* is the efficient portfolio with the highest utility. This will be found at *the point of tangency between the efficient frontier and the curve with the highest possible utility for a given investor.* For the more conservative investor, the highest utility is at the point where the curve U_2 just touches the efficient frontier, X in Figure 19–13. The other investor, because he is less risk averse, would choose portfolio Y, which has both higher expected returns and higher risk than portfolio X. Since Y lies on the U_1 curve, we know that the conservative investor does *not* feel that the additional return is enough to compensate for the additional risk, since $U(X) = U_2 > U_1 = U(Y)$ *for this investor*. Similarly, we know the less conservative investor *does* feel that the added expected return is sufficient compensation for the added risk, since $U'(X) = U_1' < U_2' = U'(Y)$. Thus, given their respective attitudes toward risk and return, it is perfectly logical that these two investors will choose different portfolios from the efficient set.

Capital Market Theory

This theory basically begins where the generalized Markowitz efficient frontier ended. It is assumed that investors have examined the set of *all risk assets* and derived the *aggregate* efficient frontier. Further, it is assumed that investors are rational utility maximizers such that they would choose a portfolio of risky assets on the efficient frontier at the point where their utility map was tangent to the efficient frontier as shown in Figure 19–13. Investors who act in this manner are referred to as Markowitz efficient investors. Because capital market theory builds upon the Markowitz portfolio model, this theory requires all the assumptions noted previously *plus* the additional set discussed below.

Assumptions of Capital Market Theory

1. All investors are Markowitz efficient investors who want to be somewhere on the efficient frontier.

2. Any amount of money can be borrowed or lent at the risk-free rate of return (RFR).

3. All investors have homogeneous expectations; i.e., all investors estimate identical probability distributions for future rates of return.

4. All investors have the same one period time horizon, e.g., one month, six months, one year.

5. All investments are infinitely divisible; i.e., it is possible to buy or sell fractional shares of any asset or portfolio.

6. There are no taxes or transactions costs involved in buying or selling assets.

7. There is no inflation and no change in interest rates, or, if inflation occurs, it is assumed that it is fully anticipated so all returns reflect the change.

8. Capital markets are in equilibrium.

The major factor that allowed the development of capital market theory was the recognition of the effect of introducing the concept of a risk-free asset. Assuming the existence of such an asset made it possible to extend the Markowitz portfolio theory and to derive a generalized theory of capital asset pricing under conditions of uncertainty. This extension has generally been attributed to William Sharpe.[26] Therefore we will begin with a discussion of the risk-free asset and the effect of combining a risk-free asset with other risky assets.

Risk-Free Asset

We have defined a *risky* asset as one about which *there is uncertainty regarding the future return.* Further, we have measured this uncertainty by the variance or standard deviation of returns. *A risk-free asset is one for which there is no uncertainty regarding the expected rate of return;* i.e., the standard deviation of returns is equal to zero ($\sigma_{RF} = 0$). Such an asset should provide a rate of return that is consistent with this characteristic and this return should be equal to the long-run real growth rate of the economy with some effect of short-run liquidity. In other words, the RFR is approximately equal to the long-run real growth rate of the economy.

Covariance with the Risk-Free Asset

The reader will recall that the covariance between two sets of returns is equal to:

$$Cov_{ij} = \sum_{i=1}^{n} (R_i - E(R_i)) (R_j - E(R_j)) \big| n$$

Because the returns for the risk-free asset are certain, $\sigma_{RF} = 0$, which means $R_i = E(R_i)$ during all periods. Therefore, when computing the covariance between the risk-free asset and *any* risky asset or portfolio of assets, the expression for the risk-free asset will always be equal to zero and the product will equal zero. Therefore, *the covariance between any risky asset or portfolio of risky assets and a risk-free asset is zero.* Because $r_{ij} = Cov_{ij}\sigma_i\sigma_j$, *the correlation between any risky asset and the risk-free asset is zero.*

Combining the Risk-Free Asset and a Risky Portfolio

An important question is, what happens to the average rate of return and standard deviation when a risk-free asset is combined with a portfolio of risky assets such as exist on the Markowitz efficient frontier?

Expected Return Similar to the expected return for a portfolio of two risky assets, *the expected return is the weighted average of the two returns* as follows:

---

[26] William F. Sharpe, "Capital Asset Prices: A Theory of Market Equilibrium Under Conditions of Risk," *Journal of Finance,* Vol. 19, No. 4 (September, 1964), pp. 425–442.

$$E(R_{port}) = W_{RF}(RFR) + (1 - W_{RF})E(R_i)$$

where

W_{RF} = the proportion of the portfolio invested in a risk-free asset

$E(R_i)$ = the expected rate of return on risky portfolio i.

Standard Deviation Recall that the expected variance for a two asset portfolio is:

$$E(\sigma^2_{port}) = W_1^2\sigma_1^2 + W_2^2\sigma_2^2 + 2W_1W_2r_{12}\sigma_1\sigma_2$$

substituting, this becomes:

$$E(\sigma^2_{port}) = W^2_{RF}\sigma^2_{RF} + (1 - W_{RF})^2\sigma_i^2 + 2W_{RF}(1 - W_{RF})r_{RFi}\sigma_{RF}\sigma_i$$

but we know that:

$$\sigma^2_{RF} = 0;\ r_{RFi} = 0.$$

Therefore:

$$E(\sigma^2_{port}) = (1 - W_{RF})^2\sigma^2_i \text{ (all other terms equal zero)}$$

$$E(\sigma_{port}) = \sqrt{(1 + W_{RF})^2\sigma_i^2} = (1 - W_{RF})\sigma_i$$

Therefore, the standard deviation of a portfolio that combines the risk-free asset and a portfolio of risky assets is *the linear proportion of the standard deviation of the risky asset portfolio.*

Therefore, *both* the expected return *and* the standard deviation of return for such a portfolio are *linear* combinations, which means the alternative portfolio returns and risks are represented by a *straight line* between the two assets. A graph depicting portfolio possibilities when the risk-free asset is combined with alternative risky portfolios on the Markowitz efficient frontier is contained in Figure 19–14.

It is possible to attain any point along the straight line RFR-A by investing some portion of your portfolio in the risk-free asset (W_{RF}) and the remainder ($1 - W_{RF}$) in the risky asset portfolio at point A on the efficient frontier. This set of portfolio possibilities dominates all risky asset portfolios below point A because there is a portfolio along this line that has equal variance but a higher rate of return than the portfolio on the original efficient frontier has. Likewise, it is possible to attain any point along the line RFR-B by investing in some combination of the risk-free asset and the risky asset portfolio at point B. Again, these combinations dominate all portfolio possibilities below point B (including line RFR-A).

Figure 19–14
Portfolio Possibilities Combining Risk-Free Asset and Risky Portfolios on Efficient Frontier

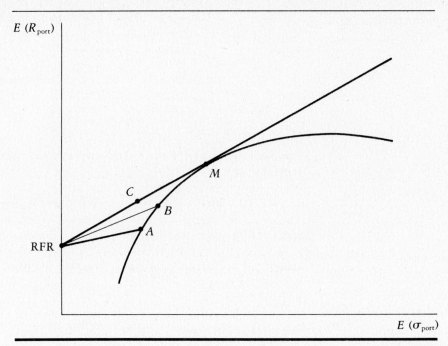

It is possible to draw further lines from the RFR to the efficient frontier at higher and higher points until you reach the point of tangency which is set at point M. The set of portfolio possibilities along line RFR-M dominates *all* portfolios below point M. You could attain a risk and return combination at point C (which is midway between the RFR and point M) by investing one half of your portfolio in the risk-free asset (lending money at the RFR) and the other half in the risky portfolio at point M.

A Leveraged Portfolio

An investor may want to attain a return above point M and also be willing to accept higher risk. One alternative would be to invest in one of the risky asset portfolios on the efficient frontier above point M. A second alternative is to add *leverage* to the portfolio by *borrowing* money at the risk-free rate and investing the proceeds in the risky asset portfolio at point M. Assuming an investor does this, what effect will it have on the return and risk for the portfolio? If the investor is able to *borrow* an amount equal to *50 percent* of his original wealth, W_{RF} is not a positive fraction, but a negative 50 percent (i.e., $W_{RF} = -0.50$). The effect on the expected return is as follows:

$$E(R_{port}) = W_{RF}(RFR) + (1 - W_{RF})E(R_m)$$

$$= -0.50(RFR) + (1 - (-0.50))E(R_m)$$

$$= -0.50(RFR) + 1.50E(R_m)$$

As shown, the return will increase in a *linear* fashion along the line RFR-M because the gross return increases by 50 percent, but it is necessary to pay interest (at the RFR) on the money borrowed.

The effect on the standard deviation of the portfolio is similar.

$$E(\sigma_{port}) = (1 - W_{RF})\sigma_m$$

$$= (1 - (-0.50))\sigma_m = 1.50\sigma_m$$

Therefore, *both return and risk increase in a linear fashion along the original line RFR-M,* and this extension dominates everything below the line on the original efficient frontier. Thus, this "new" efficient frontier is the straight line from the RFR tangent to point M. This line is referred to as the *capital market line (CML).*

As was shown in the discussion of portfolio theory, when two assets were *perfectly correlated,* the set of portfolio possibilities between them were on a *straight line.* Therefore, because it is a straight line, *all the portfolios on the CML are perfectly positively correlated.* This positive correlation is also intuitive because, as shown, all the portfolio possibilities are a combination of risky portfolio M and either borrowing or lending at the risk-free rate, so all variability is caused by the variability of the M portfolio. The only difference is the *magnitude* of the variability because of the proportion of the risky asset in the total portfolio.

The Market Portfolio

Because portfolio M is the tangent portfolio that gives the highest portfolio possibility line, everybody will want to invest in this risky asset portfolio and borrow or lend to be somewhere on the CML. Because *all* investors want this portfolio of risky assets as part of their total portfolio, *all* risky assets *must* be in this portfolio. If a risky asset was not in this portfolio, it would have no demand and, therefore, no value. Because the market is in equilibrium, *all assets are included in this portfolio in proportion to their market value.* If this were not true, prices would adjust until the value of the asset was consistent with its proportion in portfolio M. If a higher proportion of an asset than was justified by its value was included in portfolio M for any reason, the excess demand for this asset would cause an increase in its price until its value was consistent with the proportion. This portfolio of all risky assets is referred to as the *market portfolio.*

The market portfolio does *not* include only common stocks, but *all* risky assets such as bonds, options, real estate, coins, stamps, etc. Since the market portfolio contains *all* risky assets, it is a *completely diversified* portfolio. Because of this, all unsystematic risk of individual assets in the portfolio is diversified away in the M portfolio. The only risk is the systematic risk caused by macro-economic variables that influence all risky assets. This systematic risk is measured by the standard deviation of returns of the market portfolio. This market variability (systematic risk) can change over time as the macro-economic variables that affect the valuation of risky assets change.

Measure of Diversification
All portfolios on the CML are perfectly positively correlated, which means that all portfolios on the CML are perfectly correlated with the market portfolio. This implies a *measure of complete diversification.*[27] Specifically, a portfolio that is completely diversified will be perfectly correlated with the market portfolio (i.e., $R^2 = +1.00$). This is also logical because complete diversification requires the elimination of all unsystematic risk and, if all that is left is systematic risk, such a completely diversified portfolio should be perfectly correlated with the market portfolio that only has systematic risk.

Separation Theorem
Given the existence of the CML, everyone should invest in the *same* risky asset portfolio, the M portfolio. The only difference among individual investors should be in the financing decision they make, which depends upon their risk preferences. If they are relatively risk averse, they will lend some part of their portfolio at the RFR and invest the remainder in the market portfolio; if they prefer more risk, they will borrow and invest everything in the market portfolio. The CML becomes the efficient frontier of portfolios, and investors decide where they want to be along this efficient frontier as shown in Figure 19–15. This division of the *investment decision and the financing decision is referred to* as the separation theorem and was developed by Tobin.[28]

Risk in a CML World
The relevant risk measure for risky assets is *their covariance with the M portfolio.* This covariance with the market portfolio is referred to as the stock's *systematic risk.* One can see why it is this covariance that is important if one considers the following.

1) In the Markowitz portfolio discussion it was noted that the relevant risk consideration for a security being added to a portfolio is its average covariance with all other assets in the portfolio. Because the only relevant portfolio is the M portfolio, the important consideration for any risky asset is its average covariance with all the stocks in the M portfolio or simply *the stock's covariance with the market portfolio.* This then is the relevant risk measure for an individual risky asset.

---

[27] James Lorie, "Diversification: Old and New," *Journal of Portfolio Management,* Vol. 1, No. 2 (Winter, 1975), pp. 25–28.

[28] James Tobin, "Liquidity Preference as Behavior Towards Risk," *Review of Economic Studies,* Vol. 25 (February, 1958), pp. 65–85.

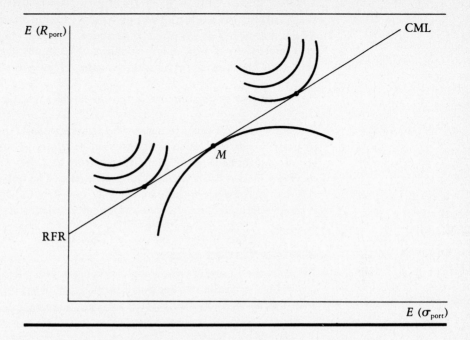

Figure 19–15
Choice of Optimal Portfolio Combinations on the CML

$E(R_{port})$

CML

M

RFR

$E(\sigma_{port})$

2) Alternatively, because all individual risky assets are a part of the M portfolio, one can describe individual asset returns as related to the returns for the M portfolio with the following linear model:

$$R_t = a_i + b_i R_{mt} + e$$

where:

R_{it} = return for asset i during period t

a_i = constant term for asset i

b_i = slope coefficient for asset i

R_{mt} = return for M portfolio during period t

e = random error term

Its variance of returns could be described as:

$$Var(R_{it}) = Var(a_i + b_i R_{mt} + e)$$

$$= Var(a_i) + Var(b_i R_{mt}) + Var(e)$$

$$= 0 + Var(b_i R_{mt}) + Var(e)$$

but $Var(b_iR_{mt})$ is the variance due to the variance of the market return which is referred to as *systematic* variance. $Var(e)$ is the residual variance, also referred to as *unsystematic* variance or "unique" variance because it is caused by the unique features of the asset. Therefore:

$$Var(r_{it}) = (\text{Systematic Variance}) + (\text{Unsystematic Variance})$$

We know that all unsystematic variance is *eliminated* in a completely diversified portfolio such as the market portfolio. Therefore, the unsystematic variance is *not* relevant to investors and they should not expect to receive added returns for assuming this risk. The only variance that is relevant is the systematic variance that *cannot* be diversified away because it is attributable to macro-economic factors that affect *all* risky assets.

Security Market Line

Because the relevant risk measure for an individual risky asset is its covariance with the market portfolio (Cov_{im}), we can draw the risk-return relationship as shown in Figure 19–16.

Figure 19–16
Graph of Security Market Line

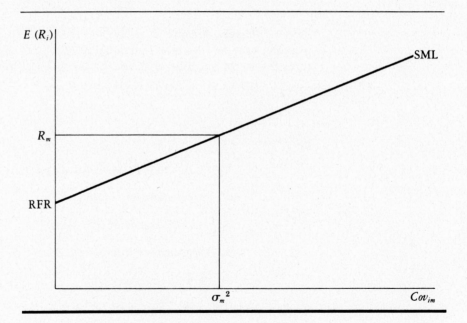

The market return (R_m) should be consistent with its own risk, which is the market variance (recall that the covariance of any asset with itself is its own variance: $Cov_{ii} = \sigma^2$). The equation for this line is:

$$E(R_i) = RFR + \frac{R_m - RFR}{\sigma_m^2} (Cov_{im})$$

$$= RFR + \frac{Cov_{im}}{\sigma_m^2} (R_m - RFR)$$

but Cov_{im} / σ_m^2 = beta (β_i), so this can be stated

$$E(R_i) = RFR + \beta_i (R_m - RFR)$$

Beta is a *normalized* measure of systematic risk; the covariance is normalized by the market portfolio covariance. Therefore, if β_i is above 1.0 the asset is higher risk than the market is. Now the SML graph can be expressed as shown in Figure 19–17.

Figure 19–17 **Graph of Security Market Line with Normalized Systematic Risk**

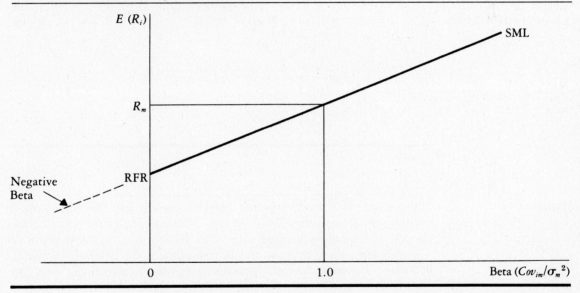

Therefore, the expected rate of return for a risky asset is determined by the RFR plus a risk premium that is a function of the *systematic* risk of the asset (β_i), and the prevailing market risk premium ($R_m - RFR$). In equilibrium, *all* individual risky assets and all portfolios should plot on the SML; i.e., all assets should be priced such that their expected rate of return is consistent with their systematic risk. Any security that plots *above* the SML would be considered underpriced because its expected return would be too high in terms of its expected systematic risk. The opposite would be true for assets that plot below the SML.

The Characteristic Line

The systematic risk input for an individual risky asset is derived from the following regression model that is referred to as the asset's characteristic line with the market portfolio.

$$R_{it} = a_i + \beta_i R_{mt} + \epsilon$$

$$\beta_i = \text{Cov}_{im} / \sigma_m^2$$

$$a_i = \bar{R}_i - \beta_i \bar{R}_m$$

The characteristic line is the line of best fit through a scatter graph of rates of return for the individual asset and the market portfolio as shown in Figure 19–18.

Figure 19–18
**Graph of
Characteristic Line**

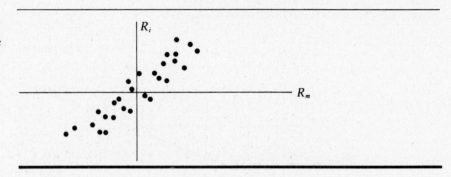

Summary

The purpose of this chapter has been to present the basic Markowitz portfolio model and the Capital Asset Pricing Model (CAPM) in detail. Initially, we briefly discussed why investors diversify and how portfolio managers diversified prior to the introduction of the Markowitz model. Following a presentation of the assumptions of the portfolio model, we dealt in detail with covariance and correlation because of the importance of these concepts to the development of the portfolio model.

The formula for the determination of the risk of the portfolio was presented and its use for a two asset portfolio under several sets of risk, return, and correlation assumptions demonstrated. It was shown that the crucial variable determining the risk of the total portfolio is the correlation between the assets in the portfolio. Given this basic understanding of the factors that influence the return and risk of a portfolio, we derived the efficient frontier for a three asset portfolio. It was shown that, based upon their utility function, investors will differ in regard to the portfolio they select along the efficient frontier.

Our discussion of the Capital Asset Pricing Model began with a definition of a risk-free asset and showed that the correlation and covariance of any asset with the risk-free asset is zero. It was then shown that any combination of an asset and the risk-free asset generated a linear return and a linear risk function. Combining the risk-free asset with any portfolio on the Markowitz efficient frontier produced a series of straight lines, with the dominant line a point of tangency with the efficient frontier. This dominant line is referred to as the capital market line (CML) and the portfolio at the point of tangency is the market portfolio of all risky assets (M). Because all investors will want to invest in this market portfolio, it was shown that the investment decision and the financing decision can be separated and that the financing decision is consistent with the risk preferences of the investor. Also, because the market portfolio is the only relevant portfolio, the important risk measure for an individual risky asset is its covariance with the market portfolio. When the covariance of an asset is normalized by the market variance, we derive the well-known beta measure of systematic risk. Finally, the security market line (SML) was presented and discussed and an individual security's characteristic line defined.

Questions

1. Why do most investors hold diversified portfolios?.

2. What is covariance and why is it important in portfolio theory?

3. Why do most assets of the same type show positive covariances of returns with each other? Would you expect this to be true of covariances of returns between *different* types of assets (e.g., returns on treasury bills and General Motors common stock, or commercial real estate)? Why or why not?

4. Why are investors' utility curves important in portfolio theory?

5. Explain why the efficient frontier takes its characteristic shape.

6. Define each of the following terms and explain the importance of each in determining the efficient frontier:
   a. isomean lines
   b. isovariance curves
   c. the critical line.

7. Explain how the optimal portfolio is chosen. Will it always be a diversified portfolio, or could it be a single security? Explain your answer.

8. If you are considering two assets with the following:

$$E(R_1) = .15 \qquad E(R_2) = .20$$
$$E(\sigma_1) = .10 \qquad E(\sigma_2) = .20$$
$$r_{12} = +0.5$$

what will be the weights, the expected return, and expected risk of the minimum variance portfolio which can be formed from these two assets?

9. Define a risk-free asset.

10. What is the covariance between a risk-free asset and a portfolio of risky assets? Explain your answer.

11. Why is the set of points between the risk-free asset and a portfolio on the Markowitz efficient frontier a straight line? Explain.

12. Show graphically and explain why the line from the RFR that is tangent to the efficient frontier is the dominant set of portfolio possibilities.

13. Define the market portfolio and discuss its characteristics.

14. Discuss leverage and indicate what it does to the CML.

15. Why is the CML considered the "new" efficient frontier?

16. Define complete diversification in terms of Capital Market Theory.

17. How would you *measure* the extent of diversification of a portfolio? Discuss the rationale for this answer.

18. Define systematic and unsystematic risk. Which of these is relevant to an investor attempting to determine his required return for the asset? *Why* is this the relevant risk?

19. Briefly discuss and show why beta is referred to as "normalized" risk or an index of risk.

20. You are given the following set of market conditions: RFR $= .08$; $R_m = .14$. Compute the $E(R_i)$ for the following risky assets:

       A. $B_i = 1.30$ B. $B_i = 0.75$ C. $B_i = 1.05$

21. Given the information in Question 20, draw a graph of the SML and plot the three securities.

22. An analyst estimates the following regarding three securities:

	B_i	$E(R_i)$
A.	1.40	.15
B.	0.80	.13
C.	1.05	.14

Given the SML in Question 20, are the stocks undervalued or overvalued? Show this graphically. Discuss what you would expect to happen to the price of each security during the subsequent period. *Why* will this occur?

References

Evans, John L. and Archer, Stephen H. "Diversification and the Reduction of Dispersion: An Empirical Analysis." *Journal of Finance,* Vol. 24, No. 1 (December, 1968).

Fama, Eugene F. "Risk, Return and Equilibrium: Some Clarifying Comments." *Journal of Finance,* Vol. 23, No. 1 (March, 1968).

Francis, Jack C. and Archer, Stephen H. *Portfolio Analysis,* 2nd ed. Englewood Cliffs, New Jersey: Prentice–Hall, Inc., 1979.

Gaumnitz, Jack E. "Maximal Gains from Diversification and Implications for Portfolio Management." *Mississippi Valley Journal of Business and Economics,* Vol. 6, No. 3 (Spring, 1971).

Jensen, Michael C. "Capital Markets: Theory and Evidence." *The Bell Journal of Economics and Management Science,* Vol. 3, No. 2 (Autumn, 1972).

Mandelbrot, Benoit. "New Methods in Statistical Economics." *Journal of Political Economy,* Vol. 71, No. 5 (October, 1963).

Mandelbrot, Benoit. The Variation of Certain Speculative Prices." *Journal of Business,* Vol. 36, No. 4 (October, 1963).

Mandelbrot, Benoit. "The Variation of Some Other Speculative Prices." *Journal of Business,* Vol. 40, No. 4 (October, 1967).

Markowitz, Harry. "The Optimization of Quadratic Function Subject to Linear Constraints." *Naval Research Logistics Quarterly,* Vol. 3 (March–June, 1956).

Markowitz, Harry. "Portfolio Selection." *Journal of Finance,* Vol. 3, No. 1 (March, 1952).

Markowitz, Harry. *Portfolio Selection: Efficient Diversification of Investments.* New York: John Wiley and Sons, Inc., 1959.

Martin, A. D., Jr. "Mathematical Programming of Portfolio Selections." *Management Science,* Vol. 1, No. 2 (January, 1955).

Mossin, J. "Equilibrium in a Capital Asset Market." *Econometrica,* Vol. 34, No. 4 (October, 1966).

Mossin, J. "Security Pricing and Investment Criteria in Competitive Markets." *American Economic Review,* Vol. 59, No. 5 (December, 1969).

Sharpe, William F. "Capital Asset Prices: A Theory of Market Equilibrium Under Conditions of Risk." *Journal of Finance,* Vol. 19, No. 4 (September, 1964).

Tobin, James. "Liquidity Preference as Behavior Towards Risk." *Review of Economic Studies,* Vol. 25 (February, 1958).

Appendix 19–A
Proof That Minimum Portfolio Variance Occurs with Equal Weights When Securities Have Equal Variances

When $E(\sigma_i) = E(\sigma_2)$, we have

$$E(\sigma^2_{port}) = W_1{}^2 E(\sigma_1)^2 + (1-W_1)^2 E(\sigma_1)^2 + 2W_1(1-W_1)r_{12}E(\sigma_1)^2$$

$$= E(\sigma_1)^2 \left[W_1{}^2 + 1 - 2W_1 + W_1{}^2 + 2W_1 r_{12} - 2W_1{}^2 r_{12} \right]$$

$$= E(\sigma_1)^2 \left[2W_1{}^2 + 1 - 2W_1 + 2W_1 r_{12} - 2W_1{}^2 r_{12} \right]$$

For this to be a minimum

$$\frac{\partial E(\sigma^2_{port})}{\partial W_1} = 0 = E(\sigma_1)^2 \left[4W_1 - 2 + 2r_{12} - 4W_1 r_{12} \right]$$

Assuming $E(\sigma_1)^2 > 0$, this implies

$$4W_1 - 2 + 2r_{12} - 4W_1 r_{12} = 0$$

$$4W_1(1-r_{12}) - 2(1-r_{12}) = 0$$

From which

$$W_1 = \frac{2(1-r_{12})}{4(1-r_{12})} = \frac{1}{2}$$

regardless of r_{12}. Thus, if $E(\sigma_1) = E(\sigma_2)$, $E(\sigma^2_{port})$ will *always* be minimized by choosing $W_1 = W_2 = 1/2$, regardless of the value of r_{12}, except when $r_{12} = +1$ (in which case $E(\sigma_{port}) = E(\sigma_1) = E(\sigma_2)$). This can be verified by checking the second order condition

$$\frac{\partial^2 E(\sigma_{port}^2)}{\partial W_1^2} > 0.$$

$$E(\sigma^2_{port}) = W_1{}^2 E(\sigma_1)^2 + (1-W_1)^2 E(\sigma_2)^2 + 2W_1(1-W_1)r_{12}E(\sigma_1)E(\sigma_2)$$

$$= W_1{}^2 E(\sigma_1)^2 + E(\sigma_2)^2 - 2W_1 E(\sigma_2) + W_1{}^2 E(\sigma_2)^2$$
$$+ 2W_1 r_{12} E(\sigma_1)E(\sigma_2) - 2W_1{}^2 r_{12} E(\sigma_1)E(\sigma_2)$$

If $r_{12} = -1$, this can be rearranged and expressed as

$$E(\sigma^2_{port}) = W_1{}^2 [E(\sigma_1)^2 + 2E(\sigma_1)E(\sigma_2) + E(\sigma_2)^2]$$

$$- 2W_1[E(\sigma_2)^2 + E(\sigma_1)E(\sigma_2)] + E(\sigma_2)^2$$

$$= W_1{}^2 [E(\sigma_1) + E(\sigma_2)]^2 - 2W_1 E(\sigma_2)[E(\sigma_1) + E(\sigma_2)] + E(\sigma_2)^2$$

$$= \{W_1[E(\sigma_1) + E(\sigma_2)] - E(\sigma_2)\}^2$$

We want to find the weight, W_1, which will reduce $E(\sigma^2_{port})$ to *zero*, therefore:

$$W_1[E(\sigma_1) + E(\sigma_2)] - E(\sigma_2) = 0$$

Which yields

$$W_1 = \frac{E(\sigma_2)}{E(\sigma_2) + E(\sigma_2)}, \text{ and } W_2 = 1 - W_1 = \frac{E(\sigma_1)}{E(\sigma_1) + E(\sigma_2)}.$$

Chapter 20

Subsequent Developments in Portfolio Theory and Capital Market Theory

There is little question that the most significant and most popular developments in portfolio theory since the Markowitz mean-variance approach (hereafter E-V) have been the "diagonal model" introduced by Sharpe[1] (and various multi-index approaches which have evolved from it) and the closely related Capital Asset Pricing Model.[2] There have, however, been several other interesting approaches in the past 25 years. Given some of the recent disenchantment with the Capital Asset Pricing Model,[3] and some evidence that stock price changes and returns may not be as "well-behaved" as previously thought,[4] it is worthwhile to examine some of these other approaches.

---

[1] William F. Sharpe, "A Simplified Model for Portfolio Analysis," *Management Science,* Vol. 9, No. 2 (January, 1963), pp. 277–293.

[2] See William F. Sharpe, "Capital Asset Prices: A Theory of Market Equilibrium Under Conditions of Risk," *Journal of Finance,* Vol. 19, No. 3 (September, 1964), pp. 425–442; John Lintner, "Security Prices, Risk and Maximal Gains from Diversification," *Journal of Finance,* Vol. 20, No. 4 (December, 1965), pp. 587–615; and J. Mossin, "Equilibrium in a Capital Asset Market," *Econometrica,* Vol. 34, No. 4 (October, 1966), pp. 768–783.

[3] For example, see E. F. Fama and J. D. MacBeth, "Risk, Return and Equilibrium: Empirical Tests," *Journal of Political Economy,* Vol. 81 (1973), pp. 607–636; "Tests of the Multiperiod Two-Parameter Model," *Journal of Financial Economics,* Vol. 1 No. 1 (May, 1974), pp. 43–66. Also, see Richard Roll, "A Critique of the Asset Pricing Theory's Tests," *Journal of Financial Economics,* Vol. 4, No. 2 (March, 1977), pp. 129–176; Richard Roll, "Ambiguity When Performance Is Measured by the Securities Market Line," *Journal of Finance,* Vol. 33, No. 4 (September, 1978), pp. 1051–1069.

[4] For example, see Benoit Mandelbrot, "Stable Paretian Random Functions and the Multiplicative Variation of Income," *Econometrica,* Vol. 29, No. 4 (October, 1961), pp.

For convenience, the alternative approaches will be divided into two basic categories: those which merely suggest the substitution of some *other* risk measure in place of variance (or standard deviation), and those which represent more radical departures from the E-V approach. Some require a substantial amount of mathematics to be used effectively, but this discussion will focus on the concepts involved, using a minimum of mathematics, and allow the reader the option of obtaining more details in the references mentioned.

After discussing the *concepts* involved, we will make some comments on the approaches and briefly discuss some of the empirical work done on them, especially the studies comparing efficient sets derived by using the various methods. This section will be brief and basically summary in nature. The reader is directed to the references for detailed discussions of methodology and proofs of various generalizations.

The final section of the chapter contains a review of some of the important extensions of the "original" Capital Asset Pricing Model. Again, we sacrifice completeness to concentrate on the concepts involved and direct the interested reader to selected references for further elaboration.

Techniques Using Other Risk Measures

The Mean-Semivariance (E-S) Approach

This approach, which was originally suggested by Markowitz[5] as an alternative to E-V, uses semivariance as a risk measure. Semivariance is a measure only of variation *below* some target level of return. This target level could be the expected return, zero return, the investor's required rate of return, or any other fixed return level. The measure is intuitively appealing, since it indicates *only* the "downside risk", or risk of falling short of some desired return. On the other hand, the *variance* approach implicitly assumes that very large returns (relative to $E(R)$) are just as undesirable as very small returns.

For a single asset with possible returns $R_1, R_2, \ldots, R_n$ with probabilities $P_1, P_2, \ldots, P_n$, respectively, the semivariance about some fixed point h could be expressed as:

$$S_h = \sum_{i=1}^{n} P_i Y_i$$

517–543; "New Methods in Statistical Economics," *Journal of Political Economy*, Vol. 71, No. 5 (October, 1963), pp. 421–440; "The Variation of Certain Speculative Prices," *Journal of Business*, Vol. 36, No. 4 (October, 1963), pp. 394–419; and "The Variation of Some Other Speculative Prices," *Journal of Business*, Vol. 40, No. 4 (October, 1967), pp. 393–413. Also, see Eugene F. Fama, "The Behavior of Stock Market Prices," *Journal of Business*, Vol. 38, No. 1 (January, 1965), pp. 34–105.

[5] Harry Markowitz, *Portfolio Selection: Efficient Diversification of Investment* (New York: John Wiley and Sons, Inc., 1959).

where

$$Y_i = \begin{cases} (Ri - h)^2 & \text{if } Ri < h \\ 0 & \text{otherwise} \end{cases}$$

For the special case in which the distribution of returns is symmetric and $h = E(R)$, S_h will be $\sigma^2/2$, so nothing would be gained by using the semivariance instead of the variance. If the distribution is *not* symmetric, or if $h \neq E(R)$, E-V and E-S could give quite different results. Figure 20–1 shows two distributions, both of which have the same expected return and variance. The risk as measured by the semivariance about $E(R)$ is indicated by the shaded area in each case.

Figure 20–1 **Example of Two Distributions with Equal E(R) and E(σ), but Unequal Semivariances**

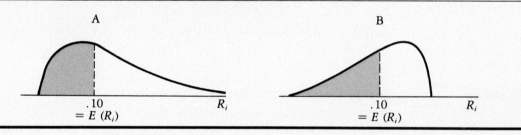

In the E-S approach, a portfolio is efficient if (1) no other portfolio has a lower expected semivariance of return with the same (or higher) expected return, or (2) no other portfolio has a higher expected return with the same (or lower) expected semivariance of return. Thus, the criterion is the same as it is with E-V, except that S has replaced V.

Baumol's Expected Gain—Confidence Limit (E-L) Criterion

Baumol[6] suggested that it may be unreasonable to employ the variance (or standard deviation) of returns as a risk measure when the expected returns differ substantially. Consider two hypothetical portfolios whose returns are assumed to be normally distributed with $E(R)$ and $E(\sigma)$ as shown in Figure 20–2. Neither portfolio dominates the other according to E-V since

$$E(R_B) > E(R_A), \text{ but}$$

$$E(\sigma_B) > E(\sigma_A).$$

---

[6] W. J. Baumol, "An Expected Gain—Confidence Limit Criterion for Portfolio Selection," *Management Science*, Vol. 10, No. 1 (October, 1963), pp. 174–182.

Figure 20–2 **Example of Two Distributions with Unequal E(R) and E(σ)**

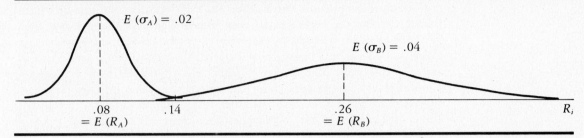

Still, it is inconceivable that an investor would ever choose A over B. With B, there is a probability of approximately .001 of earning a return of *less* than 14 percent, while the probability of earning that *high* a return with A is only about .007.

To circumvent such a problem, Baumol suggested that the appropriate risk measure for a given portfolio (or security) should be a "lower confidence limit" (L) for the investor's return:

$$L = E - k\sigma,$$

where k is some appropriately chosen value consistent with the investor's risk preferences. The more conservative the investor, the higher the value of k, and thus the more important the "kσ" becomes in relation to E for a given alternative. Since L represents a "floor" on expected return, a larger L is desirable and a portfolio is considered E-L efficient if there is no other portfolio which offers a higher E without reducing L.

As Baumol demonstrated, the E-L efficient set must be a subset of the E-V efficient set. The smaller the value of k, the more the original E-V set will be reduced in arriving at the E-L set.

The Mean-Entropy (E-H) Approach

The concepts of variance, standard deviation, and confidence intervals are generally familiar to students by the time they encounter portfolio theory. Entropy, on the other hand, is a measure that is probably known only to those with backgrounds in engineering, and thus it will require more discussion.

Entropy is a measure of uncertainty which is commonly used in information theory. We will not discuss information theory in much detail, but only sufficiently to enable the student to understand what entropy is used to measure. We will deal with what is called the *technical level* of information. At this level, the *importance* of information is *not* considered, but we do attempt to measure the *magnitude* of information conveyed.

The simplest way to describe information is as something achieved through the use of *messages* which can convey some fact to the recipient, e.g., that some given event has (or has not) occurred. If you had been uncertain about the event's occurrence *prior* to receipt of the message, then you have gained *information* by receiving the message. Suppose you feel that there is a 75 percent chance that International Harvester's earnings will increase this year. You receive a "message" in the form of a company announcement (or an annual report) which says that earnings per share increased by $.12 over their level last year. This represents information. Previously, you only felt the chances were three out of four that it *would* happen, and now you *know* that it *did* happen.

The *amount of information gained* by the receipt of a message depends upon how unsure the recipient was of the event's occurring. If you felt quite confident that the event would occur, you receive relatively little information from the fact that it actually did. If the event was highly unexpected, a message stating that it did occur would convey substantial information. To return to the International Harvester example, suppose the actual earnings were $.12 lower than last year's. Since you expected earnings to increase with a probability of .75, the message that earnings decreased conveys more information than a message which merely confirmed your feelings would have. In essence, you could consider the amount of informaton gained to be a function of how "surprised" you are by the contents of the message.

Since new information can have such a profound effect on stock market prices, it is intuitively appealing to seek ways of measuring information directly. There are many ways of doing this. As you might expect, a widely used tool is a function of the event's *probability*. The *lower* the original probability, the *greater* the amount of information conveyed by a message that the event has occurred. Nearly any inverse function could be used, but the most common is that suggested by Shannon,[7] who defined *the information contained in a message that event j has occurred as*

$$h = \log \frac{1}{P_j} = -\log P_j$$

where P_j is the prior probability of event j's occurrence. The specific units of measure are dependent upon the base of the logarithm; base 2 is most common in information theory,[8] and the resulting units are generally called

---

[7] C. E. Shannon, "A Mathematical Theory of Communication," *Bell System Technical Journal,* Vol. 27, No. 3 (July, 1948), pp. 379–423.

[8] This is true at least in its finance/investments applications. When natural logarithms are used, the resulting units are normally called "nits", and the basic units with common logarithms are called Hartley units.

"bits". In a binary situation (two equally likely outcomes), such as flipping a fair coin, the amount of information conveyed by learning the outcome is one bit:

$$h = \log_2\left(\frac{1}{.5}\right) = \log_2(2) = 1$$

$$h = -\log_2(.5) = -(-1) = 1$$

The function h is shown graphically in Figure 20–3. Notice the rapid increase in the amount of information conveyed when P_j gets very small. Also, given the previous discussion, it makes sense that h = 0 when $P_j = 1$. If you are *certain* that something is going to happen ($P_j = 1$), the fact that it *does* happen conveys *no* information (h = 0).

Figure 20–3
Amount of Information Contained in a Message (h) as a Function of the Event's Prior Probability (P_j)

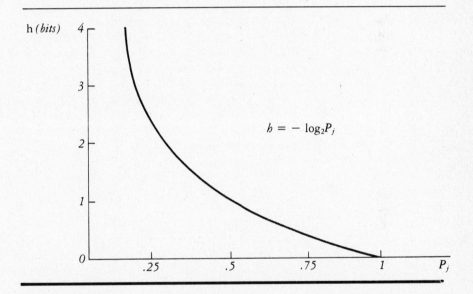

Now that we have a measure of the amount of information gained from a direct message,[9] the concept of entropy may be introduced. Entropy is the

---

[9] Here, we are concerned only with *direct* messages (which are also assumed to be reliable), though information theory measures may also be applied to *indirect* messages. A direct message states that a specific event has occurred; an indirect message is one which does not tell of the actual occurrence of an event, but contains previously unknown information which could affect the recipient's assessment of the probabilities. In the International Harvester example used earlier, a management forecast released half way through the year (or the first six months' operating report) would be an example of an *indirect* message. You still would not know what fiscal year earnings would be, but might adjust the prior probability of an earnings increase upward or downward, depending upon the news.

expected information gain from a direct message which has not yet been received. Consider the simple case in which only one of two possible events may occur (e.g., EPS increase or do not increase). This would be identical to the situation in which a *single* event either will occur (with probability P) or will not occur (with probability 1−P). In this situation, a reliable message that the event has occurred will convey −log P units of information. The prior probability that this will be the content of the message is P. Similarly, a reliable message that the event did *not* occur will convey −log (1 − P) units of information, and the probability that this message will be received is 1 − P. The *entropy* is merely the *expected value of the information gain* before the message is received, which is

$$H = -P \log P - (1 - P) \log (1 - P)$$

in this case.

When there are n possible mutually exclusive outcomes, each with probability P_j (j = 1, 2, . . . , n), such that

$$\sum_{j=1}^{n} P_j = 1,$$

entropy can be defined as

$$H = -\sum_{j=1}^{n} P_j \log P_j$$

H could be regarded as a measure of the mean uncertainty, which serves as a measure of dispersion similar to the variance. A portfolio is E-H efficient if (1) no other portfolio offers a higher expected return (E) with the same (or lower) entropy (H), or (2) no other portfolio offers a lower H with the same (or higher) E.

If the distribution of returns is known, entropy can be directly estimated from the variances.[10] However, entropy is always independent of the mean, *regardless* of the distribution, while this is not always true of the variance. This "distribution-free" quality of entropy is particularly desirable, though it has little relevance if rate of return distributions are normal.[11]

---

[10] For an example, see W. R. Garner and W. J. McGill, "The Relation Between Information and Variance Analyses," *Psychometrika,* Vol. 21, No. 3 (September, 1956), pp. 219–228.

[11] Philippatos and Gressis have shown that E-V and E-H efficiency criteria are equivalent for uniform and normal distributions. See George C. Philippatos and Nicolas Gressis, "Conditions of Equivalence Among E-V, SSD, and E-H Portfolio Selection Criteria: The Case for Uniform, Normal and Lognormal Distributions," *Management Science,* Vol. 21, No. 6 (February, 1975), pp. 617–625.

The "Safety First" Criterion

Roy[12] suggests that a risk averse individual will attempt to reduce, to the greatest extent possible, the chance of a "disaster" occurring. A disaster, in the context of the Safety First criterion, is achieving a gross return (or holding period return) that is below some specified disaster level, d. Roy suggests that investors will seek to minimize the probability of falling below this disaster level.

If we assume that we can estimate the expected *gross* return, $E(R_i)$, and standard error of this return σ_i for all portfolios (or single assets), we cannot generally determine the exact probability

$$P(R_i < d),$$

but we can get an upper bound on this probability using Tchebysheff's inequality:[13]

$$P\left(\left| R_i - E(R_i) \right| \geq E(R_i) - d\right) \leq \frac{\sigma^2}{[E(R_i) - d]^2}$$

Since one would assume that the investor would not consider alternatives where $E(R_i) < d$, and would not be concerned with cases where $R_i > E(R_i)$, we can eliminate the absolute value operator and rewrite this as:

$$P[E(R_i) - R_i \geq E(R_i) - d] \leq \frac{\sigma^2}{[E(R_i) - d]^2}$$

from which

$$P(R_i \leq d) \leq \frac{\sigma^2}{[E(R_i) - d]^2}$$

Thus, minimizing $P(R_i \leq d)$ is equivalent to minimizing its upper boundary

$$\frac{\sigma^2}{[E(R_i) - d]^2}$$

which is equivalent to *maximizing* $\dfrac{E(R_i) - d}{\sigma}$. If R_i is normally distributed, this procedure would minimize the probability of disaster; if the distribution is not normal, the procedure produces only an approximation.

---

[12] A. D. Roy, "Safety First and the Holding of Assets," *Econometrica*, Vol. 20, No. 3 (July, 1952), pp. 431–449.

[13] The development follows Roy's, but its notation differs from his. For a further discussion of Tchebysheff's inequality see, Alexander Mood and Franklin A. Graybill, *Introduction to the Theory of Statistics* (2nd edition) (New York: McGraw–Hill, 1963), pp. 147–148.

Figure 20–4 shows a graph of the procedure. We are essentially *maximizing* the *slope* of a straight line from point d [$E(R_i) = d$, $\sigma = 0$] to some feasible $E(R_i)$, σ_i combination. Points in the feasible region along the line dA clearly are not optimal, since other feasible opportunities lie *above* this line. The line with the steepest slope will be the line from point d tangent to the feasible set. In Figure 20–4, this is the line dBC, with the optimum portfolio located at point B. By choosing this portfolio, we will have made the upper boundary of P ($R_i \leq d$) as small as possible. Any line from d with a steeper slope will not intersect with any feasible alternative.

Figure 20–4
Graph of the Safety First Criterion

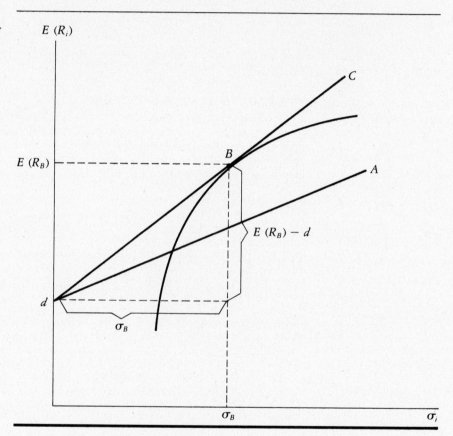

The higher the disaster level for the investor, the smaller the maximum slope will be. If the disaster level is too high, the criterion becomes useless, since the slope would be < 1, which would imply (with a slope of .8):

$$P\ (R_i \leq d) \leq \frac{1}{(.8)^2} = 1.5625$$

This is clearly useless, since we know that

$$P(R_i \leq d) \leq 1,$$

regardless of d.

Levy and Sarnat have shown[14] that, if d is the gross return on a riskless asset, E-V and Safety First will lead to the same result. That is, optimal *unleveraged* portfolios will be identical under this condition.

Decision Theory Approach

Mao and Sarndal[15] note that the E-V model is based on subjective estimates of future returns from different investments. Presumably, these estimates would be somewhat dependent upon the general level of business activity. Since this also implies that the investor assigns some probability to each possible state of the business environment, Mao and Sarndal suggest using statistical decision theory to make explicit the probabilities involved.

The simplest application of this would be one in which only two states of nature are possible.[16] Let state θ_1 represent favorable business conditions and θ_2 represent unfavorable business conditions. Also, assume that the investor's prior probabilities for these states are that:

$$P(\theta_1) = p$$

$$P(\theta_2) = q$$

and that he holds the following beliefs about the returns, variances, and covariances under each state of nature:

θ_1	θ_2
$E(R_1 \mid \theta_1)$	$E(R_1 \mid \theta_2)$
$E(\sigma_1^2 \mid \theta_1)$	$E(\sigma_1^2 \mid \theta_2)$
$E(Cov_{ij} \mid \theta_1)$	$E(Cov_{ij} \mid \theta_2)$

Suppose that the investor performs an experiment which gives additional information about the state of nature. Perhaps he obtains forecasts of the

---

[14] H. Levy and M. Sarnat, "Safety First—An Expected Utility Principle," *Journal of Financial and Quantitative Analysis,* Vol. 7, No. 3 (June, 1972), pp. 1829–1834.

[15] James C. T. Mao and Carl E. Sarndal, "A Decision Theory Approach to Portfolio Selection," *Management Science,* Vol. 12, No. 8 (April, 1966), pp. 323–333.

[16] Though Mao and Sarndal do not state the condition explicitly, the approach does not make much sense unless the states of nature are defined in such a way that they are mutually exclusive (i.e., only *one* state of nature can occur) and collectively exhaustive (all possible occurrences are included in one of the defined states).

Gross National Product over the next year from groups of econometric models. Let us denote the experimental outcome z. Now the prior probabilities, p and q, can be revised in light of the experimental outcome, z, through use of Bayes' Theorem to give

$$p^* = P(\theta = \theta_1 | z) = \frac{P(z | \theta_1)p}{P(z | \theta_1)p + P(z | \theta_2)q}$$

$$q^* = P(\theta = \theta_2 | z) = \frac{P(z | \theta_2)q}{P(z | \theta_1)p + P(z | \theta_2)q}$$

We have done nothing that affects the conditional estimates for portfolio returns, variances, and covariances under the two states $[E(R_i | \theta_1)$, $E(\sigma_i^2 | \theta_1)$, etc.]; all we have done is revise the probabilities of the states of nature themselves.

If we have m possible admissible portfolios which can be formed from the original n securities, we can construct the payoff matrix shown in Table 20–1. *Admissible* portfolios are merely those which are not dominated by any other portfolio. In Table 20–1, $U(\Pi_j, \theta_i)$ indicates the utility that will result if the investor chooses portfolio Π_j and the state of nature turns out to be θ_i. A portfolio Π_k is *dominated* by Π_n if it has lower utility in both states, that is,

$$U(\Pi_n, \theta_i) \geq U(\Pi_k, \theta_i) \quad \text{for } i = 1,2.$$

If this occurs, Π_k would never be preferred to Π_n, and thus is not admissible. In the more general case, there could be r different (mutually exclusive and collectively exhaustive) states of nature, and the payoff matrix would include r rows. Then the condition for dominance would include the above inequality for $i = 1, 2, \ldots, r$.

Table 20–1
Payoff Matrix for Decision Theory Approach with Two States of Nature

States of Nature	Portfolios				
	Π_1	Π_2	Π_3	. . .	Π_m
θ_1	$U(\Pi_1,\theta_1)$	$U(\Pi_2,\theta_1)$	$U(\Pi_3,\theta_1)$	. . .	$U(\Pi_m,\theta_1)$
θ_2	$U(\Pi_1,\theta_2)$	$U(\Pi_2,\theta_2)$	$U(\Pi_3,\theta_2)$	. . .	$U(\Pi_m,\theta_2)$

The strategy is to choose the portfolio which maximizes the weighted average of the payoffs, using p* and q* as weights. Given that the payoffs are stated as utilities, this is equivalent to choosing the portfolio which maximizes expected utility.

Decision theory can also be used as a supplement to the basic Markowitz portfolio model to help select the optimal portfolio for a specific investor from the set of portfolios on the efficient frontier. The original Markowitz formulation for deriving the efficient set can be stated as a quadratic programming problem:

$$\text{minimize } \sigma^2_{\text{port}} = \Sigma\Sigma W_i W_j \text{Cov}_{ij}$$

$$\text{subject to: } \Sigma W_i E(R_i) = E(R_{\text{port}})$$

$$\Sigma W_i = 1$$

$$W_i \geq 0$$

This will generate the entire efficient set, not just one optimal portfolio.

Farrar[17] has suggested an alteration of the Markowitz quadratic programming formulation which will allow one to choose the optimal portfolio. He suggests substituting an objective function

$$\text{maximize } E(R_{\text{port}}) - A \, \sigma^2_{\text{port}}$$

subject to the same constraints as above. In this case, A is a coefficient of risk aversion. If this risk aversion coefficient is included, the optimal portfolio will be generated without having to combine the Markowitz efficient set with the investor's utility curves. The decision theory approach is really an extension of the Farrar formulation, when expressed in quadratic programming form as:

$$\text{maximize } \Sigma W_i[p^*E(R_i|\theta_1) + q^*E(R_i|\theta_2)]$$

$$- A\Sigma\Sigma W_i W_j[p^*E(\text{Cov}_{ij}|\theta_1) + q^*E(\text{Cov}_{ij}|\theta_2)]$$

subject to the normal constraints.[18]

In the case of two states of nature, as we have been assuming for simplicity, Mao and Sarndal demonstrate a graphical solution, as shown in Figure 20–5.[19] Portfolios located along arc eF are admissible. The optimal

---

[17] Donald E. Farrar, *The Investment Decision Under Uncertainty* (Englewood Cliffs, N.J.: Prentice–Hall, Inc., 1962).

[18] In more general terms, if there are n securities and r possible states of nature, the objective function could be written as:

$$\text{maximize } \sum_{i=1}^{n} W_i \left[\sum_{k=1}^{r} {}_{Pk^*} E(R_i|\theta_k) \right] - A \sum_{i=1}^{n} \sum_{j=1}^{n} W_i W_j \left[\sum_{k=1}^{r} {}_{Pk^*} E(\text{Cov}_{ij}|\theta_k) \right]$$

where P_k^* is the revised probability, $P(\theta = \theta_k|Z)$.

[19] Figure 20–5 is, with minor notational changes, the same as Chart 2, page 329, in the Mao and Sarndal paper.

---

portfolio, Π_0, is at the point of tangency between the set of admissible portfolios and a line with a slope of $- p^*/q^*$.[20]

Figure 20–5
Graph of Decision Theory Approach with Two States

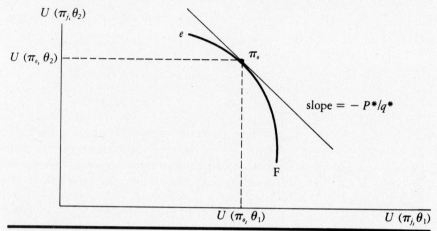

Source: Adapted with permission from James C. T. Mao and Carl E. Sarndal, "A Decision Theory Approach to Portfolio Selection," *Management Science*, Vol. 12, No. 8 (April, 1966), p. 329.

Multidimensional Portfolio Analysis

The traditional E-V approach assumes that investors base decisions solely on expected return and risk (standard deviation or variance of return). While this may be an adequate model for many investors, it is possible that some perceive a certain desirability in, for example, positive skewness. The E-V model ignores skewness and thus would not be adequate for an investor whose utility curves are based upon more than the first two moments of the probability distribution of expected returns.

William Jean did much of the pioneering work in the extension of portfolio analysis to include more than two moments.[21] While much of his contribution has been mathematical in nature and extends to n dimensions, we will concentrate here on only three dimensions (i.e., mean-variance-skewness criteria) and try to demonstrate, primarily with graphs, some of the differences from E-V which result when skewness is introduced.

As a measure of skewness, Jean used

$$m_3 = [E(R_i - \bar{R})^3]^{1/3}$$

[20] Since both p* and q* are > 0, we assume that Mao and Sarndal's "line with slope p*/q*" should have been "line with slope − p*/q*." The line obviously has a negative slope.

[21] William H. Jean, "The Extension of Portfolio Analysis to Three or More Parameters," *Journal of Financial and Quantitative Analysis*, Vol. 6, No. 1 (January, 1971), pp. 505–515; and "More on Multidimensional Portfolio Analysis," *Journal of Financial and Quantitative Analysis*, Vol. 8, No. 3 (June, 1973), pp. 475–490.

Assuming that a risk-free asset is available with return R_f, and that a proportion a (a $\geq$ 0) is invested in a risky portfolio with expected return $E(R_k)$ and standard deviation $\sigma(R_k)$, we would have, for a given value of a

$$E = a\ E(R_k) + (1 - a)R_f$$

$$\sigma = a\ \sigma(R_k)$$

These are essentially the conditions for points along the capital market line in E,σ-space, if we ignore skewness. If we add skewness, and assume portfolio k has skewness $m_3(R_k)$, we can also add the condition

$$m_3 = a\ m_3(R_k)$$

Figure 20–6 shows the resulting three-dimensional portrayal of the risky efficient set, which may be shaped somewhat like the outer surface of a bowl that has been cut in half. Portfolios with the same σ and m_3 but *negative* E will be dominated by points with *positive* E, thus only half of the "bowl" represents efficient risky portfolios.

With the introduction of a risk-free asset (E = R_f, σ = 0, m_3 = 0), the line $R_f\ R_m\ Z$ represents the capital market line (CML). It is tangent to the risky efficient set in the E-σ plane (the dotted line, where m_3 = 0). This, however, assumes that the investor has no skewness preference. An investor who prefers positive skewness would more likely choose a portfolio along R_f $R_n\ Y$, a line tangent to the risky efficient set at R_n. R_m and R_n are risky portfolios; the segments $R_f\ R_m$ and $R_f\ R_n$ represent a combination of lending at R_f and investing part of total wealth in the appropriate risky portfolio (R_m or R_n); and the segments R_mZ and R_nY represent borrowing at R_f to invest in risky assets (i.e., leveraged portfolios).

Figure 20–7 shows the projection of these two lines in E-σ space. $R_f\ R_m\ Z$ is the standard CML, but points along $R_f\ R_n\ Y$ are *dominated* by the CML in E-σ space, *even though they are perfectly logical choices for an investor with skewness preference.* Thus, we no longer have a unique CML in E-σ-m_3 space and, as a result, the separation principle no longer holds. The feasible set in three dimensions is a surface resembling part of a cone (as before, the half corresponding to E < 0 will be omitted) formed by lines from R_f tangent to the risky efficient set at various points. The situation is demonstrated graphically in Figure 20–8. Even if investors possess homogeneous expectations about distributions of security returns, and if constant and equal borrowing and lending rates are assumed, investors will not necessarily choose the same combination of risky securities in E-σ-m_3 space. Thus, *there is no longer a unique market portfolio once skewness preference is allowed as a possibility.* The rays from R_f in Figure 20–8 will continue indefinitely if borrowing is allowed. If not, the conic section would be truncated at a set of points such as R_n and R_m.

Figure 20–6
**Efficient Set in
E-σ-m₃ Space**

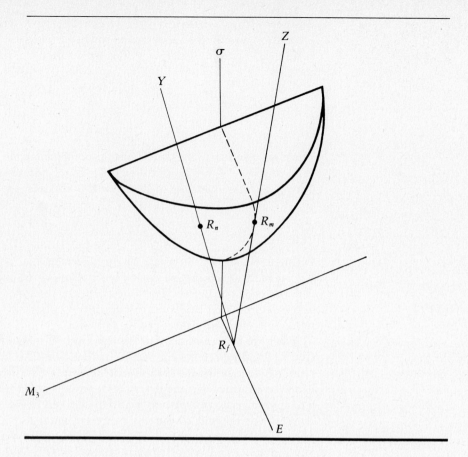

Figure 20–7
**Projection of
E-σ-m₃ Efficient
Portfolios in E-σ
Space**

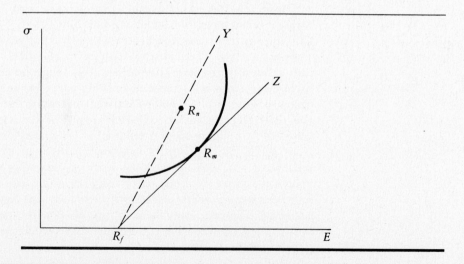

Figure 20–8
**Efficient Set in
E-σ-m₃ Space with a
Risk-Free Asset**

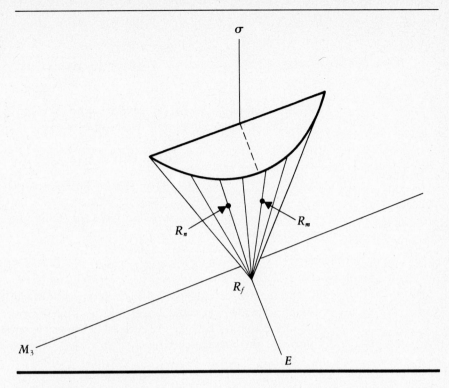

Stochastic Dominance

Rather than working with a specified number of statistical moments of a probability distribution of returns, as in E-V or the multidimensional approach, the stochastic dominance approach encompasses the *entire distribution of returns*.[22] Some of the earliest theoretical work in the area was done by Quirk and Saposnik.[23]

Suppose we are considering two probability distributions of returns,[24] f(x) and g(x) where f(x) ≠ g(x). Let

---

[22] In this sense, one might consider stochastic dominance to be a limiting case of multidimensional portfolio analysis as the number of moments, n, approaches infinity. That is, specifying all the finite moments of a probability density function (pdf) is the statistical equivalent of specifying the pdf itself. There *is* a difference, however, in the utility assumptions under the two approaches, with those under stochastic dominance being less restrictive.

[23] J. P. Quirk and R. Saposnik, "Admissibility and Measurable Utility Functions," *Review of Economic Studies,* Vol. 29, No. 79 (February, 1962), pp. 140–146.

[24] In the discussion which follows, we will assume that the pdf's are *continuous* functions. Analogous definitions could easily be made for *discrete* functions that are completely defined within a closed interval [a,b].

$$F_1(R) = \int_{-\infty}^{R} f(x)dx, \text{ and}$$

$$G_1(R) = \int_{-\infty}^{R} g(x)dx.$$

These functions, F_1 and G_1, represent the cumulative probability functions for $f(x)$ and $g(x)$, respectively. In other words,

$$F_1(R) = P(X \leq R) \text{ for pdf } f(x)$$

$$G_1(R) = P(X \leq R) \text{ for pdf } g(x)$$

According to *first degree stochastic dominance* (FSD), $f(x)$ is said to *dominate* $g(x)$ if, and only if,

$$F_1(R) \leq G_1(R) \text{ for all R}, \ -\infty < R < \infty,$$

with *strict inequality* holding for at least one value of R. That is, F_1 and G_1 may coincide over some range of values, but F_1 must be $< G_1$ somewhere and F_1 can *never* be $> G_1$. Figure 20–9 shows two possible cases of FSD. In case A, the curves never touch;[25] in case B, they coincide over part of the range of values of R. In *both* cases, $f(x)$ dominates $g(x)$ by FSD. The *FSD efficient set* consists of all those portfolios which are *not dominated by any other portfolio according to FSD.*

FSD is a very strict condition and is seldom satisfied by distributions of security returns. In examining Case A, we can see why $F_1(R) \leq G_1(R)$ for all R is desirable. For *any* point R_0 (any potential level of return), there is always a higher (or at least as high) probability of falling *below* R_0 with $g(x)$ than with $f(x)$. The probability *of exceeding* R_0 is always greater (or at least as great) with $f(x)$ than it is with $g(x)$. Thus any investor who prefers more wealth to less $\left(\frac{\partial U(R)}{\partial R} > 0 \right)$ will find FSD a logical selection criterion, regardless of the *specific* form of his utility function.

In most cases, $F_1(R)$ and $G_1(R)$ will cross within some range of values of R. A typical case might resemble that shown in Figure 20–10. At all points $R \leq R_0$, $F_1(R) \leq G_1(R)$, but at points above R_0, $F_1(R) \geq G_1(R)$. Thus, the conditions of FSD are *not* satisfied. However, if the area between the curves *below* R_0 (labeled Y in Figure 20–10) is larger than the area between the curves *above* R_0 (labeled Z), $f(x)$ will dominate $g(x)$ according to *second degree stochastic dominance* (SSD). Let

$$F_2(R) = \int_{-\infty}^{R} F_1(x)dx, \text{ and}$$

---

[25] Except beyond some point where $P(X < R) = 1.0$ for both $f(x)$ and $g(x)$, if such a point exists.

Figure 20–9 **Two Possible Examples
of First Degree Stochastic Dominance**

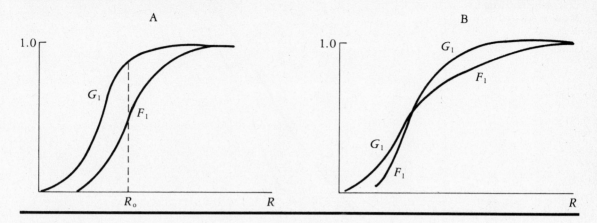

A

B

Figure 20–10
**Example of a Case
in which FSD is
Not Present**

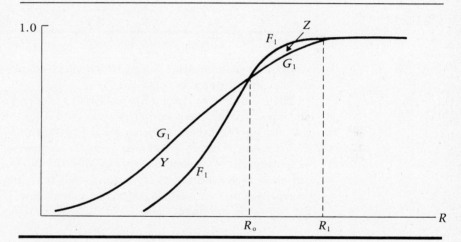

$$G_2(R) = \int_{-\infty}^{R} G_1(x)dx.$$

Then f(x) is said to *dominate* g(x) *by SSD* if, and only if, $F_2(R) \leq G_2(R)$ *for all R, with strict inequality for at least one R.*

Since F_2 and G_2 are merely the areas underneath $F_1(R)$ and $G_1(R)$, respectively, f(x) will dominate g(x) if area Y in Figure 20–10 is greater than area Z. The "SSD curves" would resemble those in Figure 20–11. Up to point R_0, the two curves are getting farther and farther apart, since G is adding to its area faster than F is. Beyond R_0, the curves start to draw closer together. Beyond point R_1, both $F_1(R)$ and $G_1(R)$ are the same, and thus the same area

Figure 20-11
**SSD Comparison
Corresponding to
Figure 20-10**

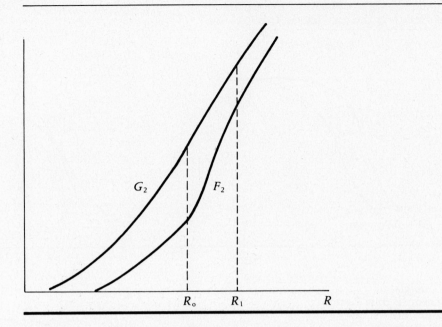

is added for each increment in R, which means that $F_2(R)$ and $G_2(R)$ will be parallel lines beyond point R_1.

There is no reason that $F_1(R)$ and $G_1(R)$ cannot cross several times. If they do, however, FSD tells us nothing, and SSD may or may not show one dominating the other. As with FSD, the *SSD efficient set* consists of *all portfolios not dominated by any other portfolio according to SSD.*

In the event of "multiple crossings" of $F_1(R)$ and $G_1(R)$, SSD comparison *may* show $F_2(R)$ and $G_2(R)$ crossing as well. If so, neither FSD nor SSD is present. In this case, *third degree stochastic dominance* (TSD) might show that f(x) or g(x) is dominant. Let

$$F_3(R) = \int_{-\infty}^{R} F_2(x)dx$$

$$G_3(R) = \int_{-\infty}^{R} G_2(x)dx$$

Then f(x) dominates g(x) by TSD if, and only if, $F_3(R) \leq G_3(R)$ *for all R, with strict inequality for at least one R.* F_3 and G_3 represent the areas under F_2 and G_2, respectively.

One could extend stochastic dominance rules beyond the third degree with the general conditions:

$$F_n(R) = \int_{-\infty}^{R} F_{n-1}(x)dx$$

$$G_n(R) = \int_{-\infty}^{R} G_{n-1}(x)dx$$

with f(x) dominating g(x) by nth degree stochastic dominance if, and only if, $F_n(R) \leq G_n(R)$ *for all R, with strict inequality for at least one R.* Nearly all empirical work, however, has focused on nothing beyond TSD, with most concentrating on SSD.

SSD is consistent with the maximization of expected utility for any utility function exhibiting increasing utility with increasing return $\left(\dfrac{\partial U}{\partial R} > 0\right)$ and diminishing marginal utility $\left(\dfrac{\partial^2 U}{\partial R^2} < 0\right)$. These utility restrictions are less severe than, for example, the assumption of quadratic utility usually associated with E-V portfolio analysis. TSD will be consistent with maximization of expected utility if we add the condition $\dfrac{\partial^3 U}{\partial R^3} > 0$.

Growth Optimum Model (Geometric Mean Criterion)

Under this criterion,[26] it is assumed that the goal of the investor is to maximize his terminal wealth ratio,

$$\text{maximize } W^n = \frac{\text{wealth at end of n periods}}{\text{initial wealth}}$$

Under this approach, the particular *sequence* of one period returns by which an investor reaches W^n is irrelevant, which implies that *ex post* risk measures typically used are also irrelevant. In an *ex post* sense

$$W^n = \prod_{t=1}^{n} R_t,$$

where R_t = holding period return in period t. Suppose we consider a simple case in which n = 2 and $W^n = W^2 = 2.25$. The *sequence* of returns is quite different, as are the arithmetic mean returns ($\bar{R}$ or E(R)) and standard deviations (σ_R), yet all are *identical* under the criterion of maximizing W^n, even though "risk" varies from zero to a very large number.[27]

---

[26] Early work in this area was done by Henry A. Latané, "Criteria for Choice Among Risky Ventures," *Journal of Political Economy,* Vol. 67, No. 2 (April, 1959), pp. 144–155. Also, see Henry A. Latané and Donald L. Tuttle, "Criteria for Portfolio Building," *Journal of Finance,* Vol. 22, No. 3 (September, 1962), pp. 359–373.

[27] σ_R is computed assuming the observations constitute a population rather than a sample.

	R_1	R_2	W^n	$\overline{R}$	σ_R
A	1.500	1.500	2.25	1.5000	—0—
B	2.000	1.125	2.25	1.5625	.4375
C	1.125	2.000	2.25	1.5625	.4375
D	3.000	0.750	2.25	1.8750	1.1250
E	0.750	3.000	2.25	1.8750	1.1250

Latané and Tuttle demonstrate that a strategy of investing in portfolios with the highest geometric mean return is almost certain to result in a higher terminal wealth position than any significantly different strategy would, when repeated investment over a relatively large number of periods is possible. Maximization of W^n is equivalent to maximizing $\sqrt[n]{W^n} = W$ (assuming initial wealth > 0 and terminal wealth ≥ 0).

A comparable *ex ante* formulation would be the geometric mean of the probability density function of returns

$$G = \prod_{j=1}^{m} R_j{}^{P^j},$$

where P_j = probability of occurrence of R_j. Since

$$W = \left(\prod_{t=1}^{n} R_j \right)^{1/n} = \left(\prod_{j=1}^{m} R_j{}^{n_j} \right)^{1/n},$$

where n_j is the number of times R_j occurs,

$$W = \prod_{j=1}^{m} R_j{}^{n_j/n}$$

But, as n becomes very large, $\frac{n_j}{n} \to P_j$ and thus $W \to G$. Therefore, the geometric mean return is regarded as a rational criterion for portfolio selection decisions, and the portfolio with the highest expected geometric mean return is the optimal portfolio.

Comparisons of the Methods

The methods that have been discussed vary quite a bit in many respects. Most assume a single period horizon, but some assume a longer horizon. Some are designed to derive an entire efficient set, others designate a single optimal portfolio. Some examine a single parameter (geometric mean), others are two parameter measures, and still others include more than two parameters of the return distribution (or the entire distribution). With some, the investor must make many estimates; others require relatively few. Needless to say, the differences are, in some cases, quite striking.

Even with all the differences, however, there are some similarities. In addition, there are some problems with and criticisms of these methods which were not mentioned earlier and which should be noted. E-V and E-H efficient frontiers tend to be quite similar, at least for common stocks.[28] The E-L criterion tends to eliminate the low risk-low return end of the E-V risky efficient set, which is of little use anyway, once we allow for lending at a riskless rate, since the CML tends to eliminate the same portion of the risky E-V frontier. Similarly, the Safety First criterion essentially produces the capital market line if the disaster level chosen is the gross return on a risk-free asset. Further, most empirical studies comparing E-S, SSD, and E-V (together or in pairs) indicate that the three are similar for the high risk-high return part of the efficient frontier, but can differ substantially on the low risk-low return portion of the risky frontier, which is largely irrelevant if we allow for a risk-free asset. E-S and SSD tend to be more similar than E-S and E-V, or SSD and E-V are, primarily because both E-S and SSD regard *downside risk* as important, while E-V does not distinguish between variations above and below the mean.

The stochastic dominance criterion seems conceptually superior to the other single period approaches, especially if it is possible that the variance does not exist for the return distributions (which would affect E-V, E-S, E-L, and Safety First). One drawback with stochastic dominance is that you must estimate the entire *distribution* of returns for each asset under consideration. Also, no algorithms exist for forming efficient portfolios, given the distribution estimates for individual assets. Thus, stochastic dominance may be an excellent method for *evaluating after the fact performance,*[29] but is not particularly easy to use to form portfolios.

The geometric mean criterion seems to implicitly assume that the pdf of returns is stationary over time, which is questionable. If it is *not,* one would need some way of estimating changes over the investment horizon to use the model as a before the fact criterion. Assuming stationarity over *one* period is not much of a problem; stationarity over n periods, where n is reasonably large, could be a quite different matter.

Hopefully, future research will solve some of the problems and develop better estimation methods for determining inputs to various portfolio theory techniques. Some such research is already in progress and more interest will probably be generated as this work continues. In addition to the sources specifically mentioned in footnotes, the reference list includes several papers and books which build upon the conceptual foundations covered here. Many of the supplemental references also include empirical

---

[28] For example, see George C. Philippatos and Charles J. Wilson, "Entropy, Market Risk, and the Selection of Efficient Portfolios," *Applied Economics,* Vol. 4, No. 3 (September, 1972), pp. 209–220.

[29] For example, see O. Maurice Joy and R. Burr Porter, "Stochastic Dominance and Mutual Fund Performance," *Journal of Financial and Quantitative Analysis,* Vol. 9, No. 1 (January, 1974), pp. 25–31.

studies which provide more detail on the methodologies and results than were presented in this brief summary. The interested reader is encouraged to consult these references for further elaboration.

Recent Developments in Capital Market Theory

The Capital Asset Pricing Model is stated in terms of expectations:

$$E(R_i) = RFR + \beta_i[E(R_m) - RFR]$$

In observing returns over time, however, expectations do not always hold and thus observed returns, R_{it}, in period t will not necessarily equal what would be expected during the period, R_{mt}, the security's β_i, and the current risk free rate, RFR_t. Nevertheless, if the CAPM is essentially valid, we would expect to observe a relationship of the form:

$$R_{it} = RFR_t + \beta_i(R_{mt} - RFR_t) + e_{it}$$

where e_i is the residual variation, a measure of the security's deviation from its conditional expected return in period t. Since these residuals are presumably independent, the average residual over time should approach zero, and we should have

$$\overline{R}_i = \overline{RFR} + \beta_i(\overline{R}_m - \overline{RFR}) + e_i$$

These last two relationships form the essential basis for most early tests of the CAPM, either in the form stated or in "excess return" form. Statistical testing generally involved a two step process:

(1) Derive estimates of β_i, $(\hat{\beta}_i)$, from a series of regressions of the form:

$$R_{it} = \hat{\alpha}_i + \hat{\beta}_i R_{mt} + \epsilon_{it}$$

(2) Combine these $\hat{\beta}_i$ with the average returns, $\overline{R}_i$, over some test period to estimate:

$$\overline{R}_i = \gamma + \hat{\beta}_i \delta + u_i$$

If the CAPM is essentially valid, we would expect to find

$$\gamma = \overline{RFR} \text{ and}$$

$$\delta = \overline{R}_m - \overline{RFR}$$

Unfortunately, however, most tests found that γ was *greater than* the average risk-free rate and δ was *less than* the average excess market return over the period. This finding, among other things, led to the development of various extensions of the "original" CAPM.

The "Zero-Beta" or "Two Factor" Model

Black, Jensen, and Scholes[30] suggested that a model of the form

$$R_{it} = (1 - \beta_i)R_{zt} + \beta_i R_{mt} + e_{it}$$

is more appropriate in describing the process generating actual returns. This is very similar to the original CAPM, in rewritten form, except that RFR_t has been replaced by R_{zt}, which represents the return on what Black, Jensen, and Scholes call the "beta-factor," and others have called the "zero-beta portfolio." Z is, in essence, a portfolio of assets whose returns are uncorrelated with the market portfolio, i.e., $Cov(R_{zt}, R_{mt}) = 0$. Since

$$\beta_z = \frac{Cov(R_{zt}, R_{mt})}{\sigma_m^2}$$

this implies that $\beta_z = 0$; thus the name "zero-beta portfolio." Z is the zero-beta portfolio with the smallest σ_z.

The "Four-Factor" Model

Fama and MacBeth,[31] in an extension of the Black-Jensen-Scholes study, found that a model of the form:

$$R_{it} = \gamma o_t + \gamma 1_t \beta_i + \gamma 2_t \beta_t^2 + \gamma 3_t \overline{\sigma_i(e)} + \epsilon_{it}$$

where

β_i^2 = average β^2 for all securities in portfolio i

$\overline{\sigma_i(e)}$ = average residual standard deviation for all securities in portfolio i

represents the data better than the simple two factor model does. The *average* values of $\gamma 2_t$ and $\gamma 3_t$ are not significantly different from zero, but *individual period values* were at times. This implies that nonportfolio risk and

---

[30] Fischer Black, Michael C. Jensen, and Myron Scholes, "The Capital Asset Pricing Model: Some Empirical Tests," in Michael C. Jensen, *Studies in the Theory of Capital Markets* (New York: Praeger Publishers, 1972), pp. 79–121.

[31] E. F. Fama and J. D. MacBeth, "Risk, Return, and Equilibrium: Empirical Tests," *Journal of Political Economy,* Vol. 81, No. 3 (May–June, 1973), pp. 607–636.

---

nonlinearities *do* occur in a random fashion from period to period. An *expectational* model tested over long periods in which these random occurrences can "average out," would not need the two additional factors, but they *are* useful in explaining what happens across time.

The "Three-Factor" Model

Assuming a different conceptual framework than that employed in the previous models, Merton[32] derived an expectational model which includes RFR, R_m, and the return on the portfolio, R_N, which is perfectly negatively correlated with *changes* in the risk-free interest rate ΔRFR. While the *form* of the three-model is quite similar to that of models just discussed, the assumptions under which it is applied make it quite different.

Other Work in Capital Market Theory

The majority of the other work done in the area has been directed at various statistical problems with the CAPM (in its various forms). The statistical background needed to understand most of this literature is beyond what we assume the typical reader has, thus we will not attempt to provide any explanation or exposition of the research; instead, we mention only the primary areas covered and direct the interested and qualified reader to selected references.

Fama[33] gives an excellent discussion of some of the problems, and suggested "solutions" if the underlying probability distributions of returns are not normal. Other studies address the problem of the CAPM with skewness in return distributions.[34] Still others are concerned with problems of stationarity in the parameters of the model,[35] heteroscadasticity

---

[32] Robert C. Merton, "An Intertemporal Capital Asset Pricing Model," *Econometrica,* Vol. 41, No. 3 (September, 1973), pp. 867–887.

[33] Eugene F. Fama, "Portfolio Analysis in a Stable Paretian Market," *Management Science,* Vol. 11, No. 1 (January, 1965), pp. 404–419.

[34] For example, see C. F. Lee, "Functional Form, Skewness Effect, and the Risk-Return Relationship," *Journal of Financial and Quantitative Analysis,* Vol. 12, No. 1 (March, 1977), pp. 55–72.

[35] S. L. Meyers, "The Stationarity Problem in the Use of the Market Model of Security Price Behavior," *The Accounting Review,* Vol. 48, No. 2 (April, 1973), pp. 318–322; F. J. Fabozzi and J. C. Francis, "Stability Tests for Alphas and Betas over Bull and Bear Market Conditions," *Journal of Finance,* Vol. 32, No. 4 (September, 1977), pp. 1093–1099; R. Reback, "The Single Index Model for Portfolio Selection With Unstable Parameters," *Journal of Bank Research,* Vol. 5, No. 1 (Spring, 1974), pp. 35–37; and Marshall E. Blume, "Betas and Their Regression Tendencies," *Journal of Finance,* Vol. 30, No. 3 (June, 1975), pp. 785–795.

(i.e., constant variance) in the model used to estimate betas,[36] and in other estimation problems.[37]

A more detailed discussion than was given here of the alternative forms of the CAPM, written by Jensen,[38] provides an excellent theoretical background and summary of earlier work on the subject. A critique by Roll[39] includes many of the theoretical and empirical shortcomings of earlier and more recent research.

Questions

1. Discuss semivariance and explain why it has intuitive appeal as a measure of risk for investors.

2. What is the rationale for the use of risk measures that are based on information theory in evaluating investments?

3. What basic advantages are claimed for the decision theory approach (as compared to E-V)?

4. What are the primary advantages of the multidimensional approach? *For what type of investor* might this approach be more relevant than E-V is?

5. Some authors contend that stochastic dominance is conceptually superior to E-V. Do you agree with this statement? Why or why not?

6. The geometric mean criterion assumes that the investor seeks to maximize the ratio of ending wealth. This implies that *ex post* risk measures are irrelevant. Do you agree with this assumption? Why or why not?

7. Several methods of deriving the risky efficient frontier were discussed. Which of them are most similar to each other and why? Which are most dissimilar and why? Which are easiest to use and why?

8. How were early tests of the CAPM typically constructed and what did the results tend to show?

---

[36] J. D. Martin and R. C. Klemkosky, "Evidence of Heteroscadasticity in the Market Model," *Journal of Business,* Vol. 48, No. 1 (January, 1975), pp. 81–86; and A. Belkaoui, "Canadian Evidence of Heteroscadasticity in the Market Model," *Journal of Finance,* Vol. 32, No. 4 (September, 1977), pp. 1320–1324.

[37] G. M. Frankfurter, H. E. Phillips, and J. P. Seagle, "Bias in Estimating Portfolio Alpha and Beta Scores," *Review of Economics and Statistics,* Vol. 56, No. 3 (August, 1974), pp. 412–414; and C. F. Lee, "Performance Measure, Systematic Risk, and Errors-in-Variables Estimation Method," *Journal of Economics and Business,* Vol. 29, No. 2 (Winter, 1977), pp. 122–127.

[38] Michael C. Jensen, "Capital Markets: Theory and Evidence," *The Bell Journal of Economics and Management Science,* Vol. 3, No. 2 (Autumn, 1972), pp. 357–398.

[39] Richard Roll, "A Critique of the Asset Pricing Theory's Tests: Part I: On Past and Potential Testability of the Theory," *Journal of Financial Economics,* Vol. 4, No. 1 (March, 1977), pp. 129–176.

---

9. Briefly discuss the differences between each of the following:
a. "original" CAPM
b. two factor (zero-beta) model
c. three factor model, and
d. four factor model

References

Angell, James W. "Uncertainty, Likelihoods, and Investment Decisions." *Quarterly Journal of Economics,* Vol. 74 (February, 1960).

Baumol, W. J. "An Expected Gain-Confidence Limit Criterion for Portfolio Selection." *Management Science,* Vol. 10, No. 1 (October, 1963).

Belkaoui, A. "Canadian Evidence on Heteroscadasticity in the Market Model." *Journal of Finance,* Vol. 30, No. 3 (June, 1975).

Black, Fischer, Jensen, Michael C., and Scholes, Myron. "The Capital Asset Pricing Model: Some Empirical Tests." In Jensen, Michael C. (editor). *Studies in the Theory of Capital Markets.* New York: Praeger Publishers, 1972.

Blume, Marshall E. "Betas and Their Regression Tendencies." *Journal of Finance,* Vol. 30, No. 3 (June, 1975).

Blume, Marshall E. and Friend, Irwin. "A New Look at the Capital Asset Pricing Model." *Journal of Finance,* Vol. 28, No. 1 (March, 1973).

Elton, Edwin J. and Gruber, Martin J. "Portfolio Theory When Investment Relatives are Lognormally Distributed." *Journal of Finance,* Vol. 29, No. 4 (September, 1974).

Fabozzi, F. J. and Francis, J. C. "Stability Tests for Alphas and Betas Over Bull and Bear Market Conditions." *Journal of Finance,* Vol. 32, No. 4 (September, 1977).

Fama, Eugene F. "The Behavior of Stock Market Prices." *Journal of Business,* Vol. 38, No. 1 (January, 1965).

Fama, Eugene F. "A Note on the Market Model and the Two-Parameter Model." *Journal of Finance,* Vol. 28, No. 5 (December, 1973).

Fama, Eugene F. "Portfolio Analysis in a Stable Paretian Analysis." *Management Science,* Vol. 11, No. 1 (January, 1965).

Fama, Eugene F. and MacBeth, J. D. "Risk, Return, and Equilibrium: Empirical Tests." *Journal of Political Economy,* Vol. 81, No. 3 (May–June, 1973).

Fama, Eugene F. and MacBeth, J. D. "Tests on the Multiperiod Two-Parameter Model." *Journal of Financial Economics,* Vol. 1, No. 1 (May, 1974).

Fama, Eugene F. and Roll, Richard. "Some Properties of Symmetric Stable Distributions." *Journal of the American Statistical Association,* Vol. 63, No. 323 (September, 1968).

Farrar, Donald E. *The Investment Decision Under Uncertainty.* Englewood Cliffs, New Jersey: Prentice–Hall, Inc., 1962.

Frankfurter, G. M., Phillips, H. E., and Seagle, J. P. "Bias in Estimating Portfolio Alpha and Beta Scores." *Review of Economics and Statistics,* Vol. 56, No. 3 (August, 1974).

Garner, W. R. and McGill, W. J. "The Relation Between Information and Variance Analysis." *Psychometrika,* Vol. 21, No. 3 (September, 1956).

Georgescu-Roegen, N. *Entropy Law and the Economic Process.* Cambridge, Massachusetts: Harvard University Press, 1971.

Hadar, J. and Russell, W. R. "Rules for Ordering Uncertain Prospects." *American Economic Review,* Vol. 59, No. 1, (March, 1969).

Hakansson, Nils H. "Capital Growth and the Mean-Variance Approach to Portfolio Selection." *Journal of Financial and Quantitative Analysis,* Vol. 6, No. 1 (January, 1971).

Hakansson, N. H. and Liu, Tien-Ching. "Optimal Growth Portfolios When Yields are Serially Correlated." *Review of Economics and Statistics,* Vol. 52, No. 4 (November, 1970).

Hogan, William W. and Warren, James M. "Computation of the Efficient Boundary in the E-S Portfolio Selection Model." *Journal of Financial and Quantitative Analysis,* Vol. 7, No. 4 (September, 1972).

Hogan, William W. and Warren, James M. "Toward the Development of an Equilibrium Capital Market Model Based on Semivariance." *Journal of Financial and Quantitative Analysis,* Vol. 9, No. 1 (January, 1974).

Jean, William H. "The Extension of Portfolio Analysis to Three or More Parameters." *Journal of Financial and Quantitative Analysis,* Vol. 6, No. 1 (January, 1971).

Jean, William H. "More on Multidimensional Portfolio Analysis." *Journal of Financial and Quantitative Analysis,* Vol. 8, No. 3 (June, 1973).

Jensen, Michael C. "Capital Markets: Theory and Evidence." *The Bell Journal of Economics and Management Science,* Vol. 3, No. 2 (Autumn, 1972).

Johnson, Keith H. and Burgess, Richard C. "The Effects of Sample Sizes on the Accuracy of EV and SSD Efficiency Criteria." *Journal of Financial and Quantitative Analysis,* Vol. 10, No. 5 (December, 1975).

Joy, O. Maurice and Porter, R. Burr. "Stochastic Dominance and Mutual Fund Performance." *Journal of Financial and Quantitative Analysis,* Vol. 9, No. 1 (January, 1974).

Latané, Henry A. "Criteria for Choice Among Risky Ventures." *Journal of Political Economy,* Vol. 67, No. 2 (April, 1959).

Latané, Henry A. and Tuttle, Donald L. "Criteria for Portfolio Building." *Journal of Finance,* Vol. 22, No. 3 (September, 1967).

Lee, C. F. "Functional Form, Skewness Effect, and the Risk-Return Relationship." *Journal of Financial and Quantitative Analysis,* Vol. 12, No. 1 (March, 1977).

Lee, C. F. "On the Relationship Between Systematic Risk and the Investment Horizon." *Journal of Financial and Quantitative Analysis,* Vol. 11, No. 5 (December, 1976).

Lee, C. F. "Performance Measure, Systematic Risk, and Errors-in-Variables Estimation Method." *Journal of Economics and Business,* Vol. 29, No. 2 (Winter, 1977).

Lee, C. F. and Lloyd, W. P. "The Capital Asset Pricing Model Expressed as a Recursive System: An Empirical Investigation." *Journal of Financial and Quantitative Analysis,* Vol. 11, No. 2 (June, 1976).

Levy, H. and Hanoch, G. "Relative Effectiveness of Efficiency Criteria for Portfolio Selection." *Journal of Financial and Quantitative Analysis,* Vol. 5, No. 1 (March, 1970).

Levy, H. and Sarnat, M. "Alternative Efficiency Criteria: An Empirical Analysis." *Journal of Finance,* Vol. 25, No. 4 (December, 1970).

Levy, H. and Sarnat, M. "Safety First—An Expected Utility Principle." *Journal of Financial and Quantitative Analysis,* Vol. 7, No. 3 (June, 1972).

Lintner, John. "Security Prices, Risk, and Maximal Gains from Diversification." *Journal of Finance,* Vol. 20, No. 4 (December, 1965).

Lloyd, W. P. and Lee, C. F. "Block Recursive Systems in Asset Pricing Models." *Journal of Finance,* Vol. 31, No. 4 (September, 1976).

Mandelbrot, Benoit. "New Methods in Statistical Economics." *Journal of Political Economy,* Vol. 71, No. 5 (October, 1963).

Mandelbrot, Benoit. "Stable Paretian Random Functions and the Multiplicative Variation of Income." *Econometrica,* Vol. 29, No. 4 (October, 1961).

Mandelbrot, Benoit. "The Variation of Certain Speculative Prices." *Journal of Business,* Vol. 36, No. 4 (October, 1963).

Mandelbrot, Benoit. "The Variation of Some Other Speculative Prices." *Journal of Business,* Vol. 40, No. 4 (October, 1967).

Mao, James C. T. and Sarndal, Carl E. "A Decision Theory Approach to Portfolio Selection." *Management Science,* Vol. 12, No. 8 (April, 1966).

Markowitz, Harry. *Portfolio Selection: Efficient Diversification of Investment.* New York: John Wiley and Sons, Inc., 1959.

Martin, J. D. and Klemkosky, R. C. "Evidence of Heteroscadasticity in the Market Model." *Journal of Business,* Vol. 48, No. 1 (January, 1975).

Merton, Robert C. "An Intertemporal Capital Asset Pricing Model." *Econometrica,* Vol. 41, No. 3 (September, 1973).

Meyers, S. L. "The Stationarity Problem in the Use of the Market Model of Security Price Behavior." *The Accounting Review,* Vol. 48, No. 2 (April, 1973).

Morgan, I. G. "Prediction of Return With the Minimum Variance Zero Beta Portfolio." *Journal of Financial Economics,* Vol. 2, No. 4 (December, 1975).

Mossin, J. "Equilibrium in a Capital Asset Market." *Econometrica,* Vol. 34, No. 4 (October, 1966).

Philippatos, George C. and Gressis, Nicolas. "Conditions of Equivalence among E-V, SSD, and E-H Portfolio Selection Criteria: The Case for Uniform, Normal and Lognormal Distributions." *Management Science,* Vol. 21, No. 6 (February, 1975).

Philippatos, George C. and Wilson, Charles J. "Entropy, Market Risk, and the Selection of Efficient Portfolios." *Applied Economics,* Vol. 4, No. 3 (September, 1972).

Porter, R. Burr. "An Empirical Comparison of Stochastic Dominance and Mean-Variance Portfolio Choice Criteria." *Journal of Financial and Quantitative Analysis,* Vol. 8, No. 4 (September, 1973).

Porter, R. Burr. "Semivariance and Stochastic Dominance: A Comparison." *American Economic Review,* Vol. 64, No. 1 (March, 1974).

Porter, R. Burr and Carey, Kenneth J. "Stochastic Dominance as a Risk Analysis Criterion." *Decision Sciences,* Vol. 5, No. 1 (January, 1974).

Porter, R. Burr and Gaumnitz, Jack E. "Stochastic Dominance vs. Mean Variance: An Empirical Evaluation." *American Economic Review,* Vol. 62, No. 3 (June, 1972).

Porter, R. Burr, Wart, J. R., and Ferguson, D. L. "Efficiency Algorithms for Conducting Stochastic Dominance Tests on Large Numbers of Portfolios." *Journal of Financial and Quantitative Analysis,* Vol. 8, No. 1 (January, 1973).

Quirk, James P. and Saposnik, R. "Admissibility and Measurable Utility Functions." *Review of Economic Studies,* Vol. 29, No. 79 (February, 1962).

Reback, R. "The Single Index Model for Portfolio Selection with Unstable Parameters." *Journal of Bank Research,* Vol. 5, No. 1 (Spring, 1974).

Roll, Richard. "Ambiguity When Performance Is Measured by the Securities Market Line." *Journal of Finance,* Vol. 33, No. 4 (September, 1978).

Roll, Richard. "A Critique of the Asset Pricing Theory's Tests." *Journal of Financial Economics,* Vol. 4, No. 2 (March, 1977).

Roll, Richard. "Evidence on the 'Growth Optimum' Model." *Journal of Finance,* Vol. 28, No. 3 (June, 1973).

Roy, A. D. "Safety First and the Holding of Assets." *Econometrica,* Vol. 20, No. 3 (July, 1952).

Shannon, C. E. "A Mathematical Theory of Communication." *Bell System Technical Journal,* Vol. 27, No. 3 (July, 1948).

Shannon, C. E. and Weaver, W. *The Mathematical Theory of Communication.* Urbana, Illinois: The University of Illinois Press, 1964.

Sharpe, William F. "Capital Asset Prices: A Theory of Market Equilibrium Under Conditions of Risk." *Journal of Finance,* Vol. 19, No. 3 (September, 1964).

Sharpe, William F. "A Simplified Model for Portfolio Analysis." *Management Science,* Vol. 9, No. 2 (January, 1963).

Theil, H. *Economics and Information Theory.* Chicago: Rand McNally, 1967.

Whitmore, G. A. "Third-Degree Stochastic Dominance." *American Economic Review,* Vol. 60, No. 3 (June, 1970).

Young, William E. and Trent, Robert H. "Geometric Mean Approximations of Individual Security and Portfolio Performance." *Journal of Financial and Quantitative Analysis,* Vol. 4, No. 2 (June, 1969).

Chapter 21   *International Diversification*

The reader is fully aware of the importance of diversification for reducing the risk of the portfolio and also knows that the important factor when selecting an asset for diversification purposes is the covariance of the asset with all other assets in the portfolio. Further, with the CAPM it is shown that the relevant covariance is that between the asset and the market portfolio of *all risky assets in the economy.* In the search for investment assets that have low covariance with the market portfolio, increasing attention has been paid to international capital markets because of the *a priori* expectation that the covariance between international securities and United States securities should be very low. Hence, one should consider adding such investments to a portfolio composed of domestic stocks.

It is with this assumption that we will deal in the following chapter. Following a brief discussion of why international diversification should be beneficial, we will review several studies that have examined the historical relationships between U.S. and foreign securities and the effects of international diversification.

Why International Diversification?

Because the objective of any diversification is to reduce the overall variance of a portfolio, one must ask why foreign securities should be expected to have low covariance with a portfolio of U.S. risky assets. Although the market portfolio used in the CAPM is *theoretically* supposed to contain all risky assets available, the investor is typically concerned with risky assets in the United States. Further, it has been noted on several occasions that almost all empirical studies of the CAPM have used the Standard & Poor's

500 Composite Index as a proxy for the market portfolio. This is a gross understatement of the market portfolio since the S&P 500 Index only includes common stocks and almost all of them are stocks listed on the NYSE. Given this orientation, it is important to demonstrate that foreign securities *should* be included in domestic portfolios. The true market portfolio should be a *total world portfolio* to derive the maximum benefits of diversification.

This discussion leads us back to our assumption of low covariance between the returns for domestic and foreign securities. To see why this expectation is reasonable, one should consider the basic dividend valuation formula

$$P = \frac{D_1}{K-g}$$

The relevant variables are expected dividend (D_1), the required rate of return (K), and the expected growth rate for dividends (g). It is contended that these variables differ significantly between countries and for different securities in the various countries. Because K and g are the most important variables, we will concentrate on them.

Differences in Required Return (K)

K is a function of the economy's risk-free rate of return, the expected inflation in the economy, and a risk premium for the uncertainty involved. It has been shown that the risk-free rate is basically determined by the real growth rate in the economy and, in the short-run, by the tightness or ease in the capital markets. Different countries have experienced different rates of growth during the past several decades as demonstrated by the high rate of growth in Japan and Germany. The rates of growth are *not synchronized*. Further, there are differences in the short-run ease or tightness of the capital markets in different countries. Therefore, one would expect differences in the *level* of the RFR and also somewhat independent *changes* in the RFR for various countries.

There has been a great deal written about differences in rates of inflation in different countries caused by monetary policy.[1] Because the monetary policy in different countries has generally been decided independently, the rates of inflation for each country have been unique and *changes* in the inflation rates have also been different, although one might expect greater interrelationships because of increased international trade.

The risk premium can either be estimated using internal characteristics (business risk, financial risk, and liquidity risk) or external market risk (covariance with market portfolio). Because this discussion is concerned

---

[1] In this regard see Beryl W. Sprinkel, *Money and Markets* (Homewood, Ill.: Richard D. Irwin, 1971), Chapter 7.

with why the covariance with the market portfolio should be low, it is appropriate to consider the relationship among the internal characteristics. Since we are interested in *changes* in stock prices (as they affect rates of return), we will consider whether *changes* in the relevant risk variables are independent. Recall that business risk is a function of sales volatility and operating leverage. One would therefore generally expect *changes* in business risk for firms in different countries to be unique because the factors that affect domestic sales, such as fiscal policy and monetary policy, are independent, so changes in sales volatility should be relatively independent. Similarly, the degree of operating leverage (DOL) is a function of how close a firm is operating to its break even point. Again, because sales are generally independent, the DOL will be unique and changes in this variable for firms in different countries should not be consistently related. Therefore, because changes in sales volatility and changes in operating leverage are not related, you should *not* expect changes in business risk to be related.

Financial risk is a function of the proportion of debt in the financial structure, and is typically measured in terms of the debt/total capital ratio or interest coverage. Firms within an economy typically would decide how much debt to employ based upon the tax laws (the higher the corporate tax rate, the greater the tax advantage of debt versus equity), earnings stability (with greater stability it is possible to employ more debt), and the expected rate of inflation (a higher rate of inflation would prompt more firms to become net debtors). The factors determining the desired level of financial leverage are generally independent and *changes* in these factors are unique, so *changes* in the level of financial risk for different countries should be relatively independent.

Liquidity risk is the uncertainty regarding the ability to buy or sell an asset quickly at a known price. The liquidity of an asset is a function of the number of investors who own and trade the asset, i.e., the volume of trading in the asset. In turn, the amount of trading in common stocks or other financial assets is influenced by the general economic climate in a country and, again, one would not expect consistency between countries. This expectation is borne out by differences in trading volume on different national exchanges. For example, there have been instances in which trading in Japan was extremely heavy while volume on U.S. exchanges was relatively light. Therefore, because trading volume changes are unique, we should expect changes in liquidity risk to be independent for different countries.

Therefore, if all else is held constant and the required return on international risky assets changes independently from that on U.S. securities, the returns for U.S. and foreign risky assets should have a low covariance. The level of covariance will depend upon the relationship between the economies involved. As an example, one would expect a higher covariance between U.S. and Canadian securities than between U.S. and Italian stocks.

Independent Changes in the Growth Rate

It can similarly be argued that the major factors determining the growth rate (g) are generally independent between countries. The growth rate is a function of the retention rate and the return on equity. One would expect changes in the retention rate to vary between countries based upon differences in their tax structure, the investment opportunities in the country, and the availability of external capital in the country's capital markets. Because all of these factors differ between countries and change independently, changes in the retention rate should be unique to a given nation. The return on equity (ROE) is determined by equity turnover and the profit margin. The equity turnover, in turn, is heavily influenced by sales growth, retention policy, and changes in the debt-equity financing ratio. All of these factors differ between countries. The profit margin depends upon such factors as capacity utilization, unit labor cost, inflation, exports, and imports. Again, the two major factors are capacity utilization and unit labor cost, and both of these are clearly variables that are internal to the economy and, therefore, changes in these variables for alternative nations should be relatively independent.

Therefore, almost all of the determinants of growth are unique and differ for different countries. Moreover, *changes* in these variables are generally determined by internal conditions, and these conditions are expected to be independent. Similar to the changes in K, the degree of independence will vary depending upon the economic ties between the countries.

The covariance between the returns for securities in *different* countries should therefore be much lower than the covariance of returns for companies *within* a country. Because changes in these variables cause changes in security prices, *these price changes should be relatively independent* and international diversification should be useful.

Empirical Studies of International Diversification

Since 1968, a number of studies have examined the effect of international diversification empirically and attempted to answer questions regarding the real benefits of such diversification.

Grubel Studies

One of the first of such studies was done by Herbert G. Grubel, who showed the benefit of diversification between the securities of different countries, using the Markowitz portfolio model, and assuming less than perfect correlation between returns.[2] He analyzed rates of return (adjusted for

---

[2] Herbert G. Grubel, "Internationally Diversified Portfolios: Welfare Gains and Capital Flows," *American Economic Review,* Vol. 58, No. 5 (December, 1968), pp. 1299–1314.

changes in the exchange rate) of monthly stock price indicator series in 11 major countries during the period 1959–1966. The countries included were: USA, Canada, the United Kingdom, West Germany, France, Italy, Belgium, the Netherlands, Japan, Australia, and South Africa. The rates of return, standard deviation, and correlation with the U.S. index are shown in Table 21–1.

Table 21–1
Rates of Return and Standard Deviation from Investing in Foreign Capital Market Averages 1959–1966

	Per cent Per Annum (1)	Value of $100 at End of Period (2)	Standard Deviation (3)	Correlation (R) with USA (4)
USA	7.54	178.92	47.26	1.0000
Canada	5.95	158.82	41.19	0.7025[a]
United Kingdom	9.59	208.00	65.28	0.2414[a]
West Germany	7.32	175.95	94.69	0.3008[a]
France	4.27	139.69	49.60	0.1938[a]
Italy	8.12	186.74	103.33	0.1465
Belgium	1.09	109.02	37.56	0.1080
Netherlands	5.14	149.33	86.34	0.2107[a]
Japan	16.54	340.21	92.52	0.1149
Australia	9.44	205.75	34.87	0.0585
South Africa	8.47	191.60	61.92	− 0.1620

[a] Statistically significant at the 5 percent level.
Source: Herbert G. Grubel, "Internationally Diversified Portfolios: Welfare Gains and Capital Flows," *American Economic Review,* Vol. 58, No. 5 (December, 1968), p. 1304. Reprinted by permission.

Japan had the highest rate of return during the period, but also one of the largest standard deviations. More important though, this index had very low correlation with the U.S. index (.1149) indicating that securities from Japan would be a good addition to a portfolio composed of U.S. securities. Australia had the lowest correlation (.0585) with the U.S. index and the South African index had a *negative* correlation (−.1620). This negative correlation is probably caused by heavy involvement in gold mining. The reader will recall from Chapter 12 that the gold mining industry was the only one with a negative beta. One would expect all of these foreign indexes to be excellent additions to a domestic portfolio.

Grubel derived hypothetical portfolios using all 11 countries, and using only the eight countries in the Atlantic Community. The results clearly showed that *diversification among the assets from the 11 countries permitted investors to attain higher rates of return or lower variance than would be attained with a portfolio of only U.S. stocks.* Also, if an investor limited himself to investments in securities from the Atlantic Community countries, and thereby ignored Japan, South Africa, and Australia, his opportunities for gains from diversification were reduced considerably.

A subsequent study by Grubel and Fadner was concerned with three questions regarding international diversification.[3] The first involved an analysis of international diversification as compared to intra-national diversification. Second, they dealt with the effect of holding periods on the correlations, and third, they examined the effect of fluctuations in the exchange rate on the variance of returns. The analysis involved 51 U.S. industry stock price indexes, 28 industry indexes from the U.K., and 28 West German indexes. The authors dealt with weekly data for the period from January 1, 1965 to June 30, 1967.

The initial correlations involved percentages of price changes adjusted for changes in exchange rates. The effect of inter and intra-national diversification was initially examined in terms of the average correlation coefficient between all pairs *within* a country compared to all pairs *between* countries. For weekly and monthly holding periods, the differences were quite dramatic and definitely significant. For monthly data, the average correlation *within* the countries was about .50, while the average correlation *between* the countries was about .12. They also examined the correlation among pairs of identical industries from the three countries. It was hypothesized that the correlations would be proportional to the amount of importing and exporting done. The results indicated that correlations between identical industries in the U.S. and the U.K. were generally higher than similar correlations between industries in the U.S. and West Germany. The U.S.–U.K. correlations were larger in 13 of the 18 comparisons, and the average U.S.–U.K. correlation was .49 compared to an average correlation for the U.S.–West German industries of .32. There was also support for the hypothesis that the correlations were influenced by the proportion of importing and exporting done by the industry.

The effect of different holding periods was examined by analyzing the differences in correlations for weekly rates of returns, monthly returns, and quarterly returns. It was hypothesized that the correlation would be positively related to the holding period, since, in the long-run, some unique characteristics briefly affecting returns would be overpowered by the underlying real valuation factors such as growth and profits. The results strongly supported the hypothesis since the average intra-national correlations increased from .40 for weekly periods to .57 for quarterly holding period returns, while the inter-national correlations went from about .06 for weekly holding periods, to .32 for quarterly holding periods. These results imply some reduction in the benefits of international diversification with longer holding periods.

Finally, the effect of fluctuations in the exchange rate on return variability was examined by comparing the correlation of returns with and without adjustments for exchange rates. During the relatively short period of

---

[3] Herbert G. Grubel and Kenneth Fadner, "The Interdependence of International Equity Markets," *Journal of Finance*, Vol. 26, No. 1 (March, 1971), pp. 89–94.

analysis, there were only small changes in exchange rates, so the fact that there were *no* significant differences caused by exchange rates is not too surprising.

Levy–Sarnat Study[4]

The purpose of the Levy–Sarnat study was to present estimates of potential gains from international diversification for the period 1951–1967, employing annual returns for 28 countries. An analysis of returns adjusted for exchange rate changes produced a wide range of mean returns (+17.8% to −1.5%) and standard deviations. After deriving the efficient set of portfolios, they utilized the concept of a market opportunity line developed by Sharpe and employed four borrowing and lending rates (2, 3, 4, and 6 percent), to generate four optimal portfolios. Although 28 countries were considered, only 9 were included in at least one of the optimal portfolios. Investments in the U.S. and Japan accounted for 50–70 percent of the optimal portfolios, with additional investments in developing or borderline countries such as Venezuela, South Africa, New Zealand and Mexico. Most of these were included because of the *low or negative correlation* they had with other countries in the sample.

The benefits to American investors of alternative diversification schemes were shown by deriving efficient frontiers using selected samples. As shown in Figure 21–1, if you invested in only developing countries, only common market countries, or only Western European countries, there is a *loss* relative to investing solely in the U.S. When Japan and South Africa are included, there is a significant improvement; i.e., there is a continuous reduction in variance as the opportunity set is broadened until the best frontier is derived when all 28 countries are considered. Canada was not included in any of the optimal portfolios because of its high correlation with the U.S. and its low rate of return. It was pointed out that, in a truly perfect capital market, an optimal portfolio would contain some of every country's stock. If it did not, the price of the omitted stock should decline until it entered at least one portfolio. Since this does not happen, it was surmised that restrictions on international trade and capital flows do make a difference.

Agmon Studies

The first article by Agmon dealing with international diversification considered whether international stock markets were segmented as suggested by previous authors, or whether there was support for the notion of one

---

[4] Haim Levy and Marshall Sarnat, "International Diversification of Investment Portfolios," *American Economic Review*, Vol. 60, No. 4 (September, 1970), pp. 668–675.

Figure 21–1
**Alternative
Efficient Frontiers
When Stocks
from Different
Countries Are
Considered**

A – 28 Countries
B – 16 High Income Countries
C – 11 Western European
        Countries
D – 5 Common Market
        Countries
E – 9 Developing Countries
F – United States

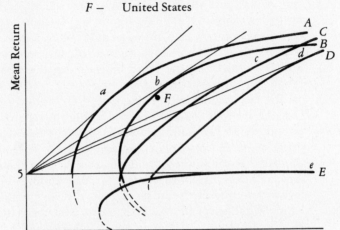

Source: Haim Levy and Marshall Sarnat, "International Diversification of Investment Portfolios," *American Economic Review,* Vol. 60, No. 4 (September, 1970), p. 673. Reprinted by permission.

multinational perfect capital market.[5] The author initially argued that earlier studies simply examining correlations were insufficient, and it would be preferable to use the Capital Asset Pricing Model, in which the marginal contribution made by an additional asset is considered, to determine the benefits of diversification. Agmon also argued against the use of composite market indicator series since he contended that whether they represent *all* possible combinations of investments is not certain. While true in theory, it is unlikely that the market indicator series are so poor that they would account for the substantial differences in returns found by other authors.

Following a brief explanation of the CAPM, the author used the model to test the consistency of international share price movements within the one market (multinational) hypothesis. This involved relating the percent of price series for the United Kingdom (U.K.), Germany, and Japan to a United States index (the Fisher Index). The test included 55 *monthly* observations for the period 1961–1966. The three slope coefficients were

---

[5] Tamir Agmon, "The Relations Among Equity Markets: A Study of Share Price Co-Movements in the United States, United Kingdom, Germany and Japan," *Journal of Finance,* Vol. 27, No. 4 (September, 1972), pp. 839–855.

positive and significant with a range from .42 to .71. At the same time, the r^2 ranged from .11 to .37, which would certainly not be considered very substantial. Even with these low r^2 and slope coefficients, Agmon contended that the one market hypothesis was not rejected.

He subsequently examined the relationship between individual stocks from each of the foreign countries and the U.S. market index. While the average slope coefficients for U.S. and German stocks was substantial and very significant, the slope coefficients for U.K. and Japanese stock were rather low (about .36) and *not* significant. In addition, the average r^2 for the U.K. was only .03 and for Japan only .009. While this would apparently indicate that the market is segmented, Agmon contends that the poor results for the U.K. and Japan indicate that these countries "specialize" in producing capital with a given risk level.

The next segmentation test looked for differences in the price of risk between the four countries by examining the relationship between average rates of return for the various series relative to the beta coefficients derived using the U.S. index as the market series. The one market hypothesis implies that the intercept and slope coefficients should be *identical* for the four countries. Agmon pointed out that almost all results had very low levels of significance, but he did not discuss the differences between the various intercepts and slope coefficients which were the test of the hypothesis. The intercepts for these foreign countries had different values *and* they had *different signs*. The intercept for the U.K. was insignificantly positive, the German intercept was negative and almost significant, and the Japanese intercept was significant and negative. In addition, the U.K. slope was negative and insignificant, while the other two were positive but not significant. Agmon points out that the U.S. results were also relatively poor, but does not mention the relevant differences. (He did not report the intercepts in the U.S. test.)

The final test was an examination of the simultaneity of stock price changes in which it was hypothesized that a one market model implies simultaneous price changes. Unfortunately, Agmon used monthly stock prices that require significant leads or lags. The results tended to support the one market hypothesis since major changes were simultaneous. The use of monthly data obviously biased the results since, even if one believes in a segmented market, it is difficult to imagine a lag of a month in price adjustments. Agmon concluded that the evidence presented is *not inconsistent* with the one market hypothesis, but acknowledged that more data and better tests are needed to establish the validity of the hypothesis.

While the first Agmon article concluded that there was no evidence denying the *possibility* of a multinational market, his second article began by asserting that the first had shown that one multinational market exists.[6]

[6] Tamir Agmon, "Country Risk: The Significance of the Country Factor for Share Price Movements in the United Kingdom, Germany and Japan," *Journal of Business,* Vol. 46, No. 1 (January, 1973), pp. 24–32.

Beyond this questionable beginning, the purpose of the paper was to examine individual stock price fluctuations "unique" to the country of origin. The sample included 145 individual stocks from the United Kingdom, Germany, and Japan during the 55 months from July, 1961 to January, 1966.

The initial test related stock prices indexes for each of the three countries to a U.S. index and to the index for the other countries. The results indicated that the strongest relationship was with the U.S. index and there was generally insignificant correlation among the other indexes. This was interpreted by Agmon as indicating that the U.S. market is the connecting link among the three markets but there was very little *direct* relationship among them. He then derived a country factor to explain intra-national changes using a two step process. First, each country's index was regressed against the U.S. index and *the residuals were used as an estimate of the net "country" factor.* Then the stock for each country was regressed against the U.S. index and against the country factor. The results indicated that another systematic factor, associated with the stock's own country, did exist. In fact, the "own" country coefficient was always *more significant* than the U.S. coefficient. Hence, a significant "own country" factor unique to the country apparently was stronger than any relationship with U.S. securities.

To determine whether the second systematic factor was, in fact, *unique* to a country, the returns for each stock were related to a U.S. index and to the residuals for each of the country indexes (the four country factors derived earlier). The results showed clearly that the major factor explaining price movements was the stock's *own country factor,* next in importance was the U.S. factor (which was statistically insignificant in two of three cases), and last was the other countries' unique factor (which was insignificant). A subsequent attempt to explain the common characteristics matched each foreign stock with a U.S. stock with a similar coefficient relative to the U.S. index. These similar U.S. stocks were then regressed against the U.S. index and the appropriate foreign index. The results showed a significant relation to the U.S. index and almost *no* remaining relation with the foreign country factor. Agmon concluded that this is further evidence that *each stock's country factor is unique to the country.*

The final question concerned the country factor and the potential benefits of international diversification. It was demonstrated quite clearly by Agmon that *different countries had unique country risks and that these unique risks were generally independent.* This independence was demonstrated again when the author showed that the country factors (the residuals) have either very low positive correlations (.04 and .07), or negative correlation ($-.15$). Based upon this evidence, Agmon states that "once the U.S. factor is removed, the non-U.S. country indices are virtually independent of each other."[7] This independence seems to indicate that there should be *substan-*

---

[7] Agmon, "Country Risk," p. 29.

tial benefits to international diversification because previously it had been shown that this unique country factor was the most important explanatory variable for the stocks considered. Therefore, if this unique component could be diversified away, these foreign securities should be very low risk stocks for a U.S. investor. This line of reasoning, that seems to follow from the Capital Asset Pricing Model, leaves us with a final statement from Agmon that is as confusing as his first statement: "The country factors are found to be *virtually independent of each other,* so that the potential gains from international diversification, *if any, are small*"[8] (emphasis added).

Lessard Study[9]

In this study, the sample was limited to four countries at approximately the same level of economic development (Colombia, Chile, Argentina, and Brazil). While, in general, one would expect stocks within a country to move together, it was contended by Lessard that this comovement should be *stronger* in less developed countries because of their unique problems. Also, the common movements of different countries are probably unrelated to each other because the problems and events in a given country would outweigh any common events of importance between the countries. This notion of independence of unique country returns was supported by the Agmon study.[10] The Lessard study was concerned with three specific questions: (1) how strong were the common elements for stocks within these four countries? (2) were the individual common elements for each of the countries related or independent? (3) what were the specific benefits of international diversification compared to diversification within countries? The sample consisted of quarterly returns on 110 common stocks from the four countries for the period December, 1958 to December, 1968.

To derive the common element of variance and the independence of the common elements, the author employed factor analysis. The extent to which returns in individual countries move together was determined by principal component analysis applied to the four samples for three different time periods. In all cases, the proportions of total variance explained by the first component of returns for each of the countries was *larger* than generally found in the United States, ranging from .40 to .73 compared to an average of about 30 percent in the U.S. This finding supports the contention that *stocks within an undeveloped capital market have a large common component.* An analysis of the correlation of first components did not show any consistent patterns; there did *not* seem to be any systematic relationships between the major movements in the various stock markets.

---

[8] Ibid., p. 29.

[9] Donald R. Lessard, "International Portfolio Diversification: A Multivariate Analysis for a Group of Latin American Countries," *Journal of Finance,* Vol. 38, No. 3 (June, 1973), pp. 619–633.

[10] Agmon, "Country Risk."

To confirm that there were major components for each country that were independent, Lessard analyzed the covariance matrix of all 110 stocks. The results confirmed that the returns in each country could be explained by a market factor, and *the market factors were independent of each other.* Of the 110 stocks, only six were closely related to another country's market factor, and all 110 were related to their own country factor.

Given the strong country factors and the independence of the country factors, it was contended that potentially large gains could be derived from international diversification. To estimate the gains, Lessard compared the return and variance of returns for intra-national portfolios to the returns and variances possible from international portfolios. When naively diversified portfolios were constructed (equal amounts of each stock), the four nation portfolio dominated all single country portfolios with few exceptions. Assuming a risk-free rate of less than 6 percent, *the four nation portfolio was dominant.*

When efficient portfolios were constructed using past data, the international portfolio dominated all except Brazil and, again assuming almost any reasonable risk-free rate (below 13 percent), *the international portfolio was best.*

Finally, the four country portfolio was compared to investing in an all U.S. portfolio, in this case, the S&P 500 Index. The results indicated that investing equal amounts in the four countries compared favorably to investing in the U.S. portfolio. From 1958–1963, the Latin country portfolio was superior; from 1963–1968 the U.S. investment was superior; and for the full ten year period neither was obviously dominant. The Latin American portfolio would be best assuming a risk-free rate *above* 1.40 percent a year. Unfortunately, Lessard did not consider diversifying *with* the U.S. Such an analysis obviously would have shown further benefits. The results do indicate, however, that international diversification is beneficial even among developing countries in a single geographical area.

French Mutual Funds[11]

McDonald examined the investment performance of internationally diversified portfolios by analyzing the performance of French mutual funds for the period 1964–1969. The reason French funds were analyzed is that they typically represent investment in both domestic French stocks and foreign stocks, with the bulk of the latter being securities listed on the NYSE. Also, the funds are typically managed by French banks that have superior access to company information. The results supported the concept of international diversification since the Sharpe reward-to-variability measure indicated that the all-French fund had the lowest performance ratio, while

---

[11] John G. McDonald, "French Mutual Fund Performance: Evaluation of Internationally Diversified Portfolios," *Journal of Finance,* Vol. 28, No. 5 (December, 1973), pp. 1161–1180.

the fund with the *most* international diversification had the highest performance ratio. Other measures of performance gave about the same relative rankings of performance.

Joy et al. Study[12]

A study by Maurice Joy and others considered the fundamental structure of comovements in the returns in major international equity markets, and also analyzed *changes* in these relationships over time. The authors examined weekly stock market index levels for 12 countries over the period 1963–1972 inclusive. The countries included were: Australia, France, Switzerland, Austria, Italy, the United Kingdom, Belgium, Japan, the United States, Canada, the Netherlands, and West Germany.

Adjusted and unadjusted rates of return were computed. The correlation matrix of weekly index rates of return for the entire ten year period is shown in Table 21–2. The top half contains the correlation among unadjusted returns, while the bottom half contains the correlation among adjusted returns. Although there are a few significant positive correlations, *most of the correlations are very low,* as shown by the average correlations between rates of return for all 66 pairs of countries of only .139 and .133 for unadjusted and adjusted rates respectively. This supports the previous studies which contended that *there are substantial risk reduction possibilities through international diversification.* It is also noteworthy that there was little difference between the results with adjusted and unadjusted rates of return.

The authors used analysis of variance (ANOVA) to test the time effect (do the correlations change over time?) and the country effect (are the correlations between various pairs of countries different?). The results indicated that *both the time and country effects were significant.* This means that there are different correlations between countries and, therefore, it is important to determine the specific relationship with the country being considered. The significant time effect indicates that the relationships do change over time, so the *ex post* correlation coefficients may not be as useful as one would like in developing portfolios. This instability also means that it may be necessary to readjust the portfolios over time. These results were confirmed with a nonparametric test. A test of whether the correlations change over rising and declining U.S. stock market periods likewise indicated significant differences. The comovements were significantly greater during declining market periods, which implies that international diversification possibilities are *not* the same during different market periods.

The final analysis examined the possible existence of time trends in the relationships (i.e., have the correlations increased over time?). The mean correlations between the 66 pairs of countries during each of the years is shown in Table 21–3.

---

[12] O. Maurice Joy, Don B. Panton, Frank K. Reilly, and Stanley A. Martin, "Comovements of Major International Equity Markets," *The Financial Review* (1976), pp. 1–20.

Table 21–2 Ten Year Correlations of Weekly Rates of Return of Twelve Major International Equity Markets

	Australia	Austria	Belgium	Canada	France	Italy	Japan	Netherlands	Switzerland	U.K.	W. Germany	U.S.	
Australia		−.022	.112	.147	.062	.018	.062	.127	.173	.173	.091	.161	
Austria	.013		.044	.026	.061	.050	.024	.058	.038	.081	.102	.020	
Belgium	.117	.044		.229	.241	.073	.101	.270	.221	.128	.216	.232	
Canada	.167	.058	.179		.150	.061	.180	.369	.278	.162	.226	.643	
France	.082	.069	.177	.163		.030	.083	.158	.144	.037	.177	.097	Unadjusted Rates of Returns
Italy	.022	.011	.079	.060	.012		.129	.119	.155	.074	.066	.021	
Japan	.086	.071	.086	.192	.106	.102		.176	.143	.080	.128	.076	
Netherlands	.134	.038	.232	.361	.158	.098	.167		.293	.157	.342	.349	
Switzerland	.173	.045	.164	.289	.148	.174	.192	.283		.067	.243	.245	
U.K.	.171	.034	.093	.146	.039	.078	.110	.131	.002		.035	.125	
W. Germany	.106	.072	.186	.201	.153	.050	.113	.357	.207	.030		.171	
U.S.	.137	.027	.205	.634	.107	.002	.092	.344	.242	.096	.163		

Adjusted Rates of Returns

Source: O. Maurice Joy, Don B. Panton, Frank K. Reilly, and Stanley A. Martin,
"Comovements of International Equity Markets," *The Financial Review* (1976), p. 5.
Reprinted by permission.

Table 21–3
Mean Correlations of Weekly Rates of Return for the Indices of Twelve Major Equity Markets, Years 1963–1972

	1963	1964	1965	1966	1967	1968	1969	1970	1971	1972
$\bar{\Theta}_t$ (adjusted)	.066	.115	.121	.115	.070	.121	.177	.280	.130	.135
$\bar{\Theta}_t$ (unadjusted)	.081	.113	.188	.115	.068	.125	.215	.271	.126	.151

Source: O. Maurice Joy, Don B. Panton, Frank K. Reilly, and Stanley A. Martin,
"Comovements of International Equity Markets," *The Financial Review* (1976), p. 11.
Reprinted by permission.

A parametric trend regression analysis tended to support the notion of a significant positive trend in the correlations. The results from a non-parametric ANOVA test were even more supportive of *a significant positive trend*. These results also affirm the conclusion that international equity market comovement was increasing during the period 1963–1972. The study also analyzed the trend in individual pairs of countries. The yearly correlations for the U.S. adjusted returns and those of the other eleven countries are contained in Table 21–4. The results for all the countries indicated that significantly more than half the trends were positive (about 70 percent), but only a few (seven out of 66) were statistically significant. For the U.S., five of the trends were negative while six were positive, but only one of the positive trends was significant. Therefore it appears that the possibility of reducing portfolio risk through international diversification has been declining over time, *but the trend is very gradual*.

Table 21–4 **Observed Correlations Between Adjusted Weekly Rates of Return of the United States (Dow Jones Industrial Average) and Adjusted Weekly Rates of Return for Eleven Major Equity Markets, Years 1963–1972**

	1963	1964	1965	1966	1967	1968	1969	1970	1971	1972	$\bar{Q}_i$
U.S.-Australia	.080	.090	.037	.323	.095	.122	.036	.213	.193	.178	.137
U.S.-Austria	.088	.309	.044	−.001	−.077	−.057	.022	−.124	−.038	.100	.027
U.S.-Belgium	.370	.328	.502	.276	−.001	.131	.168	.455	.032	−.211	.205
U.S.-Canada	.649	.563	.727	.761	.687	.668	.429	.760	.440	.651	.634
U.S.-France	.068	.007	.185	.243	.108	.071	.181	.071	.001	.137	.107
U.S.-Italy	−.024	−.116	−.104	−.006	−.128	−.025	−.020	.183	.254	.005	.002
U.S.-Japan	.203	.029	.033	−.189	−.053	.208	.232	.353	−.059	.164	.092
U.S.-Netherlands	.165	.227	.359	.403	.492	.467	.197	.439	.396	.294	.344
U.S.-Switzerland	.080	.233	.201	.282	.099	.299	.233	.556	.269	.172	.242
U.S.-United Kingdom	.022	−.040	.043	.124	−.078	.091	−.007	.417	.087	.297	.096
U.S.-W. Germany	.188	.125	.420	.049	−.030	.169	.154	.462	.053	.041	.163

Source: O. Maurice Joy, Don B. Panton, Frank K. Reilly, and Stanley A. Martin, "Comovements of International Equity Markets," *The Financial Review* (1976), p. 14. Reprinted by permission.

Conclusions and Implications

Based upon the results of the several studies discussed, it is possible to derive several major conclusions regarding the usefulness of international diversification, and to derive some implications of these findings for the portfolio manager.

Level of Correlation The results consistently indicate a *much lower* level of correlation between the stocks of *different* countries than for stocks *within* a country. This implies that there are substantial benefits to be derived from international diversification, as was demonstrated in several of the articles discussed.

It was also shown that *the correlation differs between countries* depending upon their level of development and the level of interdependence of their economies. The relationship between less developed countries and highly developed countries is clearly less than average simply because the undeveloped countries have unique economic problems such that their economies do not move together and the rates of return on their stocks are not associated. Therefore, for purposes of diversification, such undeveloped countries are excellent candidates for investment. The correlations were not stable over time so it is not possible to simply use past correlations to develop future portfolios. It will also be necessary to adjust the portfolios over time to reflect expected changes in the relationships.

Finally, there have been results that indicate a positive trend in some of the correlations. This would imply that there will be less benefit derived from international diversification in the future. The trend is gradual and is not positive for all combinations. This means that a portfolio manager should examine each country on an individual basis and make an appropriate decision based upon the past relationship, recent trends, and his assessment of the future relation between the countries involved.

Obstacles to International Diversification

Previous studies have generally indicated that the benefit of international diversification stems from the low correlation between foreign and domestic stocks. Even though international investment may involve some problems owing to the instability of relationships between the securities, these are relatively minor and no more of a problem than dealing with unstable betas for individual U.S. stocks is. Therefore, given the clear advantages of international diversification and the limited theoretical problems, why do individuals and institutions in the U.S. not invest more in foreign securities? The purpose of this section is to discuss the reasons.

The chief obstacle is the fact that international capital markets are clearly not perfect. The major characteristics of perfect markets are complete and costless information, zero transaction costs, and complete liquidity.

Availability of Information

A *set* of obstacles to foreign investment are subsumed under this general heading. The first is the *availability of information* on individual companies, industries, and economies. American investors take for granted an enormous set of data that is simply not available in many other countries, especially in some less developed nations. The numerous sources of economic data, organizations like the Federal Reserve System and the Commerce Department, simply do not exist. Further, we have a number of private sources of industry data, companies like Standard & Poor's, Moody's, Value Line, and industry trade associations that do not exist elsewhere. Finally, analysts in the U.S. are almost overwhelmed each year by annual reports, quarterly reports, and IOK reports. Again, *almost none* of this is available in *most* foreign countries. For analysts and portfolio managers accustomed to a plethora of information, it is difficult to make decisions under the conditions noted above.

There is a further problem of *interpretation of the data* received because reporting standards in many countries are different from those used here. Investors often complain about the different accounting techniques used by American firms, techniques that can seriously affect reported income. These differences are minor compared to the variations employed in many foreign countries. What, then, does the analyst do with the Japanese or German earnings figure to make it comparable to a U.S. figure?

Finally, there are timing problems because of *reporting lags*. How long will it take until figures are publicly available? In many instances, the lag is substantial compared to what it is in the U.S. Further, once figures are available, it may be a while until they are reported in the U.S. Clearly, this lag could be very important in the price adjustment process.

Liquidity

Liquidity is generally defined as the ability to buy or sell an asset quickly without the price changing significantly from what it was during a previous transaction, assuming no new information has entered the market. In earlier chapters we have discussed this concept extensively as it relates to the notion of a tiered market and the effect of liquidity on an investment's required rate of return. Liquidity is important for any investment and is especially crucial to large institutional investors who need to establish major positions in an investment if it is going to be worthwhile. As noted, because of this need for liquidity, a tiered market does exist within the U.S., and probably will continue to exist. Unfortunately, the liquidity of most foreign stocks is *substantially below* that of most U.S. stocks listed on an exchange. Although there are some stocks with good trading volume and liquidity, *the great majority of foreign stocks experience only limited trading and substantial volatility.* Therefore, it is conceivable that a number of foreign stocks could be acquired by individuals. In contrast, only a *very limited* number of foreign stocks have the necessary liquidity to be considered by institutional investors.

Transaction Costs

One must also consider the above average transaction costs involved in a foreign trade. These include commission costs (that will probably be above average), transfer taxes, and all the other costs involved in placing the order and securing the certificate.[13]

Alternatives to Direct Investment

Assume that an investor acknowledges that it is a good idea to invest in foreign securities and yet is also aware of the problems; what alternatives are available? For an individual investor an obvious solution would be to purchase shares in an investment company that specializes in foreign securities, such as the Japan Fund. This would solve the problems of lack of information and liquidity since such funds are completely liquid at their net asset value if they are open-end funds (i.e., the fund will acquire all shares at the net asset value) or relatively liquid if they are closed-end funds that trade on the secondary market like other stocks (e.g., the Japan Fund is closed-end but typically trades in excess of 50,000 shares a day based upon an examination of volume during 1978). Unfortunately, there are only a few international funds and they typically concentrate their portfolio in one country or geographic area. Hence it might be necessary to invest in several of them to derive the full benefits.

---

[13] An article by Anna Marjos indicates that many of these problems have declined in recent years with the growth of American Depository Receipts (ADR's). See Anna Marjos, "How to Invest Abroad," *Barron's* (July 24, 1978), p. 9.

Institutions can solve the information problem by either investing on the basis of advice from an institution in a desirable country or by establishing a research office in the country. The major remaining unsolved problem is liquidity. The lack of liquidity may mean it is necessary to limit the commitment to international stocks or possibly limit the number of stocks that can be considered to those with active markets. This latter suggestion is similar to what institutions have done in domestic stocks. Recently another alternative has been offered by an investment company that is going to establish a Japanese Index Fund to invest in a large cross section of Japanese stocks.[14] The initial concept is to limit the sale to institutions by requiring a minimum purchase of $250,000.

Summary

This chapter was concerned with an analysis of the benefits and potential problems involved in international diversification. Our initial discussion considered the reasons why there should be a relatively low level of correlation between securities from different countries, based upon the dividend valuation model. Because almost all the relevant valuation variables are not related, one should not expect the rates of return to be correlated.

The bulk of the chapter contained a discussion of several studies that have presented the theoretical arguments in favor of international diversification and have also empirically examined the concept. The results consistently indicated that international diversification should be beneficial although the correlations between countries change over time. There was also some evidence of an increase in the correlations among securities from various countries, but the trend was small and did not apply to all countries.

Although there are theoretical and empirical reasons for international diversification, it is clear that the concept is not without problems. The main obstacles are the availability of information, the reliability of the information received, the time lag in getting the information, a substantial liquidity problem with many securities, and higher transaction costs.

An alternative to direct investment by individuals is acquiring shares of an investment company that concentrates in foreign stocks. Institutions can invest through local experts, but the liquidity problem is difficult to avoid. Clearly the liquidity problem is greater for foreign stocks than it is in our domestic market, and will probably limit the available universe of foreign stocks that can be considered.

---

[14] "Nomura Sets Fund of Japanese Stocks for U.S. Investors," *Wall Street Journal*, March 8, 1978, p. 28.

1. What is the purpose of international diversification? Why should portfolio managers invest in foreign securities?

2. Discuss in some detail why international diversification should work. Specifically, why would you expect low correlation in the rates of return for domestic and foreign securities?

3. Would you expect a difference in the correlation of returns between U.S. and various foreign securities? Why? Be specific.

4. Using a source of international statistics, compare the percent changes in the following economic data for Japan, West Germany, Italy, Canada, and the U.S. for a recent year:
A. aggregate output (GNP)
B. inflation
C. corporate earnings
D. money supply growth
What were the differences, and which country or countries differed most from the U.S.?

5. Using a recent edition of *Barron's,* examine the weekly percentages of change in the stock price indexes for Japan, West Germany, Italy, Canada, and the U.S. For each of three weeks, which foreign series moved most closely with the U.S. series; which series was most divergent from the U.S. series? What would this indicate to you regarding international diversification?

6. What were the empirical findings regarding changes in the correlations *over time* between the stock price series for various countries? What are the implications of these results for a portfolio manager interested in international diversification?

7. Would you expect there to be a trend in the correlations between U.S. stock price series and the stock price series for different countries? Why or why not, and what would influence such a trend?

8. What were the empirical findings regarding the trend in correlations among foreign stocks over time? What are the implications of this for the portfolio manager interested in international diversification?

9. Briefly discuss the major problems involved in international diversification. Which of the problems is greatest for individuals; which is most important to institutions? Why?

10. Aside from direct investment in foreign stocks, what alternatives are available to an individual for foreign investment? What alternatives can be used by institutions? Discuss each briefly.

References

Agmon, Tamir. "Country Risk: The Significance of the Country Factor for Share Price Movements in the United Kingdom, Germany and Japan." *Journal of Business,* Vol. 46, No. 1 (January, 1973).

Agmon, Tamir. "The Relations Among Equity Markets: A Study of Share Price Co-Movements in the United States, United Kingdom, Germany and Japan." *Journal of Finance,* Vol. 27, No. 4 (September, 1972).

Bergstrom, Gary L. "A New Route to Higher Returns and Lower Risks." *Journal of Portfolio Management,* Vol. 2, No. 1 (Fall, 1975).

Garrone, Francois and Solnik, Bruno. "A Global Approach to Money Management." *Journal of Portfolio Management,* Vol. 2, No. 4 (Summer, 1976).

Grubel, Herbert G. "Internationally Diversified Portfolios: Welfare Gains and Capital Flows." *American Economic Review,* Vol. 58, No. 5 (December, 1968).

Grubel, Herbert G. and Fadner, Kenneth. "The Interdependence of International Equity Markets." *Journal of Finance,* Vol. 26, No. 1 (March, 1971).

Joy, Maurice, Panton, Don, Reilly, Frank K., and Martin, Steve. "Co-Movements of Major International Equity Markets." *The Financial Review* (1976).

Lessard, Donald, R. "International Portfolio Diversification: A Multivariate Analysis for a Group of Latin American Countries." *Journal of Finance,* Vol. 28, No. 3 (June, 1973).

Levy, Haim and Sarnat, Marshall. "International Diversification of Investment Portfolios." *American Economic Review,* Vol. 60, No. 4 (September, 1970).

McDonald, John G. "French Mutual Fund Performance: Evaluation of Internationally Diversified Portfolios." *Journal of Finance,* Vol. 28, No. 5 (December, 1973).

Marjos, Anna. "How to Invest Abroad," *Barron's* (July 24, 1978).

Solnik, Bruno H. "Why Not Diversify Internationally Rather Than Domestically?" *Financial Analysts Journal,* Vol. 30, No. 4 (July–August, 1974).

Chapter 22

Evaluation of Portfolio Performance

Investors have always been interested in evaluating the performance of their portfolios. Even if they do their own analysis, it is both expensive and time consuming to analyze and select stocks for a portfolio, so the individual must determine whether the time and effort were well spent. For an individual or company paying a professional money manager, it is imperative to be able to evaluate his performance and determine whether the results justify the cost of the service. Given the obvious importance of the topic, it is noteworthy that there was little rigorous work in the area prior to the mid-1960's.

It is the purpose of this chapter to outline the evaluation of a portfolio. Initially we will consider what is required of a portfolio manager and discuss how performance was evaluated before portfolio theory and the CAPM were developed. This is followed by a discussion of three major portfolio performance evaluation techniques that consider return and risk (referred to as *composite performance measures*), including applications of these techniques to determine the performance of mutual funds. Some observers have examined these three composite measures of performance and risk and presented evidence that the measures were biased in favor of low risk portfolios. These findings are not universally accepted and, therefore, we will examine the arguments pro and con. Finally, an article by Fama that presents techniques allowing performance to be examined in greater detail is discussed.

What Is Required of a Portfolio Manager?

When evaluating the performance of a portfolio manager, two major factors should be considered:

1. the ability to derive above average returns for a given risk class

2. the ability to diversify (eliminate all unsystematic risk from the portfolio).

In terms of return, the first requirement is obvious, but the necessity of considering *risk* in this context was not always immediately apparent. Risk was typically not dealt with prior to the 1960's, when work in portfolio theory showed its significance. In terms of modern theory, superior risk-adjusted returns can be derived *either* through superior timing or superior stock selection. If a portfolio manager can do a superior job of predicting market turns, he can change his portfolio composition to anticipate the market, investing in a completely diversified portfolio of high beta stocks during a rising market, and in a portfolio of low beta stocks during a declining market, thereby deriving above average risk-adjusted returns. If a portfolio manager and his analysts are able to consistently select under-valued securities for a given risk class, he would also be able to derive above average risk-adjusted returns.

The second factor to consider in evaluating a portfolio manager is his ability to diversify completely. The market only pays returns on the basis of systematic (market) risk. Therefore, investors should not expect to receive returns for assuming unsystematic risk, because this nonmarket risk can be eliminated in a diversified market portfolio of risky assets. Investors consequently want their portfolio to be completely diversified, which means eliminating unsystematic risk. The level of diversification can be judged on the basis of the correlation between the portfolio returns and the returns for a market portfolio; a completely diversified portfolio is perfectly correlated with the market portfolio, which is, in turn, completely diversified.

It is important to be constantly aware of these two requirements of a portfolio manager because some portfolio evaluation techniques take into account one requirement and not the other, and one evaluation technique implicitly takes both into account, but does not differentiate between them.

Composite Performance Measures

Initially investors evaluated portfolios almost entirely on the basis of the rate of return. They were clearly aware of the notion of risk and uncertainty, but did not know how to quantify risk, so they could not consider it explicitly. Developments in portfolio theory in the early 1960's enabled investors to quantify risk in terms of the variability of returns, but there was still no composite measure; it was necessary to consider both factors separately. This is basically the approach used in several early studies.[1] The

---

[1] Irwin Friend, Marshall Blume, and Jean Crockett, *Mutual Funds and Other Institutional Investors* (New York: McGraw–Hill, 1970).

idea was to put portfolios into similar risk classes based upon some measure of risk such as variance of return, and then to directly compare the rates of return for alternative portfolios *within* a risk class.

The Treynor Measure

The first composite measure of portfolio performance (including risk) was developed by Jack Treynor in an article in the *Harvard Business Review*.[2] Treynor recognized that one of the major problems in evaluating portfolio managers was deriving a means of measuring the risk for a portfolio, in the case he dealt with, mutual funds. He contended that there were two components of risk: risk produced by general market fluctuations, and risk resulting from unique fluctuations in the particular securities in the portfolio. To identify the first risk (market fluctuations as related to the portfolio), Treynor introduced the *characteristic line* which defines the relationship between the rates of return for a portfolio over time and the rates of return for an appropriate market portfolio. After discussing some scatter plots of rates of return, he noted that the *slope* of the characteristic line measures the *relative volatility* of the fund's returns in relation to aggregate market returns. In current terms, this slope is the fund's beta coefficient. The higher the slope, the more sensitive the fund is to market returns and the greater its market risk.

The deviations from the characteristic line indicate *unique* returns for the fund relative to the market. These unique portfolio returns are attributable to the unique returns on individual stocks in the portfolio. *If* the fund is properly diversified, these unique returns for individual stocks should *cancel out*. Therefore, deviations from the characteristic line are an indication of the ability of the portfolio manager to properly diversify. The higher the correlation of the fund with the market, the less the unique risk and the better diversified is the portfolio. Because Treynor was not interested in this aspect of portfolio performance, there was no further consideration of the measure of diversification.

Measure of Performance

Treynor was interested in generating a measure of performance that would apply to all investors irrespective of their risk preferences. Based upon developments in capital market theory, he introduced the notion of a risk-free asset that could be acquired by all investors, and he argued that this risk-free asset could be combined with different funds to form a straight *portfolio possibility line*. In a graph, he showed that rational, *risk averse investors would always prefer portfolio possibility lines that have a larger slope* because such high slope lines would place the investor on a higher indif-

---

[2] Jack L. Treynor, "How to Rate Management of Investment Funds," *Harvard Business Review*, Vol. 43, No. 1 (January–February, 1965), pp. 63–75.

ference curve. It was shown that the slope of the *portfolio possibility line* (designated T) is equal to:[3]

$$T = \frac{Ri - RFR}{Bi}$$

where

Ri = the average rate of return for portfolio i during time period i

RFR = the average rate of return on a risk-free investment during time period i

Bi = the slope of the fund's characteristic line which indicates the fund's relative volatility.

With this specification, the larger the T value, the larger the slope and the more preferable the fund is for *all* investors, irrespective of their risk preferences. One can view the numerator of this ratio (Ri − RFR) as the *risk premium* and the denominator as the measure of risk. Therefore, the total expression indicates the fund's *return per unit of risk* and, obviously, all risk averse investors would prefer to maximize this value. The risk variable is *systematic risk* and, as such, indicates nothing about diversification. In fact, this formulation implicitly assumes that the portfolios are perfectly diversified so that systematic risk is the relevant risk measure. When this T value for a fund is compared to a similar measure for the aggregate market, this measure indicates whether the fund would plot above the SML.

Treynor points out that this measure of performance is *not* affected by changing the RFR. The T values may change, but the *ranking* of funds will *not* change. It is possible to have negative T values if the fund has a return below the RFR and a positive beta. Such a value would simply indicate extremely poor management. Alternatively, the author has seen an instance in which the T value was negative because the *beta* was negative and the numerator was not negative.[4] This was an indication of *very good* performance. Normally one would expect a fund with a negative beta to experience a rate of return below the RFR so the numerator *and* the denominator would be negative and the T value would be positive.

The Sharpe Measure[5]

The Sharpe composite measure of portfolio performance follows closely from the author's earlier work on the Capital Asset Pricing Model

---

[3] The terms used in the formula differ from those used by Treynor but are consistent with our earlier discussion.

[4] The instance was the performance by an international mutual fund heavily involved with gold stocks.

[5] William F. Sharpe, "Mutual Fund Performance," *Journal of Business,* Vol. 39, No. 1, Part 2 (January, 1966), pp. 119–138.

(CAPM).[6] He assumed that all investors are able to borrow or lend at the risk-free rate, and that all investors share the same set of expectations. Under these conditions, all *efficient* portfolios will fall along a straight line of the form:

$$ER_i = RFR + b\sigma_i$$

where

ER_i = the expected rate of return on portfolio i

RFR = the risk-free rate of return

   b = the risk premium which will be positive since investors are assumed to be risk averse

σ_i = the standard deviation of returns for portfolio i.

Given this capital market line (CML) and the assumption that investors can borrow or lend at the risk-free rate, an investor can attain any point on the line

$$ER = RFR + \left(\frac{ER_i - RFR}{\sigma_i} \right)$$

This means that any portfolio will give rise to a complete linear set of E, σ combinations, as shown in the capital asset discussion. In such a case, the best portfolio will be the one giving the best boundary, which is the portfolio with the highest ratio of $(ER_i - RFR)/\sigma_i$. If another portfolio is efficient, it must lie along the common line and give the same ratio. In order to use this theory to test *ex post* returns, it is necessary to progress from expectations to average rates of return and the actual standard deviation of returns for alternative portfolios. Therefore, in practice, the Sharpe measure (designated S) is stated as follows:

$$S = \frac{R_i - RFR}{V_i}$$

where:

R_i = the average rate of return for portfolio i during a specified time period

RFR = the average risk-free rate that prevailed during the time period

V_i = the standard deviation of the rate of return during the time period.

---

[6] William F. Sharpe, "Capital Asset Prices: A Theory of Market Equilibrium Under Conditions of Risk," *Journal of Finance,* Vol. 19, No. 4 (September, 1964), pp. 425–442.

This measure can be used to rank the performance of mutual funds or other portfolios, but this ranking will *not* be affected by changes in the RFR since they will affect all values. Also, by computing the measure for the aggregate market, this measure can likewise be used to examine the performance of portfolios relative to the aggregate market.

Treynor Versus Sharpe Measure

The Sharpe measure uses the standard deviation of returns as the measure of risk, while the Treynor measure employs beta (systematic risk). The Sharpe measure, therefore, implicitly evaluates the portfolio manager on the basis of return performance, but *also* takes into account how well diversified the portfolio was during this period. If a portfolio is perfectly diversified (does not contain any unsystematic risk), the two measures would give identical rankings because the total variance of the portfolio would be the systematic variance. If a portfolio is poorly diversified, it is possible for it to have a high ranking on the basis of the Treynor measure, but a much lower ranking on the basis of the Sharpe measure. Any difference should be directly attributable to the poor diversification of the portfolio. Therefore, the two measures provide *complementary* but *different* information and *both measures should be derived.* As pointed out by Sharpe, if one is dealing with a well diversified group of portfolios, such as mutual funds, the two measures will provide very similar rankings. Because Sharpe felt the variability due to unsystematic risk was probably transitory, he felt that the Treynor measure might be a better measure for predicting future performance, and his results generally confirmed this expectation.

The Jensen Measure[7]

The Jensen measure is similar to the measures already discussed in that it is based upon the Capital Asset Pricing Model (CAPM). All versions of the CAPM indicate the following expression for the expected one period return on any security or portfolio:

$$E(R_j) = RFR + B_j \left[E(R_m) - RFR \right]$$

where:

$E(R_j)$ = the expected return on security or portfolio j

RFR = the one period risk-free interest rate

B_j = the systematic risk for security or portfolio j

$E(R_m)$ = the expected return on the market portfolio of risky assets.

---

[7] Michael C. Jensen, "The Performance of Mutual Funds in the Period 1945–1964," *Journal of Finance*, Vol. 23, No. 2 (May, 1968), pp. 389–416.

It has been shown that the single period models can be extended to a multiperiod world in which investors have heterogeneous horizons and trading takes place continuously.[8] Therefore, the equation above can be generalized as follows:

$$E(R_{jt}) = RFR_t + B_j\left[E(R_{mt}) - RFR_t\right]$$

Each of the expected returns and the risk-free return are different for different periods. Therefore, we are concerned with the time series of expected rates of return for security j or portfolio j. Moreover, assuming that the asset pricing model is empirically valid, it is possible to express the expectations formula in terms of *realized* rates of return as follows:

$$R_{jt} = RFR_t + B_j\left[R_{mt} - RFR_t\right] + U_{jt}$$

This indicates that the *realized* rate of return on a security or portfolio should be a linear function of the risk-free rate of return during the period, plus some risk premium that is a function of the security's systematic risk during the period, plus a random error term.

If the risk-free return is subtracted from both sides we have:

$$R_{jt} - RFR_t = B_j\left[R_{mt} - RFR_t\right] + U_{jt}$$

This indicates that the risk premium earned on the jth security or portfolio is equal to B_j times a market risk premium plus a random error term. In this form, one would not expect an intercept for the regression if all assets and portfolios were in equilibrium. If a portfolio manager is a superior forecaster, he will consistently select undervalued securities and his risk premiums will therefore exceed those implied by the market; i.e., he will have consistently positive random errors. To detect such superior performance, it is necessary that the regression not be constrained to go through the intercept (i.e., force it to be zero). If we allow for a possible nonzero constant, this equation becomes:

$$R_{jt} - RFR_t = \alpha_j + B_j\left[R_{mt} - RFR_t\right] + U_{jt}$$

Given this equation, the α_j indicates whether the portfolio manager is superior or inferior in market timing or stock selection. If he is superior, the α will be a *significant positive value;* if he is inferior, α will be a *significant negative value,* indicating that the manager consistently underperformed the market. Finally, if the portfolio manager has no forecasting ability, which means his performance is equal to a naive buy-and-hold policy, the α will be insignificantly different from zero.

---

[8] Michael C. Jensen, "Risk, The Pricing of Capital Assets, and the Evaluation of Investment Portfolios," *Journal of Business,* Vol. 42, No. 2 (April, 1969), pp. 167–247.

This measure is very useful because it allows the investigator to determine whether the abnormal returns are *statistically significant* (positive or negative). Also, the α represents the average incremental rate of return on the portfolio per unit of time which is attributable to the manager's ability to derive above average returns *adjusted for risk.* These superior risk-adjusted returns can be caused by the fact that the manager is good at predicting market turns, or because he has the ability to forecast the behavior of prices of individual issues in the portfolio.

The Jensen formulation requires a different RFR to be used for each time interval during the sample period. If one is examining the performance of a fund manager over a ten year period using yearly intervals, it is necessary to examine the annual returns for the fund for each year, less the return on risk-free assets for each year, and to relate this to the annual return on the market portfolio less the same risk-free rate. This contrasts with other techniques that examine *the average returns for the total period* for all variables (the fund, the market, and the risk-free asset). Also, the Jensen measure, like the Treynor measure, does *not* evaluate the ability of the portfolio manager to diversify, because it only examines risk premiums in terms of *systematic* risk. When evaluating the performance of a group of well-diversified portfolios like mutual funds, this is probably a fairly legitimate assumption. In Jensen's analysis of mutual fund performance, it was shown that assuming diversification was valid since the correlations of the funds with the market typically exceeded .90.

Application of Performance Measures

In order to demonstrate how one applies these measures, we selected 20 open-end mutual funds for which data was available for the 15 year period 1962–1976. The specific results for the first fund (Affiliated Fund, Inc.) are contained in Table 22–1. The returns are the total returns for each year computed as follows:

$$R_{it} = \frac{EP_{it} + Div_{it} + Cap.Dist._{it} - BP_{it}}{BP_{it}}$$

where:

R_{it} = total return on fund i during year t

EP_{it} = ending price for fund i during year t

$Cap. Dist._{it}$ = capital gain distributions made by fund i during year t

Div_{it} = dividend payment made by fund i during year t

BP_{it} = beginning price for fund i during year t.

As computed, these returns do not take into account any sales charge by the funds. Given the fund's results for each year, and the aggregate market (represented by the S&P 500), it is possible to compute the composite measures presented at the bottom of the table. As shown, the arithmetic average annual rate of return for Affiliated was above that for the market (8.43 vs. 7.65), and the fund's beta was below 1.00 (0.889). Therefore, the Treynor measure for the fund was *above* the same measure for the market (3.837 vs. 2.630). Likewise, the standard deviation of returns was below the market's (16.53 vs. 17.26), so the Sharpe measure for the fund was also above the measure for the market (.206 vs. .152). Finally, the regression of the fund's annual risk premium ($R_{it} - RFR_t$) and the market's annual risk premium ($R_{mt} - RFR_t$) indicated a positive intercept (constant) value of 1.081 that was not statistically significant. If the value was significant, it would have indicated that Affiliated, on average, earned a risk-adjusted annual rate of return that was about one percent above the market average.

Table 22–1
Example of Computation of Portfolio Evaluation Measures Using Affiliated Fund, Inc.

Year	R_{it}	R_{mt}	RFR_t	$R_{it} - RFR_t$	$R_{mt} - RFR_t$
1962	−8.9	−8.8	2.8	−11.7	−11.6
1963	18.2	21.2	3.2	15.0	18.0
1964	16.1	17.6	3.6	12.5	14.0
1965	11.7	12.3	4.0	7.7	8.3
1966	−6.5	−10.0	4.9	−11.4	−14.9
1967	22.0	23.7	4.3	17.7	19.4
1968	17.1	10.8	5.3	11.8	5.5
1969	−14.6	−8.0	6.7	−21.3	−14.7
1970	1.7	3.2	6.4	−4.7	−3.2
1971	8.0	14.1	4.3	3.7	9.8
1972	11.5	18.7	4.1	7.4	14.6
1973	−5.8	−14.5	7.0	−12.8	−21.5
1974	−15.6	−26.0	7.9	−23.5	−33.9
1975	38.4	36.9	5.8	32.6	31.1
1976	33.2	23.6	5.0	28.2	18.6

$\bar{R}_i = 8.43$ $\sigma_i = 16.53$ $\bar{B}_i = 0.889$ $R_{im}^2 = .891$

$\bar{R}_m = 7.65$ $\sigma_m = 17.26$ $\overline{RFR} = 5.02$

$T_i = \dfrac{8.43 - 5.02}{0.889} = 3.837$ $S_i = \dfrac{8.43 - 5.02}{16.53} = .206$ $T_m = \dfrac{7.65 - 5.02}{1.00} = 2.630$

$S_m = \dfrac{7.65 - 5.02}{17.26} = .152$

$R_{it} - RFR_t = 1.081 + 0.889 \, (R_{mt} - RFR_t)$

Overall Results An analysis of the overall results in Table 22–2 indicates that they are generally consistent with the findings of earlier studies, even though our sample selection was rather casual because it was only made for demonstration purposes. The mean return for all the funds was quite close to the market return (7.61 vs. 7.65). If *only* the rate of return was considered, 12 of the 20 funds performed better than the market did.

The R^2 for a portfolio with the market fund can be used as a measure of diversification, and the closer it is to 1.00, the more perfectly diversified it is. Although the average R^2 is reasonably good at .794, the range is quite large, from .437 to .985. This indicates that a number of funds are not well-diversified.

The two risk measures (standard deviation and beta) likewise show a wide range, but are generally consistent with expectations. Specifically, 14 of the 20 funds had a standard deviation that was larger than the market's, and the mean was also larger (20.48 vs. 17.26). This larger standard deviation is consistent with the lack of complete diversification. Only seven of the funds had a beta above 1.00, but the average beta is above one (1.013).

The performance of individual funds was very consistent for alternative measures. Using the Sharpe measure, eight of the 20 funds had a higher value than the market did; using the Treynor measure, nine of the 20 funds were above the market, while the Jensen measure indicated that nine of the 20 had positive intercepts, but only four of the positive intercepts were statistically significant. The mean values for all of the composite measures were below the figure for the aggregate market. These results indicate that, on average, this sample of funds did not perform as well as the market did.

Finally, an analysis of the ranks of the funds, using the alternative measures, indicates *almost identical rankings,* as shown by the ranks in parentheses. The specific rank correlations are:

Sharpe–Treynor: .992

Sharpe–Jensen: .994

Treynor–Jensen: .990

An analysis of the individual funds is left to the reader, but it should include a consideration of each of the components: return, risk (both standard deviation and beta), and the R^2 as a measure of diversification. One might expect the best performance to be generated by funds with low diversification since these funds are apparently attempting to beat the market by being "unique" in their selection or timing.

Potential Bias of One Parameter Measure
A study done by Friend and Blume reviewed the various one parameter measures and indicated to what extent they were consistent with the

Table 22–2 Performance Measures for 20 Selected Mutual Funds: 1962–1976

	Return	σ	Beta	R²	Sharpe		Treynor		Jensen	
1. Affiliated Fund, Inc.	8.43	16.53	0.889	.891	.206	(4)	3.837	(4)	1.081	(5)
2. Anchor Growth Fund, Inc.	4.31	25.05	1.167	.669	-.028	(19)	-.608	(19)	-3.782	(20)
3. Dividend Shares, Inc.	6.50	15.38	0.869	.985	.096	(13)	1.702	(15)	-.815ᵃ	(14)
4. Energy Fund, Inc.	8.31	19.19	0.967	.783	.171	(6)	3.402	(6)	.754	(6)
5. Fidelity Fund, Inc.	7.70	15.98	0.883	.941	.168	(7)	3.036	(7)	.342	(8)
6. Fundamental Investors, Inc.	4.98	18.01	0.984	.920	-.002	(18)	-.041	(18)	-2.642ᵃ	(18)
7. Guardian Mutual Fund	9.87	17.25	0.944	.923	.281	(2)	5.140	(3)	2.368ᵃ	(2)
8. Istel Fund, Inc.	9.10	16.79	0.678	.503	.243	(3)	6.018	(2)	2.240	(3)
9. Lexington Research Fund, Inc.	7.89	20.31	1.104	.911	.141	(9)	2.600	(10)	-.020	(10)
10. Mass. Investors Growth Stock Fund	5.34	18.90	0.934	.752	.017	(17)	0.343	(17)	-2.177	(17)
11. Oppenheimer Fund, Inc.	8.93	20.94	1.032	.749	.187	(5)	3.787	(5)	1.189	(4)
12. Philadelphia Fund, Inc.	8.09	18.69	1.023	.923	.164	(8)	3.001	(8)	.385	(7)
13. T. Rowe Price Growth Stock Fund	5.52	19.14	0.982	.812	.026	(16)	0.509	(16)	-2.101	(16)
14. The Putnam Growth Fund, Inc.	6.83	18.93	0.980	.799	.096	(13)	1.847	(14)	-.768	(13)
15. Scudder Special Fund, Inc.	8.37	29.58	1.410	.700	.113	(12)	2.376	(12)	-.338	(12)
16. Security Equity Fund, Inc.	14.41	30.18	1.137	.437	.311	(1)	8.261	(1)	6.327	(1)
17. Sigma Investment Shares, Inc.	7.48	17.89	0.956	.880	.137	(11)	2.573	(11)	-.068	(11)
18. Technology Fund, Inc.	7.69	19.07	0.984	.821	.140	(10)	2.712	(9)	.083	(9)
19. Value Line Special Situations Fund	8.54	39.93	1.689	.552	.088	(15)	2.084	(13)	-.865	(15)
20. Wellington Fund, Inc.	3.98	11.89	0.652	.926	-.087	(20)	-1.717	(20)	-2.793ᵃ	(20)
Means	7.61	20.48	1.013	.794	.123		2.543		-.080	
S&P 500	7.65	17.26	1.000	1.000	.152		2.630		0	
90-day T-Bill Rate	5.02	1.48								

ᵃ Significant at .05 level
Rank in parentheses

CAPM.[9] They pointed out that, theoretically, the three one-parameter measures of performance should be independent of corresponding measures of risk because the performance measures specifically consider risk—i.e., they are *risk-adjusted* measures. This may *not* be true if one or more of the following conditions pertain:

1. The assumptions underlying the market line theory are invalid.
2. The actual distributions of return and risk differ substantially from *ex ante* expectations.
3. Measurement errors caused biased estimates of the relation between risk and return.
4. There are real systematic differences among the risk-adjusted performances of portfolios.

The authors analyzed the relationship between the one parameter measures of performance and risk by examining the performance and risk measures for 200 random portfolios. These portfolios were selected from among 788 common stocks listed on the New York Stock Exchange during the period January, 1960 through June, 1968. The 200 random portfolios included 50 individual portfolios consisting of 25 securities, and 50 portfolios consisting of 50, 75, and 100 stocks respectively. An equal investment in each stock was assumed. The three composite performance measures were computed for each of the 200 random portfolios, and these performance measures were regressed against two measures of portfolio risk. The two measures of risk were the beta coefficients for the portfolios, and the standard deviation of portfolio returns. *In all cases, the risk-adjusted performance measure was highly correlated with risk.* There was a significant *inverse* relationship between the performance measure and the risk measure (the risk adjusted performance of low risk portfolios was better than the comparable performance for high risk portfolios). The authors contend that, for the period covered, the best way of insuring good performance was to select a low risk portfolio. To determine whether the analysis was consistent for periods prior to 1960, the authors examined the results reported by Jensen in his *Journal of Finance* article covering the period 1945 to 1964. Variables for this time period were estimated using annual, rather than monthly, data. Friend and Blume related the Jensen measure to corresponding beta coefficients for the portfolio as reported by Jensen. Again the results indicated that the risk-adjusted performance and risk were *inversely correlated* to a high degree, with the riskiest portfolios performing much worse than the less risky portfolios did. The results of the regression test by Friend and Blume can be seen in Table 22–3. The results

---

[9] Irwin Friend and Marshall Blume, "Measurement of Portfolio Performance Under Uncertainty," *American Economic Review*, Vol. 60, No. 4 (September, 1970), pp. 561–575.

Table 22–3
Regressions of One Parameter Performance Measures on Risk Random Portfolios, January 1960–June 1968

Performance Measure	=	a	+	b Risk Measure	$\bar{R}^2$	Standard Error
1) S	=	0.2677 (45.50)	−	0.0557 X_1 (−9.17)	0.2944	0.0215
2) S	=	0.2724 (42.00)	−	1.3614 X_2 (−9.01)	0.2871	0.0216
3) T	=	0.0134 (45.10)	−	0.0039 X_1 (−12.82)	0.4510	0.0011
4) T	=	0.0136 (39.82)	−	0.0921 X_2 (−11.59)	0.4012	0.0011
5) J	=	0.0028 (11.34)	−	0.0018 X_1 (−7.13)	0.2004	0.0009
6) J	=	0.0029 (10.42)	−	0.0429 X_2 (−6.61)	0.1768	0.0009
7) S'	=	0.2648 (44.57)	−	0.0741 X_1' (−12.04)	0.4199	0.0214
8) S'	=	0.2714 (41.49)	−	1.8356 X_2' (−11.91)	0.4146	0.0215
9) T'	=	0.0130 (44.98)	−	0.0046 X_1' (−15.29)	0.5391	0.0010
10) T'	=	0.0133 (39.92)	−	0.1097 X_2' (−13.99)	0.4946	0.0011
11) J'	=	0.0345 (31.04)	−	0.0311 X_1' (−27.03)	0.7857	0.0040
12) J'	=	0.0372 (29.80)	−	0.7698 X_2' (−26.16)	0.7745	0.0041

Source: Irwin Friend and Marshall Blume, "Measurement of Portfolio Performance Under Uncertainty," *American Economic Review*, Vol. 60, No. 4 (September, 1970), p. 566. Reprinted by permission.

S represents the Sharpe measure of performance; T represents the Treynor measure of performance; J represents the Jensen measure of performance; X_1 represents the *beta* coefficient of a random portfolio; X_2 represents the standard deviation of portfolio return; R^2 represents the coefficient of determination adjusted for degrees of freedom.

The figures in parentheses are t-values. The unprimed variables are calculated using monthly relatives; the primed variables using the logarithm of the monthly relatives.

of the comparison with the Jensen performance measure are contained in the scatter plot in Figure 22–1.

Because these results indicated a biased relationship between the one parameter measures and the overall risk of the portfolios, the authors dealt with which of the four factors mentioned earlier was responsible for the bias. They considered the several assumptions that underlie the market line theory as potential causes, and concluded that the most important assumption violated, which would explain the bias, is the unrealistic assumption of equal borrowing and lending rates. Investors in risky portfolios do not have

Figure 22–1
**Scatter Diagram
of Jensen's
Peformance
Measure[a] on Risk
January 1960–
June 1968**

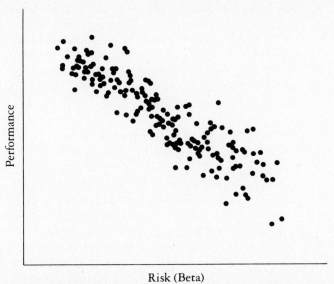

Performance

Risk (Beta)

[a] Using *log relatives*.

Source: Irwin Friend and Marshall Blume, "Measurement of Portfolio Performance Under
Uncertainty," *American Economic Review,* Vol. 60, No. 4 (September, 1970), p. 567.
Reprinted by permission.

the option of increasing their return for a given level of risk by moving to a
portfolio containing additional stocks financed by borrowing at the risk-
free lending rate. As a consequence, the risk-adjusted returns received by
investors in high risk portfolios would be below the returns received by
those investing in low risk portfolios, because the assumption of being able
to *lend* at the risk-free rate is legitimate, but the assumption of being able to
borrow at this rate is not.

Another explanation of the bias is that the actual distributions of return
and risk differ substantially from prior expectations. To examine this
possibility, the total period was broken down into two segments, January,
1960 through March, 1964, and April, 1964 through June, 1968. The
latter segment corresponds to a period of speculative fervor and rapidly
rising stock prices. During the first segment most of the tendencies that
characterized the total period are observed in even stronger form; there was
a *more significant negative correlation* between performance and risk measures.
For the second segment, however, the situation was reversed and the
correlations between performance and risk measures are *significantly positive*
and the slope coefficients are sizable. These differential results can be
explained by a difference between actual and expected returns. During the
second period, risky portfolios did not perform as badly as usual because the
high risk portfolios earned more than expected during this period of
speculative fever.

The authors concluded that improved measures of portfolio performance could be obtained by adjusting the various measures for the potential bias that existed during that particular period. However, even this assumption would give somewhat uncertain results and Friend and Blume contend that it is probably preferable, given the present stage of knowledge, to use the traditional two separate parameters (the rate of return and the risk) to measure portfolio performance, rather than the more elegant, but possibly more dangerous, composite measures.

Alternative View Regarding Bias

A later paper by Robert Klemkosky considered this bias and tested it on a number of actual portfolios.[10] The Klemkosky study examined the relationship between composite performance measures and risk measures using *actual* mutual fund data for the period 1966–1971, in contrast to the *random* portfolio data used by Friend and Blume. The data consisted of quarterly rates of return for 40 mutual funds during the 24 quarter period 1966–1971. The author derived the three composite measures as developed by Sharpe, Treynor, and Jensen, but also added two measures that computed the excess return above the risk-free rate similar to those used by Sharpe and Treynor but which utilized as risk proxies the semistandard deviation and the mean absolute deviation.

The results indicated that the composite performance measures were biased in a *positive* direction. There was a *positive* relationship between the performance derived by the mutual funds and the risk involved. This was especially true for the Treynor and Jensen measures. The performance measures incorporating the mean absolute deviation and the semistandard deviation as risk proxies were less biased than the three measures derived from the Capital Asset Pricing Model were. Because the time period for this study included a very strong bear market in 1969–1970, and a declining market in 1971, it is unlikely that the *ex post* returns were higher than *ex ante* expectations, or that *ex post* risk was lower than *ex ante* values. It was concluded that the normal bias may *not* be an inverse relationship between the composite performance measures and the risk measures, but that, in fact, there might be a positive relationship.

Comment on Jensen Study

An article by Mains commented on Jensen's study of mutual fund performance.[11] Mains was concerned with biases introduced because of the way Jensen computed rates of return for the mutual funds and the measures of risk used in the study. There was *no criticism* of Jensen's general methodol-

---

[10] Robert C. Klemkosky, "The Bias in Composite Performance Measures," *Journal of Financial and Quantitative Analysis,* Vol. 8, No. 3 (June, 1973), pp. 505–514.

[11] Norman E. Mains, "Risk, the Pricing of Capital Assets, and the Evaluation of Investment Portfolios: Comment," *Journal of Business,* Vol. 50, No. 3 (July, 1977), pp. 371–384.

ogy for evaluating portfolio performance. The only concern was with the empirical estimates used to evaluate mutual fund performance.[12]

Components of Investment Performance

In addition to the performance measures developed by Treynor, Sharpe, and Jensen, Fama suggested a somewhat finer breakdown of performance.[13] As is true with earlier measures, the underlying philosophy of Fama's evaluation was that the returns on managed portfolios can be judged relative to those of "naively selected" portfolios with similar levels of risk. The technique begins by using the simple one period version of the two parameter model and all the perfect market assumptions. The author briefly derives the *ex ante* market line which indicates that the equilibrium relationship between expected return and risk for any security j is

$$E(\tilde{R}_j) = R_f + \left[\frac{E(\tilde{R}m) - R_f}{\sigma(\tilde{R}m)} \right] \frac{Cov.(\tilde{R}j, \tilde{R}m)}{\sigma(\tilde{R}m)}$$

Cov.(Rj, Rm) is the covariance between the returns for security j and the return on the market portfolio. According to this equation, the expected return on security j is the riskless rate of interest, R_f, plus a risk premium that is $[E(\tilde{R}m) - R_f]/\sigma(\tilde{R}m)$, called the market price per unit of risk, times the risk of asset j which is $[cov. (\tilde{R}_j, \tilde{R}m)]/\sigma(\tilde{R}m)$.

This market line relationship should hold for portfolios as well as for individual assets. This *ex ante* model assumes completely efficient markets in which prices fully reflect all available information. Assuming a portfolio manager believes that the market is not completely efficient, and that he can make better judgments than the market can, then an *ex post* version of this market line can provide a benchmark for the manager's performance. Given that the risk variable, $cov.(R_j, Rm)/\sigma(Rm)$, can be denoted B_j, the *ex post* market line is as follows:

$$Rx = R_f + \left(\frac{Rm - R_f}{\sigma(Rm)} \right) Bx$$

This *ex post* market line provides the benchmark used to evaluate "managed" portfolios in a sequence of more complex measures.

---

[12] A recent article by Roll points out ambiguities with the performance measures because of problems with estimates of the security market line. See Richard Roll, "Ambiguities When Performance Is Measured by the Securities Market Line," *Journal of Finance,* Vol. 33, No. 4 (September, 1978), pp. 1051–1069.

[13] Eugene F. Fama, "Components of Investment Performance," *Journal of Finance,* Vol. 27, No. 3 (June, 1972), pp. 551–567.

Evaluating Selectivity   Assuming Ra is the return on the portfolio being evaluated and Rx(Ba) is the return on the combination of the riskless asset f and the market portfolio m that has risk Bx equal to Ba, the risk of the portfolio being evaluated, the performance is as follows:

$$\text{Selectivity} = \text{Ra} - \text{Rx(Ba)}$$

As shown in Figure 22–2, selectivity is a measure of how well the chosen portfolio did relative to a naively selected portfolio of equal risk. This measure indicates any difference from the *ex post* market line and is similar to the other measures, most specifically Treynor's.

It is also possible to examine *overall performance* in terms of selectivity, considered above, and the returns from assuming risk, as follows:

$$\begin{array}{cccc} \text{Overall} & & & \\ \text{Performance} = & \text{Selectivity} & + & \text{Risk} \\ [\text{Ra} - \text{R}_f] = & [\text{Ra} - \text{Rx(Ba)}] & + & [\text{Rx(Ba)} - \text{R}_f] \end{array}$$

As shown in figure 22–2, overall performance is the total return above the risk-free return and includes the return that *should* have been received for accepting the portfolio risk (Ba). This "expected" return is equal to [Rx(Ba) − Rf]. Any excess over this expected return is due to selectivity.

Evaluating Diversification The difference between the Treynor and Sharpe measures is that the former uses systematic risk (Bi), and the latter, total risk (σ_i). If a portfolio is *completely* diversified and, therefore, (by definition) does not have any unsystematic risk remaining, then its *total* risk will equal its systematic risk and the two techniques will give equal rankings. However, if a portfolio manager attempts to select undervalued stocks and, in the process, gives up some diversification, it is possible to generate another measure of the added return that will be necessary to justify this decision. The portfolio's selectivity is made up of *net selectivity* plus diversification as follows:

$$\begin{array}{cc} \text{Selectivity} & \text{Diversification} \\ [\text{Ra} - \text{Rx(Ba)}] = \text{Net Selectivity} + & [\text{Rx}(\sigma(\text{Ra})) - \text{Rx(Ba)}] \end{array}$$

or

$$\begin{array}{cc} \text{Selectivity} & - \quad \text{Diversification} \\ \text{Net Selectivity} = [\text{Ra} - \text{Rx(Ba)}] - & [\text{Rx}(\sigma(\text{Ra})) - \text{Rx(Ba)}] \end{array}$$

$$= \text{Ra} - \text{Rx}(\sigma(\text{Ra}))$$

where $\text{Rx}(\sigma(\text{Ra}))$ is the return on the combination of the riskless asset f and the market portfolio m that has return dispersion equivalent to that of the

Figure 22–2 **An Illustration of the Performance Measures**

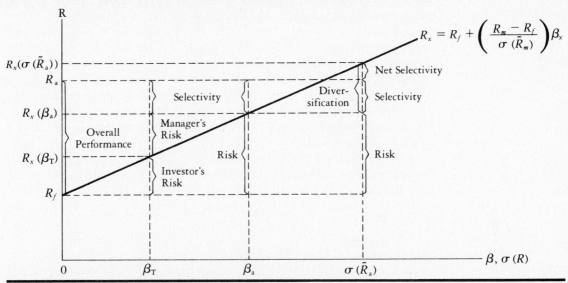

Source: Eugene F. Fama, "Components of Investment Performance," *Journal of Finance,*
Vol. 27, No. 3 (June, 1972), p. 588. Reprinted by permission.

portfolio being evaluated. Therefore, the diversification measure indicates the *added* return that must be derived to justify any loss of diversification in the portfolio. The term emphasizes the fact that diversification is the elimination of all unsystematic variability. If the portfolio is completely diversified so that total risk (σ) is equal to systematic risk (β), then the $Rx(\sigma(Ra))$ would be the same as $Rx(Ba)$, and the diversification term would equal zero. A comparison of the added return because of poor diversification and the R^2 for the funds with the market should confirm the use of the R^2 as a measure of diversification. The *higher* the R^2, the better diversified the portfolio and the *lower* the added required return to compensate for poor diversification. Because the diversification measure is always non-negative, net selectivity will always be equal to or less than selectivity (they will be equal when the portfolio is completely diversified). There may be cases in which the investor is not concerned with diversification of the portfolio being evaluated, so this particular breakdown will not be important and only gross selectivity will be considered.

Evaluating Risk It is possible to evaluate risk if it is assumed that the investor has a target level of risk for his portfolio equal to B_T. Under such an assumption, the overall performance due to risk (the total return above the risk-free return) can be assessed as follows:

$$\text{Risk} = \text{Manager's Risk} + \text{Investor's Risk}$$
$$[Rx(Ba) - R_f] = [Rx(Ba) - Rx(B_T)] + [Rx(B_T) - R_f]$$

$Rx(B_T)$ is the return on the naively selected portfolio with the target level of market risk (B_T). If the portfolio risk is equal to the target risk ($Ba = B_T$), then there is no manager's risk. If there is a difference between Ba and B_T, then the manager's risk is the return the manager must earn due to his decision to accept risk (Ba) which is different from the risk desired by the investor (B_T). The investor's risk is the return expected because the investor stipulated some positive level of risk. This evaluation can be done only if the client has specified his desired level of market risk, which is usually the case with pensions and profit sharing plans. Unfortunately, it is not possible to apply the measure for *ex post* evaluations, because the desired risk level is typically not available.

Fama made some further breakdowns in terms of timing ability, but these require an estimate of the expected market return during the period which is usually not available. Therefore, we will not discuss these measures but, if market return estimates are available, it is suggested that they be considered.

Application of Fama Measures

Several of the components of performance suggested by Fama can be used in *ex post* evaluation, as shown in Table 22–4. Overall performance is the excess return derived above the risk-free return (i.e., the return above 5.02 percent). All but two of the mutual funds considered experienced positive overall performance. The next step is to determine how much the portfolio (fund) should receive for the systematic risk that it contained, using the following expected return equation for this period:

$$E(R_i) = 5.02 + B_i(7.65 - 5.02)$$
$$= 5.02 + B_i(2.63)$$

The required return for risk is simply the latter expression: $B_i(2.63)$. The required return for risk for Affiliated Fund was: $0.889(2.63) = 2.34$ percent. *The return for selectivity is the difference between overall performance and risk.* If the overall performance exceeds the required return for risk, the portfolio has experienced a positive return for selectivity. The results indicate that Affiliated had an average annual return of 1.07 percent for selectivity $(3.41 - 2.34)$. A total of nine funds had positive returns for selectivity. Although some funds had positive overall performance, their required return for risk exceeded this figure, giving them negative returns for selectivity.

The next three columns indicate the effect of diversification on performance. The diversification term indicates the required return for not being completely diversified (i.e., total risk above systematic risk). If a fund's total risk is equal to its systematic risk, then the ratio of its total risk to the market's total risk will equal its beta; if this is not the case, then the ratio of total risk will be greater than the beta and will indicate the added return

Table 22-4 Components of Performance for 20 Selected Mutual Funds: 1962-1976

	Overall Performance	Selectivity	Risk	Net Selectivity	Selectivity	Diversification
1. Affiliated Fund, Inc.	3.41	1.07	2.34	0.89	1.07	.18
2. Anchor Growth Fund, Inc.	−0.71	−3.78	3.07	−4.53	−3.78	.75
3. Dividend Shares, Inc.	1.48	−.81	2.29	−.86	−.81	.05
4. Energy Fund, Inc.	3.29	.75	2.54	.37	.75	.38
5. Fidelity Fund, Inc.	2.68	.36	2.32	.24	.36	.12
6. Fundamental Investors, Inc.	0.04	−2.63	2.67	−2.78	−2.63	.15
7. Guardian Mutual Fund	4.85	2.37	2.48	2.22	2.37	.15
8. Istel Fund, Inc.	4.08	2.30	1.78	1.52	2.30	.78
9. Lexington Research Fund, Inc.	2.87	−.03	2.90	−.22	−.03	.19
10. Mass. Investors Growth Stock Fund	0.32	−2.14	2.46	−2.56	−2.14	.42
11. Oppenheimer Fund, Inc.	3.91	1.20	2.71	.72	1.20	.48
12. Philadelphia Fund, Inc.	3.07	.38	2.69	.22	.38	.16
13. T. Rowe Price Growth Stock Fund	0.50	−2.08	2.58	−2.42	−2.08	.34
14. The Putnam Growth Fund, Inc.	1.81	−.77	2.58	−1.07	−.77	.30
15. Scudder Special Fund, Inc.	3.35	−.36	3.71	−1.16	−.36	.80
16. Security Equity Fund, Inc.	9.39	6.40	2.99	4.79	6.40	1.61
17. Sigma Investment Shares, Inc.	2.46	−.05	2.41	−.27	−.05	.22
18. Technology Fund, Inc.	2.67	.08	2.59	−.24	.08	.32
19. Value Line Special Situations Fund	3.52	−.92	4.44	−2.56	−.92	1.64
20. Wellington Fund, Inc.	−1.04	−2.75	1.71	−2.85	−2.75	.10

required because of incomplete diversification. In the case of Affiliated, the ratio of total risk was:

$$\frac{\sigma_i}{\sigma_m} = \frac{16.53}{17.26} = .958$$

This compares to the fund's beta of .889, indicating that the fund is not completely diversified, which is consistent with the R^2 of .891 (see Table 22–2). The fund's required return given their standard deviation is:

$$R_i = 5.02 + .958(2.63)$$

$$= 7.54$$

Their required return for systematic risk was 7.36. The difference of 0.18 (7.54 − 7.36) is the added return required because of less than perfect diversification. As can be seen in Table 22–2, Dividend Shares, Inc. has an

R^2 of .985 and, therefore, a required diversification return of only 0.05 percent. In contrast, Security Equity Fund has an R^2 of .437, and a required diversification return of 1.61 percent. This required diversification return is subtracted from the selectivity return to arrive at *net* selectivity. Affiliated had a gross selectivity of 1.07 and a diversification of 0.18, indicating a return for *net* selectivity of 0.89 which would indicate that, even accounting for the added cost of not being completely diversified, the Fund's performance was above the market line. Security Equity Fund, on the other hand, obviously decided against diversification in favor of specific selections. Even after a substantial required return for not being diversified (1.61), its return for net selectivity was almost 5 percent. Eight of the funds had positive net selectivity returns.

Application of Evaluation Techniques

The answers generated using these performance measures are only as good as the data inputs. Therefore it is necessary to be careful in computing the rates of return and take proper account of all inflows and outflows. More important, it is necessary to use judgment in the evaluation process. Just as Rome was not built in a day, it is not possible to properly evaluate a portfolio manager on the basis of performance during a quarter or even a year. The evaluation should extend over a number of years and cover *at least* a full market cycle. This will make it possible to determine whether there is any difference in performance during rising or declining markets.

Summary

This chapter was intended as a discussion of portfolio performance evaluation and of the several techniques that can be used in making such an evaluation. The first major goal of portfolio management is to derive rates of returns that equal or exceed the returns on a naively selected portfolio with equal risk. The second goal is to attain complete diversification. Prior to the development of capital market theory, portfolio managers were only judged on the basis of the rate of return they achieved, with no consideration of risk. Risk was later considered, but in a not very rigorous manner. Since 1965, three major techniques have been derived, based upon the Capital Asset Pricing Model, which provide a *composite* measure of performance. The first was developed by Treynor to measure the excess returns earned per unit of *systematic* risk. The Sharpe measure indicates the excess return per unit of *total* risk. The third technique, developed by Jensen, likewise is used to evaluate performance in terms of the systematic risk involved, but the measure also makes it possible to determine whether the difference in risk-adjusted performance (good or bad) is statistically significant.

The application of the evaluation techniques to a selected sample of 20 mutual funds indicated the importance of considering both risk and return because the different funds presented a wide range of total risk and systematic risk. We also discussed how differences in diversification could influence the rankings generated using different performance measures. The rank correlations among the alternative measures were extremely high, about .99.

A paper by Friend and Blume contended that the various composite measures provided biased results; i.e., there was an inverse relationship between the risk of the portfolio and its composite performance. A subsequent paper by Klemkosky indicated a completely different bias. Therefore, it appears that there may be some biases but the direction is unknown. More important, the biases probably would seldom change the ranking. A paper by Mains commented on the empirical results derived by Jensen, but was not concerned with flaws in his theory.

Finally, in addition to the three composite measures, a paper by Fama discussed ways to break down the composite return and derive measures related to risk and diversification in addition to measuring overall performance. An analysis of 20 mutual funds, using the component breakdown, showed how much of a fund's overall performance was due to accepting higher risk and how much (positive or negative) was attributable to selection. It was also possible to pinpoint the added return required for loss of diversification, and this coincided with the correlation coefficient discussed earlier.

It is important for investors to evaluate their own performance and the performance of hired managers. The various techniques discussed here provide theoretically justifiable measures, but they all differ slightly. The author feels strongly that *all the measures should be used* in the evaluation process because they provide different information. An evaluation of a portfolio manager should also be done *a number of times* over *different market environments* before a final judgment is reached.

Questions

1. Assuming you are managing your own portfolio, do you think you should evaluate your own performance? Why or why not? Against what would you compare your performance?

2. What are the two major factors that should be considered when evaluating a portfolio manager? What should the portfolio manager be trying to do?

3. What can a portfolio manager do to try to derive superior risk-adjusted returns?

4. What is the purpose of diversification according to the CAPM? How

can you measure whether a portfolio is completely diversified? Explain why this measure makes sense.

5. Prior to the development of composite portfolio performance measures, how could you evaluate portfolio performance taking risk into consideration?

6. Define the Treynor measure of portfolio performance. Discuss this measure in terms of what it indicates (what does it measure?).

7. Assume that during the past ten year period the risk-free rate was 4 percent and three portfolios had the following characteristics:

Portfolio	Return	Beta
A	.11	1.10
B	.09	0.90
C	.14	1.20

Compute the T value for each portfolio and indicate which portfolio had the best performance. Assume you are told that the market return during this period was 10 percent; how did these managers fare relative to the market?

8. Define the Sharpe measure of performance and discuss what it tells.

9. Assume the three portfolios in Question 7 have standard deviations of .14, .10, and .20 respectively. Compute the Sharpe measure of performance. Is there any difference in the ranking achieved using the Treynor versus the Sharpe measure? Discuss the probable cause.

10. Why is it suggested that both the Treynor and Sharpe measures of performance be employed? What additional information is provided by a comparison of the rankings achieved using the two measures?

11. Define the Jensen measure of performance and indicate whether it should produce results similiar to those produced using the Treynor or Sharpe methods. Why?

12. Define overall performance. Assume that you are told a fund had an overall performance figure of 5 percent; does that mean the manager is superior? Why or why not? Discuss.

13. You are told that a fund had an overall performance of $-.50$ percent. Could the manager of this fund have a positive selectivity value? Why or why not? If so, under what conditions?

14. Define the diversification term. Under what conditions will this term equal zero?

15. Define net selectivity. If a portfolio had a negative selectivity value, could it have a positive net selectivity measure? Under what conditions?

16. You are told that a portfolio has an R^2 with the market of .95, and a selectivity value of 2.5 percent. Would you expect the portfolio to have a positive net selectivity value? Discuss why.

References

Blume, Marshall. "The Assessment of Portfolio Performance." Unpublished Ph.D. dissertation, University of Chicago, 1968.

Carlson, Robert S. "Aggregate Performance of Mutual Funds, 1948–1967." *Journal of Financial and Quantitative Analysis,* Vol. 5, No. 1 (March, 1970).

Evaluation and Measurement of Investment Performance. Seminars on Portfolio Management, Financial Analysts Research Foundation, Charlottesville, Va., 1977.

Fama, Eugene. "Components of Investment Performance." *Journal of Finance,* Vol. 27, No. 3 (June, 1972).

Fama, Eugene. "Risk, Return, and Equilibrium." *Journal of Political Economy,* Vol. 79, No. 1 (January–February, 1971).

Friend, Irwin and Blume, Marshall. "Measurement of Portfolio Performance Under Uncertainty." *American Economic Review,* Vol. 60, No. 4 (September, 1970).

Friend, Irwin, Blume, Marshall, and Crocket, Jean. *Mutual Funds and Other Institutional Investors.* New York: McGraw–Hill, 1970.

Horowitz, Ira. "The 'Reward-to-Variability' Ratio and Mutual Fund Performance." *Journal of Business,* Vol. 39, No. 4 (October, 1966).

Jensen, Michael C. "The Performance of Mutual Funds in the Period 1945–1964." *Journal of Finance,* Vol. 23, No. 2 (May, 1968).

Jensen, Michael C. "Risk, the Pricing of Capital Assets, and the Evaluation of Investment Portfolios." *Journal of Business,* Vol. 42, No. 2 (April, 1969).

Klemkosky, Robert C. "The Bias in Composite Performance Measures." *Journal of Financial and Quantitative Analysis,* Vol. 8, No. 3 (June, 1973).

Klemkosky, Robert C. "How Consistently Do Managers Manage?" *Journal of Portfolio Management,* Vol. 3, No. 2 (Winter, 1977).

Mains, Norman E. "Risk, the Pricing of Capital Assets, and the Evaluation of Investment Portfolios: Comment." *Journal of Business,* Vol. 50, No. 3 (July, 1977).

Measuring the Performance of Pension Funds. Park Ridge, Illinois: Bank Administration Institute, 1968. A supplement, *Risk and the Evaluation of Pension Fund Performance* was written by Eugene Fama.

Sharpe, William F. "Mutual Fund Performances." *Journal of Business,* Vol. 39, No. 1, Part 2 (January, 1966).

Smith, Keith V. and Tito, Dennis A. "Risk-Return Measures of Ex-Post Portfolio Performance." *Journal of Financial and Quantitative Analysis,* Vol. 4, No. 5 (December, 1969).

Treynor, Jack L. "How to Rate Management of Investment Funds." *Harvard Business Review,* Vol. 43, No. 1 (January–February, 1965).

Part 6   *Alternative Investments*

Introduction to Part 6

This section only contains three chapters, but obviously could be a book unto itself. Therefore, it was necessary to select for further discussion those investments that would be of greatest interest to the reader. The first chapter is devoted entirely to the area of stock options because of the substantial growth in this area since the opening of the Chicago Board Options Exchange in 1973. Further, it is felt that the creation of highly marketable options will allow investors to develop portfolios with risk and return characteristics that were not possible before. Therefore, the reader should be aware of what is available and the results of alternative investment strategies.

Chapter 24 contains a brief discussion of three further alternatives: convertible bonds, warrants, and commodities. There is no logical relationship among these three investment instruments except that all should be considered by investors.

The final chapter of the book considers an alternative to analyzing and selecting investments yourself, investment companies. After a basic explanation of the concept of investment companies and a description of the major forms, we will examine the many types available, from money market funds that only invest in short-term fixed income securities, to high growth common stock funds and options funds. It should be clear that almost any investment objective can be met by investing in one or several investment companies. A review of several studies that examined the performance of investment companies indicated that they have generally not performed as well as a naive buy-and-hold policy. Finally, it is pointed out that even though the typical investment company does not outperform the market, it is capable of fulfilling a number of other functions that are of importance to an investor.

Chapter 23 **Stock Options**

Stock Options

Options give the holder the right to buy or sell a security at a specified price during a designated period of time. There are two specific types: *call options* give the owner the right to *purchase* a given number of shares of a stock at a specified price during a given time period (usually from three to nine months); *put options* give the holder the right to *sell* a given number of shares of a security at a specified price during a given time interval. Put and call options have been available to investors on the OTC market for a number of years, but have only become widely accepted and used as an investment vehicle since the Chicago Board Options Exchange (CBOE) was established. As a result of actions by the CBOE and, later, exchanges which began to list options, there has been a large volume of options trading by individual and institutional investors. Another major reason for the increased interest in options is that they provide a substantial range of investment alternatives for all types of potential investors from the most speculative to the very conservative.

Recent History of Options Trading

For a number of years it has been possible to buy and sell put and call options in the over-the-counter market via individual investment firms that were members of the Put and Call Association. Through the individual firms in this association, investors could negotiate specific put and call options on given shares of stock. The arrangements were very flexible and also somewhat disorganized. An investor who wanted to buy an option would go to one of these dealers and indicate the stock he wanted to buy and the time period he was interested in. The dealer would find an interested investor and the parties would then negotiate individually on the price of the options. Because the amount of secondary trading was limited, it was usually difficult to sell the call again.

The environment changed dramatically when the CBOE was established on April 26, 1973 and began trading options on 16 stocks. The options exchange made numerous innovations in the trading of options on listed securities, such as:

1. *The creation of a central marketplace* with regulatory, surveillance, disclosure, and price dissemination capabilities.

2. *The introduction of a Clearing Corporation* as the guarantor of every CBOE option. Standing as the opposite party to every trade, by making an offsetting transaction the Clearing Corporation enables buyers and sellers of options to terminate their positions in the market at any time.

3. *The standardization* of expiration dates (most CBOE options expire in January, April, July, and October, others in February, May, August, and November) and the standardization of exercise prices (the price per share at which the stock can be acquired upon exercise of the option).

4. *The creation of a secondary market.* While an option is a contract guaranteeing the buyer the right to purchase stock at the agreed upon price, the majority of option buyers sell their options on the exchange either for a profit or to reduce loss. Before the options exchange was established, the buyers and sellers of over-the-counter options were essentially committed to their positions until the expiration date if the option was not exercised.

Operation of the CBOE

Readers are well aware of how a market is made on the New York and other stock exchanges. The specialist is at the center of the stock market and has two functions: (1) as a broker who maintains the limit order book and, (2) as a market-maker who buys and sells for his own account to ensure the operation of a "fair and orderly" market for investors. Recall the concern that the specialists had monopoly information in the form of the limit order book and also a monopoly position as the sole market-maker in a security. One might therefore expect stock specialists to derive above average returns, which they do.

Apparently the CBOE was aware of the potential problems of the stock exchange arrangement and attempted to avoid them. The limit order book on the CBOE is handled by an individual (a "board broker") who is *not* a market-marker so the two functions are separate. The board broker handles the limit order book and accepts *only* public orders on the book. In addition, the limit order book *is public!* Above the trading post there is a video screen that gives figures for the last trade, the current bid and ask for each of the options, and the limit orders on the book. The other major difference is that *there are competing market-makers for all options.* These members, designated market-makers, can *only* trade for themselves and are not allowed to handle public orders. As an example, there are four members of the CBOE who are specifically designated as primary market-makers for IBM. Each of the market-makers is assigned three or four "primary" options and another three or four options for which they are "secondary" market-makers, and they are required to concentrate 70 percent of their trading activity in their primary issues. As is the stock exchange specialist, they are expected to provide liquidity for individual and institutional investors. Given the existence of several market-makers for each option, one would expect more funds to be available for trading, and superior markets because of the added competition.

The third category of CBOE members are floor brokers who execute all types of orders for their customers. These floor brokers are very similar to floor brokers on the stock exchanges.

Volume of Trading

The CBOE started with options on 16 stocks. This number was gradually expanded and was over 100 by 1976. The American Stock Exchange began trading options on January 13, 1975, and had options on over 65 stocks by June, 1977. Options trading was also introduced on the Philadelphia Exchange (June 29, 1975), the Pacific Exchange (April 9, 1976), and the Midwest Exchange (December 10, 1976). As of June, 1977, there were options on 36 stocks traded on Philadelphia, options on 29 stocks on the Pacific, and options on 15 on the Midwest. The total number of stocks with listed options exceeded 200 by the middle of 1977. As one might expect, the 200 options are on stocks of large companies that enjoy active secondary markets.

The growth in trading volume has been phenomenal. During the first full month of trading on the CBOE (May, 1973), the number of contracts traded totalled about 31,000. By early 1978, the total number traded on all five exchanges for each month consistently exceeded three million.

Competing Markets for Options

When the ASE established trading in options in January, 1975, it was with 15 stocks that *were not* being traded on the CBOE. The point is that originally there was a very conscious effort by the exchanges *not* to establish competing markets, and this practice was continued when the Philadelphia Exchange began trading in options.

This changed late in 1976 when the ASE established a market in MGIC which was then traded on the CBOE. In February, 1977, the ASE started a market in National Semiconductor, a very active issue on the CBOE.[1] The

---

[1] For an extended discussion of what transpired, see Kevin J. Hamilton, "Options: The Dual Trading War," *Institutional Investor,* Vol. 11, No. 6 (June, 1977), pp. 30–32; and

response by the CBOE was to begin trading in six ASE issues: Merrill Lynch, Digital Equipment, Burroughs, Disney, Du Pont, and Tandy. The competition appeared to reduce the spread for these issues and increase their liquidity. There was a major effort by members of both exchanges to draw volume in the competitive issues because many of the brokerage houses usually did not check both markets when placing an order, but would select one of them as the "primary" exchange for an issue and channel all orders for the issue to this exchange. In fact, some observers felt that professional traders inflated the volume. Several months after the competition began, it appeared that the CBOE was dominant in National Semiconductor, Burroughs, Digital Equipment, and Du Pont, while the ASE was drawing the major flow of orders in Merrill Lynch, Disney, and Tandy.

Although the competition apparently created a better market for these issues, there was concern on two counts. First, the other regional exchanges that started options markets (Pacific, Philadelphia, and Midwest) were concerned that the two larger options exchanges (CBOE and ASE) would begin trading in their more active issues, and it was doubtful whether these smaller exchanges could compete on an even basis with the two larger exchanges. Even the two large exchanges were anxious about what would happen when the NYSE began trading options. The NYSE had applied for permission to establish an options market in early 1977, and planned to start later in the year. The other exchanges were concerned that the NYSE would begin by selecting the most active options from *all* the exchanges, and there was no doubt that the NYSE would be a formidable competitor.

During late 1977 the increasing competition stopped abruptly when the SEC ruled that no further options could be added to *any* exchanges while trading practices on the exchanges were being investigated. All exchanges were frozen and the NYSE was not allowed to begin trading.

Initially, all option trading on exchanges was in call options. As of June 1, 1977, the SEC allowed each of the exchanges to begin trading in five put options. The existence of put options increases the potential number of trading strategies.

Terminology

Given the unique nature of the options market, it is hardly surprising to find that it has developed its own terminology.

The Option Premium is the price paid for the option itself. It is what a buyer must pay for the ability to acquire the stock at a given price during some period in the future. The average premium on a newly issued option with the market price of the stock in question close to the option price is

---

Jonathon R. Laing and Richard E. Rustin, "Options Trading War May Afford a Preview of a National Market," *Wall Street Journal,* May 27, 1977, p. 1.

---

typically about 10 percent of the value of the stock. The premium on a six month option to buy a stock for 30 dollars, when the stock is selling for about 30 dollars, would be about 3 dollars.

The exercise price (or striking price) is the price at which the stock can be acquired. If the stock is currently selling for 38 dollars a share, one might specify an exercise price of 40 dollars a share, meaning that the holder of the option can buy the stock for 40 dollars for the duration of the option. The intervals for exercise prices are determined by the price of the stock involved. For stocks selling under 50 dollars, the exercise prices are set at 5 dollar intervals: e.g., $35, $40, $45. For stocks selling between 50 and 100 dollars, they are set at 10 dollar intervals, e.g., $60, $70, $80. Finally for stocks selling for over 100 dollars a share, the intervals are 20 dollars, e.g., $120, $140, $160. The initial exercise prices are set at the interval closest to the current market price of the stock. In a case of a stock selling for 43 dollars at the time the option is established, the exercise price would be set at 45 dollars. If the stock declines to 41 dollars a share, another option would be established at 40 dollars a share. In contrast, if the price increased to 48 dollars a share, an option would be established at 50 dollars.

The expiration date is the date on which the option expires or the last date on which the option can be exercised. In July the exchange might establish a September option which means that the holder of this option can purchase the stock at any time between July and September when the option expires. The expiration dates are designated by month, while the actual date of expiration is *the third Saturday in each month that is specified.* A September option would expire on the close of business on the third Saturday in September. Actual trading in the option would cease at the close of the market on the Friday before this third Saturday.

Beyond these basic items of terminology, there are two general phrases used extensively in the trade. One of them is the term *"in the money option,"* which is an option with a *market price for the stock that is in excess of the exercise price for the option.* Assume that the exercise price of an option was 30 dollars and the stock was currently selling for 34 dollars a share. This would be an "in the money option" meaning that the market price ($34) exceeded the exercise price ($30) and so the option had an instrinsic value of at least four dollars a share. The "out of the money option" has *an exercise price above the market price for the stock.* An example would be an option with an exercise price of 30 dollars for a stock that is currently selling at 22 dollars a share. In this instance, an investor may be willing to pay something for the option based on the *possibility* of the stock price increasing. The option itself has no intrinsic value because it provides the ability to buy a stock for 30 dollars a share at a time when it is possible to buy the stock in the open market at only 22 dollars.

A Sample Quotation

Referring to Figure 23–1, assume that in early October, 1978, you were considering acquiring a call option in Eastman Kodak (EK). The stock is currently priced at 60⅜. The arrow (1) indicates that you could buy a "Kodak January 50" for 12. This means that you would pay $12.00 a share for the right to buy a share of Eastman Kodak at $50 a share between the time of the purchase and the expiration of the option during the third week in January. This is an "in the money" option; it has an intrinsic value of 10⅜. If you wanted an option that expired in April, 1979, it would cost 12¼ a share; the extra $0.25 is the cost of the additional three months.

You could also acquire a "Kodak April 70" (arrow 2) for $3.375 a share. This is an "out of the money option" because the option exercise price of 70 dollars exceeds the current market price of $60.375. The investor may be willing to pay this $3.375 based upon an expectation that the price of EK will approach or exceed 70 dollars by the third week in April, 1979.

It is also possible to buy or sell a put option in Eastman Kodak. It is one of the five options listed this way on the CBOE. In this case, all those with prices below $60.375 are "out of the money" and the only "in the money" put is the 70 dollar option (arrow 3). It is "in the money" because it allows the owner to *sell* a stock with a market value of 60⅜ for 70 dollars. Its intrinsic value is therefore at least $9.625. Again, the longer term put option has greater value.

Alternative Trading Strategies

With the introduction of put options, the number of strategies available to an investor has become enormous and the range of complexity is substantial. In this section, we will not attempt to cover all the strategies, but will limit our discussion to the major alternatives and refer the reader to articles and books that describe the more sophisticated techniques. Most trading involves the strategies discussed in this chapter. Also, in order to understand the more sophisticated strategies, it is necessary to understand the basic techniques because the more advanced methods build upon these.

Buying Call Options

Investors buy call options because they expect the price of the underlying stock to increase during the period prior to the expiration of the option. Given this expectation, the purchase of an option will yield a large return on a small dollar investment. When considering the purchase of a call option, there are several alternatives available in terms of the exercise price relative to the market price. One can purchase an out of the money option, an at the money option, or an in the money option. Probably the riskiest is an out of the money option because it is clearly possible to lose everything that has been invested if the stock price does not rise enough to equal or exceed the

Figure 23–1
Quotations from Chicago Board Options Exchange

Chicago Board

Option	&	price	Oct Vol.	Oct Last	Jan Vol.	Jan Last	Apr Vol.	Apr Last	N.Y. Close
Alcoa		.. 40	41	6½	15	6⅞	a	a	45¾
Alcoa		...45	181	1¾	9	3¾	6	5⅜	45¾
Alcoa		...50	130	⅜	22	1¾	11	2¾	45¾
Am Exp		30	130	5	a	a	b	b	34⅞
Am Exp		35	330	¾	305	2 5-16	a	a	34⅞
Am Exp		40	1	1-16	9	⅝	5	1 5-16	34⅞
Am Tel		55	10	7	a	a	a	a	62⅛
Am Tel		.60	366	2⅛	318	2⅞	74	3⅜	62⅛
Am Tel		.65	28	1-16	58	7-16	108	1	62⅛
Atl R		.. 45	10	8¼	a	a	14	9¾	53⅜
Atl R		...50	140	3⅜	97	4¾	10	6¼	53⅜
Atl R		...60	2	1-16	60	1 1-16	19	2	53⅜
Avon	p	... 45	a	a	116	9-16	b	b	55
Avon		... 50	46	5⅛	33	6⅜	24	7⅝	55
Avon	p	.. 50	674	5-16	273	1 11-16	59	2¾	55
Avon		... 60	246	¼	283	1¾	91	2⅝	55
Avon	p	.. 60	340	5½	44	6¼	16	7⅜	55
BankAm		25	87	2⅛	25	3	26	3½	27
BankAm		30	133	⅛	104	¾	61	1⅜	27
Beth S		. 20	39	3¾	20	4¼	11	5	23¾
Beth S		. 25	163	¼	183	1 5-16	71	2 3-16	23¾
Beth S		. 30	20	1-16	51	5-16	51	15-16	23¾
Bruns		.. 15	327	1 7-16	151	2 5-16	120	2⅞	16½
Bruns		.. 20	212	1-16	202	⅝	84	1⅛	16½
Burl N		. 35	12	8⅛	10	9	a	a	43⅛
Burl N		. 40	20	3½	15	4⅝	a	a	43⅛
Burl N		. 45	38	½	28	2	1	3⅛	43⅛
Burrgh		..70	39	7⅞	a	a	a	a	78
Burrgh		80	48	1½	4	5	3	6½	78
Burrgh		. 90	5	⅛	8	1⅞	a	a	78
Citicp		...20	7	6¼	a	a	5	6¾	26¼
Citicp		.. 25	278	1½	75	2½	58	3⅜	26¼
Citicp		.. 30	102	⅛	121	11-16	61	1¼	26¼
Delta		.. 40	6	8	13	9½	b	b	48⅛
Delta		.. 45	31	4	20	6	a	a	48⅛
Delta		.. 50	160	1⅛	25	3⅞	14	5½	48⅛
Delta		.. 60	169	⅛	68	1 3-16	20	2¼	48⅛
Dig Eq		. 40	12	9⅛	a	a	a	a	48⅞
Dig Eq		45	49	4½	7	6⅜	a	a	48⅞
Dig Eq		50	100	1 5-16	36	3⅝	18	5⅜	48⅞
Disney		. 35	8	7¼	25	8	4	8¾	42⅝
Disney		..40	47	3¼	11	5	a	a	42⅝
Disney		. 45	311	⅝	34	2 9-16	10	3¾	42⅝
Dow Ch		.20	5	8½	a	a	a	a	28¼
Dow Ch		25	288	3⅜	101	4⅛	758	4⅝	28¼
Dow Ch		30	456	3-16	143	1 5-16	60	2 1-16	28¼
du Pnt		.100	7	29	b	b	b	b	127¾
du Pnt		110	17	19	5	19¼	5	21	127¾
du Pnt		.120	48	8½	17	11½	a	a	127¾
du Pnt		.130	289	1 13-16	64	5⅞	a	a	127¾
Eas Kd		.45	5	15¼	4	16¼	b	b	60⅜
Eas Kd	p	• .45	a	a	5	¼	b	b	60⅜
①→ Eas Kd		.50	118	10¼	25	12	8	12¼	60⅜
Eas Kd	p	50	330	1-16	201	⅞	71	1½	60⅜
Eas Kd		.60	1810	2	671	5	130	6⅜	60⅜
Eas Kd	p	60	1897	1 13-16	291	4¼	55	5½	60⅜
②→ Eas Kd		.70	669	1-16	493	1⅝	198	3⅜	60⅜
③→ Eas Kd	p	70	362	9¾	246	10⅝	5	11⅞	60⅜
Exxon		.. 40	1	12	a	a	a	a	52⅛
Exxon		..45	352	6⅞	9	7½	5	7¾	52⅛
Exxon		..50	2171	2⅛	488	3⅝	68	4⅜	52⅛
F N M		15	72	2¾	63	2⅞	1	3⅜	17¾
F N M		20	59	1-16	28	½	15	¾	17¾
Fluor		... 35	6	4⅜	a	a	a	a	39
Fluor		...40	40	¾	22	2¾	4	3⅝	39
Fluor		.. 45	b	b	10	1	5	1⅞	39
Ford		... 40	4	5⅝	a	a	a	a	45½
Ford		... 45	77	1 3-16	39	2¼	11	3	45½
Ford		... 50	82	1-16	66	¾	8	1 5-16	45½
Ford		... 60	a	a	5	1-16	b	b	45½
Gen El		. 45	1	7¾	a	a	b	b	52⅞
Gen El		. 50	20	2⅞	a	a	a	a	52⅞
Gen El		55	169	⅜	78	1 11-16	10	2 7-16	52⅞
Gen El		60	14	1-16	11	⅝	3	1 3-16	52⅞
G M		... 50	1	13½	3	13⅜	a	a	63⅛
G M	p	... 50	a	a	a	a	189	1	63⅛
G M		60	132	3⅝	83	4⅝	42	4¾	63⅛
G M	p	... 60	410	7-16	124	2½	94	3¾	63⅛
G M		70	28	1-16	108	⅝	52	1⅜	63⅛
G M	p	... 70	44	7	24	8⅞	20	10	63⅛
Gt Wst		..15	1	14½	b	b	b	b	30
Gt Wst		25	53	4½	38	5⅜	20	6	30
Gt Wst		30	68	¾	7	2¼	64	3⅜	30
Gt Wst		35	169	⅛	124	¾	25	1½	30
Glf Wn		10	71	4½	5	5	13	5¼	14½
Glf Wn		15	542	5-16	345	1⅛	170	1⅝	14½
Halbtn		..60	5	12½	17	13¼	a	a	71⅞
Halbtn		..70	300	2 15-16	66	6⅜	15	8¼	71⅞
Halbtn		..80	b	b	171	2⅜	20	3¾	71⅞
Homstk		25	a	a	5	12⅝	b	b	37⅜
Homstk		.30	5	7⅞	4	7⅞	2	9⅝	37⅜
Homstk		.35	88	3	13	5½	5	6¼	37⅜
Homstk		.40	250	9-16	197	2 7-16	49	3⅜	37⅜
Homstk		45	5	1-16	b	b	b	b	37⅜

Listed Options Quotations

Friday, September 29, 1978

Closing prices of all options. Sales unit usually is 100 shares. Security description includes exercise price. Stock close is New York or American exchange final price. p-Put option. o-Old shares.

Option	&	price	Nov Vol.	Nov Last	Feb Vol.	Feb Last	May Vol.	May Last	N.Y. Close
Gn Dyn		.70	15	13	a	a	a	a	82¼
Gn Dyn		.80	40	6	a	a	20	10⅝	82¼
Gn Dyn		90	142	2¼	5	5⅜	33	7¼	82¼
Gen Fd		25	40	8⅛	a	a	b	b	33¼
Gen Fd		30	90	3½	a	a	a	a	33¼
Gen Fd		.35	104	⅜	1	1⅛	16	2⅛	33¼
Hewlet		..60	69	28	b	b	b	b	87⅞
Hewlet		..70	138	18	13	19	b	b	87⅞
Hewlet		. 80	51	8¾	45	10	45	12½	87⅞
Hewlet		. 90	87	2¾	36	5¼	14	7¼	87⅞
Hewlet		100	30	⅜	39	2	2	3⅞	87⅞
H Inns		..15	106	13½	9	13⅜	b	b	28¼
H Inns		. 20	363	9¼	94	9½	14	10¼	28¼
H Inns		. 25	2542	5½	662	6¾	88	7½	28¼
H Inns		. 30	3707	2¾	1002	4¼	·187	5¼	28¼
H Inns		. 35	2483	1 1-16	281	2 5-16	149	2 15-16	28¼
Honwll		..50	64	14⅝	a	a	b	b	64⅜
Honwll	p	. 50	35	⅛	301	15-16	b	b	64⅜
Honwll		..60	352	6⅜	63	8⅛	a	a	64⅜
Honwll	p	60	930	1 11-16	307	3⅞	12	4¾	64⅜
Honwll		. 70	750	1 5-16	95	3½	14	4⅞	64⅜
Honwll	p	70	446	7	27	8¾	3	9½	64⅜
Honwll		. 80	1	⅛	100	1¼	19	2 5-16	64⅜
Honwll	p	..80	3	15⅜	a	a	a	a	64⅜
In Flv		.. 20	a	a	10	5½	b	b	24⅝
In Flv		..25	21	1⅜	64	2½	4	3½	24⅝
In Flv		..30	4	3-16	5	11-16	a	a	24⅝
J Manv		25	27	7⅛	b	b	b	b	31¾
J Manv		.30	75	2⅞	13	3⅛	a	a	31¾
J Manv		35	136	½	24	1 3-16	1	1⅞	31¾
MGIC		...20	2	5¼	a	a	a	a	25
MGIC		...25	10	1 11-16	3	2¾	a	a	25
MGIC		...30	a	a	a	a	50	2¼	25
Mobil		...60	2	10¾	21	10⅞	56	11⅜	70¼
Mobil		.. 65	45	6	15	6½	a	a	70¼
Mobil		...70	79	1⅞	199	3½	20	4⅜	70¼
N Semi		20	23	7⅞	b	b	b	b	27¾
N Semi		.25	278	3⅞	106	5⅜	21	6⅛	27¾
N Semi		.30	634	1 7-16	339	3	30	4⅛	27¾
N Semi		.35	119	½	122	1½	62	2⅜	27¾
Occi		... 20	140	1 3-16	163	2⅛	109	2 13-16	20
Occi		... 25	135	⅛	101	11-16	147	1 3-16	20
Raythn		. 40	3	8½	a	a	b	b	47½
Raythn		. 45	5	3¾	4	5⅜	a	a	47½
Raythn		50	67	1 7-16	42	3½	2	4⅜	47½
Raythn		. 60	51	¼	9	1 3-16	a	a	47½
Rynlds		..50	6	11⅞	a	a	a	a	62⅜
Rynlds		..60	46	3	13	4⅝	a	a	62⅜
Rynlds		..70	a	a	39	1⅛	5	2	62⅜
Slumb		.. 70	10	21¼	a	a	b	b	90⅝
Slumb		..80	26	11¾	111	14	6	16½	90⅝
Slumb		..90	318	4½	75	8¼	89	10	90⅝
Slumb		100	258	1	245	3⅝	20	5½	90⅝
Skylin		.. 10	a	a	3	4½	4	4¾	13¾
Skylin		..15	109	9-16	92	1¼	89	1⅝	13¾
Skylin		...20	6	⅛	a	a	b	b	13¾
Southn		..15	68	½	5	11-16	2	1	15¼
Southn		..20	a	a	10	1-16	20	1-16	15¼
St Ind		.. 45	3	7¾	a	a	a	a	53⅛
St Ind		.. 50	102	3¼	3	4¼	a	a	53⅛
St Ind		.. 60	a	a	2	½	11	1 7-16	53⅛
Tx Glf		..20	16	2⅜	1	3⅝	a	a	22⅛
Tx Glf		..25	10	7-16	5	15-16	7	1⅞	22⅛
U A L		..25	11	14⅛	5	14½	b	b	39
U A L		..30	61	9	14	10⅛	b	b	39
U A L		..35	442	6	148	7	13	8	39
U A L		..40	814	3	233	4¾	22	5⅞	39
U A L		..45	520	1¼	194	2¾	1	3¾	39
U Tech		. 35	15	9	b	b	b	b	43½
U Tech		. 40	31	4⅞	a	a	b	b	43½
U Tech		.45	177	1 13-16	34	3⅝	30	4⅝	43½
U Tech		.50	177	⅝	58	1 13-16	89	2 15-16	43½
U Tech		60	20	1-16	5	⅝	a	a	43½
J Walt		..30	18	3	50	3⅞	a	a	31¾
J Walt		..35	70	7-16	25	1½	a	a	31¾
Willms		..15	6	5⅜	a	a	b	b	19½
Willms		. 20	253	15-16	97	1⅞	42	2½	19½
Willms		. 25	39	1-16	41	9-16	50	15-16	19½
Total volume			122,211			Open	interest		2,347,759

The (a) in the Kodak line indicates no trading in this option; a (b) indicates no option was offered.

Source: *Wall Street Journal,* October 2, 1978. Reprinted by permission of The Wall Street Journal,

exercise price. At the same time, the rate of return can be very large and the initial investment is the lowest of the three alternatives.

Consider the following example (without taking commissions into account). In June, when Avon is selling for 55 dollars a share, an Avon October 60 call option is selling for 2 dollars a share. Assuming you expect a sharp increase in the price of Avon during the next four months, you would pay 200 dollars for the option. If you are correct, and the Avon stock goes to 65 dollars within this period (an 18 percent increase in price), the option will become an in the money option and have an intrinsic value of five dollars, and it could sell for more if there is any time left to the option. At this point, you could sell the option for 500 dollars and enjoy a 150 percent return on the option during a period when the increase in stock price was only 18 percent. If the stock price never got above 60, the option would be worthless when it expired and you would have lost the full 200 dollars.

You could also acquire an in the money option on the stock. This differs from the out of the money option because it requires a larger investment (the option has an intrinsic value *and* a time value). At the same time, the price of the underlying stock does not have to increase much for you to enjoy a return. Assume that in June you buy a Avon October 50 at 6¾. This option has an intrinsic value of five dollars and a time value of about $1.75. In the near future, assume the stock goes to $59. The option will then have an intrinsic value of nine dollars and, even if the time value declines to one dollar, the option should be selling for about ten dollars. Therefore, on a 7.3 percent increase in the stock price (59 vs. 55), the option has a return of 53.8 percent (10 vs. 6½). If the stock price declined to below 50, you would lose the full investment. If the price declined but was still above 50, the option would only have its intrinsic value at expiration and your gain or loss would be figured accordingly.

Writing Covered Call Options[2]

In contrast to buying call options, which is considered quite speculative, a strategy of writing call options is generally considered to be quite conservative. An option writer enters into a contract to deliver 100 shares of a stock at a predetermined exercise price during some specified time interval. When a writer enters into such a contract ("sells a call"), he can either own the stock (sell a covered option) or not own the stock (sell an uncovered, "naked," option). The option writer is typically looking for extra income from the stock (the premium he receives which also gives him some downside protection). At the same time, the option writer gives *up* a certain

---

[2] For further readable discussions of writing strategies, see *The Merrill Lynch Guide to Writing Options* (New York: Merrill Lynch, Pierce, Fenner and Smith, Inc.); and *Option Writing Strategies* (Chicago: The Chicago Board Options Exchange, 1975).

amount of upside potential on the stock if it rises above the exercise price and is called away.

Assume that in June you acquired 100 shares of Avon stock at 55 dollars a share. You could sell an Avon October 60 for about two dollars a share (sell a "covered" option). This would give you extra income ($200) or you could consider it as downside protection because your *net* price is now 53 dollars (55 − 2). If the stock does not change price between the middle of June and October (approximately four months), you have an additional 200 dollars that you would not have had otherwise (a 3.6 percent return during the four month period). If the stock increases to 61 and is called away, you have sold it at a profit of five dollars per share and you still have the premium. Your return (before dividends) during the period was seven dollars (a $2 premium plus the $5 capital gain), which would be 12.7 percent for the four months (7/55). As noted, if the stock goes to 65 dollars, you have given up the gain above 60 dollars because of the option. Therefore, you are protected on the downside by the lower net price, but also restricted on the upside by the exercise price. If an option writer wants to get out of his contract, all he has to do is *buy* a comparable call option on the exchange and the two contracts cancel each other.

Writing Options in Different Markets
Your option writing strategy should differ depending upon the general market environment (stable, rising, declining) and your outlook for the stock. If the market is *very stable* you would simply continue to sell options over time as a supplement to your dividend income. The only unique aspect of this arrangement would be that, if it is an out of the money option or at the money option, you would want to consider closing out your position (buying an option to offset your written option) prior to expiration so you can sell another one sooner. This is based on the assumption that the option price gets pretty low near its maturity because it has no intrinsic value and its time value declines.

If the market is *declining,* the sale of a call somewhat offsets the decline in price (i.e., the net cost of the stock is lower). After the stock has declined along with the market, the investor must decide whether he still wants to own the stock. If he does, he should write another call at a lower call price. Assume you bought a stock at 58 dollars and sold a 60 call. The stock then declines to 53. If you still want to own the stock, you would sell another call at 55.

Finally, assume that the stock price *increases* because of a market rise or for internal reasons. Again you must decide whether you want to continue to own the stock or let it be called away. Assume you bought the stock at 45 dollars, sold a 50 dollar option, and the stock subsequently went to 52 dollars. If you are satisfied with the five dollar capital gain plus the premium received, you might allow the stock to be called away and put the money into another stock. In contrast, if you feel there is further potential in the stock, you could simply buy back your option at 50 dollars and sell another at 55 dollars. You would have lost on the repurchase of the first option, but you would have made it up on the second option and you still own the stock.

Option Spreads

In contrast to simply buying or selling an option, it is possible to enter into a spread and do both. The purpose is to reduce the risk of a long or short position in the option for a stock. There are two basic types of spread. A *price spread* (or vertical spread) involves buying the call option for a given stock, time, and price, and selling a call option for the same stock and time at a different price, e.g., buy an Avon October 50 and sell an Avon October 60. A *time spread* (or horizontal spread) involves buying and selling an option for the same stock and price, but the time differs, e.g., buying an Avon October 50 and selling an Avon January 50.

Bullish Spreads

These are spreads that you would consider if you were bullish on the underlying stock. Assume you are optimistic regarding the outlook for Avon and want to enter into a price spread that will reduce the risk of such a transaction. The situation is as follows regarding October options (numbers rounded):

Avon 50 October	7
Avon 60 October	2

Because you are bullish, you would buy the Avon 50 and sell the Avon 60 for a net cost of 5 ($500) which is also your maximum loss. Assuming you are correct, and the stock goes from 55 to 65, the October 50 would be worth about 15 (only its intrinsic value) and the October 60 would sell for about 6 (a slight premium over intrinsic value). If you closed out both positions, you would obtain the following results:

October 50: bought at 7, sold at 15—gain 8
October 60: sold at 2, bought at 6 —loss 4
Overall   —gain 4

If the stock had declined dramatically, your maximum loss would have been 500 dollars even though both options were worthless when they expired.

Bearish Spreads

If an investor is bearish on a stock or on the market, he would buy the higher priced option and sell the lower priced option. Returning to Avon, you would:

Sell October 50 at 7
Buy October 60 at 2

This would generate an immediate gain of 500 dollars. If you are correct, and the stock declines to below 50, both options will be worthless when they expire and you will have the 500 dollar return. If you were wrong, and the stock goes to 65 as discussed under the bullish spread, you would have the following:

October 50: sold at 7; bought at 15—loss 8
October 60: bought at 2; sold at 6   —gain 4
                          Overall   —loss 4

This loss of 400 dollars compares favorably with possible loss of 800 dollars or much more if you did not have some offset from the spread. At some very high price the two options will have a difference of 10, so your maximum loss is 500 dollars ($1000 gross loss less $500 gain on original transaction).

There are numerous other potential transactions for almost any possible set of risk-return desires. This discussion served only to introduce you to the basic transactions that are used in all subsequent strategies.

Valuation of Call Options

There are five figures needed to calculate the value of an American call option,[3] assuming the stock does not pay a dividend (this assumption will later be dropped.) The five figures are: (1) the stock price, (2) the exercise price, (3) the time to maturity, (4) the interest rate, and (5) the volatility of the underlying stock.

Market Price—Exercise Price The relationship between these two prices is obviously important because it determines whether the option is in the money and, therefore, whether the option has an intrinsic value, or if it is out of the money and hence has only speculative value. In addition, some of the other variables are influenced by the relationship between the market price and the exercise price.

Time to Maturity A major component of value of an option is its time to maturity. All other factors being equal, *the longer the time to maturity, the greater the value of the option* because the span of time during which gains are possible is longer. The longer option allows investors to reap all benefits of a shorter option and also provides added time after the short option has expired. It appears that this time value of the option is greatest when the market price and exercise price are the same. If the market price is below the exercise price (out of the money) it will take some of the time before the market price reaches the exercise price and the option begins to have

---

[3] An American call option can be exercised at *any time* prior to the expiration date; a European option can only be exercised *on* the expiration date.

exchange value. If the option is significantly in the money, for a given increase in the stock price, the percent of gain would be less than it would be when the market and exercise prices are almost equal. Therefore, an investor who acquires an at the money option pays less than he would for an in the money option, and will gain more if the stock price increases.

The Interest Rate When an investor acquires an option, he buys control of the underlying stock for a period of time, but his downside risk is limited to the cost of the option. On the upside, he has the potential to gain at an accelerating rate because of the leverage involved. The option is therefore similar to buying on margin, except that there is no explicit interest charge. The higher the market interest rate, the greater the saving from using options, and the greater the value of the option. Therefore, there is a *positive* relationship between the market interest rate and the value of the call option.

Volatility of Underlying Stock Price In most cases, one considers a high level of stock price volatility as an indication of greater risk and, therefore, this reduces value, all other factors being equal. In the case of call options on a stock, the opposite is true; there is a *positive* relationship between the volatility of the underlying stock and the value of the call option. This is because, with greater volatility, there is greater potential for gain on the upside, and the downside protection of the option is also worth more.

Derivation of Valuation Formula

Black and Scholes developed a formula for deriving the value of American call options in a classic article published in 1973.[4] Merton later refined the Black–Scholes formula under less restrictive assumptions.[5] The resulting formula is as follows:

$$Po = [P_s] [N(d_1)] - [E] [antiln\ (- rt)] [N(d_2)]$$

where:

Po = the market value of the option

P_s = the current market price of the underlying common stock

$N(d_1)$ = the cumulative density function of d_1 as defined below

---

[4] Fischer Black and Myron Scholes, "The Pricing of Options and Corporate Liabilities," *Journal of Political Economy,* Vol. 81, No. 3 (May/June, 1973), pp. 637–654.

[5] Robert C. Merton, "The Theory of Rational Option Pricing," *Bell Journal of Economics and Management Science,* Vol. 4, No. 1 (Spring, 1973), pp. 141–183.

E = the exercise price of the call option

r = the current annualized market interest rate for prime commercial paper

t = the time remaining before expiration (in years, e.g., 90 days = .25)

$N(d_2)$ = the cumulative density function of d_2 as defined below

$$d_1 = \left[\frac{\ln(P_s/E) + (r + .5\sigma^2)t}{\sigma(t)^{\frac{1}{2}}} \right]$$

$$d_2 = d_1 - [\sigma(t)^{\frac{1}{2}}]$$

where:

$\ln(P_s/E)$ = the natural logarithm of (P_s/E)

σ = the standard deviation of the annual rate of return on the underlying stock.

Implementing the Formula

Although the formula appears quite forbidding, almost all the required data are observable. The major inputs are: current stock price (P_s), exercise price (E), the market interest rate (r), the time to maturity (t), and the standard deviation of annual returns (σ). The *only* variable that is not observable is the volatility of price changes as measured by the standard deviation of returns (σ). Therefore, this becomes the major factor that must be estimated and is the variable that will cause a difference in the estimated market value for the option. Black, in a subsequent article, made several observations regarding this estimate.[6] First, he noted that knowledge of past price volatility should be helpful, but *more* is needed because *the volatility for individual stocks changes over time.* This should not come as a surprise because a stock's volatility can change either because the market's volatility changes and the stock's beta is constant, or the market's volatility is constant and the individual stock's beta changes over time. Finally, it is possible for both variables to change. Therefore, given a historical estimate of the stock's volatility, the analyst should concentrate on determining the *direction* of the change; will the stock's volatility increase or decrease during the period prior to expiration? Given the variables determining volatility, one should first consider the future direction of *market* volatility; is there any reason to expect an increase or decrease in market volatility in the short run?

---

[6] Fischer Black, "Fact and Fantasy in the Use of Options," *Financial Analysts Journal*, Vol. 31, No. 4 (July–August, 1975), pp. 36–41 *et. seq.*

Second, what do you expect to happen to the stock's beta in the future? This could be affected by industry factors or internal corporate variables, e.g., any future changes in business risk, financial risk, or liquidity.

The other variable that requires some attention is the interest rate. The idea is to use a rate that corresponds to the term of the option. The most obvious is the rate on prime commercial paper that is quoted daily in *The Wall Street Journal* for different maturities ranging from 30, 60, and 90 to 240 days.

To demonstrate the formula, consider the following example. All the values except stock price volatility are observable. In the case of volatility, the historical measure is given, but it is also assumed that the analyst expects the stock's volatility to increase.

An Example of Option Valuation Variables

$$P_s = \$36.00$$

$$E = \$40.00$$

$$r = .10 \text{ (the rate on 90 day prime commercial paper)}$$

$$t = 90 \text{ days---.25 year}$$

$$\text{Historical } \sigma = .40$$

$$\text{Expected } \sigma = .50 \text{ (analysts expect an increase in stock beta because of a new debt issue)}$$

Table 23–1 contains the detailed calculations for the option assuming the historical volatility ($\sigma = .40$). Table 23–2 contains the same calculations except that we assume volatility is higher ($\sigma = .50$).

These results indicate the importance of estimating stock price volatility; given a 25 percent increase in volatility (.50 vs. .40), there is a 53 percent increase in the value of the option. Because everything else is observable, this is the variable that will differentiate estimates.

Efficiency of Options Market

A study by Galai investigated the pricing mechanism of call options and tested the efficiency of the CBOE shortly after it was established.[7] Efficiency was tested against the Black–Scholes option pricing model and is

---

[7] Dan Galai, "Tests of Market Efficiency on the Chicago Board Options Exchange," *The Journal of Business,* Vol. 50, No. 2 (April, 1977), pp. 167–195.

Table 23–1
**Calculation of
Option Value
($\sigma = .40$)**

$$d_1 = \left[\frac{\ln (36/40) + (.10 - .5(.4)^2).25}{.4(.25)^{\frac{1}{2}}} \right]$$

$$= \left[\frac{-.1054 + .045}{.2} \right]$$

$$= -.302$$

$$d_2 = -.302 - [.4(.25)^{\frac{1}{2}}]$$

$$= -.302 - .2$$

$$= -.502$$

$$N(d_1) = .3814$$

$$N(d_2) = .3079$$

$$P_0 = [P_s] [N(d_1)] - [E] [\text{antiln} (- rt)] [N(d_2)]$$

$$= [36] [.3814] - [40] [\text{antiln} (- .025)] [.3079]$$

$$= 13.7304 - [40] [0.9753] [.3079]$$

$$= 13.7304 - 12.0118$$

$$= 1.7181$$

based on a "hedging" strategy, in which a position in an option is matched with a position in the underlying stock (i.e., a fully covered option) so as to eliminate the risk of the aggregate position. There are two phases to the tests of market efficiency. The first is concerned with whether a specified trading rule can be used to separate profitable from unprofitable investments. Such an analysis indicates the power and accuracy of the trading rule. The second phase determines whether it is possible to use the trading rule to generate above normal risk-adjusted profits *in a real world environment,* since it is possible to use a rule to detect undervalued securities, but it cannot be used to predict future behavior in an efficient market. The analysis also examines changes in efficiency over time.

The data were daily prices for each option on the CBOE from April 26, 1973 to November 30, 1973 (152 trading days). During this time period, there were 245 options on 32 underlying stocks. Galai used T-bill rates and commercial paper rates as estimates of r. For the estimates of the standard deviation, he used estimates derived by Scholes and two historical series, one for 1972 and another for the last 30 trading days.

The first *ex post* hedging test examined an option on the first day it was

Table 23–2
**Calculation of
Option Value
($\sigma = .50$)**

$$d_1 = \left[\frac{\ln(36/40) + (.10 + .5(.5)^2).25}{.5(.25)^{1/2}} \right]$$

$$= \frac{-.1054 + .05625}{.25}$$

$$= -.1966$$

$$d_2 = -.1966 - [.5(.25)^{1/2}]$$

$$= -.1966 - .25$$

$$= -.4466$$

$$N(d_1) = .4199$$

$$N(d_2) = .3275$$

$$P_0 = [36][.4199] - [40][\text{antiln} - .025][.3275]$$

$$= 15.1164 - [40][0.9753][.3275]$$

$$= 15.1164 - 12.7764$$

$$= 2.34$$

available to determine whether it was underpriced or overpriced based upon the relationship of the market price to the price estimated using the B–S model. If the option was overpriced (underpriced), it was sold (bought) at the market price, and *this position was maintained for the life of the option.* Each day it was assumed the position was liquidated at the closing price and immediately re-established. Two versions were considered: one assumed that all prices were those prices estimated by the model; the other used actual closing prices to compute returns. Although none of the returns for any option were significant for the second version, the average returns using the estimated prices were significant.

The second *ex post* test was similar except that it involved the assumption that the option position could be changed daily depending upon the relationship of the market price and the model price. The average results with this test were much higher than those from the earlier tests and indicated that *the model was able to differentiate quite well between overpriced and underpriced options.* In addition, an analysis of returns over two 75-day trading periods indicated that the profitable opportunities did *not* deteriorate over time.

The tests were later performed with different estimates for the risk-free and the variance rate, and it was concluded that the qualitative results were unchanged. The model was also tested using 2, 3, 4, and 5 day holding periods, taking transaction costs into account. Assuming a one percent transaction cost, *all* the *ex post* returns were eliminated.

Earlier tests ignored the dividends on the stocks. When the portfolios were derived based upon the dividend yield, the results indicated superior performance for the low dividend stocks, as compared to the performance of high dividend portfolios, and the excess returns did not decline over time. When the author adapted the option pricing model specifically for dividends, using a formula developed by Black, the *ex post* hedge returns were substantially higher. Apparently the dividend correction made the hedging strategy more effective to use in locating profitable opportunities.

Next, the author conducted an *ex ante* hedging test, which was similar to the previous test except that it was applied to past data, which is a better reflection of the *actual* opportunities available to the trader. This test is implemented by lagging the execution of the trading by one day, i.e., based upon the value and price on day t, the option is bought or sold on day t + 1. The returns were much lower, and the number of options with significant returns declined dramatically. It was concluded that, if the future is like the past, there is less than a 50 percent chance of obtaining a return of more than three dollars per option/per day.

An analysis of portfolios based upon dividend yield provided evidence that profit opportunities still might have existed in the CBOE for a market-maker to exploit. Although individual hedges have not yielded significant profits on average, profits were achieved in the portfolio context. *The author concluded that the results of the* ex ante *tests suggest that the CBOE might not have been perfectly efficient during the period investigated and abnormal profit opportunities did exist.* Further, the profits did *not* decline over time.

Because "spreading" is used extensively by market-makers, Galai tested this strategy. Spreading involves selling the option considered to be overpriced and buying one that is underpriced. The spreading decision is based upon the relative values derived from the B–S pricing model. Initially, the author always sold the short maturity and bought the long maturity option. The results indicate small, insignificant average returns, which does not support the general belief that short maturity options are overpriced relative to long maturity prices. Galai then allowed the B–S model to determine how the spread should be carried out and the results were quite good. This indicates that the model was able to differentiate on average between good and bad investments.

The final test is an *ex ante* analysis of the spreading model. Based upon prices and values on day t, a spreading transaction is carried out on day t + 1. Because so many market-makers use this strategy, it was hypothesized that the returns from this *ex ante* test would be small. The results generally confirmed these expectations; the average returns were reduced by half, relative to the *ex post* returns.

Galai's main conclusions were: (1) the trading strategies based on the B–S model performed well in the tests when the hedges were based on the model's evaluation of prices versus the market prices; (2) the market did not seem perfectly efficient to market-makers because some of the returns from a realistic trading rule were positive. When transactions costs were considered, almost all positive returns disappeared, which means these above normal returns are *not* available to the public; (3) the dividend adjustment was important; (4) the tests of a time spreading strategy provided results similar to the hedging results; (5) the results did *not* generally indicate that the market became more efficient over time based upon an analysis of the first half of the sample period versus the second half. The whole test was conducted during the period shortly after the establishment of the CBOE, so this conclusion may be somewhat premature.

Analysis of Risks and Returns from Covered Calls

A recent study by Merton, Scholes, and Gladstein is probably the most complete in terms of results and also in relating the results to expectations based upon factors that determine the value of call options.[8] They discussed the determinants of option pricing as related to the Black–Scholes valuation model and showed what returns will be derived from options with different characteristics under varying stock return conditions. The bulk of the paper presents the results of a simulation for a group of 130 stocks that have options traded on the CBOE and the 30 stocks in the Dow-Jones Industrial Average. The simulation involved the risk and returns for a fully covered call option program as compared to returns from owning the stock alone during the period July, 1963 to December, 1975. The pricing of the options was based on the values generated with the Black–Scholes valuation model.

The analysis covered 25 semiannual holding periods during the twelve and a half years between July 1, 1963 and December 31, 1975. The returns reported are all half-year results and assume dividends are reinvested, but do *not* consider taxes and transaction costs. The portfolios are equal dollar weighted for each stock.

The authors, after dealing with the characteristics of call options, discussed their pricing, considering the five variables discussed earlier in the chapter. In a brief discussion of some earlier studies that employed the B–S model to test the efficiency of the options market, the authors noted that differences between the model price and the market price of options were found, but they were not great and to uncover discrepancies required accurate estimates of the variance of the stock returns. Because of the general accuracy of the valuation model (that was tested again later in the paper) the authors chose to simulate the strategies using option prices

---

[8] Robert C. Merton, Myron S. Scholes, and Mathew L. Gladstein, "A Simulation of the Returns and Risk of Alternative Option Portfolio Investment Strategies," *Journal of Business*, Vol. 51, No. 2 (April, 1978), pp. 183–242.

generated by the model rather than actual market option prices. This made it possible to consider a period prior to 1973 when the CBOE was founded.

In the simulation it was assumed that all options had six months to expiration and all options were held to expiration. This may not be optimal in many instances because it is often best to exercise an option before the expiration date, but this is offset by a dividend adjustment in the formula. The variance was estimated in terms of the sample variance of the previous six months of daily logarithmic price changes. The article included a plot of the average option premium for different ratios of exercise price to stock price (.9, 1.0, 1.1, 1.2). The results of the plot indicated that the premiums were clearly *not* constant over the period, and actually showed a fairly strong upward trend. It was noted that this positive trend is caused by the importance of stock price variance in the formula, and there had been an increase in return volatility during this period. Also, rising interest rates had an effect.

All the options were for six month periods. Hence, the simulation covered four strategies with the only difference being the ratio of exercise price (E) to market price of the stock (S). The four E/S ratios are .90 (in the money), 1.00 (at the money), 1.1 (out of the money), and 1.2 (deep out of the money). It was assumed that an investor bought 100 shares of the stock and wrote a six month option on the shares. The option premium was used to reduce the stock investment. The ending value was the stock value, plus the dividends received on the stock, less the cost of reacquiring the option if it had any value at the expiration date (i.e., the difference between the exercise price and the market price).

All four strategies were considered "bullish" because they all gain from an increase in the stock price although the effect differs. Also, the in the money options had the least return volatility (smaller losses on the downside and lower maximum returns on the upside). The large out of the money option had the greatest return volatility of the four option strategies, although the volatility was not as great as it was with the straight stock position. Therefore, it was shown that any *covered call position involves a lower risk than a pure stock position does, and, within the call strategies, an investor writes more out of the money options as he becomes more bullish.* Because of the nature of the return patterns, fully covered option writing will produce results superior to those for the stock during periods of small increases or decreases in the stock price.

Results of Simulation

In terms of the variability of returns, the results were generally consistent with our previous discussion. The returns from the deep out of the money option strategies were more volatile than those from the other option categories. At the same time, *all option strategies were less volatile than a pure stock position was.* These results, shown in Table 23–3, indicate higher volatility and higher returns for the all stock portfolio. Apparently, the

Table 23–3 **Summary Statistics for Rate-of-Return Simulations, Fully Covered Strategies, July 1963–December 1975**

	Exercise Price = .9 Stock Price	Exercise Price = 1.0 Stock Price	Exercise Price = 1.1 Stock Price	Exercise Price = 1.2 Stock Price	Stock
	136-Stock Sample				
Average rate of return (%)	3.3	3.7	4.5	5.3	7.9
Standard deviation (%)	4.9	7.1	9.3	11.2	16.6
Highest return (%)	14.6	19.3	24.7	30.4	54.6
Lowest return (%)	−9.9	−14.4	−17.4	−19.2	−21.0
Average compound return (%)	3.0	3.4	4.1	4.7	6.7
Growth of $1,000 ($)	2,171	2,328	2,719	3,162	5,043
Coefficient of skewness	−.63	−.48	−.26	−.01	.73
	DJ Stock Sample				
Average rate of return (%)	2.9	2.9	3.2	3.5	4.1
Standard deviation (%)	3.7	6.2	8.6	10.4	13.7
Highest return (%)	12.3	16.9	22.9	29.5	49.1
Lowest return (%)	−5.4	−9.2	−11.9	−13.8	−16.4
Average compound return (%)	2.8	2.7	2.9	3.0	3.3
Growth of $1,000 ($)	1,992	1,942	2,040	2,103	2,226
Coefficient of skewness	−.22	−.21	.04	.35	1.25

Source: Robert C. Merton, Myron S. Scholes, and Mathew L. Gladstein, "A Simulation of the Returns and Risk of Alternative Option Portfolio Investment Strategies," *Journal of Business,* Vol. 51, No. 2 (April, 1978), p. 207. Copyright © 1978 by The University of Chicago Press. Reprinted by permission of The University of Chicago Press.

covered option strategies experience less volatility and higher returns when stock prices either decline or increase by small amounts, but the returns on the option strategy suffer when stock prices increase substantially. Therefore, the returns reflect not only the strategy employed, but they also indicate what happened to the underlying stocks during the period. In the simulation, because the stock returns were sufficiently positive, the all stock portfolio did best, followed by the most bullish option strategy. If the stock returns were different, the rankings would have been different.

An analysis of how sensitive the returns are to deviations in the premium from the value specified by the B–S valuation model indicates that such deviations change the *mean* rate of return, but not the shape of the distribution. Excessive premiums increase the average returns for an option writing strategy. An analysis of returns from the option strategies, using the *actual* market prices for the options compared to the returns using prices generated by the B–S valuation model, indicated how good the valuation model is and, therefore, whether the simulation results are realistic. This comparison was carried out for the period April, 1973 to December, 1975. Based upon the results, the authors concluded, "While the fully-covered returns are higher using market prices, the difference is small."[9] The average percent premium (i.e., option price to stock price ratio) was 11.7 percent for the market option prices and 11.2 percent for the model generated prices. For the out of the money options, the average premiums were 7.5 percent for market prices and 7.1 percent for the model generated prices. These market prices were derived during the early days of the CBOE and, therefore, may have been higher than expected. Because the model appears to derive option prices that are very similar to market prices, the returns estimated from the simulation should be quite similar to the returns that would be derived using actual market prices.

The authors contended that the investor who writes options against a portfolio of stocks will reduce his risk at the expense of also reducing his rate of return. Because the expected value of the option is heavily dependent on the expected volatility of the underlying stock, if an analyst can do a superior job of estimating the return volatility of the stock, then it should be possible to select overpriced options. The returns from consistently selling these overpriced options should be above normal on a risk-adjusted basis. *The crucial talent is the ability to do a superior job of estimating the variance of the individual security.*

Summary

Our discussion began by dealing with the recent history of options trading, starting with the establishment of the CBOE in April, 1973. The reasons for the growth and expansion of this market segment were reviewed and we discussed the growing competition between exchanges dealing in options. The basic terminology for options was presented and quotations explained. This was followed by a discussion of alternative trading strategies, including the purchase of call options under different market conditions, and, finally, the use of spreads under various market expectations.

A section on the valuation of call options dealt with the major variables that influence the value of a call option and the direction of the effect. This was followed by a presentation of the classic Black–Scholes (B–S) valuation model and a demonstration of its application that indicated the importance of the estimate of stock price volatility.

The chapter finished with a discussion of two very important articles on options. A study by Galai of the efficiency of the options exchange indicated the usefulness of the B–S valuation model in selecting undervalued options, and also provided evidence that the market was not completely efficient. A study by Merton, Scholes, and Gladstein indicated what the return distribution should look like for alternative options and then empirically simu-

---

[9] Merton *et al.*, "A Simulation of the Returns," p. 213.

lated the distribution of returns using the B–S valuation model. The results confirmed their expectations that the writing of fully covered call options was a conservative strategy compared to the direct purchase of stock.

The point made throughout the chapter is that the growing acceptance of options (put and call) has provided investors with a greater number of investment alternatives.

1. Define a call option; a put option.

2. How is the CBOE different from the original over-the-counter option market? Discuss the major factors that differentiate them.

3. What are the factors that motivate an exchange to begin trading in an option? Are you surprised that the ASE began to compete with the CBOE on certain options? Why or why not?

4. Define the following terms:
   a. premium
   b. exercise price
   c. expiration date
   d. in the money option
   e. at the money option
   f. out of the money option

5. Differentiate between selling a fully covered call and a "naked" call. Give an example of why the sale of an uncovered call is much riskier.

6. There are five variables that you need to estimate the value of a call option. List and discuss each of them and indicate *why* each is important and how it influences the value, e.g., when this value increases it causes an increase in the value of the option because . . .

7. It has been contended that the sale of a fully covered option is a *conservative* investment strategy. Explain why this is so in terms of the possible distribution of returns on such a strategy. Use an example if it will help.

8. Assume you are bullish on the outlook for the stock market. Look up a four to six month option that is at the money in *The Wall Street Journal*. Assume the stock increases by 15 percent. Indicate approximately what will happen to your option and compute the percent return on the option purchase.

9. Describe a "spread." Discuss why investors engage in spreads. Is the risk higher or lower than that for simply writing a call option?

10. Pick out a stock option on the CBOE and discuss what you would do to write a *bullish* price spread.
    a. Describe what will happen if the stock goes up by 20 percent.
    b. Describe what will happen if the stock declines by 20 percent.

11. Select an option listed on the American Stock Exchange and discuss how you would enter into a price spread assuming you were *bearish* on the stock.

   a. Describe what will happen if the stock price increases by 25 percent.

   b. Describe what will happen if the stock price declines by 30 percent.

12. a. Describe the test for efficiency of the CBOE used by Galai.

   b. Why is the analysis considered a test of the semi-strong EMH?

13. According to the Merton–Scholes–Gladstein study, which is the most aggressive option writing strategy? Why is this so? Is their expectation supported by the empirical results? How?

References

Articles

Black, Fischer. "Fact and Fantasy in the Use of Options." *Financial Analysts Journal,* Vol. 31, No. 2 (July–August, 1975).

Black, Fischer and Scholes, Myron. "The Pricing of Options and Corporate Liabilities." *Journal of Political Economy,* Vol. 81, No. 3 (May–June, 1973).

Black, Fischer and Scholes, Myron. "The Valuation of Option Contracts and a Test of Market Efficiency." *Journal of Finance,* Vol. 27, No. 2 (May, 1972).

Boness, A. J. "Elements of a Theory of Stock Option Value." *Journal of Political Economy,* Vol. 72, No. 2 (April, 1964).

Brody, Eugene D. "Options and the Mathematics of Defense." *Journal of Portfolio Management,* Vol. 1, No. 2 (Winter, 1975).

Chicago Board Options Exchange. "Option Spreading." Chicago, 1975.

Chicago Board Options Exchange. "Option Writing Strategies." Chicago, 1975.

Chicago Board Options Exchange. "Tax Considerations in Using CBOE Options." Chicago, 1975.

Chicago Board Options Exchange. "Understanding Options." Chicago, 1977.

Connelly, Julie. "How Institutions are Playing the Options Game." *Institutional Investor,* Vol. 7, No. 2 (February, 1972).

Cox, John C. and Ross, Stephen A. "The Valuation of Options for Alternative Stochastic Processes." *Journal of Financial Economics,* Vol. 3, No. 1, 2 (January–March, 1976).

Galai, Dan. "Pricing of Options and the Efficiency of the Chicago Board Options Exchange." Unpublished Ph.d. dissertation, University of Chicago, March 1975.

Galai, Dan. "Tests of Market Efficiency and the Chicago Board Options Exchange." *Journal of Business,* Vol. 50, No. 2 (April, 1977).

Gould, J. P. and Galai, D. "Transaction Costs and the Relationship Between Put and Call Prices." *Journal of Financial Economics,* Vol. 1, No. 2 (July, 1974).

Hausman, W. H. "Theory of Option Strategy Under Risk Aversion." *Journal of Financial and Quantitative Analysis,* Vol. 3, No. 3 (September, 1968).

Hettenhouse, George W. and Puglisi, Donald. "Investor Experience With Put and Call Options." *Financial Analysts Journal,* Vol. 31, No. 4 (July–August, 1975).

Katz, Richard C. "The Profitability of Put and Call Option Writing." *Industrial Management Review,* Vol. 5, No. 3 (Fall, 1963).

Kruizenga, Richard J. "Profit Returns from Purchasing Puts and Calls." In Cootner, Paul, ed. *Random Character of Stock Market Prices.* Cambridge, Massachusetts: MIT Press, 1964.

Merton, Robert C. "The Relationship Between Put and Call Option Prices: Comment." *Journal of Finance,* Vol. 28, No. 1 (March, 1973).

Merton, Robert C. "Theory and Rational Option Pricing." *The Bell Journal of Economics and Management Science,* Vol. 4, No. 1 (Spring, 1973).

Merton, Robert C., Scholes, Myron S., and Gladstein, Mathew L. "A Simulation of Returns and Risk of Alternative Option Portfolio Investment Strategies." *Journal of Business,* Vol. 51, No. 2 (April, 1978).

Miller, Jerry D. "Effects of Longevity on Value of Stock Purchase Warrants," *Financial Analysts Journal,* Vol. 27, No. 6 (November–December, 1971).

Puglisi, Donald J. "Rationale for Option Buying Behavior: Theory and Evidence." *Quarterly Review of Economics and Business,* Vol. 14, No. 1 (Spring, 1974).

Reback, Robert. "Risk and Return in CBOE and AMEX Option Trading." *Financial Analysts Journal,* Vol. 31, No. 4 (July–August, 1975).

Roenfeldt, Rodney L., Cooley, Philip L., and Gombola, Michael J. "Market Risk and Return Characteristics of CBOE Options." Unpublished.

Smith, Clifford W., Jr. "Option Pricing: A Review." *Journal of Financial Economics,* Vol. 3, No. 1 (January–March, 1976).

Smith, Keith V. "Option Writing and Portfolio Management." *Financial Analysts Journal,* Vol. 24, No. 3 (May–June, 1968).

"Some New Approaches to Playing the Options Game." *Institutional Investor,* Vol. 8, No. 5 (May, 1975).

Stoll, Hans R. "The Relationship Between Put and Call Option Prices." *Journal of Finance,* Vol. 24, No. 5 (December, 1969).

Wellemeyer, Marilyn. "The Values in Options." *Fortune* (November, 1973).

Books

Asen, Robert. *How to Make Money Selling Stock Options.* West Nyack, New York: Parker, 1970.

Auster, Rolf. *Option Writing and Hedging Strategies.* Hicksville, New York: Exposition Press, 1975.

Bokron, Nicholas. *How to Use Put and Call Option.* Springfield, Massachusetts: John Magee, Inc., 1975.

Clasen, Henry, Jr. *Dow-Jones–Irwin Guide to Put and Call Options.* Homewood, Illinois: Dow-Jones–Irwin, 1975.

Filler, Herbert. *Understanding Put and Call Options.* Springfield, Massachusetts: John Magee, 1972).

Gastineau, Gary. *Stock Options Manual.* New York: McGraw–Hill, 1975.

Gross, LeRoy. *The Stockbroker's Guide to Put and Call Option Strategies.* New York: Institute of Finance, 1974.

Malkiel, Burton and Quandt, Richard. *Strategies and Rational Decisions in the Securities Options Market.* Cambridge, Massachusetts: M.I.T. Press, 1969.

Miller, Jarrot T. *Options Trading.* Chicago: Henry Regnery Co., 1975.

Noddings, Thomas C. *CBOE Call Options: Your Daily Guide to Portfolio Strategy.* Homewood, Illinois: Dow-Jones—Irwin, 1975.

Platnick, Kenneth. *The Option Game: Puts and Calls and How to Play Them.* New York: Communi—Concepts, Inc., 1975.

Rosen, Lawrence R. *How to Trade Put and Call Options.* Homewood, Illinois: Dow-Jones—Irwin, 1974.

Zieg, Kermit C., Jr. *The Profitability of Stock Options.* Larchmont, New York: Investors Intelligence, 1970.

Chapter 24   *Alternative Investments*

In previous chapters we examined in detail a number of investment instruments including common stocks, bonds, and options. In this chapter, we will consider some perhaps less orthodox and certainly less familiar alternatives. These include a very popular hybrid, convertible bonds, that have the characteristics of both bonds and common stocks. These securities have advantages for both the issuing firm and the investor, especially if issued by growth companies. The second alternative is common stock warrants which, while similar to put options, have some unique features that make them desirable for investors *and* for the companies that issue them. Finally we will turn to an area that is typically separated from common stock investments, commodities. In addition to discussing techniques of commodity investment, we will examine similarities and differences between investing in commodities and investing in common stock, a comparison that may be surprising for the similarities it uncovers.

Convertible Securities

A convertible security is one that gives the holder the right to convert one type of security into a stipulated amount of another type of security at the investor's discretion. Typically, but not invariably, the security is convertible into common stock, but it could be into preferred stock, or into a special class of common stock. The most popular convertible securities are convertible bonds and convertible preferred stock.

Convertible Bonds

A convertible bond is usually a subordinated[1] fixed income security that can be converted into a stated number of shares of common stock of the company that issued the bond. The initial conversion price is generally above the current price of the common stock. Assume a company's common stock is selling for 36 dollars a share. The company might decide to sell a subordinated convertible bond that matures in 20 years and is convertible into common stock at 40 dollars a share. If the bonds are 1,000 dollar par value, this would mean the bond is convertible into 25 shares of common stock (1,000 ÷ 40). Because convertible bonds are generally considered to be an attractive investment (for reasons to be discussed), their interest rate is typically below the required return on the firm's straight debentures. In this case, assume an 8 percent coupon.

Advantages to Issuing Firms

Issuing convertible bonds is considered desirable for a company for several reasons. First, as stated, the interest cost is lower than it is on straight debt, and the extent of the saving on interest depends upon the growth prospects of the firm. In most cases, it is a minimum of one half percent (50 basis points) and can be much higher. This is true even though convertible bonds are riskier than straight debentures are because they are subordinated. The subordination feature has led bond rating agencies to consistently rate subordinated issues one class lower than a firm's straight debentures.[2] Therefore, the savings over a comparably rated bond are even more than the 50–100 basis points suggested.

Another advantage is that these bonds are "potential common stock." The bond holder may decide to convert on his own, or the firm will make it possible to force conversion in the future by including a call feature on the bonds. This "future common" feature may be desirable for a firm that currently needs equity for an investment, but does not want to issue common stock directly because of the potential dilution before the investment begins generating earnings. After the investment generates earnings, the stock price should rise above the conversion value and the firm can force conversion by calling the bond. To understand this, consider the example of the bond convertible into stock at 40 dollars a share (25 shares of common stock). Assume that the bond is callable at 108 percent of par ($1,080), and that two years after the issue was sold the common stock had gone from 36 to 45 dollars a share because earnings have risen. Given the conversion feature, the bond has a *minimum* market value of $1,125 (25 × $45). At this point, if the firm decides that it wants to get the convertible bond off the

---

[1] Subordinated means that the claims of the bond holders are junior to the claims of other debenture holders in terms of interest and claims on assets of the firm in the event of default.

[2] See George E. Pinches and Kent A. Mingo, "A Multivariate Analysis of Industrial Bond Ratings," *Journal of Finance,* Vol. 28, No. 1 (March, 1973), pp. 1–18.

balance sheet, it would simply issue a call for the bonds at 108 ($1,080). All the bond holders should convert because the stock they would receive is worth $1,125.

Advantages to Investor

We have mentioned that convertible bonds have special features that cause them to have coupon rates substantially below what one would expect on the basis of the quality of the issue. In spite of this, there are significant advantages to investing in convertible bonds: *they provide the upside potential of common stock, and the downside protection of a bond.* The upside potential can be seen from the example above. The bond is convertible into 25 shares of common stock, so, as soon as the price of the common stock exceeds 40 dollars a share, the price of the bond should move in concert with the price of the common stock because it has intrinsic value (conversion value) above its par value. At this point, as long as the stock goes up in value, the price of the bond will increase by at least the same amount. In most cases, the bond will sell above its conversion value because it offers downside protection and interest payments on it may exceed the dividend payments (as will be explained shortly).

The downside protection is derived because, irrespective of what happens to the stock, the price of the bond will not decline below what it would be for a straight bond. To continue our example, assume that this 8 percent subordinated bond is rated A by the rating services (the company's regular debentures are rated AA). Also assume that the firm's earnings decline so that the price of common stock declines to 25 dollars a share. At this point, the bond has a conversion value of 625 dollars (25 × $25). Would you expect the bond to decline to 625 dollars? The answer is probably not because it still has value as a bond. The bond is an A rated security with an 8 percent coupon. If it is assumed that this is an 18 year bond and comparable A rated bonds are currently selling to yield 9 percent, the price of the bond will decline below par but will not decline to 625 dollars. In this case, the price will decline to about $938.80 (.9388 of par).[3] While the stock declined about 30 percent (from 36 to 25), the bond only declined about 6 percent (from $1,000 to $938.80).

In addition to the upside potential–downside protection they offer, convertible bonds are also desirable because they have *higher current return than common stocks do.* Assume that the stock had an annual dividend of $1.50 a share. This would be a 4.17 percent yield, which is reasonable, but would be less than what the investor would get from the bond. Total dividend on the 40 shares of stock would be 60 dollars a year (40 × $1.50), compared to the interest income of 80 dollars a year from the bond. Obviously the bond would be preferable until the dividend on the stock was raised to two dollars a share. Even then, the bond would probably be

---

[3] This is the price of an 18 year, 8 percent coupon bond priced to yield 9 percent.

preferred because it offers downside protection, and because the 80 dollar interest is contractual, while the 80 dollar dividend could be reduced if earnings decline. Therefore, the investor would probably wait until the common stock dividend reached $2.50 or $3.00 a share before he would convert to take advantage of the higher yield.

An advantage that has been lost was the potential for leverage on convertible bonds. Prior to the 1970s, investors could borrow on convertible bonds at about the same rate that they could borrow on straight debentures, about 80 percent. This made it possible to invest in convertibles with little cash and use the interest on the bond to partially offset the interest on the loan. Currently, the margin on convertible bonds is the same as the margin on common stock.

Convertible bonds are, therefore, a desirable investment alternative because they offer upside potential, downside protection, and, typically, higher current income than common stocks. This yield advantage is especially true for issues of growth companies that pay low dividends and have substantial potential for price increases. In such cases, institutions are willing to accept substantially lower interest than they accept on straight bonds.

Warrants

A warrant is an option to buy a stated number of shares of common stock at a specified price at any time during the life of the warrant. The reader will probably recognize this definition as being quite similar to the description of a call option, but there are several important differences. First, the life of a warrant is much longer than the term of a call option. The typical call option on the CBOE is for from three to nine months. In contrast, a warrant generally has an original term to maturity of at least two years, and many are much longer (there are a few perpetual warrants). A second major difference is that *warrants are issued by the company issuing the stock,* the stock involved is acquired from the company, and the proceeds from the sale are new capital that goes to the issuing firm.

In general, warrants are used by companies as "sweeteners" for bond issues or other stock issues because they are options that could have value if the stock price increases as expected. At the same time, the warrant can provide a major source of new equity capital for the company.

Consider the following example. The Bourke Corporation is going to issue 10 million dollars in bonds but knows that, within the next five years, it will also need an additional 5 million dollars in new external equity (in addition to expected retained earnings). One way to help the bond issue, and also, possibly, sell the stock, is to attach warrants to the bonds. If Bourke common stock is currently selling at 45 dollars a share, the firm may decide to issue three year warrants to acquire the company's common stock at 50 dollars a share. Because it wishes to raise 5 million dollars, it must issue warrants for 100,000 shares ($5 million ÷ $50). Assuming the bonds will have a par value of 1,000 dollars, the company will sell 10,000 bonds and each bond will have 10 warrants attached to it (each warrant is for one share). Assuming the company is successful, and the market price on the common stock reaches 55 dollars a share over the three years, the warrants will have an intrinsic value of five dollars each ($55 − $50), and all of the warrants will probably be exercised prior to their expiration. The result is the sale of 100,000 shares of common stock at 50 dollars a share while the company pays no explicit commission cost, although there are administrative costs.

The value of a warrant is determined in a manner similar to that used for call options because the only difference to the investor is the longer term (an investor does not care whether he buys the stock from another investor or directly from the firm). As is true for a call option, an important feature of a warrant is the leverage it provides. The leverage is probably greatest for an at the money warrant. Assume that the stock is selling for 49 dollars and the warrant for 50 dollars is selling for two dollars on the basis of its speculative appeal. If the stock goes to 55 dollars (a 12 percent increase), the warrant will go to *at least* five dollars, which is its intrinsic value. This represents a 150 percent increase. Assuming the warrant will sell at six dollars, which is a small premium over its intrinsic value, the increase in the value of the warrant would be 200 percent versus a 12 percent increase in the stock price. This is a nice return for a small investment.

As is true for a call option, a major factor determining the price of a warrant is the *length of time to maturity* (the longer the term, the greater the value). It is because of their long term to expiration that warrants will have value even when they are deep out of the money (e.g., a 50 dollar warrant will have value even though the stock is selling for 40 dollars). Another positive factor is the *volatility of the stock price* (the more volatile, the greater the premium). The reader should recall from the discussion of options that volatility is a very important factor because the value of a warrant is greatly affected by this variable.

A warrant would be adversely affected by the payment of a dividend because this is subtracted from the total value of a firm, and the warrant holder does not receive the dividend. Once an investor has analyzed the stock and decided that it could experience an increase in value over the next several years, he should find out whether the firm has any warrants outstanding, because this might allow him to control a large amount of the stock for a fairly long period (possibly several years) with a modest investment.[4]

---

[4] For a further discussion on warrant pricing, see John P. Shelton, "The Relation of the Price of a Warrant to the Price of Its Associated Stock," *Financial Analysts Journal*, Vol. 23, No. 4 (July–August, 1967), pp. 88–99.

Commodities Trading

Commodity futures trading has been a relatively neglected area of investment because it is generally not considered in basic investment courses. As a result, many feel that commodity trading is a highly specialized area that should not be considered by the "typical" investor. In order to put it in perspective, we will consider the similarities and differences between trading in common stocks and trading in commodities, and then deal with commodity futures trading in detail.

Similarities in Trading Practices

1. For both areas of investment there are highly organized exchanges. This is in contrast to other investment alternatives such as real estate, coins, or stamps, for which the trading markets are highly fragmented on a geographical basis.

2. Trading on a given exchange is limited to specified stocks or commodities. Just as the New York and American Stock Exchanges will only allow trading in "listed" stocks, each of the commodity exchanges limits trading to specified commodities.

3. Only "members" can trade on an exchange (stock or commodity), either for themselves or for others.

4. The mechancis of buying and selling stocks or commodities are quite similar. In both cases, you give an order to your local broker, who then sends it to the floor of the exchange where a member of the exchange executes the order through the stock specialist or in the appropriate pit.

5. With the exception of the OTC segment of the stock market, both markets are basically auction markets. This is in contrast to other investment markets in which trading is mainly carried out on a negotiated basis.

6. There is substantial similarity in the types of orders used on the exchanges. In both "market" orders, stop orders, and limit orders are frequently used.

7. Because they have highly organized exchanges and communication networks, both areas of investment enjoy substantial liquidity. This ability to turn investments into cash almost instantaneously at a fairly certain price contrasts sharply with the situation for other investments.

8. In both areas some investors base their decisions on the "fundamentals" of supply and demand, and there are "chartists" who are mainly, and almost totally, dependent upon past price movements for indications of future price movements.

Differences in Stock and Commodity Trading Practices

1. One of the major differences is that there is much greater leverage in commodity trading. While the current margin requirement on stocks

is 50 percent, the requirements on commodity futures range between 10 and 20 percent. Not only is more leverage available, but it is also universally used in trading commodities while in stocks leverage is rather limited. In addition, not all common stocks are eligible for margin trading.

2. There are interest charges on the money borrowed to acquire stocks but there are no interest charges on the difference between the total value and the margin for a commodity future contract. The reason is that the commodity contract is a *future* contract and, therefore, no funds are required until the date on which the contract is actually scheduled for delivery.

3. While there is a commission charged for the purchase and another charged for the sale of the stock, commissions on commodities are only paid on a completed contract (purchase and sale). The commissions also tend to be smaller in terms of the total value of the contract.

4. Stock prices are free to fluctuate without limit. In contrast, there is a daily limit on the amount of change allowed each commodity and, once it reaches this limit, trading is stopped for the day.

5. One of the major problems facing the stock market in recent years has been the stock certificate and the stock transfer procedure. This is not a problem in commodity trading since there are no certificates and the transferring is only done through the Commodity Clearing Corporation.

6. In the stock market, there is a clearing corporation but the dealers are on each side of the trade. In the commodities market, the clearing corporation actually takes the other side in all transactions.

7. Even though there are organized exchanges in both areas, there are no specialists in commodities. When a trade is desired, a member of the commodity exchange simply goes to the appropriate "pit" and makes it known he has an order and all interested traders respond.

8. When an investor wants to sell a stock short, it cannot be done on a down tick; he must wait until there is a trade at the previous price or an up tick (an increase). There is no such tick requirement for commodity short selling.

9. Trading in commodities is simpler than stock trading because there are no dividends to worry about and nothing similar to stock splits. As a result, the price changes reflect all rates of return.

10. About five percent of trading in the NYSE is in odd lots (sales or purchases of less than 100 shares). In contrast, there are typically no odd lot contracts available in commodity trading. Because of the substantial leverage available, it is really not necessary.

11. There are differences in sources of information. While the major source of information about specific firms is the company itself, the

major source of information for major commodities is the U.S. Department of Agriculture. Because of this, there is less of a problem with "inside information" in commodities since the government is scrupulous about any possible leaks.

12. Many of the previously mentioned differences produce a substantially different "typical" holding period for the two investment alternatives. The holding period for commodities seldom exceeds 90 days and almost certainly cannot exceed a year because the contracts are deliverable within that period. In contrast, stocks can be held almost indefinitely and the average holding period is probably close to a year.

13. Supposedly there are differences in price volatility. While the commodity market is known for greater price volatility, it is not altogether certain whether this reputation is attributable to greater *price* movement, or greater *return* variability due to the greater leverage available in commodity trading.

Trading Commodity Futures

The best way to understand what is involved in commodity trading is to trace the steps from a decision to trade through an actual trade. Assume that, based upon our previous discussion and some other reading, you decide to become involved in trading commodity futures. At this point, one possible approach would be to select one or several commodities and begin to analyze them. Although there are about 30 different commodities that you could trade, few traders ever attempt to trade more than five or six at a time. To get an idea of what is currently available, you might look at *The Wall Street Journal* "Future Prices" section as shown in Figure 24–1. Based upon further reading and discussions with a commodities broker, you decide that you will trade wheat on the Chicago Board of Trade (CBT). Each commodity is generally traded in "contracts" that vary by the commodity involved. In the case of wheat, a contract is 5,000 bushels and this is designated in the *Wall Street Journal.* The contract for corn and soybeans is also 5,000 bushels. Assuming you are talking about a March, 1979 wheat contract, the price is 338 cents, or $3.38, a bushel. Therefore, the total value of the contract is $16,900 (5,000 $\times$ $3.38).

How to Analyze? Now that you have selected a commodity to trade, you must decide how you are going to go about making your decisions. Similar to stock investors, commodity investors are basically divided between fundamentalists and technicians. *Fundamentalists* attempt to analyze changes in the supply and demand for the commodity. Factors influencing supply would include the amount of acreage planted, the weather during the growing season in the major areas for the crop in question and the carry over of the crop from the previous season. Regarding demand, the analyst would consider the domestic demand for the product based upon secular population growth, but also demand for animal feed. In addition, a

Figure 24–1
Commodity Quotations in *The Wall Street Journal*

Futures Prices

Friday, September 29, 1978

	Open	High	Low	Close	Change	Season's High	Season's Low
–GRAINS AND FEEDS–							
WHEAT (CBT)–5,000 bu.; cents per bu.							
Dec	344	344	341	342½-¾	–1¼to1	355	273¾
Mar 79	339	339¼	336½	337¾-338	–¾to½	354	280¾
May	333½	334	331¼	332¾-333	–¾to½	351	297½
July	322¼	322½	319¾	321	–1½	340	287½
Sept	....	....	....	324n	–2	327	290½
Dec	....	....	....	329n	–3	331	326
Sales Thurs: 8,433 contracts.							
WHEAT (K.C.)–5,000 bu.; cents per bu.							
Dec	320½	322	320	321-320¾	+1to¾	332½	269
Mar 79	319½	319½	317	318-317¾	–½to¾	336½	274½
May	316	316½	314¼	315½	–½	336½	290½
July	313	314	311¾	312½	–1	322	284
Sales Thurs.: 4,045 contracts.							
WHEAT (MPLS)–5,000 bu.; cents per bu.							
Dec	317	317	314½	315½-¼	–1to1¼	335½	277¼
Mar 79	319	319	317½	318½	–1¾	339½	294½
May	323	323	322	322½	–1¼	334	298
July	323½	323¾	323½	323¾	–¼	323¾	298½
Sales Thurs.: 1,349 contracts.							
CORN (CBT)–5,000 bu.; cents per bu.							
Dec	226	226¾	225¼	226-226½	unch to+½	277	216
Mar 79	236¼	236½	235	236-236½	+¼to¾	283¼	224
May	242¾	243½	241¼	242¾-243½	+¾to1½	286½	230½
July	246	246½	244½	246½	+1	288	233
Sept	248½	249	247	248¾	+1	255	236
Dec	249	250	249	250	+½	250	244
Sales Thurs.: 29,048 contracts.							
SOYBEANS (CBT)–5,000 bu.; cents per bu.							
Nov	655	656½	647½	650-652	–3¾to1¾	686	535
Jan 79	663	663	655½	658½-659	–2¼to1¾	689	560
Mar	670	671½	664½	667-666½	–2¾to3¼	694	577
May	675	676	669	672-672½	–1¾to1¼	697	606
July	676	677	670½	672-672½	–2to1½	697	607
Aug	670	670½	664½	666	–2½	690	608
Sales Thurs.: 22,964 contracts.							
SOYBEAN MEAL (CBT)–100 tons; $ per ton							
Oct	170.30	171.00	169.80	170.50-.30	– .20to.40	182.80	150.50
Dec	174.80	174.80	173.60	174.00-.20	– .20to unch	181.00	155.80
Jan79	176.00	176.00	175.00	175.60-.70	unch to+.10	181.00	155.90
Mar	178.00	178.00	177.00	177.50-.30	unch to–.20	182.00	161.00
May	179.00	179.00	178.20	178.50	– .50	183.00	165.00
July	180.20	180.20	179.20	179.50	– .50	184.50	166.00
Aug	180.50	180.50	179.20	179.50	– .50	184.50	174.00
Sales Thurs.: 9,016 contracts.							
SOYBEAN OIL (CBT)–60,000 lbs.; cents per lb.							
Oct	25.45	25.50	25.15	25.30-.25	– .10to.15	27.28	18.40
Dec	24.80	25.00	24.60	24.75-.71	– .10to.14	26.43	18.50
Jan 79	24.65	24.75	24.37	24.50	– .15	25.95	19.10
Mar	24.45	24.55	24.15	24.25-.20	– .17to.22	25.60	19.30
May	24.30	24.30	23.91	24.10	– .08	25.15	20.90
July	24.00	24.05	23.70	23.90	....	24.90	21.10
Aug	23.60	23.75	23.55	23.60	....	24.75	21.25
Sales Thurs.: 8,373 contracts.							
OATS (CBT)–5,000 bu.; cents per bu.							
Dec	144½	144¾	142	142¼-½	–2to1¾	167¾	127¾
Mar 79	151½	151½	149¼	149½	–1¾	170	135
May	153½	153½	151¼	151½-¼	–1¾to2	172	137½
July	152¾	152¾	151	151½	–1¼	154	143½
Sales Thurs.: 523 contracts.							
OATS (WPG)–20 metric tons; $ per ton							
Oct	73.10	74.10	73.10	74.10b	+1.00	81.30	67.50
Dec	73.80	74.00	73.80	74.00a	+ .80	80.00	68.10
Mar 79	73.90	73.90	73.90	73.90a	+ .70	73.90	68.30
May	73.90	74.00	73.80	73.90a	+ .50	74.00	69.10
July	....	....	....	73.90b	+ .40	73.50	69.70
Est. sales 170; sales Thurs.: 820 contracts.							
RAPESEED (WPG)–20 metric tons; $ per ton							
Sept	329.50	338.50	329.50	338.50b	– .50	342.00	246.50
Nov	289.00	289.00	285.00	285.40	–2.60	305.00	258.00
Jan79	285.50	285.50	283.00	283.00-.10	–3.0to2.9	302.50	257.60
Mar	282.00	282.00	278.70	278.70b	–2.30	290.50	255.20
June	282.00	282.00	278.70	278.70a	–2.30	288.00	255.60
Est. sales 1,870; sales Thurs.: 4,155 contracts.							
RYE (WPG)–20 metric tons; $ per ton							
Oct	99.20	99.20	93.50	93.50	–4.80	113.80	88.80
Nov	....	....	....	97.00a	–2.00	112.20	89.50
Dec	101.00	102.50	97.50	99.00	– .50	112.10	87.00
May79	101.80	105.20	100.30	100.30	–2.00	105.20	92.20
Est. sales 540; sales Thurs.: 1,267 contracts.							
Jan 79	44.00	44.15	43.90	44.15	+ .05	44.25	42.05
Sales Thurs.: 177 contracts.							
–FOODS AND FIBER–							
FRESH EGGS (CME)–22,500 doz.; cents per doz.							
Oct	50.30	51.00	50.10	50.20-.50	– .15to+.15	55.00	49.90
Nov	54.60	55.90	54.60	55.70-.80	+1.1to1.2	60.75	53.75
Dec	58.05	58.80	58.00	58.70	+ .70	62.25	57.50
Jan 79	...	....	....	54.60n	....	57.00	54.60
Feb	52.00	52.00	52.00	52.00	+ .05	56.00	51.40
Est. sales 214; sales Thurs.: 93 contracts.							
MAINE POTATOES (NYM)–50,000 lbs.; cts. per lb.-s							
Nov	5.13	5.17	5.13	5.17	+ .04	5.68	4.75
Mar 79	5.81	5.82	5.80	5.85	+ .05	6.77	5.60
Apr	6.20	6.20	6.14	6.23	+ .04	7.19	5.95
May	7.10	7.18	7.06	7.17	+ .06	8.59	6.75
Est. sales 1,127; sales Thurs.: 1,561 contracts.							
COFFEE (CSE)–37,500 lbs.; cents per lb.							
Dec	147.50	149.75	147.00	149.50-.75	+1.3to1.55	172.00	99.90
Mar79	137.50	139.50	137.50	139.25-.50	+1.64to1.89	167.50	93.75
May	131.85	134.00	131.50	132.50b	+1.25	163.50	94.00
July	129.50	131.00	128.50	130.50b	+ .69	163.13	92.00
Sept	128.50	129.00	128.50	131.50a	+1.12	158.75	90.00
Dec	126.00	126.00	126.00	128.50a	+2.75	137.00	92.50
Est sales 610; sales Thurs.: 1,106 contracts.							
SUGAR, WORLD (CSE)–112,000 lbs.; cents per lb.							
Oct	8.98	9.20	8.88	9.00-.01	– .06to.05	10.50	6.05
Jan 79	9.15	9.20	9.08	9.08-.10	– .02to unch	10.73	6.30
Mar	9.26	9.28	9.20	9.28-.24	– .02to.06	11.03	6.55
May	9.37	9.51	9.34	9.37-.38	– .08to.07	11.23	6.70
July	9.54	9.66	9.50	9.50	– .11	10.99	6.87
Sept	9.69	9.84	9.69	9.69	– .07	10.15	7.05
Oct	9.84	9.96	9.79	9.83	– .05	9.96	7.15
Jan 80	9.89	9.89	9.89	9.75b	– .15	9.90	9.89
Est. sales 5,215; sales Thurs.: 6,844 contracts.							
COCOA (CEX)–30,000 lbs.; cents per lb.-s							
Dec	165.50	168.25	165.25	167.85	+ .85	175.75	113.55
Mar79	165.50	167.70	165.25	167.10	+ .40	173.00	111.50
May	164.30	166.70	164.20	166.00	+ .70	170.40	110.50
July	163.50	163.50	163.50	164.25	+ .55	168.00	118.30
Sept	161.25	161.25	161.25	162.25	+ .55	165.25	116.60
Dec	158.00	158.50	158.00	158.75	+ .45	161.75	121.50
Est. sales 482; sales Thurs.: 1,348 contracts.							
ORANGE JUICE (CTN)–15,000 lbs.; cents per lb.							
Nov	110.50	110.50	108.20	108.20-.30	– .75to.65	128.50	85.45
Jan79	100.30	100.35	98.00	98.00-.10	–1.20to1.10	119.00	81.00
Mar	98.00	98.30	96.00	96.25	–1.10	116.60	80.15
May	97.75	97.75	96.00	96.00-.40	–1.05to.65	104.25	80.15
July	96.10	96.10	96.10	96.10	– .80	100.20	80.20
Sept	96.75	97.00	96.10	96.00b	– .80	99.30	95.00
Jan80	91.00	91.00	90.15	90.00b	– .50	95.50	89.50
Est sales 1,000; sales Thurs.: 457 contracts.							
COTTON (CTN)–50,000 lbs.; cents per lb.							
Oct	63.40	63.40	63.10	63.20b	– .15	68.40	53.16
Dec	65.70	65.72	65.40	65.50-.60	– .17to.07	66.45	53.80
Mar 79	67.80	67.86	67.60	67.70-.80	– .27to.17	68.25	54.90
May	68.95	69.04	68.80	69.00	– .20	69.04	58.35
July	69.28	69.37	69.10	69.40b	– .10	69.50	61.75
Oct	66.00	66.10	66.00	66.20b	...	67.10	64.00
Dec	66.00	66.25	65.95	66.15-.25	– .08to+.02	66.30	64.50
Mar 80	....	....	....	66.50b	– .25	66.50	65.85
Est. sales 4,050; sales Thurs.: 5,611 contracts.							

Source: *Wall Street Journal,* October 2, 1978. Reprinted by permission of The Wall Street Journal, © Dow Jones & Company, Inc., 1978. All rights reserved.

growing aspect of demand is that from *foreign* countries. Hence, it is necessary to consider foreign supply and demand for the commodity and its residual impact on our market.

Some investors adhere to *technical analysis* which contends that future price movements can be predicted on the basis of past price changes and volume changes, and some investors consider a combination of fundamental and technical analysis. It appears that there is a stronger preference for the technical approach in commodity analysis than there is in stock analysis, although there is a fair amount of empirical support for random changes in commodity prices.[5] Based upon either analytical technique or a combination of the two, it is assumed that you have decided to acquire two contracts of March, 1979 wheat on the CBT.

The Transaction After making the decision, you call your commodities broker and place a market order. Like a common stock transaction, the order is transmitted to the firm's representative on the floor of the CBT and this floor broker then proceeds to the wheat pit and calls out that he wants to buy two March, 1979 contracts. After bargaining with several other brokers or traders, he completes the transaction at $3.38 a bushel. The total value of the two contracts (10,000 bushels) is $33,800. If we assume that the current margin on wheat is 15 percent, it would be necessary to transmit $5,070 (.15 × $33,800) to the broker. Because each contract is for 5,000 bushels, each one cent change is worth 50 dollars on the contract or 100 dollars, to you, the investor because you have two contracts. Since you put up only 15 percent of the contract, one may ask where the remaining 85 percent comes from. The answer is that it is not necessary to have the full amount at this time because it is a *future* contract and delivery will not take place until March, 1979. The $5,070 is really a "good faith" deposit to protect the broker in case the market goes against the investor.

After the purchase, the investor can enter a stop-loss order, as is done with stocks, or simply watch the market closely. One difference between trading stocks and commodities is that limits are placed on the daily price changes of each commodity. These limits ensure that no major price change occurs due to an unexpected catastrophe. The limit allows time for new investors or speculators to enter the market. The limit on wheat is ten cents a bushel up or down from the previous close. Assuming a close at $3.38, wheat could not go beyond $3.28 or $3.48 the next day.

Assume that, after a month, the price of wheat has increased to $3.50 a bushel and you decide you want to take your profit. You call your broker and close out your March, 1979 long position in wheat by *selling* two contracts on the market. Again, the broker calls his representative on the floor of the CBT who sells two contracts at $3.50 a bushel. Your position is cleared and your return is as follows:

---

[5] Holbrook Working, "Prices of Cash Wheat and Futures at Chicago Since 1883," *Wheat Studies,* Vol. 2, No. 3 (November, 1934), pp. 75–134; Arnold B. Larson, "Measurement of a Random Process in Futures Prices," in Paul Cootner, ed., *The Random Character of Stock Market Prices* (Cambridge, Mass: The MIT Press, 1964), pp. 219–230.

Bought 2 March, '79 Contracts at $3.38	$33,800
Sold 2 March, '79 Contracts at $3.50	35,000
Gross Profit	1,200
Less estimated round trip commission ($24/contract)	48
Net Profit	$1,152

Rate of Return = 1,152/5,070 = 22.7%

Summary

The purpose of this chapter was to analyze three investment alternatives not considered previously. The discussion of convertible bonds included the advantages to the corporation, but emphasized the desirable attributes for an investor including upside potential, downside protection, and high current income. Such securities are especially attractive if issued by growth companies. The several very important differences between warrants and call options were discussed. The longer term of warrants can provide companies with an opportunity for financing.

Our discussion of the similarities between trading in commodities and in stocks also pointed out some important differences between the two. Our final topic was the specific steps an investor would go through when investing in commodities. Our coverage of commodities is considered an introduction to the area, and the interested reader is referred to the further work on the subject listed at the end of the chapter.

Questions

1. Describe how a firm "forces conversion" of a convertible bond. What conditions must exist?

2. The Baron Corporation debentures are rated Aa by Moody's and are selling to yield 8.75 percent. Their subordinated convertible bonds are rated A by Moody's and are selling to yield 8.40 percent. Explain why this is so.

3. Describe the upside potential of convertible bonds. Why do convertible bonds also provide downside protection?

4. Assume a convertible bond's conversion value is substantially above par, why would the bond holder continue to hold the bond rather than converting?

5. What advantage does a warrant have over a call option for a corporation?

6. Discuss two similarities between trading commodities and trading common stocks.

7. Discuss two differences between trading commodities and trading common stocks.

8. Discuss one advantage that commodities have over stocks; an advantage that stocks have over commodities.

9. Based upon prices listed in *The Wall Street Journal,* compute the value of a contract in soybeans for delivery in about six months (or whatever is closest to this). Assuming a 15 percent margin, compute what you must deposit with your broker.

10. Given conditions in Question 9, compute your return if prices increase by 10 percent and if they decline by 10 percent.

References

Ayres, Herbert F. "Risk Aversion in the Warrant Market." *Industrial Management Review,* Vol. 5, No. 1 (Fall, 1963).

Baumol, William J., Malkiel, Burton G., and Quandt, R. E. "The Valuation of Convertible Securities." *Quarterly Journal of Economics,* Vol. 80, No. 1 (February, 1966).

Brigham, Eugene F. "An Analysis of Convertible Debentures: Theory and Some Empirical Evidence." *Journal of Finance,* Vol. 21, No. 1 (March, 1966).

Gold, Gerald. *Modern Commodity Futures Trading.* New York: Commodity Research Bureau, Inc., 1959.

Harlow, Charles V. and Teweles, Richard J. "Commodities and Securities Compared." *Financial Analysts Journal,* Vol. 28, No. 5 (September–October, 1972).

Pease, Fred. "The Warrant—Its Powers and Its Hazards." *Financial Analysts Journal,* Vol. 19, No. 1 (January–February, 1963).

Poensgen, Otto H. "The Valuation of Convertible Bonds." *Industrial Management Review,* Vol. 7, No. 1 (Fall, 1965); and Vol. 7, No. 2 (Spring, 1966).

Samuelson, Paul. "Rational Theory of Warrant Pricing." *Industrial Management Review,* Vol. 6, No. 2 (Spring, 1965).

Shelton, John P. "The Relation of the Price of a Warrant to the Price of Its Associated Stock." *Financial Analysts Journal,* Vol. 23, No. 3 (May–June, 1967); and Vol. 23, No. 4 (July–August, 1967).

Soldofsky, Robert M. "Yield-Risk Performance of Convertible Securities." *Financial Analysts Journal,* Vol. 27, No. 2 (March–April, 1971).

Sprenkel, Case M. "Warrant Prices as Indicators of Expectations and Preferences." *Yale Economic Essays,* Vol. 1, No. 2 (Fall, 1961).

Teweles, Richard J., Harlow, Charles V., and Stone, Herbert L. *The Commodity Futures Trading Guide.* New York: McGraw–Hill, Inc., 1969.

"The Dangerous Bull in the Commodity Market." *Fortune* (July, 1973).

Van Horne, James C. "Warrant Valuation in Relation to Volatility and Opportunity Cost." *Industrial Management Review,* Vol. 10, No. 3 (Spring, 1969).

Weil, Roman L., Segall, Joel E., and Green, David, Jr. "Premiums on Convertible Bonds." *Journal of Finance,* Vol. 23, No. 3 (June, 1968).

Chapter 25 | *Investment Companies*

Up until fairly recently, most texts on investments were limited in their discussion of investment companies. This was due to the assumption that most readers would prefer to make their own investment decisions. However, recent studies of efficient capital markets have indicated that it is difficult for an individual investor to outperform the aggregate market averages, making professionally managed investment companies an appealing alternative. In addition, there are a number of different types of investment companies, offering a wide variety of options to the investor in terms of risk and return. Therefore, the reader should be aware of what investment companies are, how they operate, what types of companies there are, and how they have performed in the past. These are the topics of our concluding chapter.

We will begin by defining investment companies, discussing their basic management organization, and describing the major types of companies. These different types, ranging from very conservative to common stock funds, are the subject of the second section. In the third section, some studies that have examined the historical performance of mutual funds, using the composite performance measures dealt with in Chapter 22, will be discussed. The final section deals with sources of information on investment companies.

Investment Company Defined

An investment company is a pool of funds belonging to many individuals that is used to acquire a collection of individual investments such as stocks, bonds, and other publicly traded securities. As an example, 10 million shares of an investment company might be sold to the public at 10 dollars a share, for a total of 100 million dollars. Assuming that this is a common stock fund, the managers of the company might then invest the funds in the stock of companies like American Telephone and Telegraph, General Motors, IBM, Xerox, and General Electric. As a result, each of the individuals that bought shares of the investment company would own a percentage of the total portfolio of the investment company. In other words, they would have acquired shares of a diversified portfolio of securities. The value of the investor's shares depends upon what happens to the portfolio of assets acquired by the managers of the fund. If we assume no transactions are made, and the total market value of all the stocks in the portfolio increased to 105 million dollars, then the per share value of each of the original shares would be $10.50 ($105 \div 10$ million shares). This figure is referred to as the *net asset value (NAV)* and is equal to the total market value of all the assets of the fund divided by the number of shares of the fund outstanding.

Management of Investment Companies

The investment company is typically a corporation whose major assets are the portfolio of marketable securities. The *management* of the portfolio and most of the other administrative duties related to the company and its portfolio of securities are handled by a *separate* management company hired by the board of directors of the investment company. While this is the legal description, the actual management usually begins with a group of managers or an investment advisor who start an investment company and select a board of directors for the fund that will then hire the investment advisory firm as the fund manager. The contract between the investment company (fund) and the management company indicates the duties of the management company and the fee it will receive for these services. Major responsibilities include *research, portfolio management,* and *administrative duties* such as issuing securities and handling redemptions and dividends. The fee is generally stated in terms of a percent of the value of the fund. Fees typically range from one-quarter of one percent to one-half of one percent of the total value, with a sliding scale as funds get larger. As an example, assuming that a fund had a total market value of 200 million dollars and a one-half of one percent fee, the management company would receive $100,000 to perform all the duties mentioned. If the management company has to pay out less than $100,000 in salaries and other costs, it will make money. Because there are substantial economies of scale involved in money management, it is in the interest of the management company to have the fund get larger. If the fund grew to 500 million dollars, and the fee scale did not change, the management company would receive $250,000, and it is likely that management expenses would not increase very much because it does not cost much more to manage a 500 million dollar fund than it does a 200 million dollar fund.

The concept of economies of scale is the reason that many management companies start *several* funds with different characteristics.[1] This allows the management group to appeal to many different types of investors, provides the investors with the flexibility to switch between funds, and increases the total capital managed.

Open-End vs. Closed-End Funds

Investment companies are begun like any other company—by selling an issue of common stock to a group of investors. In the case of an investment company, the proceeds are used to purchase the securities of other publicly held companies rather than buildings and equipment. The difference between an open-end investment company (often referred to as a mutual fund) and a closed-end investment company is how they operate *after* the initial public offering is sold.

A closed-end investment company operates like any other public firm since its stock is bought and sold on the regular secondary market and the market price of the investment company shares is determined by supply and demand. There are typically no further shares offered by the investment company, and it does *not* repurchase the shares on demand. There are *no* subsequent additions to the investment company unless it makes another public sale of securities. Also, there is *no withdrawal* of funds unless the investment company decides to repurchase its stock, which is quite unusual.

There are two prices of importance for shares of a closed-end investment company. The first is the *net asset value* (NAV) for the shares which is computed as discussed earlier. The investment company's net asset value is computed twice a day, based upon prevailing market prices for the securities in the portfolio. The second price is the *market price* of shares in the fund, which is determined by the relative supply and demand for investment company stock in the market. When buying or selling shares of a closed-end investment company, the investor pays this *market* price plus or minus a regular trading commission. It is very important to recognize that *the two prices (NAV and market price) are almost never the same!* The long-run historical relationship has been that the market price for closed-end investment companies is from 5 to 20 percent *below* the net asset value. Figure 25–1 contains a list of closed-end funds from *Barron's* (they are currently referred to as "Publicly Traded Funds"). As shown, only 2 of the 27 funds were selling at a premium over net asset value. A lingering question has been why these funds sell at a discount, and why the discounts differ between

---

[1] For an interesting discussion of cases in which insurance companies acquired management companies, see David Armstrong, "Were Mutual Funds Worth the Candle?" *Journal of Portfolio Management,* Vol. 2, No. 4 (Summer, 1976), pp. 46–51.

Figure 25–1
Sample Quotations on Publicly Traded Funds

PUBLICLY TRADED FUNDS

	N.A. Value	Stk Price	% Diff
Diversified Common Stock Funds			
Adams Express	14.64	12⅜	−15.5
Baker Fentress	67.16	46	−31.5
Gen'l Amer Inv	14.06	10¾	−23.5
Lehman	13.73	10⅜	−24.4
Madison	18.59	13⅞	−25.4
Niagara Share	13.28	11¼	−15.3
Overseas Sec	4.49	3⅜	−24.8
Tri-Continental	22.92	18⅞	−17.6
US & Foreign	21.46	15⅞	−26.0
Specialized Equity and Convertible Funds			
Am Gn Cv	24.81	17½	−29.5
bASA	23.67	28¾	+21.5
Bancroft Conv	23.88	17¾	−25.7
Castle Conv	24.83	21	−15.4
Central Sec	8.13	6⅝	−18.5
Chase Conv	11.63	8¾	−24.8
Claremont	12.47	9⅛	−26.8
CLAS	(−7.31)	½	.....
aDrexel Util	20.87	18⅝	−10.8
Japan Fund	16.82	11⅝	−30.9
Nat'l Aviation	31.36	26	−17.1
New American Fd	22.90	19	−17.0
Pete & Res	24.19	22½	− 7.0
RET Inc C	2.71	2¼	−17.0
S-G Sec Inc	1.98	2⅛	+ 7.3
Source	20.22	16¼	−19.6
Value Line	4.19	2½	−40.3

a-Ex-Dividend. b-As of Thursday's close. z-Not available.

Source: *Barron's Weekly,* October 23, 1978, p. 92. Reprinted by permission.

funds. Of even more importance are the returns available to investors from funds that sell at large discounts since, given the fact that an investor is acquiring a portfolio at a price below market value, the returns from such an investment would be expected to exceed average returns.[2]

Open-end investment companies are funds for which shares continue to be bought and sold *after* the initial public offering is made. They stand ready to *sell* additional shares at the *net asset value* of the fund with or without a sales charge. In addition, open-end investment companies stand ready to buy back shares of the fund (redeem shares) at the *net asset value* at any time with or without a redemption fee.

Open-end mutual funds have enjoyed substantial growth during the post-war period, as shown by the figures in Table 25–1. As can be seen, there was a steady increase in the number of funds until 1973, followed by a decline in 1974 and 1975 due to mergers. The growth in the number of funds resumed in 1976 and 1977. The market value of the assets of the funds has not grown due to an overall decline in stock prices and redemptions by fund stockholders. Clearly, open-end funds account for a substan-

---

[2] Eugene J. Pratt, "Myths Associated with Closed-End Investment Company Discounts," *Financial Analysts Journal,* Vol. 22, No. 3 (July–August 1966), pp. 79–82; Julian L. Simon, "Does 'Good Portfolio Management' Exist?" *Management Science,* Vol. 15, No. 6 (February, 1969), pp. B308–B319; Morris Mendelson, "Closed-End Fund Discounts Revisited," *The Financial Review* (Spring, 1978), pp. 48–72.

Table 25-1
**Open-End
Investment
Company Assets
1945-1977**

Year-End	Number of Reporting Funds[a]	Assets (billions of dollars)	Year-End	Number of Reporting Funds[a]	Assets (billions of dollars)
1945	72	$1.3	1960	161	17.0
1946	74	1.3	1961	170	22.8
1947	80	1.4	1962	169	21.3
1948	87	1.5	1963	165	25.2
1949	91	2.0	1964	160	29.1
1950	98	2.5	1965	170	35.2
1951	103	3.1	1966	182	34.8
1952	110	3.9	1967	204	44.7
1953	110	4.1	1968	240	52.7
1954	115	6.1	1969	269	48.3
1955	125	7.8	1970	361	47.6
1956	135	9.0	1971	392	55.0
1957	143	8.7	1972	410	59.8
1958	151	13.2	1973	421	46.5
1959	155	15.8	1974	416	34.1
			1975	390	42.2
			1976	404	47.6
			1977	427	45.0

Source: *Mutual Fund Fact Book* (Washington, D.C.: Investment Company Institute, 1978). Reprinted by permission.

[a] The figures are for "conventional" funds, money market funds are *not* included.

tial portion of investment assets and provide a very important service for almost 9 million accounts.

Load vs. No-Load Open-End Funds

One distinction between open-end funds is whether they charge a sales fee when the fund is initially offered. In the case of a *load fund,* the offering price for a share is equal to the net asset value of the share *plus* a sales charge, typically 7.5–8.0 percent of the NAV. Therefore, assuming an 8 percent sales charge ("load"), an individual investing $1,000 in such a fund would only receive $920 worth of stock. In such cases, the funds generally do *not* charge a redemption fee, which means the shares can be redeemed at their net asset value. Therefore, the funds are typically quoted in the paper with a bid and ask price. The bid price is the redemption price and is equal to the net asset value of the shares. The ask price is the offering price and is equal to the net asset value divided by .92. The percent of the load typically declines with the size of the order.

There is no initial sales charge on *a no-load fund,* so the shares are sold at their net asset value. In some instances, there is a small redemption charge on these funds (one-half of one percent). When examining the prices of mutual funds listed in *The Wall Street Journal,* the reader will see the bid price is listed as net asset value and, in the case of a no-load fund, in the offering price column, there is the designation NL (no-load). A number of no-load funds have been established in recent years. The mutual fund listing in *The Wall Street Journal* indicated about 110 no-load funds quoted. A directory of such funds is available from an industry association.[3]

Types of Investment Companies Based Upon Portfolio Make-Up

Common Stock Funds

Some funds invest almost solely in common stocks, as contrasted to those that invest in preferred stocks, bonds, etc. Within this category of common stock funds there are wide differences in terms of whether their emphasis is on the common stock of "growth" companies, or on the stock of companies in specific industries (e.g., Chemical Fund, Oceanography Fund), or certain areas (e.g., Technology Fund). In some instances, funds will even concentrate their investments in given geographic areas (e.g., Northeast Fund, Heart of America Fund). Within the general category of common stock funds *there is a very wide variety of types of funds to suit almost any taste or investment desire.* Therefore, the first decision an investor must make is whether he wants a fund that only invests in common stock, and then he must consider the type of common stock desired.

Balanced Funds

Balanced funds contain a combination of common stock *and* fixed income securities which could include government bonds, corporate bonds, convertible bonds, or preferred stock. The idea is to balance the commitment of the fund and not restrict the portfolio to only one kind of security. Therefore, managers diversify outside of the stock market. The ratio of stocks to fixed income securities will vary by fund, as stated in the prospectus for the fund. Given the balanced nature of these funds, one would expect them to have a beta factor less than one, which means they would not rise as much as the aggregate stock market will rise during bull markets, but they also should not decline as much during bear markets.

Bond Funds

As indicated by the title, bond funds are concentrated in various types of bonds in order to generate high current income with a minimum of risk. As is true of common stock funds, there is a difference in the bond investment policy of different funds. Some concentrate in only high-grade corporate bonds, while others hold a mixture of investment grades. Some portfolio managers may engage in more trading of the bonds in the portfolio. In addition to corporate bond funds, a change in the tax law in 1976 made it possible to establish *municipal bond* funds. A number of these funds have been established and provide investors with monthly interest checks that

---

[3] No-Load Mutual Fund Association, Inc., Valley Forge, Pa., 19481.

are exempt from federal income taxes (some of the interest may be subject to state and local taxes).

Money Market Funds

Another relatively recent addition to the universe of investment companies is money market funds. These funds were initiated during 1973, when interest rates on short-term money market securities were at record levels. Managers of these funds attempt to provide current income and safety of principal by investing in short-term securities such as treasury bills, bank certificates of deposit, bank acceptances, and commercial paper. The intent is to provide a diversified portfolio of such investments to investors who are concerned with liquidity and safety. They became popular during a period when short-term rates were high, and many conservative investors, who normally invest in savings accounts or savings and loan shares, were considering switching into money market securities because the yields had risen substantially above the ceiling allowed banks and savings and loan associations.

As of the end of 1974, there were 15 money market funds worth 1.7 billion dollars reporting to the industry's trade association, The Investment Company Institute. By the end of 1977, there were 50 such funds with a value of 3.9 billion dollars, and they experienced further substantial growth during 1978 to over six billion dollars. This growth was recorded during a period when the net assets of all open-end mutual funds remained relatively constant. There was a demand for money market funds, and the investment company industry responded accordingly.

Breakdown by Fund Characteristics

The figures in Table 25–2 break down the funds in terms of how they market their funds and by their investment objectives. Wholesale-retail means that these funds are sold through brokers while direct selling means that the fund has its own sales force. The figures on methods of distribution attest to *the substantial growth of no-load funds* in absolute terms (they almost doubled during the period) and in relative terms; they increased from about 11 percent of the total to almost 20 percent. These figures reflect the creation of new no-load funds and the conversion of some load funds to no-load funds.

The breakdown by investment objective indicates a shift in investor emphasis and a response to this shift by the investment company industry. While the aggressive growth funds have remained relatively constant in absolute dollar value and as a percent of the total, there has been a notable movement from growth, growth and income, and balanced funds into the income and bond funds. The data also reveal investor interest in the new municipal bond funds. Finally, almost one percent of the total is in option income funds which specialize in writing covered call options.

Table 25–2 **Total Net Assets by Fund Characteristics**

	1975		1976		1977	
	Dollars	%	Dollars	%	Dollars	%
Total Net Assets	42,178.7	100.0	47,581.8	100.0	45,049.2	100.0
Method of Distribution						
Wholesale-Retail	27,296.1	64.7	30,088.4	63.2	25,969.1	57.6
Direct Selling	9,305.8	22.1	10,168.3	21.4	9,136.9	20.3
No-Load	4,601.6	10.9	6,026.9	12.7	8,764.8	19.5
Other	975.2	2.3	1,298.2	2.7	1,178.4	2.6
Investment Objective						
Aggressive Growth	2,011.4	4.8	2,202.7	4.6	2,212.5	4.9
Growth	13,680.3	32.4	13,855.8	29.1	11,652.7	25.9
Growth and Income	16,703.8	39.6	18,233.3	38.3	16,098.1	35.7
Balanced	5,099.4	12.1	4,898.6	10.3	4,108.9	9.1
Income	2,468.5	5.9	4,589.6	9.7	4,364.3	9.8
Bond	2,215.3	5.2	3,255.5	6.8	3,999.3	8.8
Municipal Bond	(a)	—	546.3	1.2	2,276.3	5.1
Option Income	(b)	—	(b)	—	337.1	0.7

(a) Did not exist prior to 1976.
(b) Did not exist prior to 1977.

Source: *Mutual Fund Fact Book* (Washington, D.C.: Investment Company Institute, 1978). Reprinted by permission.

Dual Funds

Dual funds are special purpose closed-end funds that issue two classes of stock, income shares and capital shares. An investor in a dual fund indicates whether he wants the income shares or the capital shares. Holders of the income shares receive a stated dividend income from *all* investments, but they give up potential capital gain. Investors in the capital shares do not receive any income during the life of the fund, but receive the capital value of all the shares at the end of the life of the fund.

Problems can arise for these funds if they are not balanced in terms of the proportion of income to capital appreciation stocks. Additional problems can arise if stock prices decline, in which case the income required on the remaining capital is above normal expectations.[4] The data in Table 25–3 indicate the status of some of the funds as of June, 1978. Like the closed-end fund, these funds sell at deep discounts from their NAV.[5]

[4] See John P. Shelton, Eugene F. Brigham, and Alfred E. Hofflander, Jr., "An Evaluation and Appraisal of Dual Funds," *Financial Analysts Journal,* Vol. 23, No. 3 (May–June 1967), pp. 131–139; and James A. Gentry and John R. Pike, "Dual Funds Revisited," *Financial Analysts Journal,* Vol. 24, No. 2 (March–April 1968), pp. 149–157.

[5] For a recent analysis and evaluation of dual funds, see Robert Litzenberger and Howard B. Sosin, "The Structure and Management of Dual Purpose Funds," *Journal of Financial Economics,* Vol. 4, No. 1 (May, 1977), pp. 203–230; "The Performance and Potential of Dual Purpose Funds," *Journal of Portfolio Management,* Vol. 4, No. 3 (Spring, 1978), pp. 56–68; "The Theory of Recapitalizations and the Evidence of Dual Purpose Funds," *Journal of Finance,* forthcoming.

	Table 25–3	
	Dual Purpose Funds Friday, June 9, 1978	

Following is a weekly listing of the unaudited net asset value of dual purpose, closed-end investment funds' capital shares as reported by the companies as of Friday's close. Also shown is the closing listed market price or the dealer-to-dealer asked price of each fund's capital shares, with the percentage of difference.

	Capital Shares Price	NAV Capital Shares	% Difference
Am DualVest	9⅜	10.94	− 14.3
Gemini	22⅞	29.48	− 22.4
Hemisphere	2	0.75	66.7
Income and Cap	6¾	8.94	− 24.5
Leverage	15⅝	20.19	− 22.6
Pegasus Inco&Cap	9¼	8.16	13.4
Putnam Duo Fund	8⅜	11.34	− 23.9
Scudder Due-Vest	8¼	10.74	− 23.2
Scudder D-V Exch	20	29.89	− 33.3

Source: *Barron's Weekly,* June 12, 1978, p. 91. Reprinted by permission.

Performance of Investment Companies

A number of studies have examined the historical performance of mutual funds for a variety of reasons. One is that the funds are a prime example of what can be accomplished by professional money managers. Another very important reasons is that data on the funds are available for a long period. Consequently, two of the three major portfolio evaluation techniques were derived in connection with a study of mutual fund performance.

Sharpe Study

A study of mutual funds done by Sharpe includes a discussion of the CAPM and a derivation of performance measure based upon the fact that all efficient portfolios will be on the CML.[6] Therefore, the best portfolios are those with the highest value of the ratio:

$$S_i = \frac{R_i - RFR}{V_1}$$

where:

R_i = average rate of return on fund i

RFR = risk-free rate

V_i = standard deviation of rates of return for fund i

---

[6] William F. Sharpe, "Mutual Fund Performance," *Journal of Business,* Vol. 39, No. 1, Part 2 (January, 1966), pp. 119–138.

This is also referred to as the reward-to-variability ratio (R/V), because the numerator is the risk premium (R_i − RFR) and the denominator is the total variability of returns. Sharpe used the measure to evaluate the performance of 34 open-end mutual funds during the period 1944–1963. The rate of return included price change, dividend, and capital distribution, which is considered a *net* return because it is calculated after the costs of administration and management have been subtracted. It does *not* include the load fee. The reward-to-variability ratio (R/V) for the sample of funds varied from .43 to .78 compared to the DJIA's performance of .667. For the total period, the performance of only 11 of the 34 funds was superior to that of the DJIA. Sharpe compared the ranks of the various funds during the first part of the sample period (1944–1953) to the rank during the second half (1954–1963) to determine the ability to predict performance. The results indicated some relationship (rank correlation of 0.36), but it was felt that the predictions were imperfect. It was generally concluded that past performance in terms of the R/V ratio was not the best predictor of future performance. Sharpe also predicted rank using the Treynor measure, and showed that the Treynor measure, which only considers systematic risk, is a better predictor. (The rank correlation between the two periods was .454.)

The amount of consistency in ranking could be attributable to the consistent performance of the managers (good or bad) *or* consistent differences in expense ratio (e.g., certain funds could always be low because they spend too much on research and administration). Therefore, Sharpe examined the relationship between performance and the expense ratio. The results indicated that *good performance was associated with low expense ratios*; the rank correlation coefficient was .505. There was only a slight relationship between size and performance.

Because it is important for an investor to know his risk class, Sharpe analyzed the consistency of the variability of returns over time. The results indicate a reasonable amount of consistency, with the rank correlation between periods being .528.

Finally, Sharpe analyzed *gross* performance with expenses added back to the returns. This comparison indicated that 19 of the 34 funds did better than the DJIA. He concluded:

it appears that the average mutual fund manager selects a portfolio at least as good as the Dow-Jones Industrials, but that the results actually obtained by the holder of mutual fund shares (after the costs associated with the operations of the fund have been deducted) fall somewhat short of those from the Dow-Jones Industrials.[7]

Jensen Study

A study by Jensen developed a portfolio evaluation technique from the CAPM as shown in Chapter 22 and then used this performance measure to

---

[7] Sharpe, "Mutual Fund Performance," p. 137.

evaluate 115 open-end mutual funds during the period 1945–1964.[8] The basic performance model is:

$$R_{it} - RFR_t = \alpha_i + \beta_i (R_{mt} - RFR_t)$$

where:

R_{it} = rate of return for fund i during the time period t

RFR_t = risk-free rate during the time period t

α_i = the abnormal return for fund i allowing for the systematic risk of the portfolio

β_i = the systematic risk for fund i (Cov_{im}/σ_m^2)

R_{mt} = rate of return for the market portfolio during time period t.

If the α_i for a fund is a statistically significant positive value, it indicates that the fund has experienced abnormally good returns during the period involved, allowing for the systematic risk of the portfolio. This superior performance can be due to the ability of the manager to consistently select undervalued stocks or to do a superior job of predicting market turns.

The summary results for the 115 mutual funds, using all the data available for the period 1945–1964, indicated that the mean alpha value (α_i) was −.011, with a minimum of −.078, and a maximum of .058. This indicates that, on average, the funds earned 1.1 percent less per year than they should have earned for their level of systematic risk. The frequency distribution of the alphas is contained in Figure 25–2. Note that these returns are *net* of expenses (i.e., after deducting expenses). There was also an analysis of *gross* returns with expenses added back each year. In this instance, the average alpha (α) was −.004. Therefore, on the basis of *net* returns, 39 funds (34 percent) had a positive alpha and 76 had a negative alpha. Using gross returns, 48 funds (42 percent) had positive alphas, and 67 had negative alphas. The results with gross returns indicate the forecasting ability of all the funds, because they do not penalize the funds for operating expenses. All the funds have to do is cover the brokerage commissions. The preponderance of negative alphas indicates the inability to forecast well enough to cover commissions.

Because data were not available for all the funds for the full 20 years, a later analysis examined the total sample for the ten years 1955–1964. The analysis of *gross* returns indicated an average alpha of −.001 and an almost even split for funds. Given the various alpha values, how many are statistically significant? An analysis of the 115 funds indicated 14 funds had *significant negative* alphas and only three had significant positive alphas. An analysis of 56 funds for which data was available for the full 20 years

---

[8] Michael C. Jensen, "The Performance of Mutual Funds in the Period 1945–1964," *Journal of Finance*, Vol. 23, No. 2 (May, 1968), pp. 389–416.

Figure 25–2 **Frequency Distribution of Estimated Intercepts ($\hat{\alpha}$) for 115 Mutual Funds for All Years Available for Each Fund. Fund Returns Calculated *Net* of All Expenses**

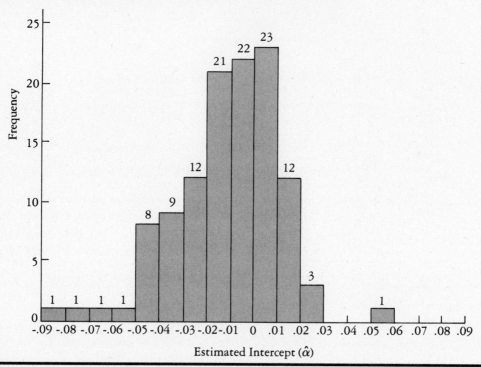

Source: Michael C. Jensen, "The Performance of Mutual Funds in the Period 1945–1964," *Journal of Finance,* Vol. 23, No. 2 (May, 1968), p. 404. Reprinted by permission.

indicated that none of them had substantial forecasting ability. Jensen concluded:

The evidence on mutual fund performance discussed above indicates not only that these 115 mutual funds were *on average* not able to predict security prices well enough to outperform a buy-the-market-and-hold policy, but also that there is very little evidence that any *individual* fund was able to do significantly better than that which we expected from mere random chance.[9]

Mains Comment

A comment by Mains on the Jensen study questioned several of the estimates made by Jensen that apparently biased the results against the mutual funds.[10] The specific objections were:

---

[9] Jensen, "The Performance of Mutual Funds," p. 415.

[10] Norman E. Mains, "Risk, the Pricing of Capital Assets, and the Evaluation of Investment Portfolios: Comment," *Journal of Business,* Vol. 50, No. 3 (July, 1977), pp. 371–384.

1. Jensen assumed that all dividend payments and capital distributions were made at the end of the year for the funds and for the market. Mains felt that the returns for the funds were underestimated as a result.

2. When Jensen computed the gross returns by adding back expenses, he likewise assumed all of this was done at the year end rather than throughout the year. Again this results in an understatement of gross returns for the funds.

3. Jensen computed the systematic risk for the funds for a 20 year period and, when he subsequently examined the performance over the last ten years, he assumed that the systematic risk for the funds during the ten year period was the same as it was for the 20 year span. Although Jensen's test for stability showed significant correlation, it was shown that risk was generally lower during the later period, and this could definitely influence the results, given the importance of the systematic risk in the performance measure. An overstatement of systematic risk would cause an understatement of fund performance.

To test the effect of these objections, Mains examined the performance of 70 funds (all in the Jensen sample) using monthly rates of return for the ten year period 1955–1964 and adjusted for the biases. Comparing the basic returns, the Mains subsample had a slightly higher return and lower risk. Because of these differences, the Mains monthly data produced an annual performance measure, using net returns, of 0.09 (not significantly different from zero) compared to an average performance measure of −0.62 for Jensen's data. In addition, 40 of the funds had positive alphas and 30 were negative. One would probably interpret this as an even split using net returns.

To derive gross returns, Mains added back expenses and an estimate of brokerage commissions on a monthly basis. It was noted that expenses and commissions averaged about one percent a year for all the funds, but the effect varied widely. Using gross returns, the annual average alpha for the Mains sample was 1.07, which indicates abnormal returns of 10.7 percent above expectations. Fifty-five of the funds posted positive alphas and 15 had negative values. This compared to an average alpha of 0.009 for the full Jensen sample with 60 of the 115 having positive results.

The author contended that, after the Jensen results are corrected for several biases, the performance of the funds on a net return basis is neutral. Further, on the basis of gross returns, the results indicate that the majority of fund managers demonstrated above average performance owing either to stock selection or timing ability, and these results do not support the strong form efficient market hypothesis.

Carlson Study

Carlson examined the overall performance of mutual funds during the period 1948–1967, with an emphasis on analyzing the effect of the market series used and the difference in results depending on the time period.[11] After providing evidence of a linear risk-return relationship, the author categorized the funds as one of three types: (1) diversified common stock, (2) balanced funds, and (3) income funds. When each of the fund groups are compared to "the market," using a return to total variability measure, it is shown, in Table 25–4, that the results are heavily dependent upon which market series is used: the S&P 500, the NYSE composite, or the DJIA. For the total period, almost all the fund groups outperformed the DJIA, but only a few had *gross* returns that were better than those for the S&P 500 or the NYSE composite. Using net returns, *none* of the groups did better than the S&P 500 or the NYSE composite. It was also noted that the balanced and income funds were consistently inferior to the full common stock funds, which indicates that the fund's objective did make a difference. An analysis of various ten year subperiods showed that the relative results were clearly dependent on the time interval examined.

Table 25–4 **Index Comparisons— Mutual Funds vs. the Market, 1948–1967**[a]

Index	No. of Funds		Riskless Return R*	Mean Return $\bar{R}$	Variability Standard Deviation V	Performance θ
	1948	1967				
Balanced fund—gross	23	25	2.92	9.92	9.22	0.7595
Common stock fund—gross	33	136	2.92	13.66	14.61	0.7352
S&P Stock Price Index			2.92	13.34	14.71	0.7086
NYSE Composite Index			2.92	13.02	14.49	0.6971
Common stock fund—net	33	136	2.92	12.89	14.63	0.6811
Balanced fund—net	23	25	2.92	9.15	9.22	0.6762
Dow-Jones Industrial Average			2.92	12.39	14.51	0.6526
Income fund—gross	6	17	2.92	11.01	12.79	0.6328
Income fund—net	6	17	2.92	10.24	12.79	0.5725

[a] Returns for each market index include estimated dividends. The riskless rate, R*, is the average annual rate of return for United States Government 9 to 12 month certificates.
Source: Robert S. Carlson, "Aggregate Performance of Mutual Funds, 1948–1967," *Journal of Financial and Quantitative Analysis,* Vol. 5, No. 1 (March, 1970), p. 8.
© March, 1970. Reprinted by permission.

Carlson examined the computation of systematic risk for the funds, and contended that investigators should consider using an index of common stock funds because the correlation with such an index is superior to that with the S&P 500. Such a practice would also eliminate some adjustments that have to be made relative to the S&P 500. Finally, he showed that,

---

[11] Robert S. Carlson, "Aggregate Performance of Mutual Funds, 1948–1967," *Journal of Financial and Quantitative Analysis,* Vol. 5, No. 1 (March, 1970), pp. 1–32.

---

during this 20 year period, the computed alpha relative to the S&P 500 was positive and about 59 percent of the funds had a positive alpha (the author did not indicate how many are "significant").

The author's final analysis considered the factors related to performance during this period. Although there was consistency over time for return or risk taken alone, there was *no* consistency in the risk-adjusted performance measure. Less than one-third of the funds that experienced above average performance during the first half did so in the second half. An analysis of five year periods indicated there was *more* consistency for the shorter intervals than there was for ten year intervals. Of substantial interest was the fact that consistency *declined* over time. Carlson also analyzed performance relative to size, expense ratios, and a new funds factor. The results indicated *no* relationship with size or the expense ratio. On the other hand, there was a relationship between performance and a measure of new cash into the fund. This relationship with new cash inflows was not related to age. There was no difference in performance of new versus old funds. Finally, he examined the performance of eight no-load funds compared to that of the other 74 funds. The results indicated that the no-loads experienced a significantly *higher* performance measure, but the conclusion must be tentative because the sample was limited.

The results indicated that the total sample did slightly better than average for the whole period, but the author contended that the results are heavily dependent on the market series used and the time period examined. Further, past performance was not generally found to be related to later performance. Finally, size and the expense ratio did not influence performance, but new cash flow did, and the few no-load funds examined experienced superior performance.

McDonald Study

A study by McDonald examined the performance of a sample of 123 mutual funds using monthly returns for the period 1960–1969.[12] In addition to an analysis of the performance of the total group, the author was concerned with performance relative to the stated objective of the fund. Each fund was categorized according to objective: (1) maximum capital gain, (2) growth, (3) income-growth, (4) balanced, and (5) income. The results indicated that there was a positive relationship between stated objectives and measures of beta and total variability. The risk measures increased as objectives became more aggressive. The second question concerned the relationship between objectives and the average monthly excess return, without considering risk. Again, the results were generally as one would expect since the returns increased with the aggressiveness of the objective except at the lower end where the income fund return was slightly higher than the

---

[12] John G. McDonald, "Objectives and Performance of Mutual Funds, 1960–1969," *Journal of Financial and Quantitative Analysis,* Vol. 9, No. 3 (June, 1974), pp. 311–333.

balanced fund return. Given the earlier results with risk and return taken alone, it should not be a surprise that there was a positive relationship between return and either systematic risk or total variability. The relationship was especially strong when the author combined several funds in a risk class.

The third consideration was the relationship between fund objective and overall risk-adjusted performance as indicated by the Sharpe, Treynor, and Jensen measures. The results shown in Table 25–5 indicate that, for all the composite performance measures, *the portfolios with the more aggressive objectives appeared to outperform the more conservative funds during this period.* On the question of overall fund performance relative to the aggregate market, four measures were considered: excess return alone plus the three composite performance measures. One-third of the funds had an excess return above the market's, and the mean excess return for all the funds was below the market's. This was not too surprising because the average beta was only .92. The analysis using the Treynor measure indicated an average value for all the funds of 0.518 versus 0.510 for the market, and approximately half the funds had a value above the market's. The results with the Jensen measure indicated that 67 of 123 (54 percent) had positive alphas during this period, and the average alpha was 0.052 percent per month which is about one-half of one percent a year above expectations. Only six of the funds had a statistically significant alpha, which is what one would expect on the basis of chance. Finally, the results with Sharpe's measure indicated that two-thirds of the funds had a performance measure below the market value (0.133), and the mean value for all the funds was below the market (0.112 vs. 0.133). The poorer performance with the Sharpe measure was due to the fact that the funds did not diversify completely.

The final question was the relationship between the market line that prevailed during the period (based upon the risk-free return and the market return) and the fund line during the period, as indicated by the relationship between risk and return for the sample of funds. If the market was in equilibrium, the two lines should coincide. The results showed that the fund line was *steeper* than the market line. This means that the low risk portfolios did *not* do as well as expected relative to the market line, and the high risk funds did better than expected on a risk-adjusted basis. It was noted that the difference in the slope is not significant. However, the difference in slope is contrary to that found by Friend and Blume[13] and consistent with the difference indicated in the Klemkosky study.[14] These results support the notion that, although there may be a bias in the composite performance measures, *the direction of the bias is unknown.*

---

[13] Irwin Friend and Marshall Blume, "Measurement of Portfolio Performance Under Uncertainty," *American Economic Review,* Vol. 60, No. 4 (September, 1970), pp. 561–575.

[14] Robert C. Klemkosky, "The Bias in Composite Performance Measures," *Journal of Financial and Quantitative Analysis,* Vol. 8, No. 3 (June, 1973), pp. 505–514.

Table 25–5 **Objectives and Performance**

Objective of Fund	Risk		Performance Measures			
	Systematic Risk (Beta)	Total Variability (Std. Dev.)	Mean Monthly Excess Return (%)	Sharpe[a] Measure	Treynor[b] Measure	Jensen[c] Measure
Maximum Capital Gain	1.22	5.90	.693	.117	.568	.122
Growth	1.01	4.57	.565	.124	.560	.099
Growth-Income	.90	3.93	.476	.121	.529	.058
Income-Growth	.86	3.80	.398	.105	.463	.004
Balanced	.68	3.05	.214	.070	.314	−.099
Income	.55	2.67	.252	.094	.458	−.002
Sample Means	.92	4.17	.477	.112	.518	.051
Market-based Portfolios	—	—	—	.133	.510	0
Stock Market Index	1.00	3.83	.510	.133	.510	0
Bond Market Index[d]	.18	1.42	.093	.065	.516	Not Available

[a] Reward-to-variability ratio: mean excess return divided by the standard deviation of fund return.
[b] Reward-to-volatility ratio: mean excess return divided by beta.
[c] Alpha: estimated constant from least-squares regression of fund excess returns on market excess returns (Jensen's delta).
[d] Proxy measure based on arithmetic means of results for Keystone B-1 and B-4 funds, with returns adjusted for .042 percent per month average management fee.

Source: John G. McDonald, "Objectives and Performance of Mutual Funds, 1960–1969," *Journal of Financial and Quantitative Analysis,* Vol. 9, No. 3 (June, 1974), p. 319.
© June, 1974. Reprinted by permission.

Klemkosky on Consistency

A study by Klemkosky specifically examined the question of the consistency of performance by mutual fund managers.[15] The author analyzed the risk-adjusted performance for a sample of 158 mutual funds using monthly data for the eight year period 1968–1975. In order to test consistency, Klemkosky compared the ranking using the Sharpe and Treynor measures for adjacent two year periods and the two four year periods. The results indicated some consistency in the four year periods, but relatively low consistency between the adjacent two year periods (only one of the three correlations was significant). As a test of consistency with the Jensen measure, Klemkosky analyzed the proportion of funds that had positive or negative alphas in adjacent periods. Again, there was no significant association in the proportion of positive and negative alphas between successive

[15] Robert C. Klemkosky, "How Consistently Do Managers Manage?" *Journal of Portfolio Management,* Vol. 3, No. 2 (Winter, 1977), pp. 11–15.

two year periods. In contrast, there was consistency for the two four year periods, mainly due to the great consistency in the negative results.

The author concluded that the investor should exercise caution in using past performance (either relative to other funds or to the market) to predict future performance. This is especially true for short periods of time.

Implications of Performance Studies

Assume that you had your own personal portfolio manager and consider the functions you would want him to perform for you. Some of these we talked about in the portfolio performance chapter. The list would probably include:

1. determine your risk-return preferences and develop a portfolio that will be consistent with your desires

2. diversify the securities in your portfolio in order to eliminate unsystematic risk

3. control your portfolio in order to maintain the diversification and ensure that you remain in your desired risk class. At the same time, allow flexibility so you can shift between investment instruments if you desire

4. attempt to derive a risk-adjusted performance record that is superior to aggregate market performance. As noted, this can be done by either consistently selecting undervalued stocks or by proper timing of market swings. For some investors, assuming that they have other diversified investments, they may be willing to sacrifice diversification for this superiority

5. administer the account, keep records of costs, provide timely information for tax purposes, and reinvest dividends, if desired.

The reader will recognize that most of the performance studies were concerned with number four—risk-adjusted performance. Still, it seems appropriate to consider all of the functions in order to put performance into perspective.

The first function of *determining* your risk preference is *not* performed by mutual funds. However, once you have determined what you want, it is clear that the industry provides a large variety of funds that can meet almost any goal in the area of marketable securities. The empirical studies indicated that *the funds were generally consistent in meeting their stated goals;* i.e., the risk and returns *were* consistent with the stated objectives.

The second function is to diversify your portfolio in order to eliminate unsystematic risk. One of the major benefits of mutual funds is *instant diversification*. This is especially beneficial to the new, small investor who does not have the resources to acquire 100 shares of 10 or 12 different issues and thereby reduce unsystematic risk. With most mutual funds, it is possible to start with about $1,000 and acquire a portfolio of securities that is correlated about .90 with the market portfolio (about 90 percent diversified). As noted in the studies, there is a range of diversification, but typically some three-quarters of the funds in any sample have a correlation about .90, so *most funds provide excellent diversification* especially if they state this as an objective.

The third function is to maintain diversification and keep you in your desired risk class. Mutual funds have been quite good in terms of the stability of their correlation with the market. This is not too surprising since, once you have a reasonably well diversified portfolio, it is difficult to change its make-up substantially. Further, the evidence is quite strong regarding the consistency of the risk class. Recall that even the studies that indicated there was not much consistency in risk-adjusted performance did generate results that indicated *consistency in risk alone.* Finally, on the flexibility to change investment instruments, the initiation of a number of funds by a given management company does help accomplish this goal. For a small service charge (five to ten dollars), these investment groups will typically allow an investor to shift between their funds simply by calling the fund. Therefore, it is possible to shift from an aggressive stock fund to a money market fund for much less than it would cost you if you did it yourself.

The fourth function is to derive a record of risk-adjusted performance that is superior to the aggregate market (i.e., naive buy-and-hold). I am sure the reader will not be surprised when I conclude that the news on this function is not very good. A reasonable summary of the evidence is that, on average, the results achieved by portfolio managers through their ability to select securities or time the market are *about as good as* or only *slightly better* than would be achieved with a naive buy-and-hold policy. This conclusion is based upon evidence using *gross* returns. Unfortunately, the evidence regarding *net* returns, which is what the investor receives, indicates that the majority of funds do *not* do as well as a naive buy-and-hold policy. A reasonable estimate is that the shortfall in performance is about one percent a year which is roughly the average cost of expenses and commissions. For the investor who would like to find one of the superior funds, the news is likewise not very encouraging. Most studies show a lack of consistency in performance over time except among funds that consistently do not perform well. Apparently if the poor performance is due to excessive expenses, this state of affairs will continue, so such funds should be avoided. In general, an investor should not expect to consistently enjoy superior risk-adjusted performance from investment in a mutual fund.

The final objective is administration of the account. This is a major benefit of most mutual funds, since they allow automatic reinvestment of dividends with no charge and consistently provide a record of total cost. Further, each year they supply a statement which indicates the dividend income and capital gain distribution for tax purposes.

Most investors have a set of functions they want their portfolio manager to perform. *Typically, mutual funds can help the investor accomplish four of the five at a cost lower in terms of time and money than it would be if they did it on their own.* Unfortunately the price of this is about one percent a year in loss of performance. The studies we discussed did not take into account the sales load of many funds, which also detracts from performance. An obvious way to avoid this loss is to acquire a no-load fund, since the limited evidence to date indicates that their performance is about equal to that of the load funds.

Sources of Information

Given the wide variety of types and number of funds available, it is important to be able to determine the performance of various funds over time and derive some understanding of their goals and management philosophy.

Daily quotations on a large number of open-end funds are contained in *The Wall Street Journal.* A more comprehensive weekly list of quotations and the dividend income and capital gain for the past 12 months are carried in *Barron's,* which also includes a quarterly update on performance over the past ten years for a number of funds. *Barron's* contains a list of closed-end funds with current net asset values, current market quotes on the funds, and indicated percent of difference between the two figures. As mentioned, the market price is typically about 5–20 percent below the net asset value. Finally, for those interested in dual funds, *Barron's* contains a list of nine dual funds, giving their current net asset value, market quotation, and the percent of difference between the two. The discounts on these funds are generally close to 20 percent.

The major source of comprehensive historical information is an annual publication issued by Arthur Wiesenberger Services entitled *Investment Companies.* This book is published each year and currently contains vital statistics for over 535 mutual funds arranged alphabetically. The description of each fund includes: a brief history, investment objectives and portfolio analysis, statistical history, special services available, personnel, advisors and distributors, sales charges, and a hypothetical $10,000 investment charted over 10 years for major funds. A sample page for the Technology Fund is contained in Figure 25–3. In addition, the Wiesenberger book contains a summary table that lists the annual rates of return and price volatility for a number of funds. Recently, Wiesenberger has added two additional services. Every three months the firm publishes *Management Results* which is an update on the long-term performance of over 400 mutual funds, arranged alphabetically according to the investment objective of the fund. Every month the firm also publishes *Current Performance and Dividend Record* which contains the dividend and short-run per-

Figure 25–3
Sample Page from
Investment
Companies

TECHNOLOGY FUND, INC.

Organized in 1948 as Television Fund, Technology Fund became Television-Electronics Fund in 1951 and adopted its present name in January 1968. On December 10, 1976, the name of the fund's adviser (then Supervised Investors Services, Inc.) was changed to Kemper Financial Services, Inc., a wholly owned subsidiary of Kemper Corp., an insurance and financial services holding company.

Under the policy revised in early 1968, the fund invests primarily in securities of companies expected to benefit from technological advances and improvements in such fields as aerospace, astrophysics, chemistry, electricity, electronics, geology, mechanical engineering, metallurgy, nuclear physics and oceanography. Management may, however, seek investment opportunities in virtually any industry in which they may be found. An advisory board provides information of a technical nature relating to new inventions and developments.

At the end of 1977, the fund had 90% of its assets in common stocks, of which a significant proportion was concentrated in five industry groups: information service industries (12.4% of assets), petroleum service and electronics (each 8.4%), conglomerates (7.2%), and aerospace & aircraft (7.1%). The five largest individual in-vestments were IBM (5.3% of assets), Studebaker-Worthington (4.7%), Schlumberger (3.7%), American International Reinsurance (3.5%), and Mapco (3.3%). The rate of portfolio turnover during the latest fiscal year was 20.5% of average assets. Unrealized appreciation was 1.4% of calendar year-end assets.

Special Services: An open account system serves for accumulation and automatic dividend reinvestment. Minimum initial investment is $100; subsequent investments must be at least $25. Income dividends are invested at net asset value. Plan payments may be made by way of pre-authorized checks against the investor's checking account. Arrangements may be made for payroll deduction. A monthly or quarterly withdrawal plan is available without charge to accounts worth $5,000 at the offering price; payments may be of any designated amount. Shares may be exchanged for those of other funds in the Kemper Financial group without service fee. Tax-deferred retirement plans are available for corporations and the self-employed, as well as Individual Retirement Account plans. A one-time account reinstatement privilege is available to redeeming shareholders within a specified time.

Statistical History

			AT YEAR-ENDS			% of Assets in			ANNUAL DATA				
Year	Total Net Assets ($)	Number of Share-holders	Net Asset Value Per Share ($)	Offer-ing Price ($)	Yield (%)	Cash & Equiv-alent	Bonds & Pre-ferreds	Com-mon Stocks	Income Div-idends ($)	Capital Gains Distribu-tion ($)	Expense Ratio (%)	Offering Price ($) High	Low
1977	358,694,594	70,491	7.14	7.80	2.5	8	2*	90	0.20	0.10	0.60	8.31	7.17
1976	432,029,805	76,716	7.58	8.28	2.3	3	6*	91	0.19	—	0.59	8.42	6.82
1975	416,490,321	86,336	6.20	6.78	2.8	6	3*	91	0.19	—	0.64	7.42	5.12
1974	338,514,102	91,141	4.67	5.12	3.5	12	3*	85	0.18	—	0.67	7.01	4.66
1973	489,644,043	96,032	6.21	6.81	2.2	8	2*	90	0.15	—	0.57	8.47	6.30
1972	665,133,022	100,312	7.66	8.39	1.6	6	4*	90	0.14	0.36	0.56	9.24	8.02
1971	667,760,452	106,008	7.47	8.14	2.1	5	6*	89	0.18	0.30	0.54	9.02	7.06
1970	617,992,236	109,703	6.91	7.53	2.6	10	6	84	0.20	0.10	0.59	8.12	5.80
1969	631,010,166	108,777	7.34	8.00	2.3	13	6	81	0.20	0.74	0.54	9.95	7.75
1968	432,029,805	77,716	7.58	9.91	1.4	12	5*	83	0.16	1.76	0.56	11.93	9.48
1967	579,966,741	109,065	10.22	11.14	1.3	11	4	85	0.16	1.12	0.59	12.48	9.38

* Includes a substantial proportion in convertible issues.

Directors: John Hawkinson, Pres.; Thomas R. Anderson, Vice President; David W. Belin; Lewis A. Burnham; Russell H. Matthias, Harry C. De Muth; Earl D. Larsen; Matthew W. Powers; Christian G. Schmidt; Reuben Thorson. Advisory Board: Dr. William L. Everitt; Dr. Frederick E. Terman; Dr. Jerome B. Wiesner.

Investment Adviser: Kemper Financial Services, Inc. (Supervised Investors Services, Inc.). Compensation to the Adviser is ½ of 1% annually of average daily net assets on first $215 million; 0.375% on the next $335 million; 0.30% on the next $250 million; and 0.25% on all assets over $800 million.

Custodian and Transfer Agent: United Missouri Bank of Kansas City N.A., Kansas City, MO 64141.

Shareholder Service Agent: Data-Sys-Tance, Inc., Kansas City, MO 64141.

Distributor: Kemper Financial Services, Inc., 120 South La Salle Street, Chicago, IL 60603.

Sales Charge: Maximum is 8½% of offering price; minimum is 1% at $1 million. Reduced charges begin at $10,000 and are applicable to combined purchases of the fund and other of the Kemper Mutual Funds.

Dividends: Income dividends are paid in cash or shares quarterly in the months of February, May, August and November. Capital gains, if any, are paid optionally in shares or cash in November.

Shareholder Reports: Issued quarterly. Fiscal year ends October 31. Current prospectus effective in March.

Qualified for Sale: In all states and DC.

Address: 120 South LaSalle St., Chicago, IL 60603.

Telephone: (312) 346-3223.

An assumed investment of $10,000 in this fund, with capital gains accepted in shares and income dividends reinvested, is illustrated below. The explanation on Page 162 must be read in conjunction with this illustration.

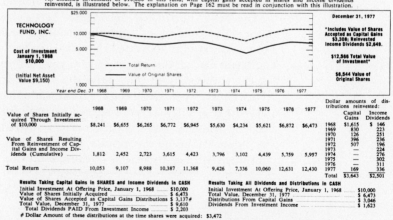

	1968	1969	1970	1971	1972	1973	1974	1975	1976	1977
Value of Shares Initially acquired Through Investment of $10,000	$8,241	$6,655	$6,265	$6,772	$6,945	$5,630	$4,234	$5,621	$6,872	$6,473
Value of Shares Resulting From Reinvestment of Capital Gains and Income Dividends (Cumulative)	1,812	2,452	2,723	3,615	4,423	3,796	3,102	4,439	5,759	5,957
Total Return	10,053	9,107	8,988	10,387	11,368	9,426	7,336	10,060	12,631	12,430

Dollar amounts of distributions reinvested:

	Capital Gains	Income Dividends
1968	$1,615	$ 146
1969	830	223
1970	126	251
1971	396	236
1972	507	196
1973	—	224
1974	—	276
1975	—	302
1976	—	311
1977	169	336
Total	$3,643	$2,501

Results Taking Capital Gains in SHARES and Income Dividends in CASH
Initial Investment At Offering Price, January 1, 1968 .... $10,000
Value of Shares Initially Acquired .... $ 6,473
Value of Shares Accepted as Capital Gains Distributions .... $ 3,137#
Total Value, December 31, 1977 .... $ 9,610
Total Dividends PAID From Investment Income .... $ 2,203
Dollar Amount of these distributions at the time shares were acquired: $3,472

Results Taking All Dividends and Distributions in CASH
Initial Investment At Offering Price, January 1, 1968 .... $10,000
Total Value, December 31, 1977 .... $ 6,473
Distributions From Capital Gains .... $ 3,046
Dividends From Investment Income .... $ 1,623

Source: *Investment Companies* (Boston, Mass.: Arthur Wiesenberger Companies Services, 1978), p. 414. Reprinted with permission from Wiesenberger Investment Companies Service, Thirty-eighth edition, copyright 1978. Warren, Gorham & Lamont, Inc., 210 South Street, Boston, Mass. All rights reserved.

formance of over 400 funds. The funds are listed alphabetically with the objective indicated.[16]

Another source of analytical historical information on funds is *Forbes*, a biweekly financial publication that usually contains information about individual companies and their investment philosophy. In addition, the magazine conducts an annual survey of mutual funds in August. A sample page is contained in Figure 25–4. As shown, the survey not only considers recent and 10 year returns, but also indicates sales charge and the annual expense ratio for each fund.

Because of the interest in mutual funds, United Business Service Company publishes a semimonthly service called *United Mutual Fund Selector*. Each issue contains several articles on specific mutual funds or classes of mutual funds (e.g., municipal bond funds). The first issue of each month contains a four page supplement entitled, "Investment Company Performance Comparisons," that gives recent and historical changes in NAV for load and no-load funds. A sample page is contained in Figure 25–5.[17]

Summary

The purpose of this chapter was to describe the general characteristics of investment companies and discuss the historical performance of mutual funds. The first section defined investment companies and discussed typical management arrangements. A breakdown of types of investment companies, including closed-end, open-end, load, no-load, and dual funds was then considered. This was followed by a discussion of the wide variety of funds available. Almost any investment objective or combination of objectives can currently be matched by some investment companies.

The major portion of the chapter was a discussion of the results of a number of studies examining the historical performance of mutual funds. Most of the studies indicated that less than half the funds did as well as the aggregate market did on a risk-adjusted basis using net returns, while the results with gross returns generally indicated an average risk-adjusted return about equal to the market's, and about half the funds did better than the market did. There were also some studies that indicated performance was superior when gross returns were considered. Following a discussion of the implications of the results for an individual investor, the chapter concluded with a discussion of sources of information on mutual funds.

---

[16] These services are currently published by Wiesenberger Investment Companies Services, 210 South Street, Boston, Massachusetts, 02111.

[17] This service is available from United Business Service Company, 210 Newbury St., Boston, Mass., 02116.

Figure 25–4
Sample Fund Page from *Forbes*

FUND RATINGS–1978

Performance Ratings			Investment Results						
In UP Markets	In DOWN Markets		Latest 12 Months Gain	10-Year Average Annual Growth Rate	Latest 12 Months Dividend Return	Total Assets 6/30/78 In Millions	% Change 1978 vs. 1977	Maximum Sales Charge	Annual Expenses Per $100
		Standard & Poor's 500 Stock Average	-4.9%	-1.3%	5.3%				
C	D	FORBES Stock Fund Average	0.5%	-2.1%	3.6%				
		STOCK FUNDS (LOAD)							
C	D	Affiliated Fund	-8.3%	-0.1%	5.0%	$1,445.5	-11.8	7.25	$0.41
A+	B	AMCAP Fund	33.3	2.9	1.6	65.4	18.5	8.50	0.93
•D	•A	American Birthright Trust (started 5/70)	-1.7	—	none	48.5	30.0	8.50	1.50
B	F	American General Capital Growth Fund	4.6	-7.0	2.6	155.7	-10.3	8.50	0.65
•B	•C	American General Venture Fund (started 10/70)	36.3	—	0.2	13.2	29.4	8.50	1.32
D	A	American Growth Fund	10.3	0.9	2.3	15.6	4.0	7.25	1.50
C	B	American Insurance & Industrial Fund	2.6	5.3	2.9	11.2	9.8	8.50	1.00
D	•D	American Leaders Fund (started 2/69)	-5.9	—	4.1	16.2	-19.4	6.50	1.33
C	B	American Mutual Fund	4.9	1.3	4.8	339.6	0.1	8.50	0.60
A	C	American National Growth Fund	23.8	1.6	2.5	25.9	25.7	8.50	0.84
C	•D	American Option & Equity Fund* (started 1/69)	-7.9	—	1.8	3.1	-3.1	8.50	1.52
C	F	Anchor Growth Fund	4.5	-7.2	3.2	167.4	-13.0	7.25	0.65
D	C	Axe-Houghton Stock Fund	0.5	-2.3	1.0	68.4	-15.6	8.50	0.91
C	•F	Berkshire Capital Fund (started 12/68)	-7.0	—	3.6	5.1	-12.1	8.50	1.44
A	•D	BLC Growth Fund (started 10/69)	10.4	—	2.3	9.1	5.8	8.50	1.02
C	•B	BLC Income Fund (started 10/69)	-4.1	—	5.5	10.8	0.0	8.50	0.97
D	D	Bondstock Corp	3.7	-3.7	4.0	17.5	-9.3	8.50	0.82
B	F	Boston Mutual Fund (started 1/69)	2.7	-3.7	2.5	3.3	-15.4	8.50	1.02
C	C	Broad Street Investing Corp	-3.7	1.1	5.0	308.1	-9.6	7.25	0.45
B	D	Brown Fund	2.3	-1.5	2.5	3.4	3.0	7.25	1.42
B	D	Bullock Fund	-1.8	-0.4	3.8	137.3	-9.4	8.50	0.72
C	F	Capital Fund of America	20.4	-4.5	2.0	94.4	3.1	8.50	0.94
B	D	The Cardinal Fund	7.5	-1.1	3.4	12.3	-6.1	8.50	1.00
A	D	Century Shares Trust	0.6	1.2	3.1	65.5	-7.6	7.25	0.57
A	F	CG Fund	4.6	-0.5	2.5	118.1	-4.8	7.50	0.71
A+	A	Charter Fund	21.4	7.3	1.1	15.5	14.8	8.50	1.78
B	F	Chase Frontier Capital Fund of Boston	15.2	-7.6	0.5	12.4	-6.1	8.50	1.51
C	F	The Chase Fund of Boston	-1.6	-8.0	3.7	28.4	-14.2	8.50	0.96
B	•F	Chase Special Fund of Boston (started 7/69)	10.1	—	1.0	10.0	-8.3	8.50	1.51
B	C	Chemical Fund	5.2	0.5	2.9	739.0	-3.8	8.50	0.53
D	D	The Colonial Fund	-4.6	-3.8	5.3	82.7	-17.5	8.50	0.79
C	F	Colonial Growth Shares	-1.5	-4.9	2.6	58.5	-15.0	8.50	1.09
B	D	Common Stock Fund of State Bond and Mtge Co	-1.4	-2.3	2.9	34.9	-6.4	8.50	1.17
D	D	Commonwealth Fund Indenture of Trust Plans A & B	-5.9	-5.3	6.9	14.4	-20.0	7.50	0.61
D	C	Commonwealth Fund Indenture of Trust Plan C	-7.3	-3.1	6.3	40.1	-13.6	7.50	0.74
D	D	Composite Fund	7.6	-3.1	2.7	23.9	-14.3	7.00	0.94
B	B	Comstock Fund	15.2	1.4	3.1	95.5	20.3	8.50	0.89
C	C	Corporate Leaders Tr Fund Certificates, Series "B"	-9.9	-0.7	5.5	43.8	-10.6	†	0.13
B	D	Country Capital Investment Fund	-0.5	-1.8	2.8	40.6	-1.7	7.50	0.91
D	C	Decatur Income Fund	-6.6	-0.4	6.1	246.1	-10.7	8.50	0.80

• Fund rated for two periods only; maximum allowable rating A.
* Formerly American Equity Fund.
† Fund not currently selling new shares; existing shares traded over-the-counter.

Source: Reprinted by permission of *Forbes* Magazine from the August 21, 1978, issue.

Figure 25–5
Sample Page from United Mutual Fund Selector

Investment Company Performance Comparisons

(This four-page supplement appears in the first issue of every month)

NO-LOAD FUNDS

% Change in Net Asset Value *

	7 Mo. 1978	Year 1977	Year 1976	5 Yrs. 1973-77	% Yield°	Type (Policy)
★ Acorn Fund	+18.0	+18	+64	+ 44	2.0	AG(S)
Advance Investors	+ 9.1	−11	+ 4	§	1.3	G(S)
Afuture Fund	+18.9	+ 4	+19	− 19	0.0	AG(S)
Allstate Enterprises Fund	+ 9.0	− 5	+ 8	− 31	2.2	G(S)
Alpha Fund	+11.5	− 4	+23	− 29	2.2	AG(S)
American Heritage Fund	+20.4	+16	+22	− 47	0.0	AG(He)
Am. Investors Fund	+20.2	+ 5	+35	0	1.2	AG(S)
Armstrong Associates	+30.6	− 1	+44	− 2	0.0	G(S)
Babson (D.L.) Income Tr.	+ 1.1	+ 3	+11	+ 23	7.0	I(Fx)
★ Babson (David L.) Inv.	+11.1	− 7	+14	− 14	2.8	G(S)
Beacon Hill Mutual	+12.5	+ 1	+11	− 18	0.7	G(S)
Capamerica Fund	+ 9.8	+ 9	+28	+ 44	5.9	GI(SFx)
Capital Shares	+16.9	+ 7	+43	− 3	1.4	G(S)
Columbia Growth Fund	+18.1	0	+31	+ 8	1.8	AG(S)
Commerce Income Shs.	+ 2.9	− 6	+21	− 8	6.3	GI(SFx)
†Companion Fund	+ 9.5	− 3	+21	− 13	3.0	G(S)
Contrafund	+14.7	−10	+36	+ 34	2.7	AG(S)
deVegh Mutual Fund	+ 7.1	− 4	+16	− 3	3.2	G(S)
Dodge & Cox Stock Fund	+13.1	− 6	+22	+ 5	3.6	G(S)
Drexel Burnham Fund	+16.3	− 4	+24	− 21	3.8	GI(SFx)
Dreyfus Number Nine	+28.3	+ 7	+39	+ 24	1.1	G(S)
Dreyfus Special Income	+ 3.3	+ 6	+19	+ 27	7.5	IG(FxS)
Dreyfus Third Century	+19.2	+13	+24	+ 34	1.2	G(S)
Edie Special Growth Fund	+26.4	+ 8	+ 7	− 34	0.6	AG(S)
Energy Fund	+ 8.1	+ 2	+32	+ 35	3.1	G(S)
Evergreen Fund	+39.5	+25	+49	+ 74	1.1	AG(S)
Explorer Fund	+23.1	+28	+17	− 11	0.1	AG(S)
Fidelity Aggressive Income	+ 4.2	§	§	§	10.3ᵃ	I(Fx)
Fidelity Corporate Bond	+ 1.1	+ 6	+17	+ 31	8.6	I(Fx)
★ Fidelity Equity-Income	+17.4	+ 5	+44	+ 56	5.0	IG(SFx)
Fidelity Thrift Trust	+ 1.5	+ 3	+25	§	7.2	I(Fx)
Financial Dynamics	+16.0	+ 8	+31	+ 8	2.7	AG(S)
Financial Industrial	+ 9.4	+ 3	+29	+ 20	4.2	GI(CS)
★ Financial Ind. Income	+ 6.6	+ 4	+40	+ 69	5.6	IG(CS)
First Index Inv. Tr.	+ 8.1	− 8	§	§	4.3	GI(S)
First Multifund	+ 7.6	− 6	+20	− 17	0.0	AG(Fn)
44 Wall Street	+45.0	+17	+47	+ 24	0.0	AG(S)
Fd. for U.S. Gv. Sec.	+ 0.6	+ 1	+13	+ 28	7.3	I(Fx)
G.T. Pacific Fund	+38.6	§	§	§	1.0	G(SJa)
General Electric S&S	+11.7	− 8	+14	− 30	3.7	G(S)
General Securities	+20.7	− 3	+36	+ 25	1.8	G(S)
Growth Industry Shares	+21.3	− 3	+17	− 20	1.7	G(S)
★ Guardian Mutual	+11.9	− 1	+35	+ 38	3.6	GI(S)
Hamilton Income	+10.5	− 3	+44	+ 71	5.2	I(SFx)
Hartwell Growth Fund	+27.0	+17	+25	− 7	0.0	AG(S)
Hartwell Leverage Fund	+29.8	+17	+35	+ 34	0.0	AG(S)
Herold Fund	+10.3	− 2	+17	− 31	0.0	AG(S)
Ind. Fund of America	+22.7	+ 1	+21	− 33	0.0	AG(S)
Ivest Fund	+17.4	+ 1	+15	− 32	1.7	AG(S)
Ivy Fund	+ 8.4	− 7	+18	− 27	2.0	G(S)
Janus Fund	+24.7	+ 4	+20	+ 10	1.0	AG(S)
★ Johnston Mutual	+ 9.6	− 5	+17	− 20	3.3	G(S)
Lindner Fund	+28.6	+30	+53	+ 72	1.0	G(S)
Loomis-Sayles Cap. Dev.	+34.4	− 1	+19	− 19	1.9	G(S)
Loomis-Sayles Mutual	+ 8.2	− 4	+16	− 2	4.7	Ba(SFx)
★ Mathers Fund	+19.9	+14	+44	+ 16	2.4	AG(S)
Morgan Growth	+19.8	+ 7	+19	0	2.2	G(S)
★ Mutual Shares	+19.8	+15	+55	+139	1.8	AG(SFx)

% Change in Net Asset Value *

	7 Mo. 1978	Year 1977	Year 1976	5 Yrs. 1973-77	% Yield°	Type (Policy)
Nassau Fund	+ 2.7	− 8	+20	− 12	4.5	GI(S)
National Industries	+ 9.8	− 2	+29	− 3	2.1	GI(S)
NEA Mutual	+ 6.2	− 7	+15	− 18	4.4	G(S)
Neuwirth Fund	+14.8	− 2	+18	− 24	2.3	AG(S)
Newton Growth Fund	+15.9	+ 2	+19	− 35	2.0	G(S)
Newton Income	+ 0.1	− 5	+24	− 3	5.3	I(FxS)
Nicholas Fund	+28.0	+20	+23	− 31	1.7	AG(S)
★ Northeast Investors	− 0.3	+ 6	+21	+ 38	9.1	I(Fx)
Oceanographic & Growth	+ 2.8	0	+12	− 17	4.1	AG(FxS)
One Hundred Fund	+23.4	+ 2	+20	− 42	1.5	G(S)
One William Street	+12.8	− 4	+17	− 8	2.2	GI(S)
★ Partners Fund	+19.4	+ 7	+31	+ 24	2.6	AG(SC)
Penn Square Mutual	+11.0	− 6	+33	+ 41	4.5	G(S)
Pennsylvania Mutual	+31.6	+23	+49	+ 12	0.0	AG(S)
Pilot Fund	+ 7.6	− 2	+24	+ 8	2.0	AG(S)
★ Pine Street Fund	+ 7.9	− 4	+25	+ 17	5.0	GI(SC)
★ Price (T.R.) Growth Stock	+16.3	− 7	+13	− 27	1.2	G(S)
★ Price New Era Fund	+10.0	− 4	+21	+ 2	2.8	G(S)
Price New Horizons Fund	+28.5	+13	+11	− 35	0.9	AG(S)
Price New Income Fund	+ 1.8	+ 5	+14	§	7.9	I(Fx)
PRO Fund	+24.0	+ 7	+17	− 42	4.1	G(S)
Rainbow Fund	+10.8	+20	+30	− 37	0.0	AG(S)
Revere Fund	+ 9.7	− 4	+32	− 42	0.9	AG(S)
Scudder, St. & Clark Com.	−14.2	− 2	+25	− 8	3.0	G(S)
Scudder Development	+39.6	+28	+20	− 22	0.8	AG(S)
Scudder Income Fund	+ 1.3	0	+24	+ 2	7.5	Ba(FxS)
Scudder International	+20.6	− 1	+ 6	− 2	1.7	G(SFo)
★ Scudder Special Fund	+28.1	+ 8	+24	− 25	1.4	AG(S)
Selected Am. Shares	+ 4.1	0	+20	− 13	5.7	GI(SFx)
Selected Special Shares	+ 9.1	− 7	+16	− 13	2.6	AG(S)
Sequoia Fund	+24.2	+19	+71	+112	1.5	G(S)
★ Sherman Dean Fund	+37.8	+ 3	+32	+ 31	0.0	AG(S)
Spectra Fund	+30.7	+ 7	+30	− 33	0.1	AG(S)
State Farm Balanced	+11.3	+ 4	+24	+ 18	4.0	Ba(SFx)
State Farm Growth	+15.0	+ 3	+39	+ 32	2.6	G(S)
Steadman Am. Industry	−12.5	− 1	+ 5	− 42	2.7	AG(SFx)
Steadman Associated Fund	+ 2.8	+ 5	+23	+ 19	7.5	IG(Fx)
Steadman Investment	+ 2.6	− 6	+37	− 6	3.4	GI(SFxC)
Stein Roe & Farnham						
Balanced Fund	+ 8.0	− 6	+15	− 11	3.9	Ba(SFx)
Cap. Opportunities	+15.2	+ 6	+25	− 13	1.9	G(SC)
Stock Fund	+10.2	− 9	+16	− 18	2.8	G(S)
Stratton Growth Fund	+15.7	+ 2	+40	+ 22	2.6	G(S)
Trustees' Equity	+12.4	− 3	+14	− 28	2.2	G(S)
Tudor Hedge Fund	+28.8	+ 7	+24	− 7	0.0	AG(He)
20th Century Growth	+51.8	+14	+61	+ 41	0.0	AG(S)
20th Century Income	+43.6	+25	+28	+ 67	1.2	GI(S)
Unified Growth Fund	+18.7	+ 1	+20	− 29	1.9	G(S)
Unified Mutual Shares	+ 9.0	− 4	+25	− 12	4.6	GI(SC)
United Services Fund	+24.9	+39	−41	− 79	6.0	G(SGo)
USAA Capital	+10.2	− 6	+ 8	− 43	2.5	G(S)
Weingarten Equity	+33.9	+19	+16	− 3	0.5	AG(S)
★ Wellesley Income Fund	+ 3.5	+ 4	+23	+ 35	8.0	I(FxS)
Wellington Fund	+ 5.7	− 5	+23	+ 7	5.4	Ba(SFx)
Westminster Bond Fund	+ 1.6	+ 5	+15	§	7.9	I(Fx)
★ Windsor Fund	+14.1	+ 1	+45	+ 44	4.1	GI(S)
Wisconsin Income	− 0.4	− 5	+23	− 6	6.9	IG(FxS)

Source: *United Mutual Fund Selector* (Boston, Mass.: United Business Service Co., August 11, 1978), p. 119. Reprinted by permission.

Questions

1. How do you compute the net asset value of an investment company?

2. Discuss the difference between an open-end investment company and a closed-end investment company.

3. What are the two prices of importance to a closed-end investment company? How do these prices typically differ?

4. What is the difference between a load and no-load fund?

5. What are the differences between a common stock fund and a balanced fund? How would you expect their risk and return characteristics to compare?

6. Why would anyone buy a money market fund?

7. What is the purpose of dual funds? What are some potential problems for these funds? What has been the typical relationship between NAV and market price?

8. Do you care about how well a mutual fund is diversified? Why or why not? How could you quickly measure the extent of diversification?

9. Why is the stability of risk for a mutual fund important to an investor? Discuss. What is the empirical evidence in this regard—i.e., is the risk measure for mutual funds generally stable?

10. Do you feel the performance of mutual funds should be judged on the basis of return alone or on a risk-adjusted basis? Why? Discuss using examples.

11. Define the net return and gross return for a mutual fund. Discuss how you would compute each of these.

12. A. As an investor in a mutual fund, is net return or gross return relevant to you?
B. As an investigator attempting to determine the ability of mutual fund managers to select undervalued stocks or project market returns, which return is relevant: net or gross?

13. You are told that, on the basis of the Treynor composite measure of performance, about half the mutual funds did better than the market and on the basis of the Sharpe measure only 35 percent did better than the market. Explain in detail *why* this happened.

14. Based upon the numerous tests of mutual fund performance, you are convinced that only about half of them do better than a naive buy-and-hold policy. Does this mean you would forget about investing in them? Why or why not?

15. A. You are told that Fund X experienced above average performance over the past two years. Do you think it will continue over the next two years? Why or why not?
B. You are told that Fund Y experienced consistently poor performance over the past two years. Would you expect this to continue over the next two years? Why or why not?

References

Bogle, John C. "Mutual Fund Performance Evaluation." *Financial Analysts Journal,* Vol. 26, No. 6 (November–December, 1970).

Carlson, Robert S. "Aggregate Performance of Mutual Funds 1948–1967." *Journal of Financial and Quantitative Analysis,* Vol. 5, No. 1 (March, 1970).

Friend, Irwin, Blume, Marshall, and Crockett, Jean. *Mutual Funds and Other Institutional Investors.* New York: McGraw-Hill, 1970.

Friend, Irwin, Brown, F. E., Herman, Edward S., and Vickers, Douglas. A Study of *Mutual Funds.* Report of the Committee on Interstate and Foreign Commerce, 87th Congress, 2nd session, August 28, 1962.

Gaumnitz, Jack E. "Appraising Performance of Investment Portfolios." *Journal of Finance,* Vol. 25, No. 3 (June, 1970).

Gentry, James A. and Pike, John R. "Dual Funds Revisited." *Financial Analysts Journal,* Vol. 24, No. 2 (March–April, 1968).

Greeley, Robert E. "Mutual Fund Management Companies." *Financial Analysts Journal,* Vol. 23, No. 5 (September–October, 1967).

Horowitz, Ira. "A Model for Mutual Fund Evaluation." *Industrial Management Review,* Vol. 6, No. 3 (Spring, 1965).

Horowitz, Ira. "The Reward-to-Variability Ratio and Mutual Fund Performance." *Journal of Business,* Vol. 39, No. 4 (October, 1966).

Horowitz, Ira and Higgins, Harold B. "Some Factors Affecting Investment Fund Performance." *Quarterly Review of Economics and Business,* Vol. 3, No. 1 (Spring, 1963).

Investment Companies. Boston, Massachusetts: Arthur Wiesenberger Services, published annually.

Jensen, Michael C. "The Performance of Mutual Funds in the Period 1945–1964." *Journal of Finance,* Vol. 23, No. 2 (May, 1968).

Litzenberger, Robert H. and Sosin, Howard B. "The Performance and Potential of Dual Purpose Funds." *Journal of Portfolio Management,* Vol. 4, No. 3 (Spring, 1978).

Litzenberger, Robert H. and Sosin, Howard B. "The Structure and Management of Dual Purpose Funds." *Journal of Financial Economics,* Vol. 4, No. 1 (May, 1977).

Litzenberger, Robert H. and Sosin, Howard B. "The Theory of Recapitalizations and the Evidence of Dual Purpose Funds." *Journal of Finance,* forthcoming.

Levy, Haim and Sarnat, Marshall. "The Case for Mutual Funds." *Financial Analysts Journal,* Vol. 28, No. 2 (March–April, 1972).

Marks, Lawrence J. "In Defense of Performance." *Financial Analysts Journal,* Vol. 18, No. 6 (November–December, 1962).

McDonald, John G. "Objectives and Performance of Mutual Funds, 1960–1969." *Journal of Financial and Quantitative Analysis,* Vol. 9, No. 3 (June, 1974).

Mills, Harlan D. "On the Measurement of Fund Performance." *Journal of Finance,* Vol. 25, No. 5 (December, 1970).

"Mutual Funds Make a Comeback." *Dun's Review* (February, 1978).

Netter, Joseph, II. "Dual-Purpose Funds." *Financial Analysts Journal,* Vol. 23, No. 4 (July–August, 1967).

Pratt, Eugene J. "Myths Associated with Closed-End Investment Company Discounts." *Financial Analysts Journal,* Vol. 22, No. 4 (July–August 1966).

Sharpe, William F. "Mutual Fund Performance." *Journal of Business, Supplement on Security Prices,* Vol. 39, No. 1 (January 1966).

Shelton, John P., Brigham, Eugene F., and Hofflander, Alfred E. "An Evaluation and Appraisal of Dual Funds." *Financial Analysts Journal,* Vol. 23, No. 3 (May–June, 1967).

Simonson, Donald G. "The Speculative Behavior of Mutual Funds." *Journal of Finance,* Vol. 27, No. 2 (May, 1972).

Treynor, Jack L. "How to Rate Management of Investment Funds." *Harvard Business Review,* Vol. 43, No. 1 (January–February 1965).

Treynor, Jack L. and Mazuy, Kay K. "Can Mutual Funds Outguess the Market?" *Harvard Business Review,* Vol. 24, No. 4 (July–August, 1966).

Williamson, Peter J. "Measuring Mutual Fund Performance." *Financial Analysts Journal,* Vol. 28, No. 6 (November–December, 1972).

Name Index[1]

---

[1]All page references are for footnotes. An asterisk appearing with a page number indicates a text reference as well.

Horrigan, James O., 426
Horton, Joseph J., Jr., 476
Hurt, Ron, 179

Ibbotson, Roger G., 38,* 173–174,
    513, 515, 516, 518

Jaffe, Jeffrey, 184
Jaffee, Dwight M., 251,* 252
Jahnke, William W., 305*
Jean, William H., 582*
Jen, Frank C., 477*
Jensen, Michael C., 171,* 186, 593,
    595,* 625,* 626, 629,* 633,*
    634,* 694,* 695, 696
Joehnk, Michael D., 429, 431, 458,
    477, 486, 487, 489, 519*
Johnson, Glenn L., 310,* 311, 312
Jones, Charles P., 179
Jordan, Jerry L., 248
Joy, O. Maurice, 179,* 264, 283, 591,
    612,* 613, 614

Kaplan, Mortimer, 429
Kaplan, Robert S., 178*
Karnosky, Denis S., 15, 289
Katz, Steven, 521
Kaufman, George C., 491
Keller, Myron, 35
Kendall, Maurice G., 168
Keran, Michael W., 251,* 282
Kerrigan, Thomas J., 402
Kessel, Reuben A., 307, 308, 483
King, Benjamin F., 190, 230,* 231,*
    318*
Kisor, M., 366
Klemkosky, Robert C., 186, 187, 595,
    634,* 700,* 701*
Kochin, Levis A., 252,* 282
Kripotos, Spero L., 405
Kwitny, Jonathan, 43

Laing, Jonathon R., 33, 651
Langbein, John H., 196
Largay, J. A., 173*
Larson, Arnold B., 682
Latané, Henry A., 179,* 316, 317, 589
Lee, C. F., 594, 595
Leibowitz, Martin L., 459, 489, 501,
    504
Leroy, Stephen F., 474

Lessard, Donald R., 34, 610*
Leuthold, S. C., 128
Levy, Haim, 579, 606*
Levy, Robert A., 189, 320,* 394, 405
Lindahl-Stevens, Mary, 217
Lindvall, John R., 429
Lintner, John, 264, 570
Little, I. M. D., 264
Litzenberger, Robert H., 179,* 692
Livingston, Miles, 319*
Logue, Dennis E., 33
Longstreet, J. R., 57
Loomis, Carol J., 93, 130
Lorie, James H., 35,* 36, 93, 129, 184,
    194,* 229, 264, 513, 558
Lyons, John F., 284

Macaulay, Frederick R., 489
MacBeth, J. D., 570, 593
McClintick, David, 284
McCulloch, J. Huston, 478
McDonald, John G., 33, 173–174,
    611,* 699,* 701
McDougall, Duncan M., 269
McEnally, Richard W., 179,* 490
McGill, W. J., 576
Mains, Norman E., 634,* 696*
Malkiel, Burton G., 191, 283, 288,
    348, 366,* 367,* 386, 478, 479,
    482, 488
Mandelbrot, Benoit, 530, 570
Mao, James C. T., 384,* 579,* 581, 582
Marjos, Anna, 616
Markowitz, Harry, 18,* 161,* 193,*
    208,* 209, 213,* 214,* 215,*
    529,* 543, 571
Marquardt, Raymond, 31
Martin, John D., 474, 520, 595
Martin, Peter, 285
Martin, Stanley A., 612, 613, 614
Martina, A. D., Jr., 543
Mayor, Thomas H., 402
Meisselman, David, 482
Mendelson, Morris, 57, 688
Mennis, Edmund A., 475
Merton, Robert C., 594,* 659, 665,
    667, 668
Meyers, Stephen L., 231,* 318,* 594
Miller, E., 57
Miller, Merton H., 4, 253,* 261, 262,*
    287, 346,* 374
Miller, Norman, 126
Miller, Roger L., 516, 517
Mills, Robert H., 477

Solomon, Ezra, 283,* 287, 346,* 374
Sosin, Howard B., 692
Sprinkel, Beryl W., 250,* 251, 256,*
    601
Stigler, George J., 372
Stoll, Hans R., 173–174
Stone, Herbert L., 30
Sunder, Shyam, 178*
Sutch, Richard, 482

Tabell, A. W., 189
Tabell, E. W., 189
Teweles, Richard J., 29, 30
Thackray, John, 98
Thompson, Donald J., II, 19
Tinic, Seha M., 56, 104, 112
Tobin, James, 558
Townsend, James E., 313*
Treynor, Jack L., 186, 622, 623, 625,*
    629,* 636,* 694*
Tuttle, Donald L., 179, 274, 276, 277,*
    316, 317, 589
Tysseland, Milford S., 317*

Van Horne, James C., 16, 17, 174,*
    175, 264, 283, 474, 479, 490,
    516

Walter, James E., 65
Weeden, Donald E., 108
Weil, Roman L., 490, 491, 513
Welles, Chris, 88, 95, 96, 98, 110
Wert, James E., 477*
West, Richard R., 56, 95, 104, 112,
    173*
West, Stan, 126
Weston, J. Fred, 16, 17, 57
Whitbeck, V. S., 288, 366
White, Reba, 444
White, Shelby, 108
Whitehead, John G., 109
Wilson, Charles J., 591
Wilt, Glenn A., Jr., 27
Winjum, James, 34
Winjum, Joanne, 34
Working, Holbrook, 682
Wright, David, 98, 285*

Ying, Louis, 175
Yohe, William P., 15, 289

Zarnowitz, Victor, 242*
Zeller, Thomas, 334*
Zinbarg, Edward D., 208, 475

Subject Index

Earnings multiple (cont.),
in estimating market returns, 266–281
and growth rate, 292–294
in industry analysis, 333–341
and required rate of return, 281–292
Earnings,
economy and industry correlation of,
228–229
estimating procedure for, 266–281
Economic analysis. *See* Aggregate economic analysis
Economic Indicators, 140
Economic indicator series. *See* Indicator series
Economic Report of the President, 141–142
Economy,
growth rate and risk-free rate in,
12–13
and money supply, 248–250
Efficient frontier,
and critical line, 546–551
derivation of for multi-asset portfolio,
543–551
for foreign securities, 607
and investor utility, 551–553
Markowitz's, 211–213
Sharpe's, 213–215
Efficient market hypothesis,
and bonds, 520–522
fair game model of, 163–164
and fundamental analysis, 190–195
and portfolio analysis, 193–199
semi-strong form of, 166–167, 171–183
strong form of, 167, 183–189
and technical analysis, 189–190
weak form of, 165–166, 167–170
Entropy, 573–576
Equal weighted portfolio, 36–37
Equipment trust certificates, 441–442
Equity securities, 27–28, 32–34, 60–71
Equity trusts, 30
Exchange, pure rate of, 5
Exchanges. *See* Securities exchanges
Expected-gain–confidence limit risk measure, 572–573
External efficiency, market, 56

Fact Book, New York Stock Exchange,
144
Fair game model, 163–164
Farm real estate returns, 41–43

Federal Financing Bank, 422 n
Federal Home Loan Bank bonds, 436 n
Federal National Mortgage Association issues, 436 n
Federal Reserve Bank publications,
142–143
Federal Reserve Bulletin, 140
Federal Reserve Monthly Chart Book, 141
FIFO, 178–179
Financial Analysts Journal, 155
Financial institutions, 28
and block trades, 81–82
exchange membership of, 88
and ownership of NYSE stocks, 83–85
trading of, vs. individual trading,
82–84
Financial Management, 155
Financial Review, 156
Financial risk, 17, 18
in company analysis, 362
for foreign securities, 602
Financial World, 154
First-in-first-out (FIFO), 178–179
Fitch's Rating Service, 425
Fixed commissions, 86–88
Fixed income investments, 25–27
Floor brokers, 72
Flower bonds, 433
Forbes, 706, 707
Foreign competition, 276–277
Foreign institutions' stock holdings, 85
Foreign investments,
for diversification, 33–34
empirical studies of, 603–615
listing of on ASE, 63
obstacles to, 615–617
rationale for, 600–615
Fourth market, 70–71
commissions in, 87–88, 100–101
Fundamental analysis, 190–195, 393
Futures contracts, 29–30, 41–43, 680–683

Gaines, Reis and Company, 106
General Motors, 65
Geometric mean criterion for risk measure, 589–590
Geometric mean return, 42, 48–50
Ginnie Mae, 435, 436–437, 522
Give-ups, 86, 97
Government National Mortgage Association (GNMA) bonds, 435, 436–437, 522

Subject Index
721

Investment companies, 655
exchange membership of, 88
information sources on, 704–706
liquidity requirements for, 112
management of, 656–657
NYSE stock holdings of, 83–85
open-end and closed-end, 687–690,
692–693
performance studies of, 693–704
rate of return from, 186–188
types of, 690–691
Investment Dealers Digest, 445

Journal of Business, 156
Journal of Finance, 155
*Journal of Financial and Quantitative
Analysis,* 155
Journal of Financial Economics, 155
Journal of Portfolio Management, 155

Kingston, Boye and Southwood, 106–
107

Labor costs and profit margin, 274–275
Lagging economic indicators, 243
Land as investment, 31–32
Last-in-first-out (LIFO), 178–179
Leading economic indicators, 242–243,
246–248
Lending at risk-free rate, 214
Leveraged portfolio, 556–557
LIFO, 178–179
Limit orders, 72–73, 74
Liquidity,
and block trades, 89–92
for bonds, 432
definition of, 17
in the good market, 55–56
institutional requirements for, 112
investments with low, 34–35
Liquidity risk, 17–18
for bonds, 432
in company analysis, 363–364
for foreign securities, 602

Macroeconomic market analysis, 239–
258
Management Results, 704
Market, 54–56
Market analysis. *See* Aggregate market
analysis

Market indicator series. *See* Indicator
series
Market orders, 72
Market portfolio of risky assets, 18, 215,
557–558
Market risk estimates, 232
May Day, 89
Mean-entropy risk measure, 573–576
Mean-semivariance risk measure, 571–
572
Merrill Lynch, Pierce, Fenner and Smith,
Inc., 71
Microeconomic market analysis, 261–297
Midwest Stock Exchange, 65–66, 100,
650–651
Mitchum, Jones and Templeton, 106
M. J. Meehan and Company, 107
Money market funds, 691
Money supply, 248–257
Moody's publications, 149, 425–428,
444–445
Mortgage-backed bonds, 442
Mortgage trusts, 30
M portfolio, 18, 215, 557–558
Multidimensional portfolio analysis,
582–585
Municipal bonds, 26, 59, 422, 423,
437–440, 510 n
Mutual funds,
information sources on, 704–706
open-end vs. closed-end, 687–690,
692–693
performance studies of, 693–704
portfolio performance evaluation of,
627–635, 638–640
rate of return on, 186–188
types of, 690–691
Mutual savings banks, 85

NASD, 67
NASDAQ, 67–69
NASDAQ Price Indicator Series, 126–
127, 130–132
National Association of Securities Dealers
(NASD), 67
National Association of Securities Dealers
Automatic Quotations
(NASDAQ), 67–69
National Bureau of Economic Research
(NBER), 241–243
National Market System, 102–111
National Quotation Bureau Average, 124
NBER, 241–243
Negotiated commissions, 88–89, 95–102

Risk premium (cont.),
    curve of for bonds, 517
    definition of, 5
    and earnings multiple, 282–285
    for foreign securities, 601–602
    and portfolio theory, 18–19
Risky asset portfolios, 554–558
Robb, Peck, McCooey and Company, 106
Rule 390, 107–111
Rule 394, 107 n

Safety first risk measure, 577–579
Safeway Stores, 350–365
Sales forecast,
    in company analysis, 350–354
    in industry analysis, 324–328
Salomon Brothers index, 39
Savings accounts, 25
Savings, negative, 4–5
Seasoned new issues, 57–58
Secondary markets,
    bond markets as, 58–59
    equity markets as, 60–71
    and liquidity risk, 17
Securities and Exchange Commission
        publications, 143
Securities exchanges,
    institutional membership in, 88
    and listing effect on prices, 174–175
    membership categories in, 71–72
    national, 60–65
    over-the-counter, 66–69
    regional, 65–66
Security Market Line (SML), 217–218,
        560–562
Semi-strong form efficient market hy-
        pothesis, 166–167, 171–183,
        520–521
Semivariance as risk measure, 571–572
Separation theorem, 558
Short sales, 73
Skewness, portfolio, 582–585
SML, 217–218, 560–562
Strong form efficient market hypothesis,
        167, 183–189
Soft dollars, 86, 96–97
Spear, Leeds and Kellogg, 107
Specialists, 71
    and block trades, 89–91
    competition among on the NYSE,
        104, 106–107
    functions of, 74–75
    income of, 75–77

Specialists (cont.)
    rate of return for, 184–185
    and Rule 390, 110
Speculative companies and stocks, 348–
        349
Spokane Stock Exchange, 66
Spot contracts, 29
Stamps as investment, 35
Standard & Poor's bond ratings, 425–428
Standard & Poor's indexes, 28, 41–43
    correlation of with other series, 130–
        132
    returns on, vs. index funds, 196–197
Standard & Poor's publications, 145,
        146, 148, 150–151, 444
Standard deviation,
    for foreign securities, 604
    of portfolio, 208–211, 564–565, 566
    and risk-free assets, 555–556
    in risk measurement, 10–11, 530 n
Statistical Abstract of the United States, 142
Statistical Bulletin, 143
Stochastic dominance, 585–589
Stock analysis, individual,
    and efficient markets, 191–192
    information sources for, 147–156
Stock exchanges. *See* Securities exchanges
Stock options. *See* Options
Stock prices,
    cyclical patterns in, 229–230
    and leading indicators, 246–248
    market and industry effect on, 230–
        232
Stock splits,
    DJIA adjustment for, 121–122
    effect of on rates of return, 171–173
Stop buy orders, 74
Stop loss orders, 73–74
Strong form efficient market hypothesis,
        167, 183–189
Supply and demand, 14, 56
Survey of Current Business, 140
Systematic risk, 18–19
    and Capital Market Line, 558–560
    in company analysis, 364–365
    definition of, 18, 215
    in industry analysis, 320–323
    normalized, 216–218, 561
    in portfolio performance evaluation,
        622–623

Tax exemptions,
    on agency issues, 421, 434–435,
        436 n

Tax exemptions (cont.),
    on municipal bonds, 26, 437–439,
        510 n
    on preferred stocks, 27
    on Treasury issues, 433
    and valuation, 470–472
Tax rate,
    in industry analysis, 331–332
    in profit margin analysis, 278–279
Tax swaps, 503–506
Tchebysheff's inequality, 577
Technical analysis, 189–190, 394–407
Technical trading rules. See Trading rules
Third market, 69–70, 86–87, 99–101
Three C's, 89–91
Tiered market, 92–94, 111–112, 197–
    198
Trading rules,
    and stock price and volume tech-
        niques, 402–407
    tests of, 166, 169–170
    types of:
        breadth of market, 400–402
        contrary opinion, 397–399
        follow the smart money, 399–400
        short interest, 402
Trading symbols, 68 n
Trading turnover, 85 n
Transactions costs, 56, 194–195
Transportation companies, 28
Treasury Bulletin, 444
Trust funds, 85

Uncertainty, 7, 16–18
Unemployment rate and profit margin,
    277
United Mutual Fund Selector, 706, 708
Unweighted price indicator series, 128–
    130

U.S. Government securities:
    agency issues, 421, 422, 434–437
    bonds, 37–43, 59, 421, 422, 423–424
    Treasury bills, 12, 13, 17, 38–43,
        233–236
Utility companies, 28, 41–43
    bond yields for, 12
Utilization rate, 274

Valuation,
    of bonds, 455–466
    of call options, 659–668
    determinants of, 261–262
    of growth stocks, 384–389, 391
    macroeconomic techniques of, 239–
        257
Value Line Investment Survey, 149, 153
Value Line OTC Special Situations Service,
    154
Value weighted indicator series, 125–128
Value weighted portfolio, 36–37
Variable rate notes, 442–443
Variance. See Standard deviation
Varo, Inc., 63–64

Wall Street Journal, 144, 704
Warrants, 32, 63, 676–677
Weak form efficient market hypothesis,
    165–166, 168–170, 520
Wells Fargo Investment Advisors, 196–
    197
World events and stock prices, 175–176

Xerox, 27–28

Yield curve, 478–485